Software Design and Data Structures in Turbo Pascal

Elliot B. Koffman
Temple University

Bruce R. Maxim
University of Michigan-Dearborn

 Addison-Wesley Publishing Company

Reading, Massachusetts ▪ Menlo Park, California ▪ New York
Don Mills, Ontario ▪ Wokingham, England ▪ Amsterdam ▪ Bonn
Sydney ▪ Singapore ▪ Tokyo ▪ Madrid ▪ San Juan ▪ Milan ▪ Paris

To our families with much appreciation for their love and support:
Caryn, Richard, Deborah, and Robin Koffman
Norma Jean, Benjamin, and Katherine Maxim

Sponsoring Editor:	Lynne Doran Cote
Production Supervisors:	David Dwyer, John Walker
Production Services:	Beth Stephens
Art Coordinator:	Dick Morton
Text and Cover Designer:	Darci Mehall, Aureo Design
Artist:	Jim Hubbard, Professional Art Services
Compositor:	Compset Inc.
Senior Manufacturing Manager:	Roy Logan

Library of Congress Cataloging-in-Publication Data
Koffman, Elliot B.
  Software design and data structures in Turbo Pascal / Elliot B.
Koffman, Bruce R. Maxim.
     p.   cm.
  ISBN 0-201-15624-5
  1. Software engineering. 2. Data structures (Computer science)
3. Turbo Pascal (Computer file)   I. Maxim, Bruce R.   II. Title.
QA76.758.K68   1994
005.7'3—dc20   93-37679
                                                     CIP

ISBN 0-201-15624-5

1 2 3 4 5 6 7 8 9 0–CRW–97969594

PREFACE

This text covers software engineering and data structures topics traditionally covered in a first course in data structures with emphasis on data abstraction and the use of abstract data types (ADTs). Our selection of topics has been heavily influenced by the recommendations of the ACM Computing Curricula Task Force for CS2[1] and the recent report of the ACM/IEEE-CS Joint Curriculum Task Force.[2] It assumes that the student is familiar with the material normally covered in an introductory computer science course in Pascal or Turbo Pascal. High school mathematics is sufficient mathematics background for most of the material in this book. A limited knowledge of discrete mathematics, however, is desirable for certain sections.

Object-oriented programming is introduced early in Chapter 1 and used throughout the text. We introduce several ADTs and describe their implementations as Borland's Pascal objects encapsulated in units. Although the text uses Borland's Pascal compiler for MS-DOS, which is known as Turbo Pascal (version 7.0), it can also be used with any version of Turbo Pascal that supports objects and units (versions 5.0 and later). The book can also be used with Borland's Pascal compiler for Windows, if you insert the statement

```
uses WinCRT;
```

immediately after the program statement.

Overview

The first third of the text discusses software engineering concepts and reviews and consolidates the built-in data structures of Pascal introduced in the first programming course. Chapters 1 and 2 are motivational and discuss

---

[1] Recommended Curriculum for CS2; Koffman, E., Stemple, D., and Wardle, C.; *Communications for the ACM 28;* vol. 8, 1985, pp. 815–818.
[2] Computing Curricula 1991, *Report of the ACM/IEEE-CS Joint Curriculum Task Force,* Tucker, A.B. (ed.), ACM Press and IEEE Computer Society Press 1991.

all aspects of the system life cycle including analysis, design, testing, and verification. Chapter 3 reviews the built-in data types of Pascal and discusses object hierarchies and inheritance. Recursion is covered in Chapter 4 as part of this "review-and-consolidate" section.

In the second third of the text, students will be introduced to stacks, queues, and lists as abstract data types and learn how to use each ADT (provided as a Borland Pascal unit on a program disk) to solve real problems. They will also see how to implement each of these ADTs in contiguous storage (using arrays) and as linked lists. Chapter 7 introduces pointer types and a List Abstract Data Type. It shows how to implement stacks, queues, and ordered linked lists as descendants of a general list. At this point, the fundamentals of object-oriented programming and the basic CS2 data structures and software engineering topics have been covered.

The last third of the text completes the coverage of data structures and algorithms with binary trees, binary search trees, general trees, AVL trees, and graphs. There are also separate chapters on searching and sorting, although some search and sort algorithms will already have been introduced through earlier examples. Chapter 12 finishes the discussion of the object-oriented programming paradigm, discussing polymorphism, virtual methods, and inheritance.

Organization of the Book

The textbook begins with an overview of software engineering and design concepts (Chapters 1 and 2) that will be integrated throughout. Chapter 1 presents a general introduction to software engineering and program design. It includes the solution to a large case study that illustrates the phases of the software life cycle. The chapter also introduces abstract data types and shows how to implement them as Borland Pascal objects encapsulated within units.

Chapter 2 discusses aspects of program documentation that are beneficial to understanding, reusing, and testing software including preconditions and postconditions. The chapter discusses how to trace programs and introduces the topic of program verification through the use of assertions and loop invariants. It also covers aspects of program testing and shows how to debug programs in Turbo Pascal. It ends with a discussion of algorithm efficiency, Big O notation, and timing programs.

Chapter 3 reviews the built-in data structures of Pascal—arrays, records, and strings—and discusses applications of these data structures. It also introduces object inheritance and shows how variant records can be more easily implemented as a family of objects.

Chapter 4 discusses recursion. There are several examples of recursive modules, and the chapter concludes with a discussion of backtracking.

Chapters 5–7 introduce abstract data types that are important for computer science students: lists, ordered lists, stacks, and queues. These ADTs are described, and a variety of applications using these data types are provided including expression evaluation and waiting-line simulation. We discuss how to implement these ADTs using arrays and linked lists. After introducing a general list object, Chapter 7 shows how to implement ordered lists, stacks, and queues as descendants of this list object.

Chapter 8 covers binary trees and binary search trees. It shows how a binary tree can be used to store expressions and how to traverse binary trees. We implement both a binary tree object and a binary search tree object, which is a descendant of a binary tree.

Chapter 9 covers advanced aspects of trees and introduces graphs. Balanced trees and AVL trees are discussed. Other topics include general trees, heaps, and priority queues.

Chapter 10 presents a discussion of various search algorithms (linear, binary, and hashing) and compares their efficiency. It includes a discussion of hashing and implementation of a hash table ADT. It concludes with a discussion of searching through indexes and B-trees.

Chapter 11 discusses sorting including quadratic sorts (selection, insertion, and bubble) and N log N sorts (MergeSort, QuickSort, and HeapSort).

Chapter 12 completes coverage of the object-oriented programming paradigm discussing polymorphism, operator overloading, and virtual methods.

Pedagogical Features

We employ several pedagogical features to enhance the usefulness of this book. Some of these features are discussed below.

End-of-section Exercises

Most sections end with a number of self-check exercises and short programming exercises. These include exercises that require analysis of program fragments as well as short programming exercises. Answers to most self-check exercises appear in the back of the book (Appendix D). Solutions to the programming exercises appear in the solutions manual.

End-of-Chapter Exercises

Each chapter ends with a set of quick-check exercises with answers. There are also chapter review exercises with solutions appearing in the solutions manual.

End-of-Chapter Projects

Each chapter contains a number of programming projects. Most chapters include one or two special project pairs for which the second member of the project in the pair requries a modification of the first project in the pair. Selected project solutions appear in the solutions manual.

Case Studies and Examples

The book contains a large number of programming examples. Whenever possible, examples contain complete programs or procedures rather than incomplete program fragments. Most chapters contain one or more substantial case studies that are solved following the software development method. Object-oriented programming is used in examples throughout this text.

Error Discussions and Chapter Review

At the end of every chapter, common programming errors are discussed, and major points from the chapter are reviewed and summarized.

Directory:
File:

Programming Examples Available on Diskette or On-Line

For many figures and end-of-chapter programming projects throughout the book, case studies, programming examples, and source code are available on diskette and on Internet. Look for the diskette icon as shown in the margin for the directory and filename of these items.

Appendixes, Source Code, and Supplements

Separate appendixes cover the Turbo Pascal environment, language elements, compiler directives, and syntax diagrams. An on-line instructor's manual, solutions manual, and source code are available for this edition. For additional information, send electronic mail messages to koffCS2@aw.com. To obtain an information file, type information on the subject line and send information in the body of the text.

Acknowledgements

The principle reviewers were most essential in suggesting improvements and finding errors. They include Jacobo Carrasquel, Carnegie-Mellon University; Paul Buis, Ball State University; Mary Lou Hines, University of Missouri-Kansas City; Stephen Krebsbach, South Dakota State University; Jeff Parker, Agile Networks; Dana Richards; and Charles M. Williams, Georgia State University.

The personnel at Addison-Wesley responsible for the production of this book worked diligently to meet a very demanding schedule. Our editor, Lynne Doran Cote, was closely involved in all phases of this project. Ably assisted by Maite Suarez-Rivas, Lynne did an excellent job of coordinating the writing and reviewing process and trying to keep us on a very tight schedule. David Dwyer and John Walker supervised the production of the book, while Katherine Harutunian coordinated the development of the manuscript. We are grateful to all of them for their fine work.

Philadelphia, PA   E.B.K.
Dearborn, MI   B.R.M.

TABLE OF CONTENTS

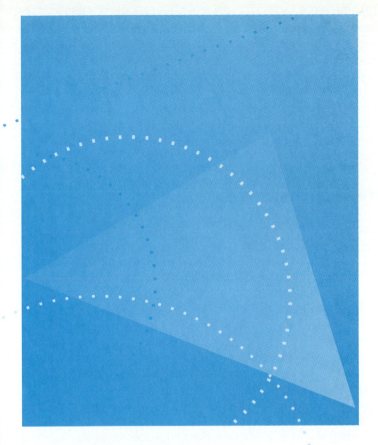

Introduction to Software Engineering

In your first course in programming methods, you probably wrote a lot of small programs that solved particular programming problems but otherwise had little general use. Since you survived the first course in programming methods and have come back for more, we assume that you want to learn more about computer science and programming.

This chapter discusses software engineering, the tools and techniques that professional programmers in industry use to facilitate the design and maintenance of large-scale programs. Our discussion will focus on some principles of software engineering that have proved useful for designing large program systems.

We will describe the different phases of a software project. We will discuss how to modularize a large project so that individual pieces can be implemented by different programmers and at different times. We will also discuss how to write software modules to simplify their reuse in other projects.

As part of this process, we will introduce the concepts of data abstraction and abstract data types. We will show how abstract data types enable us to encapsulate a data type along with operators for that type. Finally, we will show how objects in Borland Pascal enable us to easily implement abstract data types and how units enable us to write the code for an abstract data type in a separately compilable file.

1.1   The Software Challenge

Programming in college is somewhat different from programming in the real world. In college, an instructor generally gives you the problem specification. In many cases, the problem specification is ambiguous or incomplete, and interaction between the instructor and the class is necessary so that the students can pin down the details.

In the real world, the impetus for a software project comes from users of an existing software product or potential users of a new software product. The users see a need for improving an existing product or for computerizing an operation that is being done manually. This need is communicated to the individual(s) responsible for providing software support in the organization (normally called *systems analysts*).

Because the users often do not fully understand a computer's capabilities, the initial specification for a software product may be incomplete. The specification is clarified through extensive interaction between the users of the software and the systems analyst. Through this interaction, the systems analyst determines precisely what the users want the proposed software to do, and the users learn what to expect from the software product. This way, there are no surprises in the end.

Although it might seem like common sense to proceed in this manner, very often a software product does not perform as expected. The reason is usually a communication gap between those responsible for the product's design and its eventual users; generally, both parties are at fault. To avoid this possibility, it is imperative that a complete, written description of the *requirements specification* for a new software product be generated at the beginning of the project and that both users and designers sign the document.

1.2   The Software Life Cycle

The requirements specification is the first step in developing a new software system. The steps involved in the initial development and continued operation of a software system comprise the *software life cycle* (SLC):

1. Requirements specification
    Prepare a complete and unambiguous problem statement.
2. Analysis
    Understand the problem.
    Evaluate alternative solutions.
    Choose the preferred solution.
3. Design
    Perform a top-down design of the system.
    For each module, identify major data structures and associated proce-
    dures.
4. Implementation
    Write algorithms and pseudocode descriptions of individual procedures.
    Code the solution.
    Debug the code.
5. Testing and validation
    Test the code, and validate that it is correct.
6. Operation, follow-up, and maintenance
    Run the completed system.
    Evaluate its performance.
    Remove new bugs as they are detected.
    Make required changes to keep the system up to date.
    Validate that changes are correct and do not adversely affect the
    system's operation.

We will consider Steps 1 through 4 in the rest of this chapter; Step 5 will be the subject of the next chapter. The *engineering and scientific method* for solving problems specifies that problem analysis should always precede problem solution (synthesis). The first two steps of the SLC are the analysis part, and the next two steps (design and implementation) are the synthesis part.

The SLC is iterative. During the design phase (Step 3), problems may arise that make it necessary to modify the requirements specification. Similarly, during implementation (Step 4), it may become necessary to reconsider decisions made in the design phase. The systems analyst and users must approve all changes.

Once the system is implemented, it must be thoroughly tested before it enters its final step (operation and maintenance). It is possible to identify necessary system changes in both these steps that require repetition of earlier steps of the SLC. These changes may be to correct errors identified during testing or to accommodate changes required by external sources (for example, a change in the federal or state tax regulations).

There are varying estimates of the percentage of time spent on each step. For example, a typical system might require a year to proceed through the first four steps, three months of testing, then four years of operation and maintenance. Keeping these figures in mind, you can see why it is so important to design and document software in such a way that it can be easily maintained. This is especially important because the person who maintains the program might not have been involved in the original program design or implementation.

Requirements Specification

In the real world, the systems analyst works with the software users to clarify the detailed system requirements. Some of the questions that need to be answered deal with the format of the input data, the desired form of any output screens or printed forms, and the need for data validation. You often need to mimic this process by interrogating your instructor or graduate assistant to determine the precise details of a programming assignment.

For example, assume that your instructor has given you the following incomplete specification of a programming assignment.

PROBLEM ▼

Write an interactive telephone directory program that will contain a collection of names and telephone numbers. The user should be able to insert new entries in the directory, retrieve an entry in the directory, or change a directory entry.

Some of the questions that come to mind and might require clarification are the following:

1. Is there an initial list of names and numbers to be stored in the directory beforehand, or are all entries inserted at the same time?
2. If there is an initial list, is it stored on a file, or should it be entered interactively?
3. If the initial directory is stored on a file, is the file a text file (file of characters) or a binary file (file of binary values)?
4. If the file is a text file, are there any formatting conventions (for example, the name starts in column 1 and the phone number starts in column 20)? Are the name and number on the same data line or on separate lines?
5. Is the final directory stored in main memory or as a file in secondary memory? If a file, is it a sequential file or a direct access file? What are the access methods?
6. Can there be more than one number associated with a particular name? If so, should the first number be retrieved, the last number, or all numbers?
7. Is there a limit on the length of a name? How are the names stored (for example, *last, first* or *first last*)?
8. Are phone numbers stored as numbers or strings? Do they contain area codes? Are there any special characters in a phone number such as hyphens and parentheses? Should we check for illegal characters in a number or for a number that is too short or too long?

9. Should the names be stored in alphabetical order or in the sequence in which they were entered into the directory?
10. Do you need a printed list of names and phone numbers for the directory, and how should that list be formatted?
11. Is it possible to change a person's name as well as the person's phone number?
12. When a number is retrieved, should both the person's name and number be displayed or just the number? What form should this display take?
13. What action should be taken if a "new" entry has the same name as a person already in the directory? Should this be flagged as an error?

As you can see, the initial problem statement leaves plenty of questions unanswered. To complete the requirements specification, you should answer these questions and more. Many of the questions deal with details of input data, handling of potential errors in input data, and formats of input data and output lists.

ANALYSIS OF THE PROBLEM ▼

Once the system requirements are specified, the analysis stage begins. Before you can embark on the design of a program solution, make sure that you completely understand the problem. If the requirements specification has been carefully done, this will be easy. If any questions remain, they should be cleared up at this time.

The next step is to evaluate different approaches to the program design. As part of this investigation, the systems analyst and users may consider whether there are commercial software packages that can be purchased to satisfy their requirements as an alternative to developing the software in-house. They must also determine the impact of the new software product on existing computer systems and what new hardware or software will be needed to develop and run the new system. They determine the feasibility of each approach by estimating its cost and anticipated benefits. The analysis phase culminates with the selection of what appears to be the best design approach.

Although your choices will be more constrained in your coursework, you will often need to determine whether to use a personal computer or a main-frame, select a programming language for implementation, and determine the structure and organization of internal data and external data files. Some factors that should be considered in evaluating each design approach are the memory requirements for the program and its data and the requirements for on-line storage of data on a hard disk.

DESIGN ▼

Once you understand the problem and have selected the overall approach to the design, it is time to develop a high-level design of the system. Professional software engineers use several design methodologies (e.g., top-down, bottom-up, rapid prototyping) in their work. In this text, we will emphasize the top-down approach to software design.

The top-down approach to software design (also called *stepwise refinement*) instructs us to start at the top level (the original problem) and divide it into subproblems. For each subproblem, we identify a subsystem with the responsibility of solving that subproblem. We can use a *structure chart* to indicate the relationship between the subproblems (and subsystems). For example, a structure chart for our telephone directory problem is shown in Fig. 1.1.

Figure 1.1 shows the two top levels of the structure chart: the original problem and its major subproblems. Each of these subproblems may be further refined and divided into still smaller subproblems. Figure 1.2 shows that to solve the subproblem "Read the initial directory," we must be able to "read an entry" and "store an entry in the directory." Figure 1.3 shows that to solve the subproblem "Retrieve and display an entry," we must be able to "read a name from a user," "find the name in the directory," "get the entry data from the directory," and "display an entry to a user."

Figure 1.1 indicates that we can solve the original problem (Level 0) by providing solutions to four Level 1 subproblems. Figures 1.2 and 1.3 represent the solutions to two Level 1 subproblems in terms of six Level 2 subproblems. For obvious reasons, this approach to problem solving is also called *divide and conquer*.

The second part of the design step of the SLC is to identify the major data structures and procedures for each subproblem. We will use procedural and data abstraction to accomplish this as described in the next section. A subproblem's data structures and procedures together are considered a *program module*, or simply a module.

Exercises for Section 1.2   **Self-Check**

1. List the six steps of the software life cycle. Which step is usually the longest?
2. Draw a structure chart showing the refinement of the subproblem "Insert a new entry."

Figure 1.1
Structure Chart for the
Telephone Directory
Problem

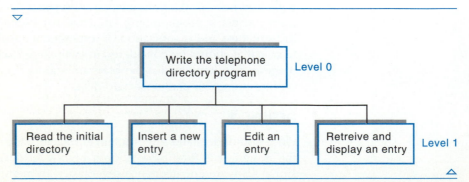

Figure 1.2
Refinement of "Read the initial directory"

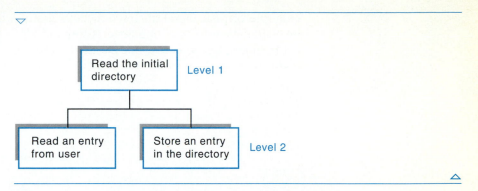

1.3   Using Abstraction to Manage Complexity

Abstraction is a powerful technique that helps programmers (or problem solvers) deal with complex issues in a piecemeal fashion. The dictionary defines *abstraction* as the act or process of separating the inherent qualities or properties of something from the actual physical object to which they belong. One example of the use of abstraction is the description of a program variable (for example, Name and TelNumber) as a storage location in memory for a data value. We need not be concerned with the details of the physical structure of memory; we don't need to know this to use variables in programming.

Procedural Abstraction

In your first course in programming, you practiced *procedural abstraction,* which is the philosophy that procedure development should separate the concern of *what* is to be achieved by a procedure from the details of *how* it is to be achieved. In other words, you can specify what you expect a procedure to do, then use that procedure in the design of a problem solution before you know how to implement the procedure. As an

Figure 1.3
Refinement of "Retrieve and display an entry"

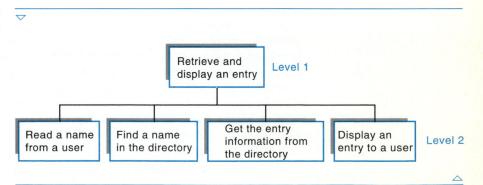

example of procedural abstraction, let's assume that we have procedures available to perform all the Level 2 steps in Fig. 1.3. We can write the Pascal fragment below to retrieve an entry from the directory using these procedures.

```
ReadName ( );              {reads a name}
FindEntry ( );             {sets "pointer" to name if found}
if name is found then  {"pointer" set to name}
  begin
    GetEntry ( );          {retrieves entry from directory}
    DisplayEntry ( )   {displays the entry just retrieved}
  end
else                       {"pointer" not set to name}
  WriteLn ('Search for ', TargetName, 'did not succeed')
```

There are five procedure call statements in the above fragment, including the call to procedure `WriteLn`. The parameter lists would have to be filled in later.

Data Abstraction

In this course, we will make extensive use of another type of abstraction: data abstraction. The idea of data abstraction is to specify the data objects for a problem and the operations to be performed on these data objects without being overly concerned with how they (the data objects) will be represented and stored in memory. We can describe what information is stored in the data object without specifying how the information is organized and represented. This is the *logical view* of the data object, in contrast to its *physical view,* which is the actual internal representation in memory. Once we understand the logical view, we can use the data object and its operators in our programs; however, we (or someone else) will eventually have to implement the data object and its operators before we can run any program that uses them.

You have already practiced data abstraction in that you have used the `Real` data type to represent real numbers without knowing much about the internal representation of this data type on a computer. The Pascal data type `Real` is an abstraction for the set of real numbers. The Pascal data type `Real` represents only a small subset of the real numbers. The computer hardware limits the range of real numbers that can be represented (e.g., positive real numbers in the range 10^{-39} to 10^{38} for IBM personal computers), and not all real numbers within the specified range can be represented on a digital computer. Because not all real numbers can be represented exactly, the results of manipulating real numbers are often only approximations to the actual result. However, for many programming applications, the approximations are close enough to the true results that we can usually use the data type `Real` and its Pascal operators (+,-,*,/,:=,<=,<, and so on), without knowing the details of their implementation.

Information Hiding

One advantage of procedural abstraction and data abstraction is that they enable the designer to make implementation decisions in a piecemeal fashion. The designer can postpone making decisions about the actual internal representation of the data objects and the implementation of its operators. At the top levels of the design, the designer focuses on how to use a data object and its operators; at the lower levels of design, the designer works out the implementation details. In this way, the designer can control or reduce the overall complexity of the problem.

If the details of a data object's implementation are not known when the higher-level module is implemented, the higher-level module can access the data object only through its operators. From a software engineering viewpoint, this is an advantage rather than a limitation. It allows the designer to change his or her mind at a later date and possibly choose a more efficient method of internal representation or implementation. If the higher-level modules reference a data object only through its operators, the higher-level module will not have to be rewritten and might not even need to be recompiled. The process of "hiding" the details of a low-level module's implementation from a higher-level module is called *information hiding*.

As an example of how information hiding works, let's see how we might access the name part of a new entry (called `MyEntry`) for our directory. If we assume that `MyEntry` is a record with a field called `Name`, we could use the qualified identifier

`MyEntry.Name`

As implementation proceeds, we might change our minds and decide to use an array of two strings to hold each entry's name and telephone number. In this case, we would have to go back and change the above reference (and all similar references) to

`MyEntry [1]`

It is much cleaner to hide the structure of an entry and instead use an operator (procedure or function) to retrieve the name string. If function `GetName` is an operator that extracts the name string from its parameter, the statement

`AName := GetName(MyEntry)`

will return the name string stored in `MyEntry` and assign it to `AName` regardless of the internal representation chosen for an entry. If we decide to change the internal representation, we have to change only the body of function `GetName`. We will not need to change any of the higher-level modules that call `GetName`, although we may have to recompile them.

The rest of this chapter assumes that you are familiar with record and array processing in Pascal. If you need to review this material, refer to Sections 3.1 and 3.3.

Self-Check

1. How does information hiding relate to procedural abstraction?
2. How does the logical view of a data object differ from its physical view?

1.4 Abstract Data Types

One of the goals of software engineering is to write *reusable code,* which is code that can be reused in many different applications, preferably without having to be recompiled. One way in which we can do this is to *encapsulate* or combine a data object together with its operators in a separate program module. As we discussed in the previous section, we can manipulate the data object in new programs by calling the operator procedures and functions contained in this module without being concerned about details of their representation and implementation. In this way, we use the module like a building block to construct new application programs. The combination of a data object together with its operators is called an *abstract data type* (ADT).

Figure 1.4 shows a diagram of an abstract data type. The data stored in the ADT are hidden inside the oval wall. The bricks around this wall are used to indicate that these data cannot be accessed except by going through the ADT's operators.

A primary goal of this text is to show you how to write and use abstract data types in programming. As you progress through this course, you will create a large collection of abstract data types in your own program library. Since each abstract data type in your library will already have been coded, debugged, tested, and even compiled, the use of these ADTs will make it much easier for you to design and implement new applications programs.

Many versions of Pascal, including Borland Pascal, provide the capability of separate compilation for modules that contain abstract data types. If

Figure 1.4
Diagram of an ADT

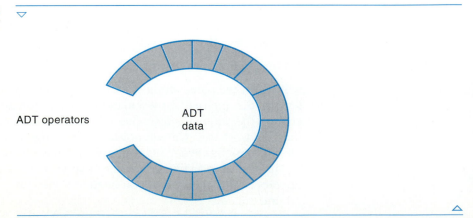

ADT operators

ADT data

we compile the abstract data type, then we can link its executable code with other programs that use it. If we were careful to include a fairly complete set of operator procedures in the abstract data type, the module containing the abstract data type will not have to be recompiled for each new application.

An abstract data type normally consists of two parts: its specification and its implementation. The *specification part* describes the structure of the data object and the capabilities of its operators. The specification part contains all the information that Pascal needs to link the abstract data type to another program. It also contains the information that a potential user of the abstract data type needs to know. The *implementation part* contains the actual implementation of the operators, which are hidden from users of the abstract data type. Development of two ADT specifications is described next.

CASE STUDY   ## Setting Up a Telephone Directory

In this section, we will illustrate how to use data abstraction and abstract data types to help design the solution to a programming problem.

PROBLEM ▼

We want to store in our computer a simple telephone directory that we can use for storage and retrieval of names and numbers. The telephone directory contains a growing collection of names and telephone numbers. Initially, we want to create the directory by entering the names and numbers of people whom we frequently call from a data file. Later, we would want to be able to insert new names and numbers, change some numbers, and retrieve selected telephone numbers.

INPUT/OUTPUT REQUIREMENTS ▼

Earlier, we discussed some questions that would have to be answered to complete the requirements specification for this problem. Most of the questions dealt with input and output considerations. We will list the answers to these questions next.

Inputs

Initial Phone Directory

Each name and number will be read from separate lines of a text file. The entries will be read one after the other until all entries are read.

Additional Entries

Each entry is typed by the user at the keyboard when requested.

Outputs

Individual Phone Numbers

The name and number of each person selected by the program user are displayed on separate output lines.

Current Phone Directory

The name and number of all entries in the directory are written on separate lines of a text file.

DATA STRUCTURE DESIGN ▼

There are really two distinct but related data objects to consider: the directory as a whole and each individual entry. We can define each of these data objects as an abstract data type.

The operations that you might want to perform on an individual entry are the following.

Operators for Data Entry Object

▶ Read and store data for a new entry.
▶ Display an existing entry.
▶ Check the name of an entry.
▶ Retrieve the name of an entry.
▶ Retrieve the phone number of an entry.

The operations that you might want to perform on the directory as a whole are the following.

Operators for the Directory Object

▶ Create a new directory.
▶ Read all the original entries into the directory from a text file.
▶ Insert a new entry in the directory.
▶ Edit an entry in the directory.
▶ Delete an entry from the directory.
▶ Find a particular entry in the directory.
▶ Write the directory contents to a text file.

The data entry object contains the operators required for our particular application—a telephone directory. In contrast, the directory object is a general object that could be used in many different applications. Although we are using it to store a telephone directory in this case, it could be used to house other lists of information. To emphasize the generic nature of this object, we will refer to it as a linear list from now on. Next, we provide a more formal specification for the two data objects, Entry and LinearList.

SPECIFICATION FOR ADT ENTRY ▼

Each entry consists of a person's name and a telephone number. We will assume that both of these data items are character strings. Not every version of Pascal allows strings to be read or displayed using procedures `Read` or `Write`, so we will include ADT operators for these tasks. Table 1.1 provides a specification for an ADT entry. The descriptions of the operators use the following parameters:

```
AnEntry is type Entry
AName is a name string
ANumber is a phone number string
```

Table 1.1
Specification for
ADT Entry

Operators

Init (var AnEntry, AName, ANumber)

Stores `AName` and `ANumber` in `AnEntry`.

ReadEntry (var AnEntry)

Reads a name and phone number from the keyboard into an entry.

DisplayEntry (AnEntry)

Displays a name and phone number on the terminal screen.

EqualName (AnEntry, AName)

(function) Tests whether `AName` is the name of `AnEntry`.

GetName (AnEntry)

(function) Retrieves the name associated with an entry.

GetNumber (AnEntry)

(function) Retrieves the number associated with an entry.

Operators `Init` and `ReadEntry` are used to store data in an entry. Operator `DisplayEntry` displays an entry. Operators `GetName` and `GetNumber` retrieve the data values stored in an entry.

SPECIFICATION FOR ADT LINEARLIST ▼

The telephone directory is a collection of items of type `Entry`. As part of the directory, we want to maintain a count of the number of entries currently in the directory. We will also maintain a pointer, called a *cursor,* that keeps track of our place in the directory. The position of the cursor at any time represents the "internal state" of the directory. At any instant, we can access only the entry selected by the cursor (called the *active entry*). Table 1.2 shows the specification for the telephone directory abstract data type. The descriptions of the operators use the following parameters:

```
Directory (type LinearList)
AnEntry (type Entry)
```

Table 1.2
LinearList Abstract
Data Type

Operators

Create (var Directory)

Creates a directory that is initially empty, sets the count of entries to zero, and initializes the cursor to the first available directory position.

ReadLinearList (var Directory)

Reads the original entries from a text file and stores them in the directory in the order in which they were read, counting the number of entries stored. After the last entry is stored, the cursor points to the next available directory position.

Insert (var Directory, AnEntry)

Inserts a new entry at the end of the directory, advancing the cursor to the next available directory position and increasing the count of entries by one.

WriteLinearList (Directory)

Writes all directory entries to a file. The entries are written in the order stored, and each entry is written on two separate lines of the file.

GetEntry (Directory, var AnEntry)

Retrieves the entry that is currently at the cursor position. The cursor position and count are unchanged.

PutEntry (var Directory, AnEntry)

Stores `AnEntry` into `Directory` at the position selected by the cursor over-writing the entry at that position. The cursor position and count are unchanged.

GetCount (Directory)

(function) Returns the count of entries in `Directory`.

Operators for Moving and Testing the Cursor

GoFirstEntry (var Directory)

Moves the cursor to the first entry in the directory.

GoLastEntry (var Directory)

Moves the cursor to the last entry in the directory.

Table 1.2
LinearList Abstract
Data Type
(*Cont.*)

> ### *GoNextEntry (var Directory)*
>
> Moves the cursor to the next entry in the directory.
>
> ### *GoFindEntry (Directory, AnEntry)*
>
> Moves the cursor to the entry with the same name as `AnEntry`. Cursor will point to the first available position following the last directory entry if `AnEntry` is not found in the directory.
>
> ### *EndOfLinearList (Directory)*
>
> (function) Tests the cursor position. Returns True if the cursor points to a position after the last entry in the directory; returns `False` if the cursor points to an entry in the directory. The function returns True after execution of operator `CreateLinearList`, `ReadLinearList`, `WriteLinearList`, or `Insert`.

Operators `GoFirstEntry`, `GoLastEntry`, `GoNextEntry`, and `GoFindEntry` in Table 1.2 are used to change the internal state of the directory by moving the cursor. For example, operator `GoFirstEntry` moves the cursor to the first entry in the directory; operator `GoNextEntry` advances the cursor from its current position to the next entry in the directory.

Function `EndOfLinearList` is a Boolean function that tests whether the cursor has passed the last entry in the directory (returns True if it has; otherwise, returns False). The function should return a value of True right after the directory is created, after all original entries are read, and after an insertion at the end of the directory. We cannot access the cursor position or move the cursor in any way except through the use of the directory operators. Note that there is no operator `GetCursor` because we have no need to access the cursor value.

USING THE ABSTRACT DATA TYPE OPERATORS ▼

To show how these operators work, we will describe how to perform a few different operations on a phone directory named `MyDirectory` (type LinearList).

First, to build a new directory, we should use the operator sequence

```
CreateLinearList (MyDirectory);
ReadLinearList (MyDirectory)
```

To read a new entry into variable `MyEntry` (type `Entry`) and insert it at the end of `MyDirectory`, we can use the operator sequence

```
ReadEntry (NextEntry);
InsertEntry (MyDirectory, NextEntry)
```

Operator `ReadEntry` reads the new entry, and operator `InsertEntry` inserts it in the directory as shown in Fig. 1.5. The original directory appears on the left, and the new directory appears on the right.

Figure 1.5

Inserting an Entry at the
End of a Directory

```
              Bill    555-123-4567              Bill    555-123-4567
              Sam     555-123-5678              Sam     555-123-5678
              Carol   555-123-6789              Carol   555-123-6789
Cursor →                                        Robin   555-222-3333
                                     Cursor →
                                              after ReadEntry,
                                                    InsertEntry
```

To change the phone number associated with a particular entry (for example, to change Sam's number to 555–123–1111), we can use the sequence

```
ReadEntry (Target);
GoFindEntry (ADirectory, Target);
if not EndOfDirectory(ADirectory) then
  PutEntry (ADirectory, Target)
```

Operator ReadEntry reads Sam's name and new telephone number into Target. Operator GoFindEntry moves the cursor to the directory entry for Sam. Sam is in the directory, so function EndOfLinearList returns False (not EndOfLinearList is True), and operator PutEntry places Sam's name and new number in the directory. Figure 1.6 shows the effect of GoFindEntry and PutEntry.

If we want to retrieve a particular entry from the directory (for example, Bill's data), we can use the operator sequence

```
Init (Target, 'Bill', '');
GoFindEntry (ADirectory, Target);
if not EndOfDirectory(ADirectory) then
  begin
    GetEntry (ADirectory, Target);
    GetNumber (Target, PhoneNumber)
  end
```

We use operator Init to define a target entry whose name is Bill and whose number is the null string (''). Operator GoFindEntry moves the cursor to Bill's entry if it is in the directory; otherwise, operator GoFindEntry

Figure 1.6

Changing Sam's Phone
Number

```
              Bill    555-123-4567                 Bill    555-123-4567
Cursor →Sam   555-123-5678       Cursor →Sam       555-111-2222
              Carol   555-123-6789                 Carol   555-123-6789
              Robin   555-222-3333                 Robin   555-222-3333

         after GoFindEntry         after PutEntry
```

moves the cursor past the last entry in the directory. If Bill's entry is found (EndOfLinearList is False), GetEntry retrieves the entry, and GetNumber retrieves its phone number.

Notice that we can describe how to use these operators to manipulate our directory without having the slightest idea how the directory is actually represented in memory and how the operators are implemented. This is the whole idea of data abstraction and information hiding. The operator descriptions do not rely on any particular representation of the directory. This means that we can use them in the same way regardless of the choices made later for the internal representation of the directory or the implementation of its operators.

One of the limitations of using standard Pascal to implement abstract data types is that it does not allow separate compilation of program modules. In standard Pascal, reusing a program module involves using an editor to copy the desired program text into a new program source file and then recompiling the program as a single file. In the next two sections, we describe two Borland Pascal language features that facilitate the implementation of abstract data types: units and objects. We will discuss units first.

Exercises for Section 1.4

Self-Check

1. What are the two components of an abstract data type?
2. How is information hiding related to data abstraction?

1.5 Procedure Libraries and Units

As you progress through this course, you will write many Pascal programs and procedures. You should try to keep each new procedure as general as possible so that you can reuse it in other applications. You will eventually build up a sizable library of your own procedures. Reusing tried and tested procedures is always much more efficient than starting from scratch; each new procedure that you write will have to be thoroughly tested and debugged, requiring a lot of startup time in every case. The procedures in your personal library will already have been tested; using these procedures over and over again will save you time.

As an example, it would be useful to have a set of procedures available for performing some common data entry operations. Since procedure ReadLn cannot be used to read Boolean values, it would be useful to have our own procedure, say, ReadLnBool, for this purpose. Procedure ReadLnBool should read a character value and return either True or False on the basis of the data character. ReadLnBool should certainly be included in a programmer's library.

In many situations, we would like a data value to lie within a specific sub-range of values. For example, we might like to enter a character that is an uppercase letter or an integer in the range −10 to +10. We can write a procedure called `EnterInt` to accomplish the latter operation. You could easily write similar procedures, called `EnterChar` and `EnterReal`, for the other standard data types of Pascal. These procedures would be useful additions to a programmer's library.

The Borland Pascal unit facilitates the collection of a group of useful procedures into a library. A `unit` is a program module that may be separately compiled. If a unit consists of a collection of procedures, the procedures in the unit can be reused by other programs (called *clients*) without having to be recompiled. Borland Pascal will automatically link the object code for any procedures that are needed in a specified unit to the object code for the new program just before program execution.

Figure 1.7 shows a Borland Pascal unit called `MyTools` with the two procedures that we just discussed. The details of the procedures are not important now; concentrate on the unit structure. A unit resembles a Pascal program. Like a Pascal program, it can be compiled, but it cannot be executed. The first line of a unit begins with the reserved word `unit` instead of

Figure 1.7
Unit `MyTools`

Directory: CHAP 1
File: MYTOOLS.PAS

```
unit MyTools;
{
  Contains library of useful procedures.
}
interface
  procedure ReadLnBool (var BoolVal, Success {output} : Boolean);
  {
    Reads a Boolean value (represented by a T or F) into
    BoolVal and sets the flag Success.
    Pre : None
    Post: BoolVal is set to True if T or t is read; otherwise,
          BoolVal is set to False. Success is set to True only
          if one of the four characters T, t, F, or f is read.
  }

  procedure EnterInt (MinN, MaxN {input} : Integer;
                      var N {output} : Integer;
                      var Success {output} : Boolean);
  {
    Reads an integer between MinN and MaxN into N.
    Pre : MinN and maxN are assigned values.
    Post: Returns in N first data value between MinN and MaxN
          and sets Success to True if MinN <= MaxN is True;
          otherwise, N is not defined and Success is set to False.
  }
```

▷ ▷ ▷ ▷ ▷

```
implementation
  procedure ReadLnBool (var BoolVal, Success {output} :
    Boolean);
    var
      NextChar : Char;    {a data character}
  begin {ReadLnBool}
    Write ('Type T or F> ');
    ReadLn (NextChar);
    BoolVal := (NextChar = 'T') or (NextChar = 't');
    Success := BoolVal or (NextChar = 'F') or (NextChar = 'f')
  end; {ReadLnBool}

  procedure EnterInt (MinN, MaxN {input} : Integer;
                      var N {output} : Integer;
                      var Success {output} : Boolean);
  begin {EnterInt}
    if MinN <= MaxN then
      begin
        {no valid value in N as yet}
        Success := False;
        {keep reading until valid number is read}
        while not Success do
          begin
            Write ('Enter an integer between ');
            Write (MinN :3, ' and ', MaxN :3, '> ');
            ReadLn (N);
            Success := (MinN <= N) and (N <= MaxN)
          end {while}
      end {valid range}
    else
      begin
        WriteLn ('Error - empty range for EnterInt');
        Success := False
      end {bad range limits}
  end; {EnterInt}

end. {MyTools}
```

program, and the last line of a unit is end. A unit consists of an interface section followed by an implementation section.

The *interface section* of a unit begins with the reserved word interface. It is called the *public part* of a unit because it contains all the information that a programmer needs to know to use the unit. It also contains all declarations that the Turbo Pascal compiler requires to check that the procedures of a unit are being called correctly by a client program or another unit.

The identifiers that are declared in the interface section can be referenced outside of the unit, so they are considered *visible*. Any constant, type, and variable declarations are written by using the usual Pascal syntax. For function and procedures, only the headings and documentation appear in the interface section.

The *implementation section* contains complete declarations for functions and procedures. Additional identifiers may also be declared in the implementation section. These new identifiers are not visible outside the unit. Consequently, the implementation section is called the *private part* of the unit, and the procedure and function bodies and any new identifiers are *hidden* from the client.

The end of a unit is indicated by the line

```
end.
```

There is no need to have a corresponding `begin` unless the unit has an initialization section. The *initialization section* is optional and is used to assign initial values to any variables that are declared in the unit. If present, the initialization section is always executed before any client of the unit. This is the reason why two units cannot be clients of one another.

The syntax display for a Borland Pascal unit follows. The example shows a unit consisting of a procedure and function for swapping two numbers and retrieving the larger of the two items.

SYNTAX DISPLAY

Unit Definition

Form:
```
unit unitname;

interface
  uses unit list;
  public declarations;

implementation
  uses unit list;
  private declarations;

  initialization section

end.
```
Example:
```
unit TwoItems;

interface
  procedure SwapTwo (var X, Y {input/output} : Real);
  {Swaps two real values.}

  function GetLarger (X, Y : Real) : Real;
  {Returns the larger of its two arguments.}

implementation
  procedure SwapTwo (var X, Y {input/output} : Real);
    var Temp : Real;
    begin {SwapTwo}
      Temp := X;
      X := Y;
      Y := Temp
    end; {SwapTwo}
```

```
function GetLarger (X, Y : Real) : Real;
begin {GetLarger}
  if X > Y then
    GetLarger := X
  else
    GetLarger := Y
end; {GetLarger}

end. {TwoItems}
```

Interpretation: Unit *unitname* is a separate program module that can be compiled to disk and then used by other units or programs. The *interface section* may contain *public declarations*. Identifiers declared in the interface section can be referenced by any program or unit that lists *unitname* in its uses statement. Only procedure headers appear in the interface section; the full procedure declarations appear in the *implementation section*.

The *implementation section* may contain its own declarations (called *private declarations*). Any additional identifiers that are declared in the implementation section cannot be referenced outside unit *unitname*.

If present, the *initialization section* starts with the reserved word begin, and it is used to initialize any variables declared in the unit. It executes before the client program.

Notes: A semicolon should not appear after the interface or implementation line.

The uses Statement

The client of a unit may be a program or another unit. A client program or client unit must list all units that it references in a uses statement. The client can reference only the public identifiers of units listed in its uses statement. When it appears in a client program, the uses statement must come directly after the program statement.

When it appears in a client unit, a uses statement may come directly after the interface line, after the implementation line, or after both. If a unit is listed in a uses statement after the interface line, its public identifiers may be referenced anywhere in the client unit. If a unit is listed in a uses statement after the implementation line, its public identifiers may be referenced only in the implementation part of the client unit. A unit can be listed in only one uses statement in a client unit.

SYNTAX DISPLAY

uses **Statement**

Form: uses *unitlist;*
Example: uses Printer, Crt, EnterData;
Interpretation: The uses statement instructs the Turbo Pascal compiler to link the previously compiled units, listed in *unitlist,* to the program unit being compiled. When the uses statement appears in a program, it must be the first statement after the program statement. A uses statement may appear right after the interface and implementation lines of a unit.

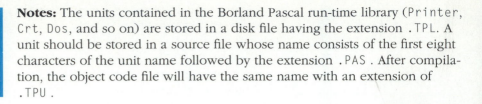

Notes: The units contained in the Borland Pascal run-time library (`Printer`, `Crt`, `Dos`, and so on) are stored in a disk file having the extension `.TPL`. A unit should be stored in a source file whose name consists of the first eight characters of the unit name followed by the extension `.PAS`. After compilation, the object code file will have the same name with an extension of `.TPU`.

We have mentioned that it is possible to include both variable and type declarations in units. This would seem to make units the ideal means by which to implement ADTs. As we will discuss in the next section, Borland Pascal units by themselves do not provide enough protection to prevent direct access of the ADT data without calling the ADT operators.

Exercises for Section 1.5   *Programming*

1. Add a procedure `EnterReal` to unit `MyTools` that reads a real data value between a specified range of real numbers.
2. Write a client program that tests the procedures from unit `MyTools`.

1.6 Object-Oriented Programming

Object-oriented programming (OOP) has become very popular in the past few years. One important reason for this is that object-oriented programming facilitates writing reusable programming modules. A second reason is the availability of objects in languages like Borland Pascal, Object Pascal, and C++.

Borland Pascal allows the programmer to encapsulate a data type declaration, along with declarations for operators that manipulate variables of this type, into an indivisible whole known as an *object*. As we will show in Chapter 3, objects may be defined in a hierarchical manner with descendant types inheriting attributes from their ancestral types. Objects are a natural means of implementing abstract data types.

A major application of object-oriented programming has been the development of reusable modules used in constructing graphical user interfaces (GUIs). Borland Pascal is distributed with an object library known as Turbo Vision. Turbo Vision contains the library of objects that Borland uses to construct the user interface for Borland Pascal's integrated development environment.

Programmers rely on abstraction as their primary tool for dealing with the complex task of writing a large computer program. You may have discovered in your previous programming work that you could often begin the task of writing a new program by editing a program that you had written previously or by modifying a program in the text. Many computer scientists have wondered why software construction cannot be more like the construction of physical objects, which are typically assembled by using off-the-shelf components. Using the data-typing mechanisms found in procedural programming languages (like standard Pascal), programmers cannot develop completely reusable software components that do not rely on at least some implementation knowledge. Programming languages that contain object definition facilities allow programmers to develop software that can be reused more easily.

Let's consider the shortcomings of Borland Pascal units as a means of implementing abstract data types. If a variable of type LinearList is declared in a client module, it is available to all routines within the scope of the client module. This means that the contents of this variable can be manipulated directly by any routine without importing or using any of its data type operators. We can place the directory variable declaration in the implementation part of the `LinearListADT` unit to prevent direct access to its contents, but then a client module could use only one variable of this type. If we did not use objects and we want to change our directory entry type, we would have to recompile both ADT units. Without objects, the directory operator names must be unique, which means that two units containing different operator names are required to use directories with two different types of entries in the same client program.

Languages that support object-oriented programming attempt to overcome these shortcomings by focusing on data values instead of data operations. The object-oriented view is that the data should be fixed and that the client program will send a message to a given piece of data to tell it what needs to be done without being concerned about how the operation is to be carried out. For example, in a graphics program, it is reasonable to assume that each graphical object should know how to draw itself on the screen regardless of how it has been implemented. Each graphical object is free to respond to a draw message in its own way.

In this same spirit, object-oriented programming languages allow *name overloading,* which leads to improved program readability by allowing operator names to have multiple meanings in the same program. For example, an operator push can mean one thing to a stack (Chapter 5) and something completely different to a robot arm. Object types can be defined so that their data elements can be manipulated only by their operators (known as *methods*). This makes objects ideally suited as a means of implementing abstract data types. Object-oriented programming languages also allow groups of related object types (or *classes*) to be defined in such a way that the features common to each object type can be reused (or *inherited*) rather than copied and edited as we have to do with units.

Although a complete discussion of *object-oriented design* (OOD) is beyond the scope of this text, we do introduce and use OOD concepts as needed throughout the book. For example, we cover inheritance in Section 3.5. Next we list the steps in object-oriented design methodology.

1. Identify the objects and define services to be provided by each.
2. Identify the interactions among objects in terms of services required and services provided.

3. Establish the visibility of each object in relation to other objects.
4. Determine the interface for each object.
5. Implement each object.

Unlike traditional software design, there is no sharp division between the analysis and design phases. In fact, in object-oriented design, programmers often follow the prototyping design practice of designing a little, implementing a little, and testing a little rather than attempting to build a complete piece of software all at once.

In the next section of this text, we will introduce some of the object-oriented programming features found in Borland Pascal and show how they can be used to implement two abstract data types. Object types can provide better protection against unauthorized access of ADT data. ADTs implemented as Borland Pascal objects are also more highly reusable than ADTs implemented as ordinary units.

Exercises for Section 1.6   *Self-Check*

1. How do the object-oriented software design steps differ from the steps of the software development method discussed in Section 1.2?
2. List the shortcomings of Borland Pascal units as a means for implementing abstract data types.

1.7   Encapsulating Objects in Units

An object type enables us to encapsulate data fields and operators (called *methods*) in a single type declaration. The type declarations in Fig. 1.8 contain a declaration for object type `Entry`, which represents an entry in our telephone directory. Object type `Entry` begins with a list of headers for the object's *method members* (`ReadEntry`, `Init`, and so on). These methods are the operators that can be called to process a variable (called an object instance) of type `Entry`. In Fig. 1.8, the reserved word `private` precedes the declaration of the object's *data members* (`Name` and `Number`).

The reserved word `private` separates the object's public part from its private part. The identifiers in the public part, the object's method members, may be referenced by clients of the abstract data type so they are visible outside the object. The identifiers in the private part, the data members, can be referenced only within the abstract data type or by its methods, so they are hidden from all clients of the abstract data type. Notice that there must be a semicolon after the last method member and after the last data member.

It is possible to declare private method members, which can be used only by other methods declared in the same unit and cannot be used directly by a client program. It is also possible to have public data members, which are

```
type
  Entry = object
          procedure Init (AName, ANumber {input} : string);
          procedure ReadEntry;
          procedure DisplayEntry;
          function GetName : string;
          function GetNumber : string;
          function EqualName (AName : string) : Boolean;

      private
        Name,
        Number : string;
      end; {Entry}
```

accessible to a client program without using any of the object's methods. However, this is contrary to our purpose in encapsulating an object inside a unit.

Figure 1.9 shows a diagram of object type Entry as described in Fig. 1.8. As with any ADT, an external module can access the object's data members only through its method members.

You might notice that the procedure headers in Fig. 1.8 do not correspond exactly with the operator descriptions shown in Table 1.1. For example, the method header

```
procedure ReadEntry;
```

is used for method ReadEntry. However, in Table 1.1, we described operator ReadEntry as

Figure 1.9
Sketch of Object Type
Entry

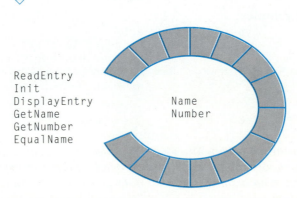

```
ReadEntry
Init
DisplayEntry          Name
GetName               Number
GetNumber
EqualName
```

```
ReadEntry (var AnEntry): Reads a name and phone number into
an entry.
```

In this description, the variable parameter `AnEntry` represents the telephone entry to be read by `ReadEntry` and returned to its caller. No parameter list is shown in the method header for `ReadEntry` in Fig. 1.8 because we always precede a method with the name of the object instance to which it is being applied. Therefore we would use the call

```
AnEntry.ReadEntry
```

to read a name and phone number into object instance `AnEntry` instead of passing `AnEntry` as a parameter to `ReadEntry`. For this reason, all references to parameter `AnEntry` have been omitted from the parameter lists in Fig. 1.8. In object-oriented programming terminology, we say that method `ReadEntry` is sending a *message* to object instance `AnEntry`.

The following method calls could be used to read an entry from the keyboard into object instance Pres (type Entry) and check whether that entry contains the telephone number of the President inaugurated in 1993: 'Clinton, Bill'.

```
Pres.ReadEntry;
if Pres.EqualName('Clinton, Bill') then
   WriteLn ('The president"s telephone number is ',
            Pres.GetNumber)
else
   WriteLn ('The entry just read is not Clinton, Bill"s');
```

SYNTAX DISPLAY

Object Type Declaration

```
type object type = object
                 data member list;
                 method heading list;
               private
                 data member list;
                 method heading list;
               end;
```

Examples:

```
type Point = object
                 procedure Init (X1, Y1 : Real);
                 function DistanceOrigin : Real;
                 function GetX : Real;
                 function GetY : Real;

             private
                 X, Y : Real;
             end; {Point}
```

Interpretation: The identifier *object type* is an object with method members (described in the *method heading list*) and data members (described in the *data member list*). The *data member list* is similar to the *field list* appearing in a record type declaration. The *method header list* consists of a list of procedure and function headers only.

The reserved word `private` indicates that the method members and data members that follow are for internal use only and cannot be referenced outside the unit in which the object type is declared. When declared in a unit, the object type declaration appears in the *interface section* of the unit, and the complete method declarations appear in the *implementation section* of the unit, as discussed next.

Declaring Objects in Units

The unit is an ideal program structure for implementing abstract data types. Figure 1.10 shows a Borland Pascal unit, `EntryADT`, which implements an entry for the telephone directory as an abstract data type. The unit's interface section corresponds to the specification part of an ADT, and the implementation section corresponds to the implementation part of an ADT.

The interface section contains the object type declaration shown in Fig. 1.8 including all its method headers. Except for private identifiers, the identifiers declared in the interface section (object type `Entry` and its methods) are visible outside the unit. The identifiers declared in the private part of object type `Entry` (data members `Name` and `Number`) are not visible outside of the unit.

Figure 1.10
Unit `EntryADT`

Directory: CHAP 1
File: ENTRYADT.PAS

```
unit EntryADT;

interface

{Insert declaration for object type Entry. See Fig. 1.8 }

implementation

  procedure Entry.Init (AName, ANumber {input} : string);
  {
   Stores AName and ANumber into an entry.
   Pre : AName and ANumber are defined.
   Post: AName and ANumber are stored in an instance of
         object type Entry.
  }
  begin {Init}
    Name := AName;
    Number := ANumber
  end; {Init}
```

▷ ▷ ▷ ▷ ▷

```
procedure Entry.ReadEntry;
{
 Reads a name and phone number into an entry.
 Pre : None
 Post: Two strings are read into an instance of object
       type Entry.
}
begin {ReadEntry}
  Write ('Name >');
  ReadLn (Name);
  Write ('Number >');
  ReadLn (Number)
end; {ReadEntry}

function Entry.GetNumber : string;
{Returns value of object data member Number.}
begin {GetNumber}
  GetNumber := Number
end; {GetNumber}

function Entry.GetName : string;
{Returns value of object data member Name.}
begin {GetName}
  GetName := Name
end; {GetName}

procedure Entry.DisplayEntry;
{Displays values of data members Name and Number.}
begin {DisplayEntry}
  WriteLn ('Name is ', Name);
  WriteLn ('Number is ', Number);
end;

function Entry.EqualName (AName : string) : Boolean;
{Tests whether AName matches object data member Name.}
begin {EqualName}
  EqualName := (Name = AName)
end; {DisplayEntry}

end. {EntryADT}
```

The implementation section contains complete declarations for object `Entry`'s method members. The object type, `Entry`, *qualifies* each method header in the implementation section (e.g., `Entry.ReadEntry`). The object data member or field names (`Name` and `Number` for type `Entry`) appear without qualification in the method declarations. When each method is called, the object instance that activates the method will be specified. For example, if we use the method call

```
Pres.Init ('Washington, George', 'unlisted')
```

the assignment statement

```
Name := AName;
```

in `Init` will assign the string 'Washington, George' (value of `AName`) to the `Name` field of object instance `Pres`.

Preconditions and Postconditions

Each method declaration begins with a series of comment lines that describe the result of the method's call and conditions that must be true before and after the method is called. The comment line labeled Pre : (for *precondition*) describes the condition that must be true before the method is called; the comment line labeled Post: (for *postcondition*) describes the condition that must be true after the method execution is completed.

You might say that the preconditions and postconditions serve as an informal contract between the method member and any program that uses it. The precondition indicates any expectations the method may have with respect to its parameters. The postcondition tells what the method does and what will happen to its parameters if the precondition is met. All bets are off if the precondition is not met. Therefore the calling program must check to make sure that all actual parameters satisfy the method preconditions before each call. The use of explicit preconditions and postconditions provides valuable documentation to another programmer who might want to use the method.

Unit for LinearListADT

The final step is to implement an abstract data type to house our telephone directory. The interface section can be easily written by referring to the specification given in Table 1.2. We will discuss the interface section (see Fig. 1.11) next.

The first line of the interface section

```
uses EntryADT; {imports object type Entry and its methods}
```

indicates that unit `LinearListADT` is a client of unit `EntryADT`. Next we declare the constant `MaxEntry` (100) and object type `LinearList`. The object declaration shows 12 public method members and three private data members. The first data member (`Entries`) is an array that is used to store the individual directory entries. The two integer data members represent the number of items currently in the directory (`Count`) and the current position in the directory (`Cursor`). The implementation section (see Fig. 1.12) provides declarations for the method members.

Procedure `CreateLinearList` simply sets the count of entries to zero and sets the cursor to 1. `CreateLinearList` should be called before reading the initial entries into a directory.

Figure 1.11
Interface Section for
`LinearListADT`

Directory: CHAP 1
File: LINEARLI.PAS

▽

```
unit LinearListADT;

interface
  uses EntryADT; {imports object type Entry and its methods}

const
  MaxEntry = 10;

type
  EntryRange = 1..MaxEntry;
  EntryArray = array [EntryRange] of Entry;

  LinearList = object
                procedure CreateLinearList;
                procedure ReadLinearList;
                procedure Insert (AnEntry {input} : Entry);
                function GetCount : Integer;
                procedure GetEntry (var AnEntry {output} : Entry);
                procedure PutEntry (AnEntry {input} : Entry);
                procedure WriteLinearList;
                procedure GoFindEntry (AnEntry {input} : Entry);
                procedure GoFirstEntry;
                procedure GoNextEntry;
                procedure GoLastEntry;
                function EndOfLinearList : Boolean;

              private
                Entries : EntryArray;    {array of entries}
                Count : Integer;         {number of entries}
                Cursor : Integer;        {current position in array}
              end; {LinearList}
```

△

Procedure `ReadLinearList` reads the directory name of the file containing the directory into string variable `FileName`, associates that name with the internal file variable `InFile` (type `Text`), and resets that file. Next, `ReadEntry` reads a pair of data strings from the input file into `InName` and `InNumber`, and the statements

```
InEntry.Init (InName, InNumber);
Next := Next + 1;
Entries[Next] := InEntry
```

store these data strings in `InEntry` (type `Entry`) and in the next element of the array of entries. Notice that the reference to method `Init` must be

```
implementation

  procedure LinearList.CreateLinearList;
  {
   Creates an initially empty linear list.
   Pre : None.
   Post: Count is 0 and Cursor set to first available position.
  }
  begin {CreateLinearList}
    Count := 0;
    Cursor := 1
  end; {CreateLinearList}

  procedure LinearList.ReadLinearList;
  {
   Reads a data file into a linear list.
   Pre : File exists and list is initialized and empty.
   Post: Data file entries stored in list in the order read,
         Count set to number of entries read, and Cursor set to
         next available list position.
  }
    var
      Next : Integer;          {next subscript for a new entry}
      InEntry : Entry;         {a new entry}
      InFile : Text;           {internal file variable}
      FileName : string[12];   {directory name of input file}
      InName : string;         {each entry name}
      InNumber : string;       {each entry number}

  begin {ReadLinearList}
    WriteLn ('Enter the name of the text file that');
    Write ('contains the linear list >');
    ReadLn (FileName);
    Assign (InFile, FileName);
    Reset (InFile);
    Next := 0;
    while not EOF(InFile) do
      begin
        ReadLn (InFile, InName);
        ReadLn (InFile, InNumber);
        InEntry.Init (InName, InNumber);
        Next := Next + 1;
        Entries[Next] := InEntry
      end; {while}

    Count := Next;
    Cursor := Next + 1
  end; {ReadLinearList}

  procedure LinearList.Insert (AnEntry {input} : Entry);
  {
```

▷ ▷ ▷ ▷ ▷ ▷

```
   Inserts entry AnEntry into a linear list.
   Pre : List exists and Cursor points to available position
         at end of list.
   Post: Inserts new entry at end of list, increases Count
         by 1, and advances Cursor to next list position.
}
begin {Insert}
  Count := Count + 1;
  Entries[Count] := AnEntry;
  Cursor := Count + 1
end; {Insert}

function LinearList.GetCount : Integer;
{Returns the count of entries in linear list}
begin {GetCount}
  GetCount := Count
end; {GetCount}

procedure LinearList.GoFindEntry (AnEntry {input} : Entry);
{
 Searches linear list for entry with same name as AnEntry.
 Pre : List has been initialized and AnEntry defined.
 Post: If found, that entry becomes the active entry pointed
       to by Cursor; otherwise Cursor points to position
       following end of list.
}
var
  Found : Boolean;
  Next : Integer;

begin {GoFindEntry}
  Found := False;
  Next := 1;
  while (not Found) and (Next <= Count) do
    if AnEntry.EqualName(Entries[Next].GetName) then
      Found := True
    else
      Next := Next + 1;

  {Define Cursor value}
  Cursor := Next
end; {GoFindEntry}

procedure LinearList.GoFirstEntry;
{
 Makes the first entry of a linear list the active entry.
 Pre : List initialized and non-empty.
 Post: Cursor points to list position 1.
}
begin {GoFirstEntry}
  Cursor := 1
end; {GoFirstEntry}
```

▷ ▷ ▷ ▷ ▷

```
procedure LinearList.GoNextEntry;
{
 Advances the cursor to the next entry of list.
 Pre : List is initialized and non-empty.
 Post: Cursor value incremented by 1.
}
begin {GoNextEntry}
  Cursor := Cursor + 1
end; {GoNextEntry}

procedure LinearList.GoLastEntry;
{
 Makes the next position following the last linear list
 entry the active entry.
 Pre : List initialized and non-empty.
 Post: Cursor points to next available position following the
       last list entry.
}
begin {GoLastEntry}
  Cursor := Count + 1
end; {GoLastEntry}

function LinearList.EndOfLinearList : Boolean;
{
 Returns true if the cursor has passed the last entry
 of a linear list.
}
begin {EndOfLinearList}
  EndOfLinearList := (Cursor > Count)
end; {EndOfLinearList}

procedure LinearList.GetEntry (var AnEntry {output} : Entry);
{
 Returns the active entry of a linear list through AnEntry.
 Pre : List initialized and Cursor points to valid list entry.
 Post: Entry pointed by Cursor copied to AnEntry.
}
begin {GetEntry}
  AnEntry := Entries[Cursor]
end; {GetEntry}

procedure LinearList.PutEntry (AnEntry {input} : Entry);
{
 Stores AnEntry into linear list at the active entry.
 Pre : List is initialized and Cursor points to valid list
       position.
 Post: AnEntry overwrites list entry stored in position
       pointed to by Cursor.
}
begin {PutEntry}
  Entries[Cursor] := AnEntry
end; {PutEntry}
```

▷ ▷ ▷ ▷ ▷ ▷

```
procedure LinearList.WriteLinearList;
{
 Writes the linear list to the screen.
 Pre : List initialized.
 Post: List entries displayed on screen in the order stored.
}
  var
    AnEntry : Entry;

begin {WriteLinearList}
  GoFirstEntry;                    {start with first entry}
  while not EndOfLinearList do
    begin
      GetEntry (AnEntry);          {access current entry}
      AnEntry.DisplayEntry;
      GoNextEntry                  {advance to next entry}
    end {while}
end; {WriteLinearList}

end. {LinearListADT}
```

△

qualified by object instance `InEntry` because `Init` is a method of object `Entry`, not object `LinearList`. After storing the last entry, `ReadEntry` stores the count of entries in `Count` and advances `Cursor` just past the last entry.

Procedure `Insert` reads one new entry into `AnEntry` and increments the count of entries. The statement

```
Entries[Count] := AnEntry;
```

places the new entry at the end of the current directory.

The if statement in procedure `GoFindEntry` uses the condition

```
AnEntry.EqualName(Entries[Next].GetName)
```

to compare the name field of the directory entry selected by `Next` with the target name stored in `AnEntry`. Method `GetName` retrieves the name field of the selected entry, and method `EqualName` performs the comparison. If a match occurs, `Found` is set to True, and loop exit occurs. After loop exit, `Cursor` points to the directory with the same name as `AnEntry`. If there is no match, loop exit occurs when `Next` passes `Count`.

Procedure `WriteLinearList` calls several other methods. The while loop

```
while not EndOfLinearList do
  begin
    GetEntry (AnEntry);      {access current entry}
    AnEntry.DisplayEntry;
    GoNextEntry              {advance to next entry}
  end {while}
```

calls three methods from object type `LinearList` and one (method `DisplayEntry`) from object type `Entry`. In the loop body, the call to method `GetEntry` stores the current directory entry in object instance `AnEntry` (a local variable). Method `DisplayEntry` displays the entry just retrieved. Method `GoNextEntry` advances the cursor to the next entry. Before each loop repetition, method `EndOfLinearList` tests whether the cursor has passed the last directory entry. Notice that object instance `AnEntry` is a parameter of method `GetEntry` (a method of object type `Directory`) but is used to qualify method `DisplayEntry` (a method of object type `Entry`). Be sure you understand the reason for this.

The remaining methods are relatively straightforward, so we will not discuss them.

Program Style

Referencing an ADT's Methods Inside the ADT

Procedure WriteLinearList is the only procedure in unit LinearListADT that makes extensive use of the other methods declared in that unit. We did this for two reasons: to simplify the implementation of WriteLinearList and to provide further illustration of how to use the other methods.

Remember that a client module can reference private data members of an object instance of type LinearList only by using the object's methods. However, methods (operators) declared inside LinearListADT may reference individual fields directly or through other operators declared earlier in LinearListADT. It is generally more efficient to reference the fields directly; however, using the other methods often leads to more readable and more flexible code.

CASE STUDY

Using the LinearList Object

To illustrate how we can use the abstract data type in a new applications program, let's write a main program to control access to the telephone directory. The main program will supply the user with a menu of possible operations. The user will select one option at a time from the menu of choices. Each option selected will be coded by using the methods associated with the two abstract data types: `EntryADT` and `LinearListADT`. The additional data requirements and the main program algorithm (written in pseudocode) follow.

Additional Data Requirements

Problem Inputs

```
Choice : Integer    {the user's selection}
The name of the file containing the directory
```

Problem Output

```
The menu displayed as a numbered list
```

Algorithm for Main Program

```
repeat
  Read the user's choice into Choice
  case Choice of
    0 : Show the menu
    1 : Read and create the initial directory
    2 : Insert a new entry in the directory
    3 : Display the count of items in the directory
    4 : Edit an entry in the directory
    5 : Display the number for a name in the directory
    6 : Write the directory to an output file
    7 : Quit the program
  end {case}
until the user's choice is 7 (quit)
```

We show the main program in Fig. 1.13. The uses statement

```
uses
  EntryADT, LinearListADT;
```

Figure 1.13
Program RunDirectory

Directory: CHAP 1
File: RUNDIREC.PAS

```
program RunDirectory;

  {import object types Entry and Directory}
  uses
    EntryADT, LinearListADT;

  var
    NextEntry, Target : Entry;
    Directory : LinearList;
    Choice : Integer;
    TargetName : string;
    TargetNumber : string;

  procedure DisplayMenu;
  begin {stub}
    WriteLn ('Display the menu here')
  end; {stub}

begin {RunDirectory}
  repeat
    WriteLn;
```

▷ ▷ ▷ ▷ ▷

```
WriteLn ('Enter the number of your selection:');
    Write ('Enter 0 to display the menu >');
    ReadLn (Choice);

    case Choice of
      0 : DisplayMenu;

      1 : begin
            Directory.CreateLinearList;
            Directory.ReadLinearList
          end; {1}

      2 : begin
            WriteLn ('Enter the data for the new entry:');
            NextEntry.ReadEntry;
            Directory.Insert (NextEntry)
          end; {2}

      3 : WriteLn ('The number of entries is ',
                    Directory.GetCount);

      4 : begin
            WriteLn ('Enter the name and new number:');
            Target.ReadEntry;
            Directory.GoFindEntry (Target);
            if not Directory.EndOfLinearList then
              Directory.PutEntry (Target)
            else
              begin
                TargetName := Target.GetName;
                WriteLn (TargetName, ' is not in the directory')
              end {else}
          end; {4}

      5 : begin
            Write ('Enter the name whose number you desire >');
            ReadLn (TargetName);
            Target.Init (TargetName, '');
            Directory.GoFindEntry (Target);
            if not Directory.EndOfLinearList then
              begin
                Directory.GetEntry (Target);
                TargetNumber := Target.GetNumber;
                WriteLn ('The number is ', TargetNumber)
              end
            else
              WriteLn (TargetName, ' is not in the directory')
          end; {5}

      6 : Directory.WriteLinearList;

      7 : WriteLn ('Exiting run directory program')
    end {case}
  until Choice = 7
end.  {RunDirectory}
```

provides the name of the two ADTs that are linked to this program. The object types Entry and Directory are declared in these ADTs along with all the methods called in the case statement.

Figure 1.13 contains a *stub* for procedure DisplayMenu that simply writes a message indicating that the menu is displayed. The completed procedure will consist of a collection of WriteLn statements and is left as an exercise. We will discuss the use of stubs for testing programs in Chapter 2.

Figure 1.14 shows a sample run of the program RunDirectory.

Figure 1.14
Sample Run of Program
`RunDirectory`

```
Enter the number of your selection:
Enter 0 to display the menu >0
Display the menu here

Enter the number of your selection:
Enter 0 to display the menu >1
Enter the name of the text file that
contains the linear list >phone.dat

Enter the number of your selection:
Enter 0 to display the menu >3
The number of entries is 3

Enter the number of your selection:
Enter 0 to display the menu >5
Enter the name whose number you desire >Sam
The number is 555-123-5678

Enter the number of your selection:
Enter 0 to display the menu >2
Enter the data for the new entry:
Name >Robin
Number >555-222-3333

Enter the number of your selection:
Enter 0 to display the menu >6
Name is Bill
Number is 555-123-4567
Name is Sam
Number is 555-123-5678
Name is Carol
Number is 555-123-6789
Name is Robin
Number is 555-222-3333

Enter the number of your selection:
Enter 0 to display the menu >7
Exiting run directory program
```

Exercises for Section 1.7   ***Self-Check***

1. Why would you want to use the reserved word private in an object type declaration?
2. What is the purpose of including preconditions and postconditions in a method's comments?

Programming

1. Write procedure DisplayMenu for program RunDirectory.

CHAPTER REVIEW

In this chapter we discussed the software engineering process. We introduced the software life cycle (SLC) and described its steps:

1. Requirements specification
2. Analysis
3. Design
4. Implementation
5. Testing and validation
6. Operation, follow-up, and maintenance

We also reviewed procedural abstraction and data abstraction as two tools for managing program complexity. In particular we described the use of a special module called an abstract data type (ADT), which encapsulates a data object together with its operators. We introduced Borland Pascal units and Borland Pascal object types as two methods for making ADTs more readily reusable in client programs.

Review of Steps for Using Abstract Data Types

In the last few sections, we discussed how to use Borland Pascal units to implement abstract data types. Next, we summarize the steps that you should follow to create and use an ADT.

1. Create a new unit that contains an abstract data type. Save the unit in a source file whose name is the same as the unit name and has an extension of `.PAS`.
2. Compile the file containing the abstract data type to disk. Borland Pascal will save the object code in a file with the same name as the source file but with the extension `.TPU`.
3. Write a client program that uses this abstract data type. Be sure to place a `uses` statement as the first statement of the client program. If the client is a unit, place the `uses` statement after the client's `interface` or `implementation` line.
4. Compile and run the client program or unit. Borland Pascal links the object code (i.e., machine language code) for the abstract data type to the object code of the client, creating an executable file with extension `.EXE`.

To perform Step 2, select Disk (instead of Memory) as the destination of the object code file for the unit. This selection should be made from the compile submenu before the compilation step is performed. To do this, first choose Destination from the Compile submenu and then change the destination from Memory to Disk (see Fig. 1.15) by clicking the left mouse button. When you perform Step 4, the new . EXE file will also be stored on disk. If you do not wish to save this file on disk, you can change the destination back to Memory before performing Step 4.

Quick-Check Exercises

1. The six steps of the software life cycle are listed below in arbitrary order. Place them in their correct order.
   testing and verification, design, analysis, implementation
   requirements specification, operation and maintenance
2. How can the use of program libraries increase a programmer's productivity?
3. Name the two sections of an abstract data type. Where is the data declaration found? Where are the procedure declarations?
4. Objects can be declared as local identifiers in procedures. True or false?
5. How do Borland Pascal object type declarations differ from record type declarations?
6. In object-oriented programming, what is name overloading?

Answers to Quick-Check

1. Requirements specification, analysis, design, implementation, testing and verification, operation and maintenance.

Figure 1.15
Selecting Disk as an
Object File Destination

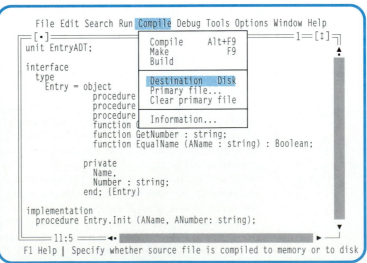

2. By allowing reuse of existing procedures that have already been debugged and tested instead of reinventing the same procedures over and over again.
3. Specification and implementation; specification section; implementation section.
4. False.
5. Object type declarations can contain method header declarations and the reserved word `private`.
6. Allowing an identifier name to have two different meanings in the same program.

Review Questions

1. Explain why the principle of information hiding is important to the software designer.
2. Define the terms *procedural abstraction* and *data abstraction*.
3. How do method preconditions and postconditions differ from one another?
4. List the steps of the object-oriented design method.
5. Define an object `Player` for the positions on a baseball team (pitcher, catcher, infield, outfield) with methods for reading and writing `Player` objects.
6. Define an object to implement an abstract data type `Money` that has methods for arithmetic operations (addition, subtraction, multiplication, and division) on real numbers having exactly two digits to the right of the decimal point, as well as methods for reading and writing `Money` objects.

Programming Projects

1. Create a Borland Pascal unit containing a set of library procedures (or functions) that can be used to determine the following information for an integer parameter:
   a. Is it a multiple of 7, 11, or 13?
   b. Is the sum of the digits odd or even?
   c. What is the square root value?
   d. Is it a prime number?

   Write a client program that tests your library procedures using the following input values: 104, 3773, 13, 121, 77, and 3075.

Directory: CHAP 1
File: PROJ1_2.PAS

2. Write a Borland Pascal unit `ColorADT`, containing the object type declaration for `ColorType` with methods for reading and writing colors (red, yellow, green, blue, black, brown, orange, purple, and white) and testing instances of `ColorType` for equality. Write a client program to test `ColorADT`.

Directory: CHAP 1
File: PROJ1_3.PAS

3. Each month a bank customer deposits $50 into a savings account. Assume that the interest rate is fixed and is a problem input. The interest is calculated on a quarterly basis. For example, if the account earns 6.5% annually, it earns one fourth of the 6.5% investment every three months. Write a program to compute the total amount in the account and the interest accrued for each of the 120 months of a 10-year period. Assume that the rate is applied to all funds in the account at the end of a quarter, regardless of when the deposits were made.

   Print all values accurate to two decimal places. The table that your program prints when the annual interest rate is 6.5% should begin as follows:

MONTH	INVESTMENT	NEW AMOUNT	INTEREST	TOTAL SAVINGS
1	50.00	50.00	0.00	50.00
2	100.00	100.00	0.00	100.00
3	150.00	150.00	2.44	152.44
4	200.00	202.44	0.00	202.44
5	250.00	252.44	0.00	252.44
6	300.00	302.44	4.91	307.35
7	350.00	357.35	0.00	357.35

Your solution should make use of an `Account` object that contains account information for a single month and has methods for initializing, updating, and displaying its data fields.

4. Redo Programming Project 3, adding columns to allow comparison of interest compounded monthly (one twelfth of the annual rate every month) with continuously compounded interest. The formula for compounded interest is

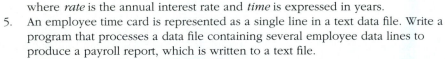

$$amount = principle * e^{rate * time}$$

where *rate* is the annual interest rate and *time* is expressed in years.

Directory: CHAP 1
File: PROJ1_5.PAS

5. An employee time card is represented as a single line in a text data file. Write a program that processes a data file containing several employee data lines to produce a payroll report, which is written to a text file.

Each data line has the following form:

Positions	Data
1–4	Employee identification number
5	blank
6–7	Number of regular hours (whole number)
8	blank
9–14	Hourly rate (dollars and cents)
15	blank
16–17	Number of dependents
18	blank
19–20	Number of overtime hours (whole number)

Define an object type `Employee` that has the data fields listed above plus data fields `GrossPay` and `NetPay` as defined below:

$$gross\ pay = (regular\ hours + overtime\ hours * 1.5) * rate$$

$$federal\ tax = 0.14 * (gross - 13 * dependents)$$
$$social\ security = 0.052 * gross$$
$$net\ pay = gross - (federal\ tax + Social\ Security)$$

6. Write a menu-driven program that contains options for creating the data file to be processed by the payroll program described in Programming Project 5 (the user should be prompted to enter several time cards from the keyboard), displaying the time cards in the file on the system printer, adding new time cards to the end of an existing data file, deleting a time card from the file by ID number, and quitting the program.

Algorithm Correctness and Efficiency

This chapter discusses program correctness and efficiency. It begins with a discussion of program bugs and how they might be avoided by careful program design. It describes how to use other members of a programming team to help detect errors in logic before they become part of the code. As in all other situations in life, early detection leads to the best results.

The chapter discusses program testing in some detail. It discusses the generation of a proper test plan and the differences between top-down, bottom-up, and integration testing. It also describes the use of drivers and stubs.

There is also a discussion of formal verification of programs. Although we are still far from being able to prove that a program is correct using mathematical techniques, we can still borrow some of these ideas to help document our programs and to increase our confidence that critical parts of programs, such as loops, operate as intended.

Finally, we discuss algorithm efficiency and introduce big-O notation. The use of big-O notation lets us compare the relative efficiency of algorithms.

2.1 Program Bugs

It does not really matter whether a program runs efficiently if it does not do what it is supposed to do. One way to show that a program is correct is through testing. However, it is difficult to determine how much testing should be done. Very often, errors appear in a software product after it is delivered, causing great inconvenience. Some notable software errors in operational programs have caused power brownouts, telephone network saturation, and space flight delays.

Proper design and testing can help to eliminate many program bugs. However, there are situations in which it is impossible to test a software product before it is used. Examples are software that controls a missile and software that prevents a meltdown in the event of a malfunction in a nuclear power plant. For such software products, you must rely on proper design techniques to reduce the likelihood of error.

This chapter is about program errors or *bugs* and how to avoid them. Program bugs can be eliminated by careful design and/or by careful debugging and testing after the program is written. Obviously, it is much easier to eliminate bugs by design rather than by removing them later through debugging and testing. There are really three kinds of errors that you might encounter.

▶ syntax errors
▶ run-time errors
▶ logic errors

Syntax Errors

Syntax errors are mistakes in your use of the grammar (or syntax) of the Pascal language, for example, using = as an assignment operator instead of := . The Pascal compiler will detect most syntax errors during compilation and will require you to correct them before it can successfully compile your program.

Although rare in Pascal, it is possible to use incorrect syntax in a statement and have that error go undetected by the compiler. If this happens, your statement will be syntactically correct but semantically incorrect (i.e., the compiler will interpret it incorrectly). This will result in the computer performing a different operation from the one you intended. For this reason, you should carefully check the syntax of each statement that you write and not rely entirely on the compiler to detect syntax errors.

Run-time Errors

Run-time errors occur during program execution. A run-time error occurs when the computer attempts to perform an invalid operation. Table 2.1 shows some examples of common run-time errors. A run-time error will cause your program to halt execution and display a run-time error. This is a "good news, bad news" situation. The good news is that the error has been detected. The bad news is that your program has crashed and is no longer executing.

Table 2.1

Run-time Errors

Division by zero	Attempting to divide by zero
Out-of-range error	Attempting to store an out-of-range value in a variable
Reading an invalid data item	Attempting to read a nonnumeric data item into an integer variable or a real data item into an integer variable
Reading beyond the end of file	Attempting to perform a read operation after the end of a file has been reached

Division by Zero

Many run-time errors can be prevented by defensive programming. If `Count` represents the count of items being processed and it is possible for `Count` to be zero, use an if statement to *guard* the statement

```
Average := Sum / Count
```

so that the division operation will not be performed when `Count` is zero. One way to do this is as follows.

```
if Count = 0 then
  WriteLn ('Count is zero - average is not defined')
else
  begin
    Average := Sum / Count;
    WriteLn ('The average value is ', Sum :2:1)
  end; {if}
```

Range-Check Errors

A range-check error occurs when a program attempts to assign an out-of-range value to a variable. Included in the declarations

```
const
  Min = 1;
  Max = 500;

type
  SmallInt = Min..Max;
  ScoreArray = array [SmallInt] of Integer;
```

```
var
  I : Integer;
  Scores : ScoreArray;
```

is a subrange type, `SmallInt`, that is a subrange of the integers (from 1 to 500). We use subrange `SmallInt` as the subscript type in the declaration for array type `ScoreArray`.

We also declare an array `Scores` (type `ScoreArray`) and an `Integer` variable `I`. The subscripted variable `Scores[I]` uses `I` as an array subscript. A range-check error would occur if we referenced this variable when the value of `I` was less than 1 or greater than 500.

If `I` is always used as a subscript to array `Scores`, we can cause the range-check error to be detected as soon as an incorrect value is stored in `I` by declaring `I` to be type `SmallInt` instead of type `Integer`. This also enables the compiler to catch some out-of-range values. For example, the assignment

```
I := 501; {out-of-range constant}
```

would result in a constant out of range syntax error.

```
var
  I : SmallInt;
  Scores : ScoreArray;
```

The advantage of doing this is that we are alerted to the range-check error as soon as it occurs rather than later when the array reference occurs.

Inserting Code to Prevent Range-Check Errors

Range-check errors can be prevented by using an if statement to validate a value before assigning it to a variable. If variable `IRawData` is type `Integer`, the following if statement ensures that the value of `IRawData` is within range before it is assigned to `I` (type `SmallInt`).

```
if IRawData < Min then
  begin
    WriteLn (IRawData, ' < ', Min, '- reset to ', Min);
    IRawData := Min
  end
else if IRawData > Max then
  begin
    WriteLn (IRawData, ' > ', Max, '- reset to ', Max);
    IRawdata := Max
  end; {if}
I := IRawData;   {assign in-range value to I}
```

You can also use a library procedure to ensure that only a valid data value is read into `IRawData`. The statements

```
Write ('Enter an integer between ', Min, ' and ', Max, '> ');
EnterInt (Min, Max, IRawData, Success);
```

Figure 2.1
Procedure EnterInt

Directory: CHAP 2
File: MYTOOLS.PAS

```
procedure EnterInt (MinN, MaxN {input} : Integer;
                        var N {output} : Integer;
                        var Success {output} : Boolean);
{
Reads an integer between MinN and MaxN into N.
Pre : MinN and MaxN are assigned values.
Post: Returns in N first data value between MinN and MaxN
        and sets Success to True if MinN <= MaxN is True;
        otherwise, N is not defined and Success is set to False.
}
begin {EnterInt}
  if MinN <= MaxN then
    begin
      {no valid value in N as yet}
      Success := False;
      {Keep reading until valid number is read}
      while not Success do
        begin
          Write ('Enter an integer between ');
          Write (MinN :3, ' and ', MaxN :3, '> ');
          ReadLn (N);
          Success := (MinN <= N) and (N <= MaxN)
        end {while}
    end {valid range}
  else
    begin
      WriteLn ('Error - empty range for EnterInt');
      Success := False
    end {bad range limits}
end; {EnterInt}
```

call procedure EnterInt (shown earlier in unit MyTools) to read an integer value between its first two parameters (Min and Max) into its third parameter (IRawData). Recall that if Min > Max, the value of IRawData will be undefined, and Success will be False. Figure 2.1 shows procedure EnterInt.

Borland Pascal's R Compiler Option

In Borland Pascal, we can determine whether range-checking is performed during run-time by setting a compiler option. A compiler option is set by using a special comment called a *compiler option directive* or through the options menu (select the Compiler Options dialog box and place an X in the check box for range checking). When the compiler directive

{$R+}

appears in a program, range checking is turned on and will be included in all code generated from that point on. The compiler directive

{$R-}

may be used later in the program to turn range checking off, although we don't recommend this.

Each compiler option has a default value (− for off, + for on). The default value for range checking is −, which means that Borland Pascal does not normally perform range checking. We recommend that you set range checking on during debugging. Further, we recommend that you begin all programs that process an array or string with the {$R+} compiler directive so that range checking is performed during normal production runs as well as debugging.

Reading an Incorrect Type of Data Item

Entering data of the wrong type can also cause an invalid data format error. If the program's prompt messages are clear, this kind of error is less likely. However, the program user may still type in the wrong data and not be aware of it. For example, a program user might type in 340O as an integer value, pressing the letter O by mistake instead of a zero. Or the user might type in 3405.0 instead of the integer 3405.

The obvious way to correct this kind of error is to read each data item into a string variable and then convert the string to a numeric value. This can be tedious; however, Borland Pascal provides a type conversion procedure, Val, which simplifies this process. Val converts a string (its first parameter) to a real or integer value based on the data type of its second parameter. If the string satisfies the Pascal syntax for a valid number of the specified type, the third parameter is set to zero; otherwise, the third parameter indicates the position in the string of the first nonnumeric character. Procedure Val is discussed further in Section 3.6.

Figure 2.2 shows procedure ReadInt (in unit MyTools), which reads an integer variable as a string and returns the corresponding integer value in its first parameter.

Attempt to Read Beyond the End of a File

In reading data from a file, any of the errors described in this section can occur. It is also possible to attempt to read more data items than were provided in the data file, which would cause an attempt to read beyond end of data file error.

The most common cause of this error is a data entry loop that is repeated one more time than it should be. We can minimize the chances of this kind of error if we always use a while loop that checks for an end of file before performing a read operation as shown next.

Figure 2.2
Procedure ReadInt

Directory: CHAP 2
File: MYTOOLS.PAS

```
procedure ReadInt (var IntNum {output} : Integer);
{
 Uses Borland Pascal procedure Val to convert string read from
 key board to an integer value.
 Pre : None.
 Post: IntNum contains first valid integer value typed by
       user.
}
var
  NumStr : string; {input string }
  Error : Integer; {position of first invalid error position}

begin {ReadInt}
  repeat
    ReadLn (NumStr);                     {read numeric string}
    Val (NumStr, IntNum, Error);  {convert to integer value}
    if Error <> 0 then               {test for invalid characters}
      begin
        WriteLn (NumStr);            {mark first bad character}
        WriteLn ('^' : Error);
        WriteLn ('Invalid character at position ', Error);
        Write ('Try again > ')
      end
  until Error = 0   {exit if no bad character positions}
end; {ReadInt}
```

```
while not EOF(DataFile) do
  begin
    Read (DataFile, NextItem);
    Process (NextItem)              {process the data item}
  end; {while}
```

This loop continues to read data items from file DataFile until the end of
the file is reached.

   If there are extra characters (including blanks) at the end of the last data
line, an error could occur. In this case, the end-of-file will not be detected after the last data value has been read, so one more read operation will be at-
tempted. If DataFile is a Text file (a file of characters separated into lines),
it is better to use

```
ReadLn (DataFile, NextItem)
```

when NextItem is type Integer, Char, Real, or string and only one data
item is supposed to be read from each line.

   An attempt to read beyond the end of data file error may occur when multiple data items are being read from each line of a Text file. For example, if
InFile is a Text file and the statement

```
Read (InFile, Item1, Item2, Item3)
```

is used in a while loop similar to the one shown earlier, three data items will be read from each data line. Let's assume that line 3 of the following data file contains a typing error: 0 in the third column instead of a blank.

line #	Data File
1	34 56 78
2	63 47 96
3	12045 89
4	43 67 92
5	45 67 88

The first two data lines will be read correctly, but the third read operation will take its third data item (43) from data line 4. The fourth read operation will take its first two data items (67 and 92) from line 4 and its third data item (45) from data line 5. In standard Pascal, the fifth read operation will cause an attempt to read beyond end of data file error because there is no third data item. Not all versions of Borland (or Turbo) Pascal detect this error.

Exercises for Section 2.1   **Programming**

1. Write a program to test procedure `ReadInt`.
2. Write a program to test the Pascal compiler that you are using for this course to see whether it can identify an attempt to read beyond the end of the data file.

2.2   Desk Checking and Program Walkthroughs

Once you have removed all syntax errors and run-time errors, a program will execute through to normal completion. However, that is no guarantee that the program does not contain logic errors. Because logic errors do not usually cause an error message to be displayed, they frequently go undetected.

Logic errors can be difficult to detect and isolate. If the logic error occurs in a part of the program that always executes, then each run of the program may generate incorrect results. Although this sounds bad, it is actually the best situation because the error is more likely to be detected if it occurs frequently. If the value that is being computed incorrectly is always displayed, it will be easy to find the logic error. However, if this value is part of a computation and is not displayed, it will be very difficult to track down the error and the section of code that is responsible.

The worst kind of logic error is one that occurs in a relatively obscure part of the code that is infrequently executed. If the test data set does not exercise this section of code, the error will not occur during normal program testing. Therefore the software product will be delivered to its users with a hidden bug. Once that happens, detecting and correcting the problem becomes much more difficult.

Logic errors arise during the design phase and are the result of an incorrect algorithm. One way to reduce the likelihood of logic errors is to carefully check the algorithm before implementing it. This can be done by hand-tracing the algorithm, carefully simulating the execution of each algorithm step and comparing its execution result to one that is calculated by hand.

Hand-tracing an algorithm is complicated by the fact that the algorithm designer often anticipates what an algorithm step should do without actually simulating its execution. Because the algorithm designer knows the purpose of each step, it requires quite a bit of discipline to carefully simulate each individual algorithm step, particularly if the algorithm step is inside a loop. For this reason, programmers often work in teams to trace through an algorithm. The algorithm designer must explain the algorithm to the other team members and simulate its execution with the other team members looking on. This procedure is called a *structured walkthrough*.

In tracing through an algorithm, it is important to exercise all paths of the algorithm. It is also important to check special conditions and *boundary conditions,* to make sure that the algorithm works for these cases as well as the more common ones. For example, if you are tracing an algorithm that searches for a particular target element in an array, you should make sure that the algorithm works for all the following cases.

▶ The target element is not in the array.
▶ The target element is the middle element of the array.
▶ The target element is the first array element.
▶ The target element is the last array element.
▶ The array has only one element.
▶ The array is empty (zero elements).
▶ There are multiple occurrences of the target element.

The techniques discussed in this section are applicable to testing the completed program as well as the algorithm. We discuss program testing next.

Exercises for Section 2.2   ***Self-Check***

1. Why is it a good idea to use the structured walkthrough approach in hand-tracing an algorithm?
2. List two boundary conditions that should be checked when testing procedure `EnterInt` (see Fig. 2.1).

2.3 Testing Strategies

Preparations for Testing

After a program has been written and debugged, it must be thoroughly tested before it can be delivered as a final software product. Although testing is done after the software is completed, it is beneficial to develop a test plan early in the design stage.

Some aspects of a test plan include deciding how the software will be tested, when the tests will occur, who will do the testing, and what test data will be used. We will discuss these components of the test plan throughout the section. If the test plan is developed early in the design stage, testing can take place concurrently with the design and coding. Again, the earlier an error is detected, the easier and less expensive it will be to correct.

Another advantage of deciding on the test plan early is that this will encourage programmers to prepare for testing as they write their code. A good programmer will practice *defensive programming* and include code that detects unexpected or invalid data values. For example, if a procedure has the precondition

```
Pre : N greater than zero
```

it would be a good idea to place the if statement

```
if N <= 0 then
   WriteLn ('Invalid value for parameter N-', N :1);
```

at the beginning of the procedure. This if statement will provide a diagnostic message if the parameter passed to the procedure is invalid.

Similarly, if a data value being read from the keyboard is supposed to be between 0 and 40, a defensive programmer would use procedure `EnterInt` from unit `MyTools`:

```
WriteLn ('Enter number of hours worked:');
EnterInt (0, 40, Hours, Success);
```

As discussed earlier, the first and second parameters of `EnterInt` define the range of acceptable values for its third parameter, while the fourth parameter `Success` is set to False if `EnterInt` is called with an invalid range.

Debugging Tips for Program Systems

Most of the time, you will be testing program systems that contain collections of procedure and function modules. We provide a list of debugging tips to follow in writing these modules.

1. Carefully document each module parameter and local identifier, using comments as you write the code. Also describe the module operation, using comments.

2. Leave a trace of execution by printing the module name as you enter it.
3. Print the values of all input and input/output parameters upon entry to a module. Check that these values make sense.
4. Print the values of all module outputs after returning from a module. Verify that these values are correct by hand computation. For procedures, make sure that all input/output and output parameters are declared as variable parameters.
5. Make sure that a module stub assigns a value to each of its outputs.

You should plan for debugging as you write each module rather than afterward. Include the output statements required for Steps 2 through 4 in the original Pascal code for the module. When you are satisfied that the module works as desired, you can remove the debugging statements. One efficient way to remove them is to change them to comments by enclosing them with the symbols {, }. Sometimes it is better to use the comment symbol pair (*, *) to comment out debugging code, since Borland Pascal does not allow comments to contain the symbol pair {, } (which would occur if any of your debugging code contained comments). If you have a problem later, you can remove the symbols (*, *) again, thereby changing the comments to executable statements.

Another approach to turning debugging statements on and off is to use a Boolean constant (say `Debug`) that is declared in the main program. The declaration

```
const
  Debug = True;  {turn debugging on}
```

should be used during debugging runs, and the declaration

```
const
  Debug = False; {turn debugging off}
```

should be used during production runs. Within the main program body and its procedures, each diagnostic print statement should be part of an if statement with `Debug` as its condition. If procedure `Process` begins with the following if statement, the `WriteLn` statements will execute only during debugging runs (`Debug` is True) as desired.

```
if Debug then
  begin
    WriteLn ('Procedure Process entered');
    WriteLn ('Input parameter StartBal has value ',
            StartBal :4:2)
  end; {if}
```

Developing the Test Data

The test data should be specified during the analysis and design phases. During the analysis phase, the systems analyst is very concerned with the relationship between the system inputs and outputs. There should be system test data to check for all expected system inputs as well as unanticipated data. The test plan should also specify the expected system behavior and outputs for each set of input data.

Who Does the Testing

Normally, testing is done by the programmer, by other members of the software team who did not code the module being tested, and by the final users of the software product. It is extremely important not to rely only on programmers for testing a module. Some companies have special testing groups who are expert at finding bugs in other programmers' code. The reason for involving future users is to determine whether they have difficulty in interpreting prompts for data. Users are more likely to make data-entry errors than are the other members of the programming or testing teams.

Black Box versus White Box Testing

There are two basic ways to test a completed module or system: *black box* or *specification-based* testing and *white box* or *glass box* testing. In black box testing, we assume that the program tester has no idea of the code inside the module or system. The tester's job is to verify that the module does what its specification says that it does. For a procedure, this means ensuring that the procedure's postconditions are satisfied whenever its preconditions are met. For a system or subsystem, this means ensuring that the system does indeed satisfy its original requirements specification. Because the tester cannot look inside the module or system, he or she must prepare sufficient sets of test data to ensure that the system outputs are correct for all valid system inputs. Also, the module or system should not crash when it is presented with invalid inputs. Black box testing is most often done by a special testing team or by program users instead of the programmers.

In glass box or white box testing, the tester has full knowledge of the code for the module or system and must ensure that each and every section of code has been thoroughly tested. For a selection statement (if or case), this means checking all possible paths through the selection statement. The tester must determine that the correct path is chosen for all possible values of the selection variable, taking special care at the boundary values where the path changes. For example, a boundary for a payroll program would be the value of hours worked that triggers overtime pay.

For a loop, the tester must make sure that the loop always performs the correct number of iterations and that the number of iterations is not off by one. Also, the tester should verify that the computations inside the loop are correct at the boundaries—that is, for the initial and final values of the loop control variable. Finally, the tester should make sure that the module or system still meets its specification when a loop executes zero times. The tester should make every effort to ensure that it is very unlikely that there are circumstances under which the loop would execute forever.

Top-down Testing

As the number of statements in a program system grows, the possibility of error also increases. If you keep each module to a manageable size, the likelihood of error will increase much more slowly. It will also be easier to read and test each module. Finally, avoiding the use of global variables will minimize the chance of harmful side effects that are always difficult to locate.

Not all the methods for a particular unit will be completed at the same time. However, we can still test the unit and its completed methods if we use a stub in place of each method that has not yet been completed. A *stub* has the same header as the procedure or function that it replaces; however, the body just prints a message indicating that the module was called. Figure 2.3 shows a stub for method `WriteDirectory` shown earlier in Fig. 1.12.

Besides displaying an identification message, a stub will assign easily recognizable values (e.g., 0 or 1) to any module outputs to prevent execution errors caused by undefined values. If a client program calls one or more stubs, the message printed by each stub when it is called provides a trace of the call sequence and allows the programmer to determine whether the flow of control within the client program is correct. The process of testing a client program in this way is called *top-down testing*.

Bottom-up Testing

When a module is completed, it can be substituted for its stub. However, before doing this, you should perform a preliminary test of the module because it is easier to locate and correct errors when dealing with a single module rather than a complete program system. We can test a new module by writing a short driver program. A driver program declares any necessary object instances and variables, assigns values to any of the module's inputs (as specified in the module's preconditions), calls the module, and displays the values of any outputs returned by the module.

Figure 2.3
Stub for Method
Directory.
WriteDirectory

```
procedure Directory.WriteDirectory;
{
  Stub for method which writes directory to screen.
  Pre : Directory initialized.
  Post: Directory entries displayed on screen in the order
        stored.
}
begin {WriteDirectory}
  WriteLn ('Stub for Directory method WriteDirectory')
end; {WriteDirectory}
```

Figure 2.4
Driver Program for Testing
Method `ReadEntry`

Directory: CHAP 2
File: TESTREAD.PAS

```
program TestReadEntry;
{
 Driver program tests ReadEntry.
 Tested : March 20, 1993

 Imports object type Entry, methods:
 ReadEntry, GetName, GetNumber
}
uses EntryADT;

  var
    AnEntry : Entry;

begin {TestReadEntry}
  AnEntry.ReadEntry;
  WriteLn ('Name field is ', AnEntry.GetName);
  WriteLn ('Number field is ', AnEntry.GetNumber)
end. {TestReadEntry}
```

Don't spend too much time creating an elegant driver program; you will discard it as soon as the new module is tested. Figure 2.4 shows a driver program to test method `ReadEntry` in unit `EntryADT` (see Fig. 1.9).

Once you are confident that a module works properly, you can substitute the module for its stub in the unit. The process of separately testing individual modules before inserting them in a unit is called *bottom-up testing*.

By following a combination of top-down and bottom-up testing, the programming team can be fairly confident that the complete program system will be relatively free of errors when it is finally put together. Consequently, the final debugging sessions should proceed quickly and smoothly.

Integration Testing

Another aspect of testing a system is called *integration testing*. In integration testing, the program tester must determine whether the individual components of the system that have been separately tested (using either top-down, bottom-up, or some combination) can be integrated with other like components. Each phase of integration testing will deal with larger units, progressing from individual modules through units and ending with the entire system. For example, after two units are completed, integration testing must determine whether the two units can work together. Once the entire system is completed, integration testing must determine whether that system is compatible with other systems in the computing environment in which it will be used.

Exercises for Section 2.3   **Self-Check**

1. Explain why a procedure interface error would not be discovered during white box testing.
2. Devise a set of data to test procedure `EnterInt` (Fig. 2.1) using:
    a. white box testing
    b. black box testing

2.4   Debugging Techniques

We mentioned earlier that one way to debug a program is to insert extra `WriteLn` statements to display intermediate results during program execution. If the program executes interactively, you can look at these results each time the program pauses for input and compare them against hand-calculated values. If the program executes in batch mode, you will have to wait until the program completes its execution before checking any intermediate results.

A better approach is to utilize the debugger that is part of the Borland Pascal environment. The debugger enables you to execute your program one statement at a time (*single-step execution*) while observing changes made to selected variables or expressions. As each statement executes, you can compare the values of variables that have been placed in a special *Watches* window with their expected values.

The Watches Window

Before beginning single-step execution, you must place the variables that you wish to observe in the Watches window. The easiest way to do this is to move the edit cursor to any occurrence of the variable in the program and then press Ctrl-F7. This will cause a dialogue box labeled Add Watch to pop up containing the name of the selected variable in its Watch expression field (see Fig. 2.5). If you press Enter or select OK, this variable will be added to the Watches window. You can also get an Add Watch window to pop up by going through the Debug menu and selecting Add Watch (see Fig. 2.6). If the variable in the Expression field of the Add Watch window is incorrect, you can edit it and press Enter when done.

You should place variables that represent intermediate results in the Watches window. Also, loop control variables should be placed in the Watches window. You can add variables at any time that program execution pauses, and you might want to have different variables and expressions in the Watches window at different points in the program.

You can insert expressions in the same way that you insert variables. One approach is to type in the expression when the Add Watch dialog box pops up. A second approach is to move the edit cursor to the first character in the expression before causing the Add Watch dialog box to pop up. The variable or literal at the edit cursor will appear in the Watch expression field. Pressing

Figure 2.5
Add Watch Dialog Box

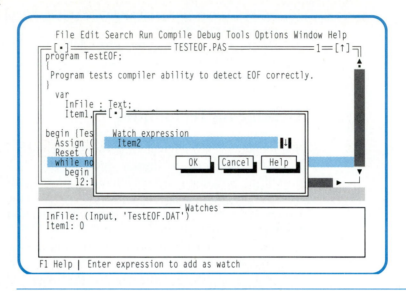

the right arrow key will move additional characters from the expression into the Watch expression field. Press Enter or select OK when done.

You can delete individual variables or expressions from the Watches window when they are no longer needed. To do this, highlight an item to be

Figure 2.6
Selecting Add Watch
from the Debug Menu

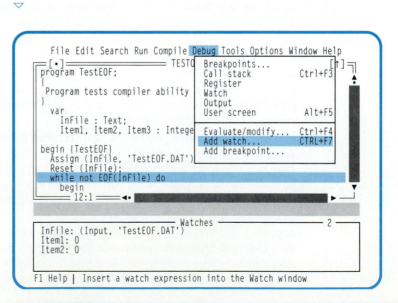

deleted by using your mouse cursor. Next, press the Delete key on the keyboard to remove the highlighted item from the Watches window. To remove all variables or expressions, close the Watches window.

You can use the F6 function key as a toggle to switch between the Edit window and the Watches window. You can also display both windows on the screen if you reduce the size of the Edit window.

Single-Step Execution

The purpose of placing variables and expressions in the Watches window is to enable you to observe changes to these items as your program executes. One way to accomplish this is to use single-step execution. To specify single-step execution, select the Trace into option from the Run menu (or press F7). An *execution bar* will appear over the `begin` line of the main program. If you continue to press F7, the statement under the execution bar will execute, and the execution bar will advance to the next program statement (see Fig. 2.7).

A second method of specifying single-step execution is to select the Step over option from the Run menu (or press F8). These two modes operate in the same way except when the next statement is a procedure or function call. If you press F8 (Step over), the debugger will execute the whole procedure or function body, stopping at the first statement after the return from the module. If you press F7 (Trace into), the debugger will single-step through the statements in the body.

Figure 2.7
Debugger Execution Bar

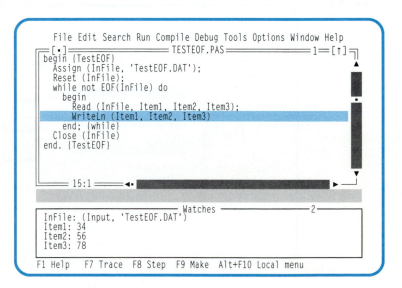

```
   File Edit Search Run Compile Debug Tools Options Window Help
 =[■]================ TESTEOF.PAS ================1═[↑]═┐
 begin {TestEOF}                                        ▲
   Assign (InFile, 'TestEOF.DAT');
   Reset (InFile);
   while not EOF(InFile) do
     begin
       Read (InFile, Item1, Item2, Item3);
       WriteLn (Item1, Item2, Item3)
     end; {while}
   Close (InFile)
 end. {TestEOF}

                                                        ▼
 == 15:1 ==== ◄■                                    ■ ►
 
 ================ Watches ================2
  InFile: (Input, 'TestEOF.DAT')
  Item1: 34
  Item2: 56
  Item3: 78

  F1 Help   F7 Trace   F8 Step   F9 Make   Alt+F10 Local menu
```

Setting Breakpoints

Another way to use the debugger is to separate your program into executable chunks or sections by setting *breakpoints*. When you select Run (or press Ctrl-F9), the program will execute from the point at which it has stopped to the next breakpoint. When the program pauses again, you can check the values of all items in the Watches window and add any new variables or expressions whose values you wish to see.

A programmer may use breakpoints in combination with single-step execution to locate errors. By executing from breakpoint to breakpoint, the programmer can find the section where a particular error has occurred. Then by reexecuting that section using single-step execution, the programmer can find the individual statements that are in error.

There are two ways to set and remove breakpoints. The easiest approach is to move the edit cursor to a statement where you would like to set a breakpoint. Then press Ctrl-F8 (Toggle breakpoint), and a highlight bar denoting a breakpoint will appear over that statement. If the statement is already a breakpoint and you press Ctrl-F8, the highlight bar (and breakpoint) will disappear.

The second approach is to use the Debug menu. First move the edit cursor to the location of the new breakpoint and pull up the Debug menu. Select Add Breakpoint to bring up the Add Breakpoint dialog box shown in Fig. 2.8. If you select the condition field, you can specify a condition under which this breakpoint will be activated. If you select the Pass count field, you can spec-

Figure 2.8
Add Breakpoint
Dialog Box

s

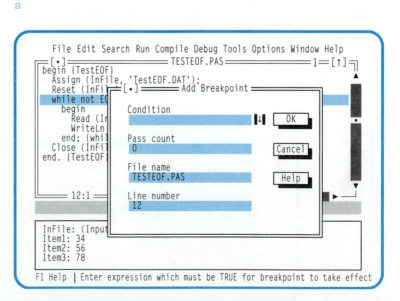

a

Figure 2.9
Breakpoints Dialog Box

s

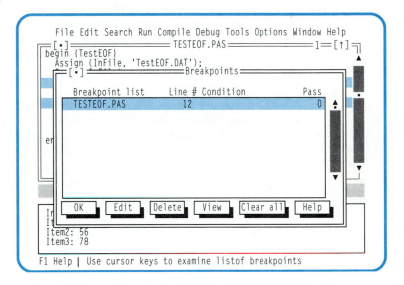

```
      File Edit Search Run Compile Debug Tools Options Window Help
   =[•]============ TESTEOF.PAS ================1=[↑]┐
   begin {TestEOF}                                   ▲
     Assign (InFile, 'TestEOF.DAT');
   ┌=[•]===================Breakpoints================

      Breakpoint list      Line # Condition          Pass
      TESTEOF.PAS              12                        0   ▲


   er




              OK      Edit    Delete    View    Clear all    Help

   I
   I
   Item2: 56
   Item3: 78

   F1 Help | Use cursor keys to examine listof breakpoints
```

a

ify the number of loop repetitions to allow before the breakpoint is activated. Select OK to actually set the breakpoint.

If you chose the Breakpoints option from the Debug menu, a Breakpoints dialog box will pop up as shown in Fig. 2.9. Details of all of the breakpoints set in your program will appear in the list of breakpoints. You can highlight any breakpoint in this list and then use the buttons as specified next.

v   OK closes the Breakpoints dialog box.
v   Edit enables you to modify the breakpoint's condition or pass count field.
v   Delete removes the breakpoint.
v   View shows you the statement where the breakpoint is set without moving the execution bar.
v   Clear all removes all breakpoints.

As an alternative to setting breakpoints in advance, you can move the edit cursor to a statement where you would like to begin single-step execution. If you then press F4, Borland Pascal will execute all statements from the current one up to the one selected by the edit cursor. After execution pauses, you can select single-step execution. When you wish to return to normal execution, either press Ctrl-F9 (Run) or move the edit cursor to the next stopping point and press F4 again.

Restarting the Debugger

If you are in the middle of a debugging session and want to start over again from the beginning of your program, select Program Reset (Ctrl-F2) from the Run menu. This reinitializes the debugging system and positions the execution bar over the begin line of the main program. It also closes any open files, clears the execution stack of any procedure calls, and releases any storage used by your program.

Before loading a new program into the Borland Pascal environment after a debugging session, select Program Reset to be certain that the computer memory used by your old program is available for use by your new program. It is important to note that neither loading a new program into the Borland Pascal system nor selecting Program Reset removes any of the expressions displayed in the Watch window or clears any of the program breakpoints. To remove the watch expressions from the Watch window, close the Watch window. To clear all breakpoints, select the Clear all button shown in Fig. 2.9. You should do this before loading a new program into the Borland Pascal environment.

Borland Pascal will offer to restart the debugging session if you make any changes to a program's statements during debugging. For example, if you make a change to a program statement using an Edit command and then press one of the execution command keys (F7, F4, or Ctrl-F9), Borland Pascal will display an Information dialog box with the message Source has been modified. Rebuild? If you type Y, your program will be compiled again, the execution bar will be placed on the begin line of the main program, and the debugger will be reinitialized (as it would following a Program Reset). If you type N, you will continue the current debugging session, and the changes made to your program will have no effect until you recompile your program. Table 2.2 contains a summary of the debugger keys that we have discussed in this section. A more complete discussion of the debugger appears in the Borland Pascal User's Guide.

Table 2.2
Borland Pascal Debugger Hot Keys

Ctrl-F2	Reset debugging environment
Ctrl-F7	Opens Add Watch dialog box
Ctrl-F8	Toggle breakpoint
Ctrl-F9	Resume normal execution
F4	Execute to cursor position
F6	Switch between windows
F7	Single-step execution: trace into procedures
F8	Single-step execution: step over procedure calls

2.5 Formal Methods of Program Verification

In Section 2.3, we described some aspects of program and system testing. We stated that testing should begin as early as possible in the design phase and continue through system implementation. Even though testing is an extremely valuable tool for providing evidence that a program is correct and meets its specifications, it is very difficult to know how much testing is enough. For example, how do we know that we have tried enough different sets of test data or that all possible paths through the program have been executed?

For these reasons, computer scientists have developed a second method of demonstrating the correctness of a program. This method is called *formal verification,* and it involves the application of formal rules of logic to show that a program meets its specification. By carefully applying formal rules, we can determine that a program meets its specification just as a mathematician proves a theorem by using definitions, axioms, and previously proved theorems. Although formal verification works well on small programs, it is more difficult to apply effectively on very large programs or program systems.

A thorough discussion of formal verification is beyond the scope of this book. However, we will introduce two key concepts, assertions and loop invariants, and we will use them to help document and clarify some of the program modules that appear in the book.

Assertions

An important part of formal verification is to document a program using *assertions,* logical statements about the program that are "asserted" to be true. An assertion is written as a comment, and it describes what is supposed to be true about the program variables at that point.

EXAMPLE 2.1 ▼

The next program fragment contains a sequence of assignment statements, each followed by an assertion.

```
A := 5;       {assert: A = 5}
X := A;       {assert: X = 5}
Y := X + A;   {assert: Y = 10}
```

The truth of the first assertion, $\{A = 5\}$, follows from executing the first statement with the knowledge that 5 is a constant. The truth of the second assertion, $\{X = 5\}$, follows from executing $X := A$ with the knowledge that A is 5. The truth of the third assertion, $\{Y = 10\}$, follows from executing $Y := X + A$ with the knowledge that X is 5 and A is 5. In this fragment, we used assertions as comments to document the change in a program variable after each assignment statement executes.

The task of a person using formal verification is to prove that a program fragment meets its specification. For the fragment above, this means proving that the final assertion or *postcondition,* $\{Y = 10\}$, follows from the initial presumption or *precondition,* {5 is a constant}, after the program fragment executes. The assignment rule is critical to this process. If we know that $\{A = 5\}$ is true, the assignment rule allows us to make the assertion $\{X = 5\}$ after executing the statement $X := A$. ▲

SYNTAX DISPLAY

The Assignment Rule

```
{P(A)}
X := A;
{P(X)}
```

Explanation: If P(A) is a logical statement (assertion) about A, the same statement will be true of X after the assignment statement

```
X := A
```

executes.

Preconditions and Postconditions Revisited

For our purposes, it will suffice to use assertions as a documentation tool to improve our understanding of programs rather than as a means of formally proving them correct. We have already used assertions in the form of preconditions and postconditions to document the effect of executing a procedure or function. A procedure's precondition is a logical statement about its input parameters. A procedure's postcondition may be a logical statement about its output parameters, or it may be a logical statement that describes the change in *program state* caused by the procedure execution. Any of the following activities represents a change in program state: changing the value of a variable, writing additional program output, or reading new input data from a data file or the keyboard.

EXAMPLE 2.2 ▼

The precondition and postcondition for procedure `EnterInt` (see Fig. 2.1) are repeated next.

```
procedure EnterInt (MinN, MaxN {input} : Integer;
                    var N {output} : Integer;
                    var Success {output} : Boolean);
{
 Reads an integer between MinN and MaxN into N.
 Pre : MinN and MaxN are assigned values.
 Post: Returns in N the first data value between MinN and MaxN
       and sets Success to True if MinN <= MaxN is true;
       otherwise, N is not defined and Success is set to
       False.
}
```

The precondition tells us that input parameters `MinN` and `MaxN` are defined before the procedure begins execution. The postcondition tells us that the procedure's execution assigns the first data value between `MinN` and `MaxN` to the output parameter N whenever

```
MinN <= MaxN is true.  ▲
```

Verifying an if Statement

Verification of an if statement requires us to consider what happens when the if statement condition is true and what happens when it is false. Formally, the semantics of the if statement look like

```
{P}
if B then
    {P₁} S₁ {Q₁}
else
    {P₂} S₂ {Q₂}
{Q}
```

The semantics of the if statement say if the Boolean expression B evaluates to True, then execute statement S_1; when the Boolean expression evaluates to false, execute statement S_2. Each of the statements S_1 and S_2 have their own preconditions and postconditions, which are logically related to the if statement precondition {P} and postcondition {Q}.

EXAMPLE 2.3 ▼

The following program fragment could be used to compute the absolute value of some variable X.

```
{assert: X has an initial value}

if X >= 0 then
    {assert: X >= 0}
    Y := X
    {assert: (X >= 0) and (Y = X)}
else
    {assert: X < 0}
    Y := -X
    {assert: (X < 0) and (Y = -X)}

{assert: ((X >= 0) and (Y = X)) or ((X < 0) and (Y = -X))}
```

The assertion "X has an initial value" is the precondition to the whole if statement. The assertions surrounding the statement

```
Y := X
```

were determined by using our knowledge of the formal semantics of the assignment and the if statement. The semantics of the if statement tell us that we cannot execute the statement

```
Y := X
```

unless X >= 0. To determine the precondition for the statement

```
Y := -X
```

the semantics of the if statement tell us that we need to negate the Boolean condition

```
X >= 0
```

to get

```
X < 0
```

To complete the postcondition that we need for the else clause statement, we use our understanding of the semantics of assignment statements. The postcondition for the whole if statement is constructed by using the Boolean operator or combining the postconditions for the statements following each of the assignment statements. In this case, our postcondition is equivalent to the mathematical definition of the absolute value of X, which is what we were seeking to verify. ▲

Loop Invariant

Loops are a very common source of program errors. It is often difficult to determine that a loop body executes exactly the right number of times or that loop execution causes the desired change in program variables. A special type of assertion, a *loop invariant,* is used to help prove that a loop meets its specification. A loop invariant is a logical statement involving program variables that is true before the loop is entered, true after each execution of the loop body, and true when loop termination occurs. It is called an invariant because it is a relationship that remains true as loop execution progresses.

As an example of a loop invariant, let's examine the following loop, which accumulates the sum of the integers 1, 2, . . . , N, where N is a positive integer and Sum, I, and N are type Integer.

```
{
 Accumulate the sum of integers 1 through N in Sum.

 assert: N >= 1
}
Sum := 0;
I := 1;
while I <= N do
   begin
      Sum := Sum + I;
      I := I + 1
   end; {while}

{assert: Sum = 1 + 2 + 3  . . . + N - 1 + N}
```

The first assertion, $\{N >= 1\}$, is the precondition for the loop, and the last assertion is its postcondition.

We stated that the loop invariant must be true before the loop begins execution and after each loop repetition. Since it traces the loop's progress, it should be a logical statement about the loop control variable I and the accumulating sum.

Figure 2.10
Sketch of a
Summation Loop

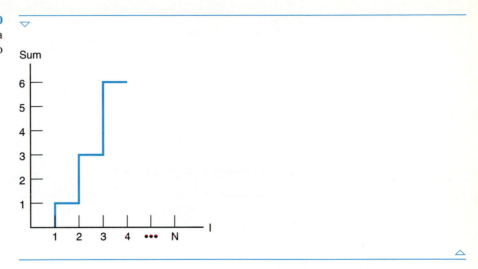

Figure 2.10 sketches the loop's progress for the first four iterations of the loop. At the end of the fourth iteration, I is 4 and Sum is 6—the sum of all integers less than 4 (1 + 2 + 3). When loop repetition finishes, I will be N + 1 and Sum will contain the desired result, (1 + 2 + 3 + ... + N). Therefore we propose the invariant

`{invariant: I <= N + 1 and Sum := 1 + 2 + . . . + I - 1}`

This means that inside the loop, I must be less than or equal to N + 1 and that after each loop repetition, Sum is equal to the sum of all positive integers less than I.

You might be wondering why the first part of the invariant is I <= N + 1 instead of I <= N. This is because the loop invariant must be true after the last iteration of the loop too. Since the last step taken in the loop body is to increment I, the last value assigned to I just before loop exit is N + 1.

The loop invariant must also be true before loop execution begins. At this point, I is 1 and 1 <= N + 1 is true for N >= 1 (the precondition). Also, the invariant requires that the value of Sum be equal to the summation of all positive integers less than 1. Because Sum is initialized to 0, this is also the case.

In program verification, the loop invariant is used to prove that the loop meets its specification. For our purposes, we will use the loop invariant to document what we know about the loop's behavior, and we will place it just before the loop body as shown:

```
{
 Accumulate the sum of integers 1 through N in Sum.

 assert: N >= 1
}
Sum := 0;
```

```
I := 1;
while I <= N do
  {invariant: I <= N + 1 and Sum := 1 + 2 + . . . + I - 1}
  begin
    Sum := Sum + I;
    I := I + 1
  end; {while}

{assert: (I = N + 1) and (Sum = 1 + 2 + 3 + . . . + N - 1 + N)}
```

Loop Invariants as a Design Tool

Some computer scientists recommend writing the loop invariant as a preliminary step before coding the loop. The invariant serves as a specification for the loop, and it can be used as a guide to help determine the loop initialization, the loop repetition condition, and the loop body. For example, we can write the following loop invariant to describe a summation loop that adds N data items:

```
{invariant:
  Count <= N and
  Sum is the sum of all data read so far
}
```

From the loop invariant, we can determine that:

▶ The loop initialization is

```
Sum:= 0.0;
Count:= 0;
```

▶ The loop repetition test is

```
Count < N
```

▶ The loop body is

```
Read (Next);
Sum:= Sum + Next;
Count:= Count + 1;
```

Given all this information, it becomes a simple task to write the summation loop (see Programming Exercise 2 at the end of this section).

Invariants and the for Statement

Since the loop invariant states what we know to be true about a loop after each iteration, we should be able to write an invariant for a for statement as well as a while statement. However, the loop control variable in a for statement is undefined after loop exit occurs. So that the loop invariant will remain true, we will assume that the loop control variable in a for statement is incremented just before loop exit and retains its final value.

```
{assert: N >= 1}
Sum := 0;
for I := 1 to N do
   {invariant: I <= N + 1 and Sum := 1 + 2 + . . . + I - 1}
   Sum := Sum + I;

{assert: Sum = 1 + 2 + 3 + . . . + N - 1 + N}
```

More Loop Invariants

This section provides more examples of the use of assertions and loop invariants to document a loop. Studying these examples should help you understand how to write invariants.

EXAMPLE 2.4 ▼

Figure 2.11 shows a sentinel-controlled while loop that computes the product of a collection of data values. Loop exit occurs after reading in the sentinel value (value of Sentinel). The loop invariant indicates that Product is the product of all values read before the current one and that none of these values was the sentinel. The preconditions and postconditions for the loop are written as assertions.   ▲

Figure 2.11
Sentinel-controlled Loop
with an Invariant

```
{
 Compute the product of a sequence of data values.

 assert: Sentinel is a constant
}
Product := 1;
WriteLn ('When done, enter ', Sentinel :1, ' to stop.');
WriteLn ('Enter the first number> ');
ReadLn (Num);
while Num <> Sentinel do
   {invariant:
      Product is the product of all prior values read into Num
      and no prior value of Num was the sentinel
   }
   begin
      Product := Product * Num;
      WriteLn ('Enter the next number> ');
      ReadLn (Num)
   end; {while}

{assert:
   Product is the product of all numbers
   read into Num before the sentinel
}
```

Selection Sort with Assertions and Loop Invariants

This section discusses a fairly intuitive (but not very efficient) algorithm called the *selection sort*. To perform a selection sort of an array with N elements (subscripts 1,...,N), we locate the smallest element in the array and then switch the smallest element with the element at subscript 1, thereby placing the smallest element at position 1. Then we locate the smallest element remaining in the subarray with subscripts 2,...,N and switch it with the element at subscript 2, thereby placing the second smallest element at position 2. Then we locate the smallest element remaining in subarray 3,...,N and switch it with the element at subscript 3, and so on.

Figure 2.12 traces the operation of the selection sort algorithm. The column on the left shows the original array. Each subsequent column shows the array after the next smallest element is moved to its final position in the array. The subarray under the color screen represents the portion of the array that is sorted after each exchange occurs. Note that it will require at most N − 1 exchanges to sort an array with N elements. The algorithm follows.

```
Selection Sort Algorithm
1. for Fill := 1 to N-1 do
      2.   Find the position of the smallest element
           in subarray with subscripts Fill..N.
      3.   if Fill is not the position of the smallest element then
           4.   Switch the smallest element with the one at
                position Fill.
```

To refine Step 2 of the selection sort algorithm, we need a loop that "searches" for the smallest element in the subarray with subscripts Fill..N. This loop must save the index of the smallest element found so far and com-

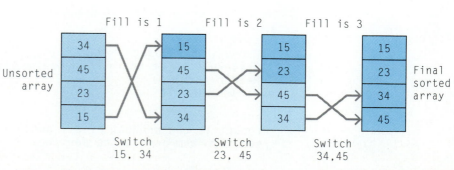

Figure 2.12
Trace of the Selection Sort

pare each new element to the smallest so far. If a new element is smaller than the smallest so far, the index of the new element is saved.

```
Step 2 Refinement
2.1  Initialize the position of the smallest so far to Fill.
2.2  for Next := Fill + 1 to N do
       2.3 if the element at Next < the smallest so far then
             2.4 Reset the position of the smallest so far to
                 Next.
```

Procedure `SelectSort` in Fig. 2.13 implements the selection sort algorithm for its array parameter `SArray`. Local variable `IndexOfMin` holds the location of the smallest exam score found so far in the current subarray. After each execution of the inner for loop, procedure `Switch` is called to exchange the elements with subscripts `IndexOfMin` and `Fill`, provided that `IndexOfMin` and `Fill` are different. After the execution of procedure `SelectSort`, the array elements will form an increasing sequence.

Directory: CHAP 2
File: SELECTSO.PAS

Figure. 2.13
Procedure `SelectSort`

```
procedure Switch (var Num1, Num2 {input/output} : Integer);
{Switches values of Num1 and Num2.
 Pre : Num1 and Num2 are defined.
 Post: Num1 is old Num2, and Num2 is old Num1.
}
  var
    Temp : Integer;              {temporary value}

begin {Switch}
  Temp := Num1; {assert: Temp = Num1}
  Num1 := Num2; {assert: Temp = Num1 and Num1 = Num2}
  Num2 := Temp  {assert: Temp = Num1 and Num2 = Temp}
end; {Switch}

procedure SelectSort (var SArray {input/output} : SortArray;
                          N {input} : Word);
{
 Sorts the data in array SArray.
 Pre : 1 <= N <= declared size of SArray and
       subarray SArray[1..N] is defined.
 Post: The values in array SArray are in increasing order.
}
  var
    Fill,    {index of element being filled with next smallest score}
    Next,                  {element being compared to smallest so far}
    IndexOfMin : Word;                       {index of smallest so far}
```

▷ ▷ ▷ ▷ ▷ ▷

```
begin {SelectSort}
  for Fill := 1 to N - 1 do
    begin
      {invariant:
          The elements in SArray[1..Fill - 1] are arranged in
          increasing order and Fill <= N.
      }

      {Find the position of the smallest element in SArray[Fill..N]}
      IndexOfMin := Fill;
      for Next := Fill + 1 to N do
        {invariant:
            The element at IndexOfMin is the smallest
            in SArray[Fill..Next - 1] and Next <= N - 1
        }
        if SArray[Next] < SArray[IndexOfMin] then
          IndexOfMin := Next;

      {assert: element at IndexOfMin is smallest in SArray[Fill..N]}

      {Exchange elements with subscripts Fill and IndexOfMin}
      if IndexOfMin <> Fill then
        Switch (SArray[Fill], SArray[IndexOfMin])
    end {for Fill}
end; {SelectSort}
```

The loop invariant for the outer loop

```
{invariant:
    The elements in SArray[1..Fill-1] are arranged in
    increasing order and Fill <= N.
}
```

summarizes the progress of selection sort. The subarray whose elements are in their proper place is shown under the color screen in Fig. 2.14. The remaining elements are not yet in place and are all larger than SArray[Fill-1].

Figure 2.14
Partially Sorted SArray

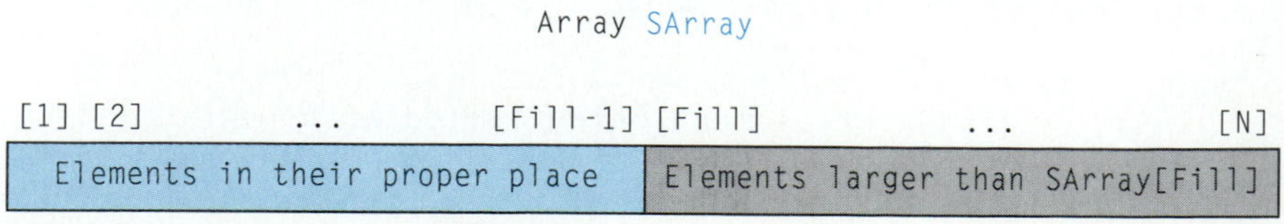

Array SArray

[1] [2]	...	[Fill-1] [Fill]	...	[N]

Elements in their proper place	Elements larger than SArray[Fill]

During each pass, the portion of the array under the color screen grows by one element, and `Fill` is incremented to reflect this. When `Fill` is equal to N, the first N − 1 elements will be in their proper place, so `SArray[N]` must also be in its proper place.

Exercises for Section 2.5   **Self-Check**

1. Write the loop invariant and the assertion following the loop for the while loop in procedure `EnterInt` (Fig. 2.1).
2. What other assertions should be added to procedure `EnterInt` to facilitate its verification?
3. For procedure `SelectSort`, explain the loop invariant for the inner for loop, and sketch its meaning.
4. Trace the execution of the selection sort on the following list. Show the array after each exchange occurs. How many exchanges are required? How many comparisons?
   10 55 34 56 76 5
5. How could you get the array elements in descending order (largest value first)?

Programming

1. Another method of performing the selection sort is to place the largest value in position N, the next largest value in position N − 1, and so on. Write this version.
2. Write a function that returns the count (N) of the number of nonzero digits in an arbitrary `Integer` (`Number`). Your solution should include a while loop for which the following is a valid loop invariant:

   ```
   {invariant:
       0 <= Count <= N and Number has been
       divided by 10 Count times.
   }
   ```

   and the following assertion would be valid following the loop:

   ```
   {assert: Count = N}
   ```

3. Write a program fragment that implements the loop whose invariant is described in the subsection entitled "Loop Invariants as a Design Tool."

2.6   Efficiency of Algorithms

There are many algorithms for searching and sorting arrays. Since arrays can have a very large number of elements, the time required to process all the elements of an array can become significant. Therefore it is important to have some idea of the relative efficiency of different algorithms. It is very difficult to get a precise measure of an algorithm or program's performance. For this reason, we normally try to approximate the effect on an algorithm of a change in the number of items, N, that it processes. In this way, we can see how an algorithm's execution time increases with N, so we can compare two algorithms by examining their growth rates.

For example, if we determine that the expression

```
T(N) = 2N² + N - 5
```

expresses the relationship between processing time and N, we say that the algorithm is an O(N²) algorithm, where O is an abbreviation for "order of magnitude." (This notation is called *big-O notation*.) When an algorithm has order of magnitude f(n), it means that there is some constant c such that the actual running time of the algorithm, T(N), is no more than c ∗ f(n). It is also the case that the growth rate of T(N) will be determined by the growth rate of the fastest-growing term (the one with the largest exponent), which in this case is the N² term. This means that the algorithm in this example is an O(N²) algorithm rather than an O(2N²) algorithm or an O(N² + N − 5) algorithm. In general, it is safe to ignore all constants in determining an algorithm's order of magnitude.

To search an array of N elements for a target, we have to examine all N elements when the target is not present in the array. If the target is in the array, we have to search only until we find it. However, it could be anywhere in the array, and it is as likely to be at the beginning of the array as at the end of the array. So on average, we have to examine N/2 array elements to locate a target value that is in an array. This means that an array search is an O(N) process, so the growth rate is linear.

To determine the efficiency of a sorting algorithm, we normally focus on the number of array element comparisons and exchanges that it requires. Performing a selection sort on an array with N elements requires N − 1 comparisons during the first pass through the array, N − 2 comparisons during the second pass, and so on. Therefore the total number of comparisons is represented by the series

```
1 + 2 + 3 + . . . + N - 2 + N - 1
```

From your mathematics courses, you might recall that the value of this series with N − 1 elements, whose first element is 1 and whose last element is N − 1, can be expressed in closed form as

$$\frac{(N - 1) * ((N - 1) + 1)}{2} = \frac{(N - 1) * N}{2} = N^2/2 - N/2$$

The number of comparisons performed in sorting an array of N elements using selection sort is always the same; however, the number of array element exchanges varies depending on the initial ordering of the array elements. During the search for the kth smallest element, the inner for loop sets IndexOfMin to the index of the kth smallest element in the array. If IndexOfMin is set to k, this means that the kth smallest element is already in its correct place, so no exchange takes place. If this never happens, there will be one exchange at the end of each iteration of the outer loop or a total of N − 1 exchanges (*worst-case situation*). If the array happens to be sorted before procedure SelectSort is called, all its elements will be in their proper place, so there will be zero exchanges (*best-case situation*). Therefore the number of array element exchanges for an arbitrary initial ordering is between zero and N − 1, which is O(N).

Because the dominant term in the expression for the number of comparisons shown earlier is $N^2/2$, selection sort is considered an $O(N^2)$ process, and the growth rate is quadratic (proportional to the square of the number of elements). What difference does it make whether an algorithm is an O(N) process or an $O(N^2)$ process? Table 2.2 evaluates N and N^2 for different values of N. A doubling of N causes N^2 to increase by a factor of 4. Since N increases much more slowly with N^2, the performance of an O(N) algorithm is not as adversely affected by an increase in N as is an $O(N^2)$ algorithm. For large values of N (say, 100 or more), the differences in performance for an O(N) and an $O(N^2)$ algorithm are significant.

Table 2.2
Table of Values of N
and N^2

N	N^2
2	4
4	16
8	64
16	256
32	1024
64	4096
128	16384
256	65536
512	262144

Other factors besides the number of comparisons and exchanges affect an algorithm's performance. For example, one algorithm may take more time preparing for each exchange or comparison than another. One algorithm might need to swap only subscript values to complete an exchange, whereas another algorithm might need to swap the array elements themselves to complete an exchange. The latter can be more time-consuming, since the amount of data that must be copied between memory locations is potentially much greater. Another measure of efficiency is the amount of memory required by an algorithm. Chapters 10 and 11 discuss additional techniques for searching and sorting that are considerably more efficient than the simple ones discussed so far.

Exercises for Section 2.6

1. Determine how many times the Write statement is displayed in each of the following fragments. Indicate whether the algorithm is O(N) or $O(N^2)$.

   a. for I := 1 to N do
       for J := 1 to N do
         WriteLn (I, J)
   b. for I := 1 to N do
       for J := 1 to 2 do
         WriteLn (I, J)
   c. for I := 1 to N do
       for J := N downto I
         WriteLn (I, J)

Programming

1. Write a program that compares the following values of Y1 and Y2 for values N up to 100 in increments of 10. Does the result surprise you?

```
Y1 = 100N + 10
Y2 = 5N² + 2
```

2.7 Timing Program Execution

An alternative way of examining algorithm performance is by measuring the time required for a program to execute. If there are several factors that can affect an algorithm's performance, you need to plan your timing experiments so that only one factor is allowed to change at a time. For example, you might suspect that the execution performance of two sorting algorithms may be affected by both size of the array and the initial order of the data being sorted. To be fair, you should examine the time required by each algorithm to sort identical copies of the same array. In your experiments, you might decide to fix the array size at some reasonably large value and then examine the times required by each algorithm to sort the array when it has one of several different initial data orderings (e.g., already sorted, inversely ordered, and randomly ordered). You also might decide to select a single initial data ordering and then examine the time required by each algorithm to sort arrays of several different sizes having that data ordering.

Computing Current Time and Elapsed Time

The Borland Pascal unit Dos contains a procedure GetTime, which allows a program to obtain the time from the computer system's internal clock. Unfortunately, GetTime returns the 24-hour time as four variables (hours, minutes, seconds, and hundredths of a second). To translate the information returned by GetTime to a more usable form, it is helpful to define a function Clock that returns the system time as the number of seconds. To make this Clock easier to reuse, we have placed Clock in a unit Timer (see Fig. 2.15).

Figure 2.15
Unit Timer

Directory: CHAP 2
File: TIMER.PAS

```pascal
unit Timer;
{
 Unit exports function Clock which returns system clock
 time in seconds.

 Imports GetTime procedure from Turbo Pascal unit Dos.
}
interface

  uses Dos; {we need GetTime from the DOS unit}

  function Clock : Real;
  {
    Converts system clock time returned by GetTime to seconds.
  }

implementation

  function Clock : Real;

    const
      SecInMin = 60.0;    {# seconds in 1 minute}
      SecInHour = 3600.0; {# seconds in 1 hour}

    var
      Hour,                {Hour returned by GetTime}
      Minute,              {Minute returned by GetTime}
      Second,              {Seconds returned by GetTime}
      Sec100th : Word;     {Hundredths of sec. returned by GetTime}
      TotalSec : Real;     {running sum - conversions}

    begin {Clock}
      {Call system time function}
      GetTime (Hour, Minute, Second, Sec100th);

      {Convert 24 hour time to seconds}
      TotalSec := Second + Sec100th / 100.0;
      TotalSec := TotalSec + Minute * 60;
      TotalSec := TotalSec + Hour * 3600;

      Clock := TotalSec {return time in seconds}
    end; {Clock}

end. {Timer}
```

Timing an algorithm involves implementing the algorithm in a Pascal program that is a client of unit Timer. By saving the values returned by Clock before and after algorithm execution, it is possible to compute its execution time. The algorithm's execution time is obtained by subtracting the time execution begins from the time execution terminates as shown in Fig. 2.16.

You need to be very careful in comparing the execution times of algorithms run on two different computer systems, since execution times are influenced by both the characteristics of the computer hardware and the operating system used. For example, execution times measured on multi-user systems (such as local area networks) are greatly affected by the number of people using the computer system (or network) at any given time.

You also need to be careful in comparing the execution times of algorithms that depend on communication with external devices such as printers or disk drives. If you are not careful, you could end up timing the operational speed of the device rather than the execution speed of the algorithm.

Execution Profilers

Some computing systems contain programs called *execution profilers*. Some versions of Borland Pascal include an execution profiler. Typically, an execution profiler automatically counts the number of times a program's functions and procedures are called. The profiler might also keep track of how much time was spent executing each function or procedure. The execution

Figure 2.16
Skeletal Program for Computing Algorithm Execution Time

Directory: CHAP 2
File: TESTTIME.PAS

```
program TestTime;
{
  Program skeleton for timing algorithm execution.
}
  uses Timer;

  var
     StartTime,          {time algorithm execution begins}
     StopTime,           {time algorithm execution ends}
     TotalTime : Real;   {total algorithm execution time}

begin {TestTime}
   StartTime := Clock; {save system time in seconds}

   {Insert code here - for algorithm being timed.}

   StopTime := Clock; {save system time in seconds}

   {compute elapsed execution time}

   TotalTime := StopTime - StartTime;
   WriteLn ('Execution time ', TotalTime :4:2, ' seconds.')
end. {TestTime}
```

times obtained from an execution profiler are subject to many of the same limitations that we mentioned earlier. Despite these limitations, comparing execution times of algorithms can provide some insight into their relative efficiencies. This is especially useful for algorithms whose complexity (order of magnitude) cannot be determined with absolute certainty.

Exercises for Section 2.7   **Programming**

1. Compare the execution times required to compute the square roots of the numbers 1 to 10,000 using a
   a. for loop
   b. while loop
2. Modify the program that you developed in Programming Exercise 1 so that you include in the execution times the additional time required to write each square root to a disk file.

CHAPTER REVIEW

In this chapter we discussed methods of assessing program correctness and efficiency. We discussed planning for testing, selection of test teams, structured walk-throughs, black box testing, white box testing, and integration testing.

We introduced formal verification as an alternative to testing and described the use of assertions and loop invariants. In this text we will use informal logical statements about programs and loops to document our programs so that we can better understand them.

Big-O notation was introduced in this chapter as a means of assessing an algorithm's efficiency. We discussed timing algorithm execution as an alternative means of determining the efficiency of an algorithm implementation.

Quick-Check Exercises

1. What are the three broad categories of program bugs discussed in this chapter?
2. What is the purpose of desk checking an algorithm?
3. _____ testing requires the use of test data that exercise each statement in a module.
4. _____ testing focuses on testing the functional characteristics of a module.
5. Indicate which of the following may be false:

   `loop invariant, while condition, assertion`

6. The use of loop invariants is useful for which of the following?

   `loop control, loop design, loop verification`

7. Write a loop invariant for the following code segment:

```
Product := 1;
Counter := 2;
while Counter < 5 do
   begin
      Product := Product * Counter;
      Counter := Counter + 1
   end; {while}
```

8. Determine the order of magnitude for an algorithm whose running time is given by the expression

$$T(N) = 3N^4 - 2N^2 + 100N + 37.$$

Answers to Quick-Check Exercises

1. Syntax errors, run-time errors, logic errors
2. To increase the likelihood of finding program logic errors
3. White box
4. Black box
5. While condition
6. Loop design, loop verification
7. ```
   {invariant: Counter <= 0 and Product contains product of
    positive integers < Counter.
   }
   ```
8. $O(N^4)$

Review Questions

1. Describe a technique to prevent a run-time error caused by the user typing a bad character while entering a numeric value.
2. Describe the differences between top-down and bottom-up testing.
3. Briefly describe a test plan for the telephone directory program described in Chapter 1. Assume that integration testing is used.
4. Which of the following statements is incorrect?
   a. Loop invariants are used in loop verification.
   b. Loop invariants are used in loop design.
   c. A loop invariant is always an assertion.
   d. An assertion is always a loop invariant.
5. Write a procedure that counts the number of adjacent data items that are out of place in an array (assume that increasing order is desired). Include loop invariants and any other assertions necessary to verify that the procedure is correct.
6. Write a big-O expression for the following algorithm:

```
for I := 1 to N do
   for J := 1 to N do
      for K := N downto 1 do
         begin
            Sum := I + J + K;
            WriteLn (Sum)
         end; {for}
```
```

Programming Projects

Directory: CHAP 2
File: PROJ2_1.PAS

Directory: CHAP 2
File: PROJ2_2.PAS

Directory: CHAP 2
File: PROJ2_4.PAS

Directory: CHAP 2
File: PROJ2_5.PAS

1. Write a program that determines the average time required to successfully locate an integer in an array of 100 unordered integers using sequential search. Your program should also compute the average time required for a failed search in the same array. Each of your average times should be based on trials involving searching for at least 50 different numbers.

2. Add statements to Programming Project 1 that will let you determine the average number of array locations that were examined in the successful and unsuccessful searches.

3. Redo Programming Project 2 using an array of integers sorted in ascending order. Modify the sequential search algorithm to halt a search as soon as the array values are larger than the value being sought.

4. Write a program that allows you to examine the effects of array size and initial data order when selection sort operates on an array of integers. Test two different array sizes (N = 50 and N = 100) and three different array orderings (ascending order, inverse order, and random order). This should produce six test times. The Borland Pascal function `Random` may be helpful in building the randomly ordered arrays.

5. Add statements to Programming Project 4 that will let you determine the number of comparisons and exchanges that were required to sort each array.

6. Redo Programming Project 4 using an array of strings instead of an array of integers.

7. Write a set of stub methods for `LinearListADT` that could be used to test the logic of program `RunDirectory` (Fig. 1.13).

CHAPTER THREE

Arrays, Records, and Strings

There are several structured data types that are part of Borland Pascal. These include arrays, records, and strings. You were probably introduced to most, if not all, of these data types in your first programming course. In this chapter we will review these data types and discuss abstract data types for one-dimensional arrays and strings.

We will also discuss the use of *inheritance* as a means of adapting previously defined objects to meet the needs of new programming applications. Inheritance of object methods and data members allows us to write more reliable software by letting us reuse pieces of previously tested objects in the definition of new objects.

Inheritance also promotes information hiding, since a programmer needs to understand only an object's behavior and its interface to reuse it in the definition of a new object.

3.1 One-Dimensional Arrays

The one-dimensional array, or table, is often the first structured data type that most programmers encounter. You have probably written several programs that process arrays.

An array is an indexed collection of data elements that are all the same type. One array element is associated with each possible value of the array index (called the *array subscript*). For example, the declarations

```
type
    ArrayType = array [IndexType] of ElementType;

var
    A : ArrayType;
```

allocate storage for an array A whose elements are type ElementType. There will be one array element for each value in data type IndexType. For example, if IndexType is the subrange 1, . . . , 100, the array elements are denoted as A[1], A[2], . . . , A[100].

In most applications, IndexType will be a subrange of the integers. However, Pascal lets us use any ordinal type as IndexType. The following declarations declare two arrays, Codes and HeatHours, shown in Fig. 3.1. The array Codes contains characters that may be substituted for each letter of the alphabet in an encryption program. The array HeatHours contains the time in hours that our heating system was on during each day of the past week.

```
type
    Day = (Sunday, Monday, Tuesday, Wednesday,
           Thursday, Friday, Saturday);
    LetterIndex = 'A'..'Z';
    CodeArray = array [LetterIndex] of Char;
    HoursArray = array [Day] of Real;

var
    Today : Day;
    MaxHeat : Real;
    HeatHours : HoursArray;  {Array of heat usage.}
    Codes : CodeArray;       {Array of codes.}
```

The values in array Codes show that we are using the letter B as a code symbol for the letter A (Codes['A'] is B) and the letter A as a code symbol

Figure 3.1
Codes and HeatHours with
Sample Data Values

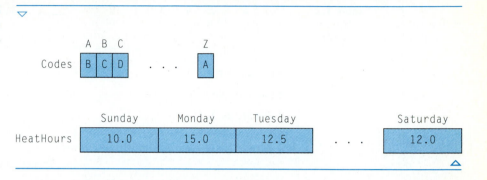

for the letter Z (Codes['Z'] is A). Array HeatHours shows that our heating system was on for 10 hours on Sunday (HeatHours[Sunday] is 10.0) and 12 hours on Saturday (HeatHours[Saturday] is 12.0).

We often use for loops to process arrays. For example the following for loop finds the largest value in the array HeatHours.

```
MaxHeat := HeatHours[Sunday]; {assume most use on Sunday}
for Today := Sunday through Saturday do
  if HeatHours[Today] > MaxHeat then
    MaxHeat := HeatHours[Today];

{assert: MaxHeat contains the largest value in HeatHours.}
WriteLn ('The largest heat usage was ', MaxHeat)
```

CASE STUDY　# Implementing an Abstract Indexed Table

Even though the array is a built-in data type in Pascal, we can describe an indexed table (or table) as an abstract data type. The basic list operations are Store and Retrieve. We can store a value in a list by specifying the value to be stored and an index value. We can retrieve a value by specifying an index value. Table 3.1 describes an indexed list. The principal difference between Table and LinearList is that Table does not require contiguous storage of data values, whereas LinearList does.

Table 3.1
Specification of
Abstract Table

Structure
A Table is an indexed collection of elements that are all the same data type; there is one array element corresponding to each value in the index type.

Operators
In the operator descriptions we will assume the following parameters:

Table 3.2
Specification for Abstract
Data Type StringADT

```
X has the same data type as the array elements.
I has the same data type as the array index.
Success is type Boolean and contains True if the operation
    completes its task successfully and False if it does not.
```

Table.Create   Creates an empty table.

Table.Init (X)   Initializes all elements of a table to X.

Table.Store (X, I)   The value in X is placed at the table
                                                         position having index I, and Success is
                                                         set to True. Otherwise, the table is
                                                         unchanged, and Success is set to False.

Table.Retrieve (var X, I, var Success)   If a value has been stored at the table
                                                         position having index I, it is returned
                                                         through X, and Success is set to True.
                                                         If a value has not been placed at the
                                                         table position with index I, X is not
                                                         defined, and Success is set to False.

Our abstract array or table has two advantages over Pascal's built-in arrays. First, it comes with an operator Init that can be used to initialize all elements of the table to the same value. Second, the Retrieve operator returns a table element value and also returns a Boolean value that indicates whether the table element value returned was meaningful. Many times we use tables that contain meaningful data in only part of the table. For example, Fig. 3.2 shows list X, which is partially filled with data; elements 1 through 5 are defined, while elements 6 through 10 are undefined. Although the situation depicted in Fig. 3.2 is most common, it is possible for a table that has not been initialized to have "holes" (undefined values) anywhere within its index range.

Figure 3.3 shows the Borland Pascal unit for an abstract array. We discuss the interface section first. For generality we will import the type declarations for IndexType and ElementType from unit IndexElementADT. We have

Figure 3.2
Partially Filled Array

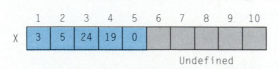

chosen to use a record with fields `Data` (type `ElementType`) and `Defined` (type `Boolean`) to represent each table element. The value of `Defined` indicates whether the table element contains meaningful data. The table itself is an object whose data member is an array of these records; its method members are the operators listed in Table 3.1.

Figure 3.3
Unit TableADT

Directory: CHAP 3
File: TABLEADT.PAS

```
unit TableADT;
{
 Abstract data type Table: contains declarations for data
 type Table and operator procedures for a Table object.
}
interface

  uses
     ElementIndexADT; {imports ElementType and IndexType}

  type
     TableElement = record
                      Data : ElementType;
                      Defined : Boolean
                    end; {TableElement}

     ElementsArray = array [IndexType] of TableElement;

     Table = object
               procedure Create;
               procedure Init
                            (X {input} : ElementType);
               procedure Store
                            (X {input} : ElementType;
                             I {input} : IndexType);
               procedure Retrieve
                            (var X {output} : ElementType;
                             I {input} : IndexType;
                             var Success {output} : Boolean);

             private
                Elements : ElementsArray;
             end; {Table}

implementation
  procedure Table.Create;
  {
    Creates an empty abstract array.
    Pre : None
    Post: Creates an empty array.
  }
```

▷ ▷ ▷ ▷ ▷ ▷

```
      var
         Index : IndexType;

   begin {Create}
      {Mark all elements as undefined.}
      for Index := Low(Elements) to High(Elements) do
         Elements[Index].Defined := False
   end; {Create}

   procedure Table.Init (X {input} : ElementType);
   {
    Initializes all elements of abstract array to X.
    Pre : Table created and X is defined.
    Post: All array elements set to X and marked as defined.
   }
      var
         Index : IndexType;

   begin {Init}
      for Index := Low(Elements) to High(Elements) do
         begin
            {Initialize all elements to X.}
            Elements[Index].Data := X;
            {Mark all elements as defined.}
            Elements[Index].Defined := True
         end
   end; {Init}

   procedure Table.Store (X {input} : ElementType;
                          I {input} : IndexType);
   {
    Stores X at index I of an abstract array.
    Pre : Table created, I and X are defined, value stored
          at Table position I is to be overwritten.
    Post: Elements[I].Data is X and Elements[I].Defined is
          True.
   }
   begin {Store}
      Elements[I].Data := X;
      Elements[I].Defined := True
   end; {Store}

   procedure Table.Retrieve (var X {output} : ElementType;
                             I {input} : IndexType;
                             var Success {output} : Boolean);
   {
    Copies to X the value stored at index I of Table.
    Pre : A Table has been created and I is defined.
    Post: Returns through X the element at index I if that
          element is defined. Sets Success to indicate
          success
          (True) or failure (False).
   }
   begin {Retrieve}
```

▷ ▷ ▷ ▷ ▷

```
    Success := Elements[I].Defined;
    if Success then
      X := Elements[I].Data
  end; {Retrieve}

end. {TableADT}
```

As shown in the implementation section, procedure Create marks all list elements as undefined; procedure Init stores the same initial value (X) in all table elements and marks them as defined. Both Create and Init use the loop header

```
for Index := Low(Elements) to High(Elements) do
```

to access all list elements. Function Low returns the lowest value in the subscript type (type IndexType) for data member Elements, and function High returns the highest value. Consequently, the local variable Index cycles through all values of data type IndexType during loop repetition, so all elements of data member Elements are accessed in sequence. Within the for loop in procedure Create, the statement

```
Elements[Index].Defined := False
```

sets the Defined field of the array element selected by Index to False because the array elements do not yet contain meaningful data.

Figure 3.4 shows a client program (with sample run) for TableADT that stores and retrieves values in list Codes. Figure 3.5 shows the declarations for ElementType and IndexType that would be needed in unit ElementIndex (see Fig. 3.5).

In Fig. 3.4 the repeat-until loop reads a sequence of letter and code symbol pairs. The if statement checks that an uppercase letter was read before attempting to store a code symbol in table Codes. After all code symbols are stored, the for loop cycles through the elements of table Codes and displays each code symbol or the string 'not defined'. For brevity the sample

Directory: CHAP 3
File: TESTTABL.PAS

Figure 3.4
Client of TableADT with
Sample Run

```
program TestTable;
{
 Program to test TableADT.
}
  uses TableADT;

  var
```

```
Codes : Table;
ChIn, ChOut, CodeSymbol : Char;
Success : Boolean;

begin {TestTable}
  Codes.Create;
  repeat
    {Get code table from user keyboard.}
    WriteLn ('Enter ** to stop -');
    Write ('or enter an uppercase letter followed by its code symbol>');
    ReadLn (ChIn, CodeSymbol);
    if ChIn in ['A'..'Z'] then
      begin
        Codes.Store (CodeSymbol, ChIn);
        Codes.Retrieve (ChOut, ChIn, Success);
        WriteLn ('For letter ', ChIn,
                 ' the code symbol is ', ChOut);
        WriteLn
      end {if}
    else
      WriteLn ('Not an uppercase letter-try again!')
  until ChIn = '*';

  {Display the array of code symbols so far}
  WriteLn (' Code Symbol');
  for ChIn := 'A' to 'Z' do
    begin
      Codes.Retrieve (ChOut, ChIn, Success);
      if Success then
        WriteLn (ChIn, ChOut :3)
      else
        WriteLn (ChIn, ' not defined')
    end {for}
end. {TestTable}

Enter ** to stop-or enter an
uppercase letter followed by its code symbol> AB

Enter ** to stop-or enter an
uppercase letter followed by its code symbol> bC
Not an uppercase letter-code not stored!

Enter ** to stop-or enter an
uppercase letter followed by its code symbol> BC

Enter ** to stop-or enter an
uppercase letter followed by its code symbol> CD

Enter ** to stop-or enter an
uppercase letter followed by its code symbol> ZA

Enter ** to stop-or enter an
uppercase letter followed by its code symbol> **
Not an uppercase letter-code not stored!
```

▷ ▷ ▷ ▷ ▷ ▷

```
   Code Symbol
A  B
B  C
C  D
D  not defined
E  not defined
 .  .  .

Z  A
```

run shows only the first five lines and the last line displayed by the for loop.

Obviously, we don't recommend that you use unit `TableADT` whenever you need to declare an array in a programming application. However, this provides a nice illustration of how you could create your own abstract data type to possibly enhance a built-in data type. Some small improvements over standard Pascal appear in `TableADT`. `TableADT` contains a method for initializing a table. The `Retrieve` method also indicates whether a meaningful value was returned.

Open Array Parameters

One of the shortcomings of standard Pascal is that functions or procedures written for one array type cannot be used with another array type. This means that if we write a procedure to sort an integer array with subscripts 1 through 100, we cannot reuse this same procedure to sort an integer array with subscripts 1 through 1000 or with subscripts `Sunday` through `Saturday` (values for enumerated type `Day`). To remove this restriction, Borland Pascal 7.0 provides open array parameters for procedures and functions.

For an open array parameter we specify only the element type and not the subscript type. Therefore an open array may correspond to any array with the required element type. In the procedure heading

```
procedure SelectSort (var SArray : array of Integer);
```

Figure 3.5
Unit `ElementIndexADT`

Directory: CHAP 3
File: ELEMENTI.PAS

```
unit ElementIndexADT;

interface
  type
    IndexType = 'A'..'Z';
    ElementType = Char;

implementation

end. {ElementIndexADT}
```

the formal parameter SArray is declared as an open array of type Integer elements.

Within the procedure body we need to reference individual elements of the array corresponding to SArray. This is complicated by the fact that the subscript type is not known when the procedure is written and may be different each time the procedure is called. Consequently, Borland Pascal assumes that the subscript lower bound is 0 and the subscript upper bound is $N - 1$, where N is the declared size of the array. Within function SelectSort the function reference High(SArray) would return the subscript upper bound.

Figure 3.6 shows procedure SelectSort, which sorts any array of integer elements. Procedure SelectSort rearranges the data in the entire array.

In the for loop with the header

```
for Fill := 0 to High(SArray) - 1 do
```

Fill takes on all values from 0 to $N - 2$, where N is the declared size of the actual array parameter. Because Fill is always positive, it is declared to be data type Word. A variable of type Word is an *unsigned integer* with a range of allowable values from 0 to 65,535.

For the following array MonthlyQuota

```
type
  Month = (January, February, March, April, May, June, July,
           August, September, October, November, December);
  QuotaArray = array [Month] of Integer;

var
  MonthlyQuota : QuotaArray;
```

we could use the procedure call

```
SelectSort (MonthlyQuota)
```

to sort all 12 values in the array.

It would be interesting to consider what changes would be required to revise procedure SelectSort to sort an instance of a table object. The procedure header would need to be changed because the elements of a table are type ElementType. Also, each reference to an array element (e.g., SArray[Next]) would have to be replaced by either a Store or a Retrieve operation. (See Programming Exercise 1.)

We could also consider adding a selection sort procedure as a method member for an abstract array object. In this case, SelectSort would not have a formal parameter list. We would reference array elements directly using the subscripted variable Elements[Next] in the implementation section of the abstract array object instead of using Store or Retrieve. (See Programming Exercise 2.)

Figure 3.6
Procedure `SelectSort`
with an Open Array
Parameter

Directory: CHAP 3
File: SELECTSO.PAS

```
procedure SelectSort
            (var SArray {input/output} : array of Integer);
{
 Sorts the data in array SArray.
 Pre : Array SArray is filled with data.
 Post: The values in array SArray are in increasing order.
}
  var
    Fill,    {index of element filled with next smallest score}
    Next,         {element being compared to smallest so far}
    IndexOfMin : Word;               {index of smallest so far}

begin {SelectSort}
  for Fill := 0 to High(SArray)-1 do
    begin
      {invariant:
          The elements in SArray[0..Fill - 1] are arranged in
          increasing order and Fill <= High(SArray)
      }

      {
       Find position of smallest element in
       Sarray[Fill..High(SArray)]
      }
      IndexOfMin := Fill;
      for Next := Fill + 1 to High(SArray) do
        {invariant:
            The element at IndexOfMin is the smallest in
            SArray[Fill..Next - 1] and Next <= High(SArray) + 1
        }
        if SArray[Next] < SArray[IndexOfMin] then
          IndexOfMin := Next;
      {
       assert: element at IndexOfMin is smallest in
       SArray[Fill..High(SArray)]
      }
      {Exchange elements with subscripts Fill and IndexOfMin}
      if IndexOfMin <> Fill then
        Switch (SArray[Fill], SArray[IndexOfMin])
    end {for Fill}
end; {SelectSort}
```

Exercises for Section 3.1

Self-Check

1. Why would you want to use the built-in array type instead of the abstract array defined by unit `TableADT`?
2. What are the advantages of using an open array type for a procedure formal parameter?

Programming

1. Rewrite `SelectSort` as a method of an indexed table object.
2. Rewrite `SelectSort` as a client procedure that sorts elements of an indexed table. Use the table Store and Retrieve operations.

3.2   Multidimensional Arrays

Pascal allows arrays of several dimensions, not just one. The following two-dimensional array Sales contains 10 rows and four columns.

```
type
   Quarter = (Summer, Fall, Winter, Spring);
   RowIndex = 1..10;
   SalesArray = array [RowIndex, Quarter] of Real;

var
   Sales : SalesArray;
   Row : Word;
   Column : Quarter;
   TotalSum, RowSum : Real;
```

Figure 3.7 shows the layout of this array.

We often use nested for loops to process multidimensional arrays. The following program fragment computes and displays the ten individual row sums and the total sum of all values stored in array Sales.

```
TotalSum := 0.0;
for Row := 1 to 10 do
   begin
      {Compute the row sum for the current row.}
      RowSum := 0.0;
      for Column := Summer to Spring do
        RowSum := RowSum + Sales[Row, Column];

      {Display the row sum and add it to the total.}
      WriteLn ('The sum for row ', Row :1, ' is ', RowSum :2:1);
      TotalSum := TotalSum + RowSum
   end; {for Row}

WriteLn ('The total sum is ', TotalSum :2:1)
```

Arrays of Arrays

Alternatively, we can declare a two-dimensional array as an array of arrays. In the following declarations, the array Sales is declared as an array of 10 elements, each of which is itself an array of four values.

```
type
   Quarter = (Summer, Fall, Winter, Spring);
   QuarterArray = array [Quarter] of Real;
   SalesArray = array [1..10] of QuarterArray;
```

Figure 3.7
Array Sales

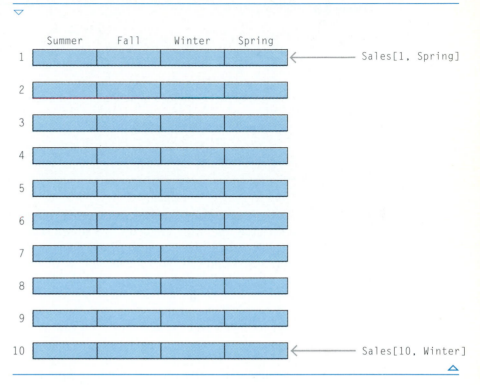

```
var
    Sales : SalesArray;        {2-D array of Sales [10 x 4] }
    SalesRow : QuarterArray;   {List of sales by quarter}
```

We can use either Sales[10, Spring] or Sales[10][Spring] to reference the last element in the last row of array Sales. We can use the subscripted variable Sales[10] to reference all four values in the last row. The statement

```
SalesRow := Sales[10]
```

copies the last row of array Sales into the list SalesRow.

Mapping an Array Reference to a Storage Location

When translating a module with the subscripted variable X[I, J], how does the compiler know how to access array element X[I, J] when it does not know what values I or J will have? The compiler must generate code that computes the actual storage location at run-time when these values are known. Instead of computing the actual storage location, it is sufficient to compute the offset of the array element with subscripts I, J from the first array element (say, X[1, 1] for simplicity).

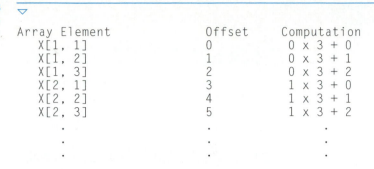

Figure 3.8
Offsets for Array X with
Dimensions [2 x 3]

```
Array Element              Offset        Computation
    X[1, 1]                0             0 x 3 + 0
    X[1, 2]                1             0 x 3 + 1
    X[1, 3]                2             0 x 3 + 2
    X[2, 1]                3             1 x 3 + 0
    X[2, 2]                4             1 x 3 + 1
    X[2, 3]                5             1 x 3 + 2
       .                   .                 .
       .                   .                 .
       .                   .                 .
```

To understand how the compiler does this, we must know something about how the array elements are stored. For a two-dimensional array the compiler stores the first row of elements in consecutive storage locations, then the second row of elements, and so on (see Fig. 3.8). The number of elements in the first row is the same as the number of columns in the array, or dim_2, the size of the second array dimension.

Figure 3.8 shows the offsets (on the right) for a two-dimensional array with two rows and five columns. You can use the formula

$$offset = (I - 1) \times dim_2 + (J - 1)$$

to compute the offset for X[I, J] where dim_2 is 3.

To actually locate array element X[I, J], the compiler must multiply the offset computed above by the number of bytes required for storing each array element. This value should then be added to the memory address of the first array element. We could use this access formula to extend our Table object to allow us to define two-dimensional abstract arrays (see Programming Project 1 at the end of this chapter).

This approach can be generalized for higher-dimensional arrays. Figure 3.9 shows how storage would be allocated to the first eight elements of array Y declared next.

Figure 3.9
Offsets for Array Y with
Dimensions [4 x 2 x 3]

```
Array Element              Offset        Computation
    Y[1, 1, 1]             0             0 x 2 x 3 + 0 x 3 + 0
    Y[1, 1, 2]             1             0 x 2 x 3 + 0 x 3 + 1
    Y[1, 1, 3]             2             0 x 2 x 3 + 0 x 3 + 2
    Y[1, 2, 1]             3             0 x 2 x 3 + 1 x 3 + 0
    Y[1, 2, 2]             4             0 x 2 x 3 + 1 x 3 + 1
    Y[1, 2, 3]             5             0 x 2 x 3 + 1 x 3 + 2
    Y[2, 1, 1]             6             1 x 2 x 3 + 0 x 3 + 0
    Y[2, 1, 2]             7             1 x 2 x 3 + 0 x 3 + 1
```

```
var
  Y : array [1..4,1..2,1..3] of Integer;
```

The following formula is used to compute the offset for array element Y[I, J, K]:

$$offset = (I - 1) \times dim_2 \times dim_3 + (J - 1) \times dim_3 + (K - 1)$$

For array Y shown in Fig. 3.9, dim_2 is 2 and dim_3 is 3.

For an array Z with n dimensions we could use the following formula to compute the offset for element Z[I1, I2, . . . , In].

$$offset = (I1 - 1) \times dim_2 \times dim_3 \ldots \times dim_n +$$
$$(I2 - 1) \times dim_3 \times dim_4 \ldots \times dim_n + \ldots + (In - 1)$$

We leave the verification of this formula to the reader.

Exercises for Section 3.2 ***Self-Check***

1. Determine the offset for array element A[2, 3, 1] if A has dimensions [4 x 5 x 3].

Programming

1. Write a function that returns the largest value in a two-dimensional array of Real values. The function should have three parameters: the array, its largest row subscript, and its largest column subscript. Assume that the row and column subscripts start at 1.
2. Assume that you already have a function that returns the largest value in a real list (one-dimensional array). Write a new function that uses the old function to find the largest value in an array of arrays.

3.3 Records and Arrays of Records

Earlier, we used the record type shown below to represent each element of a table (see Fig. 3.3). Each record of type TableElement has two *fields* named Data and Defined.

```
type
  TableElement = record
                   Data : ElementType;
                   Defined : Boolean
                 end; {TableElement}

  Clerk, Janitor : TableElement;
```

To reference a particular field of a record variable, we must use a *field selector* consisting of the record variable (also called a *qualifier*) followed by the field name. A period separates the qualifier and the field name. The field selector Janitor.Defined selects field Defined of record Janitor.

If there are frequent references to the same qualifier in a single or compound statement, we can ease our typing burden by using the with statement as shown next.

```
with Janitor do
  begin
    WriteLn (Defined);
    if Defined then
      Display (Data)
  end {with}
```

Within the body of the if statement, each occurrence of the field names Defined and Data is assumed to be qualified by record variable Janitor.

We can pass a record variable as a value or variable parameter to a procedure (e.g., procedure Display). We can also copy one record variable to another of the same type as in the following assignment statement:

```
Clerk := Janitor;
```

Mapping a Record Field Reference to a Storage Location

When translating a module with a record field reference like Janitor.Defined, how does the compiler know which memory location to access at run-time? Record field storage locations must be determined during program compilation, unlike subscripted array references, which may contain variables that do not receive their values until program run-time.

To understand what the compiler needs to do, we need to know something about how record fields are stored in memory. Record fields, like array elements, are stored in consecutive memory locations. The name of the record is associated with a location in memory called its *base address*. To access a record field, the compiler needs to know its starting location. To do this, the compiler creates a table that contains the starting location of each field expressed as its offset from the record's base address. To determine the storage location for a record field, the compiler examines this table to determine the field's offset and adds the offset to the record's base address. Figure 3.10 shows the offsets in bytes for record Bolt declared below, assuming that its base address is 1000.

```
type
  Part = record
           Num : Integer;
           Cost : Real;
           Supplier : string
         end; {Part}

var
  Bolt : Part;
```

Hierarchical Records

Records can have other records as fields. For example, the following record Student has a record field named ExamData.

Figure 3.10

Offsets and Addresses for
Field of Record Bolt

Field	Length in Bytes	Offset	Address
Num	2	0	1000
Cost	6	2	1002
Supplier	256	8	1008

```
type
  ExamData = record
                Score : Integer;
                Grade : Char
            end; {ExamData}

  Student = record
                Name : string;
                FinalExam : ExamData;
                CourseGrade : Char
            end; {Student}

var
  AStudent : Student;
```

To reference the final exam grade for AStudent, we must use the field selector `AStudent.FinalExam.Grade`, which shows that `Grade` is a field of `FinalExam`, which is itself a field of record `AStudent`.

Arrays of Records

Arrays of records are very convenient data structures. We used an array of records in our earlier implementation of an abstract array (see Fig. 3.3). In this implementation record field identifier Elements[Next].Data referenced the Data field of the array element selected by subscript Next.

As another example of an array of records, let's see how we would represent a class of students using the student record shown earlier. If we have a class of ten students, we could add the type and variable declarations below to those shown earlier.

```
type
  ClassIndex = 1..10;
  StudentArray = array [ClassIndex] of Student;

var
  MyClass : StudentArray;
```

Each element of `MyClass` would be a record of type `Student`. Figure 3.11 shows the layout of this array.

Figure 3.11
Array MyClass

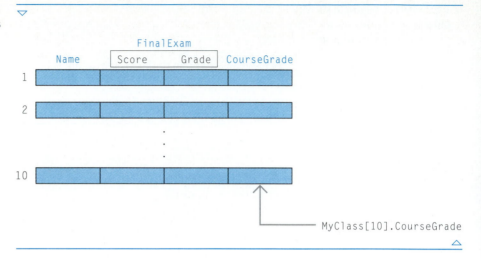

MyClass[10].CourseGrade

Each field in this array must be qualified by MyClass[*subscript*]. As shown in Fig. 3.11, the field selector MyClass[10].CourseGrade references the CourseGrade field of the last array element. The field selector MyClass[1].FinalExam.Score references the Score field of subrecord FinalExam for the first array element.

Usually, we process each record in an array of records as a composite unit. This means that we would use a procedure to read all values for a single student into a record variable (say, AStudent). Then we could assign that record variable to a particular element of array MyClass. As an example, assume that procedure ReadStudent reads data into a record of type Student. We can use the following statements to read the next student record and store these data in the Ith element of array MyClass.

```
ReadStudent (AStudent);
MyClass[I] := AStudent;
```

Exercises for Section 3.3   ***Self-Check***

1. What is being referenced by MyClass[3].Name[2]?
2. How does a two-dimensional array differ from an array of records?

Programming

1. Write procedure ReadStudent. Prompt the user to enter data from the keyboard for each record field.

3.4 Variant Records

Sometimes we would like to declare records that have several fields that are the same but also have some fields that are different. An example is a record that could be used to store a geometric figure. For all figures we would want to store the name of the figure as a string (e.g., 'circle'), its perimeter, and its area. Then for a circle we would store its radius, for a square its side length, for a rectangle its width and height, for a triangle its base and height, and so on. We can use the following record type `Figure` to do this.

```
type
   FigKind = (Circle, Rectangle, Square, Triangle);

   Figure = record
              Name : string;
              Area, Perimeter : Real;
            case Shape : FigKind of
              Circle : (Radius : Real);
              Rectangle : (Width, Length : Real);
              Square : (Side : Real);
              Triangle : (Base, Height : Real)
            end; {Figure}

var
   MyFigure : Figure;
```

The record type above actually has four fixed fields: `Name`, `Area`, `Perimeter`, and `Shape`. Shape is known as the *tag field* for variant record type Figure. The tag field is always defined as the last fixed field and must appear after the reserved word **case**. For any record variable the value of the tag field determines which of the record variants is defined. Because Shape is type FigKind, there are four possible variants, one for each value of the enumerated type `FigKind`. The variants are listed as case labels; the fields associated with each variant appear in parentheses following the corresponding case label. For example, field `Radius` (type `Real`) is associated with a record whose `Shape` field has the value `Circle`.

Figure 3.12 shows a sketch of record variable `MyFigure`. The compiler always allocates the maximum storage space that might be needed for a record variant. As shown in the figure, there is unused space when the record variable stored has a tag field of `Circle` or `Square`.

Figure 3.12
Instances of Record
Variable MyFigure

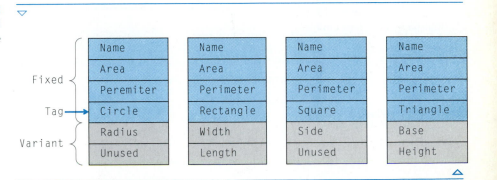

The following assignment statements store data in record variable MyFigure using the variant for a circle.

```
MyFigure.Shape := Circle;
MyFigure.Name := 'circle';
MyFigure.Radius := 1.0;
MyFigure.Area := Pi * Sqr(MyFigure.Radius);
MyFigure.Perimeter := 2 * Pi * MyFigure.Radius;
```

Often, we define the tag field first and then use a case statement to store values in the remaining fields of a record with variants. On the basis of the value stored in its tag field, the following case statement stores an appropriate string in the Name field of record MyFigure.

```
case MyFigure.Shape of
   Circle : MyFigure.Name := 'circle';
   Rectangle : MyFigure.Name := 'rectangle';
   Square : MyFigure.Name := 'square';
   Triangle : MyFigure.Name := 'triangle'
end; {case}
```

You must be careful to reference only the fields that are defined for a particular variant. For example, if the tag field value is `Circle`, it makes no sense to reference fields `Side`, `Base`, or `Width`. Pascal cannot detect this kind of error.

CASE STUDY   An Abstract Data Type for Figures

Let's say we wanted to write an abstract data type that enabled us to manipulate a variety of geometric figures. One way to do this would be to create a unit whose interface section contained a declaration for record type `Figure` and procedure headers for several of its operator procedures. The implementation section would contain complete procedure declarations. Figure 3.13 shows the interface section for unit `FigureADT`.

Figure 3.13
Interface Section of Unit
`FigureADT`

Directory: CHAP 3
File: FIGUREAD.PAS

```
unit FigureADT;
{
   Abstract data type Figure with procedures for reading
   and displaying the characteristics of type Figure.
}
interface

   type
      FigKind = (Circle, Rectangle, Square, Triangle);
```

▷ ▷ ▷ ▷ ▷

```
Figure = record
          Name : string;
          Area, Perimeter : Real;
        case Shape : FigKind of
          Circle        : (Radius : Real);
          Rectangle     : (Width, Length : Real);
          Square        : (Side : Real);
          Triangle      : (Base, Height : Real)
        end; {Figure}

procedure Create (var Fig {output} : Figure);
{Creates a figure with Name field a null string.}

procedure Init (var Fig {input/output} : Figure;
                    ShapeVal {input} : FigKind;
                    Val1, Val2 {input} : Real);
{
  Stores data in a figure.
  Pre : The figure has been created.
  Post: The fixed and variant part of a figure with tag field
        ShapeVal is defined. If the figure has one data field
        in its variant part, Val1 is stored in it and Val2 is
        ignored. Otherwise, Val1 and Val2 are stored.
}

procedure ComputePerim (var Fig {input/output} : Figure);
{
  Defines Perimeter field of Fig.
  Pre : The tag field and characteristics of Fig are defined.
  Post: Assigns value to Perimeter field.
}

procedure ComputeArea (var Fig {input/output} : Figure);
{
  Defines Area field of Fig.
  Pre : The tag field and characteristics of Fig are defined.
  Post: Assigns value to Area field.
}

function GetName (Fig {input} : Figure) : string;
{
  Retrieves the name field of Fig.
  Pre : none
  Post: The function result is Figure.Name.
}

function GetArea (Fig {input} : Figure) : Real;
{
  Retrieves the area field of Fig.
  Pre : none
  Post: The function result is Figure.Name.
}

function GetPerim (Fig {input} : Figure) : Real;
```

▷ ▷ ▷ ▷ ▷ ▷

```
{
  Retrieves the perimeter field of Fig.
  Pre : none
  Post: The function result is Figure.Name.
}

function GetFirstVar (Fig {input} : Figure) : Real;
{
  Retrieves the first variant field of Fig.
  Pre : none
  Post: The function result is the first variant field value.
}

function GetSecondVar (Fig {input} : Figure) : Real;
{
  Retrieves the second variant field of Fig.
  Pre : none
  Post: If Fig has two variant fields, the function result
        is the second variant field value; otherwise, the
        function result is undefined.
}

procedure Display (Fig {input} : Figure);
{
  Displays the characteristics of Fig.
  Pre : All fields of Fig are defined.
  Post: Displays each field of Fig.
}
```

Figure 3.14
Part of the Implementation
Section of Unit FigureADT

Directory: CHAP 3
File: FIGUREAD.PAS

```
implementation                        {operator procedures}

  procedure Create (var Fig {output} : Figure);
  begin {Create}
    Fig.Name := "
  end; {Create}

  procedure Init (var Fig {input/output} : Figure;
                  ShapeVal {input} : FigKind;
                  Val1, Val2 {input} : Real);
  begin {Init}
    with Fig do
      case ShapeVal of
        Circle :           begin
                             Shape := Circle;
                             Name := 'circle';
```

▷ ▷ ▷ ▷ ▷

```
                        Radius := Val1
                    end; {Circle}
        Rectangle : begin
                      Shape := Rectangle;
                      Name := 'rectangle';
                      Length := Val1;
                      Width := Val2
                    end; {Rectangle}
        Square :    begin
                      Shape := Square;
                      Name := 'square';
                      Side := Val1
                    end; {Square}
        Triangle :  begin
                      Shape := Triangle;
                      Name := 'triangle';
                      Base := Val1;
                      Height := Val2
                    end {Triangle}
      end {case}
end; {Init}

procedure ComputePerim (var Fig {input/output} : Figure);
begin {ComputePerim}
  with Fig do
    case Shape of
      Circle    : Perimeter := 2 * Pi * Radius;
      Rectangle : Perimeter := 2 * (Width + Length);
      Square    : Perimeter := 4 * Side;
      Triangle  : Perimeter := Base + Height +
                               Sqrt(Sqr(Base) +
                               Sqr(Height))
    end {case}
end; {ComputePerim}

procedure ComputeArea (var Fig {input/output} : Figure);
begin {ComputeArea}
  with Fig do
    case Shape of
      Circle    : Area := Pi * Radius * Radius;
      Rectangle : Area := Width * Length;
      Square    : Area := Side * Side;
      Triangle  : Area := 0.5 * Base * Height
    end {case}
end; {ComputeArea}

function GetFirstVar (Fig : Figure) : Real;
begin {GetFirstVar}
  case Fig.Shape of
    Circle    : GetFirstVar := Fig.Radius;
    Rectangle : GetFirstVar := Fig.Length;
    Square    : GetFirstVar := Fig.Side;
```

▷ ▷ ▷ ▷ ▷ ▷

```
      Triangle  : GetFirstVar := Fig.Base
    end {case}
  end; {GetFirstVar}

  function GetSecondVar (Fig : Figure) : Real;
  begin {GetSecond}
    case Fig.Shape of
      Circle    : {not defined} ;
      Rectangle : GetSecondVar := Fig.Length;
      Square    : {not defined} ;
      Triangle  : GetSecondVar := Fig.Base
    end {case}
  end; {GetSecondVar}
end. {Figure ADT}
```

△

Figure 3.14 shows part of the implementation section of FigureADT. Procedure Create sets the Name field of a new figure to the null string ("). Procedure Init stores ShapeVal into the tag field, defines the name field, and stores either Val1 or both Val1 and Val2 in the appropriate variant field(s).

The accessor functions GetName, GetArea, and so on are all pretty straightforward. Accessor function GetSecondVar returns the value stored in the second variant field. As shown, its value is not defined when the figure is a circle or square. Procedure Display displays all fields of a record of type Figure. The case statement is used to display the record's variant part.

Using FigureADT

Figure 3.15 provides a simple client program that uses FigureADT. The program creates a rectangle and a square, stores data in both records, computes the area and perimeter of each figure, and displays the figure's characteristics.

The availability of record variants allows us to store a variety of different shapes of figures using just one record type. However, the approach just illustrated has some serious limitations. Let's say we wanted to add another geometric figure, say rhombus, to our collection of simple figures. First, we would have to add another variant to record type Figure. Next, we would have to change every operator procedure, adding an extra alternative to each case statement to handle rhombuses. In general, it is better not to modify procedures that have already been implemented, tested, and in use. In the next section we will see an alternative approach that has none of these limitations.

Exercises for Section 3.4

Self-Check

1. What is the reason for including a tag field in a variant record type declaration?

Figure 3.15
Client Program
for `FigureADT` with
Sample Run

Directory: CHAP 3
File: TESTFIGA.PAS

```
program TestFigure;
{
 Program to test unit FigureADT.
}
uses FigureADT;

  var
    MySquare, MyRectangle : Figure;

begin {TestFigure}
  Create (MySquare);
  Create (MyRectangle);

  Init (MyRectangle, Rectangle, 5.0, 10.0);
  ComputePerim (MyRectangle);
  ComputeArea (MyRectangle);
  Display (MyRectangle);
  WriteLn;

  Init (MySquare, Square, 7.0, 0.0);
  ComputePerim (MySquare);
  ComputeArea (MySquare);
  Display (MySquare);
  WriteLn
end. {TestFigure}

Figure kind is rectangle
Area is 50.00
Perimeter is 30.00
Width is 10.00
Length is 5.00

Figure kind is square
Area is 49.00
Perimeter is 28.00
Side is 7.00
```

Programming

1. Write a client program for unit `FigureADT` that prompts the user to enter information for 10 figures and stores this information in an array of figures.
2. Write a procedure that uses the character ⋆ to draw a picture on the computer screen for rectangle or square variants of `Figure` type variables. Assume that one ⋆ is used for each unit of length or width.

3.5 Object Inheritance

Another way to look at the collection of figures that we have been discussing is that they are all specializations of a general figure. A general figure has properties such as name, area, and perimeter. But then each of these objects has its own special properties depending on whether it is a circle, a rectangle, and so on.

Object-oriented programming allows us to implement this representation of our collection of figures using a property called *inheritance*. Each figure type can be considered a *descendant* of a general figure object type (the *ancestor*). Just as children inherit certain characteristics from their parents, a descendant type can inherit properties of its ancestor type. A descendant type will inherit all the data members of its ancestor object and may have additional data members of its own. A descendant type will also inherit all the method members of its ancestor, but it may redefine these methods. A descendant object may also have its own additional data members.

Figure 3.16 is a sketch of a general figure object and its descendants. Rather than represent a square as a direct descendant of Figure, we have shown Square as a descendant of Rectangle (a rectangle whose length and width are the same).

Figure 3.17 is a more detailed description of this object hierarchy. It shows each object along with its method and data members. As shown, the general Figure object has three data members: Name, Area, and Perimeter. All other objects inherit these three data members and add data members of their own (e.g., Length and Width for Rectangle). The object Square does not have any data members of its own, since a square is a rectangle whose length and width are equal. Each object including the general Figure object has its own Init and Display method members. Each object, except for the general Figure object and the Square object, has its own method for computing area and perimeter. The Square object inherits these methods from Rectangle.

Figure 3.16
Ancestor Tree (Hierarchy)
for Geometric Figures

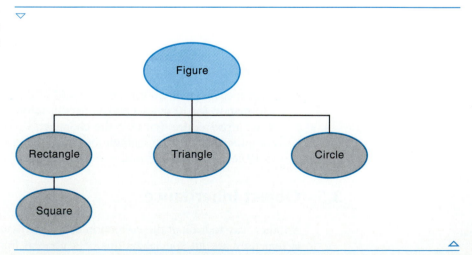

Figure 3.17
Object Hierarchy with
Method and Data Members

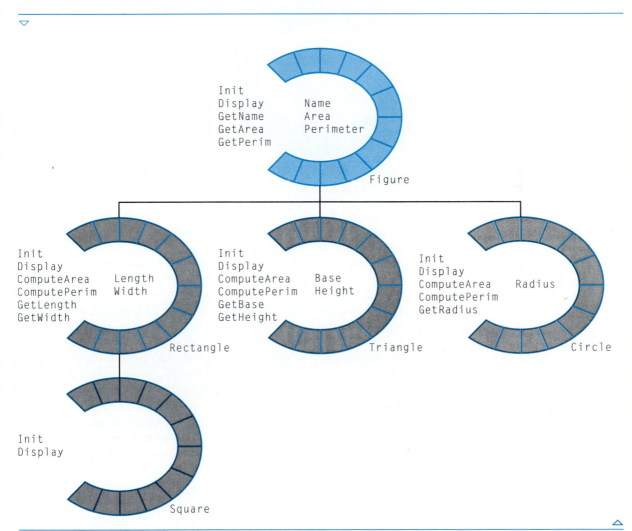

```
Init
Display        Name
GetName        Area
GetArea        Perimeter
GetPerim
                          Figure
```

```
Init
Display
ComputeArea    Length
ComputePerim   Width
GetLength
GetWidth
                  Rectangle
```

```
Init
Display
ComputeArea    Base
ComputePerim   Height
GetBase
GetHeight
                  Triangle
```

```
Init
Display
ComputeArea    Radius
ComputePerim
GetRadius
                  Circle
```

```
Init
Display

                  Square
```

Figure 3.18 shows a more complete specification of object Rectangle. In Fig. 3.18 the data and method members that are inherited are shown in italics.

Figure 3.19 shows unit FigFamilyADT. For brevity we have just shown three object types: Figure, Rectangle, and Square. In the interface section the header of the declaration for each descendant object shows its ancestor in parentheses (e.g., Rectangle = object(Figure); Square = object(Rectangle)). You may notice that the reserved word virtual follows declarations of several method headings. This tells the Borland Pascal

Figure 3.18
Object `Rectangle` with
Inherited Members
in Italics

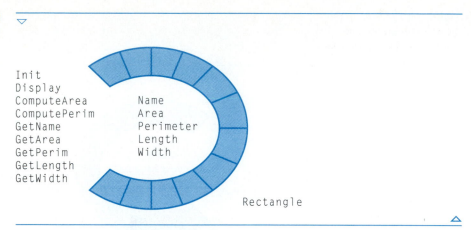

```
Init
Display
ComputeArea        Name
ComputePerim       Area
GetName            Perimeter
GetArea            Length
GetPerim           Width
GetLength
GetWidth
```

Rectangle

compiler that methods are to be treated as virtual methods rather than as static methods, which is the default method declaration.

Calls to static methods are resolved during program compilation, while calls to virtual methods are resolved at program run-time. When static methods are redefined by descendant object types, it is permissible to make changes in the method parameter lists or function return types. Virtual methods must have identical parameter lists and function return types in all descendant object types. For reasons that we will explain more fully in Chapter 12, methods that are likely to be redefined in descendant object types should be declared as virtual methods to maximize their reusability.

Objects that contain virtual methods must be explicitly initialized at run-time by calls to special methods known as *constructors*. Constructors are defined in the same way as procedures, except that the reserved word `constructor` is used in place of the reserved word `procedure`. Constructors are called in the same way as other methods. An object may have several constructors, which may be inherited. Constructors may be declared as virtual methods.

Figure 3.19
Unit `FigFamilyADT`

Directory: CHAP 3
File: FIGFAMIL.PAS

```
unit FigFamilyADT;
{
 Defines a family of Figure objects with methods for
 initializing and displaying their attributes.
}
interface
type
  Figure = object
              constructor Init;
              procedure Display;
              function GetName : string;
```

```
                    function GetArea : Real;
                    function GetPerim : Real;

             private
                Name : string;
                Area, Perimeter : Real;
             end; {Figure}

   Rectangle = object(Figure)
                constructor Init
                             (LengthVal, WidthVal {input} : Real);
                procedure Display; virtual;
                procedure ComputeArea; virtual;
                procedure ComputePerim; virtual;

                 private
                    Length, Width : Real;
                 end; {Rectangle}

   Square = object(Rectangle)
                constructor Init (SideVal {input} : Real);
                procedure Display; virtual;
              end; {Square}

implementation

  constructor Figure.Init;
  {
   Initializes Figure type objects.
   Pre : None.
   Post: Figure object initialized and data fields defined.
  }
  begin {Init}
    Name := '';
     {
      Area and Perimeter initialized to prevent run-time errors
      if accessor functions GetArea or GetPerimeter are called.
     }
     Area := 0.0;
     Perimeter := 0.0
  end; {Init}

  procedure Figure.Display;
  {
   Displays attributes of Figure type objects.
   Pre : Object initialized and all data fields defined.
   Post: Displays values of fields Name, Area, and Perimeter.
  }
  begin {Display}
     if Name = '' then
       WriteLn ('Figure is not defined')
     else
       begin
         WriteLn ('Figure is ', Name);
```

▷ ▷ ▷ ▷ ▷ ▷

```
       WriteLn ('Area is ', Area :3:1);
       WriteLn ('Perimeter is ', Perimeter :3:1)
     end {if}
end; {Display}

function Figure.GetName : string;
{Returns value of object Name field.}
begin {GetName}
  GetName := Name
end; {GetName}

function Figure.GetArea : Real;
{Returns value of object Area field.}
begin {GetArea}
  GetArea := Area
end; {GetArea}

function Figure.GetPerim : Real;
{Returns value of object Perimeter field.}
begin {GetPerimeter}
  GetPerim := Perimeter
end; {GetPerimeter}

constructor Rectangle.Init (LengthVal, WidthVal : Real);
{
 Initializes Rectangle type objects.
 Pre : None.
 Post: Rectangle object initialized and fields Name,
       Length, and Width are defined.
}
begin {Init}
  Name := 'Rectangle';
  Length := LengthVal;
  Width := WidthVal
end; {Init}

procedure Rectangle.ComputeArea;
{
 Computes area for Rectangle type objects.
 Pre : Object initialized.
 Post: Area field assigned computed value.
}
begin {ComputeArea}
  Area := Length * Width
end; {ComputeArea}

procedure Rectangle.ComputePerim;
{
 Computes perimeter for Rectangle type objects.
 Pre : Object initialized.
 Post: Perimeter field assigned computed value.
}
begin {ComputePerim}
  Perimeter := 2 * (Length + Width)
end; {ComputePerim}
```

▷ ▷ ▷ ▷ ▷

```
procedure Rectangle.Display;
{
 Displays attributes of Rectangle type objects.
 Pre : Object initialized and methods have been called to
       compute values for data fields Area and Perimeter.
 Post: Displays values of fields Name, Area, Perimeter,
       Length, and Width.
}
begin {Display}
  Figure.Display;
  WriteLn ('Width is ', Width :3:1);
  WriteLn ('Length is ', Length :3:1)
end; {Display}

constructor Square.Init (SideVal : Real);
{
 Initializes Square type objects.
 Pre : None.
 Post: Square object initialized and fields Name, Length,
       and Width are defined.
}
begin {Init}
  Name := 'Square';
  Width := SideVal;
  Length := SideVal
end; {Init}

procedure Square.Display;
{
 Displays attributes of Square type objects.
 Pre : Object initialized and methods have been called to
       compute values for data fields Area and Perimeter.
 Post: Displays values of fields Name, Area, Perimeter, and
       Width.
}
begin {Display}
  Figure.Display;
  WriteLn ('Side is ', Width :3:1)
end; {Display}

end. {FigFamilyADT}
```

The {$R+} compiler directive in a client program can be used to force each virtual method call to check the initialization status of the object instance making the call. Calling a virtual method before calling the object's constructor may cause your computer system to crash.

A number of features of the implementation section need explanation. Both procedures Rectangle.Display and Square.Display begin with a call to Figure.Display, which displays the Name, Area, and Perimeter data members of an object instance if the Name field of that object instance is defined. Procedure `Square.Init` assigns SideVal to its data members `Length` and `Width`, both of which are inherited from `Rectangle`.

Square does not have its own method to compute perimeter and area, so it inherits methods `ComputePerim` and `ComputeArea` from object `Rectangle`. Because `Width` and `Height` are set to the same value when `Square.Init` executes, the values computed by these inherited methods will be correct.

Accessor methods `GetName`, `GetArea`, and `GetPerim` are defined in object `Figure` and are inherited by all its descendants. Although not required, we initialized the fields `Area` and `Perimeter` to avoid a run-time error if accessor methods `GetArea` and `GetPerimeter` are called before these fields are defined. This could be accomplished by calling constructor `Figure.Init` as the first statement in both `Rectangle.Init` and `Square.Init`. It might also be desirable to define additional accessor methods in objects `Rectangle` and `Square` to allow access to any fields that are not present in their ancestor `Figure`.

Program Style

Advantages of Object Inheritance

There are several important advantages to using inheritance. First of all, we have minimized the effort required to introduce a new geometric figure type as each new figure has the capability of inheriting data and method members from its ancestor. For example, we were able to add object Square by providing only two new method members. Second, if we want to add a new figure (say, `Triangle` or `Circle`), we could do this without modifying the objects and methods that have already been written. Third, we could place these new objects in a separate unit and import all ancestor objects and their methods by placing the statement

```
uses FigFamilyADT;
```

in the interface section of the new unit. Then we could compile just the new unit and would not need to recompile `FigFamilyADT`.

Using FigFamilyADT

Figure 3.20 shows a client program that initializes a general figure object and a rectangle and a square object. After the objects are initialized, the areas and perimeters of the rectangle and square are computed, and their characteristics are displayed.

Object Type Compatibility

The rules of assignment compatibility have been extended to allow variables declared as instances of an object to be assigned values of another instance of the same object or any of its descendant types. For example, if F1 is a vari-

Figure 3.20
Client Program for
`FigFamilyADT` with
Sample Run

Directory: CHAP 3
File: TESTFIFA.PAS

```
program TestFigFamily;
{
 Program tests FigFamilyADT.
}
  uses FigFamilyADT;

  var
    MyFigure : Figure;
    MyRectangle : Rectangle;
    MySquare : Square;

begin {TestFigFamilyADT}
  MyFigure.Init;

  MyRectangle.Init (5.0, 10.0);    {Create a 5 x 10 rectangle.}
  MyRectangle.ComputePerim;
  MyRectangle.ComputeArea;

  MySquare.Init (7.0);             {Create a square with side 7.0.}
  MySquare.ComputePerim;
  MySquare.ComputeArea;

  MyFigure.Display; {Display general figure object instance.}
  WriteLn;

  MyRectangle.Display;    {Display Rectangle object instance.}
  WriteLn;

  MySquare.Display;            {Display Square object instance.}
  WriteLn
end. {TestFigFamilyADT}

Figure is not defined

Figure is Rectangle
Area is 50.0
Perimeter is 30.0
Width is 10.0
Length is 5.0
Figure is Square
Area is 49.0
Perimeter is 28.0
Side is 7.0
```

able of type Figure and R1 is of type Rectangle, the following is a valid as-signment statement

```
F1 := R1
```

Only the fields of R1 that were inherited from `Figure` will have their values copied to the corresponding fields of F1. Both F1 and R1 must have been initialized by appropriate constructor calls before this assignment. Because inheritance is a nonsymmetric relationship, F1 may not be assigned to R1.

The rules of assignment compatibility also apply to variable formal parameters that are declared as object types. Consequently, either F1 or R1 could be used as actual parameters in calling procedures having a formal variable parameter declared to be of type Figure.

SYNTAX DISPLAY

Descendant Object Declaration

Form: type
```
        descendant type = object(ancestor type)
                        field list;
                        method heading list;
                    private
                        field list;
                        method list
                    end;
```

Example: type
```
        Person = object
                constructor Init (N : string);
                procedure Display; virtual;
            private
                Name : string;
            end; {Person}

        Student = object(Person)
                constructor Init (N : string; R :
                Real);
                procedure Display; virtual;
            private
                GPA : Real;
            end; {Student}
```

Interpretation: The type declaration for *descendant type* must contain *ancestor type* inside parentheses following the reserved word object. The *ancestor type* must be a previously declared object type. The *descendant type* inherits all fields present in its *ancestor type*. Inherited fields may not be redefined in descendant objects. Object field identifiers must be unique within an object, all its descendants, and their methods.

The *descendant type* inherits all ancestor type methods that it does not redefine. Once a method is redefined by a *descendant type,* its scope becomes that of the *descendant type* unless the method was declared by using the virtual directive. Virtual methods must contain identical method heading declarations in all subsequent descendant type declarations.

Objects containing virtual methods need to be initialized at run-time by calling special methods known as constructors. An object may have more than one constructor, and constructors may not be virtual. Constructor declarations are similar to those of ordinary methods, except that the reserved word constructor is used in place of either function or procedure in the method heading declaration.

Notes: The {$R+} compiler directive can be used to force Borland Pascal to check the initialization status of an object before calling a virtual method. When range-checking is active, a run-time error occurs when a virtual method call is for an object not properly initialized by a constructor.

Use of Self

An object's field identifiers may not be redefined as formal parameters or local identifiers in any of the object's methods. However, it is possible for identifiers that are not part of the object to be the same as the object's field identifiers. To refer to an object field that has the same name as some other identifier in the same scope, the object field identifier can be qualified by using the identifier Self. Within a method, Self always refers to the object instance making the method call. For example, within the method Figure.ComputeArea an assignment to the object field Area could be written as

```
Self.Area := 0.0
```

Exercises for Section 3.5

Self-Check

1. Why would you need to use a constructor method to initialize an object instance?
2. What are the advantages of using object inheritance to extend object types?

Programming

1. Implement object types Circle and Triangle as descendants of object type Figure, using the declarations in unit FigureADT as a guide.
2. Write a client program to test the implementation of your object types Circle and Triangle.

3.6 Strings

Many computer applications are concerned with the manipulation of character strings or textual data rather than numerical data. For example, a word processor was used in writing this text; computerized typesetters are used extensively in the publishing of books and newspapers; "personalized" junk mail is computer generated; computers are used in the analysis of great works of literature; and finally, a Pascal program is a sequence of words and symbols that are interpreted by a compiler.

If you have used a word processor, you are familiar with the kinds of operations that we might like to perform on string data. For example, we frequently want to insert one or more characters into an existing string, delete a portion of a string (called a *substring*), overwrite or replace one substring of a string with another, search for a target substring, join two strings together to form a longer string, and so on.

Fixed-Length and Variable-Length Strings

An important characteristic of a string is its length. Standard Pascal allows us to store fixed-length strings in packed arrays of characters. If S is a variable whose type is `packed array [1..N] of Char`, there must always be exactly N characters stored in S. If we want to store a shorter string in S, we must pad it with blanks, and these extra blank characters are treated as part of the string. This means that the blank characters will appear when we display a fixed-length string or when we join one fixed-length string to another.

To make string comparison and input/output easier, the length of a string should be *variable* and should depend on its contents. Typically, the length would be between 0 and some predefined maximum value (the string's *capacity*). A variable-length string type (StringADT) is described in Table 3.2. In Borland Pascal, `string` is a reserved word, and the string abstract data type described in Table 3.2 is supported by the compiler, so we will not need to implement these operators ourselves.

Table 3.2

Specification for Abstract
Data Type StringADT

Structure

A string is an indexed list of characters. The length of a string is variable and is based on its contents. This length must be between 0 and some predefined maximum.

Operators

In the descriptions of the operators we will assume the following parameters:

```
S1, S2, . . . , Sn are all strings.
NumericString is a string that contains only numeric
characters.
Index, Size, and Error are type Integer.
NumVal should be of the same data type as the numeric
value to be returned through it.
Format is a valid format specification.
```

Length (S1)
(function) Length returns the length of its argument string.

Delete (var S1, Index, Size)

Concat (S1, S2, . . . , Sn)   (function) Returns the string composed of the concatenation of its argument strings. The number of argument strings is variable. If the result string is longer than 255 characters, only the first 255 characters will be returned.

Copy (S1, Index, Size)   (function) Returns the substring of S1 consisting of Size characters starting at position Index. If Index + Size - 1 is larger than the string length, only the remainder of the string is returned. If Index is larger than the string length, the null string (length of zero) is returned.

Table 3.2 Specification for Abstract Data Type StringADT (*Cont.*)	*Pos (S1, S2)*	(function) If string S1 is a substring of string S2, function Pos returns the location in S2 of the first occurrence of string S1. The value returned is the position in S2 of the first character of S1. If string S1 is not found, function Pos returns zero. If string S1 is the null string, function Pos returns 1.
	Delete (var S1, Index, Size)	Procedure Delete removes Size characters from string S beginning at position Index. If Size is too big, all characters from Index to the end of string S are removed.
	Insert (S1, var S2, Index)	Procedure Insert inserts string S1 into string S2; the substring that formerly began at Index will follow the string inserted. If the new string is too big, the extra characters at the right end are removed. If Index > Length(S2) is true before the insertion, string S1 is joined to the end of old string S2.
	Val (NumericString, var NumVal, var Error)	Procedure Val returns through NumVal the numeric value of the string stored in NumericString and returns 0 through Error, provided that there are no nonnumeric characters in NumericString. Otherwise, NumVal is undefined, and the value returned through Error is the position of the first nonnumeric character.
	Str (NumVal :Format, var NumericString)	Procedure Str returns the numeric value passed to NumVal as a numeric string through parameter NumericString. The Format determines the actual form and length of numeric string just as it would if used with the Write procedure.

String Length and the Null String

As we have mentioned, the working length of a string variable is dynamic and is determined by the data stored in it. This length cannot exceed the capacity for that variable. The string capacity is determined when the variable is declared.

```
var
   Ch : Char;
   FullName : string;
   BirthStone : string[10];
```

The capacity of `FullName` is 255 characters, whereas the capacity of `Birth-Stone` is only 10 characters. The assignment statement

```
BirthStone := 'Black Topaz';
FullName := '';
```

stores the string 'Black Topa' in `BirthStone` and the *null string* in `Full-Name`. The value of `Length(BirthStone)` is 10, and `Length(FullName)` is zero. The assignment statement

```
FullName := 'William Clinton';
```

stores the string on the right in `FullName`; the value of `Length(FullName)` is 15.

Characters and Strings

We can reference individual characters in a string and store them in type `Char` variables. The assignment statement

```
Ch := FullName[9];
```

stores the letter C in `Ch`. Similarly, the assignment statements

```
Ch := 'B';
FullName[1] := Ch;
```

changes the first letter of the string in `FullName` from W to B (`FullName` is 'Billiam Clinton').

We can also assign a type `Char` variable to a `string`. The assignment

```
FullName := Ch;
```

changes `FullName` to the string 'B', and Length(FullName) becomes 1. However, we cannot assign a `string` to a type `Char` variable. The assignment

```
Ch := FullName;    {invalid assignment}
```

causes a syntax error.

Substrings and Procedure Copy

It is often necessary to manipulate segments, or *substrings,* of a larger character string. For example, we might want to examine the three components (month, day, year) of the string 'Jun 25, 1995'. Procedure `Copy` can be used to do this as shown next.

Let us assume that a date string (stored in `Date`) always has the form 'MMM DD, YYYY', where the characters represented by MMM are the month name, DD the day of the month, and YYYY the year. Assuming that `Date`, `MonthStr`, `Day`, and `Year` are variable-length strings, the statement

```
MonthStr := Copy (Date, 1, 3)
```

assigns to `MonthStr` the substring of `Date` starting at position 1 and consisting of the first three characters. The statement

```
Day := Copy (Date, 5, 2)
```

assigns to `Day` the two characters representing the day of the month (positions 5 and 6). Finally, the statement

```
Year := Copy (Date, 9, 4)
```

assigns to Year the four characters representing the year (positions 9–12). If the contents of Date is 'Jun 25, 1995', the contents of the variable-length strings MonthStr, Day, and Year will become 'Jun', '25', and '1995', respectively.

EXAMPLE 3.1 ▼

Procedure PrintWords in Fig. 3.21 displays each individual word found in its parameter Sentence on a separate line. It assumes that there is always a single blank character between words.

The variable First always points to the start of the current word and is initialized to 1. During each execution of the for loop, the Boolean expression

```
Sentence[Next] = WordSeparator
```

tests whether the next character is a blank. If it is, the substring occupying positions First through Next − 1 in Sentence is copied to Word by the statement

```
Word := Copy (Sentence, First, Next - First); {get word}
```

The values of First and Next are shown below just before the fourth word of a string stored in Sentence is displayed. The value of Next − First is 5, so the substring short is displayed.

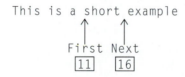

After each word is printed, First is reset to Next + 1, the position of the first character of the next word. After loop exit, the statement

```
Word := Copy (Sentence, First, Length(Sentence) - First + 1);
```

stores the last word of Sentence in Word. For the sentence above, the value of First is 17, and the value of the third parameter is (23 − 17 + 1) or 7, so the last word displayed is "example." ▲

Concatenating Strings

The Copy function is used to reference a substring of a longer string. You can use the Concat function to combine two or more strings to form a new string.

EXAMPLE 3.2 ▼

The statements below join together, or *concatenate,* their string arguments. The string result is stored in Name. For the following string contents (the symbol □ denotes a blank)

Figure 3.21
Procedure `PrintWords`

Directory: CHAP 3
File: PRINTWOR.PAS

```pascal
procedure PrintWords (Sentence {input} : string);
{
  Displays each word of a sentence on a separate line.
  Pre : Variable length string Sentence is defined and does not
        contain either leading or trailing blanks.
  Post: Each word in Sentence is displayed on a separate line.
}
  const
    WordSeparator = ' ';

  var
    Word : string;    {each word}
    SentLen,          {length of Sentence}
    First,            {first character in each word}
    Next : Word;      {position of next character}
begin {PrintWords}
  {Display each word of Sentence on a separate line.}
  First := 1;         {first word starts at position 1}
  SentLen := Length(Sentence);
  for Next := 1 to SentLen do
    begin
      if Sentence[Next] = WordSeparator then
        begin
          Word := Copy(Sentence, First, Next - First); {get word}
          WriteLn (Word);
          First := Next + 1
        end {if}
    end; {for}

  {Display last word.}
  Word := Copy(Sentence, First, Length(Sentence) - First +1);
  WriteLn (Word)
end; {PrintWords}
```

Title	First	Last
Ms.	□Bo	□Peep

the statement

```pascal
Name := Concat (Title, Last)
```

stores the string 'Ms.□Peep' in Name. The statement

```pascal
Name := Concat (Title, First, Last);
```

stores the string 'Ms.□Bo□Peep' in Name.

Fig. 3.22
Function Reverse

Directory: CHAP 3
File: REVERSE.PAS

```
function Reverse (InString : string) : string;

{Reverses the string stored in InString.}

  var
    I          : Integer;          {loop control variable}
    TempString : string;          {temporary reversed string}

begin {Reverse}
  TempString := '';              {initialize TempString}

  for I := Length(InString) downto 1 do
    TempString := Concat(TempString, InString[I]);

  Reverse := TempString          {define result}
end; {Reverse}
```

In Borland Pascal the operator + can also be used to concatenate strings. The assignment statement above can be written as

```
Name := Title + First + Last;  ▲
```

When its operands are strings, Borland Pascal interprets the operator + as "concatenate" instead of "add." Using the same operator for two different purposes is called *operator overloading*.

EXAMPLE 3.3 ▼

Function Reverse in Fig. 3.22 uses the Concat function. This function reverses the string passed to its argument string InString. The string being formed is saved in TempString, which is initialized to the null string. Characters are taken one at a time from InString, starting with the last character, and joined to the end of TempString. The first character of InString is the last character joined to TempString. Table 3.3 traces the execution of this function when InString is 'Turbo'. ▲

Table 3.3
Trace of for Loop when
InString is 'Turbo'

I	InString[I]	TempString
5	'o'	'o'
4	'b'	'ob'
3	'r'	'obr'
4	'u'	'obru'
5	'T'	'obruT'

String Search

When processing string data, we often need to locate a particular substring. For example, we might want to know whether the string 'and' appears in a sentence and, if so, where. If Target is a string of length 4 with contents 'and', the statement

```
PosAnd := Pos(Target, Sentence)
```

assigns to PosAnd the starting position of the first occurrence of 'and' in string Sentence. If the string 'Birds and bees fly all day' is stored in Sentence, the value assigned to PosAnd is 7. If the string 'and' is not in Sentence, the Pos function returns a zero value.

EXAMPLE 3.4 ▼

A compiler can determine the form of many statements by checking whether the statement begins with a reserved word. If leading blanks are removed from Statement and Target is a string of length 4 with contents 'for ', the condition

```
Pos(Target, Statement) = 1
```

is true when Statement is a for statement.

   Another task of the compiler is to extract the syntactic elements of each statement. A for statement may have the syntactic form

```
for counter := initial to final do statement
```

The first two statements that follow use the Pos function to locate the strings 'for ' and ':='. The if statement copies the substring between these symbols into the string Counter.

```
PosFor := Pos('for ', Statement);
PosAssign := Pos(':=', Statement);
if (PosFor > 0) and (PosAssign > PosFor) then
  Counter := Copy(Statement, PosFor + 4, PosAssign - PosFor - 4)
```

Because the string 'for ' has four characters, the starting position of the *counter* is at position PosFor + 4. The number of characters in the *counter* is determined by the expression PosAssign - PosFor - 4. If the string 'for ID := 1 to N do X := X + 1' is stored in Statement, then PosFor gets 1, PosAssign gets 8, and the contents of Counter is the string 'ID ' (length is 8 − 1 − 4 or 3).

```
PosFor      PosAssign      Counter
  1             8            ID#     ▲
```

Procedures Delete and Insert

Besides the string manipulation functions described so far, there are procedures to insert and delete substrings. They are illustrated next.

EXAMPLE 3.5 ▼

Assume that `Sentence` contains the string 'This is the example.' before the first procedure call. The procedure call statement

```
Delete (Sentence, 1, 5)
```

deletes the first five characters from string Sentence. The new contents of `Sentence` become 'is the example'. The procedure call statement

```
Delete (Sentence, Pos('the ', Sentence), 4)
```

deletes the first occurrence of the string 'the ' (length is 4) from `Sentence`. The new contents of Sentence become 'is example'. Finally, the statements

```
PosTarg := Pos(Target, Sentence);
if PosTarg > 0 then
  Delete (Sentence, PosTarg, Length(Target))
```

delete the first occurrence of string `Target` from `Sentence`, provided that `Target` is found. If `Target` is 'ex', the new contents of `Sentence` become 'is ample'. ▲

EXAMPLE 3.6 ▼

Assume that the contents of Sentence is the string 'is the stuff?' and the contents of `NewString` is 'Where'. The procedure call statement

```
Insert (NewString, Sentence, 1)
```

inserts the string 'Where' at the beginning of string `Sentence`, changing its contents to 'Where is the stuff?'.

   If the contents of `Target` is 'stuff' and the contents of `NewString` is '*#@!', the statements

```
PosStuff := Pos(Target, Sentence);
if PosStuff > 0 then
  Insert (NewString, Sentence, PosStuff)
```

insert the string '*#@!' in front of the string 'stuff' in `Sentence`. The new contents of `Sentence` become 'Where is the *#@! stuff?'. ▲

EXAMPLE 3.7 ▼

Procedure `Replace` in Fig. 3.23 replaces a specified target string (`Target`) in a source string (`Source`) with a new string (`Pattern`). It uses function Pos to locate `Target`, `Delete` to delete it, and `Insert` to insert `Pattern` in place of `Target`. An error message is displayed if `Target` is not found. No error message will be displayed if the string in `Pattern` cases a string overflow error. ▲

Figure 3.23
Procedure `Replace`

**Directory: CHAP 3
File: REPLACE.PAS**

```
procedure Replace (Target, Pattern : string;
                       var Source : string);
{
 Replaces first string Target in Source with Pattern if
 found.
 Pre : Target, Pattern, and Source are defined.
 Post: Source is modified.
}

 var
   PosTarg : Integer;                      {position of Target}

begin {Replace}
  PosTarg := Pos(Target, Source);       {Locate Target}
  if PosTarg > 0 then
    begin
      Delete (Source, PosTarg, Length(Target));
      Insert (Pattern, Source, PosTarg)
    end
  else
    WriteLn ('No replacement-string ', Target,
             ' not found.')
end; {Replace}
```

Converting Strings to Numbers Using Val

The `Val` procedure is used to convert a numeric string to a number (type `Integer` or `Real`), and the `Str` procedure converts a number to a numeric string. A *numeric string* is a string that satisfies the syntax requirements for a valid Pascal number (for example, '1234', '0.1234', '1.25E-6').

Assuming that `IntNum` and `Error` are type `Integer`, the procedure call statement

```
Val ('1234', IntNum, Error);
```

causes the integer value 1234 to be stored in `IntNum` and 0 in `Error`. The procedure call statement

```
Val ('12#34', IntNum, Error);
```

causes the value 3 to be returned to `Error`, which is the position of the non-numeric symbol # in the string '12#34'. In this case the value of `IntNum` is undefined.

EXAMPLE 3.8 ▼

Table 3.4 shows the results for several calls to `Val`, assuming that `RealNum` is declared type `Real` and `IntNum` and `Error` are type `Integer`. The type of the second parameter determines whether an `Integer` or a `Real` value will be returned. As shown by the last two lines, a blank cannot appear in the numeric string being converted. ▲

Table 3.4

Using the `Val` Procedure

Call to Val	Values Returned
Val ('-3507', IntNum, Error)	IntNum is -3507, Error is 0.
Val ('-3507', RealNum, Error)	RealNum is -3507.0, Error is 0.
Val ('1.23E3', RealNum, Error)	RealNum is 1230.0, Error is 0.
Val ('1.23E3', IntNum, Error)	IntNum is undefined, Error is 2.
Val ('1.23E 3', RealNum, Error)	RealNum is undefined, Error is 6.
Val (' 1.2E3', RealNum, Error)	RealNum is undefined, Error is 1.

EXAMPLE 3.9 ▼

In procedure `ReadInt` (see Fig. 2.2) we used the loop

```
repeat
  ReadLn (NumStr);
  Val (NumStr, IntNum, Error);
  if Error <> 0 then
    WriteLn ('Invalid character at position ', Error,
             '- try again > ');
until Error = 0
```

to read and store an integer value in `IntNum`. If a valid numeric string is read into `NumStr` (type string), procedure `Val` returns its numeric value in `IntNum` (type Integer). If an invalid numeric string is read, `Val` returns a nonzero value in `Error` (type `Integer`), and the loop is repeated until a valid numeric string is read. The purpose of this loop is to prevent an Invalid numeric format run-time error. If the value of `IntNum` is read directly by using the statement

```
ReadLn (IntNum);
```

the run-time error described above would occur if an invalid integer were entered by mistake. ▲

Converting Numbers to Strings Using Str

The `Str` procedure performs the inverse of the operation performed by `Val`; it converts a number to a numeric string. The procedure call statement

```
Str (345 :5, NumStr);
```

stores the string '□□345' in `NumStr` (type string), where the format :5 specifies a field width of 5. The procedure call statement

```
Str (345.162 :3:1, NumStr)
```

causes the string '345.2' to be stored in NumStr, where the format :3:1 specifies a real value rounded to one decimal place and with a minimum field width of 3.

Compatibility of String Parameters

We have been careful to declare all string parameters as data type string, which has a capacity of 255 characters. For value parameters, Borland Pascal permits an actual parameter and corresponding formal parameter to have different capacities. This means that we can pass a variable of type string[10] (capacity is 10 characters) to a procedure that requires a type string value parameter. However, for variable parameters, each actual string parameter must have the same capacity as its corresponding formal parameter. If this is not the case, a Type mismatch syntax error will occur. Also, string literals may be used as value parameters but never as variable parameters.

We can instruct Borland Pascal to consider data type string as an open string parameter using the compiler directive {$P+}. For an open string parameter the corresponding actual parameter can be any string type. Within the procedure or function the capacity of the formal parameter will be the same as that of the actual parameter.

SYNTAX DISPLAY

Open String Parameter Compiler Directive

Default: {$P-}
The $P directive controls the meaning of variable parameters declared using the string keyword. In the default state, variable parameters declared as type string are normal variable parameters, but in the {$P+} state they are open string parameters.
Note: This compiler directive is not available on versions of Borland Pascal before Version 7.0. You can use the compiler directive {$V-} to disable strict type checking of variable string parameters on these versions. However, this is not as safe as using {$P+} on Borland Pascal 7.0.

Exercises for Section 3.6   *Self-Check*

1. Determine the result of the following procedure calls and function designators. Assume that the string variables are type string[20] and that the initial contents of Temp1 are 'Abra' and those of Temp2 are 'cadabra'.
    a. Magic := Concat(Temp1, Temp2)
    b. Length(Magic)
    c. HisMagic := Copy(Magic, 1, 8)
    d. Delete (HisMagic, 4, 3)
    e. Insert (Temp1, HisMagic, 3)
    f. Pos(Temp2, Magic)
    g. Pos(Temp1, Magic)

h. Val ('1.234', RealNum, Error)
i. Str (1.234 :3:1, RealStr)

2. Source, Target, and Destin are three variables of type string[20]. Assume that Source begins with a person's last name and has a comma and one space between the last and first names (i.e., *last name, first name*). Use Pos and Copy to store the first name in Destin and the second name in Target.

Programming

1. Write a program that calls PrintWords to read in a sentence and then display each word on a separate line. Insert the necessary declarations and procedure calls.

3.7 Representing Strings

If you were using standard Pascal, which does not contain the built-in data type string, you would probably want to write your own string ADT. Most likely, you would want to provide string operators that are very similar to the ones that we described in the last section. One of the decisions that you would need to make would be how to represent the string. Most likely, you would use a record with two fields as described next. (Note that string is a reserved word in Borland Pascal, so this record declaration would not be allowed in Borland Pascal.)

```
const
  Capacity = 255;

type
  StringIndex = 1..Capacity;
  StringLength = 0..Capacity;

  String = record
             Contents : packed array [StringIndex] of Char;
             Length : StringLength;
           end; {String}
```

The array field Contents would contain the character string, and the integer field Length would contain the actual string length. Each of your string operators would be responsible for updating Length after each change to the Contents field so that the value in Length was correct for the character string currently stored in Contents.

Representing Strings in Borland Pascal

Borland Pascal uses a slightly different technique for representing a string. If Name is a string variable whose capacity is 255 characters, Borland Pascal would allocate 256 bytes of storage for Name. The string itself would be stored in the subarray `Name[1]` through `Name[255]`, and its actual length would be stored in byte `Name[0]`. The following statement shows two ways of displaying the actual length, where the `Ord` function converts the length which is stored as a "character" in `Name[0]` to an integer value.

```
WriteLn (Ord(Name[0]), Length(Name) :5)
```

Null-terminated Strings

Borland Pascal 7.0 permits a second type of string representation called a null-terminated string. A null-terminated string has no length byte; instead, it consists of a sequence of nonnull characters followed by the NULL character (represented as ^0 or Chr(0)). This is similar to the way in which Pascal views a line in a text file as being terminated by an EOLN (end of line character). There is no inherent capacity associated with a null-terminated string, but system limitations restrict null-terminated strings to a maximum of 65,535 characters (64K bytes).

A null-terminated string is declared as a zero-based character array. There are no built-in routines for handling null-terminated strings, but Borland Pascal provides a `unit` named `Strings`, which provides features similar to those already discussed for built-in strings. In the declarations below, FirstName is declared as a null-terminated string.

```
type
    ShortString = array [0..20] of Char;

var
    FirstName : ShortString;
```

The statement

```
StrCopy (FirstName, 'Princess Elizabeth'#0)
```

uses the `StrCopy` procedure in unit `Strings` to assign a string value to `FirstName`. Nineteen characters are stored in `FirstName`, the last character being NULL.

Throughout this text we will continue to use the built-in type string and its operators so we will not go into further details of using null-terminated strings.

Exercises for Section 3.7

Self-Check

1. What is a null-terminated string?
2. How does the representation of a variable-length string differ from the representation of a fixed-length character string?

3.8 A Line Editor

You have been using a text editor to create and edit Pascal programs. This is probably a fairly sophisticated *screen-oriented* editor in which special commands are used to move the cursor around the video screen and to specify edit operations. Although we cannot develop such an editor yet, we can write a less sophisticated one.

CASE STUDY   **Line Editor**

PROBLEM ▼

We need an editor to perform some editing operations on a line of text. The editor should be able to locate a specified target string, delete a substring, insert a substring at a specified location, and replace one substring with another.

Analysis

We can use Borland Pascal's string manipulation functions and procedures to perform the editing operations relatively easily. We will write a program that enters a string and then processes a series of edit commands for that string.

Data Requirements

Problem Inputs

The source string (Source : string)
Each edit command (Command : Char)

Problem Output

The modified source string (Source : string)

Initial Algorithm

```
1. Read the string to be edited into Source.
2. repeat
      3. Read an edit command.
      4. Perform each edit operation.
   until done
```

Refinements and Program Structure

Step 4 is performed by procedure DoEdit. DoEdit is responsible for calling the appropriate string operators to read any data strings and to perform the required operations. A portion of the structure chart for the line editor is shown in Fig. 3.24; the local variables and algorithm for procedure DoEdit follow.

```
Local Variables
   OldStr : string   {substring to be found, replaced, or deleted}
   NewStr : string   {substring to be inserted}
   Index : Word      {index to the string Source}
```

Figure 3.24
Structure Chart for Line
Editor Program

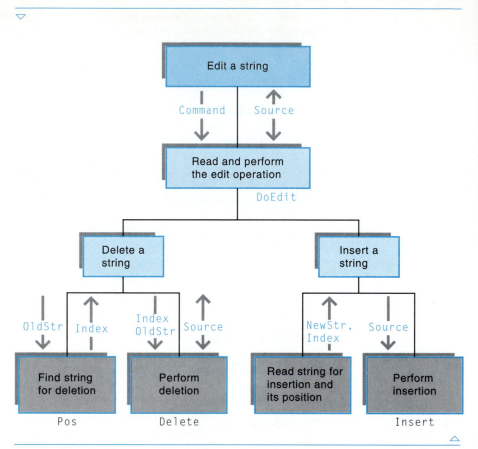

Algorithm for DoEdit

```
1. case Command of
       'D' : Read the substring to be deleted and delete it.
       'I' : Read the substring to be inserted and its
               position and insert it.
       'F' : Read substring to be found and print its position
               if found.
       'R': Read substring to be replaced and replace it with a
               new substring.
     end {case}
```

The complete program is shown in Fig. 3.25 along with a sample run. We could make program LineEdit a little easier to maintain by placing each set of user prompts, input statements, and edit action statements shown in the case in separate procedures of their own.

Figure 3.25
Text Editor Program with
Sample Run

Directory: CHAP 3
File: LINEEDIT.PAS

▽

```pascal
program LineEdit;
{
  Performs text editing operations on a source string.
}
  const
    Sentinel = 'Q';            {sentinel command}

  var
    Source : string;      {the string being edited}
    Command : Char;       {each edit command}

  {$I REPLACE.PAS}        {see Fig. 3.23}

  procedure DoEdit (Command {input} : Char;
                    var Source : string);
  {
    Performs the edit operation specified by Command.
    Pre : Command and Source are defined.
    Post: One or more data strings are read and
          Source is modified if Command is
          'D','I','F', or 'R'. If Command is 'Q'
          a message is displayed; otherwise, nothing
          is done.
  }
  var
    NewStr, OldStr : string;        {work strings}
    Index : Integer;                {index to string Source}
  begin {Do Edit}
    {Perform the operation.}
    case Command of
      'D' : begin {Delete}
              Write ('Delete what string? ');
              ReadLn (OldStr);
              Index := Pos(OldStr, Source);
              if Index > 0 then
                Delete (Source, Index, Length(OldStr))
              else
                WriteLn (OldStr, ' not found.')
            end; {Delete}
      'I' : begin {Insert}
              Write ('Insert what string? ');
              ReadLn (NewStr);
              Write ('At what position? ');
```

▷ ▷ ▷ ▷ ▷ ▷

```
                    ReadLn (Index);
                    Insert (NewStr, Source, Index)
                 end; {Insert}
        'F' : begin {Find}
                 Write ('Find what string? ');
                 ReadLn (OldStr);
                 Index := Pos(OldStr, Source);
                 if Index > 0 then
                 WriteLn (OldStr, ' found at position ',
                    Index :3)
                 else
                    WriteLn (OldStr, ' not found.')
              end; {Find}
        'R' : begin {Replace}
                 Write ('Replace what string? ');
                 ReadLn (OldStr);
                 Write ('With new string? ');
                 ReadLn (NewStr);
                 Replace (OldStr, NewStr, Source)
              end; {Replace}
        'Q' : WriteLn ('Quitting text editor.')
      else
        WriteLn (Command, ' is an invalid edit character')
      end {case}
    end; {DoEdit}

begin {LineEdit}
  {Read in the string to be edited.}
  WriteLn ('Enter the source string:');
  ReadLn (Source);

  {Perform each edit operation until done.}
  repeat
    {Get the operation symbol.}
    WriteLn;
    Write ('Enter D (Delete), I (Insert), ');
    Write ('F (Find), R (Replace), Q (Quit): ');
    ReadLn (Command);
    Command := UpCase(Command);        {convert to uppercase}

    {Perform operation}
    DoEdit (Command, Source);

    {Display latest string}
    WriteLn ('New source: ', Source)
  until Command = Sentinel
end. {LineEdit}

    Enter the source string:
    Mary had a cute little lamb.

    Enter D (Delete), I (Insert), F (Find), R (Replace), Q (Quit): f
    Find what string? cute
    cute found at position 12
```

▷ ▷ ▷ ▷ ▷ ▷

```
New source: Mary had a cute little lamb.

Enter D (Delete), I (Insert), F (Find), R (Replace), Q (Quit): i
Insert what string? very
At what position? 12
New source: Mary had a very cute little lamb.

Enter D (Delete), I (Insert), F (Find), R (Replace), Q (Quit): R
Replace old string? lamb
With new string? lamb chop
New source: Mary had a very cute little lamb chop.

Enter D (Delete), I (Insert), F (Find), R (Replace), Q (Quit): D
Delete what string? very cute
New source: Mary had a lamb chop.

Enter D (Delete), I (Insert), F (Find), R (Replace), Q (Quit): q
Quitting text editor.
New source: Mary had a lamb chop.
```

Exercises for Section 3.8

Self-Check

1. Draw the program structure chart for finding a string and replacing a string.

CHAPTER REVIEW

In this chapter we reviewed three of Borland Pascal's built-in structured data types (arrays, records, strings). We described their attributes, implementations, and uses in programming applications. We also introduced the use of object inheritance as a means of reducing the effort involved in reusing previously defined objects. Object inheritance is also an effective technique for hiding object implementation information from client programs that make use of descendant objects.

Quick-Check Exercises

1. What is the primary difference between a record and an array?
2. When should you use a variant record?
3. Write a type declaration for an array that can hold the batting averages by position (Pitcher, Catcher, FirstBase, etc.) for each of 10 teams in two leagues (American, National).
4. Write a type declaration for an array that holds 25 player records containing his or her name, salary, position, batting average, fielding percentage, and number of runs, hits, runs batted in, and errors.

5. Is it easier to compare strings stored in variables of type string or in arrays of characters?

6. Assuming that S1, S2, and S3 are all type string, what is the effect of the statement

```
S3 := Copy(S2, Pos(S1, S2), Length(S1))
```

   a. when Pos returns a nonzero value?
   b. when Pos returns a zero value?

7. What does a descendant object inherit from its ancestor?

8. When should the virtual directive be used in declaring an object method?

Answers to Quick-Check Exercises

1. The values stored in an array must all be of the same type, whereas the values stored in a record need not all be of the same type.

2. When you need a record type in which some fields are the same for all data cases and some fields need to be different for some of the data items.

3. ```
   type
       Position = (Pitcher, Catcher, FirstBase, SecondBase,
                   ThirdBase, ShortStop, LeftField, Center-
                   Field, RightField);
       League = (American, National);
       TeamIndex = 1..10;
       BatAveArray = array[League, TeamIndex, Position] or Real;
   ```

4. ```
   type
       StringType = string[20];
       Player = record
                   Name : StringType;
                   Salary : Real;
                   Place : Position;
                   BatAve, FieldPct : Real;
                   Runs, Hits, RBIs,Errors : Integer
               end; {Player}
       PlayerIndex = 1..15;
       TeamArray = array[PlayerIndex] of Player;
   ```

5. It is easier to compare two strings because you can use the relational operators. Two character arrays must be compared element by element, and there may be some problems if the arrays don't contain the same number of characters.

6. a. The first occurrence of S1 in S2 is assigned to S3.
   b. The null string is stored in S3.

7. The ancestor's data fields and methods.

8. Any time a method is likely to be redefined by a descendant object and the method heading will not need to be changed.

Review Exercises

1. Define row-major order.

2. Why should a programmer always include a tag field in the declaration of a variant record?

3. Write declarations for the array CPUArray that can hold 20 records of type CPU. Each CPU record has the following fields: IDNumber (integer), Manufacturer (10 characters), Cost (real), and Ports (integer).

4. Write a function AveCost that computes the average cost of the items stored in an array of type CPUArray. Assume that the array is passed as an open parameter.

5. Write a variant record declaration for Supplies, which consists of Paper, Ribbon, or Labels. For Paper the information needed is the number of sheets per box and the size of the paper. For Ribbon the size, color, and kind (Carbon or Cloth) are needed. For Labels the size and number per box are needed. For each supply, the cost and number on hand must be recorded.

6. Redo Review Exercise 5, but declare Supplies as a family of descendant objects. Include method stubs for reading and writing objects of each Supply type.

Programming Projects

Directory: CHAP 3
File: PROJ3_1.PAS

1. Implement an abstract two-dimensional array as an object descended from the Table object shown in Fig. 3.3. Methods Store and Retrieve will need to be declared as static methods.

2. Define a Matrix object with methods for matrix input, output, addition, subtraction, and multiplication. Write a client program to test your Matrix object.

3. Implement a FractionADT as an object that includes methods for adding, subtracting, multiplying, dividing two fractions, reducing a fraction, and computing its decimal equivalent. Use the skeletal object declaration as part of your solution.

```
type
   Fraction = object
                  .
                  .
                  .
             private
                Num, Denom : Integer;
             end; {Fraction}
```

Directory: CHAP 3
File: PROJ3_4.PAS

Directory: CHAP 3
File: PROJ3_5.PAS

4. A company wants an on-line phone directory that will allow phone numbers to be retrieved by room number as well as by name. Implement this directory as an object descended from the Table object shown in Fig. 1.12. Add methods to allow for manipulation of directory entries by room number.

5. Implement an object that uses a three-dimensional array to represent a building (floors 1 to 3, wings A and B, and rooms 1 to 5). Each entry in the array will be an object containing a person's name and phone number. Define object methods that will initialize an empty building, read data into the building, display the entire building, display a particular floor of the building, retrieve an entry for a particular room, and store a new entry in a particular room. To designate a particular room, a client program must provide the floor number, wing letter, and room number.

6. Write a menu-driven program that tests the Building object from Programming Project 5. Include procedures that display the menu choices and provide the user with help if requested.

Directory: CHAP 3
File: PROJ3_7.PAS

7. Write a program that generates the Morse code for a sentence that ends in a period and contains no other characters except letters and blanks. After reading
the Morse code into an array of strings, your program should read each word of
the sentence and display its Morse code equivalent on a separate data line. The
Morse code is as follows:

```
A .-    B -...  C -.-.  D -..   E .    F ..-.  G --.   H ....  I ..

J .---  K -.-   L .-..  M --    N -.   O ---   P .--.  Q --.-  R .-.

S ...   T -     U ..-   V ...-  W .--  X -..-  Y -.--  Z --..
```

Directory: CHAP 3
File: PROJ3_8.PAS

8. Revise the text editor discussed in Section 3.8 so that it will edit a "page" of text.
Define a `Page` object that uses an array of strings in which each array element
holds one line of text and maintains a cursor (index) to the line currently being
edited. The `Page` object should have methods for moving the cursor to the top
of the page, the bottom of the page, and up or down a specified number of
lines. The `Page` object will need methods for inserting a line before the current
line, deleting the current line, and replacing the current line. The first two commands will require moving a portion of the array of strings up or down by one
element.

9. Write a program that will read 400 characters into a 20-by-20 array. Afterward,
read in a character string of 10 characters that will be used to search the "table"
of characters. You should then display the number of times the string occurs in
the 20-by-20 array. This should include horizontal, vertical, and right-diagonal
occurrences. (Right-diagonal means going down and to the right for the search.)

CHAPTER FOUR

Recursion

A recursive procedure or function is one that calls itself. This ability enables a recursive procedure to be repeated with different parameter values. You can use recursion as an alternative to iteration (looping). Generally, a recursive solution is less efficient in terms of computer time than an iterative one because of the overhead for the extra procedure calls; however, in many instances the use of recursion enables us to specify a very natural, simple solution to a problem that would otherwise be very difficult to solve. For this reason, recursion is an important and powerful tool in problem solving and programming.

4.1 The Nature of Recursion

Problems that lend themselves to a recursive solution have the following characteristics.

▶ One or more simple cases of the problem (called *stopping cases*) have a simple, nonrecursive solution.
▶ For the other cases there is a process (using recursion) for substituting one or more reduced cases of the problem that are closer to a stopping case.
▶ The problem can eventually be reduced to stopping cases only, all of which are relatively easy to solve.

The recursive algorithms that we write will generally consist of an if statement with the following form:

```
if the stopping case is reached then
    Solve it
else
    Reduce the problem using recursion
```

Figure 4.1 illustrates what we mean by this, starting with a problem of size N. Let's assume that for any N we can split this problem into one involving a problem of size 1, which we can solve (a stopping case), and a problem of size N − 1, which we can split further. If we split the problem N times, we will end up with N problems of size 1, all of which we can solve.

EXAMPLE 4.1 ▼

As a simple example of this approach, let's consider how we might solve the problem of multiplying 6 by 3, assuming that we know our addition tables

Figure 4.1
Splitting a Problem into
Smaller Problems

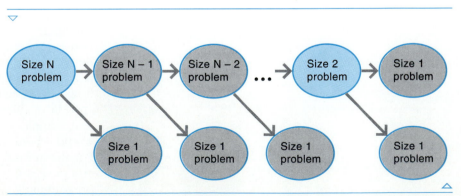

but not our multiplication tables. The problem of multiplying 6 by 3 can be split into the two problems:

1.   Multiply 6 by 2.
2.   Add 6 to the result of Problem 1.

Since we know our addition tables, we can solve Problem 2 but not Problem 1. However, Problem 1 is simpler than the original problem. We can split it into two problems 1.1 and 1.2, leaving us three problems to solve, two of which are additions.

1.   Multiply 6 by 2.   ⌐── 1.1 Multiply 6 by 1.
                         └── 1.2 Add 6 to the result.
2.   Add 6 to the result of Problem 1.

Even though we don't know our multiplication tables, we are familiar with the simple rule that M x 1 is M for any M, so by solving Problem 1.1 (the answer is 6) and Problem 1.2 we get the solution to Problem 1 (the answer is 12). Solving Problem 2 gives us the final answer (18).

Figure 4.2 implements this approach to doing multiplication as the recursive Pascal function `Multiply`. The stopping case is reached when the condition N = 1 is true. In this case the answer is M (M x 1 is M). If N is greater than 1, the statement

```
Multiply := M + Multiply(M, N - 1)    {recursive step}
```

executes, splitting the original problem into the two simpler problems:

▶   multiply M by N – 1
▶   add M to the result

Figure 4.2
Recursive Function
`Multiply`

Directory: CHAP 4
File: MULTIPLY.PAS

```
function Multiply (M, N : Integer) : Integer;
{
  Performs multiplication using + operator.
  Pre : M and N are defined and N > 0.
  Post: Returns M x N
}
begin {Multiply}
   if N = 1 then
      Multiply := M                        {stopping case}
   else
      Multiply := M + Multiply(M, N - 1)   {recursive step}
end;  {Multiply}
```

The first of these problems is solved by calling Multiply again with N - 1 as its second argument. If the new second argument is greater than 1, there will be additional calls to function `Multiply`. ▲

For now, you will have to take our word that function `Multiply` performs as desired. We will see how to trace the execution of a recursive function or procedure in the next section.

The body of function `Multiply` implements the general form of a recursive algorithm shown earlier:

```
if stopping case is reached then
   Solve it
else
   Reduce the problem using recursion
```

The recursive step in function `Multiply`

```
Multiply := M + Multiply(M, N - 1) {recursive step}
```

splits the problem of multiplication by N into an addition problem and a problem of multiplication by N - 1. Note the two different uses of identifier `Multiply` in this statement. The first assigns a value to `Multiply`; the second calls the function recursively.

Exercises for Section 4.1   **Self-Check**

1. Show the problems that are generated by the procedure call statement `Multiply (5, 4)`. Use a diagram similar to Fig. 4.1.
2. Write a pseudocode representation of a recursive algorithm that uses repetitive subtraction to divide M by N.

4.2   Tracing a Recursive Procedure or Function

Hand-tracing an algorithm's execution provides us with valuable insight into how that algorithm works. We can also trace the execution of a recursive procedure or function. We will illustrate how to do this by studying a recursive function and procedure.

Tracing a Recursive Function

In the previous section we wrote the recursive function `Multiply` (see Fig. 4.2). We can trace the execution of the function designator `Multiply(6, 3)` by drawing an *activation frame* corresponding to each call of the function. An activation frame shows the parameter values for each call and summarizes its execution.

The three activation frames generated to solve the problem of multiplying 6 by 3 are shown in Fig. 4.3. The part of each activation frame that executes

Figure 4.3
Trace of Function
`Multiply`

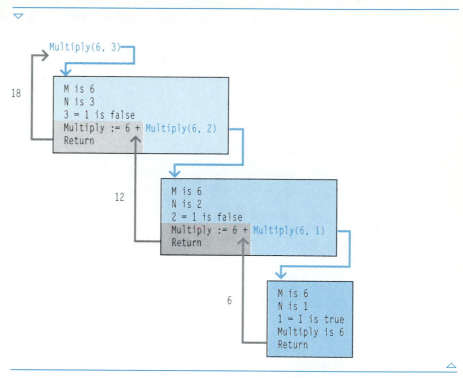

before the next recursive call is in color; the part that executes after the return from the next call is in grey. The darker the color of an activation frame, the greater the depth of recursion.

The value returned from each call is shown alongside each black arrow. The return arrow from each procedure call points to the operator + because the addition is performed just after the return.

Figure 4.3 shows that there are three calls to function `Multiply`. Parameter M has the value 6 for all three calls; parameter N has the values 3, 2, and finally 1. Since N is 1 in the third call, the value of M (6) is returned as the result of the third and last call. After return to the second activation frame, the value of M is added to this result, and the sum (12) is returned as the result of the second call. After return to the first activation frame, the value of M is added to this result, and the sum (18) is returned as the result of the original call to function `Multiply`.

Tracing a Recursive Procedure

EXAMPLE 4.2 ▼

Procedure `Palindrome` in Fig. 4.4 is a recursive procedure that reads in a string of length N and prints it out backwards. (A *palindrome* is a string of characters that reads the same backwards as forwards.) If the procedure call statement

Palindrome (5)

is executed, the five characters entered at the screen will be printed in reverse order. If the characters abcde are entered when this procedure is called, the line

abcde
edcba

will appear on the screen. The letters in color are entered as data, and the letters in black are printed. If the procedure call statement

Palindrome (3)

is executed instead, only three characters will be read, and the line

abc
cba

will appear on the screen. ▲

Like most recursive procedures, the body of procedure Palindrome consists of an if statement that evaluates a *terminating condition,* N <= 1. When

Figure 4.4
Procedure Palindrome

Directory: CHAP 4
File: PALINDRO.PAS

```
procedure Palindrome (N : Integer);
{
  Displays a string of length N in
  reverse of the order in which it is entered.
  Pre : N is greater than or equal to one.
  Post: Displays N characters.
}
  var
    Next : Char;        {next data character}

begin {Palindrome}
  if N <= 1 then
    begin {stopping case}
      Read (Next);
      Write (Next)
    end {stopping case}
  else
    begin {recursion}
      Read (Next);
      Palindrome (N - 1);
      Write (Next)
    end {recursion}
end; {Palindrome}
```

the terminating condition is true, the problem has reached a stopping case: a data string of length 1. If N <= 1 is true, the Read and Write statements are executed.

If the terminating condition is false (N greater than 1), the recursive step (following else) is executed. The Read statement enters the next data character. The procedure call statement

```
Palindrome (N - 1);
```

calls the procedure recursively with the parameter value decreased by 1. The character just read is not displayed until later. This is because the Write statement comes after the recursive procedure call; consequently, the Write statement cannot be performed until after the procedure execution is completed and control is returned back to the Write statement. For example, the character that is read when N is 3 is not displayed until after the procedure execution for N equal to 2 is done. Hence this character is displayed after the characters that are read when N is 2 and N is 1.

To fully understand this, it is necessary to trace the execution of the procedure call statement

```
Palindrome (3)
```

This trace is shown in Fig. 4.5 assuming that the letters abc are entered as data.

The trace shows three separate activation frames for procedure Palindrome. Each activation frame begins with a list of the initial values of N and Next for that frame. The value of N is passed into the procedure when it is called because N is a value parameter; the value of Next is initially undefined because Next is a local variable.

Next, the statements that are executed for each frame are shown. The statements in color are recursive procedure calls and result in a new activation frame, as indicated by the colored arrows. A procedure return occurs when the procedure end statement is reached. This is indicated by the word

Figure 4.5
Trace of Palindrome
(3)

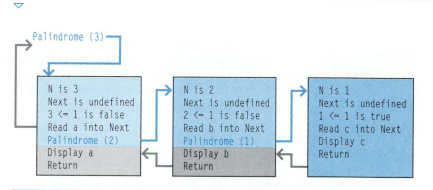

Return in Fig. 4.5 and a black arrow that points to the statement in the calling frame to which the procedure returns. Tracing the colored arrows and then the black arrows gives us the sequence of events listed below. To help you understand this figure, all the statements for a particular activation frame are indented to the same column and have the same background color.

```
Call Palindrome with N equal to 3.
  Read the first character (a) into Next.
  Call Palindrome with N equal to 2.
    Read the second character (b) into Next.
    Call Palindrome with N equal to 1.
      Read the third character (c) into Next.
      Display the third character (c).
      Return from third call.
    Display the second character (b).
    Return from second call.
  Display the first character (a).
  Return from original call.
```

As shown, there are three calls to procedure `Palindrome`, each with a different parameter value. The procedure returns always occur in the reverse order of the procedure calls; that is, we return from the last call first, then we return from the next to last call, and so on. After we return from a particular execution of the procedure, we display the character that was read into Next just before that procedure call.

Parameter and Local Variable Stacks

You may be wondering how Pascal keeps track of the values of N and Next at any given point. Pascal uses a special data structure called a *stack* that is analogous to a stack of dishes or trays. Think of the countless times you have stood in line in a cafeteria. Recall that clean dishes are often stored in a stack in a spring-loaded device that serves up one dish at a time. When you need a dish, you always remove the one that was placed on the stack most recently. This causes the next to last dish placed on the stack to move to the top of the stack. (The stack data structure is discussed further in Section 5.1.)

Similarly, whenever a new procedure call occurs, the parameter value associated with that call is placed on the top of the parameter stack. Also, a new cell whose value is initially undefined is placed on top of the stack that is maintained for the local variable Next. Whenever N or Next is referenced, the value at the top of the corresponding stack is always used. When a procedure return occurs, the value currently at the top of each stack is removed, and the value just below it moves to the top.

EXAMPLE 4.3 ▼

Let's look at the two stacks right after the first call to Palindrome. There is one cell on each stack, as shown below.

After First Call to Palindrome

```
N        Next
|3|       |?|
```

The letter a is read into Next just before the second call to Palindrome.

```
N        Next
|3|       |a|
```

After the second call to Palindrome, the number 2 is placed on top of the stack for N, and the top of the stack for Next becomes undefined again as shown below. The darker color cells represent the top of each stack.

After Second Call to Palindrome

```
N        Next
|2|        |?|
|3|        |a|
```

The letter b is read into Next just before the third call to Palindrome.

```
N        Next
|2|        |b|
|3|        |a|
```

However, Next becomes undefined again right after the third call.

After Third Call to Palindrome

```
N        Next
|1|        |?|
|2|        |b|
|3|        |a|
```

During this execution of the procedure the letter c is read into Next, and c is echo printed immediately, since N is 1 (the stopping case).

```
N        Next
|1|        |c|
|2|        |b|
|3|        |a|
```

The procedure return causes the values at the top of the stack to be removed as shown below.

After First Return

```
N        Next
|2|        |b|
|3|        |a|
```

Since control is returned to a Write statement, the value of Next (b) at the top of the stack is then displayed. Another return occurs, causing the values currently at the top of the stack to be removed.

After Second Return

N   Next
|3| |a|

Again control is returned to a `Write` statement, and the value of `Next` (a) at the top of the stack is displayed. The third and last return removes the last pair of values from the stack, and `N` and `Next` both become undefined.

After Third Return

N   Next
|?| |?| ▲

We will see how to declare and manipulate stacks ourselves in the next chapter. Since these steps are all done automatically by Pascal, we can write recursive procedures without needing to worry about the stacks.

Implementation of Parameter Stacks in Pascal

For illustrative purposes we have used separate stacks for each parameter in our discussion; however, the compiler actually maintains a single stack. Each time a call to a procedure or function occurs, all its parameters and local variables are pushed onto the stack along with the memory address of the calling statement. The latter gives the computer the return point after execution of the procedure or function. Although there may be multiple copies of a procedure's parameters saved on the stack, there is only one copy of the procedure body in memory.

Exercises for Section 4.2   **Self-Check**

1. Why is `N` a value parameter in Fig. 4.4?
2. Assume that the characters `*+-/` are entered for the procedure call statement

   `Palindrome (4)`

   What output line would appear on the screen? Show the contents of the stacks immediately after each procedure call and return.
3. Trace the execution of `Multiply(5, 4)`, and show the stacks after each recursive call.

4.3 Recursive Mathematical Functions

Many mathematical functions are defined recursively. An example is the factorial of a number n (n!).

▶   0! is 1.
▶   n! is n x (n − 1)! for n > 0.

Thus 4! is 4 x 3 x 2 x 1, or 24. It is quite easy to implement this definition as a recursive function in Pascal.

EXAMPLE 4.4 ▼

Function `Factorial` in Fig. 4.6 computes the factorial of its argument N. The recursive step

```
Factorial := N * Factorial(N - 1)
```

implements the second line of the factorial definition above. This means that the result of the current call (argument N) is determined by multiplying the result of the next call (argument N - 1) by N.

A trace of

```
Fact := Factorial (3)
```

is shown in Fig. 4.7. The value returned from the original call, `Factorial` (3), is 6, and this value is assigned to `Fact`. Be careful when using the factorial function; its value increases very rapidly and could lead to an integer overflow error (e.g., 10! is 24320).

Although the recursive implementation of function `Factorial` follows naturally from its definition, this function can be implemented easily by using iteration. The iterative version is shown in Fig. 4.8.

Note that the iterative version contains a loop as its major control structure, whereas the recursive version contains an if statement. Also, a local variable, Factorial, is needed in the iterative version to hold the accumulating product. It should be noted here that while it is very easy for us to implement `Factorial` using recursion, programmers would generally not do so. The iterative version of `Factorial` is just as easy to program and would run faster and use less computer memory. ▲

Figure 4.6
Recursive Function
`Factorial`

Directory: CHAP 4
File: FACTOR.PAS

```
function Factorial (N : Integer) : Integer;
{
  Computes the factorial of N (N!).
  Pre : N is defined and N >= 0.
  Post: Returns N!
}
begin {Factorial}
   if N = 0 then
     Factorial := 1
   else
     Factorial := N * Factorial(N-1)
end;  {Factorial}
```

Figure 4.7
Trace of Fact :=
Factorial(3)

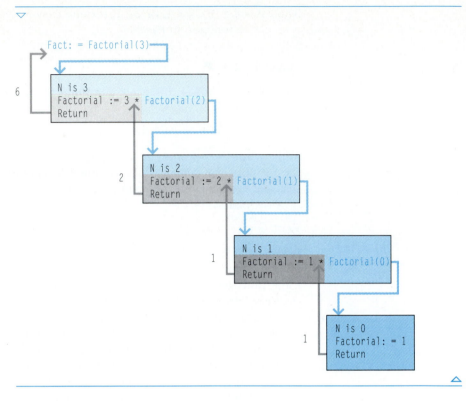

Figure 4.8
Iterative Function
Factorial

Directory: CHAP 4
File: FACTORIT.PAS

```
function Factorial (N : Integer) : Integer;
{
 Computes the factorial of N (N!).
 Pre : N is defined and N >= 0.
 Post: Returns N!
}
  var
    I,                       {loop control variable}
    Product : Integer;       {storage for accumulating product}

begin {Factorial}
  Product := 1;
  for I := 2 to N do
    Factorial := Factorial * I;

  Factorial := Product        {Define result}
end; {Factorial}
```

EXAMPLE 4.5 ▼

The `Fibonacci` numbers are a sequence of numbers that have many varied uses. They were originally intended to model the growth of a rabbit colony. Although we will not go into details of the model here, the `Fibonacci` sequence 1, 1, 2, 3, 5, 8, 13, 21, 34, . . . certainly seems to increase rapidly enough. The fifteenth number in the sequence is 610 (that's a lot of rabbits!). The `Fibonacci` sequence is defined as follows:

▶ Fib_1 is 1.
▶ Fib_2 is 1.
▶ Fib_n is $Fib_{n-2} + Fib_{n-1}$ for n > 2.

Verify for yourself that the sequence of numbers shown in the paragraph above is correct. A recursive function that computes the Nth Fibonacci number is shown in Fig. 4.9.

Although easy to write, the `Fibonacci` function is not very efficient because each recursive step generates two calls to function `Fibonacci`. As shown in Fig. 4.10, the recursive `Fibonnaci` function repeats the same calculation several times during the evaluation of the expression

```
Fib := Fibonacci(5).
```

This does not happen in an iterative implementation of the `Fibonacci` function. ▲

EXAMPLE 4.6 ▼

Euclid's algorithm for finding the greatest common divisor of two positive integers, `GCD(M,N)`, is defined recursively below. The *greatest common divisor* of two integers is the largest integer that divides them both. For example, the value of `GCD(24, 18)` is 6.

Figure 4.9
Recursive Function
`Fibonacci`

Directory: CHAP 4
File: FIBONACC.PAS

```
function Fibonacci (N : Integer) : Integer;
{
   Computes the Nth Fibonacci number.
   Pre : N is defined and N > 0
   Post: Returns the Nth Fibonacci number.
}
begin {Fibonacci}
   if (N = 1) or (N = 2) then
      Fibonacci := 1
   else
      Fibonacci := Fibonacci(N - 2) + Fibonacci(N - 1)
end;  {Fibonacci}
```

△

Figure 4.10
Evaluation of Recursive
Function Fibonacci

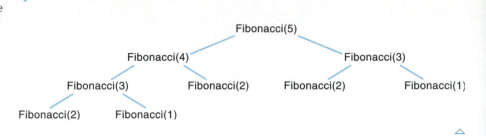

▶ GCD(M,N) is N if N divides M.
▶ GCD(M,N) is GCD(N, remainder of M divided by N) otherwise.

This algorithm states that the GCD is N if N divides M. If N does not divide M,
the answer is obtained by finding the GCD of N and the remainder of M divided by N. If M is smaller than N, the function call GCD(N, remainder of M

Figure 4.11
Euclid's Algorithm for the
Greatest Common Divisor

Directory: CHAP 4
File: FINDGCD.PAS

```
program FindGCD;
{Prints the greatest common divisor of two integers}

   var
     M, N : Integer;                    {two input items}

   function GCD (M, N : Integer) : Integer;
   {
    Finds the greatest common divisor of M and N.
    Pre : M and N are defined and both are > 0.
    Post: Returns the greatest common divisor of M and N.
   }
   begin   {GCD}
     if (M mod N = 0) then
       GCD := N
     else
       GCD := GCD(N, M mod N)
   end;   {GCD}

begin   {FindGCD}
   Write ('Enter two positive integers separated by a space: ');
   ReadLn (M, N);
   WriteLn ('Their greatest common divisor is ', GCD (M, N) :1)
end.   {FindGCD}

Enter two positive integers separated by a space: 24 84
Their greatest common divisor is 12
```

divided by N) evaluates to GCD(N, M), so GCD(18, 24) is also 6. The declaration and use of the Pascal function GCD are shown in Fig. 4.11. ▲

Exercises for Section 4.3   ***Self-Check***

1. Complete the following recursive function that calculates the value of a number (Base) raised to a power (Power). Assume that Power is positive.

```
function PowerRaiser (Base, Power : Integer) : Integer;
begin {PowerRaiser}
  if Power = _____ then
    PowerRaiser := _____
  else
    PowerRaiser := _____ * _____
end; {PowerRaiser}
```

2. What is the output of the following program? What does function Strange compute?

```
program TestStrange;

  function Strange (N : Integer) : Integer;
  begin {TestStrange}
    if N = 1 then
      Strange := 0
    else
      Strange := 1 + Strange (N div 2)
  end; {Strange}

begin {Strange}
  WriteLn (Strange(8))
end. {TestStrange}
```

3. Explain what would happen if the terminating condition for function Fibonacci were just (N = 1).

Programming

1. Write a recursive function FindSum that calculates the sum of successive integers starting at 1 and ending at N; i.e.,

    FindSum(N) = (1 + 2 + . . . + (N - 1) + N).

2. Write an iterative version of the Fibonacci function.
3. Write an iterative function for the greatest common divisor.

4.4 Recursive Procedures with Array Parameters

In this section we will examine two familiar problems and implement recursive procedures to solve them. Both problems involve processing an array.

CASE STUDY **Printing an Array Backwards**

PROBLEM ▼

Provide a recursive solution to the problem of printing the elements of an array in reverse order.

DESIGN OVERVIEW ▼

If the array X has elements with subscripts 1, . . . , N, then the element values should be printed in the sequence X[N], X[N-1], X[N-2], . . . , X[2], X[1]. The stopping case is printing an array with one element (N is 1); the solution is to print that element. For larger arrays the recursive step is to print the last array element (X[N]) and then print the subarray with subscripts 1, . . . ,N–1 backwards.

Data Requirements

Problem Inputs

```
An array of integer values (X : IntArray)
The number of elements in the array (N : Integer)
```

Problem Outputs

```
The array values in reverse order (X[N], X[N-1], . . . ,
X[2], X[1])
```

Initial Algorithm

```
1. if N is 1 then
      2.  Print X[1]
```

Figure 4.12
Procedure PrintBack

Directory: CHAP 4
File: PRINTBAC.PAS

```
procedure PrintBack (var X {input} : IntArray;
                         N {input} : Integer);
{
   Prints an array of integers (X) with subscripts 1..N.
   Pre : Array X and N are defined and N > 0.
   Post: Displays X[N], X[N-1], . . . , X[2], X[1]
}
begin   {PrintBack}
   if N = 1 then
      WriteLn (X[1])                            {stopping case}
   else
      begin   {recursive step}
         WriteLn (X[N]);
         PrintBack  (X, N-1)
      end {recursive step}
end; {PrintBack}
```

```
      else
         begin
            3. Print X[N]
            4. Print the subarray with subscripts 1..N-1
         end
```

Coding

Procedure `PrintBack` in Fig. 4.12 implements the recursive algorithm.

TESTING ▼

Given the declarations

```
type
   IndexType = 1..20;
   IntArray = array [IndexType] of Integer;

var
   Test : IntArray;
```

and the procedure call statement

```
PrintBack (Test, 3)
```

three `WriteLn` statements will be executed in the order indicated below, and the elements of Test will be printed backwards as desired.

```
WriteLn (Test[3]);
WriteLn (Test[2]);
WriteLn (Test[1])
```

To verify this, we trace the execution of the procedure call statement above in Fig. 4.13. Tracing the color arrows and then the black arrows leads to the following sequence of events:

```
Call PrintBack with parameters Test and 3.
   Print Test[3].
   Call PrintBack with parameters Test and 2.
```

Figure 4.13
Trace of `PrintBack`
`(Test, 3)`

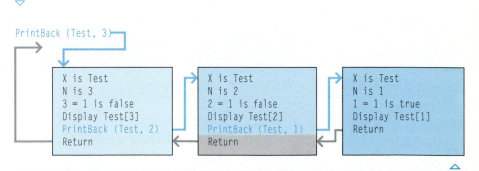

```
      Print Test[2].
      Call PrintBack with parameters Test and 1.
        Print Test[1].
        Return from third call.
      Return from second call.
    Return from original call.
```

As shown, there are three calls to procedure `PrintBack`, each with different parameters. The procedure returns always occur in the reverse order of the procedure calls; in other words, we return from the last call first, then we return from the next to last call, and so on. This time there are no statements left to execute after the returns because the recursive call

`PrintBack (X, N - 1)`

occurs at the end of the recursive step.

Procedure `PrintBack` is another example of a procedure that is easy for us to use in illustrating recursion, but we would probably not implement it as a recursive procedure in a real program. An iterative version of procedure `PrintBack`, which uses both less processing time and less computer memory, could be implemented very easily by using a for loop.

Program Style

Avoiding Value Array Parameters in Recursive Procedures

In procedure `PrintBack`, X is declared as a variable parameter even though it is used for input only. If X were a value parameter instead, each recursive call would generate a local copy of the actual array corresponding to X in each activation frame. This can result in a tremendous waste of time and memory space. For example, if X corresponds to an array with 10 elements and we want to print the entire array (N is 10), then there will be 10 activation frames—so storage space will be needed for 100 integer values. If N is 100, then storage space is needed for 100 x 100, or 10,000, integer values.

CASE STUDY   Recursive Selection Sort

PROBLEM ▼

We have discussed selection sort and implemented an iterative selection sort procedure. Because the selection sort first finds the largest element in an array and places it where it belongs, then finds and places the next largest element, and so on, it is a good candidate for a recursive solution.

Figure 4.14
PlaceLargest and
Recursive SelectSort

Directory: CHAP 4
File: SELECTSO.PAS

```
procedure PlaceLargest (var X {input/output} : array of Integer;
                        N {input} : Word);
{
 Finds the largest element in array X[0]..X[N] and exchanges
 it with the element at X[N].
 Pre : Array X and N are defined and N >= 0.
 Post: X[N] contains the largest value.
}
  var
    Temp : Integer;        {temporary copy for exchange}
    J,                     {array subscript and loop control}
    MaxIndex : Integer;    {index of largest so far}

begin {PlaceLargest}
  {Save subscript of largest element in MaxIndex.}
  MaxIndex := N;                {Assume X[N] is largest.}
  for J := N - 1 downto 0 do
    if X[J] > X[MaxIndex] then
      MaxIndex := J;                {X[J] is largest so far.}

  {assertion: MaxIndex is subscript of largest element.}
  if MaxIndex <> N then
    begin {exchange X[N] and X[MaxIndex]}
      Temp := X[N];
      X[N] := X[MaxIndex];
      X[MaxIndex] := Temp
    end {if}
end; {PlaceLargest}

procedure SelectSort (var X {input/output} : array of Integer;
                      N {input} : Word);
{
  Sorts an array of integers (X) with subscripts 0..N - 1.
  Pre : Array X and N are defined and N >= 0.
  Post: The array elements are in ascending numerical order.
}
begin {SelectSort}
  if N > 1 then
    begin {recursive step}
      {Place largest value in X[N] and sort subarray 1..N - 1.}
      PlaceLargest (X, N - 1);
      SelectSort (X, N - 1)
    end {recursive step}
end; {SelectSort}
```

DESIGN OVERVIEW ▼

The selection sort algorithm follows from the preceding description. The stopping case is an array of length 1 that is sorted by definition. Review Fig. 2.11 to see how the elements of an array are placed in their final positions by a selection sort.

Recursive Algorithm for Selection Sort

```
1.  if N is 1 then
      2. The array is sorted.
    else
      begin
        3. Place the largest array element in X[N].
        4. Sort the subarray with subscripts 0..N-1.
      end
```

CODING ▼

This algorithm is implemented as a recursive procedure at the bottom of Fig. 4.14. Procedure PlaceLargest performs Step 3 of the algorithm. The recursive procedure SelectSort is simpler to understand than the one in Fig. 2.12 because it contains a single if statement instead of nested for loops. However, the recursive procedure will execute more slowly because of the extra overhead due to the recursive procedure calls.

If N = 1, procedure SelectSort returns without doing anything. This behavior is correct because a one-element array is always sorted.

Exercises for Section 4.4   ### Self-Check

1. Trace the execution of SelectSort on an array that has the integers 5, 8, 10, 1 stored in consecutive elements.
2. For the array in Exercise 1, trace the execution of PrintBack.

Programming

1. Provide an iterative procedure that is equivalent to PrintBack in Fig. 4.12.
2. Write a recursive procedure that prints the elements in an array X[1..N] in their normal order. Use procedure PrintBack as a model for your solution.

4.5 Problem Solving with Recursion

The next case study is considerably more complicated than the preceding ones. It leads to a recursive procedure that solves the Towers of Hanoi Problem.

CASE STUDY   ## Towers of Hanoi Problem

PROBLEM ▼

The Towers of Hanoi Problem involves moving a specified number of disks that are all of different sizes from one tower (or peg) to another. Legend has it that the world will come to an end when the problem is solved for 64 disks. In the version of the problem shown in Fig. 4.15 there are five disks (labeled 1 through 5) and three towers or pegs (labeled A, B, C). The goal is to move the five disks from peg A to peg C subject to the following rules:

1.　Only one disk may be moved at a time, and this disk must be the top disk on a peg.
2.　A larger disk can never be placed on top of a smaller disk.

ANALYSIS ▼

The stopping cases of the problem involve moving one disk only (e.g., "move disk 2 from peg A to peg C"). A simpler problem than the original would be to move four disks subject to the conditions above, or three disks, and so on. Therefore we want to split the original five-disk problem into one or more problems involving fewer disks. Let's consider splitting the original problem into the following three problems:

1.　Move four disks from peg A to peg B.
2.　Move disk 5 from peg A to peg C.
3.　Move four disks from peg B to peg C.

Step 1 moves all disks but the largest to tower B, which is used as an auxiliary tower. Step 2 moves the largest disk to the goal tower, tower C. Then Step 3 moves the remaining disks from B to the goal tower, where they will be placed on top of the largest disk. Let's assume that we will be able to perform Step 1 and Step 2 (a stopping case); Fig. 4.16 shows the status of the three towers after completion of these steps. At this point, it should be clear that we can solve the original five-disk problem if we can complete Step 3.

Unfortunately, we still don't know how to perform Step 1 or Step 3. However, both of these steps involve four disks instead of five, so they are easier than the original problem. We should be able to split them into simpler problems in the same way that we split the original problem. Step 3 involves moving four disks from tower B to tower C, so we can split it into two three-disk problems and a one-disk problem:

Figure 4.15
Towers of Hanoi

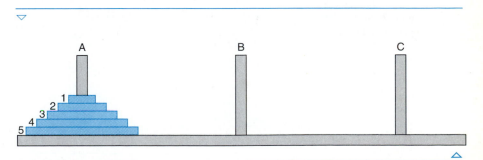

Figure 4.16
Towers of Hanoi after
Steps 1 and 2

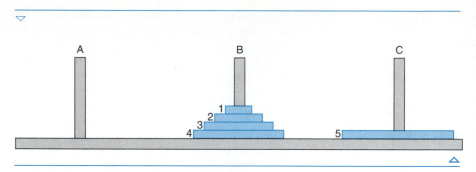

3.1 Move three disks from peg B to peg A.
3.2 Move disk 4 from peg B to peg C.
3.3 Move three disks from peg A to peg C.

Figure 4.17 shows the status of the towers after completion of Steps 3.1 and 3.2. We now have the two largest disks on peg C. Once we complete Step 3.3, all five disks will be on peg C as required. By splitting each n-disk problem into two problems involving n − 1 disks and a one-disk problem, we will eventually reach all cases of one disk, which we know how to solve.

DESIGN OVERVIEW ▼

The solution to the Towers of Hanoi Problem consists of a printed list of individual disk moves. We need a recursive procedure that can be used to move any number of disks from one peg to another, using the third peg as an auxiliary.

Data Requirements

Problem Inputs

```
The number of disks to be moved (N : Integer)
The from peg (FromPeg : 'A'..'C')
The to peg (ToPeg : 'A'..'C')
The auxiliary peg (AuxPeg : 'A'..'C')
```

Figure 4.17
Towers of Hanoi after
Steps 1, 2, 3.1, and 3.2

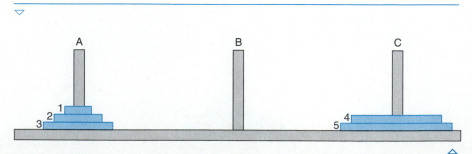

Problem Outputs

A list of individual disk moves

Initial Algorithm

```
1. if N is 1 then
       2. Move disk 1 from the from peg to the to peg
     else
       begin
         3. Move N-1 disks from the from peg to the auxiliary
            peg using the to peg.
         4. Move disk N from the from peg to the to peg.
         5. Move N-1 disks from the auxiliary peg to the to
            peg using the from peg.
       end
```

If N is 1, a stopping case is reached. If N is greater than 1, the recursive step (following else) splits the original problem into three smaller subproblems, one of which is a stopping case. Each stopping case displays a move instruction. Verify that the recursive step generates the three problems listed above Fig. 4.15 when N is 5, the *from* peg is A, and the *to* peg is C.

The implementation of this algorithm is shown as procedure Tower in Fig. 4.18. Procedure Tower has four parameters. The procedure call statement

```
Tower ('A', 'C', 'B', 5)
```

solves the problem posed earlier of moving five disks from tower A to tower C using B as an auxiliary (see Fig. 4.15).

Figure 4.18
Recursive Procedure
Tower

Directory: CHAP 4
File: TOWER.PAS

```
procedure Tower (FromPeg, ToPeg, AuxPeg {input} : Char;
                 N {input} : Integer);
{
 Moves N disks from FromPeg to ToPeg
 using AuxPeg as an auxiliary.
 Pre : FromPeg, ToPeg, AuxPeg, and N are defined.
 Post: Displays a list of move instructions to transfer
       the disks.
}
begin {Tower}
  if N = 1 then
    WriteLn ('Move disk 1 from peg ', FromPeg,
             ' to peg ', ToPeg)
  else
    begin {recursive step}
      Tower (FromPeg, AuxPeg, ToPeg, N-1);
```

▷ ▷ ▷ ▷ ▷

```
          WriteLn ('Move disk ', N :1, ' from peg ', FromPeg,
                   ' to peg ', ToPeg);
          Tower (AuxPeg, ToPeg, FromPeg, N-1)
       end {recursive step}
end;    {Tower}
```

In Fig. 4.18 the stopping case (move disk 1) is implemented as a call to procedure `WriteLn`. Each recursive step consists of two recursive calls to `Tower` with a call to `WriteLn` sandwiched between them. The first recursive call solves the problem of moving N - 1 disks to the *auxiliary* peg. The call to `WriteLn` displays a message to move disk N to the *to* peg. The second recursive call solves the problem of moving the N - 1 disks back from the *auxiliary* peg to the *to* peg.

Figure 4.19
Trace of Tower
('A','C','B',3)

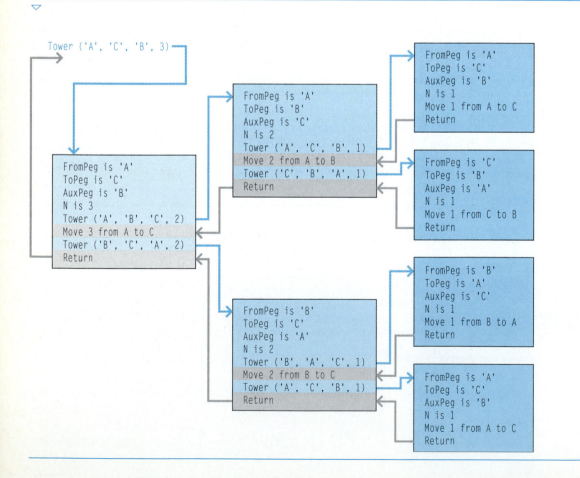

TESTING ▼

The procedure call statement

```
Tower ('A', 'C', 'B', 3)
```

solves a simpler three-disk problem: Move three disks from peg A to peg C. Its execution is traced in Fig. 4.19; the output generated is shown in Table 4.1. Verify for yourself that this list of steps does indeed solve the three-disk problem.

Table 4.1
Output generated by Tower ('A','C','B',3)

Move disk 1 from A to C
Move disk 2 from A to B
Move disk 1 from C to B
Move disk 3 from A to C
Move disk 1 from B to A
Move disk 2 from B to C
Move disk 1 from A to C

Comparison of Iteration and Recursive Procedures

It is interesting to consider that procedure Tower in Fig. 4.18 will solve the Tower of Hanoi Problem for any number of disks. The three-disk problem results in a total of seven calls to procedure Tower and is solved by seven disk moves. The five-disk problem would result in a total of 31 calls to procedure Tower and is solved in 31 moves. In general, the number of moves required to solve the n-disk problem is $2^n - 1$. Since each procedure call requires the allocation and initialization of a local data area in memory, the computer time increases exponentially with the problem size. For this reason, be careful about running this program with a value of N that is larger than 10.

The dramatic increase in processing time for larger towers is a function of this problem, not recursion. However, in general, if there are recursive and iterative solutions to the same problem, the recursive solution will require more time and space because of the extra procedure calls. We will discuss algorithm efficiency later.

Although recursion was not really needed to solve the simpler problems in this section, it was extremely useful in formulating an algorithm for the Towers of Hanoi Problem. We will see that for certain problems, recursion leads naturally to solutions that are much easier to read and understand than their iterative counterparts. In these cases the benefits gained from increased clarity far outweigh the extra cost (in time and memory) of running a recursive program.

Self-Check

1. Show the problems that are generated by attempting to solve the problem "Move two disks from peg A to peg C". Answer the same question for the problem "Move three disks from peg A to peg C". Draw a diagram similar to Fig. 4.1.
2. How many moves are needed to solve the six-disk problem?
3. Write a main program that reads in a data value for N (the number of disks) and calls procedure Tower to move N disks from A to B.

4.6 Recursive Functions with Array Parameters

The process described in the previous sections can be followed to write recursive functions. This process involves identifying the stopping cases of a problem. For the other cases we must have a means of reducing the problem to one that is closer to a stopping case.

CASE STUDY Summing the Values in an Array

PROBLEM ▼

We want to write a recursive function that finds the sum of the values in an array X with subscripts $1, \ldots, N$.

DESIGN OVERVIEW ▼

The stopping case occurs when N is 1—the sum is X[1]. If N is not 1, then we must add X[N] to the sum that we get when we add the values in the subarray with subscripts $1, \ldots, N - 1$.

Data Requirements

Problem Inputs

```
An array of integer values (X : IntArray)
The number of elements in the array (N : Integer)
```

Problem Outputs

```
The sum of the array values
```

Initial Algorithm

```
1. if N is 1 then
     2.  The sum is X[1]
   else
     begin
       3. Add X[N] to the sum of values in the subarray with
          subscripts 1..N - 1
     end
```

Figure 4.20
Using Recursive Function
FindSum

Directory: CHAP 4
File: TESTFIND.PAS

```
program TestFindSum;
{
 Tests function FindSum
}
  type
     IndexType = 1..20;
     IntArray = array [IndexType] of Integer;

  var
    N : Integer;
    X : IntArray;

  function FindSum (var X : IntArray;
                        N : Integer) : Integer;
  {
   Finds the sum of the values in elements 1..N of array X.
   Pre : Array X and N are defined and N > 0.
   Post: Returns sum of first N elements of X.
  }
  begin   {FindSum}
    if N = 1 then
      FindSum := X[1]
    else
      FindSum := X[N] + FindSum(X, N - 1)
  end;   {FindSum}

begin   {TestFindSum}
  N := 3;
  X[1] := 5; X[2] := 10; X[3] := -7;
  WriteLn ('The array sum is ', FindSum(X, 3) :3)
end. {TestFindSum}

The array sum is 8
```

CODING ▼

Function FindSum in Fig. 4.20 implements this algorithm. The result of calling FindSum for a small array (N is 3) is also shown.

TESTING ▼

Figure 4.21 shows a trace of the function call FindSum(X, 3). As before, the colored part of each activation frame executes before the next recursive function call, and each color arrow points to a new activation frame. The grey part of each activation frame executes after the return from a recursive call, and each black arrow indicates the return point (the operator +) after a function execution. The value returned is indicated alongside the arrow. The value returned for the original call, FindSum(X, 3), is 8, and this value is printed.

Figure 4.21
Trace of `FindSum(X, 3)`

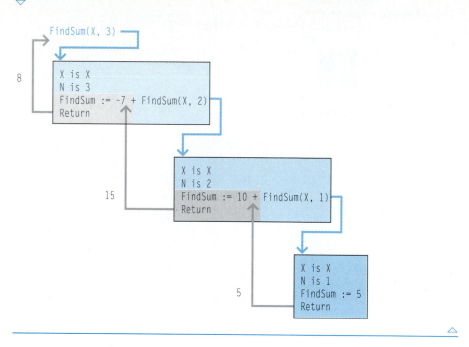

Functions that return `Boolean` values (`True` or `False`) can also be written recursively. The function result is determined by evaluating an expression (type `Boolean`) containing a recursive call. We will write recursive functions that search an array and compare two arrays.

EXAMPLE 4.7 ▼

The `Boolean` function `Member` in Fig. 4.22 returns the value `True` if the argument `Target` is in the array X with subscripts 1, . . . ,N; otherwise, it returns the value `False`. If N is 1 (the stopping case), the result is determined by comparing `X[1]` and `Target`. If N is not 1 (the recursive step), then the result is true if either `X[N]` is `Target` or `Target` occurs in the subarray with subscripts 1, . . . ,N–1. The recursive step is implemented as the assignment statement

```
Member := (X[N] = Target) or Member(X, Target, N - 1)
```

in Fig. 4.22. ▲

The function designator `Member(X, 10, 3)` is traced in Fig. 4.23 for the array X defined in Fig. 4.21. The value returned is True, since the expression `X[N] = Target` is `True` when N is 2 (the second activation frame).

Figure 4.22
Recursive Function
Member

Directory: CHAP 4
File: MEMBER.PAS

```
function Member (var X : IntArray;
                 Target,
                 N       : Integer) : Boolean;
{
 Searches for Target in array X with subscripts 1..N.
 Pre : Target, N and array X are defined and N > 0.
 Post: Returns True if Target is located in array X;
       otherwise, returns False.
}
begin {Member}
  if N = 1 then
    Member := (X[1] = Target)
  else
    Member := (X[N] = Target) or Member(X, Target, N - 1)
end; {Member}
```

Figure 4.23
Trace of Function Member

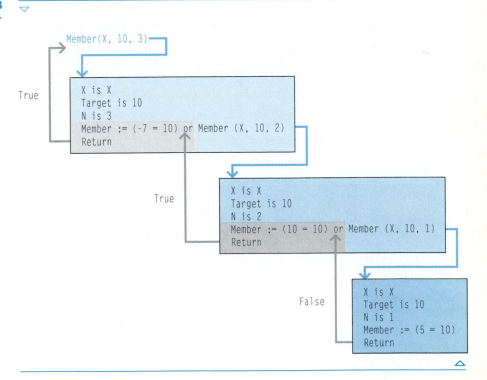

EXAMPLE 4.8 ▼

The Boolean function Equal returns the value True if two arrays, say, X and Y, of N elements are the same (i.e., X[1] = Y[1], X[2] = Y[2], . . . , X[N] = Y[N]). This function (see Fig. 4.24) looks similar to function Member. For the stopping case, single-element arrays, the function result depends on whether or not X[1] = Y[1]. For larger arrays the result is True if X[N] = Y[N] and the subarrays with subscripts 1, . . . ,N - 1 are equal.   ▲

Comparison of Iterative and Recursive Functions

It is interesting to consider the iterative version of function Member shown in Fig. 4.25. A for loop is needed to examine each array element. Without recursion it is not possible to use the function name in an expression, so a local variable, Found, is needed to represent the result so far. Before returning from the function, the final value of Found is assigned as the function result.

We could certainly improve the search function shown in Fig. 4.25. For example, we could make it more efficient by using a while loop and exiting from the loop when Found becomes True; however, the version shown in Fig. 4.25 would still execute faster than the recursive version.

Many would argue that the recursive version is aesthetically more pleasing. It is certainly more compact (a single if statement) and requires no local variables. Once you are accustomed to thinking recursively, the recursive form is somewhat easier to read and understand than the iterative form.

Some programmers like to use recursion as a conceptual tool. Once they have written the recursive form of a function or procedure, they can always translate it into an iterative version if run-time efficiency is a major concern.

Figure 4.24
Recursive Function Equal

Directory: CHAP 4
File: EQUAL.PAS

```
function Equal (var X, Y : IntArray;
                    N : Integer) : Boolean;
{
 Compares arrays X and Y with elements 1..N.
 Pre : Arrays X and Y are defined and N > 0.
 Post: Returns True if arrays X and Y are equal;
       otherwise, returns False.
}
begin {Equal}
   if N = 1 then
      Equal := X[1] = Y[1]
   else
      Equal := (X[N] = Y[N]) and Equal(X, Y, N-1)
end; {Equal}
```

Figure 4.25
Iterative Function Member

Directory: CHAP 4
File: MEMBERIT.PAS

```
function Member (var X : IntArray;
                     Target,
                     N : Integer) : Boolean;
{
 Compares arrays X and Y with elements 1..N.
 Pre : Arrays X and Y are defined and N > 0.
 Post: Returns True if arrays X and Y are equal; otherwise,
       returns False.
}
var
   Found : Boolean;                {local flag}
   I : Integer;                    {loop-control variable}

begin {Member}
   Found := False;                 {Assume Target not found.}

   {Search array X for Target.}
   for I := 1 to N do
      Found := (X[I] = Target) or Found;

   Member := Found                 {Define result.}
end; {Member}
```

CASE STUDY   Counting Cells in a Blob

This problem is a good illustration of the power of recursion. Its solution is relatively easy to write recursively; however, the problem would be much more difficult without using recursion.

PROBLEM ▼

We have a two-dimensional grid of cells, each of which may be empty or filled. The filled cells that are connected form a blob. There may be several blobs on the grid. We would like a function that accepts as input the coordinates of a particular cell and returns the size of the blob containing the cell.

There are three blobs in the sample grid below. If the function parameters represent the X and Y coordinates of a cell, the result of BlobCount(3, 4) is 5; the result of BlobCount(1, 2) is 2; the result of BlobCount(5, 5) is 0; the result of BlobCount(5, 1) is 4.

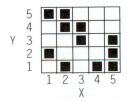

DESIGN OVERVIEW ▼

Function `BlobCount` must test the cell specified by its arguments to see whether it is filled. There are two stopping cases: the cell (X, Y) is not on the grid, or the cell (X, Y) is empty; in either case the value returned by Blob-Count is 0. If the cell is on the grid and filled, then the value returned is 1 plus the size of the blobs containing each of its eight neighbors. To avoid counting a filled cell more than once, we will mark it as empty once we have visited it.

Data Requirements

Problem Inputs

```
The grid
The X and Y coordinates of the point being visited

   (X, Y : Integer)
```

Problem Outputs

```
The number of the cells in the blob containing point X, Y
```

Initial Algorithm

```
1. if cell (X, Y) is not in the array then
     2. Return a count of 0
   else if cell (X, Y) is empty then
     3. Return a count of 0
   else
     begin
       4. Mark cell (X, Y) as empty
       5. Add 1 and see whether the blob contains any of
          the 8 neighbors of cell (X, Y)
     end
```

Function BlobCount is shown in Fig. 4.26 assuming the declarations below. The array type `BlobArray` has element values `Filled` or `Empty`. The constants `MaxX` and `MaxY` represent the largest X and Y coordinates, respectively.

```
const
   MaxX = 100;
   MaxY = 100;

type
   RowIndex = 1,,MaxX;
   ColIndex = 1..MaxY;
   ElementType = (Filled, Empty);
   BlobArray = array [RowIndex, ColIndex] of Element;
```

Function `Blob` in Fig. 4.26 implements the counting algorithm; function BlobCount simply calls the recursive function `Blob`, passing on its arguments, and returns the count computed by function Blob as its own result.

Figure 4.26
Function `BlobCount`

Directory: CHAP 4
File: BLOBCOUN.PAS

```
function BlobCount (Grid : BlobArray;
                        X, Y : Integer) : Integer;
{
 Counts the number of filled cells in the blob containing
 point (X, Y).
 Pre : Array Grid and point (X, Y) are defined.
 Post: Returns the size of the blob containing the point (X, Y).
 Calls: Blob to perform the counting operation.
}
  function Blob (var Grid {input/output} : BlobArray;
                        X, Y : Integer) : Integer;
  {
   Performs counting operation for BlobCount.
   Pre : Array Grid and point (X, Y) are defined.
   Post: Returns size of the blob containing the point (X, Y).
         Resets the status of each cell in the blob to Empty.
  }
  begin {Blob}
    if (X < 1) or (X > MaxX) or (Y < 1) or (Y > MaxY) then
       Blob := 0                        {Cell not in grid.}
    else if Grid[X, Y] = Empty then
       Blob := 0                        {Cell is empty.}
    else {cell is filled}
      begin {recursive step}
        Grid[X, Y] := Empty;
        Blob := 1 + Blob(Grid, X-1, Y+1) +
                 Blob(Grid, X, Y+1) + Blob(Grid, X+1, Y+1) +
                 Blob(Grid, X+1, Y) + Blob(Grid, X+1, Y-1) +
                 Blob(Grid, X, Y-1) + Blob(Grid, X-1, Y-1) +
                 Blob(Grid, X-1, Y)
      end {recursive step}
  end; {Blob}

begin {BlobCount}
{Call BlobCount and return its result.}
 BlobCount := Blob(Grid, X, Y)
end; {BlobCount}
```

We used two functions instead of one to protect the actual array from being modified when filled cells are reset to empty by function `Blob`. We will come back to this point shortly.

If the cell being visited is off the grid or is empty, a value of zero will be returned immediately. Otherwise, the recursive step executes, causing function `Blob` to call itself eight times; each time, a different neighbor of the current cell is visited. The cells are visited in a clockwise manner, starting with the neighbor above and to the left. The function result is defined as the sum of all values returned from these recursive calls plus 1 (for the current cell).

The sequence of operations performed in function Blob is very important. The if statement tests whether the cell (X, Y) is on the grid before testing whether (X, Y) is empty. If the order were reversed, the run-time error "out of bounds" would occur whenever (X, Y) was off the grid.

Also, the recursive step resets Grid[X, Y] to Empty before visiting the neighbors of point (X, Y). If this were not done first, then cell (X, Y) would be counted more than once, since it is a neighbor of all its neighbors. A worse problem is that the recursion would not terminate. When each neighbor of the current cell is visited, Blob is called again with the coordinates of the current cell as arguments. If the current cell is Empty, an immediate return occurs. If the current cell is still Filled, then the recursive step would be executed erroneously. Eventually, the program will run out of time or memory space; the latter is often indicated by a "stack overflow" message.

A side-effect of the execution of function Blob is that all cells that are part of the blob being processed are reset to Empty. This is the reason for using two functions. Since the array is passed as a value parameter to function BlobCount, a local copy is saved when BlobCount is first called. Only this local array is changed by function Blob, not the actual array. If the counting operation were performed in function BlobCount instead of function Blob, eight copies of this array would be made each time the recursive step was executed, and we would soon run out of memory.

....

Exercises for Section 4.6   Self-Check

1. Trace the execution of recursive function Equal for the three-element arrays X (element values 1, 15, 10) and Y (element values 1, 15, 7). Write out completely in one equivalent Boolean expression the values that function Equal is assigned through all three recursive calls. Spell out all the values that are being compared.
2. Trace the execution of function BlobCount for the coordinate pairs (1, 1) and (1, 2) in the sample grid.
3. Is the order of the two tests performed in function BlobCount critical? What happens if we reverse them or combine them into a single condition?

Programming

1. Write a recursive function that finds the product of the elements in an array X of N elements.
2. Write a recursive function that finds the index of the smallest element in an array.
3. Write the recursive function FindMin that finds the smallest value in an integer array X with subscripts 1, . . . ,N.

4.7   Backtracking

In this section we will consider a technique known as *chronological back-tracking* or just backtracking. Backtracking is a search technique that is based on systematic trial and error. To illustrate backtracking, consider the task of finding a path through a maze.

One approach to finding a path through a maze is to start down a path and follow it as far as we can. If we find the end of the maze, then we are finished. If we find a dead end instead, then we need to retrace our steps (or backtrack) until we find an opening in the walls and try one of the alternative paths that we have not tried yet. What makes backtracking different from randomly guessing is that we are systematically eliminating alternative paths as we try them. This means that we will not try exactly the same path more than once and that eventually we will try every possible path.

Problems that are solvable by using backtracking have several features in common with our maze problem. The solution to these problems can be described as a set of choices made by some arbitrary method. If at some point in time it turns out that a solution is not possible by using the current set of choices, the most recent choice made is identified and removed. If a previously untried alternative exists for that choice, it is added to the set of choices, and search continues. If no previously untried alternative exists, then the next most recent choice is examined. This process continues until either a choice with an untried alternative is found and forward progress can continue or no more choices remain to try. If a solution to the problem exists, then backtracking will find it, though it may take a very long time to do so.

CASE STUDY   Finding a Path Through a Maze

It is very natural to want to implement a backtracking algorithm recursively. We will now describe a recursive algorithm that uses backtracking to find a path through a maze.

PROBLEM ▼

Given a maze and an initial starting location, find a path to the exit location if one exists. Every maze has the same exit location (the lower right-hand corner). Only vertical and horizontal moves may be used. Diagonal moves are not allowed. If we reach a dead end, we must backtrack to find a new path to try. We cannot simply jump to a new maze location and try again.

We will assume that our maze is stored in a two-dimensional array of characters as shown in Figure 4.27. A blank character is used to mark an open space, and the character 'X' is used to mark a wall location. As we visit each empty location, we will mark it with the character '*'. When we back-

Figure 4.27
A Maze as a Two-
Dimensional Array

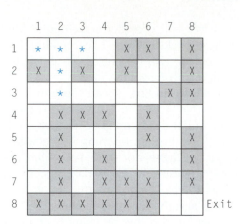

track, we will replace the '*' with a blank. In Fig. 4.27, we show a partial path for Maze[1,1] to Maze[1,2] to Maze[2,2] to Maze[3,2].

DESIGN OVERVIEW ▼

Procedure Solve must test the current location specified by its input parameters to see whether or not the path has reached the maze exit location. There are four stopping cases:

▶   Maze[Row, Col] is the exit location;
▶   Maze[Row, Col] is not part of the maze, meaning that the path includes an illegal move;
▶   Position Maze[Row, Col] has already been visited;
▶   and finally, after trying to find a path through each alternative (down, right, up, left) from the current position without reaching the exit, backtrack.

If the position Maze[Row, Col] is not the maze exit and is a legal position within the maze, then we try to find a path through each of the four adjacent Maze locations unless the exit is located first.

Data Requirements

Problem Inputs

```
The maze
The row and column location of the current maze position

    (Row, Col : Integer)
```

Problem Outputs

```
The maze with a path marked—if one was found
```

Program flag indicating whether path found or not

   (Success : Boolean)

Initial Algorithm

```
1.  if Maze[Row, Col] is exit then
      2.  Mark Maze[Row, Col] as visited
      3.  Stopping case - set Success to True
    else if Maze[Row, Col] is not part of the maze then
      4.  Stopping case - set Success to False
    else if Maze[Row, Col] has not been visited then
      begin
        5.  Mark Maze[Row, Col] as visited
        6.  if not Success and we can move down then
              7.  Move down and continue this path
        8.  if not Success and we can move right then
              9.  Move right and continue this path
       10.  if not Success and we can move up then
             11.  Move up and continue this path
       12.  if not Success and we can move left then
             13.  Move left and continue this path
       14.  if not Success then
      end
15.  Stop & Backtrack - Mark Maze[Row, Col] not visited
```

Consider what happens in the maze shown in Fig. 4.27 when Row is 3 and Col is 2. Maze[3, 2] is marked as visited (Step 5). Step 6 fails so we try Step 8. The condition for Step 8 is true, so we attempt to continue the path through position Maze[3, 3] (Step 9). Eventually, we will reach the exit point (Maze[8, 8]) through this path, so we will never have to remove the * at Maze[3, 3] or Maze[3, 2].

When Row is 3 and Col is 2, if Maze[3, 3] contained an X instead of a blank, we would be forced to continue the path to the left through point Maze[3, 1]. From Maze[3, 1], the only choice available would be to continue down column 1 through Maze[4, 1], Maze[5, 1], and so on. We would eventually reach a dead end and would have to backtrack, removing the * from Maze[7, 1], Maze[6, 1], and so on. Because there would be no untried alternatives at any point along the path we are backing up, we would remove all stars and back up to the entry point of the maze (Maze[1, 1]).

Procedure Solve is shown in Fig. 4.28 assuming the declarations below. The array Maze has element values ' ' or 'X' to represent Open spaces or Wall locations, respectively. The constant MaxSize represents the largest row or column subscript.

```
const
  MazeSize = 8;
  Open = ' ';
  Wall = 'X';

type
  MazeIndex = 1..MazeSize;
  MazeType = array [MazeIndex, MazeIndex] of Char;
```

Figure 4.28
Procedure Solve

Directory: CHAP 4
File: SOLVE.PAS

```
procedure Solve (var Maze {input/output} : MazeType;
                 Row, Col {input} : Integer;
                 var Success {output} : Boolean);
{
  Finds path through Maze if one exists.
  Pre : Maze, Row, and Col are defined.
  Post: If there is a path from [1,1] to [Row, Col], mark
        it in Maze and set Success to True; otherwise do
        nothing and set Success to False.
}
begin {Solve}
  if (Row = MazeSize) and (Col = MazeSize) then
    {Stopping case, we're there! Mark it visited}
    begin
      Maze[Row, Col] := '*';
      Success := True
    end {Maze solved}
  else if (Row < 1) or (Row > MazeSize)
          or (Col < 1) or (Col > MazeSize) then
    {Stopping case, ran off the edge of the Maze}
    Success := False
  else  if Maze[Row, Col] = Open then
    {We're on the path, look for a path to this point}
    begin
      {Tentatively mark this point as visited}
      Maze[Row, Col] := '*';

      {Try down}
      if not Success and (Maze[Row + 1, Col] = Open) then
        Solve (Maze, Row + 1, Col, Success);

      {Try right}
      if not Success and (Maze[Row, Col + 1] = Open) then
        Solve (Maze, Row, Col + 1, Success);

      {Try up}
      if not Success and (Maze[Row - 1, Col] = Open) then
        Solve (Maze, Row - 1, Col, Success);

      {Try left}
      if not Success and (Maze[Row, Col - 1] = Open) then
        Solve (Maze, Row, Col - 1, Success);

      {If deadend was reached take back the move.}
      if not Success then
        Maze[Row, Col] := Open
    end {else}
end; {Solve}
```

Procedure `Solve` begins by checking two of the stopping cases: the case in which the exit is found and the case in which the subscripts `Row` and `Col` denote positions outside the maze. Success is assigned `True` if the exit is found and `False` if `Row` and `Col` contain bad subscript values.

The next step is to check whether `Maze[Row, Col]` is an open position. If it is, then tentatively move there and store the character '*' there to mark it as visited. Now each array location adjacent to `Maze[Row, Col]` is explored one at a time as long as Success contains the value False (meaning that the exit has not already been found). Checking each adjacent array location involves a recursive call to procedure `Solve` with the subscripts of the array location being passed to procedure Solve.

If `Success` contains the value `True` after the four if statements have been executed, then the '*' is left as the value of position Maze[Row, Col]. If `Success` is `False` after checking all four positions, we will withdraw our move to `Maze[Row, Col]` by storing a blank at that position. In either case, execution of procedure `Solve` terminates, and control is returned to the caller. If the caller is the top-level module, the final value of `Success` will indicate whether or not `Maze` contains a marked path from the starting position to the exit at `Maze[MaxSize, MaxSize]`.

Exercises for Section 4.7

Self-Check

1. Trace the execution of procedure `Solve` if it is passed through the maze shown below, with starting position `Maze[1, 1]`. You may assume that the value of `MaxSize` is 3.

```
    1 2 3
  ┌─┬─┬─┐
1 │ │ │ │
  ├─┼─┼─┤
2 │ │X│ │
  ├─┼─┼─┤
3 │X│X│ │
  └─┴─┴─┘
```

2. What will be the consequences of replacing the five independent if statements in procedure Solve with the following nested if statement?

```
if not Success and (Maze[Row + 1, Col] = Open) then
  Solve (Maze, Row + 1, Col, Success)
else if not Success and (Maze[Row, Col + 1] = Open) then
  Solve (Maze, Row, Col + 1, Success)
else if not Success and (Maze[Row - 1, Col] = Open) then
  Solve (Maze, Row - 1, Col, Success)
else if not Success and (Maze[Row, Col - 1] = Open) then
  Solve (Maze, Row, Col - 1, Success)
else if not Success then
  Maze[Row, Col] := Open;
```

Programming

1. Write a driver program to test procedure `Solve` (Fig. 4.28).

4.8 Debugging Recursive Algorithms

You can use the Borland Pascal debugger to aid in debugging a recursive function or procedure. If you place a value parameter in the Watch window, you can see how that parameter's value changes during successive calls to the recursive subprogram. If your subprogram's local variables are in a Watch window, you can observe their values as you single-step through the subprogram using the F7 function key.

The Call Stack window can help to trace the execution of a recursive subprogram. Each time a procedure or function is called, the Borland Pascal debugger remembers the call by placing a record on the call stack. This record contains the subprogram name along with the values of the actual parameters used in the subprogram call. When the procedure or function is exited, its record is removed from the call stack. Whenever execution pauses during a debugging session, you can view the contents of the call stack by pressing Ctrl-F3. This opens a window similar to that shown in Fig. 4.29.

The Call Stack window contains a list of the calls to the currently active subprograms. If this list is too long to fit on the screen, use the mouse or the F6 key to move the Call Stack window, and then use the mouse or the arrow keys to scroll through the list of calls.

You can also determine the statement that is currently executing in any of the active calls. Normally, the most recent call is highlighted in the Call Stack window, and its currently executing statement is highlighted in the Edit win-

Figure 4.29
Call Stack Window

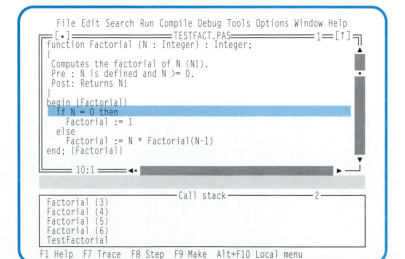

dow. If you select another call in the Call Stack window (using the arrow keys or the mouse), the Call Stack window will disappear, and the Edit window cursor will be positioned at the statement currently executing that call. You can bring back the Call Stack window by pressing Ctrl-F3 again.

4.9 Common Programming Errors

The most common problem with a recursive procedure is that it may not terminate properly. For example, if the terminating condition is incorrect or incomplete, then the procedure may call itself indefinitely or until all available memory is used up. Normally, a "stack overflow" run-time error is an indicator that a recursive procedure is not terminating. Make sure that you identify all stopping cases and provide a terminating condition for each one. Also be sure that each recursive step leads to a situation that is closer to a stopping case and that repeated recursive calls will eventually lead to stopping cases only.

The use of large arrays or other data structures as value parameters can quickly consume all available memory. Unless absolutely essential for data protection, arrays should be passed as variable parameters. Any expression such as N − 1 must be passed as a value parameter.

Sometimes it is difficult to observe the result of a recursive procedure execution. If each recursive call generates a large number of output lines and there are many recursive calls, the output will scroll down the screen more quickly than it can be read. You can cause your output to stop temporarily by printing a prompting message followed by a Read (NextChar) operation. Your program will resume execution when you enter a data character.

CHAPTER REVIEW

Many examples of recursive procedures and functions were provided in this chapter. Hopefully, studying them has given you some appreciation of the power of recursion as a problem-solving and programming tool and has provided you with valuable insight into its use. It may take some time to feel comfortable thinking in this new way about programming, but it is certainly worth the effort.

Quick-Check Exercises

1. Explain the use of a stack in recursion.
2. Which is generally more efficient, recursion or iteration?
3. What are the two uses of the function name in a recursive function?
4. Why would a programmer conceptualize the problem solution using recursion and implement it using iteration?
5. Explain the problem with value array parameters in recursion.

6. In a recursive problem involving N items, why must N be a value parameter?
7. What causes a "stack overflow" error?
8. What can you say about a recursive algorithm that has the following form?

```
if condition then
    Perform recursive step.
```

9. What does the following recursive function do?

```
function Mystery (X : IntArray;
                         N : Word) : Integer;
   var
      Temp : Integer;

begin {Mystery}
   if N = 1 then
      Mystery := X[1]
   else
      begin
        Temp :=  Mystery(X, N - 1);
        if X[N] > Temp then
           Mystery := X[N]
        else
           Mystery := Temp
      end {if}
end; {Mystery}
```

Answers to Quick-Check Exercises

1. The stack is used to hold all parameter and local variable values and the return point for each execution of a recursive procedure.
2. Iteration is generally more efficient than recursion.
3. To assign a value to the function and to call it recursively.
4. When its solution is much easier to conceptualize by using recursion but its implementation would be too inefficient.
5. A copy of the array must be pushed onto the stack each time a call occurs. All available stack memory could be exhausted.
6. If N were a variable parameter, its address would be saved on the stack, not its value, so it would not be possible to retain a different value for each call.
7. Too many recursive calls.
8. Nothing is done when the stopping case is reached.
9. Returns the largest value in array X.

Review Questions

1. Explain the nature of a recursive problem.
2. Discuss the efficiency of recursive procedures.
3. Differentiate between stopping cases and a terminating condition.
4. Write a Pascal procedure that prints the accumulating sum of ordinal values corresponding to each character in a string. For example, if the string value is 'a boy', the first value printed would be the ordinal number of a, then the sum of

ordinals for a and the space character, then the sum of ordinals for a, space, b, and so on.

5. Write a Pascal function that returns the sum of ordinal values corresponding to the characters stored in a string; however, this time exclude any space characters from the sum.

6. The expression for computing C(n, r), the number of combinations of n items taken r at a time, is

$$c(n, r) = \frac{n!}{r!(n-r)!}$$

Write a function for computing c(n, r) given that n! is the factorial of n.

Programming Projects

Directory: CHAP 4
File: PROJ4_1.PAS

1. Write a procedure that reads each row of an array as a string and converts it to a row of `Grid` to be processed by function `BlobCount` (see Fig. 4.26). The first character of Row 1 corresponds to `Grid[1,1]`, the second character to `Grid[1,2]`, etc. Set the element value to `Empty` if the character is blank; otherwise, set it to `Filled`. The number of rows in the array should be read first. Use this procedure in a program that reads in cell coordinates and prints the number of cells in the blob containing each coordinate pair.

2. A palindrome consists of a word that is spelled exactly the same when the letters are reversed, for example, such words as Level, Deed, and Mom. Write a recursive function that returns the `Boolean` value True if a word, passed as a parameter, is a palindrome.

3. Write a recursive function that returns the value of the following recursive definition:

```
F(X,Y) = X - Y                    if X or Y < 0
F(X,Y) = F(X - 1, Y) + F(X, Y - 1)  otherwise
```

Directory: CHAP 4
File: PROJ4_4.PAS

4. Write a recursive procedure that lists all of the pairs of subsets for a given set of letters. For example,

```
['A', 'C', 'E', 'G'] => ['A', 'C'], ['A', 'E'], ['A', 'G'],
                        ['C', 'E'], ['C', 'G'], ['E', 'G']
```

Directory: CHAP 4
File: PROJ4_5.PAS

5. One method of solving a continuous numerical function for a root implements a technique similar to the binary search. Given a numerical function, defined as f(X), and two values of X that are known to bracket one of the roots, an approximation to this root can be determined through a method of repeated division of this bracket. For a set of values of X to bracket a root, the value of the function for one X must be negative and the other must be positive as illustrated in Fig. 4.30, which plots f(X) for values of X between X1 and X2.

The algorithm requires that the midpoint between X1 and X2 be evaluated in the function, and if it equals zero the root is found; otherwise, X1 or X2 is set to this midpoint. To determine whether to replace X1 or X2, the sign of the midpoint is compared against the signs of the values of f(X1) and f(X2). The midpoint replaces the X (X1 or X2) whose function value has the same sign as the function value at the midpoint.

Figure 4.30
Graph of f(X)

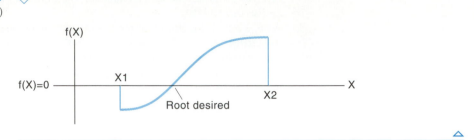

This routine can be written recursively. The terminating conditions are true when either the midpoint evaluated in the function is zero or the absolute value of X1 minus X2 is less than some small predetermined value (e.g., 0.0005). If the second condition occurs, then the root is said to be approximately equal to the last midpoint.

6. We can use a merge technique to sort two arrays. The *mergesort* begins by taking adjacent pairs of array values and ordering the values in each pair. It then forms groups of four elements by merging adjacent pairs (first pair with second pair, third pair with fourth pair, etc.) into another array. It then takes adjacent groups of four elements from this new array and merges them back into the original array as groups of eight, and so on. The process terminates when a single group is formed that has the same number of elements as the array. The mergesort is illustrated in Fig. 4.31 for an array with eight elements. Write a `MergeSort` procedure.

7. The Eight Queens Problem is a famous chess problem that has as its goal the placement of eight queens on a single chessboard so that no queen will be able to attack any other queen. A queen may move any number of squares vertically, horizontally, or diagonally. A chessboard can be represented by a two-

Directory: CHAP 4
File: PROJ4_7.PAS

Figure 4.31
Illustration of `MergeSort`

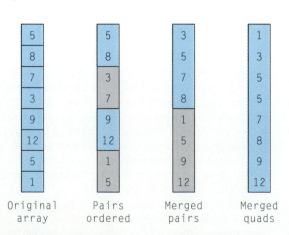

dimensional array having eight rows and eight columns. Write a program that contains a recursive routine that solves the Eight Queens Problem.

Hint: Arbitrarily choose the location for the first queen, then attempt to place the second queen in the next available open row. This process continues as long as it is possible to place queens. If a dead end is reached, the last placed queen is removed and repositioned by backtracking to the previous activation of the recursive routine and attempting to place the queen in a different location.

CHAPTER FIVE

Stacks

In Chapters 5 through 9 we introduce several abstract data types of great importance to software engineers. As each abstract data type is introduced, study its attributes and operators very carefully. Look for similarities and differences between the new abstract data type and the abstract data types that we have already discussed. This will help to identify abstract data types that are candidates for reuse via object inheritance.

When we describe alternative methods of implementing an abstract data type, pay close attention to the limitations imposed by the Borland Pascal compiler and the limitations that are present in the definition of the abstract data type itself. It is best to compare two implementations of the same abstract data type in terms of their relative execution times, the amount of memory required, and the ease with which they may be programmed.

In this chapter we illustrate how to use an abstract data type known as a stack and how to implement a stack abstract data type. When we discussed recursion in Chapter 4, we introduced the stack as a useful data structure for storing the actual parameters passed in each call to a recursive procedure or function (see Section 4.1). A stack provides a convenient mechanism for storing information (or dishes in a cafeteria); we can access only the top item in a stack, and we can do this only when data in the stack is to be accessed in the reverse order from which it was stored in the stack.

5.1 Stack Abstract Data Type

In this section we discuss a data abstraction, the stack, that is very useful in computer science applications such as writing compilers. We introduced the stack in Section 4.1 and discussed how stacks might be used to implement recursion.

A stack is characterized by the property that at any one time, only the top element of the stack is accessible. In a stack the top element of the stack is always the data value that was most recently stored in the stack. Sometimes this storage policy is known as "last in, first out," or *LIFO*. Some of the operations that we might wish to perform on a stack are summarized in Table 5.1.

Table 5.1
Specification of Abstract
Data Type Stack

Elements
A stack consists of a collection of elements that are all the same data type.

Structure
The elements of a stack are ordered according to when they were placed on the stack. Only the element that was last inserted into the stack may be removed or examined. New elements are inserted at the top of the stack.

Operators
In the descriptions of the operators we will assume the following parameters:

```
X has the same data type as the stack elements.
Success is type Boolean and indicates whether or not the
    operation succeeds.
```

Stack.CreateStack	Creates an empty stack.
Stack.Push (X, var Success)	If the stack is not full, the value in X is placed on the top of the stack, and Success is set to True. Otherwise, the top of the stack is not changed, and Success is set to False.

Table 5.1 Specification of Abstract Data Type Stack (*Cont.*)	***Stack.Pop (var X, var Success)***	If the stack is not empty, the value at the top of the stack is removed, its value is placed in X, and Success is set to True. If the stack is empty, X is not defined, and Success is set to False.
	Stack.Retrieve (var X, var Success)	If the stack is not empty, the value at the top of the stack is copied into X, and Success is set to True. If the stack is empty, X is not defined, and Success is set to False. In either case the stack is not changed.
	Stack.IsEmpty (function)	Returns True if the stack is empty; otherwise, returns False.
	Stack.IsFull	(function) Returns True if the stack is full; otherwise, returns False.

As before, we can illustrate how these operators work and use them in a client program without worrying about the details of how the stack is represented in memory. We will discuss one internal representation for a stack (StackADT) in Section 5.4 and implement the stack operators. Since we would like to be able to manipulate different types of data objects using a stack, we will use the identifier StackElement to represent the type of each stack element. Each client program must import data types StackElement from StackElementADT and Stack from StackADT before trying to use variables of these types.

A client program can allocate multiple stacks by declaring several variables of type Stack. Because StackElement can be declared only once in a program, all stacks that are used in a particular program must have the same type of element.

Procedure CreateStack must be called before a stack can be processed. CreateStack creates a stack that is initially empty. If S is declared as type Stack, the statements

```
S.CreateStack;
if S.IsEmpty then
  WriteLn ('Stack is empty')
```

display the message Stack is empty.

EXAMPLE 5.1 ▼

A stack S of character elements is shown in Fig. 5.1. This stack currently has four elements; the element '2' was placed on the stack before the other three elements; '*' was the last element placed on the stack.

For stack S in Fig. 5.1 the value of IsEmpty(S) is False. The value of IsFull(S) is False if stack S can store more than four elements; otherwise, the value of IsFull(S) is True. The procedure call statement

Figure 5.1
Stack S

S

S.Retrieve (X, Success)

stores '*' in X (type Char) without changing S. The procedure call statement

S.Pop (X, Success)

removes '*' from S and stores it in X. The new stack S contains three elements and is shown in Fig. 5.2.
    The procedure call statement

S.Push ('/', Success)

pushes '/' onto the stack; the new stack S contains four elements and is
shown in Fig. 5.3. The value of Success (type Boolean) after each of the
operations discussed above should be True. ▲

Exercises for Section 5.1   **Self-Check**

1.   Assume that the stack S is defined as in Fig. 5.3, and perform the sequence of operations below. Indicate the result of each operation and
the new stack if it is changed. Rather than draw the stack each time, use
the notation |2+C/ to represent the stack in Fig. 5.3.

```
S.Push ('$', Success);
S.Push ('-', Success);
S.Pop (NextCh, Success);
S.Retrieve (NextCh, Success);
```

Figure 5.2
Stack S After Pop
Operation

```
C
+
2
```

S

Figure 5.3
Stack S After Push
Operation

5.2 Stack Applications

In this section we study some client programs that use stacks. These programs illustrate some simple applications in which the stack abstract data type is quite useful.

CASE STUDY   **Displaying a String in Reverse Order**

PROBLEM ▼

A reading instructor is studying dyslexia and would like a program that displays a word or sentence in reverse order.

DESIGN OVERVIEW ▼

A stack of characters is a good data structure for such a program. If we first push each data character onto a stack and then pop each character and display it, the characters will be displayed in reverse order. The sequence of characters is displayed in reverse order because the last character pushed onto the stack is the first one popped. For example, the diagram in Fig. 5.4 shows the stack S after the letters in the string `'house'` are processed, beginning with the letter `'h'`. The first letter that will be popped and displayed is e, the next letter is s, and so on.

Figure 5.4
Pushing the Characters
'house' on a Stack

Data Requirements

Problem Inputs

Each data character

Problem Outputs

Each character on the stack

Program Variables

The stack of characters (S : Stack)

Algorithm

1. Create an empty stack of characters.
2. Push each data character onto a stack.
3. Pop each character and display it.
4. Indicate whether the stack is empty or full.

PROGRAM STRUCTURE ▼

The system structure chart (see Fig. 5.5) shows that procedure CreateStack performs Step 1, procedure FillStack performs Step 2, and procedure DisplayStack performs Step 3. FillStack and DisplayStack call procedures Push and Pop from StackADT. Functions IsEmpty and IsFull (from StackADT) are called to perform Step 4.

Figure 5.5
System Structure Chart for
PrintReverse

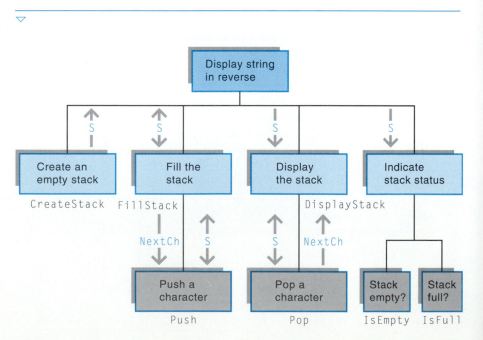

CODING THE MAIN PROGRAM ▼

The main program and its procedures are shown in Fig. 5.6. The type declarations for StackElement (type is Char) and Stack must be imported along with the stack operators. Procedures FillStack and DisplayStack are described after the program.

CODING THE PROCEDURES ▼

The repeat-until loop in procedure FillStack (see Fig. 5.7) reads each data character (at least one) into NextCh and pushes it onto the stack. The if statement displays an error message in the event that the input string is too long. This would happen if the program user entered more characters than the stack capacity before pressing Enter.

Figure 5.6
Program PrintReverse

Directory: CHAP 5
File: PRINTREV.PAS

```
program PrintReverse;
{
  Reads a sequence of characters and displays it in reverse
  order.

  IMPORT: Stack, CreateStack, Push, Pop, IsFull, IsEmpty
      from StackADT (see Section 5.4)
}
  uses StackADT;

  var
    S : Stack;                        {the stack of characters}

  {Insert FillStack and DisplayStack}
  {$I FILLSTAC.PAS}
  {$I DISPLAYS.PAS}

begin {PrintReverse}
  S.CreateStack;                      {start with an empty stack}

  {Fill the stack.}
  FillStack (S);

  {Display the characters in reverse order.}
  DisplayStack (S);

  {Display status of stack S.}
  if S.IsEmpty then
    WriteLn ('Stack is empty - operation succeeds')
  else if S.IsFull then
    WriteLn ('Stack is full - reversal failed')
end. {PrintReverse}

Enter a string of one or more characters.
Press return when done.
This is a short string.
.gnirts trohs a si sihT
Stack is empty - operation succeeds
```

```
procedure FillStack (var S {in/out} : Stack);
{
 Reads data characters and pushes them onto the stack.
 Pre : S is a stack.
 Post: Each data character read is pushed onto stack S.
 Calls: Push
}
  var
    NextCh : Char;                {the next character}
    Success : Boolean;           {flag}
begin {FillStack}
  WriteLn ('Enter a string of one or more characters.');
  WriteLn ('Press return when done.');
  repeat
    Read (NextCh);               {read next character}
    S.Push (NextCh, Success)     {push it onto stack}
  until Eoln(Input) or not Success;

  {Print an error if stack overflows.}
  if not Success then
    WriteLn ('Stack overflow error - string too long')
end; {FillStack}
```

The while loop in procedure DisplayStack (see Fig. 5.8) pops each character from the stack into NextCh and then displays it. The loop is repeated as long as characters remain on the stack (Success is True). After DisplayStack is finished, the stack should be empty.

TESTING ▼

It would be a good idea to see what happens when the stack overflows. This can be done by setting MaxStack to a small value (say, 10).

CASE STUDY **Checking for Balanced Parentheses**

One application of a stack is to determine whether an expression is balanced with respect to parentheses. For example, the expression

```
(a + b * (c / (d - e))) + (d / e)
1         2   3     321   1     1
```

```
procedure DisplayStack (var S {in/out} : Stack);
{
  Pops each stack character and displays it.
  Pre : Stack S is defined.
  Post: Each character is displayed and S is empty.
  Calls: Pop
}
  var
    NextCh : Char;                  {the next character}
    Success : Boolean;              {flag}

begin {DisplayStack}
  S.Pop (NextCh, Success);
  while Success do
    begin
      Write (NextCh);
      S.Pop (NextCh, Success)
    end; {while}
  WriteLn
end; {DisplayStack}
```

is balanced. We can solve this problem without using a stack by ignoring all characters except the symbols `"("` and `")"`. We should add 1 to a counter for each open parenthesis that follows another open parenthesis and subtract 1 for each close parenthesis that follows another close parenthesis. Since we are ignoring all other symbols, the parentheses being considered do not have to be consecutive characters. The count should begin and end at 1.

This task becomes more difficult if we allow different types of symbols to be used as parentheses. For example, the expression

`(a + b * {c / [d - e]}) + (d / e)`

is balanced, whereas the expression

`(a + b * {c / [d - e}}) + (d / e)`

is not because the subexpression [d - e} *is incorrect*.

PROBLEM ▼

The set of open parentheses includes the symbols {, [, and (. An expression is balanced if each subexpression that starts with the symbol { ends with the symbol }, and the same statement is true for the symbol pairs [,] and (,). Another way of saying this is that the unmatched open parenthesis that is nearest to each close parenthesis must have the correct shape (e.g., if } is the close parenthesis in question, then the symbol { must be the nearest preceding unmatched open parenthesis).

DESIGN OVERVIEW ▼

With stacks, this problem is fairly easy to solve. We can scan the expression from left to right, ignoring all characters except parentheses. We will push each open parenthesis onto a stack of characters. When we reach a close parenthesis, we will see whether it matches the symbol on the top of the stack. If the characters don't match or the stack is empty, there is an error in the expression. If they do match, we will continue the scan.

Data Requirements

Problem Inputs

```
The expression to be checked for balanced parentheses
  (Expression : string)
```

Problem Outputs

```
The function result indicates whether the parentheses in
  Expression are balanced
```

Program Variables

```
The stack of open parentheses (ParenStack : Stack)
A flag indicating whether parentheses are balanced
  (Balanced : Boolean)
The next character in Expression (NextCh : Char)
The index of the next character (Index : Integer)
The open parenthesis at the top of the stack (Open : Char)
The close parenthesis being matched (Close : Char)
```

Algorithm

```
1. Create an empty stack of characters.
2. Assume that the expression is balanced (Balanced is True).
3. while the expression is balanced and still in the string do
     begin
       4. Get the next character in the data string.
       5. if the next character is an open parenthesis then
             6. Push it onto the stack
           else if the next character is a close parenthesis then
             begin
               7. Pop the top of the stack
               8. if stack was empty or its top was incorrect then
                    9. Set Balanced to False.
             end
     end
10. if the expression is balanced then
      11. There is an error if the stack is not empty.
```

The if statement in Step 5 tests each character in the expression, ignoring all characters except for open and close parentheses. If the next character is an open parenthesis, it is pushed onto the stack. If the next character is a close parenthesis, the nearest unmatched open parenthesis is retrieved (by popping the stack) and compared to the close parenthesis.

CODING ▼

Figure 5.9 shows a function that determines whether its input parameter (an expression) is balanced. The if statement in the while loop tests for open and close parentheses as discussed earlier. Each open parenthesis is pushed onto stack `ParenStack`. For each close parenthesis, procedure `Pop` retrieves the nearest unmatched open parenthesis from the stack. If the stack was empty, `Pop` sets `Balanced` to `False`, causing the while loop exit. Otherwise, the case statement sets `Balanced` to indicate whether the character popped matches the current close parenthesis. After loop exit occurs, the function result is defined. It is true only when the expression is balanced and the stack is empty.

TESTING ▼

You will have to write a driver program to test function IsBalanced. The driver program will have to import the type declarations for `StackElement`

Figure 5.9
Function `IsBalanced`

Directory: CHAP 5
File: ISBALANC.PAS

```
function IsBalanced (Expression {input} : string) : Boolean;
{
 Determines whether Expression is balanced with respect
 to parentheses.
 Pre : Expression is defined.
 Post: Returns True if Expression is balanced; otherwise,
       returns False.
 Calls: CreateStack, Push, Pop and IsEmpty from StackADT.
}
   var
      ParenStack : Stack;    {the stack of open parentheses}
      NextCh,                {the next character in Expression}
      Close,                 {close parenthesis to be matched}
      Open : Char;           {open parenthesis at top of stack}
      Index : Integer;       {index to Expression}
      Balanced : Boolean;    {program flag}

begin {IsBalanced}
   ParenStack.CreateStack;          {Create an empty stack}
   Balanced := True;
   Index := 1;
   while Balanced and (Index <= Length(Expression)) do
         {invariant:
```

▷ ▷ ▷ ▷ ▷

```
      All closing parentheses so far were matched and
      Index <= Length(Expression) + 1
        }
      begin
        NextCh := Expression[Index];  {access next character}
        if NextCh in ['(', '[', '{'] then
          ParenStack.Push (NextCh, Balanced) {stack parenthesis}
        else if NextCh in [')', ']', '}'] then
          begin {close paren}
            Close := NextCh;
            {Get nearest unmatched open parenthesis}
            ParenStack.Pop (Open, Balanced);
            if Balanced then
              {Check for matching parentheses.}
              case Close of
                ')' : Balanced := Open = '(';
                ']' : Balanced := Open = '[';
                '}' : Balanced := Open = '{'
              end {case}
          end; {close paren}
        Index := Index + 1  {access next character}
      end; {while}

    {Define function result}
    if Balanced then
      IsBalanced := ParenStack.IsEmpty
    else
      IsBalanced := False
end; {IsBalanced}
```

△

(type is Char) and Stack (from StackADT). It will also have to import the
stack operators and string operators that are called by IsBalanced. Make
sure you use a variety of balanced and unbalanced expressions to test Is-
Balanced, including an expression without parentheses.

Exercises for Section 5.2   **Self-Check**

1. Trace the execution of function IsBalanced for each of the following
    expressions. Your trace should show the stack after each push or pop
    operation. Also show the values of Balanced, Open, and Close after
    each close parenthesis is processed.

    ```
    (a + b * {c / [d - e]}) + (d / e)
    (a + b * {c / [d - e}}) + (d / e)
    ```

Programming

1.   Write a main program to test function `IsBalanced`.

5.3   Evaluating Expressions

One task of a compiler is to evaluate arithmetic expressions. We will discuss one approach to expression evaluation in this section. Some of you may use calculators that evaluate postfix expressions. A *postfix expression* is one in which each operator follows its operands. We will discuss postfix expressions further in Chapter 8; for the time being, you should get a pretty good idea of what a postfix expression is by studying the examples in Table 5.2. The braces under each expression are added to help you visualize the operands for each operator. The more familiar *infix expression* corresponding to each postfix expression is shown in the middle column of the table.

Table 5.2
Table of Postfix
Expressions

Postfix Expression	Infix Expression	Value
5 6 *	5 * 6	30
5 6 1 + *	5 * (6 + 1)	35
5 6 * 10 –	(5 * 6) – 10	20
4 5 6 * 3 / +	4 + ((5 * 6) / 3)	14

The advantage of the postfix form is that there is no need to group subexpressions in parentheses or to consider operator precedence. The parentheses in Table 5.1 are for our convenience and are not required. We will write a program that evaluates a postfix expression next.

CASE STUDY ## Evaluating Postfix Expressions

PROBLEM ▼

Simulate the operation of a calculator by reading an expression in postfix form and displaying its result. Each data character will be a blank, a digit character, or one of the operator characters from the set [+, –, *, /].

DESIGN OVERVIEW ▼

Using a stack of integer values makes it easy to evaluate the expression. Our program will push each integer operand onto the stack. When an operator is read, the top two operands are popped, the operation is performed on its operands, and the result is pushed back onto the stack. The final result should be the only value remaining on the stack when the end of the expression is reached.

Data Requirements

Problem Inputs

```
The expression to evaluate (Expression)
```

Problem Outputs

```
The expression value (Result : Integer)
```

Program Variables

```
The stack of integer operands (OpStack : Stack)
A program flag indicating the result of a stack operation
  (Success : Boolean)
The next character in Expression (NextCh : Char)
The index to the next character (Index : Integer)
The next integer value in Expression (NewOp : Integer)
The two operands of an operator (Op1, Op2 : Integer)
```

Algorithm

```
1. Read the expression string.
2. Create an empty stack of integers.
3. Set Success to True.
4. while Success is True and not at the end of the expression do
     begin
         5. Get the next character.
         6. if the character is a digit then
             begin
                 7. Get the integer that starts with this digit.
                 8. Push the integer onto the stack.
             end
         else if the character is an operator then
             begin
                 9. Pop the top two operands into.
                10. Evaluate the operation.
                11. Push the result onto the stack.
             end
     end
12. Display the result
```

Figure 5.10 shows the evaluation of the third expression in Table 5.2 using this algorithm. The arrow under the expression points to the character being processed; the stack diagram shows the stack after this character is processed.

Figure 5.10
Evaluating a Postfix
Expression

Expression	Action	Stack
5 6 * 10 - ^	Push 5	5
5 6 * 10 - ^	Push 6	6 5
5 6 * 10 - ^	Pop 6 and 5, evaluate 5 * 6, push 30	30
5 6 * 10 - ^	Push 10	10 30
5 6 * 10 - ^	Pop 10 and 30, evaluate 30 − 10, push 20	20
5 6 * 10 - ^	Pop 20, stack is empty, result is 20	

Refinements

The stack operators perform algorithm Steps 2, 8, 9, 11, and 12. Steps 7 and 10 are the only algorithm steps that require refinement. Step 7 is performed by procedure GetInteger, and Step 10 is performed by function Eval. The system structure chart in Fig. 5.11 shows the data flow between these two subprograms and the main program.

CODING ▼

Main Program

The main program is shown in Fig. 5.12. Besides the operators mentioned earlier, data types Stack and StackElement must be imported into the main program.

Each time stack S is manipulated, the Boolean flag Success is set to indicate the success or failure of that operation. If Success is False, the program displays an error message and terminates the expression evaluation. If the final value of Success is True and the stack is empty, the result is displayed.

Subprograms

Procedure GetInteger (see Fig. 5.13) accumulates the integer value of a string of consecutive digit characters and returns this value through parameter NewOp. The assignment statement

Figure 5.11
System Structure Chart for
Program `PostFix`

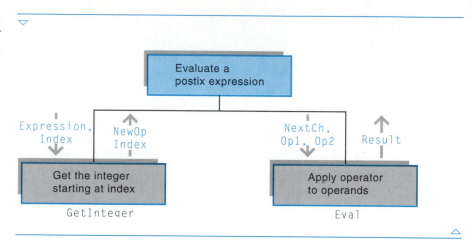

Figure 5.12
Program `Postfix` and
Sample Run

$$NewOp := (10 * NewOp) + Ord(NextCh) - Ord('0');$$

adds the numeric value of the digit character in `NextCh` to the numeric value
being accumulated in `NewOp`. For example, if the current value of `NewOp` is 15
and `NextCh` is '3', `NewOp` gets the value 153. When `GetInteger` returns to the
main program, `Index` points to the last digit of the number just processed.

Whenever an operator is encountered, the main program pops its two
operands off the stack and calls function `Eval` (see Fig. 5.14) to compute the

```
program PostFix;
{
 Evaluates a postfix expression.

 IMPORT: Stack, CreateStack, Pop, Push, IsEmpty from StackADT
         (see Section 5.4).
}
  uses StackADT;

  var
    OpStack : Stack;          {a stack of integers}
    Expression : string;      {expression to be evaluated}
    NextCh : Char;            {the next data character}
    Index : Integer;          {index of next character}
    Op1, Op2,                 {operand values from stack}
    NewOp,                    {new operand for the stack}
    Result : Integer;         {result of operator evaluation}
    Success : Boolean;        {flag for stack operation}
```

```
   {Insert GetInteger and Eval}
   {$I GETINTEG.Pas}
   {$I EVAL.PAS}

begin {Postfix}
   Write ('Enter your expression> ');
   ReadLn (Expression);

   OpStack.CreateStack;          {Create an empty stack}
   Index := 1;
   Success := True;
   while Success and (Index <= Length(Expression)) do
     {invariant:
         OpStack contains all unprocessed operands and results
         and Index <= Length(Expression) + 1
     }
     begin
       NextCh := Expression[Index];    {Get the next character}
       if NextCh in ['0'..'9'] then
         begin {digit}
           GetInteger(Expression, Index, NewOp);   {Get integer value}
           OpStack.Push (NewOp, Success);          {Push integer value}
           if not Success then
             WriteLn ('Stack overflow error')
         end {digit}
       else if NextCh in ['+','-','*','/'] then
         begin {operator}
           OpStack.Pop (Op2, Success);                    {Get last operand}
           OpStack.Pop (Op1, Success);                    {Get first operand}
           if not Success then
             WriteLn ('Invalid expression')
           else
             begin {evaluate operator}
               Result := Eval(NextCh, Op1, Op2);
               OpStack.Push (Result, Success);            {Push result}
               if not Success then
                 WriteLn ('Stack overflow')
             end {evaluate operator}
         end; {operator}
       Index := Index + 1                             {Go to next character}
     end; {while}

   if Success then
     OpStack.Pop (Result, Success);                   {Get the result}
   if Success and OpStack.IsEmpty then
     WriteLn ('Expression value is ', Result :1) {Print it}
   else
     WriteLn ('Invalid expression')
end. {Postfix}

Enter your expression> 5 6 * 10 -

Expression value is 20
```

Figure 5.13
Procedure GetInteger

Directory: CHAP 5
File: GETINTEG.PAS

▽

```
procedure GetInteger (Expression {input} : string;
                         var Index {input/output},
                             NewOp {output} : Integer);
{
 Returns in NewOp the integer whose first digit is at position Index.
 Pre : Expression and Index are defined and the character at Index is a digit.
 Post: Index points to the last digit of the number whose first digit is pointed to
       by the initial value of Index.
       NewOp is the value of that number.
}
begin {GetInteger}
  NewOp := 0;
  NextCh := Expression[Index];
  while (NextCh in ['0'..'9']) and (Index <= Length(Expression)) do
   {invariant:
       Last character in NextCh was a digit and
       Index <= Length(Expression) + 1 and
       NewOp is the numerical value of all digits processed so far
   }
    begin
      NewOp := (10 * NewOp) + Ord(NextCh) - Ord('0');
      Index := Index + 1;
      NextCh := Expression[Index]
    end; {while}
  {assert:
     NewOp is the numerical value of the substring processed and
     Index is at the end of the substring or just past it.
  }
  if not (NextCh in ['0'..'9']) then
    Index := Index - 1                    {point to the last digit}
end; {GetInteger}
```

△

result of applying the operator (passed through NextCh) to its operands (passed through Op1, Op2). The case statement in function Eval selects the appropriate operation and performs it.

TESTING ▼

You will have to import the necessary data types and procedures to test program PostFix. See what happens when the expression is not a valid postfix expression or it contains characters other than those expected.

Figure 5.14
Function Eval

Directory: CHAP 5
File: EVAL.PAS

```
function Eval (NextCh : Char;
              Op1, Op2 : Integer) : Integer;
{
  Applies operator NextCh to operands Op1, Op2.
  Pre : NextCh is an operator and Op1, Op2 are defined.
  Post: If NextCh is '+', returns Op1 + Op2, and so on.
}
begin {Eval}
  if NextCh in ['+', '-', '*', '/'] then
    case NextCh of
      '+' : Eval := Op1 + Op2;
      '-' : Eval := Op1 - Op2;
      '*' : Eval := Op1 * Op2;
      '/' : Eval := Op1 div Op2    {integer division}
    end {case}
  else
    WriteLn ('Error in operator symbol')
end; {Eval}
```

Exercises for Section 5.3

Self-Check

1. Trace the evaluation of the last expression in Table 5.2. Show the stack each time it is modified, and show how the values of NewOp and Result are changed as the program executes.

Programming

1. Modify the program to handle the exponentiation operator, which will be indicated by the symbol ∧. Assume that the first operand is raised to the power indicated by the second operand.

5.4 Implementing a Stack

In this section we discuss how we might implement a stack in Pascal. We will begin with the internal representation for a stack.

Declaration for Type Stack

The data type Stack is declared in the interface section for StackADT (see Fig. 5.15). The array data member named Items provides storage for the stack elements. Top is an index to this array, and Top selects the element at the top of the stack. We can store up to MaxStack (value is 100) elements in an object of type Stack.

The statement

```
uses StackElementADT;    {Import type StackElement}
```

imports the data type StackElement. StackElement can be a standard type or a user-defined object type with methods. To create a stack that can contain up to 100 characters, we should declare the unit shown in Fig. 5.16.

Although it would be simpler to insert this type declaration directly in StackADT, this approach is more general. It allows us to use StackADT to create a stack of any object type. To do this, we first specify the new unit StackElementADT and then compile it and unit StackADT to disk.

As always, storage is not allocated until a variable of type Stack is declared. The variable declaration

```
var
  S : Stack;
```

Directory: CHAP 5
File: STACKADT.PAS

Figure 5.15
Interface Section for Unit
StackADT

▽

```
unit StackADT;
{
 Abstract data type Stack: contains declarations for data
 type Stack and operator procedures for an object of type Stack.
}
interface

  uses StackElementADT;

  const
    MaxStack = 100;

  type
    IndexType = 1..MaxStack;
    TopRange = 0..MaxStack;
    Stack = object
              procedure CreateStack;
              procedure Push (X {input} : StackElement;
                         var Success {output} : Boolean);
              procedure Pop (var X {output} : StackElement;
                         var Success {output} : Boolean);
              procedure Retrieve (var X {output} : StackElement;
                              var Success {output} : Boolean);
              function IsFull : Boolean;
              function IsEmpty : Boolean;

            private
              Top : TopRange;
              Items : array [IndexType] of StackElement;
            end; {Stack}
```

△

Figure 5.16
Unit `StackElementADT`
for a Stack of Characters

Directory: CHAP 5
File: STACKELE.PAS

```
unit StackElementADT;

interface
  type
    StackElement = Char;

implementation
  {none - standard data type}

end. {StackElementADT}
```

allocates storage for a stack, S, of up to 100 elements of type `StackElement`. Note that the storage space for the entire stack is allocated at one time even though there won't be any objects on the stack initially.

The abstract stack S on the left in Fig. 5.17 would be represented in memory by the record shown on the right. `S.Top` is 3, and the stack consists of the subarray `S.Items[1..3]`; the subarray `S.Items[4..100]` is currently undefined. The array element `S.Items[S.Top]` contains the character value `'{'`, which is the value at the top of the stack.

We can change the capacity of a stack by redefining the constant `MaxStack`. Also, we can change the stack elements to another simple type or a structured type by changing the declaration for `StackElement` in unit `StackElementADT`. If we use the declaration

```
type
  StackElement = Integer;
```

a variable of type `Stack` will be able to store up to 100 integer values.

EXAMPLE 5.2 ▼

Figure 5.18 shows the effect of the statement

```
Push (S, '(', Success)
```

Figure 5.17
Stack Containing
Three Elements

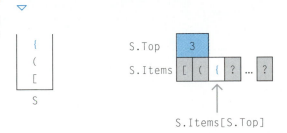

where the initial stack S is shown on the left. Before Push is executed, S.Top is 3, so S.Items[3] is the element at the top of the stack. Procedure Push must increment S.Top to 4 so that the new item ('(') will be stored in S.Items[4] as shown on the right in Fig. 5.18. ▲

Stack Operators

The stack operators manipulate the array Items using Top as an index to the array. Their implementation is fairly straightforward. You should have little difficulty in reading and understanding the stack operators shown in the implementation section of StackADT (see Fig. 5.19).

Procedure Stack.CreateStack must be called before the stack can be manipulated. In Stack.CreateStack the statement

```
Top := 0   {stack is empty}
```

initializes a stack by setting its top of stack pointer to zero.

Procedure Stack.Push increments the top of stack pointer before pushing a new value onto the stack. Procedure Stack.Pop copies the value at the top of the stack (denoted by Items[Top]) into X before decrementing the top of stack pointer. Procedure Stack.Retrieve copies the value at the top of the stack into X without changing the top of stack pointer. Functions Stack.IsFull and Stack.IsEmpty test the top of stack pointer to determine the stack status. When the value of data field Top is greater than MaxStack, there is no more room to store elements in the stack. When the value of Top is 0, the stack is empty.

Program Style

Efficiency versus Readability

Procedure Push in Fig. 5.19 uses the condition Top >= MaxStack to determine whether the stack is full. It would be more readable, but less efficient,

▶▶▶▶▶▶

Figure 5.18
Pushing '(' onto Stack S

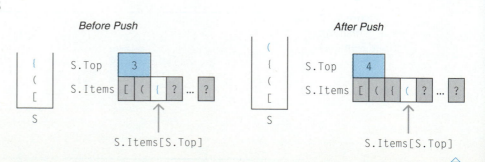

Figure 5.19
Implementation Section for
Unit StackADT

Directory: CHAP 5
File: STACKADT.PAS

```
implementation
  procedure Stack.CreateStack;
  {
   Creates an empty stack.
   Pre : None
   Post: Creates an empty stack.
  }
  begin {CreateStack}
    Top := 0                {stack is empty}
  end; {CreateStack}

  procedure Stack.Push (X {input} : StackElement;
                        var Success {output} : Boolean);
  {
   Pushes X onto a stack.
   Pre : X is defined.
   Post: Sets Success to indicate success (True) or failure
         (False) of push operation.
  }
  begin {Push}
    if Top >= MaxStack then
      Success := False      {no room on stack}
    else
      begin
        Top := Top + 1;    {increment top of stack pointer}
        Items[Top] := X;   {push X onto stack}
        Success := True
      end {if}
  end; {Push}

  procedure Stack.Pop (var X {output} : StackElement;
                       var Success {output} : Boolean);
  {
   Pops the top of a stack into X.
   Pre : A stack has been created.
   Post: Contents of X is character at top of the stack which is
         then removed from the stack. Sets Success to indicate
         success (True) or failure (False) of pop operation.
  }
  begin {Pop}
    if Top <= 0 then
      Success := False
    else
      begin
        X := Items[Top];   {pop top of stack into X}
        Top := Top - 1;    {decrement top of stack pointer}
        Success := True
      end {if}
  end; {Pop}

  procedure Stack.Retrieve (var X {output} : StackElement;
                            var Success {output} : Boolean);
```

```
{
 Copies the value at the top of the stack into X.
 Pre : A stack has been created.
 Post: Contents of X is character at top of the stack; the
       stack is unchanged. Sets Success to indicate success
       (True) or failure (False).
}
  begin {Retrieve}
   if Top <= 0 then
     Success := False
   else
     begin
       X := Items[Top];   {copy top of stack into X}
       Success := True
     end {if}
end; {Retrieve}

function Stack.IsEmpty : Boolean;
{
 Pre : A stack has been created.
 Post: Returns True if the stack is empty;
       otherwise, returns False.
}
begin {IsEmpty}
   IsEmpty := Top <= 0
end; {IsEmpty}

function Stack.IsFull : Boolean;
{
 Pre : A stack has been created.
 Post: Returns True if the stack is full;
       otherwise, returns False.
}
begin {IsFull}
   IsFull := Top >= MaxStack
end; {IsFull}

end. {StackADT}
```

to use the function Stack.IsFull to test whether a stack is full. You must use the function Stack.IsFull for this purpose in any client program that manipulates the stack because the stack's internal representation is hidden from a client program. However, it is perfectly reasonable for another stack operator to directly manipulate private data members of a stack.

Exercises for Section 5.4 **Self-Check**

1. Declare a stack of 50 student records in which each record consists of a student's name (string of 20 characters), an exam score, and a letter

grade. Can you use the operators in StacKADT to manipulate this stack?

Programming

1. Write a method SizeOfStack that returns the number of elements currently on the stack.

5.5   Additional Stack Applications

This section discusses additional applications of stacks that relate to their use in computer science. The first application is a continuation of the expression evaluation case study and shows how to use a stack to convert an expression from infix notation to postfix notation. Next, we discuss how the stack is used to implement recursion in a block-structured language like Pascal. Finally, we discuss how to use a stack to convert a recursive procedure to an iterative procedure.

Converting from Infix to Postfix

Since programmers normally write expressions in infix notation, a compiler must convert an infix expression into postfix notation before it can apply the technique of expression evaluation discussed in Section 5.3. To complete our discussion of expression evaluation, we will describe a method of doing this that makes extensive use of an operator stack as its central data structure.

CASE STUDY   Converting from Infix to Postfix

PROBLEM ▼

To complete the design of an expression evaluator, we need a set of procedures that convert infix expressions to postfix expressions. For simplicity we will assume that each operand is a single letter and that the symbol @ appears at the end of the infix expression.

DESIGN OVERVIEW ▼

Table 5.2 shows the infix and postfix form of four expressions. For each expression pair, the operands are in the same sequence; however, the placement of the operators changes in going from infix to postfix. For example, in converting A + B ∗ C to its postfix form (A B C ∗ +) we see that the three letters (operands) retain their relative ordering from the infix expression but the order of the operators is reversed (⋆ first, + second). This means that we should insert the letters in the output expression (postfix) as soon as they are reached in the input expression (infix), but the operators should be placed on a stack before being inserted in the output expression. The use of a stack enables the order of the operators + and ⋆ to be reversed as shown in the above example. The data requirements and initial algorithm for procedure `InfixToPost` follow.

Data Requirements

Problem Inputs

```
The expression to convert (Infix : string)
```

Problem Outputs

```
The postfix expression (Postfix : string)
A flag indicating success or failure (ValidInfix : Boolean)
```

Local Variables

```
The operator stack (OpStack : Stack)
The current token (Token : Char)
```

Initial Algorithm for Procedure InfixToPost

```
1. Initialize Postfix to a blank string
2. Initialize the operator stack to an empty stack
3. repeat
      4. Get the next token in Infix
      5. if the next token is an operand then
            6. Insert the operand in Postfix
         else if the next token is an operator then
            7. Process the operator
   until the sentinel operator is processed
8. Infix is valid if the sentinel operator is the only opera-
   tor on the stack
```

The repeat-until loop executes until the sentinel operator has been processed. The if statement (Step 5) differentiates between operands and operators. Step 6 inserts operands directly in `Postfix`; Step 7 executes when the next token is an operator. Step 7 (performed by procedure `DoOperator`) either pushes the operator onto the stack immediately or inserts in `Postfix` earlier operators that have been saved on the stack. After the sentinel operator is processed, Step 8 sets `ValidInfix` to `True` or `False` depending on the state of the stack. `ValidInfix` should be `True` if the only operator on the stack is the sentinel.

CODING FOR INFIXTOPOST ▼

Figure 5.20 shows procedure `InfixToPost`. The statement

```
Postfix := '';
```

Figure 5.20
Procedures `GetToken` and `InfixtoPost`

Directory: CHAP 5
File: INFIXTOP.PAS

```
procedure GetToken (Infix {input} : string;
                    var Next {input/output} : Integer;
                    var Token {output} : Char);
{
 Locates next non-blank character appearing after position
 Next in string Infix.
 Pre : Infix contains a non-blank character after position
       Next and 0 <= Next < Length(Infix).
 Post: Token contains non-blank character and Next is
       position of Token within string Infix.
}
  const
    Blank = ' ';

begin {GetToken}
  repeat
    Next := Next + 1;
    Token := Infix[Next]
  until (Token <> Blank)
end; {GetToken}

procedure InfixToPost (Infix {input} : string;
                       var Postfix {output} : string;
                       var ValidInfix {output} : Boolean);
{
 Converts infix expression stored in string Infix to postfix
 to postfix expression stored in string Postfix.
 Pre : Infix is defined.
 Post: Either Postfix contains valid postfix representation of
       infix expression contained in Infix and ValidInfix is
       True; or Postfix in undefined and ValidInfix is False.
 Calls: procedure GetToken
}
  const
    Sentinel = '@';

  var
    OpStack : Stack;
    Next : Integer;
        Token,
        TopOp : Char;
        Success : Boolean;
```

▷ ▷ ▷ ▷ ▷ ▷

```
begin {InfixToPost}
  Postfix := '';                              {initialize Postfix}
  OpStack.CreateStack;                   {start with empty stack}
  Next := 0;                          {start at beginning of Infix}

  repeat
    GetToken (Infix, Next, Token);            {get first token}
    if Token in ['A' .. 'Z'] then
      Postfix := Postfix + ' ' + Token          {insert operand}
    else if Token in ['*','/','+','-',Sentinel] then
      DoOperator (Infix, Token, OpStack, Postfix)
    else
      begin
        WriteLn ('Illegal character in expression: ', Token);
        Token := Sentinel                        {exit loop}
      end {if}
  until Token = Sentinel;

  OpStack.Pop (TopOp, Success);
  ValidInfix := Success and (TopOp = Sentinel)
                and (OpStack.IsEmpty)
end; {InfixToPost}
```

initializes Postfix to the *null string* (string of length zero). Procedure Get-Token stores in Token the next nonblank character in string Infix. The statement

```
Postfix := Postfix + ' ' + Token;
```

uses the string concatenation operator (+) to append a blank character followed by the character in Token to the end of string Postfix (for example, 'A B' + ' ' + '*' is the string 'A B *').

The last clause of the nested if statement in Fig. 5.20 executes when Token contains an illegal character. It displays an error message and resets Token to the sentinel, causing loop exit to occur.

After loop exit occurs, the stack is popped, and its contents are stored in TopOp. If the sentinel operator was the only operator remaining on the stack, ValidInfix is set to True; otherwise, ValidInfix is set to False.

PROCEDURE DOOPERATOR ▼

The relative precedence of adjacent operators determines the sequence in which they are performed. Therefore as part of the processing of each new operator, we should expect to compare its precedence with that of earlier operators stored on the stack. Each new operator will eventually be pushed onto the stack. However, before doing this, we will see whether operators that are currently on the stack have precedence equal to or higher than that of the new operator. If operators on the stack have equal or higher precedence, they should be performed first, so we will pop them off the stack and insert them in the output string (`Postfix`). When we reach a stacked operator with lower precedence, we will push the new operator onto the stack. In the following algorithm for procedure `DoOperator`, `Token` represents the new operator.

Algorithm for Procedure DoOperator

```
repeat
  if the stack is empty then
    Push Token onto the stack
  else
    if Precedence(Token) > Precedence(top of stack) then
      Push Token onto the stack
    else
      begin
        Pop OpStack into TopOp
        Insert TopOp in the output expression
      end
until Token is pushed onto the stack
```

The repeat statement executes until `Token` is pushed onto the stack. This happens in the first pass if the stack is empty or if `Token` has higher precedence than the operator on the top of the stack. Otherwise, we pop the top operator from the stack and insert it in the output string. We continue to pop and insert operators until the stack becomes empty or the operator on the top of the stack has lower precedence than `Token`. To ensure that all operators have been popped from the stack when we reach the sentinel operator, we should give the sentinel the lowest precedence.

Table 5.3 shows a trace of the conversion of the infix expression A + B * C / D @ to the postfix expression A B C * D / +. Procedure `DoOperator` is called when `Token` is an operator. Procedure `InfixToPost` processes all other characters without calling `DoOperator`. The final value of `Postfix` shows that * is performed first (operands B and C), / is performed next (operands B * C and D), and + is performed last. The stack contains the sentinel operator after the last call to `DoOperator`.

Table 5.3
Conversion of
A + B * C / D @

Token	Action	Effect on OpStack	Effect on Postfix
A	Insert A in Postfix.		A
+	Stack is empty, push + onto stack.	+	A
B	Insert B in Postfix.	+	A B
*	Precedence(`'*'`) > precedence(`'+'`), push * onto stack.	* / +	A B

Table 5.3
Conversion of
A + B * C / D @
(*Cont.*)

C	Insert C in Postfix.	$\begin{array}{c} * \\ + \end{array}$	A B C
/	Precedence('/') = Precedence('*'), pop stack, insert * in Postfix.	$\begin{array}{c} + \end{array}$	A B C *
/	Precedence('/') > Precedence('+'), push / onto stack.	$\begin{array}{c} / \\ + \end{array}$	A B C *
D	Insert D in Postfix.	$\begin{array}{c} / \\ + \end{array}$	A B C * D
@	Precedence('@') < Precedence('/'), pop stack, insert / in Postfix.	$\begin{array}{c} + \end{array}$	A B C * D /
@	Precedence('@') < Precedence('+'), pop stack, insert + in Postfix.		A B C * D / +
@	Push @ onto stack, exit DoOperator.	$\begin{array}{c} @ \end{array}$	A B C * D / +

Coding Procedure DoOperator

Procedure `DoOperator` is shown in Fig. 5.21. Procedure `DoOperator` calls function `Precedence` to determine the precedence of an operator (2 for *, /; 1 for +, −; 0 for @). It also uses local variable `TokenStacked` to determine whether the new operator in `Token` has been pushed onto the stack.

TESTING PROCEDURE INFIXTOPOST ▼

Figure 5.22 shows a driver program that tests procedures `InfixToPost` and `DoOperator`. The program begins with

`uses StackADT;`

Make sure that `StackElement` is declared as type `Char` before compiling `StackADT` to disk. Use enough test expressions to satisfy yourself that the conversion is correct for properly formed input expressions. For example, try infix expressions in which the + operator appears before and after the * operator. Also try infix expressions in which all operators have the same precedence.

If the value returned by procedure `InfixToPost` through `ValidInfix` is `True`, the driver program displays the postfix expression; otherwise, it dis-

Figure 5.21
Function Precedence
and Procedure
DoOperator

Directory: CHAP 5
File: DOOPERAT.PAS

```
function Precedence (Op {input} : Char) : Integer;
{
  Returns precedence value of valid arithmetic operator Op.
}
begin
  case Op of
    '*', '/' : Precedence := 2;
    '+', '-' : Precedence := 1;
    Sentinel : Precedence := 0
  end {case}
end; {Precedence}

procedure DoOperator (Infix {input} : string;
                      Token {input} : Char;
                      var OpStack {input/output} : Stack;
                      var Postfix {input/output} : string);
{
  Pre : Infix, Token, OpStack and Postfix are defined.
  Post: If Precedence(Token) > Precedence(top of OpStack) then
        Token is pushed onto OpStack and Postfix is unchanged;
        otherwise operator is popped off stack and concatenated
        onto the end of string Postfix.
  Calls: Function Precedence.
}
  var
    TopOp : Char;                {operator on top of stack}
    TokenStacked,                {new operator is stacked}
    Success : Boolean;           {flag for stack operators}

begin {DoOperator}
  repeat
    if OpStack.IsEmpty then
      begin {stack is empty}
        OpStack.Push (Token, Success);
        TokenStacked := True
      end {stack is empty}
    else
      begin {stack not empty}
        OpStack.Retrieve (TopOp, Success);
        if Precedence(Token) > Precedence(TopOp) then
          begin {push Token}
            OpStack.Push (Token, Success);
            TokenStacked := True
          end {push Token}
        else
          begin {pop OpStack}
            OpStack.Pop (TopOp, Success);
            Postfix := Postfix + ' ' + TopOp;
            TokenStacked := False
          end {pop OpStack}
      end {stack not empty}
  until TokenStacked

end; {DoOperator}
```

Figure 5.22
Testing InfixToPostfix

```
program TestInfixToPost;
{
 Program tests infix to post fix conversion procedures.

 Imports: StackADT.
}
  uses StackAdt;

  const
    Sentinel = '@';

  var
    Infix, Postfix : string;
    ValidInfix : Boolean;
{
Insert procedures DoOperator, GetToken, InfixToPostFix, and
function Precedence.
{

begin {TestInfixToPost}
  repeat
    Write ('Enter infix string ending with "@" > ');
    ReadLn (Infix);
    InfixToPost (Infix, Postfix, ValidInfix);
    if ValidInfix then
      WriteLn ('Postfix is ', Postfix)
    else
      WriteLn ('Improperly formed infix expression.')
  until Infix = Sentinel
end. {TestInfixToPost}
```

plays an error message. Unfortunately, procedure InfixToPost does not detect all possible errors. For example, the procedure does not detect a pair of adjacent operands or operators.

HANDLING PARENTHESES ▼

The ability to handle parentheses would be an important (and necessary) addition to the conversion procedures. Parentheses are used to separate an expression into subexpressions. We can think of an opening parenthesis on an operator stack as a boundary or fence between operators. Whenever we encounter an opening parenthesis, we want to push it onto the stack. We can think of a closing parenthesis as the terminator symbol for a subexpression. Whenever we encounter a closing parenthesis, we want to pop all operators on the stack down to the matching opening parenthesis. Neither opening nor closing parentheses should appear in the postfix expression.

To accomplish these objectives, we should modify procedure DoOperator in the following way. DoOperator should push each opening parenthesis onto the stack as soon as it is encountered. Since operators following the opening parenthesis should be evaluated before the opening parenthesis, the precedence of the opening parenthesis must be smaller than that of any other operator. When a closing parenthesis is encountered, we want to pop all operators up to and including the matching closing parenthesis, inserting all operators popped (except for the opening parenthesis) in the postfix string. Consequently, the precedence of the closing parenthesis must also be smaller than that of any other operator except for the opening parenthesis. A closing parenthesis is considered to be processed when an opening parenthesis is popped from the stack and the closing parenthesis is not placed on the stack.

Figure 5.23
Function `Precedence` and Procedure `DoOperator` Modified to Handle Parentheses

Directory: CHAP 5
File: MODIFYDO.PAS

```
function Precedence (Op {input} : Char) : Integer;
{
  Determines precedence value of valid arithmetic operator Op.
}
begin
  case Op of
    '*', '/' : Precedence := 2;
    '+', '-' : Precedence := 1;
    Sentinel : Precedence := 0;
    '(', ')' : Precedence := -1
  end {case}
end; {Precedence}

procedure DoOperator (Infix {input} : string;
                      Token {input} : Char;
                      var OpStack {input/output} : Stack;
                      var Postfix {input/output} : string);
{
  Pre : Infix, Token, OpStack and Postfix are defined.
  Post: If Precedence(Token) > Precedence(top of OpStack) then
        Token is pushed onto OpStack and Postfix is unchanged;
        otherwise operator is popped off stack and concatenated
        onto the end of string Postfix.
  Calls: Function Precedence.
}
  var
    OldOp : Char;                {operator on top of stack}
    TokenStacked,                {new operator is processed}
    Success : Boolean;           {flag for stack operations}

begin {DoOperator}
  repeat
    if (OpStack.IsEmpty) or (Token = '(') then
      begin {push Token}
```

▷ ▷ ▷ ▷ ▷

```
        OpStack.Push (Token, Success);
        TokenStacked := True
     end {push Token}
   else
     begin {stack not empty}
        OpStack.Retrieve (OldOp, Success);
        if Precedence(Token) > Precedence(OldOp) then
           begin {push Token}
              OpStack.Push (Token, Success);
              TokenStacked := True
           end {push Token}
        else
           begin {pop stack}
              OpStack.Pop (OldOp, Success);
              if OldOp = '(' then
                 TokenStacked := True      {parentheses processed}
              else
                 begin
                    Postfix := Postfix + ' ' + OldOp;
                    TokenStacked := False
                 end
           end {pop stack}
     end {stack not empty}
  until TokenStacked

end; {DoOperator}
```

In Fig. 5.23, procedure DoOperator and function Precedence are modified to handle parenthesized infix expressions. Both opening and closing parentheses are assigned a precedence of -1. The modified sections of code are shown in color. We must also change the set of operators shown in procedure InfixToPost to include parentheses.

Figure 5.24
Sample Run of
TestInToPost with
Modified DoOperator

```
Enter infix string ending with "@" > (A + B) * C / (D + E) @
Posfix is A B + C * D E + /
Enter infix string ending with "@" > A + B * C / D @
Postfix is A B C * D / +
Enter infix string ending with "@" > A * B + C @
Postfix is A B * C +
Enter infix string ending with "@" > A + B + C @
Postfix is A B + C +
Enter infix string ending with "@" > ( (A + B) @
Improperly formed infix expression.
Enter infix string ending with "@" > (A + B * C @
Improperly formed infix expression.
Enter infix string ending with "@" > @
Postfix is
```

Testing the Conversion of Infix Expressions with Parentheses

Figure 5.24 shows a sample run of the driver program using the modified procedure `DoOperator`. Note that the driver program displays an error message if there are missing or extra parentheses.

USING STACKS IN RECURSION ▼

One of the most important applications of stacks in computer science is the use of a run-time stack to facilitate the implementation of procedure calls and recursion in a block-structured language. The *run-time stack* contains one activation record for each procedure that is currently executing. With each procedure call, a new activation record is pushed onto the run-time stack. With each procedure return, an activation record is popped off of the run-time stack. At any instant the activation record for the currently executing procedure will be on the top of the run-time stack.

Figure 5.25 shows a run-time stack for a program P that has called a procedure Q. Q, in turn, has called procedure R, which has called itself recursively. There are four activation records on the run-time stack. The activation record for the second call to R is the *active record*.

Figure 5.25 shows that there are two activation records for procedure R. Each activation record may contain different values for the procedure's parameters, local variables, and the return address. The return address for the active record is the point of the recursive call in procedure R, whereas the return address in the activation record for the first call to R is the point in Q where that call occurred. When we return from the second recursive call, its activation record will be popped from the stack, and the new active record will be the activation record for the first call to R. However, if another recursive call to R occurs before the return, a third activation record for procedure R will appear on the run-time stack. The return address for the call to program P (the bottom activation record) is an address in the operating system.

USING STACKS TO ELIMINATE RECURSION ▼

Now that we understand what happens to the run-time stack when a recursive call occurs, we can implement recursive behavior by manipulating our own parameter stack. Our parameter stack will be a stack of records in which each record contains storage for the procedure's value parameters and any local variables. We will show how to do this for a special case of recursion called *tail recursion*. This technique can be adapted for general recursive procedures; however, we will leave this exercise as a programming assignment (see Programming Project 6 at the end of the chapter).

A *tail-recursive procedure* is a recursive procedure in which the last statement executed in the statement body is a recursive call to itself. The body of a tail-recursive procedure has the general form

Figure 5.25
Run-Time Stack with Four
Activation Records

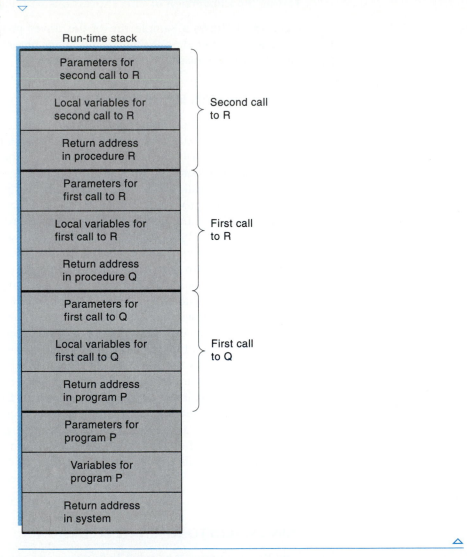

Run-time stack

Parameters for second call to R
Local variables for second call to R
Return address in procedure R

Second call to R

Parameters for first call to R
Local variables for first call to R
Return address in procedure Q

First call to R

Parameters for first call to Q
Local variables for first call to Q
Return address in program P

First call to Q

Parameters for program P
Variables for program P
Return address in system

sive procedures; however, we will leave this exercise as a programming assignment (see Programming Project 6 at the end of the chapter).

A *tail-recursive procedure* is a recursive procedure in which the last statement executed in the statement body is a recursive call to itself. The body of a tail-recursive procedure has the general form

```
if stopping condition then
   perform stopping step
else
   begin
      do something before recursive call
```

Figure 5.26
Procedure PrintBack

Directory: CHAP 5
File: PRINTBAC.PAS

```
procedure PrintBack (var X {input} : IntArray;
                         N {input} : Integer);
{
 Prints an array of integers (X) with subscripts 1..N.
 Pre : Array X and N are defined and N > 0.
 Post: Displays X[N], X[N-1], ... , X[2], X[1]
}
begin {PrintBack }
  if N = 1 then
    WriteLn (X[1])                        {stopping case}
  else
    begin {recursive step}
      WriteLn (X[N]);
      PrintBack (X, N-1)
    end {recursive step}
end; {PrintBack }
```

PrintBack prints an array in normal order. The first parameter, X, is an array type, and the second parameter, N, is an integer that represents the subscript of the element being printed.

To remove recursion, we will begin by creating a parameter stack and pushing the initial values of the procedure parameters onto the stack. Since we are implementing recursion using iteration (looping), the main control structure will be a loop that repeats until the parameter stack becomes empty. The first step in the loop body will be to pop the parameter values from the stack. Next, we will execute an if statement based on the if statement in the original recursive procedure. The recursive call will be replaced by a statement that pushes the parameters for the recursive call onto the parameter stack. Each time we repeat the loop, we will pop the top record from the parameter stack to retrieve the active values for the procedure parameters. The iterative form of a tail-recursive procedure is

```
create an empty parameter stack
push the initial parameter values on the parameter stack
repeat
  pop stack to retrieve parameter values
  if stopping condition then
    perform stopping step
  else
    begin
      do something before recursion
      push new parameter values onto stack
    end {else clause}
until the parameter stack is empty
```

Figure 5.27 shows an iterative version of procedure PrintBack after recursion removal. In simulating recursion we need to push value parameters

Figure 5.27
Procedure PrintBack
with Recursion Removed

Directory: CHAP 5
File: PRINTBIT.PAS

```
procedure PrintBack (var X {input} : IntArray;
                          N {input} : Integer);
{
 Prints an array of integers (X) with subscripts 1..N.
 Pre : Array X and N are defined and N > 0.
 Post: Displays X[N], X[N-1], . . . , X[2], X[1]
}
   var
      ParamStack : Stack;      {stack of integer values}
      Success : Boolean;

begin {PrintBack}
   ParamStack.CreateStack;
   ParamStack.Push (N, Success);
   repeat
      ParamStack.Pop (N, Success);
      if N = 1 then
        WriteLn (X[1])
      else
        begin {recursive step}
           WriteLn (X[N]);
           ParamStack.Push (N - 1, Success)
        end {recursive step}
   until ParamStack.IsEmpty
end; {PrintBack}
```

onto the parameter stack to save their values between simulated recursive procedure activations. In procedure PrintBack, only the value parameter N must be placed on the parameter stack (a stack of integers). Note that the initial value of N is pushed onto this stack when the procedure is first called; the "recursive step" pushes subsequent values of N onto the stack.

Exercises for Section 5.5

Self-Check

1. Does the order of operands change when an infix expression is translated to a postfix expression?
2. Which stack method is used to simulate the call to a recursive procedure, and which stack method is used to simulate the exit from a recursive routine?

Programming

1. Modify procedures DoOperator and Precedence (Fig. 5.23) to allow the use of ∧ as an exponentiation operator. This operator should have the highest precedence value.

2. Write a program to test the nonrecursive version of procedure `Print-Back` shown in Fig. 5.27.

5.6 Common Programming Errors

In this chapter we used an array data field to store the contents of a stack. Consequently, most stack methods manipulate an array subscript. The errors that you are most likely to encounter in working with this stack implementation are many of the same errors that you would encounter in any array programming applications. The most common error in working with arrays is an out-of-range-subscript error. The default behavior for Borland Pascal is to ignore subscript range errors, which means that you may accidentally access or even modify storage locations outside the array without your knowledge. For this reason it is very important to enable range checking using the {$R+} compiler directive when testing and debugging your stack methods. You can also reduce the likelihood of a subscript range error by being certain that client programs for your `StackADT` do not attempt to manipulate the stack array subscript directly. This is best accomplished by making the stack array field private so that it may be accessed only by using previously tested stack methods.

You also need to be certain that there are no type inconsistencies. The client programs in this chapter all made use of unit `StackADT`, which in turn made use of unit `StackElementADT`. It is important to remember to change the type declarations in unit `StackElementADT` any time you write a client program that requires a different stack element type. You need to recompile both units (`StackElementADT` and `StackADT`) to disk any time you wish to change the stack element type. The stack instances in our case studies had stack elements that were built-in types (e.g., `Char` or `Integer`), so we did not need to import `StackElementADT` into our `StackADT` client programs. When your stack element is a user-defined data type, you may need to explicitly import the declarations in unit `StackElementADT` into your client program as well. The general rule to follow is that a client program must have access to the units containing declarations for any identifiers referenced in the program code.

CHAPTER REVIEW

In this chapter we introduced the stack as an abstract data type. Stacks are used to implement recursion and expression translation. A stack is a last-in, first-out data structure. This means that the last item added to a stack is the first to be removed.

In this chapter we described an array-based implementation of a stack object. We showed how stacks may be used to balance parentheses, to evaluate arithmetic expressions, to translate infix expressions to postfix, and to remove recursion. In Chapter 7 we will discuss a stack implementation that makes more efficient use of computer memory.

Quick-Check Exercises

1. A stack is a _____-in, _____-out data structure.
2. Draw the array representation of the following stack.

```
| $ |
| * |
| & |
```

3. What is the value of S.Items[1] for the stack shown in Exercise 2?
4. What is the value of S.Top for the stack shown in Exercise 2?
5. Why should the statement S.Top := S.Top - 1 not appear in a client program of StackADT?
6. Write a program segment that uses the stack method that removes the element just below the top of the stack.
7. Write a method PopNextTop for a Stack object descendant called NewStack that removes the element just below the top of the stack.
8. Can method PopNextTop be written without using methods Stack.Pop and Stack.Push?

Answers to Quick-Check Exercises

1. last, first
2.

```
S.Top     | 3 |

S.Items   | & | * | $ |
```

3. &
4. 3
5. The client program should not be aware of the internal representation of the stack. Also, S.Top is private, and the Borland Pascal compiler will not allow the user to reference this field outside unit StackADT.
6.
```
S.Pop (X, Success);
S.Pop (Y, Success);
S.Push (X, Success);
```

7.
```
uses StackADT, StackElementADT;

NewStack = object(Stack)
              procedure PopNextTop
                          (var X {output} : StackElement;
                           var Success {output} : Boolean);
           end; {NewStack}

procedure NewStack.PopNextTop
                    (var X {output} : StackElement;
                     var Success {output} : Boolean);
```

```
begin {PopNextTop}
  Pop (X, Success);
  Pop (Y, Success);
  Push (X, Success)
end; {PopNextTop}
```

8. No, because the data fields for Stack instances are private and are not acces-
    sible to any methods that are not declared in unit StackADT.

Review Questions

1. Show the effect of each of the following operations on stack S. Assume that
    Y (type Char) contains the character '&'. What are the final values of X and
    Success (type Boolean) and the contents of stack S?

    ```
    S.CreateStack;
    S.Push ('+', Success);
    S.Pop (X, Success);
    S.Pop (X, Success);
    S.Push ('(', Success);
    S.Push (Y, Success);
    S.Pop (X, Success);
    ```

2. Assuming that stack S is implemented by using our StackADT, answer Ques-
    tion 1 by showing the values of data field Top and array data field Items after
    each operation.
3. Write a new Stack method called PopTwo that removes the top two stack
    elements and returns them as method output parameters. Use method
    Stack.Pop.
4. Answer Question 3 without using method Stack.Pop.
5. Write a procedure that uses Stack methods to make an exact copy of a stack.

Programming Projects

Directory: CHAP 5
File: PROJ5_1.PAS

Directory: CHAP 5
File: PROJ5_2.PAS

1. Write a client program that uses our stack abstract data type to simulate a
    typical session with a bank teller. Unlike most banks, this one has decided that
    the last customer to arrive will always be the first to be served. Change
    StackElement to allow it to represent information about a bank customer.
    For each customer you need to store a name, a transaction type, and the
    amount of the transaction. After every five customers are processed, display the
    size of the stack and the names of the customers who are waiting.
2. Write a program to handle the flow of an item into and out of a warehouse. The
    warehouse will have numerous deliveries and shipments for this item (a widget)
    during the time period covered. A shipment out is billed at a profit of 50 per-
    cent over the cost of a widget. Unfortunately, a different cost may be associated
    with each shipment received. The accountants for the firm have instituted a last-
    in, first-out system for filling orders. This means that the newest widgets are the
    first ones sent out to fill an order. This method of inventory can be represented
    by using a stack. Then when a shipment is received, an element is pushed onto
    the stack. When a shipment is sent out, one or more records are popped from
    the stack. Each data record will consist of

```
S or O:  shipment received or order to be sent
   Qty:  quantity shipped out
  Cost:  cost per widget (for shipment received)
Vendor:  character string: name of company sent to or
         received from
```

Write the necessary procedures to store the shipments received and to process orders. The output for an order will consist of the quantity and the total bill for all widgets in the order. *Hint:* The bill for each widget is 50 percent higher than its cost. The widgets used to fill an order may come from multiple shipments with different costs.

Directory: CHAP 5
File: PROJ5_3.PAS

3. Write a program that determines whether it is possible to travel between two cities entered by the program user on the basis of the airline routing information stored in a table. Each entry in the table contains the name of the city where a flight originates and the name of the city that is its destination. If a direct connection exists between the user's two cities, a simple search of the routing table would be sufficient. If a direct connection is not in the table, then the program would need to search for a series of shorter flights that could be combined to travel between the user's two cities.

It is possible to choose a set of flights that leads to a dead end. If this happens, you need to backtrack and try to find an alternative set of flights. A stack can be used to keep track of the order in which each city is visited. Backtracking is then accomplished by popping elements off the top of the stack.

You will want to keep track of which cities are on the stack at any given time so that you don't have the same city on the stack more than once. You might want to have a table containing the name of each city and a field indicating whether the city has been visited (is already on the stack) or has not yet been visited (is not on the stack right now).

4. Redo the maze case study from Chapter 4 without using recursion. Have your program push the coordinates of the current maze position onto the stack. When backtracking needs to be done, simply pop coordinates off the stack until you find a place that allows you to move forward again.

Directory: CHAP 5
File: PROJ5_5.PAS

5. Write a client program that uses unit StackADT to compile a simple arithmetic expression without parentheses. For example, the expression

```
A + B * C - D
```

should be compiled as the table

Operator	Operand1	Operand2	Result
*	B	C	Z
+	A	Z	Y
-	Y	D	X

The table shows the order in which the operations are performed (*, +, −) and operands for each operator. The result column gives the name of an identifier (working backwards from Z) chosen to hold each result. Assume that the operands are the letters A through F and the operators are (+, −, ∗, /).

Your program should read each character and process it as follows. If the character is blank, ignore it. If it is an operand, push it onto the operand stack. If the character is not an operator, display an error message and terminate the program. If it is an operator, compare its precedence to that of the operator on top of the operator stack. If the new operator has higher precedence than the one currently on top of the stack (or the stack is empty), the new operator should be pushed onto the operator stack.

If the new operator has the same or lower precedence, the operator on top of the operator stack must be evaluated next. This is done by popping it off the operator stack along with a pair of operands from the operand stack and writing a new line in the output table. The character selected to hold the result should then be pushed onto the operand stack. Next, the new operator should be compared to the new top of the operator stack. Continue to generate output lines until the top of the operator stack has lower precedence than the new operator or until it is empty. At this point, push the new operator onto the top of the stack, and examine the next character in the data string. When the end of the string is reached, pop any remaining operator along with its operand pair. Remember to push the result character onto the operand stack after each table line is generated.

6. Make use of a parameter stack and write an iterative version of the Towers of Hanoi Problem that we discussed in Chapter 4. Remember that procedure Tower contains two recursive calls and each will need to be simulated in your iterative procedure.

CHAPTER SIX

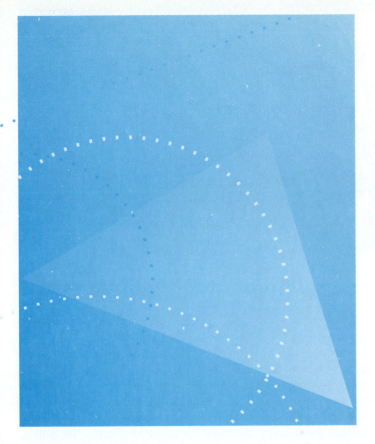

Queues

The queue is a data structure that has one important difference from a stack. A stack is called a LIFO (last-in, first-out) list because the last element pushed onto a stack will be the first element popped off. A queue, on the other hand, is a FIFO (first-in, first-out) list because the first element inserted in the queue will be the first element removed. The easiest way to visualize a queue is to think of a line of customers waiting to buy theater tickets or see a bank teller (see Fig. 6.1). Usually, the next person to be served is the one who has been waiting the longest, and latecomers are added to the end of the line. (The British people "queue up" instead of waiting in lines.)

Figure 6.1
Customers Waiting in a
Line or Queue

In computer science, queues are used in operating systems for a time-shared computer to keep track of tasks waiting for the processor. If all tasks have the same priority, the one that receives the processor is the one that has been waiting the longest. Operating systems also use queues to keep track of the list of jobs waiting to be printed.

We will describe the queue as an abstract data type and show how to use a queue to represent a list of airline passengers waiting to see a ticket agent. We will also implement an abstract data type for a queue. Finally, we will illustrate how to use a process called simulation to determine the amount of time customers spend waiting in queues.

6.1   Queue Abstract Data Type

A queue differs from a stack in that new elements are inserted at one end (the rear of the queue) and elements in the queue are removed from the other end (the front of the queue). In this way the element that has been waiting longest is removed first. In contrast, stack elements are inserted and removed from the same end (the top of the stack).

A queue of three passengers waiting to see an airline ticket agent is shown in Fig. 6.2. The name of the passenger who has been waiting the longest is McMann (pointed to by Front); the name of the most recent arrival is Carson (pointed to by Rear). Passenger McMann will be the first one removed from the queue when an agent becomes available, and pointer Front will be moved to passenger Watson. Any new passengers will follow passenger Carson in the queue, and pointer Rear will be adjusted accordingly.

Table 6.1 gives the specification for the abstract data type `Queue`. Compare it with the earlier specification for an abstract stack.

Figure 6.2
A Passenger Queue

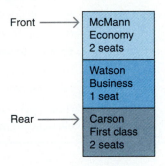

Table 6.1
Specification of Abstract
Data Type Queue

Elements

A queue consists of a collection of elements that are all the same data type.

Structure

The elements of a queue are ordered according to time of arrival. The only element that may be removed or examined at any given time is the element that entered the queue first and has been in the queue the longest. Elements are removed from the *front* of the queue and inserted at the *rear* of the queue.

Operators

In the descriptions of the operators we will assume the following parameters:

```
El (pronounced el) has the same data type as the queue
    elements.
Success is type Boolean and indicates whether the
    operation succeeds.
```

Queue.CreateQueue	Creates an empty queue.
Queue.Insert (El, var Success)	If the queue is not full, the value in El is inserted at the rear of the queue, and Success is set to True. Otherwise, the queue is not changed, and Success is set to False.
Queue.Remove (var El, var Success)	If the queue is not empty, the element at the front of the queue is removed and copied to El, and Success is set to True. If the queue is empty, El is not changed, and Success is set to False.
Queue.Retrieve (var El, var Success)	If the queue is not empty, the element at the front of the queue is copied into El, and Success is set to True. If the

	queue is empty, El is not defined, and Success is set to False. In either case the queue is not changed.
Queue.IsEmpty	(function) Returns True if the queue is empty; otherwise, returns False.
Queue.IsFull	(function) Returns True if the queue is full; otherwise, returns False.
Queue.SizeOfQueue	(function) Returns the number of elements in the queue.

We will implement `QueueADT` in Section 6.3. We will illustrate how to use a queue next. Just as we did for stacks, we will assume that the identifier `QElement` represents the type of each queue element. Each client program must import the type declarations for `QElement` and `Queue` before trying to use them.

Exercises for Section 6.1   **Self-Check**

1. Draw the queue in Fig. 6.2 after the insertion of first-class passenger Harris (three seats reserved) and the removal of one passenger from the queue. Which passenger is removed? How many passengers are left?

6.2   Queue Applications

Our application is to write a program that processes a queue of airline passengers.

CASE STUDY   **Maintaining a Queue of Passengers**

PROBLEM ▼

Write a menu-driven program that maintains a queue of passengers waiting to see a ticket agent. The program user should be able to insert a new passenger at the rear of the queue, display the passenger at the front of the queue, or remove the passenger at the front of the queue. The program will display the number of passengers left in the queue just before it terminates.

DESIGN OVERVIEW ▼

We can use the queue abstract data type and operators `Insert`, `Retrieve`, and `Remove` to process the queue. We can simplify the program by using an abstract data type, `Passenger`, that contains type declarations for an airline passenger and provides its input/output operators (`ReadPass` and `WritePass`). We will implement this abstract data type later.

Data Requirements

Problem Inputs

```
The operation to be performed (Choice : Char)
The next passenger's data (NextPass : Passenger)
```

Problem Outputs

```
The passenger at the front of the queue (FirstPass : Passenger)
```

Program Variables

```
The queue of passengers (PassQueue : Queue)
A flag for storing the result of a queue operation
  (Success : Boolean)
```

Algorithm

```
1. Initialize the queue.
2. repeat
      3. Display the menu.
      4. Read the operation selected.
      5. Perform the operation selected.
   until user is done or a queue operation fails.
6. Display the number of passengers left in the queue.
```

CODING ▼

Main Program

The main program (see Fig. 6.3) imports the type declarations for `QElement` (from `QElementADT`) and for `Queue` (from `QueueADT`). Method `Queue. CreateQueue` (from `QueueADT`) initializes the passenger queue to an empty queue. In the main program body the statement

```
Write ('Enter I(nsert), R(emove), D(isplay), or Q(uit)> ');
```

displays the menu of choices (Step 3). After the selection is read into `Choice`, the main program calls procedure `ModifyQueue` to perform Step 5. Procedure `ModifyQueue` is discussed next.

ModifyQueue

For each selection, procedure `ModifyQueue` (see Fig. 6.4) calls the operators required to manipulate the `Queue` (from `QueueADT`) and the operators needed to read or display a passenger object (from `QElementADT` via inheritance from `PassengerADT`). The main control structure is a case statement that determines which operators are called.

Figure 6.3
Program UseQueue

Directory: CHAP 6
File: USEQUEUE.PAS

```
program UseQueue;
{
 Manipulates a queue of airline passengers.

 IMPORT: Queue, CreateQueue, Insert, Remove, and Retrieve
         from QueueADT (see Section 6.3).
         QElement, ReadPass, WritePass from QElementADT
         via inheritance from PassengerADT (see Fig. 6.6).
}
  uses QElementADT, QueueADT;

  var
     PassQueue : Queue;          {a passenger queue}
     Choice : Char;              {operation request}
     Success : Boolean;          {program flag}

  {insert procedure ModifyQueue}
  {$I MODIFYQU.PAS}

begin {UseQueue}
  PassQueue.CreateQueue;        {start with an empty queue}

  {Process all requests until done.}
  repeat
     Write ('Enter I(nsert), R(emove), D(isplay), or Q(uit)> ');
     ReadLn (Choice);
     Choice := UpCase(Choice);

     {Process current request.}
     ModifyQueue (PassQueue, Choice, Success);
     WriteLn
  until (Choice = 'Q')
end. {UseQueue}
```

TESTING ▼

Before you can run program UseQueue, it will be necessary to code and compile units PassengerADT, QElementADT, and QueueADT. You can store the initial passenger list by selecting a sequence of insert operations. In the sample run of program UseQueue shown in Fig. 6.5, passenger Brown is inserted first, followed by passenger Watson. After passenger Brown is removed from the queue, the new passenger at the front of the queue (Watson) is displayed.

To test the program thoroughly, it would be necessary to attempt to display or remove a passenger after the queue is empty. Either attempt should cause the error message Queue is empty to be displayed before the program terminates. To check that there was no insertion after the queue is full, it would be necessary to redefine the queue capacity (part of the declaration for type Queue) so that the message Queue is full—no insertion appears after a small number of passenger insertions takes place.

Figure 6.4
Procedure ModifyQueue

Directory: CHAP 6
File: MODIFYQU.PAS

▽

```
procedure ModifyQueue (var Q {input/output} : Queue;
                           Choice {input} : Char;
                           var Success {output} : Boolean);
{
 Performs the operation indicated by Choice on the queue Q.
 Pre : Q has been created.
 Post: Q is modified based on Choice and Success indicates
       whether requested operation was performed.
}
  var
    NextPass,               {new passenger}
    FirstPass : QElement;   {passenger at front of queue}

begin {ModifyQueue}
  if Choice in ['I', 'R', 'D', 'Q'] then
    case Choice of
      'I' : begin {insert}
              WriteLn ('Enter passenger data.');
              NextPass.ReadPass;
              Q.Insert (NextPass, Success);
              if not Success then
                WriteLn ('Queue is full - no insertion')
            end; {insert}
      'R' : begin {remove}
              Q.Remove (FirstPass, Success);
              if Success then
                begin
                  WriteLn ('Passenger removed from queue follows.');
                  FirstPass.WritePass
                end
              else
                WriteLn ('Queue is empty - no deletion')
            end; {remove}
      'D' : begin {display}
              Q.Retrieve (FirstPass, Success);
              if Success then
                begin
                  WriteLn ('Passenger at head of queue follows.');
                  FirstPass.WritePass
                end
              else
                WriteLn ('Queue is empty - no passenger')
            end; {display}
      'Q' : begin
```

▷ ▷ ▷ ▷ ▷ ▷

```
            WriteLn ('Leaving passenger queue.');
            WriteLn ('Number of passengers in the queue is ', Q.SizeOfQueue :1)
          end {quit}
    end {case}
  else
    WriteLn ('Incorrect choice - try again.')
end; {ModifyQueue}
```

△

CODING THE ABSTRACT DATA TYPE PASSENGER ▼

Figure 6.6 shows an abstract data type that contains a declaration for object type `Passenger`. Procedures `ReadPass` and `WritePass` read and write a single passenger's record. The completion of `WritePass` is left as an exercise.

Figure 6.5
Sample Run of Program
UseQueue

▽

```
Enter I(nsert), R(emove), D(isplay), or Q(uit)> I
Enter passenger data.
Passenger Name> Brown
Class (F, B, E, S)> E
Number of seats> 2

Enter I(nsert), R(emove), D(isplay), or Q(uit)> I
Enter passenger data.
Passenger Name> Watson
Class (F, B, E, S)> B
Number of Seats> 1

Enter I(nsert), R(emove), D(isplay), or Q(uit)> I
Enter passenger data.
Passenger Name> Dietz
Class (F, B, E, S)> E
Number of Seats> 3

Enter I(nsert), R(emove), D(isplay), or Q(uit)> R
Passenger removed from queue follows.
Brown
Economy Class
 2 Seats

Enter I(nsert), R(emove), D(isplay), or Q(uit)> D
Passenger at head of queue follows.
Watson
Business Class
 1 Seat

Enter I(nsert), R(emove), D(isplay), or Q(uit)> Q
Leaving passenger queue.
Number of passengers in the queue is 2
```

△

Figure 6.6
Unit PassengerADT

```
unit PassengerADT;
{
 Abstract data type Passenger: contains declarations for object
 type Passenger and methods for reading and displaying values
 of type Passenger.
}
interface

  type
    ClassType = (FirstClass, Business, Economy,
                  StandBy, Undesignated);

    Passenger = object
                    procedure ReadPass;
                    procedure WritePass;

                    private
                      Name : string;
                      Class : ClassType;
                      NumSeats : Integer;
                    end; {Passenger}

implementation
  function ClassConvert (ClassCh : Char) : ClassType;
  {
   Converts a character to a passenger category.
  }
  begin {ClassConvert - stub}
   ClassConvert := Economy
  end; {ClassConvert - stub}

  procedure Passenger.ReadPass;
  {
   Reads values into a passenger's data members.
   Pre : None
   Post: Data are read into all the data members of a
         passenger.
  }
    var
      ClassCh : Char;      {input - character for class type}

  begin {ReadPass}
    Write ('Passenger name > ');
    ReadLn (Name);
    Write ('Class (F, B, E, S)> ');
    ReadLn (ClassCh);
    Class := ClassConvert(ClassCh);
    Write ('Number of Seats>');
    ReadLn (NumSeats)
  end; {ReadPass}

  procedure Passenger.WritePass;
```

```
        {
         Displays the data members of a passenger.
        }
        begin {WritePass - stub}
          Write ('Name: ');
          WriteLn (Name)
        end; {WritePass - stub}

  end. {PassengerADT}
```

At this point we can draw the module dependency diagram for program UseQueue (see Fig. 6.7). As shown, both UseQueue and QueueADT use unit QElementADT, and QElement uses unit PassengerADT. We will implement unit QueueADT next.

Exercises for Section 6.2   **Self-Check**

1. Draw the queue after completion of the sample run in Fig. 6.5.

Programming

1. Complete method Passenger.WritePass (see Fig. 6.6).
2. Complete function ClassConvert (in method Passenger.ReadPass) shown in Fig. 6.6.

Figure 6.7
Module Dependency
Diagram for useQueue

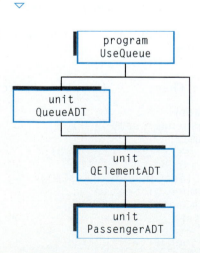

6.3 Implementing a Queue Abstract Data Type

To represent a queue, we will use an object with three Integer data members (Front, Rear, NumItems) and an array data member, Items, that provides storage for the queue elements. The declarations for a queue whose capacity is 100 elements is shown in the interface section for QueueADT (see Fig. 6.8).

The Integer fields Front and Rear are pointers to the queue elements at the front and rear of the queue, respectively. The Integer field NumItems keeps track of the actual number of items in the queue and allows us to easily determine whether the queue is empty (NumItems is 0) or full (NumItems is MaxQueue).

The statement

```
uses QElementADT;      {imports QElement}
```

Figure 6.8
Interface Section for Unit
QueueADT

Directory: CHAP 6
File: QUEUEADT.PAS

```
unit QueueADT;
{
  Abstract data type Queue: contains declarations for data type
  Queue and operator procedures for an object of type Queue.
}
interface

  uses QElementADT; {imports QElement}

  const
    MaxQueue = 100;

  type
    QNumRange = 0..MaxQueue;
    QIndex = 1..MaxQueue;
    QueueArray = array [QIndex] of QElement;

    Queue = object
            procedure CreateQueue;
            procedure Insert
                (El {input} : QElement;
                 var {output} Success : Boolean);
            procedure Remove
                (var El {output} : QElement;
                 var Success {output} : Boolean);
            procedure Retrieve
                (var El {output} : QElement;
                 var Success {output} : Boolean);
            function IsEmpty : Boolean;
```

▷ ▷ ▷ ▷ ▷

```
            function IsFull : Boolean;
            function SizeOfQueue : Integer;

        private
          Front, Rear : QIndex;
          NumItems : QNumRange;
          Items : QueueArray;
        end; {Queue}
```

imports the data type `QElement`. `QElement` can be a standard type or a user-defined object type with methods. To create a queue of airline passengers, we should declare the unit shown in Fig. 6.9. Because `Passenger` is an object type, we will use object inheritance and declare `QElement` as one of its descendant object types. If we simply used the type declaration statement

```
type
  QElement = Passenger;
```

instead, we would need to import `PassengerADT` explicitly into both `QueueADT` and its client program `UseQueue`. By declaring `QElement` as a descendant object, clients of unit `QElementADT` will not need to be concerned with importing unit `PassengerADT` in addition to unit `QElementADT`.

It makes sense to store the first queue record in element 1, the second queue record in element 2, and so on. So we should set `Front` and `Rear` to 1 when we create an initially empty queue. Each time we make an insertion, we should increment `NumItems` and `Rear` by 1. Figure 6.10 shows an instance, `Q`, of a queue that is filled to its capacity (`NumItems` is

Figure 6.9

Unit `QElementADT` for a
Queue of Passengers

Directory: CHAP 6
File: QELEMENT.PAS

```
unit QElementADT;

interface

  uses PassengerADT;

  type
    QElement = object(Passenger)
               end; {QElement}

implementation

  {none}

end. {QElementADT}
```

Figure 6.10
A Queue Filled with
Characters

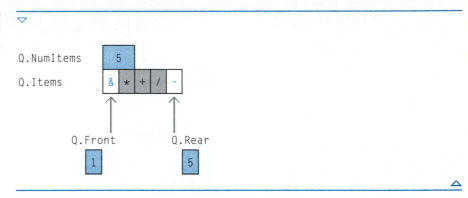

MaxQueue). The queue contains the symbols &, *, +, /, –, inserted in that order.

Because Q is filled to capacity, we cannot insert a new character. We can remove a queue element by decrementing NumItems and incrementing Front to 2, thereby removing Q.Items[1] (the symbol &). Figure 6.11 shows the queue after removal of the first element. The symbol ? in Q.Items[1] indicates that this element is no longer in the queue.

Even though the queue in Fig. 6.11 is no longer filled, we cannot insert a new character because Rear is at its maximum value. One way to solve this problem would be to shift the elements housed in the array items so that the empty cells come after Q.Rear and adjust Q.Front and Q.Rear accordingly. With a large array this can be a very time-consuming task. This kind of array shifting must be done very carefully to avoid losing track of active array elements.

A better way to solve this problem is to represent the array field Items as a circular array. In a *circular array,* the elements wrap around so that the first element actually follows the last. This allows us to "increment" Rear to 1 and

Figure 6.11
The Queue After Deletion
of the First Element

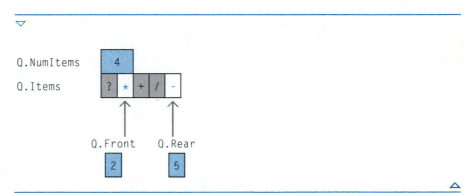

Figure 6.12
A Queue as a Circular
Array

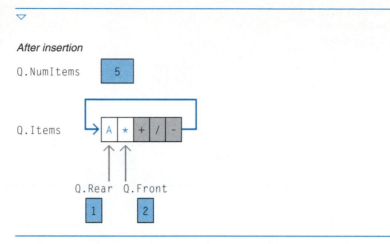

store a new character in Q.Items[1]. Figure 6.12 shows the queue after insertion of a new element (the character A). After the insertion, Front is still 2, but Rear becomes 1. The contents of Q.Items[1] changes from ? to A.

EXAMPLE 6.1 ▼

The left side of Fig. 6.13 shows the effect of removing two elements from the queue described above. As shown, there are three characters in this queue (stored in Items[4], Items[5], and Items[1]). The symbol ? in Items[2] and Items[3] indicates that the values stored in these elements have been removed from the queue. The two elements that are currently unused are shown in unshaded boxes.

Figure 6.13
The Effect of Two
Deletions and One
Insertion

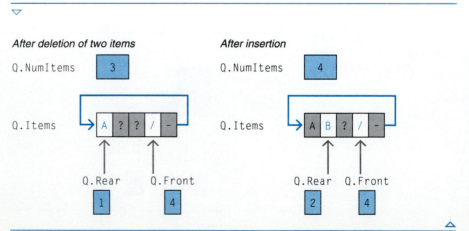

The right side of Fig. 6.13 shows the queue after insertion of a new character (B). The value of `Rear` is incremented to 2, and the next element is inserted in `Q.Items[2]`. This queue element follows the character A in `Q.Items[1]`. The value of `Q.Front` is still 4 because the character / at `Q.Items[4]` has been in the queue the longest. `Q.Items[3]` is now the only queue element that is unused. The new queue contains the symbols /, −, A, and B, in that order. ▲

Figure 6.14 shows the implementation section for the queue abstract data type (`QueueADT`).

Figure 6.14
Implementation Section for
Unit `QueueADT`

Directory: CHAP 6
File: QUEUEADT.PAS

```
implementation

  procedure Queue.CreateQueue;
  {
   Creates an empty queue.
   Pre : None
   Post: Q is initialized to a queue of zero elements.
  }
  begin {CreateQueue}
    NumItems := 0;              {queue is empty}
    Front := 1;
    Rear := MaxQueue           {queue is circular}
  end; {CreateQueue}

  procedure Queue.Insert (El {input} : QElement;
                          var Success {output} : Boolean);
  {
   Inserts El in a queue.
   Pre : The queue has been created.
   Post: If the queue is not full, increments Rear and
         inserts El. Sets Success to indicate success or
         failure.
  }
  begin {Insert}
    if NumItems = MaxQueue then
      Success := False              {queue is full}
    else
      begin {insert El}
        Rear := (Rear mod MaxQueue) + 1;       {increment Rear}
        Items[Rear] := El;
        NumItems := NumItems + 1;
        Success := True
      end {insert El}
  end; {Insert}

  procedure Queue.Remove (var El {output} : QElement;
                          var Success {output} : Boolean);
```

▷ ▷ ▷ ▷ ▷

```
{
 Removes the element at the front of the queue and copies
 it into El.
 Pre : The queue has been created.
 Post: If the queue is not empty, El contains its first
       element, Front is decremented, and Success indicates
       success or failure.
}
begin {Remove}
  if NumItems = 0 then
    Success := False     {queue is empty}
  else
    begin
      {Remove the element at the front of the queue.}
      El := Items[Front];
      Front := (Front mod MaxQueue) + 1;      {increment Front}
      NumItems := NumItems - 1;
      Success := True
    end {if}
end; {Remove}

procedure Queue.Retrieve (var El {out} : QElement;
                               var Success {out} : Boolean);
{
 Copies the value at the front of a queue into El without
 removing it.
 Pre : The queue has been created.
 Post: If the queue is not empty, El contains its first
       element and Success indicates success or failure.
}
begin {Retrieve}
  if NumItems = 0 then
    Success := False     {queue is empty}
  else
    begin
      {Retrieve the item at the front of the queue.}
      El := Items[Front];
      Success := True
    end {if}
end; {Retrieve}

function Queue.IsEmpty : Boolean;
{
 Tests for an empty queue.
 Pre : The queue has been created.
 Post: Returns True if the queue is empty;
       otherwise, returns False.
}
begin {IsEmpty}
  IsEmpty := NumItems = 0
end; {IsEmpty}

function Queue.IsFull : Boolean;
```

▷ ▷ ▷ ▷ ▷ ▷

```
{
 Test for a full queue.
 Pre : The queue has been created.
 Post: Returns True if the queue is full; otherwise,
       returns False.
}
begin {IsFull}
  IsFull := NumItems = MaxQueue
end; {IsFull}

function Queue.SizeOfQueue : Integer;
{
 Finds the number of elements in a queue.
 Pre : Q has been created.
 Post: Returns the number of elements in the queue.
}
begin {SizeOfQueue}
  SizeOfQueue := NumItems
end; {SizeOfQueue}

end. {unit QueueADT}
```

△
_____

Method `Queue.CreateQueue` must be called before any of the other methods in Fig. 6.14. `Queue.CreateQueue` sets `NumItems` to 0 and `Front` to 1 because array element `Items[1]` is considered the front of the empty queue. `Rear` is initialized to `MaxQueue` because the queue is circular.

In method `Queue.Insert` the statement

```
Rear := (Rear mod MaxQueue) + 1;                {increment Rear}
```

is used to increment the value of `Rear`. When `Rear` is less than `MaxQueue`, this statement simply increments its value by 1. But when `Rear` is equal to `MaxQueue`, this statement sets `Rear` to 1 (`MaxQueue mod MaxQueue` is 0), thereby wrapping the last element of the queue around to the first element. Since `Queue.CreateQueue` initializes `Rear` to `MaxQueue`, the first queue element will be placed in `Items[1]` as desired. ▲

In method `Queue.Remove` the element that is currently stored in `Items[Front]` is copied into `El` before `Front` is incremented. In procedure `Queue.Retrieve`, the element at `Items[Front]` is copied into `El`, but `Front` is not changed.

The number of elements in the queue is changed by methods `Queue.Insert` and `Queue.Remove`, so `NumItems` must be incremented by one in `Queue.Insert` and decremented by one in `Queue.Remove`. The value of `NumItems` is tested in both `Queue.IsFull` and `Queue.IsEmpty` to determine the status of the queue. The function method `Queue.SizeOfQueue` simply returns the value of `NumItems`.

Self-Check

1. What are the final values of `Front`, `Rear`, and the `Name` fields of `Items[1..3]` after the sample run of `UseQueue` in Fig. 6.5?
2. Provide the algorithm for the operator in Programming Exercise 1. If program `UseQueue` calls this operator, how would this affect the module dependency diagram in Fig. 6.7?

Programming

1. Write a new `Queue` method that displays the entire queue contents (from `Front` to `Rear`, inclusive).

6.4 Simulating Waiting Lines Using Queues

Simulation is a technique that is used to study the performance of a physical system by using a physical, mathematical, or computer model of the system. Through simulation the designers of a new system can estimate the system's expected performance before they actually build it. The use of simulation can lead to changes in the design that will improve the expected performance of the new system. Simulation is especially useful when the actual system would be too expensive to rebuild or too dangerous to experiment with after its construction.

A physical model of a system could be a small-scale model or a model that contained only a subset of the features of the complete system. A mathematical model would be a system of equations whose solution characterized the properties of the system. In this section we focus on the use of a computer model in simulating a physical system.

CASE STUDY   Airline Ticket Sales Simulation

PROBLEM ▼

We Fly Anywhere Airlines (WFAA) is considering redesigning its ticket counters for airline passengers. It would like to have two separate waiting lines, one for regular customers and one for frequent flyers. Assuming that only one ticket agent is available to serve all passengers, the airline would like to determine the average waiting time for both types of passengers using various strategies for taking passengers from the waiting lines (see Fig. 6.15).

As examples of different strategies for serving passengers, a democratic strategy would be to take turns serving passengers from both lines (that is, one frequent flyer, one regular passenger, one frequent flyer, and so on). (Another democratic strategy would be to serve the passenger who has been waiting in line the longest, but this would be the same as having a sin-

Figure 6.15
Passenger Waiting Lines

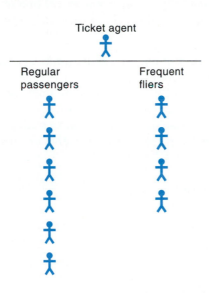

gle queue. Why?) An elitist strategy would be to serve any frequent flyer waiting in line before serving the regular passengers. We can study these strategies and all those in between by introducing a queue variable FFMax, which must be a positive integer. FFMax will represent the number of consecutive frequent flyer passengers served between regular passengers. When FFMax is 1, every other passenger served will be a regular passenger (the democratic strategy). When FFMax is 2, every third passenger served will be a regular passenger. When FFMax is as large as the queue size, any frequent flyer waiting in line will be served before any regular passenger (the elitist strategy).

DESIGN OVERVIEW ▼

Running a computer simulation is a good way to investigate the effect of different serving strategies. To run a computer simulation, we must keep track of the current time by maintaining a clock that is set to an initial time of zero. The clock time will be repeatedly incremented by one time unit until the simulation is finished. During each time interval, one or more of the events listed below may occur.

1. A new frequent flyer arrives in line.
2. A new regular passenger arrives in line.
3. The ticket agent finishes serving a passenger and begins to serve the first passenger in the frequent flyer queue.

4. The ticket agent finishes serving a passenger and begins to serve the first passenger in the regular passenger queue.
5. The ticket agent is idle because there are no passengers in either queue to serve.

The purpose of running the simulation is to determine statistics about the waiting times for frequent flyers and for regular passengers. Besides the priority given to frequent flyers, the waiting times depend on the arrival rate of each type of passenger (number of passengers per minute) and the time required to serve a passenger. In addition to statistics on waiting times, we can display a minute-by-minute trace of events occurring during each minute of the simulation.

Data Requirements

Problem Inputs

```
Arrival rate for frequent flyers expressed as number of
   arrivals per minute (FFArrivalRate : Real)
Arrival rate for regular passengers expressed as number of
   arrivals per minute (RPArrivalRate : Real)
Maximum number of frequent flyers to serve before
   switching to regular passengers (FFMax : Integer)
Time required to serve a passenger (ServeTime : Integer)
Total time of simulation (TotalTime : Integer)
Indicator of whether the minute-by-minute display will be on
   or off (ShowAll : Char)
```

Problem Outputs

```
Clock showing time that the simulation has run (Clock : Integer)
Accumulated waiting time for service for a frequent flyer
   (FFWait : Integer)
Accumulated waiting time for service for a regular passenger
   (RPWait : Real)
Minute-by-minute display of simulation events
```

Program Variables

```
Program flag indicating whether display is on or off
   (DisplayOn : Boolean)
Queue of regular passengers containing the time of arrival
   for each passenger (RPQueue : Queue)
Queue of frequent flyers containing the time of arrival
   for each passenger (FFQueue : Queue)
Time at which service will conclude for the passenger being
   served (TimeDone : Integer)
Number of frequent flyer passengers served
   (NumFFServed : Integer)
Number of regular passengers served
   (NumRPServed : Integer)
Count of frequent flyer passengers served since the
   last regular passenger (FFSinceRP : Integer)
```

Program variables `FFQueue` and `RPQueue` are two queues that represent airline passengers waiting to be served by a ticket agent. For the purpose of this simulation the only information that we need to save about each passenger is the time the passenger was inserted in the queue (an Integer). Therefore we should place the declaration

```
type
  QElement = Integer;
```

in unit `QElementADT` (see Fig. 6.9).

The algorithm for the simulation program follows. The loop at Step 5 executes once for each minute of the simulation. During each loop repetition we check whether a new arrival occurs (Steps 6 and 7) and whether to begin service for a passenger who is currently waiting in line (Steps 8 and 9).

Algorithm for Passenger Lines Simulation Program

```
 1. Enter input data.
 2. Create two empty queues.
 3. Set DisplayOn to True or False.
 4. Initialize total wait times, numbers of passengers
    served, FFSinceRP, and TimeDone to zero.
 5. for each minute of the simulation do
      begin
          6. Check whether to insert a new regular passenger
             in RPQueue and save the clock time if inserted.
          7. Check whether to insert a new frequent flyer
             in FFQueue and save the clock time if inserted.
          8. If the server is not busy then
             9. Select a new passenger to be served
                from one of the queues, remove that passenger,
                update the waiting times and passenger counts,
                update FFSinceRP and TimeDone.
      end
10. Display number of passengers served and compute and dis-
    play average waiting times for each queue.
```

STRUCTURE CHART ▼

For the algorithm above, procedure `EnterData` performs Step 1, `Initialize` performs Step 4, `CheckArrival` performs Steps 6 and 7, `StartServe` performs Step 9, and `ShowStats` performs Step 10. Figure 6.16 shows the structure chart.

CODING ▼

Main Program

Figure 6.17 shows the main program. The steps preceding the for loop correspond to Steps 1 through 4 of the algorithm. The statement

```
DisplayOn := UpCase(ShowAll) = 'Y';          {set display flag}
```

Figure 6.16
Structure Chart for the
Waiting Line Simulation

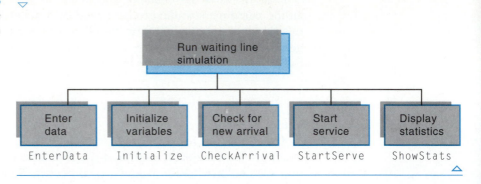

sets the display flag to activate (or deactivate) the minute-by-minute trace.
We will explain the purpose of the statement

```
Randomize;
```

when we examine procedure `CheckNewArrival`.

The for loop executes once for each minute of the simulation. It calls procedure `CheckNewArrival` twice to see whether any new arrivals should be
inserted into either queue. Next, if the condition

```
Clock >= TimeDone
```

Figure 6.17
Main Program for the
Waiting Line Simulation

Directory: CHAP 6
File: SIMULATE.PAS

```
program Simulate;
{
 Program performs simulation of customer service policies
 for two waiting lines.

 Imports: Queue object and its methods from unit QueueADT.
}
  uses QueueADT;

  var
    {problem inputs}
    FFArrivalRate, RPArrivalRate : Real;
    FFMax : Integer;
    ServeTime, TotalTime : Integer;
    ShowAll : Char;

    {problem outputs}
    Clock : Integer;
    FFWait, RPWait : Integer;

    {program variables}
    DisplayOn : Boolean;
```

▷ ▷ ▷ ▷ ▷ ▷

```
    RPQueue, FFQueue : Queue;
    TimeDone : Integer;
    NumFFServed,
    NumRPServed,
    FFSinceRP    : Integer;

  {
   insert procedures: EnterData, Initialize, CheckNewArrival,
   StartServe, and ShowStats here
  }
  {$I EnterDat.PAS}
  {$I CHECKNEW.PAS}
  {$I INITIALI.PAS}
  {$I STARTSER.PAS}
  {$I SHOWSTAT.PAS}

begin {Simulate}
  EnterData (FFArrivalRate, RPArrivalRate, FFMax, ServeTime,
            TotalTime, ShowAll);
  WriteLn;

  RPQueue.CreateQueue;      {create regular passenger queue.}
  FFQueue.CreateQueue;      {create frequent flyer queue.}

  Initialize (FFWait, RPWait, NumFFServed, NumRPServed,
             FFSinceRP, TimeDone);      {set all values to 0}
  DisplayOn := UpCase(ShowAll) = 'Y';     {set display flag}

  {Initialize pseudo random number generator}
  Randomize;

  {Perform minute by minute simulation.}
  for Clock := 0 to TotalTime do
    begin
      CheckNewArrival (RPQueue, RPArrivalRate, Clock,
                      DisplayOn, 'regular passenger');
      CheckNewArrival (FFQueue, FFArrivalRate, Clock,
                      DisplayOn, 'frequent flyer');
      if Clock >= TimeDone then
        StartServe(RPQueue, FFQueue, FFMax, Clock,
                  ServeTime, RPWait, FFWait, NumFFServed,
                  NumRPServed, FFSinceRP, TimeDone,
                  DisplayOn)
    end; {for}

  WriteLn;          {Display summary statistics next.}
  ShowStats (RPWait, FFWait, NumFFServed, NumRPServed)
end. {Simulate}
```

is true, then the ticket agent is finished with the current passenger, so it calls procedure StartServe to begin serving the next passenger. StartServe must select a queue, remove a passenger, and update several simulation variables that are passed as parameters.

Procedures EnterData, Initialize, and ShowStats

Procedures EnterData, Initialize, and ShowStats are relatively straight-forward and are shown in Fig. 6.18. Procedures EnterData and ShowStats perform all input/output operations during the simulation except for the minute-by-minute trace.

Procedure CheckNewArrival

Procedure CheckNewArrival (see Fig. 6.19) is the most interesting part of the simulation program. Its purpose is to determine whether a new arrival occurs during a given time unit and, if so, to update the appropriate passenger queue. During each time unit, CheckNewArrival is called twice, once for each passenger queue.

The arrival of passengers is considered a random event because we cannot predict with certainty the time at which passengers arrive. The arrival

Figure 6.18
Procedures EnterData, Initialize, and ShowStats

Directory: CHAP 6
File: ENTERDAT.PAS

```
procedure EnterData (var FFArrivalRate,
                         RPArrivalRate {output} : Real;
                     var FFMax, ServeTime,
                         TotalTime {output} : Integer;
                     var ShowAll {output} : Char);
{
  Prompts user for values to assign to simulation variables.
  Pre : None.
  Post: All parameters assigned values, but no input
        validation was performed by this procedure.
}
begin {EnterData};
  WriteLn ('Expected number of frequent flyer arrivals per ',
           'minute:');
  Write ('Enter a fraction less than 1.0 >');
  ReadLn (FFArrivalRate);
  WriteLn ('Expected number of regular passenger arrivals ',
           'per minute');
  Write ('Enter a fraction less than 1.0 >');
  ReadLn (RPArrivalRate);
  WriteLn ('Enter the maximum number of frequent flyers');
  Write ('served between regular passengers >');
  ReadLn (FFMax);
  Write ('Enter the average service time ',
         'rounded to the nearest minute >');
  ReadLn (ServeTime);
  Write ('Enter the total simulation time in minutes >');
  ReadLn (TotalTime);
  Write ('Display minute-by-minute trace of simulation (Y or N) >');
  ReadLn (ShowAll)
end; {EnterData}
```

rate tells us the average rate at which passengers will arrive. For example, an arrival rate of 0.25 means that, on average, 0.25 passenger will arrive every minute or, stated another way, one passenger will arrive every four minutes. However, this does not mean that passengers will arrive precisely at clock times 0, 4, 8, 12, and so on. A group of passengers may arrive in consecutive time units, and then we may not see another arrival for several more minutes. All we know is that if the simulation runs long enough, the number of passenger arrivals should be pretty close to the total simulation length times 0.25. In statistical terms, an arrival rate of 0.25 means that the probability of a passenger arrival in any given minute is 0.25, or 25%.

How do we represent the random nature of passenger arrivals in a program? One way is to use a random number generator. A *random number generator* is a function that returns a value in the range 0.0 to 1.0 in such a way that any number in this range is equally likely to occur. This means that if we call the random number generator a large number of times and count the number of values generated in each of the 10 subranges 0–0.1, 0.1–0.2, 0.2–0.3, and so on, these counts should be close in value.

Most computer languages do not have true random number generators. However, many languages do provide a pseudo–random number generator. A pseudo–random number generator produces numbers in such a way that, although the order in which they appear is not completly random, the distribution of the numbers produced is close enough to a uniform distribution that for many purposes they can be treated as if they were random. Table 6.2 shows the results from one experiment using the pseudo–random number generator in Borland Pascal. Ideally there should be 100 occurrences in each range, but the actual number of occurrences is between 92 and 110.

Table 6.2
Test of a Pseudo–Random Number Generator (Number of values in each range for 1000 trials)

Range	Occurrences
0.0–0.099999	92
0.1–0.199999	95
0.2–0.299999	99
0.3–0.399999	101
0.4–0.499999	104
0.5–0.599999	95
0.6–0.699999	92
0.7–0.799999	103
0.8–0.899999	109
0.9–0.999999	110

We can use a pseudo–random number generator to determine whether a passenger has arrived in a given minute of the simulation. The Borland Pascal function `Random` is a function with no arguments that generates a pseudo–random number. The condition

```
Random < ArrivalRate
```

compares the pseudo–random number generated to the value of ArrivalRate. Because the values being compared are in the range 0.0–1.0, the probability that this condition will be true is proportional to the value of ArrivalRate as desired. If ArrivalRate is 0.25, this condition should be true 25% of the time.

Figure 6.19 shows procedure CheckNewArrival. If the above condition is true and the queue passed as its first parameter is not full, a new passenger is inserted in that queue. The only information about a passenger that is stored in the queue is the time of arrival, which is called a *time stamp*. If DisplayOn is True, the time of arrival, the queue name, and the new queue size are displayed.

Before the first call to function Random we must execute the statement

```
Randomize;
```

Figure 6.19
Procedure
CheckNewArrival

Directory: CHAP 6
File: CHECKNEW.PAS

```
procedure CheckNewArrival (var PassQueue {input/output} : Queue;
                               ArrivalRate {input} : Real;
                               Clock {input} : Integer;
                               DisplayOn {input} : Boolean;
                               QueueName {input} : string);
{
 Determine whether a new arrival occurs during a given time unit.
 Pre : PassQueue and input parameters defined.
 Post: If new arrival and queues are not full then passenger is
       added to PassQueue; if PassQueue is full an error message
       is displayed; otherwise no change is made to PassQueue.
}
  var
    Success : Boolean;

begin {CheckNewArrival}
  if Random < ArrivalRate then
    begin {arrival}
      if PassQueue.IsFull then
        WriteLn ('Simulation error - ', QueueName, ' queue full',
                 '-reduce arrival rate or increase queue size')
      else
        begin {insert}
          PassQueue.Insert (Clock, Success);
          if Success and DisplayOn then
            WriteLn ('Time is ', Clock :1, ', ', QueueName,
                     ' arrival, new queue size is ',
                     PassQueue.SizeOfQueue :1)
        end {insert}
    end {arrival}
end; {CheckNewArrival}
```

Procedure Randomize uses the computer system clock to initialize the pseudo–random number generator (function Random) and is called in the main program (see Fig. 6.17).

Procedure StartServe

Procedure StartServe is called to select a queue and remove the first passenger from that queue. If the frequent flyer queue is not empty, StartServe selects it if either of the two following conditions is true.

▶ The number of frequent flyers who have been served since the last regular passenger is less than FFMax (FFSinceRP < FFMax).
▶ The regular passenger queue is empty (IsEmpty(RPQueue)).

Otherwise, StartServe selects the regular passenger queue if it is not empty. If both queues are empty, StartServe displays a message that the agent is idle.

After selecting a queue, StartServe (bottom of Fig. 6.20) increments FFSinceRP or resets it to zero, depending on the passenger type being served. Next, StartServe calls procedure Update (top of Fig. 6.20) to update the simulation variables that are passed as parameters. Update removes a passenger from the queue and computes that passenger's waiting time (clock time − time stamp) and adds it to the total wait time. Next, Update computes the time when the agent will be finished with this passenger and saves it in TimeDone. Update also increments the count of passengers of this type that have been served since the simulation began.

Figure 6.20
Procedures Update and StartServe

Directory: CHAP 6
File: STARTSER.PAS

```
procedure Update (var PassQueue {input/output} : Queue;
                  Clock, ServeTime {input} : Integer;
                  var TimeDone, NumServed,
                      Wait {input/output} : Integer;
                  DisplayOn {input} : Boolean;
                  QueueName {input} : string);
{
 Update removes passenger from PassQueue and updates the
 simulation variables.
 Pre : PassQueue is non-empty and all input parameters are defined.
 Post: Passenger removed from PassQueue; and TimeDone, NumServed,
       and Wait receive new values.
}
```

▷ ▷ ▷ ▷ ▷ ▷

```
var
   TimeStamp,               {time passenger was inserted in queue}
   LastWait : Integer;  {waiting time of passenger removed}
   Success : Boolean;   {Boolean flag for Remove operator}

begin {Update}
  PassQueue.Remove (TimeStamp, Success);
  LastWait := Clock - TimeStamp;
  Wait := Wait + LastWait;
  TimeDone := Clock + ServeTime;
  NumServed := NumServed + 1;
  if DisplayOn then
     WriteLn ('Time is ', Clock :1, ', serving ', QueueName,
              ' with time stamp ', TimeStamp : 1)
end; {Update}

procedure StartServe
                (var RPQueue, FFQueue {input/output} : Queue;
                 FFMax, Clock, ServeTime {input} : Integer;
                 var RPWait, FFWait,
                     NumFFServed, NumRPServed,
                     FFSinceRP, TimeDone {input/output} : Integer;
                 DisplayOn {input} : Boolean);
{
 Selects a queue and removes first passenger from queue.
 Pre : At least one of the queues RPQueue or FFQueue is non-empty
        and all other input parameters are defined.
 Post: If frequent flyer queue is not empty and either the
        number of frequent flyer < FFMax or the regular passenger
        queue is empty then frequent flyer queue is used; otherwise
        the regular passenger queue is used.
 Calls: Procedure Update.
}
begin  {StartServe}
  if (not (FFQueue.IsEmpty)) and
      ((FFSinceRP < FFMax) or (RPQueue.IsEmpty)) then
    begin {serve frequent flyer}
       FFSinceRP := FFSinceRP + 1;
       Update (FFQueue, Clock, ServeTime, TimeDone,
               NumFFServed, FFWait, DisplayOn, 'frequent flyer')
    end {serve frequent flyer}
  else if not (RPQueue.IsEmpty) then
    begin {serve regular passenger}
       FFSinceRP := 0;
       Update (RPQueue, Clock, ServeTime, TimeDone,
               NumRPServed, RPWait, DisplayOn, 'regular passenger')
    end {serve regular passenger}
  else {both queues empty}
    if DisplayOn then
       WriteLn ('Time is ', Clock :1, ', server is idle')
end; {StartServe}
```

TESTING THE SIMULATION PROGRAM ▼

Figure 6.21 shows a sample run of the simulation program with the trace turned on. To test the simulation program, you should run it a number of times with the trace turned on and verify that passengers in the frequent flyer queue have the specified priority over regular passengers. Also, make sure that the "server is idle" message is displayed only when both queues are empty. If both arrival rates are the same, check that the waiting times reflect the priority given to frequent flyers. Also see what happens when both kinds of passengers are treated equally (FFSinceRp is 1), as they are in Fig. 6.21.

Figure 6.21
Sample Run of the
Simulation Program

▽

```
Expected number of frequent flyer arrivals per minute:
Enter a fraction less than 1.0 >0.50
Expected number of regular passenger arrivals per minute
Enter a fraction less than 1.0 >0.50
Enter the maximum number of frequent flyers
served between regular passengers >1
Enter the average service time rounded to the nearest minute >2
Enter the total simulation time in minutes> 10
Display minute-by-minute trace of simulation (Y or N) >Y

Time is 0, server is idle
Time is 1, regular passenger arrival, new queue size is 1
Time is 1, serving regular passenger with time stamp 1
Time is 2, regular passenger arrival, new queue size is 1
Time is 2, frequent flyer arrival, new queue size is 1
Time is 3, regular passenger arrival, new queue size is 2
Time is 3, frequent flyer arrival, new queue size is 2
Time is 3, serving frequent flyer with time stamp 2
Time is 4, regular passenger arrival, new queue size is 3
Time is 4, frequent flyer arrival, new queue size is 2
Time is 5, frequent flyer arrival, new queue size is 3
Time is 5, serving regular passenger with time stamp 2
Time is 7, regular passenger arrival, new queue size is 3
Time is 7, frequent flyer arrival, new queue size is 4
Time is 7, serving frequent flyer with time stamp 3
Time is 8, frequent flyer arrival, new queue size is 4
Time is 9, regular passenger arrival, new queue size is 4
Time is 9, frequent flyer arrival, new queue size is 5
Time is 9, serving regular passenger with time stamp 3
Time is 10, regular passenger arrival, new queue size is 4

The number of regular passengers served was 3,
   with an average waiting time of 3.0 minutes
The number of frequent flyers served was 2,
   with an average waiting time of 2.5 minutes
```

△

When running the program, make sure that you use integer values for the total simulation time and for the service time. It is also a good idea to choose values for arrival rates and service time that keep the system from becoming saturated. The system will become saturated if the arrival rates are too large and passengers arrive more quickly than they can be served. This will result in very long queues and large waiting times. The system will become saturated if the total number of arrivals per minute (FFArrivalRate + RPArrivalRate) is greater than the number of passengers being served in a minute (1 / ServeTime).

When you are certain that the program runs correctly, you should turn off the trace and focus on the summary statistics. It is interesting to see how these values change for a particular set of arrival rates and service times. Remember, passenger arrivals are a random event, so the results should vary from one run to the next even if all input data stay the same.

Exercises for Section 6.4   **Self-Check**

1. Why is it important that procedure StartServe be called after CheckNewArrival and not before?

Programming

1. Rewrite procedure EnterData so that the program user is prompted for new values if out-of-range values are typed in.

6.5 Common Programming Errors

In this chapter we used an array field to store the contents of a queue (as we did in Chapter 5 for a stack). Consequently, many of our queue methods manipulated array subscripts. Testing your programs using the {$R+} complier directive will help you identify out-of-range subscript errors.

The client programs in this chapter all used QueueADT. Make sure that this unit is available and has been compiled to disk (file QueueADT.TPU) before you run your program. Be sure that you specify the correct data type for QElement in QElementADT and that you recompile QElementADT before compiling QueueADT. Also be certain that you use object inheritance, if appropriate, in modifying QElement.

CHAPTER REVIEW

In this chapter we introduced the queue as an abstract data type. The queue is a first-in, first-out data structure. This means that the item that has been in the queue the longest will be the first to be removed.

We described an array-based implementation of a queue object. We showed how stacks can be used to simulate reservation lists and waiting lines. In Chapter 7 we will discuss a queue implementation that makes more efficient use of computer memory.

We also discussed pseudo–random numbers. We showed how they might be used with queues to perform computer simulations of random events.

Quick-Check Exercises

1. A queue is a _____-in, _____-out data structure.
2. Would a compiler use a stack or a queue in a program that converts infix expressions to postfix expressions?
3. Would an operating system use a stack or a queue to determine which print job should be handled next?
4. Assume that a circular queue of capacity 6 contains the five characters +, *, −, &, and #. Assume that + is stored in the first position in the array used in the array representation of the queue. What is the value of Q.Front? What is the value of Q.Rear?
5. Remove the first element from the queue in Exercise 4, and insert the characters \ and %. Draw the new queue. What is the value of Q.Front? What is the value of Q.Rear?
6. Can you have two queues of real numbers in the same client program? Can you have a queue of integers and a queue of real numbers in the same client program?

Answers to Quick-Check Exercises

1. first, first
2. A stack
3. A queue
4. Q.Front is 1; Q.Rear is 5.
5.

    Q.Rear Q.Front

    Q.Front is 2; Q.Rear is 1.

6. Yes; no

Review Questions

1. Show the effect of each of the following operations on queue Q. Assume that Y (type Char) contains the character '&'. What are the final values of X and Success (type Boolean) and the contents of queue Q?

    ```
    Q.CreateQueue;
    Q.Insert ('+', Success);
    Q.Remove (X, Success);
    Q.Remove (X, Success);
    ```

```
Q.Insert ('(', Success);
Q.Insert (Y, Success);
Q.Remove (Y, Success);
```

2. Assume that queue Q is implemented by using our QueueADT but with the value of MaxQueue being 5. Show the values of data fields Front and Rear, along with array data field Items after each operation.

3. Write a new queue method called MoveToRear that moves the element that is currently at the front of the queue to the rear of the queue. The element that was second in line will be the new front element. Do this by using methods Queue.Insert and Queue.Remove.

4. Answer Question 3 without using method Queue.Insert or Queue.Remove. You will need to manipulate the queue's internal data fields directly.

5. Write a new queue method called MoveToFront that moves the element at the rear of the queue to the front of the queue, the other queue elements maintaining their relative positions behind the old front element. Do this by using methods Queue.Insert and Queue.Remove.

6. Answer Question 5 without using Queue.Insert and Queue.Remove.

Programming Projects

1. Redo Programming Project 2 from Chapter 5 assuming that widgets are shipped according to a first-in, first-out inventory system. Use our queue abstract data type to ship widgets.

Directory: CHAP 6
File: PROJ6_2.PAS

2. A dequeue might be described as a double-ended queue, that is, a structure in which elements may be inserted into or removed from either end. Implement a dequeue as a descendant object type having object type Queue as its ancestor.

Directory: CHAP 6
File: PROJ6_3.PAS

3. Write a program that simulates the operation of a busy airport that has only two runways to handle all takeoffs and landings. You may assume that each takeoff or landing takes 15 minutes to complete. One runway request is made during each five-minute time interval, and the likelihood of a landing request is the same as that of a takeoff request. Priority is given to planes requesting a landing. If a request cannot be honored, it is added to a takeoff or landing queue. Your program should simulate 120 minutes of activity at the airport. Each request for runway clearance should be time-stamped and added to the appropriate queue. The output from your program should include the final queue contents, the number of takeoffs completed, the number of landings completed, and the average number of minutes spent in each queue.

4. An operating system assigns jobs to print queues on the basis of the number of pages to be printed (fewer than 10 pages, fewer than 20 pages, or more than 20 pages but fewer than 50 pages). You may assume that the system printers can print 10 pages per minute. Smaller print jobs are printed before larger print jobs, and print jobs of the same priority are queued up in the order in which they are received. The system administrators would like to compare the time required to process a set of print jobs using one, two, or three system printers.

    Write a program that simulates processing 100 print jobs of varying lengths using one, two, or three printers. Assume that a print request is made every minute and that the number of pages to print varies from 1 to 50 pages. To be fair, you will need to process the same set of print jobs each time you add a printer.

The output from your program should indicate the order in which the jobs were received, the order in which they were printed, and the time required to process the set of print jobs. If more than one printer is being used, indicate the printer on which each job was printed.

Directory: CHAP 6
File: PROJ6_5.PAS

5. Write a menu-driven program that uses an array of queues to keep track of a group of executives as they are transferred from one department to another, get paid, or become unemployed. Executives within a department are paid on the basis of their seniority, the person who has been in the department the longest receiving the most money. Each person in the department receives $1000 in salary for each person in their department having less seniority than they have. People who are unemployed receive no compensation. Your program should be able to process the following set of commands:

```
Join <person> <department>: <person> added to
                       <department>
Quit <person>: <person> is removed from his or her
              department.
Change <person> <department>: <person> is moved from old
                department to <department> to become
                employee with least seniority.
Payroll: each executive's salary is computed and displayed
        by department in decreasing order of seniority.
```

Hint: To make searching more efficient, you might want to include a table that contains each executive's name and information on the location of the queue that contains his or her name.

CHAPTER SEVEN

Dynamic Data Structures and Lists

This chapter will discuss how Pascal can be used to create *dynamic data structures*. Dynamic data structures are data structures that expand and contract as a program executes. A dynamic data structure is a collection of elements (called *nodes*) that are records. In contrast to an array that always contains storage for a fixed number of elements, the number of records stored in a dynamic data structure changes as the program executes.

Dynamic data structures are extremely flexible. It is relatively easy to add new information by creating a new node and inserting it between two existing nodes. It is also relatively easy to delete a node.

Several examples of dynamic data structures are discussed in this chapter. These include lists, stacks, queues, and circular lists. You will learn how to store information in these data structures and how to process that information.

7.1 Pointers and the New Procedure

Before discussing dynamic data structures, we will introduce the pointer data type. We can declare variables (called *pointer variables*) whose types are pointer types. We can store the address of a data object in a pointer variable and, in this way, reference or access the data object through the pointer variable that points to it.

As an example, the type declaration

```
type
    RealPointer = ^Real;

var
    P : RealPointer;
    R : Real;
```

identifies `RealPointer` as the name of a data type. You should read the symbols "`^Real`" as "pointer to Real." The variable declaration specifies that `P` is a pointer variable of type `RealPointer`. This means that we can store the address of a type `Real` variable in `P`.

The statement

```
New (P);
```

calls the Pascal procedure `New` that allocates storage for a type `Real` value and places the address of this memory cell in pointer variable `P`. Once storage is allocated for the type `Real` value that is pointed to by `P`, we can store a value in that memory cell and manipulate it. The exact location in memory of this particular cell is immaterial.

We can represent the value of a pointer variable by an arrow drawn to a memory cell. The diagram

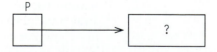

shows that pointer variable `P` points to a memory cell whose contents are unknown. This is the situation that exists just after `New (P)` is executed.

The symbols `P^` are used to reference the memory cell pointed to by pointer variable `P`. The symbol `^` (caret) is called the *dereferencing operator*. The assignment statement

```
P^ := 15.0
```

stores the `Real` value 15.0 data in memory cell P^ (the cell pointed to by P) as shown below.

The statement

```
Write (P^ :12:1)
```

displays the value (15.0) stored in memory cell P^. Note that the statements

```
P := 15.0;           {invalid assignment}
Write (P :12:1)      {invalid address display}
```

are both invalid because we cannot store a type `Real` value in pointer variable P, nor can we display the value (an address) of a pointer variable.

We are introducing pointer variables and pointer types now because they are used to create and access dynamic data structures. Later in this chapter, we will see how to use a pointer variable to reference a dynamic data structure and how to use pointer fields to connect the nodes of a dynamic data structure.

SYNTAX DISPLAY

Pointer Type Declaration

Form: type *ptype* = ^*dtype*;
Interpretation: Pointer type *ptype* is a data type whose values are memory cell addresses. A data object whose address is stored in a variable of type *ptype* must be type *dtype*.

SYNTAX DISPLAY

New Procedure

Form: New (*pvar*)
Example: New (P)
Interpretation: Storage for a new data object is allocated, and the address of this data object is stored in pointer variable *pvar*. The internal representation of this data object is determined by its data type. If *pvar* is type *ptype*, the type of the new data object is determined from the declaration for *ptype*. The symbol *pvar*^ is used to reference this data object.

Records with Pointer Fields

Since we don't know beforehand how many nodes will be in a dynamic data structure, we cannot allocate storage for a dynamic data structure in the conventional way, that is, through a variable declaration. Instead, we must allocate storage for each individual node as needed and somehow join this node to the rest of the structure.

We can connect two nodes if we include a pointer field in each node. The declarations

```
type
  String2 = string[2];

  ListPointer = ^Electric;
  Electric = record
               Current : String2;
               Volts : Integer;
               Link : ListPointer
             end; {Electric}

var
  P, Q, R : ListPointer;
```

identify `ListPointer` as a pointer type. A pointer variable of type `List-Pointer` points to a record of type `Electric` with three fields: `Current`, `Volts`, and `Link`. The `Link` field is also type `ListPointer`. We can use this field to point to the "next" node in a dynamic data structure. We will illustrate how to connect two nodes in the next section.

Note that the type declaration for `ListPointer` makes reference to the identifier `Electric`, which is not yet declared. The declaration of a pointer type is the only situation in which Pascal allows us to reference an undeclared identifier.

Variables `P`, `Q`, and `R` are pointer variables and may be used to reference records of type `Electric` (denoted by `P^`, `Q^`, and `R^`). An address can be stored in a pointer variable in one of two ways. The statements

```
New(P);
New(Q);
```

allocate storage for two records of type `Electric`. The memory address of the first of these records is stored in P, and the memory address of the second of these records is stored in Q. All three fields of these two nodes are initially undefined.

The assignment statements

```
P^.Current := 'AC'; P.Volts := 115;
Q^.Current := 'DC'; Q.Volts := 12;
```

define two fields of these nodes as shown in Fig. 7.1. The `Link` fields are still undefined. Note that it makes no difference where the arrow representing the value of a pointer variable touches its node.

Besides using a New statement, we can also use an assignment statement to store an address in a pointer variable. The *pointer assignment statement*

```
R := P;
```

copies the value of pointer variable P into pointer variable R. This means that pointers P and R contain the same memory address and therefore point to the same node, as shown in Fig. 7.2.

Figure 7.1
Nodes P^ and Q^

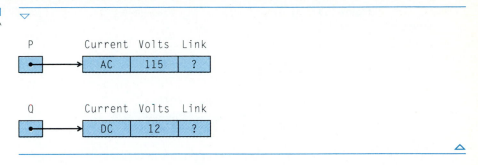

The pointer assignment statements

```
P := Q; Q := R;
```

would have the effect of exchanging the nodes pointed to by P and Q, as shown in Fig. 7.3.

The statement

```
WriteLn (Q^.Current, P^.Current);
```

displays the Current fields of the records pointed to by Q and P. For the situation depicted in Fig. 7.3 the line

```
ACDC
```

would be displayed.

The statement

```
New(Q);
```

changes the value of Q to the address of a new node, thereby disconnecting Q from its previous node. The data fields of the new node pointed to by Q are initially undefined; however, the statements

Figure 7.2
Nodes R^, P^, and Q^

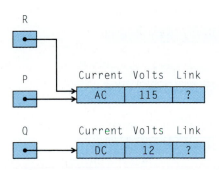

Figure 7.3
Nodes R^, Q^, and P^

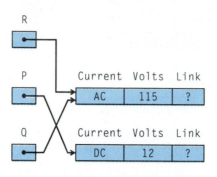

Figure 7.3
Nodes R^, Q^, and P^

```
Q^ := R;
Q^.Volts := 220;
```

copy the contents of node R^ to node Q^ and reset the Volts field to 220. Figure 7.4 shows the three nodes P^, Q^, and R^.

Pointers P, Q, and R are like subscripts in that they select a particular node or element of a data structure. However, unlike subscripts, their range of values is not declared, and their values (memory cell addresses) cannot be printed.

It is important that you understand the difference between using P and P^ in a program. P is a pointer variable (type ListPointer) and is used to store the address of a data structure of type Electric. P can be assigned a new value through a pointer assignment or execution of a New statement. P^ is the name of the record pointed to by P and can be manipulated like any other record in Pascal. The field selectors P^.Current and P^.Volts may

Figure 7.4
Nodes R^, Q^, and P^

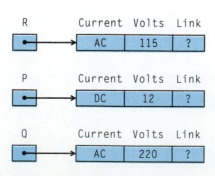

Figure 7.4
Nodes R^, Q^, and P^

be used to reference data (a string and an integer, respectively) stored in this record.

Connecting Nodes

One purpose of dynamically allocated nodes is to be able to build data structures of varying sizes. We can accomplish this by connecting individual nodes. If you look at the nodes allocated in the last section, you will see that their Link fields are undefined. Since the Link fields are type ListPointer, they can be used to store a memory cell address. The pointer assignment statement

```
R^.Link := P;
```

copies the address stored in P into the Link field of node R^, thereby connecting node R^ to node P^. Similarly, the pointer assignment statement

```
P^.Link := Q
```

copies the address stored in pointer variable Q into the Link field of node P^, thereby connecting node P^ to node Q^. The situation after execution of these two assignment statements is shown in Fig. 7.5. The arrows that represent the new values of R^.Link and P^.Link are shown in color. The label next to the arrow denotes one of the pointer assignments above.

The data structure pointed to by R now includes all three nodes. The first node is referenced by R^. The second node can be referenced by P^ or R^.Link^. Finally, the third node can be referenced by Q^, or P^.Link^, or even R^.Link^.Link^.

Figure 7.5
Connecting Nodes

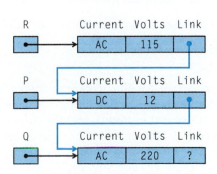

Self-Check

1. For Fig. 7.5, explain the effect of each of the following legal assignment statements.

    a. `R^.Current := 'CA'`   e. `R^.Link^.Volts := 0`
    b. `P^ := R^`   f. `P := R`
    c. `P.Current := 'HT'`   g. `R^.Link^.Link^.Current := 'XY'`
    d. `P := 54`   h. `Q^.Volts := R^.Volts`

2. The assignment statements

    ```
    R := P;    P := Q;    Q := R
    ```

    are used to exchange the values of pointer variables P and Q (type `ListPointer`). What do the following assignment statements do?

    ```
    R^.Current := P^.Current;
    P^.Current := Q^.Current;
    Q^.Current := R^.Current
    ```

Programming

1. Write a program segment that creates a collection of nodes and stores the musical scale (Do, Re, Mi, Fa, So, La, Ti, Do) in these nodes. Connect these nodes so that Do is stored in the first one, Re in the second, and so on.

7.2 Manipulating the Heap

In Section 7.1 you saw that a new record is created whenever the New procedure is executed. You may be wondering where in memory the new record is stored. Pascal maintains a storage pool of available memory cells called a *heap;* memory cells from this pool are allocated whenever procedure New is executed.

Effect of New Statement on the Heap

If P is a pointer variable of type `ListPointer` (declared in the last section), the statement

`New (P);`

allocates memory space for the storage of two characters, an integer variable, and an address. These cells are originally undefined (they retain whatever data were last stored in them), and the memory address of the first cell allocated is stored in P. The cells that have been allocated are no longer considered part of the heap. The only way to reference these cells is through pointer variable P (e.g., `P^.Current` or `P^.Volts` or `P^.Link`).

Figure 7.6
The Heap Before and After
New (P)

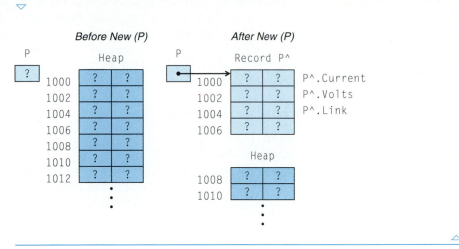

Figure 7.6 shows the pointer variable P and the heap before and after the execution of New (P). The before diagram shows pointer variable P as undefined before the execution of New (P). The after diagram shows P pointing to the first of eight bytes allocated for the new record (two bytes for the Current field, two bytes for the Volts field, and four bytes for the Link field).

As an example, if the memory cells with addresses 1000 through 2000 were originally in the heap, then after the execution of New (P) the memory cells with addresses 1000 through 1007 are no longer available to be allocated by New. The address 1000 would be stored in pointer variable P, and that cell would contain the first byte of P^.Current; memory cells 1002 and 1004 would contain the first byte of P^.Volts and P^.Link, respectively.

Returning Cells to the Heap

The procedure call statement

```
Dispose(P)
```

returns the memory cells pointed to by P to the heap. Unfortunately, in many implementations of Pascal the value of pointer variable P remains unchanged following the call to Dispose. This means that data that were formerly associated with P^ are still accessible in the heap. P is known as a *dangling reference* to this heap storage. Using P^ to access memory cells after they have been returned to the heap is a dangerous practice. The heap memory cells that were used to house the data associated with P^ may have been reallocated after they were returned to the heap, and referencing them through P may not be correct.

Often, more than one pointer will point to the same record. For this reason you must be careful in returning the storage occupied by a record to the heap. If these cells are reallocated after they are returned, errors may result if they are later referenced by another pointer that still points to them. Make sure that you have no need for a particular record before returning the storage that it occupies.

SYNTAX DISPLAY

The Dispose Procedure

Form: Dispose (*pvar*)

Example: Dispose (P)

Interpretation: The memory cells that make up the record whose address is stored in pointer *pvar* are returned to the heap. These cells may be reallocated when procedure New is called.

Exercises for Section 7.2   *Self-Check*

1.   What is a dangling reference?

Programming

1.   Do pointer values in Borland Pascal change following a call to Dispose? (*Hint:* place a pointer value in the Watch window, and see what value is displayed for the pointer variable.)

7.3   Linked Lists

This section will introduce an important data structure called a *linked list* or simply a *list*. We will see how to build and manipulate lists in Pascal.

A linked list (or list) is a sequence of nodes in which each node is linked or connected to the node following it. A list with three nodes is shown in Fig. 7.7. ListHeader is a record variable that contains a pointer to the first list element and a count of the number of elements in the list.

Each node in the list has two fields: the first field contains data, and the second field is a pointer (represented by an arrow) to the next list element. The last list element always has a diagonal line in its pointer field to indicate the end of the list.

Figure 7.7
Linked List with Three Nodes

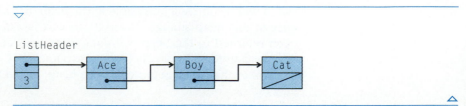

Figure 7.8
Inserting Node into
Linked List

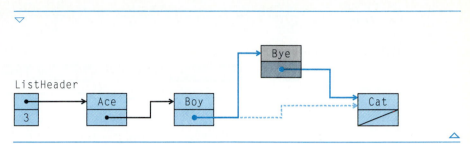

Lists are an important data structure because they can be modified easily. For example, a new node containing the string 'Bye' can be inserted
between the strings 'Boy' and 'Cat' by changing only one pointer value
(the one from 'Boy') and setting the pointer from the new node to point
to 'Cat'. This is true regardless of how many elements the list contains.
Figure 7.8 shows the list after the insertion; the old pointer values are
shown shaded in color.

Similarly, it is quite easy to delete a list element. Only one pointer value
has to be changed—the pointer that currently points to the element being
deleted. The linked list is redrawn as shown in Fig. 7.9 after deletion of the
string 'Boy' by changing the pointer from the node 'Ace'. The node containing the string 'Boy' is effectively disconnected from the list. The new list
consists of the strings 'Ace', 'Bye', and 'Cat'. Although these strings happen to be in alphabetical order, this is not required.

Representing Linked Lists by Using Pointers

The previous list is relatively easy to create in Pascal by using pointers and
dynamic allocation. In Section 7.1 we saw how to connect three nodes with
pointer fields. Although you didn't know it at the time, the data structure in
Fig. 7.5 could be considered a list of three nodes with pointer variable R as
the pointer to its head (see Fig. 7.10).

Figure 7.9
Deleting Node from
Linked List

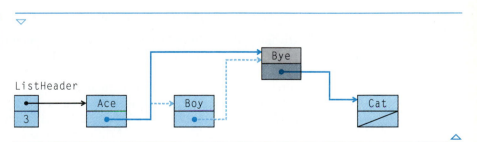

Figure 7.10
Linked List of Elements of
Type Electric

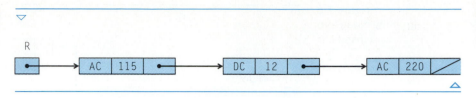

In Pascal the reserved word nil is a predefined value that may be assigned to any pointer variable. It is used to indicate that the pointer variable does not point to any memory cells on the heap. Normally, we assign this value to the pointer field of the last node in a list. After the assignment statement

```
Q^.Link := nil
```

is executed, the data structure shown in Fig. 7.10 represents a linked list of elements of type Electric. Each element has two data fields (Current and Volts) and one pointer field (Link). The pointer value nil is drawn as a diagonal line.

Traversing a List

In many list-processing operations we must process each node in the list in sequence; this is called *traversing* a list. To traverse a list, we must start at the list head and follow the list pointers.

One operation that we often perform on a data structure is displaying its contents. To display the contents of a list, we must display only the values of the information fields, not the link fields. Procedure PrintList in Fig. 7.11 displays the information fields of each node in the list shown in Fig. 7.10. The procedure call statement

```
PrintList (R)
```

displays the output lines

```
AC 115
DC 12
AC 220
```

In PrintList the statement

```
Head := Head^.Link     {advance to next node}
```

advances the pointer Head to the next list element, which is pointed to by the Link field of the current list element. This type of statement is very common in list-processing procedures and is analogous to incrementing an array subscript by 1 to advance to the next element. The while loop is exited when Head becomes nil. Since Head is a value parameter, a local copy of the pointer to the first list element is established when the procedure is entered. This local pointer is advanced; however, the corresponding pointer in the

Figure 7.11
Procedure PrintList

Directory: CHAP 7
File: PRINTLIS.PAS

```
procedure PrintList (Head {input} : ListPointer);
{
 Displays the list pointed to by Head.
 Pre : Head points to a list whose last node has a pointer
       field of nil.
 Post: The data fields of each list node is displayed.
}
begin {PrintList}
   {Traverse the list until the end is reached.}
   while Head <> nil do
     {invariant:
        No prior value of Head was nil.
     }
     begin
       WriteLn (Head^.Current, Head^.Volts :6);
       Head := Head.Link             {advance to next node}
     end {while}
end; {PrintList}
```

calling program remains unchanged. What would happen to our list if Head were a variable parameter?

Program Style

Warning About Variable Pointer Parameters

The last line above asks you to consider the effect of parameter Head being a variable parameter instead of a value parameter. We know that this will allow the procedure to change the corresponding actual parameter regardless of our intentions. In PrintList and many similar procedures the last value assigned to the pointer parameter is nil. If Head is a variable parameter, the corresponding actual parameter would be changed, thereby disconnecting it from the list that it pointed to before the procedure call. Disconnecting the node from the pointer passed as an actual parameter to a procedure has the effect of making all subsequent list nodes inaccessible to our program and thus losing the information stored in the list.

Representing Linked Lists Using Arrays

You can also represent a linked list as an array of records in which an Integer field stores the index of the next list element. Figure 7.12 shows the previous abstract list stored in an array (Circuits) whose elements are records (data type Electric). The last field of each record contains the index (subscript) of the next element. The variable R contains the subscript of the first list element. The three list nodes happen to be stored in array elements 2, 4,

Figure 7.12

Array Representation of a
Linked List

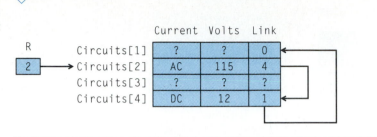

and 1, in that order, although any three elements could be used. Element 1 has a link field of 0, which indicates the end of the list.

Program Style

Storage Considerations for List Representations

Lists stored in arrays are just as easy to modify as lists that are created by using pointer variables. To insert or delete a list element, it is necessary to change only one or more subscript values. The disadvantage, however, is that memory space for the entire array must be allocated at one time. If a list is created by using pointer variables and dynamic allocation, then the size of the list in memory will grow and shrink as needed, and the storage allocated to it will change accordingly. For this reason we recommend implementing lists by using pointers.

Exercises for Section 7.3   ### Self-Check

1. For the array `Circuits` shown in Fig. 7.12, trace the execution of the following program fragment. What is printed?

    ```
    R := 2;
    while R <> 0 do
       begin
          WriteLn (Circuits[R].Current, Circuits[R].Volts);
          R := Circuits[R].Link
       end; {while}
    ```

Programming

1. Solve Programming Exercise 1 from Section 7.1 assuming that an array similar to `Circuits` is used to store the scale.

7.4   Linked List Abstract Data Type

In this section we provide the formal specification for a list abstract data type (`LinkListADT`) and show how to implement it by using pointer variables. Table 7.1 shows the formal specification.

Structure

A list consists of a linked collection of elements preceded by a header record. The header record consists of a pointer (Head) to the first list element, a pointer (Cursor) to the currently active list element, and a count of the number of elements in the list. Each list element contains an information part (type ListData) and a pointer to its successor in the list.

Operators

For the following descriptions, assume the parameters:

```
El (pronounced el) has data type ListData.
Success is a Boolean flag indicating success (True) or
   failure (False) of an operation.
Visit is a procedure type with formal parameter of
   object type ListData.
```

LinkList.CreateList	Creates an empty list. Must be called before any other operators.
LinkList.GetSize	(function) Returns the number of elements currently in the list.
LinkList.IsEmpty	(function) Returns True if the list is empty; otherwise, returns False.
LinkList.Search (El, var Success)	Searches a list to find the element that matches data element El (as determined by function ListData.-IsEqual). If found, Success is set to True, and the data member Cursor is set to point to that list element; otherwise, Cursor is not changed.
LinkList.Insert (El)	Inserts item El as the information part of a new list element pointed to by data member Cursor. The successor of the new list element is the one that was previously pointed to by Cursor. If cursor is nil, inserts El as the information part of the first list element and points Cursor to it.
LinkList.InsertAfter (El)	Inserts item El as the information part of a new list element that will be the successor of the one initially pointed to by data member Cursor and advances Cursor to the new list element. If Cursor is nil, inserts El as the information part of the first list element and points Cursor to it.

LinkList.InsertAtEnd (El)	Inserts item El as the last node in the list. If the list is empty, El is inserted as the information portion of the first node in the list. In both cases, Cursor is set to point to the node containing El.
LinkList.Retrieve (var El, var Success)	Returns through El the list element pointed to by Cursor and sets Success to True. Sets Success to False if Cursor is nil.
LinkList.Delete	Deletes the list element pointed to by Cursor, resets Cursor to point to the deleted element's successor, and returns its storage space to the heap. If Cursor is nil, no list element is deleted.
LinkList.InitCursor	Sets data member Cursor to point to the first list element. If the list is empty, Cursor is set to nil.
LinkList.Advance	Advances data member Cursor to the next list element. If Cursor is pointing to the last list element, no change is made.
LinkList.AtEnd (function)	Returns True if data member Cursor is nil or is pointing to the last list element; otherwise, returns False.
LinkList.Traverse (Visit)	Applies procedure Visit to each list element in sequence starting with the first.

Using the Linked List ADT

A number of points in Table 7.1 should be clarified. Linked list `MyList` is shown in Fig. 7.13. The information part is a string of three characters. The current list element (as denoted by `Cursor`) is the one containing the string `'Boy'`.

If `MyData` has type `ListData`, the message

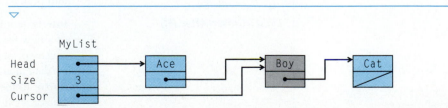

Figure 7.14
MyList After Deleting
Node

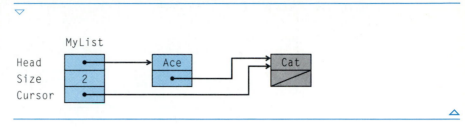

`MyList.Retrieve (MyData)`

stores string `'Boy'` in MyData, but the list will be unchanged.
The message

`MyList.Delete`

deletes the element pointed to by `Cursor`, changing the list as shown in Fig. 7.14.
The message

`MyList.InitCursor`

will reset the cursor to point to the first node, as shown in Fig. 7.15.
If MyData is type ListData and contains the string `'Cat'`, either message in Fig. 7.16 will move the cursor to the second node.
We are assuming that `Search` calls method member `ListData.IsEqual` to compare the *target string* `'Cat'` to the information part of each node, starting with the first. If `MyData` contains the string `'Boy'`, the message

`MyList.Insert (MyData)`

will insert the string `'Boy'` in the second position, changing the list back to the original form shown in Fig. 7.13 (see Fig. 7.17).
Finally, if `MyData` contains the string `'Cap'`, the message

`MyList.InsertAfter (MyData)`

changes the list as shown in Fig. 7.18. The new list element is inserted after the one currently pointed to by `Cursor`, and `Cursor` is advanced to the new list element.

Figure 7.15
MyList After Calling
InitCursor

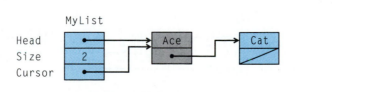

Figure 7.16
MyList *After Advancing
the Cursor*

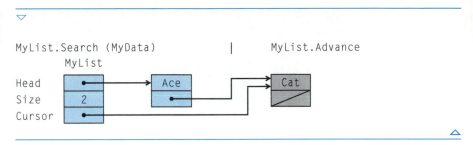

Method member Traverse processes the list elements in sequence and applies procedure parameter Visit to each list element. If Visit has a formal parameter of type ListData and calls ListData.Display (a method member that displays an object instance of type ListData), the result of MyList.Traverse on the list above would be

```
Ace
Boy
Cap
Cat
```

We will discuss procedures as parameters when we implement method member Traverse.

CASE STUDY   **Building a Linked List from Input Data**

Figure 7.19 shows a program that builds and displays a linked list consisting of string data. The list method member Insert causes the list elements to be stored in the same sequence as they would be in a stack (the last string read is stored in the first list element). To allow procedure DisplayNodeInfo to be passed as an actual parameter to method LinkList.Traverse, we tell Borland Pascal to compile it by using its far call model. To do this, we place the compiler directive far after the procedure heading.

Figure 7.17
MyList *After Call to
Insert*

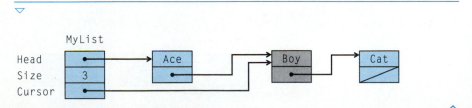

Figure 7.18
MyList After Call to
InsertAfter

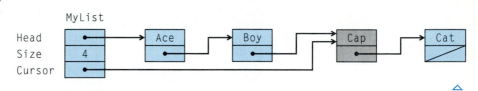

Figure 7.19
Building and Displaying a
Linked List

Directory: CHAP 7
File: LISTSTAC.PAS

```
program ListLikeStack;
{
 Builds a linked list in stack form.

 Imports: LinkList object from unit LinkListADT and
          ListData object from unit ListDataADT.
}
  uses LinkListADT, ListDataADT;

  var
    MyList : LinkList;      {list being created and displayed}
    MyData : ListData;      {input - each data element}
    Success : Boolean;      {flag - indicates search result}

  procedure DisplayNodeInfo (Info {input} : ListData); far;
  {
   Procedure to be applied to each list node by method
   LinkList.Traverse.
   Pre : Info is defined.
   Post: Display contents of one list node.

   Note: Parameter list must be compatible with declaration
         of ProcedureType in unit LinkListADT.
  }
  begin {DisplayNodeInfo}
    WriteLn ('This node contains: ');
    Info.Display
  end; {DisplayNodeInfo}

begin {ListLikeStack}
  MyList.CreateList;

  {Read and insert the list elements.}
  WriteLn ('Enter list values—use ', Sentinel, ' to stop:');
  MyData.ReadInfo;
  while MyData.GetInfo <> Sentinel do
    begin
      MyList.Insert (MyData);
      MyData.ReadInfo
    end; {while}
```

▷ ▷ ▷ ▷ ▷ ▷

```
        {Search for an element.}
        WriteLn;
        WriteLn ('Enter a string to seach for.');
        MyData.ReadInfo;
        MyList.Search (MyData, Success);
        if Success then
          begin
            Write ('Found ');
            MyList.Retrieve (MyData, Success);
            MyData.Display
          end
        else
          WriteLn ('Not found');

        {Display list size and the list.}
        WriteLn;
        WriteLn ('The size of the list is ', MyList.GetSize :1);
        WriteLn;
        WriteLn ('The list elements follow:');
        MyList.Traverse (DisplayNodeInfo)

end. {ListLikeStack}

Enter list values—use *** to stop:
Enter one list element value> abc
Enter one list element value> def
Enter one list element value> ghi
Enter one list element value> 000
Enter one list element value> 999
Enter one list element value> XXX
Enter one list element value> ***

Enter a string to seach for.
Enter one list element value> 000
Found 000
The size of the list is 6

The list elements follow:
This node contains:
XXX
This node contains:
999
This node contains:
000
This node contains:
ghi
This node contains:
def
This node contains:
abc
```

7.5 Implementing ListDataADT

In this section we write `ListDataADT`. We will not bother with a formal specification; we will simply provide the Borland Pascal unit that implements this abstract data type (see Fig. 7.20). The interface section shows that the information part of a list element is a three-character string and the string value `'***'` is reserved as a sentinel. Obviously, we can read, write, and compare strings without using these methods. However, we want to show what would be needed in general.

Figure 7.20
Unit `ListDataADT`

Directory: CHAP 7
File: LISTDAT1.PAS

```
unit ListDataADT;
{
 Implements object type ListData for a list whose list elements
 have an information field that is type string[3].
}
interface

    const
        Sentinel = '***';              {the sentinel string}

    type
        InfoType = string[3];

        ListData = object
                    procedure Init (Item {input} : InfoType);
                    procedure ReadInfo;
                    procedure Display;
                    function GetInfo : InfoType;
                    function IsEqual (Item : ListData) : Boolean;
                    function LessThan (Item : ListData) : Boolean;

                private
                    Info : InfoType;
                end; {ListData}

implementation

    procedure ListData.Init (Item : InfoType);
    {
     Initializes instance of object ListData.
     Pre : Item is defined.
     Post: Data field Info is set to Item.
    }
    begin {Init}
        Info := Item
    end; {Init}
```

▷ ▷ ▷ ▷ ▷ ▷

```
procedure ListData.ReadInfo;
{
 Prompts user to enter values to initialize data field Info
 for ListData object.
 Pre : None.
 Post: Data field Info contains input string.
}
begin {ReadInfo}
  Write ('Enter one list element value> ');
  ReadLn (Info)
end; {ReadInfo}

procedure ListData.Display;
{
 Displays data field values for instance of object ListData.
 Pre : Object is initialized.
 Post: Displays contents of Info.
}
begin {Display}
  WriteLn (Info)
end; {Display}

function ListData.GetInfo : InfoType;
{
 Returns value of data field Info.
}
begin {GetInfo}
  GetInfo := Info
end; {GetInfo}

function ListData.IsEqual (Item : ListData) : Boolean;
{
 Compares Info data field to Item.Info data field to test
 for equality.
 Pre : Object initialized and Item defined.
 Post: Returns True if Self.Info = Item.Info;
       otherwise returns False.
}
begin {IsEqual}
  IsEqual := (Info = Item.Info)
end; {IsEqual}

function ListData.LessThan (Item : ListData) : Boolean;
{
 Stub for method ListData.LessThan. Implementation left
 as programming exercise.
}
begin {LessThan}
end; {LessThan}

end. {ListDataADT}
```

If `MyData` and `Item` are instances of object type ListData, the message

```
MyData.IsEqual(Item)
```

compares the string stored in data member `MyData.Info` to the string stored in data member `Item.Info`. It returns True if the strings are equal. If `InfoType` were a record type instead of just a string type, method `IsEqual` would need to compare one field (called the *record key*) to determine whether there was a match between its parameter and the object instance that called it. The message

```
MyData.LessThan(Item)
```

returns `True` if the string in `MyData.Info` is less than the string in Item.Info.

Implementing LinkListADT

In this section we implement unit `LinkListADT`. We start with the interface section that appears in Fig. 7.21. You will notice that Object LinkList has two additional pointer fields (`Prev` and `Rear`) that point to the node that precedes `Cursor` in the list and the last node in the list, respectively. We will explain the purpose of these pointers later in this section.

Figure 7.21
Interface Section for Unit
`LinkListADT`

Directory: CHAP 7
File: LINKLIST.PAS

```
unit LinkListADT;
{
 Abstract data type LinkList: contains declarations for data
 type LinkList and its methods.
}
interface

  uses ListDataADT;        {Import object type ListData}

  type
    ListPointer = ListElement;
    ListElement = record                    {a list element}
                    ListInfo : ListData;   {information part}
                    Successor : ListPointer
                  end;

    ProcedureType = procedure (P : ListData);
```

▷ ▷ ▷ ▷ ▷ ▷

```
LinkList = object                               {a linked list}
            procedure CreateList;
            function GetSize : Word;
            function IsEmpty : Boolean;
            procedure Search
                        (El {input} : ListData;
                         var Success {output} : Boolean);
            procedure Insert (El {input} : ListData);
            procedure InsertAfter (El {input} : ListData);
            procedure InsertAtEnd (El {input} : ListData);
            procedure Retrieve
                        (var El {output} : ListData;
                         var {output} Success : Boolean);
            procedure Delete;
            procedure InitCursor;
            function AtEnd : Boolean;
            procedure Advance;
            procedure Traverse (Visit: ProcedureType);

        private
          Head, Cursor, Prev, Rear : ListPointer;
          Size : Word;
          procedure DoSearch
                        (El {input} : ListData;
                         ListHead {input} : ListPointer;
                         var Success {output} : Boolean);
        end; {LinkList}
```

Implementing the Methods for LinkListADT

We will show the implementation section in stages. Figure 7.22 shows
method members CreateList, GetSize, IsEmpty, InitCursor, Advance,
and AtEnd. All are relatively straightforward and require little explanation.
Procedure CreateList creates an empty list that contains a Size field of 0.
As shown, pointers Head, Prev, Cursor, and Rear are also set to nil when
the list is empty.

Figure 7.22
Methods CreateList,
GetSize, IsEmpty,
InitCursor, Advance,
and AtEnd

```
implementation
  procedure LinkList.CreateList;
  {
    Creates an empty list.
    Pre : None.
    Post: Head, Prev, Cursor, Rear are nil and Size is 0.
  }
```

▷ ▷ ▷ ▷ ▷ ▷

```
begin {CreateList}
  Head := nil;
  Prev := nil;
  Cursor := nil;
  Rear := nil;
  Size := 0
end; {CreateList}

function LinkList.GetSize : Word;
{
 Returns the number of elements currently in the list.
}
begin {GetSize}
  GetSize := Size
end; {GetSize}

function LinkList.IsEmpty : Boolean;
{
 Returns True if the list is empty; otherwise, returns
 False.
}
begin {IsEmpty}
  IsEmpty := (Size = 0)
end; {IsEmpty}

procedure LinkList.InitCursor;
{
 Sets Cursor to point to the first list element.
 Pre : List is defined and non-empty.
 Post: Cursor set to point to first list element and Prev set
       to nil, since first list element has no predecessor.
}
begin {InitCursor}
  Cursor := Head;
  Prev := nil
end; {InitCursor}

function LinkList.AtEnd : Boolean;
{
 Returns True if Cursor is nil or is pointing to the last
 list element; otherwise, returns False.
}
begin {AtEnd}
   if Cursor = nil then          {empty list}
      AtEnd := True
   else if Cursor^.Successor = nil then
      AtEnd := True
   else
      AtEnd := False
end; {AtEnd}

procedure LinkList.Advance;
```

▷ ▷ ▷ ▷ ▷

```
{
 Advances Cursor to the next list element.
 Pre : Object initialized.
 Post: Cursor set to next list element, Prev points to old
       Cursor position.
}
begin {Advance}
  if Cursor <> nil then
    begin
      Prev := Cursor;                {Save cursor value}
      Cursor := Cursor^.Successor {Advance to next element}
    end {if}
end; {Advance}
```

The only methods in Fig. 7.22 that may need clarification are AtEnd and Advance. AtEnd returns True if the list is empty (Cursor is nil) or if the successor of the current list element is nil. In Advance, the statement

```
Cursor := Cursor^.Successor    {Advance to next element}
```

advances Cursor to the next element or becomes nil.

Method Retrieve

Figure 7.23 shows procedure Retrieve. The statement

Figure 7.23
Method Retrieve

Directory: CHAP 7
File: LINKLIST.PAS

```
procedure LinkList.Retrieve
                      (var El {output} : ListData;
                       var Success {output} : Boolean);
{
 Retrieves linked list element pointed to by Cursor.
 Pre : Linked list initialized.
 Post: Returns through El the list element that Cursor points
       to and sets Success to True. Sets Success to False if
       Cursor is nil.
}
begin {Retrieve}
  if Cursor = nil then
    Success := False
  else
    begin
      El := Cursor^.ListInfo;     {store list data in El}
      Success := True
    end {if}
end; {Retrieve}
```

```
El := Cursor^.ListInfo; {store list data in El}
```

extracts the information part of the list element pointed to by Cursor and stores it in El. Retrieve does not modify the linked list.

Method Traverse

Figure 7.24 shows procedure Traverse. The parameter list indicates that Visit is of type ProcedureType (declared in unit LinkListADT as a procedure that has a single parameter of type ListData). The message

```
MyList.Traverse (DisplayNodeInfo)
```

causes procedure DisplayNodeInfo (part of client program) to be applied to each element of list MyList. The local pointer variable Next advances down the list until it reaches the end of the list. To be able to pass procedure DisplayNodeInfo as an actual parameter to method MyList.Traverse, Borland Pascal requires us to compile DisplayNodeInfo with the far compiler directive as shown in Fig. 7.19.

Method InsertAfter

Method InsertAfter (see Fig. 7.25) inserts item El as the information part of the list element pointed to by Cursor. There are two cases: the list is

Figure 7.24
Method Traverse

Directory: CHAP 7
File: LINKLIST.PAS

```
procedure LinkList.Traverse (Visit : ProcedureType);
{
 Applies the procedure Visit to each list element in sequence
 starting with the first.
 Pre : Linked list is initialized. Procedure Visit was compiled
       using the Borland Pascal far code model in any client
       program using unit LinkListADT.
 Post: Visit has been applied each list node.
}
 var
   Next : ListPointer;              {pointer to next list element}

begin {Traverse}
  Next := Head;                     {start with first element}
  while Next <> nil do
    begin
      {Perform procedure Visit on list node information field}
      Visit (Next^.ListInfo);
      Next := Next^.Successor       {advance down the list}
    end {while}
end; {Traverse}
```

```
procedure LinkList.InsertAfter (El {input} : ListData);
{
 Inserts item El as the information part of a new list element
 which will be the successor of the one initially pointed to
 by data member Cursor.
 Pre : List is initialized.
 Post: Advances Cursor to the new list element and set Prev
       to old value of Cursor. If Cursor is nil, inserts El
       as the information part of the first list element and
       points Cursor to it; Prev is set to nil. Increments
       Size.
}
  var
    RestOfList : ListPointer;  {sublist after insertion point}

begin {InsertAfter}
  if Cursor = nil then
    begin {empty list}
      New (Head);                    {allocate first list element}
      Cursor := Head;                      {Point Cursor to it}
      RestOfList := nil
    end {if}
  else
    begin
      {Save the new element's successor}
      RestOfList := Cursor^.Successor;
      {Link new list element to current element}
      New (Cursor^.Successor);
      Prev := Cursor;                      {save cursor position}
      Cursor := Cursor^.Successor     {set Cursor to new node}
    end; {else}

  Cursor^.ListInfo := El;             {store El in new element}
  Cursor^.Successor^ := RestOfList;   {link it to rest of list}
  Size := Size + 1;

  {Update Rear if new node is at end of list}
  if AtEnd then
    Rear := Cursor
end; {InsertAfter}
```

empty (`Cursor` is `nil`) or the list is not empty. If the list is empty, the statements

```
New (Head);        {allocate first list element}
Cursor := Head;            {Point Cursor to it}
RestOfList := nil
```

execute. Their effect is shown in Fig. 7.26.

Figure 7.26
The Effect of
`MyList.InsertAfter`
When `MyList` Is `Empty`

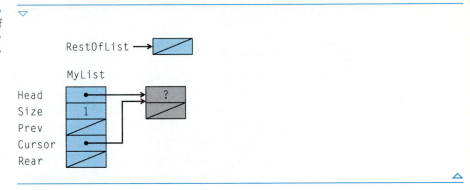

If the list is not empty, the statements labeled

```
RestOfList := Cursor^.Successor;
New (Cursor^.Successor);
Prev := Cursor;                      {save cursor position}
Cursor := Cursor^.Successor          {set Cursor to new node}
```

execute. Their effect is shown in Fig. 7.27. First, `RestOfList` is set to point to part of the list that follows the element initially pointed to by `Cursor`. Then we allocate a new list element and link it to the element pointed to by `Cursor` (data `'Ace'`). Next we set `Prev` to point to the node that was initially pointed to by `Cursor` and advance `Cursor` to the new element.

After the if statement executes, the information part and successor fields of the new node are defined by the statements

```
Cursor^.ListInfo := El;              {store El in new element}
Cursor^.Successor := RestOfList;     {link it to rest of list}
```

For Fig. 7.26 the effect is to set the `Successor` field of the new node to nil; for Fig. 7.27 the effect is to link the `Successor` field of the new element to the rest of the list. If `El` is `'Boy'`, the list would consist of the strings `'Ace'`,

Figure 7.27
The Effect of
`MyList.InsertAfter`
When `MyList` Is Not
`Empty`

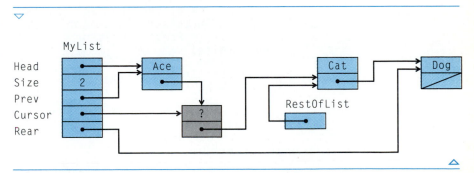

'Boy', 'Cat', and 'Dog'. Since the new node is not the last list node, Rear is not updated.

Method Insert

Next, we implement method Insert (see Fig. 7.28). Insert takes advantage of the fact that the location of the predecessor of the node pointed to by Cursor is pointed to by Prev. There are two special cases to check for that will require us to insert the new element at the head of the list. This happens if the list is empty or if Cursor is pointing to the first list element (in both cases, Cursor equals Head). In both these cases a new node is allocated, and Head must be reset to point to it. If the new node is not being inserted at the head of the list, then it must be inserted between the elements pointed to by

Figure 7.28
Method Insert

Directory: CHAP 7
File: LINKLIST.PAS

```
procedure LinkList.Insert (El {input} : ListData);
{
  Inserts item El as the information part of a new list element
  pointed to by data member Cursor.
  Pre : List object initialized and El defined.
  Post: The successor of the new list element is the one that
        was previously pointed to by Cursor. If Head is nil or
        Head equals Cursor, inserts El as the information part
        of the first list element and points Cursor to it.
}
begin {Insert}
  if Cursor = Head then
    begin {insert new Head}
      New (Head);                  {connect new element to Head}
      Head^.Successor := Cursor;   {connect it to rest of list}
      Cursor := Head;              {reset Cursor}
    end {if}
  else
    begin {insert between Prev and Cursor}
      {Allocate new node and Connect to predecessor}
      New (Prev^.Successor);
      {Link new element to rest of list}
      Prev^.Successor^.Successor := Cursor;
      Cursor := Prev^.Successor                {Reset Cursor}
    end; {else}

  Cursor^.ListInfo := El;          {store El in new element}
  Size := Size + 1;

  {Update Rear if new node at end of list}
  if AtEnd then
    Rear := Cursor
end; {Insert}
```

Figure 7.29
Inserting a List Element at
`Cursor`

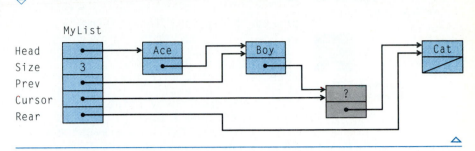

Prev and Cursor. In all three cases, `Cursor` must be reset to point to the new list element.

Figure 7.29 shows the effect of the statements

```
New (Prev^.Successor);
Prev^.Successor^.Successor := Cursor;
Cursor := Prev^.Successor                        {Reset Cursor}
```

the list containing the string `'Ace'`, `'Boy'`, and `'Cat'` if the `Cursor` was initially pointing to the node containing `'Cat'`. After the if statement executes, the information part of the new list element is defined, and `Size` is incremented to 4. Since the new node was not added to the end of the list shown in Fig. 7.29, we will not need to update `Rear`.

Method InsertAtEnd

Method `InsertAtEnd` will be useful when we want to use queuelike lists. Its implementation is shown in Fig. 7.30. There are two cases to account for in this algorithm: inserting a node into an empty list and inserting a new last node after the last node in a nonempty list. A new node inserted into an empty list is both the first and last node in the list. The statements that are required to add a new last node following the node pointed to by `Rear` are similar to those used in `InsertAfter` (Fig. 7.25) to add a new node following the node pointed to by `Cursor`.

Method Search

Procedure `Search` requires moving down the list until we reach the element whose information part matches the procedure parameter. From the programmer's perspective, many list operations are more conveniently implemented as recursive algorithms. A recursive algorithm for Search follows.

Recursive Search Algorithm

1. if the list is empty then
   2.   The target is not in the list
   else if the target matches the first list element then

Figure 7.30
Method InsertAtEnd

**Directory: CHAP 7
File: LINKLIST.PAS**

```
procedure LinkList.InsertAtEnd (El {input} : ListData);
{
 Inserts item El as the information part of a new list element
 pointed to by data member Cursor.
 Pre : List object initialized and El defined.
 Post: The successor of the new list element is the one that
       was previously pointed to by Cursor. If Head is nil or
       Head equals Cursor, inserts El as the information part
       of the first list element and points Cursor to it.
}
begin {InsertAtEnd}
  if Head = nil then                    {test for empty list}
    begin {insert new Head}
      New (Head);                       {connect new element to Head}
      Head^.Successor := nil;
      Cursor := Head                    {reset Cursor}
    end {if}
  else
    begin {insert after last node}
      {Save location of last node}
      Prev := Rear;
      {Allocate new node and Connect to predecessor}
      New (Rear^.Successor);
      {Mark last element as end of list}
      Rear^.Successor^.Successor := nil;
      Cursor := Prev^.Successor                   {reset Cursor}
    end; {else}

  Cursor^.ListInfo := El;               {store El in new element}
  Size := Size + 1;
  Rear := Cursor            {set Rear to point to new last node}
end; {InsertAtEnd}
```

3. The target has been located
else if the list has just one element then
4. The element has been checked and does not match target
else
5. Search for the target in the rest of the list

Steps 2, 3, and 4 are stopping states, and Step 5 is the recursive step. We will implement this algorithm in a helper procedure (DoSearch), which will be called by Search (see Fig. 7.31). Search simply starts DoSearch off at the head of the initial list, and DoSearch does the rest. In DoSearch the condition

```
ListHead = nil
```

checks for an empty list. If the list is empty, Success is set to False. If the list is not empty, the message

```
ListHead^.ListInfo.IsEqual(El)
```

compares the first list element to El. If there is a match, Success is set to True. The value assigned to Success is returned to Search after we unwind from the recursion. If there is no match, the condition

```
ListHead^.Successor = Head
```

checks for a one-element list. Since we have already compared its information part to El, there is no need to continue the search. If these conditions are all false, the method calls

```
Advance;
DoSearch (El, Cursor, Success)
```

search to look for El in the rest of the list after advancing the values of Cursor and Prev.

Figure 7.31

Methods DoSearch and Search

Directory: CHAP 7
File: LINKLIST.PAS

```
procedure LinkList.DoSearch (El {input} : ListData;
                             ListHead {input} : ListPointer;
                             var Success {output} : Boolean);
{
 Helper procedure called by Search to perform the work of
 the search.
 Pre : List object initialized, El is Defined, and ListHead
       points to same node as Cursor.
 Post: Returns True if the element at the head of the list
       pointed to by ListHead matches El and points data
       field Cursor to the element containing El and Prev to
       its predecessor. Returns False when the list is empty
       or contains one element that was not matched.
}
begin {DoSearch}
  if ListHead = nil then
    {Empty list — no match possible}
    Success := False
  else if ListHead^.ListInfo.IsEqual(El) then
    {Element at list head matches El}
    Success := True
  else if ListHead^.Successor = nil then
    {One element list — not matched}
    Success := False
  else
    begin
      {Search remainder of the list}
      Advance;
      DoSearch (El, Cursor, Success)
    end {else}
end; {DoSearch}
```

▷ ▷ ▷ ▷ ▷

```
procedure LinkList.Search (El {input} : ListData;
                       var Success {output} : Boolean);
{
 Searches a list to find the element that matches data element
 El (as determined by function ListData.IsEqual).
 Pre : List is initialized and El defined.
 Post: If found, Success is set to True and the data field
        Cursor is set to point to that list element and Prev
        is set to point to its predecessor; otherwise, Success
        is set to False and neither Cursor or Prev are changed.
}
begin {Search}
  {Start search at list head}
  InitCursor;
  DoSearch (El, Cursor, Success)
end; {Search}
```

Notice that the order of the conditions in `DoSearch` is extremely important. The value of `ListHead^` is undefined when `ListHead` is `nil`. We must also check for a one-element list before advancing `Cursor` and `Prev`. Figure 7.32 traces the progress of `MyList.Search` when searching for the string `'Cat'`. It shows the list whose first element (in color) is compared to `'Cat'` during each recursive call.

Method Delete

In procedure `Delete` (see Fig. 7.33) we take advantage of the fact that Prev points to the predecessor of the list element to be deleted (pointed to by `Cursor`). To perform the deletion, we must change the `Successor` field of the predecessor element. There is one special case to be considered, namely, deleting the first (and perhaps only) element from the list.

The first condition in `Delete` checks to see whether we are deleting the first list element and updates the values of `Cursor` and `Head` to accomplish the deletion. To delete a node later in the list, the statement

```
Prev^.Successor := Cursor^.Successor;
```

deletes the intended element by resetting its predecessor's Successor pointer to point to the rest of the list. The old `Cursor` value is temporarily saved in `ToBeDeleted`, and `Cursor` is advanced to the successor of the deleted element. Next, `Delete` returns the storage occupied by the deleted element to the heap and decrements `Size` by 1. If the last list element is deleted, then the value of `Rear` must be reset.

Figure 7.34 shows the effect of `Delete` on `MyList`. The element containing `'Boy'` is deleted.

Figure 7.32
Trace of `DoSearch`

Initial call: Compare 'Cat' to 'Ace'

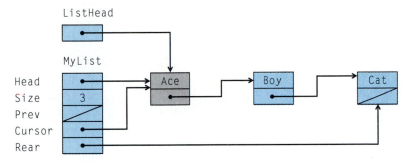

Second call: Compare 'Cat' to 'Boy'

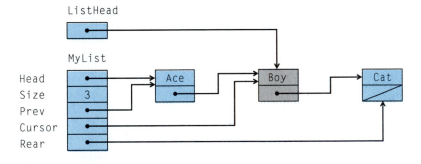

Third call: Compare 'Cat' to 'Cat' — set Success to True

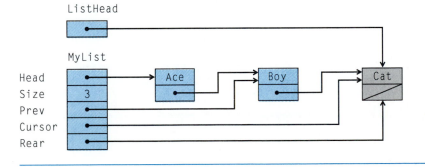

Analysis of Linked List ADT

We added the two pointer fields (`Prev` and `Rear`) to our implementation of our linked list ADT to avoid several costly searches for the predecessor of the currently active node (`Cursor`) and the final list node. `Rear` is used to speed

```
procedure LinkList.Delete;
{
 Deletes the list element pointed to by Cursor.
 Pre : List object initialized.
 Post: Resets Cursor to point to the deleted element's
       successor and returns its storage space to the heap.
       If the list is empty, no list element is deleted.
}
  var
    ToBeDeleted : ListPointer;       {Item to be deleted}

begin {Delete}
  if Size <> 0 then                  {non-empty list?}
    begin
      if Cursor = Head then          {first element}
        begin
          {Save position of node to delete}
          ToBeDeleted := Head;
          {Advance Cursor to next list position}
          Cursor := Cursor.Successor;
          {Make head point to new first node}
          Head := Cursor
        end {first element}
      else
        begin
          {Connect predecessor to rest of list}
          Prev^.Successor := Cursor.Successor;
          {Save position of Node to delete}
          ToBeDeleted := Cursor;
          {Advance Cursor to next list element}
          Cursor := Cursor^.Successor
        end; {else}

      Dispose (ToBeDeleted);         {Dispose node being deleted.}
      Size := Size - 1;

      {Update Rear if last list node was deleted}
      if Cursor = nil then
        Rear := Prev
    end {non-empty list}
end; {Delete}
```

up `InsertAtEnd` by eliminating the need to search for the last list element. Prev is used to speed up `Insert`, `InsertAtEnd`, and `Delete` by eliminating the search for the current node's predecessor. These two pointer fields (`Prev` and `Rear`) do not take up much computer memory, and maintaining them is

Figure 7.34
Deleting the List Element
Containing 'Boy'

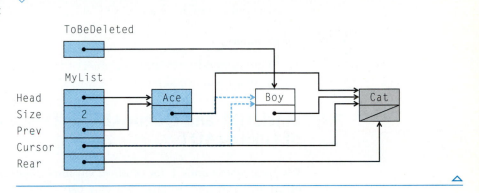

fairly easy. As we show in Table 7.2, without these two pointers, several operators (Insert, InsertAfter, Delete) that have O(1) complexity would have O(N) complexity.

Table 7.2
Complexity of Several
Linked List Operators

	With Pointers Prev and Rear	Without Pointers Prev and Rear
Search	O(N)	O(N)
Insert	O(1)	O(N)
InsertAfter	O(1)	O(1)
InsertAtEnd	O(1)	O(N)
Delete	O(1)	O(N)

Program Style

Prohibiting Direct Access to Internal List Pointers

Notice that none of the methods returns the value of Cursor directly to a client. This is as it should be. Cursor is an internal list pointer that keeps track of the current "state" of any list-processing operation. It would be a bad software practice to return internal pointers to a client program. That would allow the client to change the state or perhaps modify the list in an unauthorized or unexpected way. It is much better to require internal pointers to be referenced through methods that you supply, such as Init and Advance, so that you can control how they are used.

Exercises for Section 7.5   **Self-Check**

1. Program ListStack in Fig. 7.19 builds a LIFO list. Explain how you would have to modify it to get it to build a FIFO list.

2. How would you implement methods Insert and Delete without using data field `Prev` in object `LinkList`.

Programming

1. Write method `LessThan` for object `ListData`.
2. Write a recursive version of `LinkList.Traverse`.

7.6 StackADT and QueueADT as Descendants of LinkListADT

We have spent quite a bit of effort on implementing LinkListADT. Now this effort will pay off because we can use object LinkList as the ancestor of linked stack and queue objects.

A New Stack Object

We can consider a stack as a linked list in which all insertions and deletions take place at the list head. Figure 7.35 shows our new unit `StackADT`. Object `Stack` contains all the method members previously shown in Figs. 5.15 and 5.19 except for `IsEmpty`. `IsEmpty` is inherited from object type `LinkList`. The stack object does not contain any data members of its own.

Figure 7.35
Stack as a Descendant of
`LinkList`

Directory: CHAP 7
File: STACKADT.PAS

```
unit StackADT;
{
  Abstract data type Stack: contains declarations for object
  Stack and its methods.

  Imports: Object ListData from unit ListDataADT and object
           LinkList from unit ListDataADT.
}
interface

  uses LinkListADT, ListDataADT;

  type
    Stack = object (LinkList)
              procedure CreateStack;
              procedure Push (X {input} : ListData;
                              var {output} Success : Boolean);
              procedure Pop (var X {output} : ListData;
                             var Success {output}: Boolean);
              procedure Retrieve
                          (var X {output} : ListData;
                           var Success {output} : Boolean);
```

▷ ▷ ▷ ▷ ▷ ▷

```
            function IsFull : Boolean;
        end; {Stack}

implementation

  procedure Stack.CreateStack;
  {
   Initialize empty stack.
   Pre : None.
   Post: Stack object initialized.
  }
  begin {CreateStack}
    CreateList
  end; {CreateStack}

  procedure Stack.Push (X {input} : ListData;
                        var Success {output} : Boolean);
  {
   Pushes X onto a stack.
   Pre : X is defined.
   Post: Sets Success to indicate success (True) or failure
         (False) of push operation.
  }
  begin {Push}
    Success := True;
    InitCursor;
    Insert (X)
  end; {Push}

  procedure Stack.Pop (var X {output} : ListData;
                       var Success {output} : Boolean);
  {
   Pops the top of a stack into X.
   Pre : A stack has been created.
   Post: Contents of X is character at top of the stack which is
         then removed from the stack. Sets Success to indicate
         success (True) or failure (False) of pop operation.
  }
  begin {Pop}
    InitCursor;
    LinkList.Retrieve (X, Success);
    Delete
  end; {Pop}

  procedure Stack.Retrieve (var X {output} : ListData;
                            var Success {output} : Boolean);
  {
   Copies the value at the top of the stack into X.
   Pre : A stack has been created.
   Post: Contents of X is character at top of the stack; the
         stack is unchanged. Sets Success to indicate success
         (True) or failure (False).
  }
```

▷ ▷ ▷ ▷ ▷ ▷

```
begin {Retrieve}
  InitCursor;
  LinkList.Retrieve (X, Success)
end; {Retrieve}

function Stack.IsFull : Boolean;
{
 Tests whether it is possible to add a new element to stack.
 Pre : A stack has been created.
 Post: Returns True if the stack is full;
       otherwise, returns False.
 Calls: Borland Pascal functions SizeOf and MemAvail
}
begin {IsFull}
  {Is there enough room on the heap to allocate a list
   element}
  IsFull := SizeOf(ListElement) > MemAvail
end; {IsFull}

end. {StackADT}
```

△

The stack methods `Push`, `Pop`, and `Retrieve` are implemented by using `LinkList` methods `InitCursor`, `Insert`, `Retrieve`, and `Delete`. `InitCursor` moves the `Cursor` to the first list element (the top of the stack) before any of these operations. Next, `Push` calls `LinkList.Insert` to insert the new stack element. Methods `Pop` and `Retrieve` use `LinkList.Retrieve` to extract the data at the top of the stack. Method `Pop` calls `LinkList.Delete` to remove the top element after its information part has been retrieved.

Method `Stack.IsFull` makes use of two Borland Pascal functions (`SizeOf` and `MemAvail`) to determine whether there is enough space on the heap to store an additional stack node. Function `SizeOf` returns the number of bytes required to store a variable of the data type passed as its argument. Function `MemAvail` returns the number of bytes left on the heap. Consequently, the condition

`SizeOf(ListElement) > MemAvail`

is true when there is not sufficient space on the heap to allocate a new stack node (type `ListElement`).

A New Queue Object

It is just as straightforward to implement the `Queue` object shown in Figs. 6.8 and 6.14 in linked form. We will consider a queue to be a descendant of our `LinkList` object. This enables a queue object to inherit methods from object types `LinkList`. Since the first queue element is the one processed by queue Retrieve and `Remove` methods, we can take the same approach that we did in our `Stack` object and use inherited `LinkList` methods `InitCursor`, `Retrieve`, and `Delete`. Because we insert new elements at the end of the queue, we can use the inherited `LinkList` method `InsertAtEnd`. Figure 7.36 shows a new object type `Queue` that takes advantage of inheritance.

This certainly shows the power of object-oriented programming. We have created two new ADTs with very little effort. You should be able to run all the earlier client programs for `StackADT` and `QueueADT` with very minor modification. If the client programs had been written in a more general manner from the start, it would be necessary only to recompile and relink the client programs to the new versions of the ADTs before running them.

Figure 7.36
Unit `QueueADT`

Directory: CHAP 7
File: QUEUEADT.PAS

```
unit QueueADT;
{
 Abstract data type Queue: contains declarations for Queue
 object and its methods.

 Imports: Object ListData from unit ListDataADT and object
          LinkList from unit LinkListADT.
}
interface

  uses ListDataADT, LinkListADT;

  type
    Queue = object (LinkList)
              procedure CreateQueue;
              procedure Remove (var El {output} : ListData;
                                    var Success {output} : Boolean);
              procedure Retrieve
                                (var El {output} : ListData;
                                    var Success {output} : Boolean);
              procedure Insert (El {input} : ListData;
                                    var Success {output} : Boolean);
              function SizeOfQueue : Word;

              private
                Rear : ListPointer;
            end; {Queue}

implementation

  procedure Queue.CreateQueue;
  {
   Creates an empty queue.
```

▷ ▷ ▷ ▷ ▷ ▷

```
    Pre : None.
    Post: Queue object initialized.
}
begin {CreateQueue}
  CreateList;
  Rear := nil;            {set pointer to last queue element}
end; {CreateQueue}

procedure Queue.Remove (var El {output} : ListData;
                        var Success {output} : Boolean);
{
 Removes element from front of queue and copies it into El.
 Pre : Queue is initialized.
 Post: If queue is not empty, El contains first queue
       element, which is then removed from the queue.
       Sets Success to True if Remove is successful and
       False if not.
}
begin {Remove}
  InitCursor;
  LinkList.Retrieve (El, Success);
  Delete;
  {if last element removed reset rear queue pointer}
  if IsEmpty then
    Rear := nil;
end; {Remove}

procedure Queue.Retrieve (var El {output} : ListData;
                          var Success {output} : Boolean);
{
 Copies the value at the front of the queue into El.
 Pre : Queue has been created.
 Post: Contents of El is element at the front of the queue;
       the queue is unchanged. Sets Success to indicate
       success (True) or failure (False).
}
begin {Retrieve}
  InitCursor;
  LinkList.Retrieve (El, Success)
end; {Retrieve}

function Queue.SizeOfQueue : Word;
{
 Return number of elements housed in queue.
}
begin {SizeOfQueue}
  SizeOfQueue := GetSize
end; {SizeOfQueue}

procedure Queue.Insert (El {input} : ListData;
                        var Success {output} : Boolean);
{
 Inserts El in a queue.
 Pre : The queue has been created.
```

▷ ▷ ▷ ▷ ▷ ▷

```
      Post: Inserts El at the rear of the queue. Sets Success to
            True if insertion is successful and False if not.
      }
   begin {Insert}
     Success := True;
     InsertAtEnd (El)
   end; {Insert}

end. {QueueADT}
```

Figure 7.37 shows the "family tree" for the objects that we have created so far. It also shows a new object type, OrderList, which we will discuss in the next section.

Exercises for Section 7.6   **Self-Check**

1. Can any of the Stack or Queue methods access the LinkList data fields Head or Cursor directly?
2. Do instances of Stack or Queue objects have direct access to LinkList methods InsertAfter or Search? What does this say about information hiding and object inheritance?

Programming

1. Modify program UseStack so that it uses our new StackADT.
2. Write the implementation of Queue methods Insert and Remove if object Queue is not implemented as a descendant of our LinkList object.

7.7 Ordered Linked List ADT

Figure 7.38 shows an *ordered linked list,* that is, a linked list in which the information fields of the list elements are in increasing sequence (e.g., 123 < 300 < 456 < 600). It is often desirable to maintain data ordering as we process and update a

Figure 7.37
Family Tree of List Type
Objects

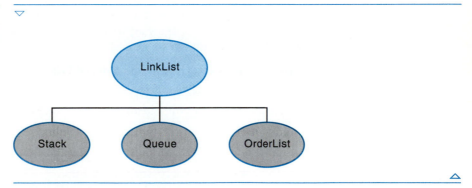

Figure 7.38
An Ordered List of Integers

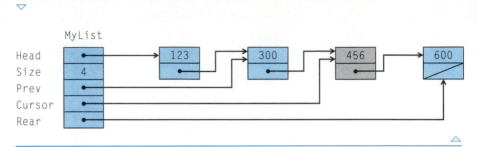

list. We can easily write an ordered list object as a descendant of object `LinkList`. All we need to do is provide a new method `Insert` that performs insertions in such a way as to maintain the increasing sequence of list data.

Let's see what's involved in inserting the data stored in object instance `E1` (type `ListData`) in the list. If `E1` contains the data item 345, we should insert `E1` into a new list element between the elements with data items 300 and 456; that is, its successor will be the element with data item 456 (current position of `Cursor`). If `E1` contains the data item 500, we should insert `E1` into a new list element that precedes the last list element; if `E1` contains the data item 666, we should insert `E1` into a new list element that follows the last list element.

Therefore to insert the data in `E1` where they belong, we must first search the list for `E1`'s successor, starting with the first list element. `E1`'s successor should be the first list element that we find whose data item is greater than or equal to the data in `E1`. When `Cursor` is at this element, we can use `LinkList.Insert` to insert `E1` in a new list element. If `E1` has no successor (there is no list element with a larger data item than `E1`) or its successor is the last list element, we must terminate the search when we reach the end of the list. At this point, we must insert `E1` either before or after the last list element, depending on whether `E1`'s data are less than (insert before) or greater than (insert after) the last list element's data.

There are two special cases: insertion into an empty list and attempting to insert an object instance `E1` whose data item is already in the list. In the case of an empty list we simply insert `E1` as the first list element without performing a search. In the case of a duplicate item we will not perform the insertion and will set a `Success` flag to False to indicate that the insertion attempt failed. The algorithm is summarized below.

Algorithm for Inserting in an Ordered List

1. if the list is empty then
    2. Insert El at list head and set Success to True.
   else
     begin
        3. Advance Cursor to the successor of El or to the end of the list.
        4. if the successor is found then
           5. Insert El at Cursor and set Success to True.

else if the element at Cursor equals El then

   6. Set Success to False.

else

   7. Insert El after the element at Cursor and set
       Success to True

end

Figure 7.39 shows unit `OrderList` with methods `FindSuccessor` (private) and `Insert`, which perform the search and insertion, respectively. We need to declare only these two new methods; all other data and method members of OrderList are inherited from `LinkListADT`. To allow lists to be ordered in either ascending or descending order, methods `FindSuccessor` and `Insert` have a functional parameter `Compare`. Function `Compare` will need to be defined in a client program and will use a `ListData` method that returns `True` if the data in `El` are to precede the data in `Compare`'s second argument.

You might be wondering why it is necessary in `FindSuccessor` (and `Insert`) to store each list element's data in `CurrentEl` before comparing them to the data in `El`. Why can't we just use a loop header like

---

Figure 7.39
Unit `OrderListADT`

Directory: CHAP 7
File: ORDERLIST.PAS

```
unit OrderListADT;
{
 Abstract data type OrderList is a linked list whose
 information fields are in increasing sequence.

 Imports: Object type ListData from unit ListDataADT and
          object type LinkList from unit LinkListADT.
}
interface

  uses LinkListADT, ListDataADT;

  type
    FunctionType = function (P, Q : ListData) : Boolean;

    OrderList = object (LinkList)
                procedure Insert
                          (El {input} : ListData;
                           Compare : FunctionType;
                           var {output} Success :
                           Boolean);
                private
                  procedure FindSuccessor
                          (El {input} : ListData;
                           var CurrentEl {output} :
                           ListData; Compare : Function Type);
                end; {OrderList}
```

▷ ▷ ▷ ▷ ▷

```
implementation
  procedure OrderList.FindSuccessor
                      (El {input} : ListData;
                       var CurrentEl {output} : ListData;
                       Compare : FunctionType);
  {
   Searches for successor of new list element. Advances
   Cursor to first element whose information part does not
   precede El's. Returns that element's information part
   through CurrentEl.
   Pre : OrderList is created and El is defined. Function
         Compare compiled in client program using far code
         model
   Post: Returns through CurrentEl the information part of
         the successor to El or the last list node. Cursor
         is at CurrentEl and El.Info succeeds CurrentEl.Info or
         Cursor is at end of list.
  }
    var
      Success : Boolean; {flag indicating retrieval result}

  begin
    InitCursor;                                {start at beginning}

    {Compare each element's data to El}
    Retrieve (CurrentEl, Success);
    while not AtEnd and
          not(Compare(El, CurrentEl) or EL.IsEqual(CurrentEl)) do
      begin
        Advance;
        Retrieve (CurrentEl, Success)    {get next element}
      end {while}
  end; {FindSuccessor}

  procedure OrderList.Insert (El {input} : ListData;
                              Compare : FunctionType;
                              var Success {output} : Boolean);
  {
   Inserts item El as the information part of a new list
   element maintaining the property of an ordered list.
   Pre : OrderList is created and El is defined. Function
         Compare compiled in client program using far code
         model.
   Post: Returns True when El.Info precedes Current.Info.
         If there is already an element that contains El,
         Success is set to False and no insertion takes
         place; otherwise, Success is set to True. In either
         case, the Cursor is positioned at the element whose
         information part is El.
  }
    var
      CurrentEl : ListData;                      {Successor to El}

  begin {Insert}
```

▷ ▷ ▷ ▷ ▷ ▷

```
if IsEmpty then
  begin
    LinkList.Insert (El);                    {insert at head}
    Success := True
  end {if}
else
  begin {Insert in non-empty list}
    {Find the element that should follow El}
    FindSuccessor (El, CurrentEl, Compare);
    {assert: Cursor points to the first element whose
             information part succeeds El.Info or Cursor
             is at the end of the list.
    }
    if CurrentEl.IsEqual(El) then
      Success := False                       {duplicate entry}
    else if not Compare(El, CurrentEl) then
      begin                          {CurrentEl is last element}
        Success := True;
        LinkList.InsertAfter (El)      {put El at end of list}
      end
        else
          begin
            Success := True;
            LinkList.Insert (El)   {insert El before CurrentEl}
          end {if}
      end {if}

  end; {Insert}

end. {OrderListADT}
```

△

```
while not AtEnd and
      not Compare(Cursor^.ListInfo, El) do
```

in the search loop? The reason is that a private data member of an object is not visible in any client of that object. Borland Pascal considers a descendant object to be another client and does not allow `OrderList` to reference `Cursor`, which is declared as a private data member of its ancestor, `LinkList`. Reference to an ancestor's private data members may be allowed in some other object-oriented languages, but it is not allowed in Borland Pascal.

CASE STUDY ⋯⋯⋯⋯⋯⋯⋯⋯⋯⋯⋯⋯ **Addition of Polynomials**

PROBLEM ▼

You are trying to develop an application program that performs polynomial arithmetic. Your task is to develop procedures for reading and displaying a polynomial in X and for finding the sum of two polynomials in X.

Figure 7.40
Storing a Polynomial in a
List Ordered by Exponent
Value

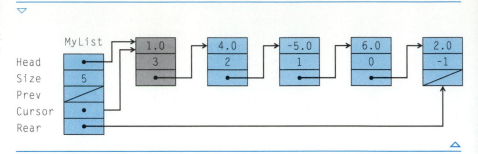

ANALYSIS ▼

An ordered linked list is an ideal data structure for storing a polynomial. Each term of the polynomial can be stored in a list element that contains a type `Real` coefficient and an Integer exponent. For example, the polynomial

$$X^3 + 4X^2 - 5X + 6 + 2X^{-1}$$

could be stored in the linked list shown in Fig. 7.40. The data stored in each term consist of a coefficient (type `Real`) and an exponent (type `Integer`), and the list elements are in increasing order by exponent value (3, 2, 1, 0, −1). Notice that the next to last list element represents the constant 6 in the polynomial above (i.e., 6 is $6X^0$).

ABSTRACT DATA TYPE LISTDATA ▼

We can declare a new abstract data type `ListData` (see Fig. 7.41) for storage of a polynomial term. It contains two data members, `Coefficient` and

Figure 7.41
Unit `ListData` for a
Polynomial Term

Directory: CHAP 7
File: LISTDAT2.PAS

```
unit ListDataADT;
{
  Implements object type ListData for a list whose list elements
  contain a polynomial term.
}
interface

  const
     Sentinel = 0.0;            {sentinel coefficient}
     PolyVariable = 'X';        {Polynomial in X}

  type
     InfoType = record
                   Coefficient : Real;
                   Exponent : Integer
                end; {InfoType}
```

▷ ▷ ▷ ▷ ▷ ▷

```
ListData = object
             procedure Init (C {input} : Real;
                             E {input} : Integer);
             procedure ReadInfo;
             procedure Display;
             function GetCoefficient : Real;
             function GetExponent : Integer;
             function IsEqual (Item : ListData) : Boolean;
             function GreaterThan (Item: ListData) : Boolean;
             function IsZero : Boolean;

           private
             Coefficient : Real;
             Exponent : Integer;
           end; {ListData}

implementation

  procedure ListData.Init (C {input} : Real;
                           E {input} : Integer);
  {
   Initializes instance of object ListData.
   Pre : C and E are defined.
   Post: Coefficient is C and Exponent is E.
  }
  begin {Init}
    Coefficient := C;
    Exponent := E
  end; {Init}

  procedure ListData.ReadInfo;
  {
   Prompts user to enter values to initialize data fields for
   ListData object.
   Pre : None.
   Post: If valid data value is read into coefficient,
         Exponent is defined.
  }
  begin {ReadInfo}
    Write ('coefficient> ');
    ReadLn (Coefficient);
    if Coefficient <> Sentinel then
      begin
        Write ('exponent (an integer)> ');
        ReadLn (Exponent)
      end {if}
  end; {ReadInfo}

  procedure ListData.Display;
  {
   Displays data field values for instance of object ListData.
   Pre : Object is initialized.
   Post: Field values Coefficient and Exponent displayed in
         polynomial term format.
  }
```

```
            begin {Display}
               if Coefficient <> 0.0 then
                  begin
                     if Coefficient < 0.0 then
                        Write ('-' :2, ' ')
                     else
                        Write ('+' :2, ' ');
                     if Abs(Coefficient) <> 1.0 then
                        Write (Abs(Coefficient) :2:1);
                     if Exponent = 1 then
                        Write (PolyVariable)
                     else if Exponent <> 0 then
                        Write (PolyVariable, '^', Exponent :1)
                  end {if}
            end; {Display}

            function ListData.GetCoefficient : Real;
            {
             Returns value of data field Coefficient.
            }
            begin {GetCoefficient}
               GetCoefficient := Coefficient
            end; {GetCoefficient}

            function ListData.GetExponent : Integer;
            {
             Returns value of data field Exponent.
            }
            begin {GetExponent}
               GetExponent := Exponent
            end; {GetExponent}

            function ListData.IsEqual (Item : ListData) : Boolean;
            {
             Compares Exponent data field to Item.Exponent field to test
             for equality.
             Pre : Object initialized and Item defined.
             Post: Returns True if Self.Exponent = Item.Exponent;
                   otherwise returns False.
            }
            begin {IsEqual}
               IsEqual := (Exponent = Item.Exponent)
            end; {IsEqual}

            function ListData.GreaterThan (Item : ListData) : Boolean;
            {
             Compares Exponent data field to Item.Exponent field to test
             whether Exponent is greater than Item.Exponent.
             Pre : Object initialized and Item defined.
             Post: Returns True if Self.Exponent > Item.Exponent;
                   otherwise returns False.
            }
            begin {GreaterThan}
```

▷ ▷ ▷ ▷ ▷ ▷

```
   GreaterThan := (Exponent > Item.Exponent)
 end; {GreaterThan}

 function ListData.IsZero : Boolean;
 {
  Test whether data Coefficient is 0.0 or not.
 }
 begin {IsZero}
   IsZero := (Coefficient = 0.0)
 end; {IsZero}

end. {ListDataADT}
```

Exponent. Its method members include the traditional methods for initializing a term, reading a term, displaying a term, and extracting the coefficient and exponent of a term. It also has methods IsEqual and GreaterThan for comparing two terms on the basis of their exponent values, since that is what determines the order of terms in the list. Function IsZero is a new method member that returns True if the polynomial's coefficient is 0.0.

The Display procedure displays a polynomial term. The sign and absolute value of the coefficient are displayed separately with a space before and after the sign. The coefficient is not displayed if its absolute value is 1.0. The polynomial variable (X) is displayed after the coefficient value if the exponent is not 0. Next, the exponent is displayed unless it is 1. The exponent is preceded by the ∧ symbol, which indicates exponentiation. Nothing is displayed if a term's coefficient is 0. The first line below shows a polynomial as we would normally write it in algebraic notation; under each term is the way it would be printed by procedure Display.

```
   X³ + 4X²    - 5X   + 6    + 2X⁻¹
 + X^3 + 4.0X^2 - 5.0X + 6.0 + 2.0X^-1
```

READING AND DISPLAYING A POLYNOMIAL ▼

We can use procedure LinkList.Traverse to display a polynomial in the form shown above. Only two tasks remain: reading and storing the terms of a polynomial and adding two polynomials.

To read and store a polynomial, we need to read each term's coefficient and exponent and store these data in an object of type ListData. Then we can use LinkList.Insert to place the new list element where it belongs in the linked list representation of the polynomial. We will allow the polynomial terms to be entered in any order, but we will not allow duplicate terms (i.e., terms with the same exponent). The algorithm for ReadPoly follows. Figure 7.42 shows procedure ReadPoly.

ALGORITHM FOR READPOLY ▼

```
1. Initialize polynomial Poly to an empty list.
2. while there are more terms do
      begin
         3. Read the next term into NextTerm.
         4. Use OrderList.Insert to insert the NextTerm.
         5. if not successful then
               display duplicate exponent message.
      end
```

ADDITION OF TWO POLYNOMIALS ▼

We can think of the addition of two polynomials as the process of inserting each term of the second polynomial (Poly2) into the first (Poly1). After we have inserted all the terms of Poly2, the modified version of Poly1 will represent the sum of the two polynomials. If there is no term in Poly1 with the same exponent as the term of Poly2 being inserted, the term of Poly2 should be inserted directly. If there is already a term of Poly1 with the same exponent as the Poly2 term (duplicate term), the rules of polynomial

Figure 7.42
Procedure ReadPoly

Directory: CHAP 7
File: READPOLY.PAS

```
procedure ReadPoly (var Poly {output} : OrderList);
{
 Reads each term of a polynomial and stores it in an ordered
 linked list.
 Pre : None.
 Post: Ordered list Poly contains polynomial with terms ordered
       by decreasing exponent value.
}
  var
     NextTerm : ListData;
     Success : Boolean;

begin {ReadPoly}
  Poly.CreateList;
  WriteLn ('Enter the terms. After the ');
  WriteLn ('last term, enter a coefficent of 0.0 to stop:');
  NextTerm.ReadInfo;
  while not NextTerm.IsZero do
     begin
        Poly.Insert (NextTerm, Compare, Success);
        if not Success then
           WriteLn ('Duplicate exponent - try again');
        NextTerm.ReadInfo
     end {while}
end; {ReadPoly}
```

addition state that this term should be replaced with one whose coefficient is the sum of the coefficients from `Poly1` and `Poly2`. Table 7.3 illustrates this process. The algorithm for procedure `AddPoly` follows the table.

Table 7.3
Trace of Polynomial
Addition

```
Poly1: +  X³ + 4X² - 5X + 6 + 2X⁻¹
Poly2: + 3X⁴ - 4X² - 2X + 3 + X⁻²
```

Next Term of Poly2	Effect
+ 3X⁴	Insert at head of Poly1.
− 4X²	Delete + 4X² in Poly1 (4 + −4 is 0).
− 2X	Replace − 5X in Poly1 with − 7X (−5X + −2X).
+ 3	Replace + 6 in Poly1 with + 9 (6 + 3).
+ X⁻²	Insert at rear of Poly1

Poly1 after Addition: + 3X⁴ + X³ − 7X + 9 + 2X⁻¹ + X⁻²

ALGORITHM FOR ADDPOLY ▼

```
1. Start at the beginning of Poly2.
2. while there are more terms in Poly2 do
      begin
          3. Retrieve the current term of Poly2.
          4. Attempt to insert current term of Poly2 in Poly1.
          5. if not successful then
              Replace coefficient of matching term in Poly1
              with the sum of the coefficients.
          6. Advance to next term in Poly2
      end
7. if Poly2 is not empty then
      8. Perform steps 3, 4, and 5 for the last term of Poly2.
```

Figure 7.43 shows procedure `AddPoly` and procedure `InsertPoly`, which performs Steps 4 and 5. To replace a term of `Poly1` with another, we simply delete the original term and then insert the replacement. The new term will automatically be inserted where it belongs in the ordered list.

TESTING THE PROCEDURES ▼

Figure 7.44 shows a client program that reads, displays, and sums the two polynomials shown in the preceding subsection. For this case study we have defined function Compare so that it uses function GreaterThan to arrange our list elements in descending order. To completely test these procedures, you should see what happens when one or both of the polynomials is an empty polynomial or when the two polynomials sum to zero (i.e., each term of `Poly1` is negated by the corresponding term of `Poly2`).

Figure 7.43
Procedures `InsertPoly`
and `AddPoly`

Directory: CHAP 7
File: INSERTPO.PAS

```
procedure InsertPoly (TermIn {input} : ListData;
                          var Poly {input/output} : OrderList);
{
 Inserts TermIn in ordered list Poly.
 Pre : TermIn defined and Poly contains polynomial with terms
       ordered by decreasing exponent values.
 Post: If TermIn has new exponent value not in Poly it is
       inserted into Poly; if TermIn has same exponent value
       as a term already in Poly their coefficient values are
       added. Terms with zero coefficients are removed from
       Poly.
}
  var
    NewCoefficient : Real;
    {Term in polynomial with same exponent as TermIn}
    CurrentTerm : ListData;
    Success : Boolean;            {indicates success of insert}

begin {InsertPoly}
  {Try to insert TermIn in polynomial}
  Poly.Insert (TermIn, Compare, Success);
  {Check for duplicate exponent value case}
  if not Success then
    begin
      {Retrieve the term whose exponent matches TermIn}
      Poly.Retrieve (CurrentTerm, Success);
      {Add term coefficient}
      NewCoefficient := CurrentTerm.GetCoefficient +
                        TermIn.GetCoefficient;
      {Delete term from polynomial if new coefficient is zero}
      if NewCoefficient = 0 then
        Poly.Delete
      else
        begin
          {Update term coefficient and replace term in Poly}
          TermIn.Init (NewCoefficient, TermIn.GetExponent);
          Poly.Delete;
          Poly.Insert (TermIn, Compare, Success)
        end {if}
    end {if}
end; {InsertPoly}

procedure AddPoly (var Poly1 {input/output} : OrderList;
                       Poly2 {input} : OrderList);
{
 Adds two polynomials.
 Pre : Poly1 and Poly2 contain polynomial terms ordered by
       decreasing exponent values.
 Post: The result is returned through Poly1.
}
```

Directory: CHAP 7
File: ADDPOLY.PAS

▷ ▷ ▷ ▷ ▷

```
      var
        CurrentTerm : ListData;        {the current term of Poly2}
        Success : Boolean;             {flag for retrieval result}

  begin {AddPoly}
    Poly2.InitCursor;                    {start at beginning of Poly2}
    while not Poly2.AtEnd do
      begin
        Poly2.Retrieve (CurrentTerm, Success); {get current term}
        InsertPoly (CurrentTerm, Poly1);    {insert it in Poly1}
        Poly2.Advance                       {go to next term}
      end; {while}

  {assert: Poly2 is empty or Poly2.Cursor is at last element.}
  if not Poly2.IsEmpty then
    begin
      Poly2.Retrieve (CurrentTerm, Success);      {get last term}
      InsertPoly (CurrentTerm, Poly1)        {insert it in Poly1}
      end {if}
  end; {AddPoly}
```

Figure 7.44
Program RunPoly with
Sample Run

Directory: CHAP 7
File: RUNPOLY.PAS

```
program RunPoly;
{
 Tests polynomial arithmetic procedures.
}
  uses OrderListADT, ListDataADT;

  var
    Poly1, Poly2 : OrderList;

  function Compare (P, Q : ListData) : Boolean; far;
  {
   Used by OrderList.Insert to determine if P precedes Q.
   Pre : P and Q defined.
   Post: Returns True if P.Info > Q.Info
  }
  begin {Compare}
    IsGreater := P.GreaterThan(Q)
  end; {Compare}

  {insert procedures AddPoly, InsertPoly, and ReadPoly here}
  {$I INSERTPO.PAS}
  {$I ADDPOLY.PAS}
  {$I READPOLY.PAS}

  procedure DisplayTerm (Info {input} : ListData); far;
  {
   Procedure to be applied to each list node by method
   LinkList.Traverse to display polynomial.
   Pre : Info is defined.
```

▷ ▷ ▷ ▷ ▷ ▷

```
            Post: Display contents of one ordered list node.
            }
          begin {DisplayTerm}
            Info.Display
          end; {DisplayTerm}

      begin {RunPoly}
        Write ('For polynomial 1 - ');
        ReadPoly (Poly1);
        WriteLn;
        Write ('For polynomial 2 - ');
        ReadPoly (Poly2);

        WriteLn;
        WriteLn ('The first polynomial is ');
        Poly1.Traverse (DisplayTerm);
        WriteLn;
        WriteLn ('The second polynomial is ');
        Poly2.Traverse (DisplayTerm);
        WriteLn;

        {Add them up and display the result.}
        AddPoly (Poly1, Poly2);
        WriteLn ('The sum of polynomials is ');
        Poly1.Traverse (DisplayTerm);
        WriteLn
      end. {RunPoly}

      For polynomial 1 - Enter the terms. After the
      last term, enter a coeffecent of 0.0 to stop:
      coefficient> 1
      exponent (an integer)> 3
      coefficient> 4
      exponent (an integer)> 2
      coefficient> -5
      exponent (an integer)> 1
      coefficient> 6
      exponent (an integer)> 0
      coefficient> 2
      exponent (an integer)> -1
      coefficient> 0

      For polynomial 2 - Enter the terms. After the
      last term, enter a coeffecent of 0.0 to stop:
      coefficient> 3
      exponent (an integer)> 4
      coefficient> -4
      exponent (an integer)> 2
      coefficient> -2
      exponent (an integer)> 1
      coefficient> 3
      exponent (an integer)> 0
      coefficient> 1
      exponent (an integer)> -2
      coefficient> 0
```

▷ ▷ ▷ ▷ ▷ ▷

```
The first polynomial is
+ X^3 + 4.0X^2 - 5.0X + 6.0 + 2.0X^-1
The second polynomial is
+ 3.0X^4 - 4.0X^2 - 2.0X + 3.0 + X^-2
The sum of polynomials is
+ 3.0X^4 + X^3 - 7.0X + 9.0 + 2.0X^-1 + X^-2
```

△

Exercises for Section 7.7 **Self-Check**

1. Explain what you would have to do to program `ListStack` (see Fig. 7.19) to get it to build an ordered linked list.
2. How would you need to modify function `Compare` to store the polynomial terms in increasing exponent order?

Programming

1. Write a polynomial subtraction procedure.
2. Replace method member ReadData with one that reads a string representing each polynomial term in the form *coefficient* X^*exponent*. Your new method should use Borland Pascal's string operators to extract the coefficient and exponent as strings and convert them to numbers.
3. The process of adding two polynomials destroys the first polynomial. If you wish to prevent this, you need to make a copy of the first polynomial before performing the addition. Write a method (for object type `LinkList`) called `CopyList` that creates a second list containing all the elements of the object instance that calls it. `CopyList` will need one parameter that represents its output list. Because `CopyList` is a method of `LinkList`, we will be able to use it to copy any list structure in our family of listlike objects.

7.8 Circular List Abstract Data Type

The linked list implementation that we have been using in this chapter is sometimes described as a *linear linked list*. Each list element except the first has a unique predecessor, and each list element except the last has a unique successor. An important limitation of this linked list implementation is that it allows us to easily access any of the elements that follow a given list element but to access none of the elements that precede the list element without starting at the beginning of the list and advancing forward. Hence we must always have a pointer to the start of the list to access any of the list elements.

Figure 7.45
Circular List

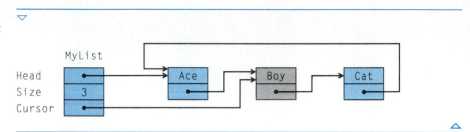

As shown in Fig. 7.45, we can alter our list implementation and make it a *circular list* by having the Successor field of the final list element point back to the first list element instead of containing nil. This allows us to start at any list node and traverse the entire list. In a true circular list, the notion of having a first or last node is not necessary for many programming applications—those that simply require that the data be stored in a ring of unordered elements.

For our purposes in this chapter we will describe the circular list as an alternative implementation of our linked list abstract type. We will assume that our circular list abstract data type will have the same operators that we discussed in Section 7.4. This means that any client module that works with our LinkListADT will work with our CircularListADT once the uses statement is modified to import the circular list type.

Using the Circular List ADT

Many of our object CircularList methods are identical to their LinkList counterparts. In fact, if we had not declared the LinkList pointer fields to be private, we could have used object inheritance to add these LinkList methods to our CircularList type. However, in the interest of maintaining data integrity we decided that clients of unit LinkListADT would not be allowed to manipulate these pointers directly. Consequently, the new CircularList methods that need to access these private data fields cannot do so. Next let us examine the effects of some of these methods on MyList shown in Fig. 7.45, which is an example of our CircularList type.

Figure 7.46
Deleting Circular List Node

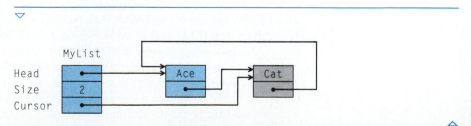

Figure 7.47
Resetting Circular List
`Cursor`

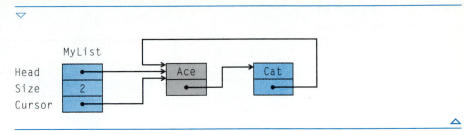

If `MyData` has type `ListData`, the message

`MyList.Retrieve (MyData)`

stores string `'Boy'` in `MyData`, but the list will be unchanged. The message

`MyList.Delete`

deletes the element pointed to by Cursor, changing the list as shown in Fig. 7.46.

Because the list is a circular list, the message

`MyList.Advance`

will reset the cursor to point from the last node to the first node, as shown in Fig. 7.47.

If `MyData` is type `ListData` and contains the string `'Cat'`, either message in Fig. 7.48 will move the cursor to the second node.

`MyList.Search (MyData)` | `MyList.Advance`

We are assuming that `Search` calls method member `ListData.IsEqual` to compare the *target string* `'Cat'` to the information part of each node, starting with the first. If `MyData` contains the string `'Boy'`, the message

`MyList.Insert (MyData)`

will insert the string `'Boy'` in the second position, changing the list back to the original form shown in Fig. 7.45 (see Fig. 7.49).

Finally, if `MyData` contains the string `'Cap'`, the message

Figure 7.48
Advancing Circular List
`Cursor`

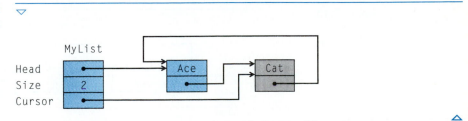

Figure 7.49
Inserting Node Into
Circular List

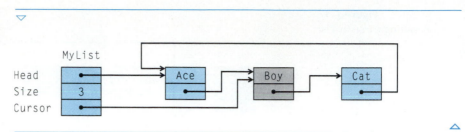

MyList.InsertAfter (MyData)

changes the list as shown in Fig. 7.50. The new list element is inserted after
the one currently pointed to by Cursor, and Cursor is advanced to the new
list element.

Method member Traverse processes the list elements in sequence and
applies procedure parameter Visit to each list element. If Visit corresponds to ListData.Display, the result of MyList.Traverse on the list
above will be

Ace
Boy
Cap
Cat

Implementing CircularListADT

In this section we describe the implementation of unit CircularListADT.
We are leaving the full implementation of unit CircularListADT as a programming project (see Programming Project 5 at the end of the chapter). If
we can make the interface section of unit CircularListADT resemble the
interface section of unit LinkListADT, we will be able to maximize the
amount of code that we can reuse. It is sometimes possible to do without
the Head pointer in a circular list field and just use Rear^.Successor to
find the first list element. We have decided to leave the Head field in our
CircularList object to increase the clarity of its method implementations.

Figure 7.50
Inserting Node
After Cursor Position

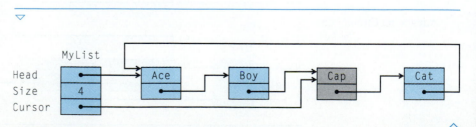

Figure 7.51
Method `Insert`

Directory: CHAP 7
File: CIRCLIST.PAS

```
procedure CircularList.Insert (El {input} : ListData);
{
 Inserts item El as the information part of a new list
 element pointed to by data member Cursor.
 Pre : Circular list object initialized and El defined.
 Post: The successor of the new list element is the one
       that was previously pointed to by Cursor. If Head
       is nil or Head equals Cursor, inserts El as the
       information part of the first list element and points
       Cursor to it.
}
begin {Insert}
   if Head = nil then
     begin {empty list}
       New (Head);                    {connect new element to Head}
       Head^.Successor := Head;           {list has one element}
       Cursor := Head;                          {reset Cursor}
       Prev := Head               {node is its own predecessor}
     end {if}
   else if Cursor = Head then
     begin {insert new head}
       New (Head);                    {connect new element to Head}
       Head^.Successor := Cursor;  {connect it to rest of list}
       Prev^.Successor := Head;             {make list circular}
       Cursor := Head                          {reset Cursor}
     end {else if}
   else
     begin
       {Insert between Prev and Cursor}
       New (Prev.Successor);
       {Connect to predecessor}
       Prev^.Successor^.Successor := Cursor;
       {Link new element to rest of list}
       Cursor := Prev^.Successor               {reset Cursor}
     end; {else}

   Cursor^.ListInfo := El;              {store El in new element}
   Size := Size + 1;
   if AtEnd then
     Rear := Cursor;
end; {Insert}
```

CircularList Methods

The implementation of method `Insert` is shown in Fig. 7.51. For this method we need to distinguish between inserting a new element in an empty list and inserting a new first list element. The methods `InsertAfter` and `InsertAtEnd` require very minor changes to the implementations of their `LinkList` counterparts.

Figure 7.52
Method Delete

Directory: CHAP 7
File: CIRCLIST.PAS

```pascal
procedure CircularList.Delete;
{
 Deletes the list element pointed to by Cursor.
 Pre : Circular list initialized.
 Post: Resets Cursor to point to the deleted element's
       successor, and returns its storage space to the heap.
       If the list is empty, no list element is deleted.
}
  var
    ToBeDeleted : ListPointer;      {Item to be deleted}

begin
  if Size = 1 then
    begin {1-element list}
      {Save old position of node to be deleted}
      ToBeDeleted := Head;
      Cursor := nil;                     {List is now empty.}
      Head := nil;
      Prev := nil;
      Dispose (ToBeDeleted);             {Return storage to heap.}
      Size := 0
    end {1-element list}
  else if (Prev <> nil) then
    begin
      {Connect predecessor to rest of list}
      Prev^.Successor := Cursor^.Successor;
      {Save old Cursor value}
      ToBeDeleted := Cursor;
      {Advance Cursor to next element}
      Cursor := Cursor^.Successor;
      {Reset Head if old head deleted}
      if Head = ToBeDeleted then
        Head := Cursor;
      {Dispose node being deleted}
      Dispose (ToBeDeleted);
      Size := Size - 1
    end;

  if IsEmpty then
    Rear := nil;
end; {Delete}
```

Method Delete

In method Delete (see Fig. 7.52) we need to deal with two special cases: a list with one element and a list whose first element is being deleted.

The first condition in Delete checks for a one-element list and sets Cursor and Head to nil to accomplish the deletion. For a longer list, the statement

```
Prev^.Successor := Cursor^.Successor;
```

deletes the intended element by resetting its predecessor's Successor pointer to point to the rest of the list. The old Cursor value is temporarily saved in ToBeDeleted, and Cursor is advanced to the successor of the deleted element. The if statement checks whether the list head was deleted (Head equals ToBeDeleted) and, if so, resets Head to point to the second list element. Next, Delete returns the storage occupied by the deleted element to the heap and decrements Size by 1. Finally, Rear is updated if the circular list is now empty.

Exercises for Section 7.8   **Self-Check**

1. What is the principal difference in the implementation of a circular list and the implementation of a linear list?

Programming

1. Implement method Traverse so that it begins list traversal from the element pointed to by Cursor, not the element pointed to by Head.
2. Rewrite method Insert using references to the pointer field Rear in place of the reference to Head.

7.9 Common Programming Errors

Make sure you use the dereferencing operator ^ where it is needed. If P is a pointer variable, P^.X should be used to reference field X of the record pointed to by P.

The New and Dispose procedures allocate and deallocate storage, respectively. Both procedures require a parameter that is a pointer variable. New (P) is correct; New (P^) is incorrect.

Several run-time errors can occur when you are traversing linked data structures. For example, if Next is supposed to point to each node in the linked list, the while statement

```
while Next <> nil do
  Write (Next^.Data);
  Next := Next^.Link
```

executes forever. That happens because the pointer assignment statement is not included in the loop body, so Next is not advanced down the list.

A run-time error can occur when the pointer Next is advanced too far down the list and Next takes on the value nil, indicating the end of the list. If pointer Next has the value nil, the while condition

```
while (Next <> nil) and (Next^.ID <> 9999) do
```

cause a run-time error because Next^.ID is undefined when Next is nil. The while condition should be changed to

```
while (Next^.Link <> nil) and (Next^.ID <> 9999) do
```

Finally, if pointer `Next` is a procedure parameter that corresponds to a list head pointer, make sure that it is a value parameter. If it is a variable parameter, the last value assigned to `Next` will be returned as a procedure result. This may cause you to lose some of the elements that were originally in the linked list.

Problems with heap management can also cause run-time errors. When you are creating a dynamic data structure, it is possible for your program to consume all memory cells on the storage heap. This situation will lead to a heap overflow run-time error.

Make sure your program does not attempt to reference a list node after the node is returned to the heap. All pointers to a node being disposed should be set to nil so that the node cannot be accessed again.

In searching or traversing a circular list, it is fairly easy to get stuck in an endless loop. If you are not careful to check that the search or traversal does, in fact, terminate, you could end up cycling through the loop "forever."

Debugging Tips

It is difficult to debug programs that manipulate pointers because the value of a pointer variable cannot be printed. If a pointer variable is displayed in the Watch window, it appears as a pair of hexadecimal numbers (segment : offset) that have little meaning to anyone who is not a systems programmer. Consequently, you will often find it more informative to trace the execution of such a program by printing (or watching) an information field that uniquely identifies the list element being processed instead of the pointer itself.

When you are writing driver programs to test and debug list operators, it often is helpful to create a sample list structure using the `New` statement to allocate several nodes, then using several assignment statements to link them into a list, as we discussed in Section 7.1. You can also use assignment statements to put information into the nodes before linking them.

CHAPTER REVIEW

We introduced several dynamic data structures in this chapter. We discussed the use of pointers to reference and connect elements of a dynamic data structure. The procedure `New` allocates additional elements of a dynamic structure. The procedure `Dispose` returns the memory cells to the heap.

We covered many different aspects of manipulating linked lists. We showed how to build or create a linked list, how to traverse a linked list, and how to insert and delete elements of a linked list.

We showed how to use object inheritance to implement stacks, queues, and ordered lists as descendants of our linked list abstract data type. We also considered a circular list implementation of our list ADT.

Quick-Check Exercises

1. Procedure _____ allocates storage for a data object referenced though a _____; procedure _____ returns the storage to the _____.
2. What is the major advantage of using pointer representations of linked lists instead of array representations?
3. It is just as easy to modify a linked list that is represented as an array as one that is represented by using pointers. True or false?
4. When an element is deleted from a linked list by using pointers, it is automatically returned to the heap. True or false?
5. All pointers to a node that is returned to the heap are automatically reset to nil so that they cannot reference the node that was returned to the heap. True or false?
6. If a linked list contains three elements with the string values 'Him', 'Her', and 'Its' and H is a pointer to the first list element, what is the effect of the following statements? Assume that the data field is ListInfo, the link field is Successor, and N and P are pointer variables.

```
N := H^.Successor;
N^.ListInfo := 'She';
```

7. Answer Exercise 6 for the following segment:

```
P := H^.Successor;
N := P^.Successor;
P^.Successor := N^.Successor;
Dispose (N);
```

8. Answer Exercise 6 for the following segment:

```
N := H;
New (H);
H^.ListInfo := 'His';
H^.Successor := N;
```

9. Is an ordered list a first-in, first-out structure, a last-in, first-out structure, or neither?
10. In a circular list, the last list element contains nil as the value of its link field. True or false?

Answers to Quick-Check Exercises

1. New; pointer; Dispose; heap
2. Storage is allocated as needed rather than all at once.
3. True
4. False; Dispose must be called.
5. False
6. Replaces 'Her' with 'She'
7. Deletes the third list element
8. Inserts a new element with value 'His' at the front of the list

9. Neither
10. False

Review Questions

1. Differentiate between dynamic and nondynamic data structures.
2. Describe a linear linked list. Explain how the pointers are used to establish links between nodes and how list traversal is facilitated.
3. Give the missing type declarations, and show the effects of each of the following statements. What does each do?

```
New (P);
P^.Info := 'ABC';
New (P^.Next);
Q := P^.Next;
Q^.Info := 'abc';
Q^.Next := nil;
```

4. Assume that the following type declaration appears in unit ListDataADT:

```
type
   InfoType = string;
```

Write a program segment for a client of unit `LinkListADT` that places the names Washington, Roosevelt, and Kennedy in successive elements of a linked list.
5. Write a program segment to insert the name Eisenhower between Roosevelt and Kennedy in the list built for Exercise 4.
6. Write a new `LinkList` method called `DeleteLast` that removes the last element of a linked list.
7. Write a version of `DeleteLast` as a CircularList method.
8. Write a procedure called `CopyList` that creates a new list that contains the same data as the list passed to a formal parameter to the procedure. Write your solution so that `CopyList` calls a recursive procedure called `DoCopy`.
9. Write a procedure to delete all list nodes containing the name Smith from the list passed as a formal parameter to the procedure.

Programming Projects

Directory: CHAP 7
File: PROJ7_2.PAS

Directory: CHAP 7
File: PROJ7_5.PAS

1. Implement a linked Stack object that is not a descendant of our object `LinkList`.
2. Implement a linked `Queue` object that is not a descendant of our object `LinkList`.
3. Do Programming Project 3 at the end of Chapter 5 using the linked implementation of `StackADT` from this chapter.
4. Do Programming Project 5 at the end of Chapter 6 using the linked implementation of `QueueADT` from this chapter.
5. Implement unit `CircularListADT` described in Section 7.8.

Figure 7.53
Table of Student Class
Schedule

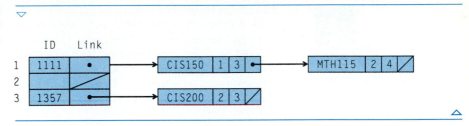

Directory: CHAP 7
File: PROJ7_6.PAS

6. Use an ordered list to maintain an airline passenger list. The main program should be a menu-driven program with options to allow the user to display the data for a particular passenger, display the entire list, create a list, insert a passenger node, delete a node, and replace the data stored in a passenger node.

7. Each student in a university takes a different number of courses, so the registrar has decided to use a linked list to store each student's class schedule and a table of students to represent the whole student body. A portion of this data structure is shown in Fig. 7.53.

   The records show that the first student (ID is 1111) is taking Section 1 of CIS 150 for three credits and Section 2 of MTH 115 for four credits, the second student (ID is 1234) is not taking any courses, and so on. Write an abstract data type for this data structure. Provide methods for creating the original table of student ID numbers, inserting a student's initial class schedule, adding a course, and dropping a course. Write a menu-driven program that uses this abstract data type.

Directory: CHAP 7
File: PROJ7_8.PAS

8. The Radix sorting algorithm uses an array of queues (numbered 0 through 9) to simulate the operation of the old card-sorting machines. This algorithm requires that one pass be made for every digit of the numbers being sorted. For example, a list of three-digit numbers would require three passes through the list. During the first pass, the least significant digit (the ones digit) of each number is examined, and the number is added to the rear of the queue whose subscript matches the digit. After all numbers have been processed, the elements of each queue, beginning with Q[0] are copied one at a time to the end of an eleventh queue before the beginning of the next pass. The process is repeated for the next most significant digit (the tens digit) using the order of the numbers in the eleventh queue. The process is repeated for the third most significant digit (the hundreds digit). After the final pass, the eleventh queue will contain the numbers in sorted order. Write a program that implements Radix sort using our linked QueueADT.

9. In preparing mailing lists it is often helpful to be able to display entries in order either by name or by Zip Code. This can be done if each list node has a pointer to the next node by name and a pointer to the next node by Zip Code. The nodes representing each person's data can then be linked in order by both name and Zip Code. There should only be one copy of each person's data (name, street address, city, state, and Zip Code). Write a menu-driven program that allows the user to display a single address label, input a single label, create an empty mailing list, insert a mailing list entry, display a mailing list in name order, and display a mailing list in Zip Code order.

Directory: CHAP 7
File: PROJ7_10.PAS

10. Pascal's set capability is limited in the number of elements that can be stored in a set. A more universal system can be implemented by using an ordered list to store the elements of a set. Implement a NewSet object as a descendant of our ordered list object. Implement methods to insert and delete integer values from a set. Also write methods needed to implement the operations set union, set intersection, and set difference. To verify the results of each operation, display the set contents before and after each operation.

CHAPTER EIGHT

Binary Trees

Chapter 7 introduced dynamic data structures including pointers, linked lists, and linked list implementations of stacks and queues. Each list node has a single pointer field connecting it to the next node. This chapter introduces a data structure called a *binary tree,* which has two pointer fields, enabling each node to be connected to two others.

The binary tree has wide application in compiler design and other computer science applications. For example, binary trees can be used to store arithmetic expressions. Binary trees are also used for storing the identifiers appearing in a program. This list of identifiers, called a *symbol table,* is constructed by the compiler as it scans each line of a program. Storing each identifier as a new entry in a binary tree the first time it is encountered can reduce significantly the time it takes to retrieve that identifier the next time it appears in the program.

8.1 Binary Trees

A binary tree is a data structure whose elements (called *nodes*) contain two pointer fields. Because one or both pointers can have the value nil, a binary tree node can point to zero, one, or two other nodes of the binary tree (its *children*). A recursive definition of a binary tree follows:

> A **binary tree** either is empty or consists of an item, called the **root item**, and two disjoint binary trees, called its **left subtree** and **right subtree**, respectively.

In this definition, the statement that the subtrees must be *disjoint* means that a node cannot be in both the left subtree and the right subtree of a particular node. This also means that a node cannot have more than one parent node. This definition does not eliminate the possibility that in some binary trees, duplicate copies of the same information may be housed in two physically distinct nodes.

Figure 8.1 shows several binary trees. Each tree element is represented by a data item (a letter, an integer, a three-letter string, or an operator symbol) and zero, one, or two pointers. The pointers are drawn as arrows pointing downward and to the left or right. The root of the tree in Fig. 8.1(a) contains the letter A. This node is the parent of the nodes containing the letters B and C.

Although we haven't shown the detailed structure of each node in Fig. 8.1, you should realize that each tree node has three components: a data part (enclosed in a circle), a left pointer (drawn as an arrow pointing down and to the left), and a right pointer (drawn as an arrow pointing down and to the right). Figure 8.2 shows a more explicit representation of the tree in Fig. 8.1(b). In Fig. 8.2 we show explicitly all three components of a node and draw a slash to indicate a pointer value of nil. In Fig. 8.1 the nil pointers were not drawn.

As shown in Fig. 8.1, trees in computer science actually grow from the top down rather than from the ground up. Family tree terminology is used to describe computer science trees. In Fig. 8.1(e) the node containing the string 'HEN' is the *parent* of the nodes containing the strings 'HAT' and 'HOG'. Similarly, the nodes 'HAT' and 'HOG' are *siblings* because they are both *children* of the same parent node. The *root* of the tree (its topmost node) is an *ancestor* of all other nodes in the tree, and they, in turn, are all *descendants* of the root node.

A tree has only one root node; however, each node in a tree may be thought of as the root of its own *subtree*. Since each node has two branches (pointers), it can spawn two subtrees, a *left subtree* and a *right subtree*. The

Figure 8.1
Examples of Binary Trees

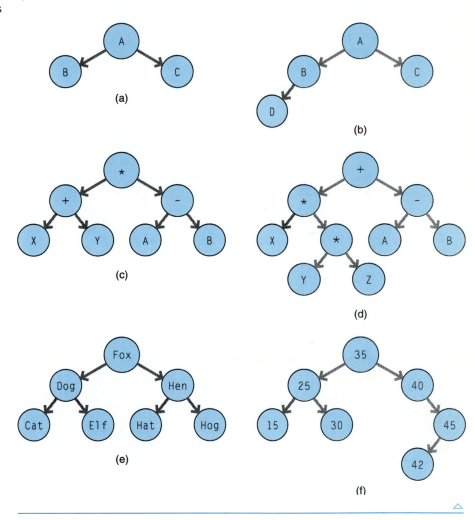

Figure 8.2
Explicit Representation of
the Tree in Fig. 8.1(b)

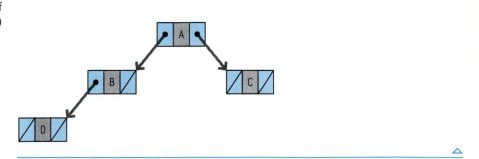

Figure 8.3
An Invalid Binary Tree

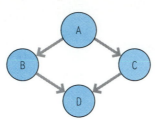

left (right) child of a node is the root node of its left (right) subtree. Either one or both of these subtrees may be empty (denoted by a pointer value of nil). A node with two empty subtrees is called a *leaf node*.

Figure 8.3 shows an invalid binary tree. The problem with the tree is that the node containing the letter D has two parents (B and C). This data structure is called a graph; it will be discussed in Chapter 9.

Height of a Tree and Level of a Node

The *height* of a tree is the length of the longest path from the root node to a leaf node (i.e., the number of branches in the longest path). The height of a tree is also one less than the number of nodes in its longest path. The heights of the trees in Fig. 8.1 and their longest paths are shown in Table 8.1. As shown, some trees have several paths that qualify as the longest path.

Table 8.1
Heights and Longest Paths of the Trees in Fig. 8.1

Tree	Height	Longest Path(s)
(a)	1	A, B; A, C
(b)	2	A, B, D
(c)	2	$\star$, + , X; $\star$, + , Y; $\star$, − , A; $\star$, − , B;
(d)	3	+ , $\star$, $\star$, Y; + , $\star$, $\star$, Z
(e)	2	FOX, DOG, CAT; FOX, DOG, ELF; FOX, HEN, HAT; FOX, HEN, HOG
(f)	3	35, 40, 45, 42

The level of a particular node indicates its relative position in the tree and is defined recursively as follows.

The *level* (or *depth*) of the root node is zero. The level of any other node is one more than the level of its parent node.

Table 8.2 shows the level of each node of the tree in Fig. 8.1 (f). There are three nodes at level 2.

Table 8.2
Level (Depth) of Each
Node of Fig. 8.1 (f)

Level	List of Nodes
0	35
1	25, 40
2	15, 30, 45
3	42

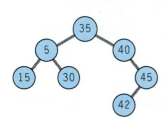

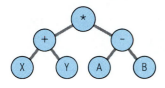

Expression Trees

Trees may be used for representing expressions in memory. For example, the expression

```
(X + Y) * (A - B)
```

could be represented by the tree in Fig. 8.1(c). Notice that the parentheses are not stored in the tree but are implied by the shape of the tree. If we assume that all operators have two operands, we can represent an expression by a binary tree whose root contains an operator and whose left and right subtrees are the left and right operands, respectively. Each operand can be a letter (X, Y, A, B, and so on) or a subexpression represented as a subtree. For example, the operator in the root is *, its left subtree represents the subexpression (X + Y), and its right subtree represents the subexpression (A – B). The root node for the left subtree contains the left subexpression operator (+), and the root node for the right subtree contains the right subexpression operator (–). All letter operands are stored in leaf nodes.

Using this reasoning, we can write the expression stored in Fig. 8.1(d) as

```
(X * (Y * Z)) + (A - B)
```

where we have inserted parentheses around subexpressions in the tree. Notice that operands (Y, Z) for the innermost subexpression (Y * Z) have the largest level value (3).

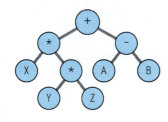

Figure 8.4
Expression Tree for
X * (Y / -Z)

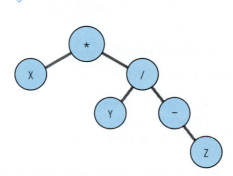

The operators for the trees shown in Figs. 8.1(c) and 8.1(d) all have two operands, so they are *binary operators*. Expressions sometimes have *unary operators,* which have only one operand (for example, unary minus). We can represent a unary operator and its operand by using a node with only a right subtree (the left subtree is empty). The expression X * (Y / −Z) could be represented by the tree in Fig. 8.4, where the operand for the unary minus operator is its right subtree.

Exercises for Section 8.1   **Self-Check**

1. What expression is stored in each of the following trees?

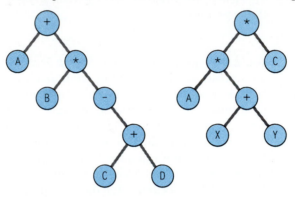

2. Draw the binary tree representation of each of the following expressions, assuming the normal rules of expression evaluation.

```
X * Y / (A + B) * C
X * Y / A + B * C
```

8.2 Traversing a Tree

To display the data stored in a tree, we need to be able to traverse the tree, or visit each node in a systematic way. The first approach that will be illustrated is called an *inorder traversal.* We provide a recursive algorithm for an inorder traversal next.

Algorithm for Inorder Traversal

1. if the tree is not empty then
    begin
        2. Traverse the left subtree
        3. Visit the root node
        4. Traverse the right subtree
    end

Recall that the left subtree of any node is the part of the tree whose root is the left child of that node. Figure 8.5 shows the order in which the nodes

Figure 8.5
Inorder Traversal of a Tree

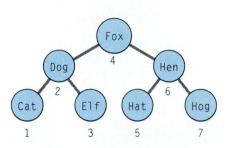

would be visited for an inorder traversal. If we assume that each node's data are displayed when it is visited, the strings will be printed in alphabetical order, as shown:

```
'CAT' 'DOG' 'ELF' 'FOX' 'HAT' 'HEN' 'HOG'
```

In Fig. 8.5 the nodes are numbered in the order in which they are visited during the inorder traversal. The first subtree traversed is the left subtree of the root node. Its left subtree (rooted at the node containing the string 'DOG') is traversed next. The next left subtree (rooted at the node containing the string 'CAT') has no left subtree; therefore the node is visited, and the string 'CAT' is displayed. The node containing 'CAT' has no right subtree; therefore we return to its ancestor node, and 'DOG' is displayed. Its right subtree consists of the leaf node containing the string 'ELF'. After 'ELF' is printed, the root node for the complete tree is visited ('FOX' is printed), and the right subtree of the root node (containing the string 'HEN') is traversed in a like manner.

Procedure Traverse in Fig. 8.6 is a recursive procedure that performs an inorder traversal of a tree and displays each node's data. We are assuming the following declarations for a tree element.

```
type
   TreePointer = ^TreeElement;
   TreeElement = record
                    TreeInfo : TreeData;
                    Left, Right : TreePointer
                 end; {TreeElement}
```

In procedure Traverse, the parameter Root represents the pointer to the root node of the tree being traversed. If the tree is empty (Root = nil), an immediate return occurs. Procedure Traverse, like most procedures that process trees, can be written much more simply with recursion than without it.

The if statement in Fig. 8.6 differs from the if statements shown in earlier recursive algorithms. Those if statements had the form

Figure 8.6
Procedure Traverse

Directory: CHAP 8
File: TRAVERSE.PAS

```
procedure Traverse (Root {input} : TreePointer);
{
  Performs an inorder traversal of a binary tree.
  Pre : Root points to a binary tree or is nil.
  Post: Displays each node visited.
}
begin {Traverse}
  if Root <> nil then
    begin {recursive step}
      Traverse (Root^.Left);       {Traverse left subtree}
      Root^.TreeInfo.Display;      {Display root value}
      Traverse (Root^.Right)       {Traverse right subtree}
    end {recursive step}
end; {Traverse}
```

```
if a stopping case is reached then
  Perform stopping step
else
  Perform recursion step
```

In a tree traversal there is nothing to do when a stopping case is reached except unwind from the recursion, so the if statement in Fig. 8.6 has the form

```
if a stopping case is not reached then
  Perform recursion step
```

Table 8.3 traces the recursive execution of procedure Traverse when the actual parameter in the original call points to the root of the tree in Fig. 8.1(c). The traversal would display the nodes in the sequence

```
X + Y * A - B
```

Except for the absence of parentheses, this is the form in which we would write the expression. The expression above is called an *infix* expression because each operator is between its two operands.

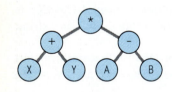

Table 8.3
Trace of Procedure
Traverse on Fig. 8.1(c)

Root	Action
Pointer to *	Traverse Left Subtree of *
Pointer to +	Traverse Left Subtree of +
Pointer to X	Traverse Left Subtree of X
nil	Return from Traversal of Left Subtree of X
Pointer to X	Display X
	Traverse Right Subtree of X
nil	Return from Traversal of Right Subtree of X

Root	Action
Pointer to X	Return from Traversal of Left Subtree of +
Pointer to +	Display +
	Traverse Right Subtree of +
Pointer to Y	Traverse Left Subtree of Y
nil	Return from Traversal of Left Subtree of Y
Pointer to Y	Display Y
	Traverse Right Subtree of Y
nil	Return from Traversal of Right Subtree of Y
Pointer to Y	Return from Traversal of Right Subtree of +
Pointer to +	Return from Traversal of Left Subtree of *
Pointer to *	Display *
	Traverse Right Subtree of *
Pointer to -	Traverse Left Subtree of -
Pointer to A	Traverse Left Subtree of A
nil	Return from Traversal of Left Subtree of A
Pointer to A	Display A
	Traverse Right Subtree of A
nil	Return from Traversal of Right Subtree of A
Pointer to A	Return from Traversal of Left Subtree of -
Pointer to -	Display -
	Traverse Right Subtree of -
Pointer to B	Traverse Left Subtree of B
nil	Return from Traversal of Left Subtree of B
Pointer to B	Display B
	Traverse Right Subtree of B
nil	Return from Traversal of Right Subtree of B
Pointer to B	Return from Traversal of Right Subtree of -
Pointer to -	Return from Traversal of Right Subtree of *
Pointer to *	Return from Original Call to Traverse

You get an interesting effect if you turn Table 8.3 sideways so that the right margin of the page is closest to you. If you focus only on the symbols in color, you will see that the relative location of each symbol on the page reflects its position in the tree. Figure 8.7 shows only the symbols in color, providing a flattened out version of the original tree.

Figure 8.7
Symbols in Color from
Table 8.3

Figure 8.8 illustrates the progress of procedure Traverse on the tree itself. The "snapshots" in the figure show the current value of parameter `Root` and the contents of the parameter stack that contains the current and previous values of `Root`. The snapshots in Fig. 8.8 correspond to the first 10 lines of Table 8.3. The parameter stack is empty in Fig. 8.8(a); after the first recursive call, it contains a pointer to $\star$ (denoted as ^ $\star$) in Fig. 8.8(b).

To clarify the meaning of an expression generated from an inorder traversal, we should insert parentheses where needed. We can do this by displaying a left parenthesis before each left traversal of a tree and by displaying a right parenthesis after returning from each right traversal. If we examine Fig. 8.8, the first four characters displayed would be (((X as a result of actions labeled (a), (b), (c), and (e). The complete traversal would display the fully parenthesized expression.

```
(((X) * (Y)) + ((A) - (B)))
```

We could eliminate the extra parentheses around the operands (e.g., (X)) by modifying the traversal procedure to display parentheses only when the symbol at the root of the current tree is an operator. Figure 8.9 shows procedure InOrder assuming that message Root^.TreeInfo.IsOperator returns True when the current tree root contains an operator.

PostOrder Traversal

Switching the sequence of the three statements in the if statement shown in Fig. 8.6 (procedure Traverse) will produce rather different results. The sequence

```
Traverse (Root^.Left);    {Traverse left subtree}
Traverse (Root^.Right);   {Traverse right subtree}
Root^.TreeInfo.Display    {Display root value}
```

displays the root node after traversing each of its subtrees; consequently, each root's data will be printed after all data in its subtrees. This is called a *postorder* traversal. The nodes in Fig. 8.1(e) would be visited in the sequence

```
CAT  ELF  DOG  HAT  HOG  HEN  FOX
```

Figure 8.8
Snapshots from the First 10
Lines of Table 10.3

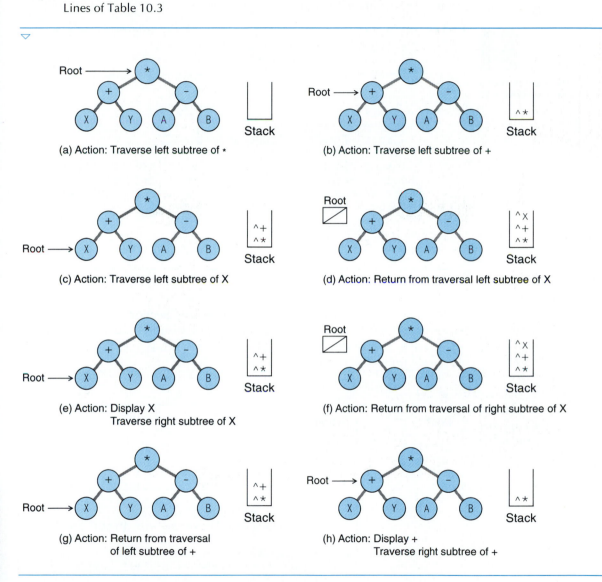

(a) Action: Traverse left subtree of *

(b) Action: Traverse left subtree of +

(c) Action: Traverse left subtree of X

(d) Action: Return from traversal left subtree of X

(e) Action: Display X
Traverse right subtree of X

(f) Action: Return from traversal of right subtree of X

(g) Action: Return from traversal
of left subtree of +

(h) Action: Display +
Traverse right subtree of +

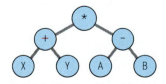

The nodes in the expression tree in Fig. 8.1(c) would be visited in the sequence

$$X \; Y \; + \; A \; B \; - \; *$$

Figure 8.9
Procedure Inorder with
Parentheses

Directory: CHAP 8
File: INORDER.PAS

```
procedure InOrder (Root {input} : TreePointer);
{
 Performs an inorder traversal of a binary expression tree.
 Pre : Root points to a binary tree or is nil.
 Post: Displays each node visited with parentheses around
         subexpressions.
}
begin {InOrder}
   if Root <> nil then
     begin {recursive step}
       if Root^.TreeInfo.IsOperator then
         Write ('(');
       InOrder (Root^.Left);        {Traverse left subtree}
       Root^.TreeInfo.Display;      {Display root value}
       InOrder (Root^.Right);       {Traverse right subtree}
       if Root^.TreeInfo.IsOperator then
         Write (')')
     end {recursive step}
   end; {InOrder}
```

This expression is called a *postfix expression* (see Section 5.3) because each operator follows its operands. The operands of + are X and Y; the operands of − are A and B; the operands of * are the two triples X Y + and A B −. Table 8.4 traces the postorder traversal of this tree.

Table 8.4
Trace of Postorder
Traversal on Fig. 8.1(c)

Root	Action
Pointer to *	Traverse Left Subtree of *
Pointer to +	Traverse Left Subtree of +
Pointer to X	Traverse Left Subtree of X
nil	Return from Traversal of Left Subtree of X
Pointer to X	Traverse Right Subtree of X
nil	Return from Traversal of Right Subtree of X
Pointer to X	Display X
	Return from Traversal of Left Subtree of +
Pointer to +	Traverse Right Subtree of +
Pointer to Y	Traverse Left Subtree of Y
nil	Return from Traversal of Left Subtree of Y
Pointer to Y	Traverse Right Subtree of Y
nil	Return from Traversal of Right Subtree of Y
Pointer to Y	Display Y

Table 8.4
Trace of Postorder
Traversal on Fig. 8.1(c)
(*Cont.*)

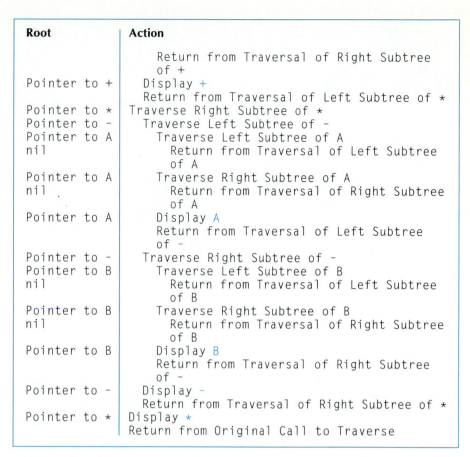

Root	Action
	Return from Traversal of Right Subtree of +
Pointer to +	Display +
	Return from Traversal of Left Subtree of *
Pointer to *	Traverse Right Subtree of *
Pointer to -	Traverse Left Subtree of -
Pointer to A	Traverse Left Subtree of A
nil	Return from Traversal of Left Subtree of A
Pointer to A	Traverse Right Subtree of A
nil	Return from Traversal of Right Subtree of A
Pointer to A	Display A
	Return from Traversal of Left Subtree of -
Pointer to -	Traverse Right Subtree of -
Pointer to B	Traverse Left Subtree of B
nil	Return from Traversal of Left Subtree of B
Pointer to B	Traverse Right Subtree of B
nil	Return from Traversal of Right Subtree of B
Pointer to B	Display B
	Return from Traversal of Right Subtree of -
Pointer to -	Display -
	Return from Traversal of Right Subtree of *
Pointer to *	Display *
	Return from Original Call to Traverse

PreOrder Traversal

Finally, the sequence

```
Root^.Info.Display;     {Display root value}
Traverse (Root^.Left);  {Traverse left subtree}
Traverse (Root^.Right)  {Traverse right subtree}
```

displays the root node before traversing its subtrees; consequently, the root node's data will be displayed before the data in its subtrees. This is called a *preorder* traversal. The preorder traversal of the tree in Fig. 8.1(e) would display the sequence

```
FOX  DOG  CAT  ELF  HEN  HAT  HOG
```

The nodes in the expression tree in Fig. 8.1(c) would be visited in the sequence

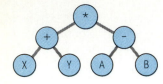

The previous expression is called a *prefix expression* because each operator precedes its operands. The operands of + are X and Y; the operands of − are A and B; the operands of * are the two triples + X Y and − A B. Table 8.5 traces the preorder traversal of this tree.

Table 8.5

Trace of Preorder Traversal on Fig. 8.1(c)

Root	Action
Pointer to *	Display *
	Traverse Left Subtree of *
Pointer to +	Display +
	Traverse Left Subtree of +
Pointer to X	Display X
	Traverse Left Subtree of X
nil	Return from Traversal of Left Subtree of X
Pointer to X	Traverse Right Subtree of X
nil	Return from Traversal of Right Subtree of X
Pointer to X	Return from Traversal of Left Subtree of +
Pointer to +	Traverse Right Subtree of +
Pointer to Y	Display Y
	Traverse Left Subtree of Y
nil	Return from Traversal of Left Subtree of Y
Pointer to Y	Traverse Right Subtree of Y
nil	Return from Traversal of Right Subtree of Y
Pointer to Y	Return from Traversal of Right Subtree of +
Pointer to +	Return from Traversal of Left Subtree of *
Pointer to *	Traverse Right Subtree of *
Pointer to −	Display −
	Traverse Left Subtree of −
Pointer to A	Display A
	Traverse Left Subtree of A
nil	Return from Traversal of Left Subtree of A
Pointer to A	Traverse Right Subtree of A
nil	Return from Traversal of Right Subtree of A
Pointer to A	Return from Traversal of Left Subtree of −
Pointer to −	Traverse Right Subtree of −
Pointer to B	Display B
	Traverse Left Subtree of B
nil	Return from Traversal of Left Subtree of B

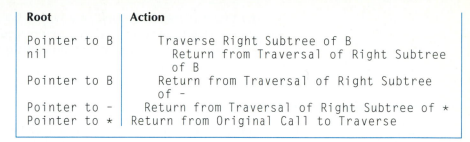

Root	Action
Pointer to B	Traverse Right Subtree of B
nil	Return from Traversal of Right Subtree of B
Pointer to B	Return from Traversal of Right Subtree of -
Pointer to -	Return from Traversal of Right Subtree of *
Pointer to *	Return from Original Call to Traverse

Table 8.5
Trace of Preorder Traversal
on Fig. 8.1(c)
(*Cont.*)

Tracing the Contour of a Tree

An easy way to determine the order in which the nodes of a tree are visited is to trace the contour of the tree, following all indentations, as shown in Fig. 8.10. Move your finger along the tree contour, starting to the left of the root node. As your finger passes under a node (indicated by an arrowhead), that node is visited in an inorder traversal (Fig. 8.10(a)). It is visited after you have traced all nodes in its left subtree and before you have started to trace the nodes in its right subtree.

As your finger passes to the right of a node, that node is visited in a postorder traversal (Fig. 8.10(b)). It is visited after you have traced its left and right subtrees. Your finger should be moving in an upward direction when a node is visited in a postorder traversal.

Figure 8.10
Tracing the Contour of
a Tree

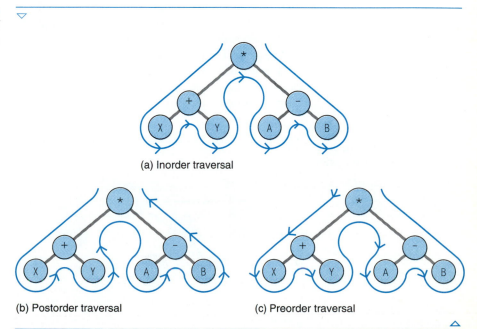

(a) Inorder traversal

(b) Postorder traversal

(c) Preorder traversal

As your finger passes to the left of a node, that node is visited in a preorder traversal (Fig 8.10(c)). It is visited before you start tracing its left subtree. Your finger should be moving in a downward direction when a node is visited in a preorder traversal.

Exercises for Section 8.2

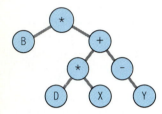

Self-Check

1. Rewrite the expressions in Self-Check Exercise 2 in Section 8.1 in prefix and postfix forms.
2. What would be printed by the inorder, preorder, and postorder traversals of the trees in Self-Check Exercise 1 in Section 8.1?
3. What would be printed by the inorder, preorder, and postorder traversals of the tree shown at left?

8.3 Binary Tree Abstract Data Type

In this section we will implement an abstract data type that contains some general methods for binary trees. The binary tree object declared in this unit will not be of much interest by itself; however, it will be an important ancestor to several descendant objects, including the binary search tree that will be described in Section 8.5.

The organization of our binary tree object will be similar to the organization that we used for our linked list object in Chapter 7. Each binary tree object will have three data members: the count of nodes in the tree (size), a pointer (Root) to the root of the tree, and a pointer (Cursor) to the most recently accessed node (the current element).

Figure 8.11 shows a sketch of a tree with 5 nodes. The information part of each node is a single character. The method members will move the Cursor down the tree, test the position of the Cursor, retrieve the data in the current element, replace the data stored in the current element, and insert a

Figure 8.11
A Tree with Five Nodes

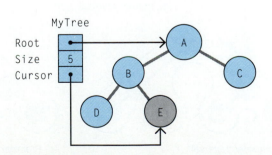

new node in one of three locations: the root of the tree, to the left of the current element, or to the right of the current element. The first insertion will be performed only when the tree is empty; for the latter two insertions the current node will become the parent of the new node. See Table 8.6.

Table 8.6

Specification of Binary Tree Abstract Data Type

Structure

A binary tree (object BinTree) is a collection of elements such that each element contains an information part (type TreeData) and pointers to its left and right subtrees. There are data members that consist of a pointer (`Root`) to the root of the binary tree, a pointer (`Cursor`) to the most recently accessed element, and a count of the number of elements in the tree.

Operators

For the following descriptions, assume the parameters:

```
El (pronounced el) has data type TreeData.
Ptr has data type TreePointer.
Success is a Boolean flag indicating success (True) or
    failure (False) of an operation.
Visit is procedure with a single formal parameter
    of object type TreeData.
```

BinTree.CreateTree	Creates an empty tree. Must be called before any other operators.
BinTree.GetSize	(function) Returns the number of elements currently in the tree.
BinTree.GetRoot	(function) Returns a pointer to the tree root.
BinTree.GetCursor	(function) Returns a pointer to the current tree node.
BinTree.IsEmpty	(function) Returns True if the tree is empty; otherwise, returns False.
BinTree.InsertAtRoot (El, var Success)	If Root is nil, inserts El as the information part of the root node and sets Cursor to the root. Otherwise, sets Success to False.
BinTree.InsertLeft (El, var Success)	Inserts item El as the information part of the root of the left subtree of the element pointed to by data member Cursor. The left subtree (if any) of the element pointed to by Cursor will become the left subtree of the new node. Cursor is advanced to point to the new node, and Success is set to

BinTree.InsertLeft (El, var Success)	True. If Cursor is nil, nothing is done, and Success is set to False.
BinTree.InsertRight (El, var Success)	Inserts item El as the information part of the root of the right subtree of the element pointed to by data member Cursor. The right subtree (if any) of the element pointed to by Cursor will become the right subtree of the new node. Cursor is advanced to point to the new node, and Success is set to True. If Cursor is nil, nothing is done, and Success is set to False.
BinTree.Replace (El, var Success)	Replaces the information part of the node pointed to by Cursor with El. If Cursor is nil, Success is set to False.
BinTree.Retrieve (var El, var Success)	Returns through El the tree element pointed to by Cursor and sets Success to True. If Cursor is nil, Success is set to False.
BinTree.InitCursor (Ptr : TreePointer)	Sets data member Cursor to the value of Ptr.
BinTree.GoLeft	Advances data member Cursor to the left child of the node pointed to by Cursor. If Cursor is nil, it is not changed.
BinTree.GoRight	Advances data member Cursor to the right child of the node pointed to by Cursor. If Cursor is nil, it is not changed.
BinTree.HasLeftTree	(function) Returns True if the node pointed to by Cursor has a left subtree; returns False if Cursor is nil or if the node pointed to by Cursor has no left subtree.
BinTree.HasRightTree	(function) Returns True if the node pointed to by Cursor has a right subtree; returns False if Cursor is nil or if the node pointed to by Cursor has no right subtree.
BinTree.InOrder (Visit)	Applies procedure Visit to each tree element of type TreeData using an inorder traversal.

Figure 8.12
The Effects of
InsertLeft and
InsertRight

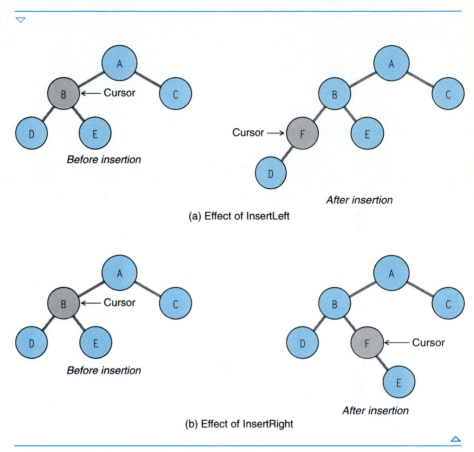

(a) Effect of InsertLeft

(b) Effect of InsertRight

The method members are all relatively straightforward with the possible exception of InsertLeft and InsertRight. InsertLeft inserts a new node to the left of the one pointed to by Cursor (the new node's parent node). The new node will become the root of the left subtree of its parent. If its parent already has a left subtree, the left subtree of the parent will become the left subtree of the new child.

Figure 8.12(a) illustrates the effect of a call to InsertLeft on the tree in Fig. 8.1(b). The new node (node F) is inserted as the left child of node B. Node F's left subtree is the former left subtree of node B. Node B's right subtree is unchanged, and new node B has no right subtree. For purposes of comparison, Fig. 8.12(b) shows the effect of InsertRight on the same tree.

Figure 8.13
Interface Section for Unit
BinTreeADT

Directory: CHAP 8
File: BINTREEA.PAS

```pascal
unit BinTreeADT;
{
 Abstract data type BinTree: contains declarations for data
 type BinTree and its methods.
}
interface

  uses TreeDataADT;          {Import object type TreeData}

  type
    TreePointer = ^TreeNode;
    TreeNode = record                        {a tree node}
                   TreeInfo : TreeData;      {information part}
                   Left,
                   Right : TreePointer
                 end; {TreeNode}

    ProcedureType = procedure (P : TreeData);

    BinTree = object
                procedure CreateTree;
                function GetSize : Word;
                function GetRoot : TreePointer;
                function GetCursor : TreePointer;
                function IsEmpty : Boolean;
                procedure InsertAtRoot
                         (El {input} : TreeData;
                          var Success {output} : Boolean);
                procedure InsertLeft
                         (El {input} : TreeData;
                          var Success {output} : Boolean);
                procedure InsertRight
                         (El {input} : TreeData;
                          var Success {output} : Boolean);
                procedure Retrieve
                         (var El {output} : TreeData;
                          var Success : Boolean);
                procedure Replace (El {input} : TreeData;
                          var Success : Boolean);
                procedure InitCursor (Ptr {input} : TreePointer);
                function HasLeftTree : Boolean;
                function HasRightTree : Boolean;
                procedure GoLeft;
                procedure GoRight;
                procedure InOrder (Visit : ProcedureType);

              private
                Root, Cursor : TreePointer;
                Size : Word;
                procedure DoInOrder (Next {input} : TreePointer;
                                     Visit : ProcedureType);
              end; {BinTree}
```

8.4 Implementing a Binary Tree ADT

Figure 8.13 shows the interface section for object type `BinTree`.

Figure 8.14 shows the implementation section for unit `BinTreeADT`. Most of the methods are quite straightforward. You may want to trace the execution of procedures `InsertRight` and `InsertLeft` carefully on the trees in Fig. 8.12 to verify that they do what is intended.

Figure 8.14
Implementation Section for
Unit `BinTreeADT`

Directory: CHAP 8
File: BINTREEA.PAS

```
implementation

  procedure BinTree.CreateTree;
  {
   Creates an empty tree. Must be called first.
   Pre : None.
   Post: Root and Cursor set to nil, Size set to 0.
  }
  begin {CreateTree}
    Root := nil;
    Cursor := nil;
    Size := 0
  end; {CreateTree}

  function BinTree.GetSize : Word;
  {
   Returns number of elements currently in tree.
  }
  begin {GetSize}
    GetSize := Size
  end; {GetSize}

  function BinTree.GetRoot : TreePointer;
  {
   Returns value of data member Root.
  }
  begin {GetRoot}
    GetRoot := Root
  end; {GetRoot}

  function BinTree.GetCursor : TreePointer;
  {
   Returns value of data member Cursor.
  }
  begin {GetCursor}
    GetCursor := Cursor
  end; {GetCursor}
```

▷ ▷ ▷ ▷ ▷

```
function BinTree.IsEmpty : Boolean;
{
 Returns True if tree is empty; otherwise returns False.
}
begin {IsEmpty}
  IsEmpty := (Size = 0)
end; {IsEmpty}

procedure BinTree.InsertAtRoot
                     (El {input} : TreeData;
                      var Success {output} : Boolean);
{
 Inserts new root node containing El into empty tree.
 Pre : Tree is initialized.
 Post: If Root is nil, inserts new root containing El and
       sets Success to True; otherwise sets Success to
       False.
}
begin {InsertAtRoot}
  if Root <> nil then
    Success := False
  else
    begin
      New (Root);
      Root^.TreeInfo := El;
      Root^.Left := nil;
      Root^.Right := nil;
      Cursor := Root;
      Size := 1;
      Success := True
    end {else}
end; {InsertAtRoot}

procedure BinTree.InsertLeft (El {input} : TreeData;
                               var Success {output} : Boolean);
{
 Inserts El into new node in left subtree of node pointed
 to by Cursor.
 Pre : Tree is initialized and El defined.
 Post: If Cursor is nil, Success is False. If Cursor
       is not nil, Success is set to True, Cursor points to
       new node containing El which is left child of old
       node pointed to by Cursor. New node's left subtree
       is the left subtree of the old node. New node's right
       subtree is empty.
}
  var
    OldLeft : TreePointer; {Pointer to old left subtree}

begin {InsertLeft}
  if Cursor = nil then
    Success := False
```

▷ ▷ ▷ ▷ ▷ ▷

```
    else
      begin
        OldLeft := Cursor^.Left;      {Save old left subtree}
        New (Cursor^.Left);           {Connect new node}
        Cursor := Cursor^.Left;       {Move Cursor to new node}
        Cursor^.TreeInfo := El;       {Store El in it}
        Cursor^.Right := nil;         {Define its right and}
        Cursor^.Left := OldLeft;      {left subtrees.}
        Size := Size + 1;
        Success := True
      end {if}
end; {InsertLeft}

procedure BinTree.InsertRight (El {input} : TreeData;
                                    var Success {output} : Boolean);
{
 Inserts El into new node in right subtree of the node
 pointed to by Cursor.
 Pre : Tree is initialized and El defined.
 Post: If Cursor is nil, Success is False. If Cursor is not
       nil, Success is set to True, Cursor points to new
       node containing El which is the child of the old node
       pointed to by Cursor. New node's right subtree is
       the right subtree of the old node. New node's left
       subtree is empty.
}
   var
     OldRight : TreePointer; {Pointer to old right subtree}

begin {InsertRight}
   if Cursor = nil then
     Success := False
   else
     begin
       OldRight := Cursor^.Right;     {Save old right subtree}
       New (Cursor^.Right);           {Connect new node}
       Cursor := Cursor^ .Right;      {Move Cursor to new node}
       Cursor^.TreeInfo := El;        {Store El in it}
       Cursor^.Left := nil;           {Define its left and}
       Cursor^.Right := OldRight;     {right subtrees}
       Size := Size + 1;
       Success := True
     end {if}
end; {InsertRight}

procedure BinTree.Retrieve (var El {output} : TreeData;
                                var Success {output} : Boolean);
{
 Returns data stored in tree node pointed to by Cursor.
 Pre : Tree initialized.
 Post: If Cursor is nil Success is False and El is not
       defined; otherwise data stored in node pointed to by
 Cursor is copied to El and Success is set to True.
```

▷ ▷ ▷ ▷ ▷

```
      }
   begin {Retrieve}
     if Cursor = nil then
       Success := False
     else
       begin
         El := Cursor^.TreeInfo;
         Success := True
       end {else}
   end; {Retrieve}

   procedure BinTree.Replace (El {input} : TreeData;
                                 var Success {output} : Boolean);
   {
    Copies data stored in El to tree node pointed to by Cursor.
    Pre : Tree initialized and El defined.
    Post: If Cursor is nil, Success is False; otherwise data
          is copied from El to node pointed to by Cursor and
          Success is set to True.
   }
   begin {Replace}
     if Cursor = nil then
       Success := False
     else
       begin
         Cursor^.TreeInfo := El;
         Success := True
       end {else}
   end; {Replace}

   procedure BinTree.InitCursor (Ptr {input} : TreePointer);
   {
    Sets data member Cursor to value of Ptr.
    Pre : Tree is initialized and Ptr defined.
    Post: Cursor set to point to Ptr node.
   }
   begin {InitCursor}
     Cursor := Ptr
   end; {InitCursor}

   function BinTree.HasLeftTree : Boolean;
   {
    Returns True if node pointed to by Cursor has left subtree;
    otherwise returns False.
   }
   begin {HasLeftTree}
     if Cursor = nil then
       HasLeftTree := False
     else if Cursor^ .Left = nil then
       HasLeftTree := False
     else
       HasLeftTree := True
     end; {HasLeftTree}
```

▷ ▷ ▷ ▷ ▷ ▷

```
function BinTree.HasRightTree : Boolean;
{
 Returns True if node pointed to by Cursor has right
 subtree; otherwise returns False.
}
begin {HasRightTree}
  if Cursor = nil then
    HasRightTree := False
  else if Cursor^.Right = nil then
    HasRightTree := False
  else
    HasRightTree := True
end; {HasRightTree}

procedure BinTree.GoLeft;
{
 Advances Cursor to point to left child of node pointed to
 by Cursor.
 Pre : Tree initialized.
 Post: If Cursor is not nil, it is set to left child of the
       node originally pointed to by Cursor; otherwise
       Cursor value is not changed.
}
begin {GoLeft}
  if Cursor <> nil then
    Cursor := Cursor^.Left
end; {GoLeft}

procedure BinTree.GoRight;
{
 Advances Cursor to point to right child of node pointed to
 by Cursor.
 Pre : Tree initialized.
 Post: If Cursor is not nil, it is set to right child of the
       node originally pointed to by Cursor; otherwise
       Cursor value is not changed.
}
begin {GoRight}
  if Cursor <> nil then
    Cursor := Cursor^.Right
end; {GoRight}

procedure BinTree.DoInOrder (Next {input} : TreePointer;
                             Visit : ProcedureType);
{
 Applies procedure Visit to each node in tree having root
 pointer Next.
 Pre : Tree initialized and Visit defined
 Post: Returns if Next is nil; otherwise, traverses left
       subtree, visits root to apply Visit, and traverses
       right subtree.
  }
```

```
      begin {DoInOrder}
        if Next <> nil then
          begin
            DoInOrder (Next^.Left, Visit);
            Visit (Next^.TreeInfo);
            DoInOrder (Next^.Right, Visit)
          end {if}
      end; {DoInOrder}

      procedure BinTree.InOrder (Visit : ProcedureType);

      {
        Applies procedure Visit to each tree element using an
        inorder traversal.
        Pre : Tree initialized; Visit defined in client program
              and compiled using Borland Pascal far code model.
        Post: Visit has been applied to each tree node.
      }
      begin {InOrder}
        DoInOrder (Root, Visit)
      end; {InOrder}

  end. {BinTreeADT}
```

△

Notice that procedure InOrder (inorder traversal) uses a private helper function DoInOrder that performs the actual traversal. In the initial call to DoInOrder, procedure InOrder passes DoInOrder a pointer to the tree root. In each recursive call, DoInOrder is passed a pointer to either the left or the right subtree of its current tree root.

CASE STUDY   Evaluation of a Binary Expression Tree

PROBLEM ▼

We would like to be able to store expressions in a binary expression tree and evaluate them.

ANALYSIS ▼

We can consider a binary expression tree as a descendant of a binary tree. Besides the methods shown earlier, we will need a new traversal method that will insert parentheses where needed (see Fig. 8.9) and methods that build a binary expression tree and that evaluate an expression stored in a binary expression tree. Figure 8.15 shows the interface section for unit BinExpTreeADT.

```
unit BinExpTreeADT;
{
  Abstract data type BinExpTree: contains declarations for data
  type BinExpTree and its methods.
}
interface

  uses TreeDataADT, BinTreeADT;  {Import object type TreeData}

  type
    BinExpTree = object (BinTree) {descendant of binary tree}
                   function Eval : Real;
                   procedure InOrder (Visit : ProcedureType);

                 private
                   procedure DoInOrder
                               (Root {input} : TreePointer;
                                Visit : ProcedureType);
                   function DoEval
                               (Root {input} : TreePointer) : Real;
                 end; {SearchTree}
```

DESIGN ▼

Figure 8.16 shows the new traversal methods. InOrder can be called by a client program to initiate the traversal. InOrder calls DoInOrder, passing it a pointer to the root of the tree. Method TreeData.Display will display each node's data without terminating the display line.

```
implementation

  procedure BinExpTree.DoInOrder (Root {input} : TreePointer;
                                  Visit : ProcedureType);
  {
    Applies procedure Visit to each tree node root Pointer Root.
    Pre : Tree initialized and Visit is defined.
    Post: Returns if Root is nil; otherwise, traverses left
          subtree, visits root to apply visit, and traverses
          right subtree.
  }
  begin {DoInOrder}
    if Root <> nil then
      begin {recursive step}
```

▷ ▷ ▷ ▷ ▷ ▷

```
          if Root^.TreeInfo.IsOperator then
            Write ('(');
          DoInOrder (Root^.Left, Visit);  {Traverse left subtree}
          Visit (Root^.TreeInfo);         {Display root value}
          DoInOrder (Root^.Right, Visit); {Traverse right subtree}
          if Root^.TreeInfo.IsOperator then
            Write (')')
      end {recursive step}
end; {DoInOrder}

procedure BinExpTree.InOrder (Visit : ProcedureType);
{
  Applies procedure Visit to each tree element using an
  inorder traversal.
  Pre : Tree initialized; Visit defined in client program and
        compiled using Borland Pascal far code model.
  Post: Visit has been applied to each tree node.
}
begin {InOrder}
  DoInOrder (GetRoot, Visit)
end; {InOrder}
```

Notice that method BinExpTree.DoInOrder calls method BinTree.GetRoot to access the pointer to the tree root. Because root is a private data member of object BinTree, object BinExpTree's methods cannot reference it directly.

Next we will focus on the evaluation methods. We can use recursion to simplify the solution to this problem. There are three cases to account for. If the binary tree root contains an operator, we must apply that operator to the result of evaluating its left and right subtrees. If the binary tree root contains an operand, the result is the value of its operand. If the binary tree being evaluated is empty, the result is zero. The last situation occurs only when the operator is unary minus because only unary minus can have just one operand (its right subtree). The algorithm for evaluating a binary expression tree follows.

Algorithm for Evaluating a Binary Expression Tree

1. if the tree is empty then
    2. the tree value is 0
else if the information part is an operand then
    3. the result is the value of the operand
else
    begin
        4. Evaluate the left subtree
        5. Evaluate the right subtree
        6. Apply the operator to the results of steps 4. and 5.
    end

CODING FUNCTION Eval ▼

We will use function `Eval` and a helper function, `DoEval`, to implement this algorithm (see Fig. 8.17). A client program can call function `Eval` to initiate the expression evaluation; function `Eval` calls `DoEval`, passing it a pointer to the tree root. Function `DoEval` implements the recursive algorithm above. It begins by pointing `Cursor` to the root of the subtree being evaluated and retrieving the data at that node. Next, `DoEval` calls method `TreeData.IsOperator` to determine whether the node contains an operator. If it does, `DoEval` calls itself recursively to evaluate the left and right subtrees of the root node using the statements

```
LeftTreeVal := DoEval(Tree.GoLeft);  {Evaluate left subtree}
RightTreeVal := DoEval(Tree.GoRight);{Evaluate right subtree}
```

The argument for each of these calls is a pointer to the root of the subtree to be evaluated in the next recursive call of `DoEval`.

Figure 8.17

Methods `Eval` and `DoEval` for `BinExpTree`

Directory: CHAP 8
File: BINEXPTR.PAS

```
function BinExpTree.DoEval (Root : TreePointer) : Real;
{
 Computes value of expression stored in expression tree
 with root stored in Root.
 Pre : Binary expression tree is initialized.
 Post: If tree is empty returns 0.0, if CurrentNode is an
       operand the operand value is returned, if it is an
       operators DoEval calls itself recursively to evaluate
       the left and right subtree of the tree whose root
       is stored in Root.
}
  var
    CurrentNode : TreeData;       {Data at current node}
    LeftTreeVal,                  {Left subtree value}
    RightTreeVal : Real;          {Right subtree value}
    Success : Boolean;            {flag}

begin {DoEval}
  InitCursor (Root);                   {Set Cursor to tree root}
  Retrieve (CurrentNode, Success);     {Retrieve root data}
  if not Success then
    DoEval := 0.0                                {Tree is empty}
  else if not CurrentNode.IsOperator then
    DoEval := CurrentNode.GetVal    {Return operand's value}
  else
    begin {operator}
      LeftTreeVal := DoEval(Root^.Left);
      RightTreeVal := DoEval(Root^.Right);
```

▷ ▷ ▷ ▷ ▷ ▷

```
        case CurrentNode.GetOperator of
          '+' : DoEval := LeftTreeVal + RightTreeVal;
          '-' : DoEval := LeftTreeVal - RightTreeVal;
          '*' : DoEval := LeftTreeVal * RightTreeVal;
          '/' : DoEval := LeftTreeVal / RightTreeVal
        end {case}
     end {operator}
 end; {DoEval}

 function BinExpTree.Eval : Real;
 {
  Computes value of expression housed in expression tree.
  Pre : Binary expression tree is initialized.
  Post: Returns value of expression stored in tree or
        0.0 if tree is empty.
 }
 begin {Eval}
   Eval := DoEval(GetRoot)        {Start at tree root}
 end; {Eval}

end. {BinExpTreeADT}
```

After the left and right subtrees are evaluated, the case statement uses the method `TreeData.GetOperator` to retrieve the operator value (a character). Next, one of four possible arithmetic operations is chosen on the basis of the operator value and is performed on the left and right subtree values.

TESTING AND VERIFICATION ▼

Before we can test these methods, we must provide object type `TreeData` and a method for building a binary expression tree. We will leave these tasks for a programming project (see Programming Project 5 at the end of the chapter). In the project description we discuss how to store a binary expression in a tree. We show how to build a different kind of binary tree in the next section.

Exercises for Section 8.4

Self-Check

1. Does our binary expression tree allow for the use of the unary minus operator? If so, how?

Programming

1. Write unit `TreeDataADT` containing the declaration of an object `TreeData` that contains an Integer data field called `Info` and methods for reading and displaying the contents of `Info`.

2. Write a client program that uses your unit `TreeDataADT` (from Programming Exercise 1) and our unit `BinTreeADT` to build and display the following tree:

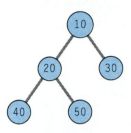

8.5 Binary Search Tree Abstract Data Type

The most important binary tree that we will study is the binary search tree. A binary search tree is a tree structure that stores data in such a way that it can be retrieved very efficiently. A binary search tree has the property that for any node, all key values less than that node's key value are in its left subtree, and all key values greater than that node's key value are in its right subtree. For example, in the binary search tree in Fig. 8.18(a) whose keys are 3 character strings, the left child of each node alphabetically precedes its parent, and the right child alphabetically follows its parent. A similar statement can be made for the integer values stored in the binary search tree in Fig. 8.18(b). (*Note:* These trees were first shown in Figs. 8.1(e) and 8.6(f).) A formal definition of a binary search tree follows.

A **binary search tree** T is a binary tree such that either T is empty or

▶ Each item in the left subtree of T is less than the root item of T.
▶ Each item in the right subtree of T is greater than the root item of T.
▶ The left and right subtrees of T are binary search trees.

Figure 8.18
Binary Search Trees

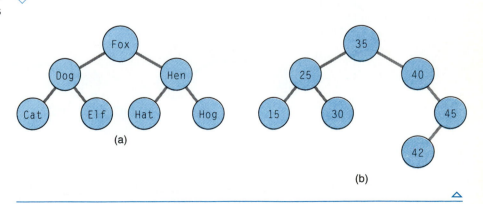

Figure 8.19
Search for 42 in a Binary
Search Tree

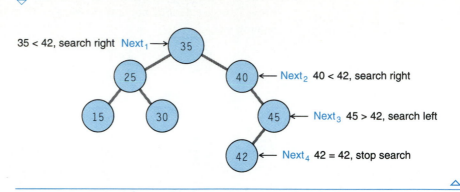

Searching a Binary Search Tree

Next we explain how we search for an item in a binary search tree. To find a particular item (say, E1), we compare E1's key to the root item's key. If E1's key is less than the root item's key, we know that E1 can only be in the left subtree, so we can ignore the right subtree. Similarly, if E1's key is greater than the root item's key, we know that item E1 can only be in the right subtree, so we can ignore the left subtree.

Figure 8.19 illustrates a search of a binary search tree that contains a collection of integer values. $Next_i$ points to the node being compared to the target item (42) during the ith comparison.

In the search in Fig. 8.19, it took four probes into the tree to find the key 42. This tree has a height of three, and it took the maximum number of probes (one plus the tree height) to locate the target key. This result does not seem very good for a tree that contains only six values. However, this is a very small tree, and there were a lot of empty spaces in it.

Figure 8.20
Fully Populated Binary
Search Trees

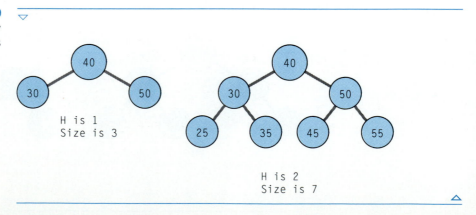

Fully Populated and Balanced Binary Trees

Figure 8.20 shows two fully populated binary search trees of height 1 and 2, where a *fully populated binary tree* has no nil pointers except at the bottom level.

Let's consider a slightly larger tree. It is possible to store $2^{10} - 1$ (or 1023) keys in a fully populated tree with height 9. Because the maximum number of probes is one more than the tree height, it would require at most 10 probes to retrieve any one of 1023 keys stored in a fully populated binary tree. To see where the number 1023 comes from, consider that we can store 3 $(2^2 - 1)$ keys in a tree of height 1, 7 $(2^3 - 1)$ keys in a tree of height 2, . . ., and $2^{H+1} - 1$ keys in a tree of height H.

Although we cannot always have fully populated trees, it is possible to always have trees that are balanced.

A **balanced tree** T is a binary tree such that either T is empty or

▶ The height of the left subtree of T (H_L) differs by at most 1 from the height of the right subtree of T (H_R); that is, $|H_L - H_R| < 1$.
▶ The left and right subtrees of T are balanced trees.

Figure 8.21 shows a balanced binary search tree in which we have included the value of $H_L - H_R$ under the key of each node. For example, for the root node, $H_L - H_R$ is 0 because its left and right subtrees have a height of 3. For the node with key 40, $H_L - H_R$ is -1 because H_L is 1 and H_R is 2. In Section 9.2 we will discuss how we keep a binary search tree balanced.

Search Efficiency for Binary Search Trees

What is the relationship between the number of keys (N) in a tree and the maximum number of probes that we have to make? If N is between 512 and 1023 and the tree is nearly full at each level, we will usually not need more than 10 probes. If we write the equation

Figure 8.21
A Balanced Binary Tree
with $H_L - H_R$

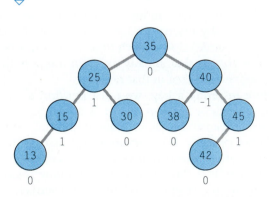

$$1024 = 2^{10}$$

and take the log to the base 2 of both sides, we get

$$\log_2 1024 = 10$$

Therefore the search process in the best case is an $O(\log_2 N)$ process. However, if the tree is not full and if it is badly unbalanced, its shape will begin to resemble that of a linear linked list, and the search algorithm in the worst case is an $O(N)$ process. Table 8.7 shows some values of N and $\log_2 N$. Each doubling of N causes $\log_2 N$ to increase by only 1.

Table 8.7
Table of N versus $\log_2 N$

Values of N	$\log_2 N$
32	5
64	6
128	7
256	8
512	9
1024	10

Of course, we will not always be dealing with full binary trees, so our search results will not always be this good. However, if we assume that the keys being stored in the tree arrive in random order, experimental results show that searching a binary search tree in its average case is an $O(\log_2 N)$ process.

How does this compare with searching a linked list? If we are assuming random arrival of keys, on average we will have to examine N/2 items in a linked list to find a particular key. Therefore searching a list is an $O(N)$ process in both its average and worst cases.

Inserting Keys in a Binary Search Tree

Before we can retrieve an item from a binary search tree, we must, of course, build the tree by inserting a list of keys in it. We must build a tree from the top (or root node) down. Each time we insert a new key, we will connect a new node to one that already exists in the tree and then store the new key and its associated data in that node.

Before inserting a key, we must perform a search similar to the one required to retrieve an item. If our search is successful, the key is already in the tree. Because we don't want duplicate entries for the same key, we should not perform an insertion in this case. If the search is unsuccessful, it will terminate at the parent of the new key. If it is smaller than its parent's key, the new key should be stored in a new node that is the root of its parent's left subtree (use method BinTree.InsertLeft); if it is larger than its par-

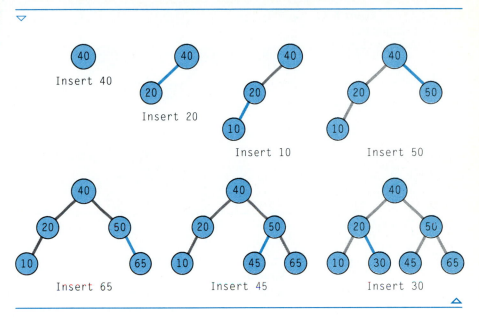

ent's key, the new key should be stored in a new node that is the root of its parent's right subtree (use method member BinTree.InsertRight). Figure 8.22 builds a tree from the following list of keys: 40, 20, 10, 50, 65, 45, 30. The search path followed in inserting a particular key is shown in color in each diagram.

We will verify the insertion path shown for the key 30 (the last diagram in Fig. 8.22). The tree searched is the one in the middle of the bottom row of Fig. 8.22. 30 is less than 40, so 30 must be in the left subtree of the root. 30 is greater than 20, so 30 must be in the right subtree of 20. Because 20 has no subtree, 30 is inserted in 20's new right subtree as shown.

The last tree in Fig. 8.22 is fully populated. It is interesting to observe how the order of key insertion affects the shape of the final tree. Let's try the same collection of keys but this time store them in increasing order: 10, 20, 30, 40, 45, 50, 65. Figure 8.23 shows the first four trees. It should be clear that all left subtrees are empty and will continue to be empty as the remaining keys are inserted. As we discussed retrieving data from this tree would be no more efficient than using a linked list.

Specification for a Binary Search Tree

Because the binary search tree object is a descendant of our general binary tree, the only new methods that we need are Search and Insert. Table 8.8 gives the specification for a binary search tree.

Figure 8.23
Inserting Keys in an
Increasing Sequence

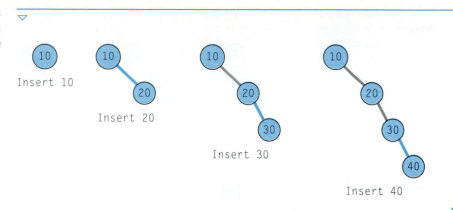

Table 8.8
Specification of
Binary Search Tree
Abstract Data Type

Structure

A binary search tree (object SearchTree) is a binary tree that consists of a collection of elements such that each element includes among its data fields a special field called the key field. The key field of each element in a binary search tree is larger than all keys in its left subtree and smaller than all keys in its right subtree. A binary search tree object has data fields that consist of a pointer (Root) to the root of the binary search tree, a pointer (Cursor) to the most recently accessed element, and a count of the number of elements in the tree.

Operators

For the following descriptions, assume the parameters:

```
Tree represents the binary search tree.
El (pronounced el) has the same data type as the tree
   elements.
Success is a Boolean flag indicating success (True) or
   failure (False) of an operation.
```

Insert (El, var Success)   Inserts item El into a binary search tree and sets Success to True. If there is already an element with the same key value as El, Success is set to False, and no insertion is performed.

Search (El, var Success)   Searches a binary search tree to find the tree node with the same key field as El. If found, sets Success to True; otherwise, sets Success to False. Advances Cursor to point to the tree node that matched El and sets Success to True. If El is not matched, sets Success to False and advances Cursor to the last tree node whose key field was probed.

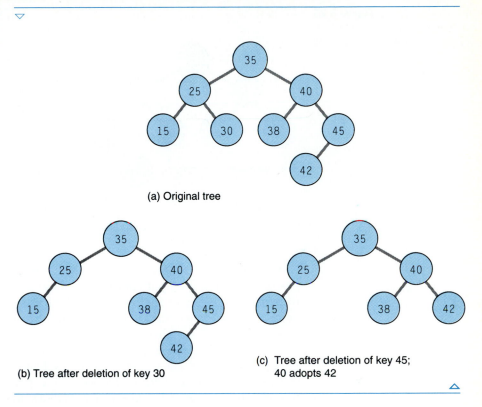

Figure 8.24
Deleting Nodes with Zero
or One Subtree

(a) Original tree

(b) Tree after deletion of key 30

(c) Tree after deletion of key 45;
40 adopts 42

Deleting a Tree Node

If you compare the binary tree and binary search tree ADTs with the linked list ADT, you may notice that there is no `Delete` method. We have not provided this method because there is generally no need to delete a node once it has been placed in a binary tree (unless the binary tree is being used to house an active database). Binary search trees can be used to store a dictionary of words or a *symbol table* (a tree of identifiers) for a particular program. If for some reason a word is no longer needed in the dictionary, it is usually less trouble to leave it in and ignore it (i.e., never retrieve it) than it is to remove it and reorganize the tree. Of course, if the tree contains lots of deleted nodes, the search efficiency will decrease markedly.

There are three cases to deal with in deleting a node's data from a binary search tree. The first two cases are relatively easy. If the node is a leaf node (i.e., has no left or right subtree), it can be deleted by setting its parent's pointer to nil. Figures 8.24(a) and 8.28(b) show a binary search tree before and after deletion of a leaf node (key 30). If the node being deleted (key 40) has only one child, it can be deleted by having its parent (the child's grandparent) adopt that child (see Figs. 8.24(b) and 8.24(c)).

Figure 8.25
Deleting a Node with Two
Nonempty Subtrees

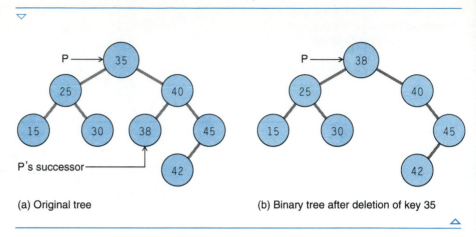

(a) Original tree

(b) Binary tree after deletion of key 35

What if the key that we wish to delete is found in a node (say, node P) that has both a left and a right child? In this case we cannot just remove node P from the tree. We must replace P's data with data stored in one of its descendants (having zero or one child nodes) and then delete that node instead. To retain the binary search tree property, we need to choose the descendant node whose key is the next larger key (after P's key) stored in the tree. The next larger key will always be found in the leftmost node of P's right subtree so that it cannot have a left child of its own. For example, if we want to delete the data in the root of the tree in Fig. 8.25(a), we would replace it with the data in the node with key 38 and then delete the node that contained key 38 (i.e., P's right subtree has key 40, and its leftmost descendant has key 38).

Why does the leftmost node in the right subtree of the node being deleted contain the next larger key? Recall what happens during an inorder traversal of a binary tree. All keys larger than the key being deleted are in its right subtree. The smallest of these keys will be the first node visited during an inorder traversal of P's right subtree, which is the right subtree's leftmost node.

In general, how do we find the leftmost node in the right subtree? We go to the right subtree and follow all left pointers until we reach a node whose left pointer is nil (the node with key 38 in Fig. 8.25(a)). It is impossible for the leftmost child to have more than one subtree (Why?), so we can easily delete the leftmost child after we move its data. Figure 8.25(b) shows the tree after we have replaced the data in its root node and deleted the child node with key 38. We will leave the implementation of this method for a programming project (see Programming Project 6 at the end of the chapter). If the node containing 38 had a right subtree, its right subtree would become the left subtree of its old parent (the node containing 40).

We can also delete a node by replacing it with the data in the node that contains the next smaller key. Self-Check Exercise 1 discusses where this key might be located in the tree.

Exercises for Section 8.5   ***Self-Check***

1. What key is in the rightmost child of the left subtree of the root node of Fig. 8.25(a)? What is the relationship between that key and the key in the root node?
2. Which two keys could be moved to the root if we wanted to delete key 38 from the tree in Fig. 8.25(b)? Draw the new trees that would result.

8.6 Implementing the Binary Search Tree ADT

Figure 8.26 shows the interface section of unit `SearchTreeADT`. We will discuss the method implementations after Fig. 8.26.

We have already discussed the algorithms for searching a binary search tree and inserting an element in a binary search tree. The search algorithm is repeated below.

Algorithm for Searching a Binary Search Tree

1. if the current node's key matches the target key then
   2. Success : = True
   else if the current node's key < target key then
      3. if the current node has no right subtree then
         4. Success : = False
      else
         5. Search the right subtree
   else if the current node has no left subtree then
      6. Success : = False
   else
      7. Search the left subtree

Figure 8.27 implements procedure `Search`. `Search` initializes `Cursor` to the tree root and calls its helper procedure `DoSearch`. `DoSearch` advances `Cursor` down the tree until it reaches the element whose key matches `El`'s (`Success` is `True`) or it reaches the node that would be `El`'s parent if `El` were in the tree (`Success` is `False`).

The algorithm for inserting a key in a tree follows. The first key is always inserted in the tree root. If the tree is not empty, we must determine whether the key is already in the tree (duplicate entry) or find its parent node.

Algorithm for Inserting a Key in a Binary Search Tree

1. if the tree is empty then
   2. Insert the first key in the tree root.

Figure 8.26
Interface Section for Unit
`SearchTree.ADT`

Directory: CHAP 8
File: SEARCHTR.PAS

```
unit SearchTreeADT;
{
 Abstract data type SearchTree: contains declarations for
 data type SearchTree and its methods.
}
interface

  uses TreeDataADT, BinTreeADT; {Import object type TreeData}

    type
      SearchTree = object (BinTree) {descendant of binary tree}
                  procedure Insert
                            (El {input} : TreeData;
                             var {output} Success : Boolean);
                  procedure Search
                            (El {input} : TreeData;
                             var {output} Success : Boolean);
                private
                  procedure DoSearch
                            (El {input} : TreeData;
                             var Success {output} : Boolean);
      end; {SearchTree}
```

    else
    begin
       3. Search for El's key in the tree, moving Cursor
           to El or to El's parent if El is missing.
      4. if El's key is in the tree then
         5. Set Success to False to indicate duplicate key.
         else if El's parent's key $<$ El's key then
        7. Insert El in its parent's right subtree.
      else
       8. Insert El in its parent's left subtree.

Figure 8.28 shows the implementation of procedure `Insert`. `Insert` calls `Search` to find the position in the tree where the new key should be inserted.

Exercises for Section 8.6

Self-Check

1. What additional `SearchTree` methods would you need to implement if `SearchTree` were not a descendant of our `BinTree` object?
2. Write a recursive algorithm for determining the height of a binary search tree.

Figure 8.27
Methods Search and
DoSearch

Directory: CHAP 8
File: SEARCHTR.PAS

▽

```
implementation

  procedure SearchTree.DoSearch (El {input} : TreeData;
                                 var Success {output} : Boolean);
  {
   Advances Cursor to node containing El.
   Pre : Binary tree is initialized and El is defined.
   Post: Success is set to True if Cursor points to tree node
         with same key as El; Success is set to False if
         Cursor points to node that would be El's parent and
         subtree which should contain El does not exist.
  }
    var
      CurrentElement : TreeData; {data in node pointed to by Cursor}

  begin {DoSearch}
    Retrieve (CurrentElement, Success); {retrieve data at Cursor}
    if not Success then
      Success := False              {error - no data retrieved}
    else if CurrentElement.IsEqual(El) then
      Success := True    {Cursor at node with El}
    else if CurrentElement.LessThan(El) then
      if not HasRightTree then
        Success := False {Cursor at the parent of missing El}
      else
        begin
          GoRight;                {move Cursor to right subtree}
          DoSearch (El, Success)       {search right subtree}
        end {search right subtree}
    else {current element's key > target key}
      if not HasLeftTree then
        Success := False {Cursor at the parent of missing El}
      else
        begin
          GoLeft;                 {move Cursor to left subtree}
          DoSearch (El, Success)       {search left subtree}
        end {search left subtree}
  end; {DoSearch}

  procedure SearchTree.Search (El {input} : TreeData;
                               var Success {output} : Boolean);
  {
   Searchs binary tree for node containing El.
   Pre : Tree is initialized and El is defined.
```

▷ ▷ ▷ ▷ ▷ ▷

```
  Post: If node containing same key field as El is found,
        Success is set to True, and Cursor set to point to tree node; otherwise
        Success is set to False.
}
begin {Search}
  InitCursor (GetRoot); {start search at tree root}
  DoSearch (El, Success)
end; {Search}
```

Figure 8.28
Method Insert

Directory: CHAP 8
File: SEARCHTR.PAS

```
procedure SearchTree.Insert (El {input} : TreeData;
                                var {output} Success : Boolean);
{
  Inserts El into binary tree.
  Pre : Binary tree is initialized and El is defined.
  Post: If El is not already stored in search tree a node
        containing El is added to tree and Success set to
        True; otherwise Success set to False.
}
  var
    CurrentEl : TreeData; {Data in node pointed to by Cursor}

begin {Insert}
  if IsEmpty then
    InsertAtRoot (El, Success) {Insert at root of empty tree}
  else
    begin {tree not empty}
      Search (El, Success);        {look for El's key in tree}
      if Success then
        Success := False       {duplicate key - no insertion}
      else
        begin {attach to parent}
          Retrieve (CurrentEl, Success);  {get parent's data}
          if CurrentEl.LessThan(El) then
            InsertRight (El, Success) {insert-right subtree}
          else
            InsertLeft (El, Success)   {insert-left subtree}
        end {attach to parent}
    end {tree not empty}
  end; {Insert}

end. {SearchTreeADT}
```

Programming

1. Write a nonrecursive implementation of the `SearchTree` method Insert.

8.7 Using a Binary Search Tree

The program in Fig. 8.29 stores a collection of integer data items in a binary search tree. It does this by repeatedly calling procedure `SearchTree.Insert` to insert the key just read at its correct position in the tree. After the tree is completed, the program displays the tree size. Finally, it performs an inorder traversal, displaying the value stored in each tree node.

Figure 8.29
Using a Binary Search Tree

Directory: CHAP 8
File: USESEARC.PAS

```
program UseSearchTree;
{
 Program builds and displays a binary tree of integers.

 Imports: SearchTree object from unit SearchTreeADT and
          TreeData object from unit TreeDataADT.
}
  uses SearchTreeADT, TreeDataADT;

  var
    MyTree : SearchTree;    {a tree}
    SentinelItem,
    AnItem : TreeData;      {each data item}
    Success : Boolean;      {flag}

  procedure DisplayNodeInfo (Info {input} : TreeData); far;
  {
   Procedure to be applied to each list node by method
   BinTree.Traverse.
   Pre : Info is defined.
   Post: Display contents of one list node.

   Note: Parameter list must be compatible with declaration
         of ProcedureType in unit BinTreeADT.
  }
  begin {DisplayNodeInfo}
    Info.Display
  end; {DisplayNodeInfo}

begin {UseSearch}
  {Initialize sentinel item of type TreeData}
  SentinelItem.Init (Sentinel);
  {Creates an empty tree}
  MyTree.CreateTree;
  {Fill the tree with data items}
  Write ('Enter tree items—enter -999 to stop> ');
```

▷ ▷ ▷ ▷ ▷ ▷

```
      AnItem.ReadInfo;
      while not AnItem.IsEqual(SentinelItem) do
        begin
          MyTree.Insert (AnItem, Success);
          if not Success then
            WriteLn ('Duplicate - not inserted');
          Write ('Enter tree items—enter -999 to stop> ');
          AnItem.ReadInfo;
        end; {while}

    {Display tree size and contents}
    WriteLn;
    WriteLn (MyTree.GetSize, ' nodes in the tree');
    WriteLn ('Tree contents in order follow:');
    MyTree.InOrder (DisplayNodeInfo)
end. {UseSearch}

Enter tree items—enter -999 to stop> 55
Enter tree items—enter -999 to stop> 60
Enter tree items—enter -999 to stop> 40
Enter tree items—enter -999 to stop> 38
Enter tree items—enter -999 to stop> 39
Enter tree items—enter -999 to stop> 57
Enter tree items—enter -999 to stop> 65
Enter tree items—enter -999 to stop> 55
Duplicate - not inserted
Enter tree items—enter -999 to stop> 59
Enter tree items—enter -999 to stop> 42
Enter tree items—enter -999 to stop> -999

9 nodes in the tree
Tree contents in order follow:
38
39
40
42
55
57
59
60
65
```

Figure 8.30 shows the binary tree created by the sample run. You should trace through the data items in Fig. 8.30 and verify that this tree is correct.

Program UseSearch calls only three methods directly: `BinTree.CreateTree`, `BinTree.InOrder`, and `SearchTree.Insert`. However, in the process of building the tree, all the methods in objects `BinTree` and `SearchTree` are called except for methods `BinTree.Replace` and `BinTree.GetCursor`.

Figure 8.30
Tree Created by a Sample
Run of Fig. 8.29

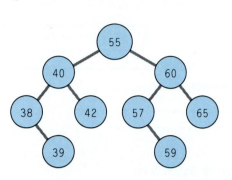

Exercises for Section 8.7   **Self-Check**

1. Write the steps described for deleting a node as a recursive algorithm.
2. How would the deletion of a node for a binary tree differ from the deletion of a node for a binary search tree?

Programming

1. Write unit `TreeDataADT` for the program in Fig. 8.29.

8.8 Common Programming Errors

The procedures in this chapter manipulate pointer fields, so review the errors described in Chapter 7. Make sure all recursive procedures do, in fact, terminate. Also, be careful in using the tree root pointer as a variable parameter. If this pointer is moved down the tree, you could lose the root of the tree.

CHAPTER REVIEW

In this chapter we discussed binary trees. We discussed the differences between in-order, preorder, and postorder traversal and showed how these traversals yield infix, prefix, and postfix expressions in traversing a binary expression tree.

We described two descendants of a binary tree: a binary expression tree and a binary search tree. We discussed how to store expressions in a binary expression tree and how to evaluate these expressions. We also introduced the binary search tree that is used to maintain an ordered collection of data. We showed how to build a binary search tree and how to retrieve an item from this tree. We learned that searching a balanced binary tree is on average an $O(\log_2 N)$ process. Figure 8.31 shows the hierarchy for objects introduced in this chapter.

Figure 8.31
Hierarchy of Tree Objects

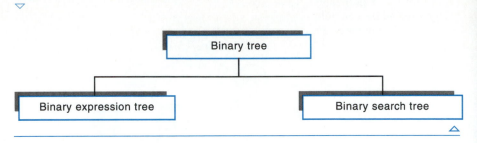

Quick-Check Exercises

1. In what direction do computer science trees grow?
2. Name three tree traversal methods, and relate them to the three forms of arithmetic expressions.
3. A node in a Pascal tree can have a maximum of two children. True or false?
4. A node in a binary search tree can have a maximum of two children. True or false?
5. What is the relationship between the left child and the right child of a binary search tree? Between the left child and the parent? Between the right child and the parent?
6. Explain when searching a binary search tree is more efficient than searching an ordered list and when it isn't.
7. Traverse the tree in Fig. 8.32 in three ways. Is this tree a binary search tree? Is it fully populated?

Answers to Quick-Check Exercises

1. From the top down
2. Inorder (infix), preorder (prefix), postorder (postfix)

Figure 8.32
Tree for Quick-Check
Exercise 7

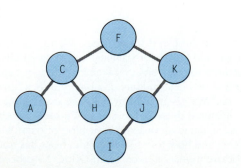

3. False
4. True
5. Left child < parent < right child
6. It is more efficient when the tree is fully populated or at least balanced
7. `Inorder:`   `A C H F I J K`
    `Preorder:`   `F C A H K J I`
    `Postorder:`   `A H C I J K F`

    It is not a binary search tree: H is in the wrong subtree of the root; it is not fully populated.

Review Questions

1. Discuss the differences between a simple linked list and a binary tree. Consider such things as numbers of pointer fields per node, search technique, and insertion algorithm.
2. How can you determine whether a node is a leaf?
3. Traverse the tree in Fig. 8.33 in inorder, preorder, and postorder.
4. Provide one data sequence that would create the binary search tree in Question 3. Are there any letters that must occur before other letters?
5. Would it be reasonable to implement `BinExpTree` as a descendant of our `SearchTree` object? Why or why not?
6. Write a recursive procedure that counts the number of leaf nodes in a binary tree.

Programming Projects

1. Do Programming Project 6 from Chapter 7 using a binary search tree to maintain an airline passenger list. The main program should be menu driven and should allow its user to display the data for a particular passenger, display the entire list, create a list, insert a node, delete a node, and replace the data for a particular passenger.

Figure 8.33
Tree for Review Question 3

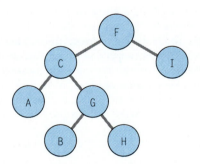

Directory: CHAP 8
File: PROJ8_2.PAS

2. In this chapter we wrote recursive procedures to perform preorder, inorder, and postorder tree traversals. A tree traversal can be written without using recursion. In this case it is necessary to push the address of a tree node that is reached during the traversal onto a stack. The node will be popped off later, when it is time to traverse the tree rooted at this node. For example, the algorithm for a nonrecursive preorder traversal is

```
1. Push nil onto the stack.
2. Assign the root node as the current node.
3. while the current node is not nil do
     begin
         4. Print the current node.
         5. if the current node has a right subtree then
             6. Push the right subtree root onto the
                 stack.
         7. if the current node has a left subtree then
             8.  Make it the current node.
           else
             9. Pop the stack and make the node removed
                 the current node.
     end
```

   In this algorithm, each right subtree pointer that is not nil is pushed onto the stack; the stack is popped when the current left subtree pointer is nil.

   Implement and test a nonrecursive procedure for preorder traversal. Write a nonrecursive algorithm for inorder traversal, and implement and test it as well.

Directory: CHAP 8
File: PROJ8_3.PAS

3. Save each word appearing in a block of text in a binary search tree. Also save the number of occurrences of each word and the line number of each occurrence. Use a queue for the line numbers. After all words are processed, display each word in alphabetical order. Along with each word, display the number of occurrences and the line number for each occurrence.

4. Store the Morse code (see Programming Project 7 in Chapter 3) in a binary tree as shown in Fig. 8.34. The symbol . should cause a branch to the left, and the symbol − should cause a branch to the right. Each node should contain the letter represented by the code symbol formed by tracing a path from the root to that node. For example, following two left branches gives us the code symbol .., which represents the letter I. The first two levels of the Morse code tree are shown in Fig. 8.34. You can consider a Morse code tree to be a descendant of a binary tree. Build the tree by reading in the Morse codes and their corresponding letters in the sequence E·, T−, I··, A·−, N−·, M−−, and so on. Insert each code and letter in the "next" tree node. After the tree is filled, read in a coded message using a space between each letter of the message and a double space between words. Translate the message into English.

Directory: CHAP 8
File: PROJ8_5.PAS

5. Complete the implementation of object `BinExpTree` by writing a method for building a binary expression tree from a string containing an infix expression and unit `TreeDataADT`. Write a client program to test your implementation `BinExpTree`.

6. Implement method `SearchTree.Delete`, which deletes a node from a binary tree.

Directory: CHAP 8
File: PROJ8_6.PAS

Figure 8.34
First Two Levels of the
Morse Code Tree

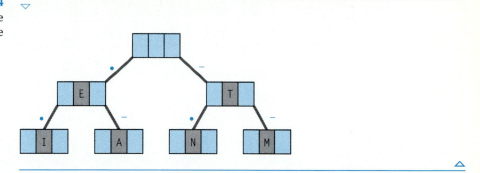

Directory: CHAP 8
File: PROJ8_7.PAS

7. Write a method `BinTree.Copy` that makes an exact duplicate of a binary tree. The new tree should have the exact same structure as the original tree. When you are done, you should have two distinct collections of nodes that represent the original tree and its duplicate. Make sure your solution does not consist of two instances of object `BinTree` that point to the same collection of nodes.

CHAPTER NINE

More Trees and Graphs

In Chapter 8 we introduced a binary search tree ADT. We use a binary search tree to store hierarchically organized data. In some cases, even though the data elements are hierarchically related to each other, the binary tree ADT operators by themselves are not adequate for the needs of the programming application. In this chapter we introduce three additional tree type data structures: *heaps, height-balanced (AVL) trees,* and *general trees.* We will examine heaps as a possible means for implementing a *priority queue.* A priority queue might be described as a data structure whose first element always contains the largest data value in the priority queue. We will not attempt to discuss full implementations of either AVL or general trees.

At the end of this chapter we will examine another data type, known as a *graph*. Graphs are more general than trees in that each node (vertex) may have an arbitrary number of immediate predecessors (parents) and successors (children). Each tree node, by contrast, is allowed to have only one parent. Computer scientists have found graphs to be very important data structures to use in the study of many areas, including information networks.

9.1 Heaps

In this section we describe an abstract data type known as a heap and discuss its use as a means of implementing a priority queue. In Chapter 11 we will discuss the use of a heap to implement a sorting algorithm known as HeapSort. A *heap* (also known as a partially ordered tree) is a binary tree that satisfies two conditions:

Figure 9.1
Several Binary Trees
Illustrating Heap
Conditions

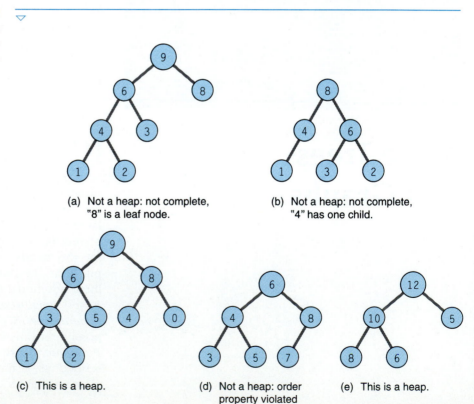

(a) Not a heap: not complete, "8" is a leaf node.

(b) Not a heap: not complete, "4" has one child.

(c) This is a heap.

(d) Not a heap: order property violated

(e) This is a heap.

1. The data value stored in any node is larger than the data value stored in either of the node's children. This condition is known as the *order property* of heaps.
2. The binary tree must be *complete*. This means that all leaf nodes in a binary tree with I levels are found on either level I or level I − 1, the leaves on level I being as far to the left as possible. This condition is called the *structure property* of heaps.

Figure 9.1 contains several binary trees, three of which are not heaps. In contrast to binary search trees, in binary trees there is no fixed ordering of a node's left and right children. For example, in Fig. 9.1(e) the node values at level 2 (8, 6) are larger than the node value 5 at level 1. This is fine because 8 and 6 are smaller than their parent node value (10). In a heap the nodes at the lowest level of a heap are filled moving from left to right. This is not true in a binary search tree.

The most important heap operations involve inserting elements into the heap and removing (or retrieving) the largest heap element (the value stored at the root node). Both operations may require some heap nodes to be moved to new locations to ensure that the resulting heap continues to be complete and properly ordered after each operation.

For example, inserting 7 into the heap in Fig. 9.1(e) would involve initially making '7' the left child of node 5 (since this is leftmost position on the lowest heap level). This violates the heap order property. We can restore the heap order property by swapping the positions of nodes 5 and 7 (see Fig. 9.2a).

Figure 9.2
Restoring Heap Order

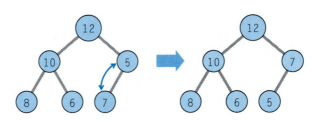

(a) Restoring heap order after inserting 7

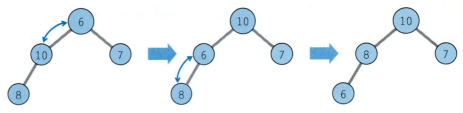

(b) Restoring heap order after deleting 12

Deleting the largest value (12) from the heap in Fig. 9.1(e) is accomplished by taking node 6 (the rightmost node in the lowest level) and temporarily placing it in the root node. The old node is pruned from the tree. To restore the heap order property, we need to swap the positions of node 6 and its largest child (10). This process is repeated (e.g., swap 6 and 8) until 6 is larger than either of its children (see Fig. 9.2b).

Table 9.1 gives the full specification for a heap.

Table 9.1
Specification of Heap
Abstract Data Type

Structure

A heap is a complete, rooted binary tree with the additional constraint that the data value stored in each node is larger than the data values stored in either of the node's children. The heap header node contains the location of the root and a count of the number of nodes that are present in the heap.

Operators

For the following descriptions, assume the parameters:

```
El has data type HeapElement.

Success is a Boolean flag indicating the success (True)
    or failure (False) of an operation.
```

Heap.CreateHeap	Creates an empty heap. Must be called before any other operator.
Heap.GetSize	(function) Returns the number of elements currently in the heap.
Heap.IsEmpty	(function) Returns True if the heap is empty and False otherwise.
Heap.Insert (El, var Success)	Inserts element El as the information portion of a node in an existing heap. Preserves heap order and structure properties following insertion. Success is set to True if the insertion was successful; otherwise, Success is False, and the heap is not altered.
Heap.DeleteMax (var El, var Success)	Removes the largest (highest-priority) element from the heap and stores its information portion in El. Preserves heap order and structure properties following deletion. Success is set to True if deletion was successful; otherwise, Success is set to False, and the heap is not altered.

Table 9.1 Specification of Heap Abstract Data Type (*Cont.*)	***Heap.RetrieveMax (var El, var Boolean)*** Returns through El the information portion of the largest heap element without altering the heap. Success is set to True if retrieval was successful and False if it was not successful.

The binary tree implementation that we discussed in Chapter 8 called for each node to contain two pointer fields to its children. This was necessary to give us the flexibility of placing nodes anywhere that we wish in the tree because binary trees are not required to be complete. However, using two pointer fields per tree node can be a wasteful use of computer memory if the binary tree is complete and the storage requirements of the tree can be determined at program compile time.

Given the requirement that a heap must be a complete binary tree, it is possible to house its data elements in a one-dimensional array and not make any use of pointer variables. However, using a one-dimensional array to house a heap also assumes that the total storage needs of the heap are known in advance. Figure 9.3 shows a one-dimensional array representation of a ten-element binary tree.

In an array representation of a binary tree the root node is assumed to be in the first array location, so A[1] would be the root node of the binary tree. If we look at any tree node in Fig. 9.3, we can write mathematical expressions that will allow us to locate its child nodes and its parent node. For a tree node having array subscript I, its left child will be located at array subscript 2 * I, and its right child will be located at position 2 * I + 1. Inciden-

Figure 9.3
Array Representation of a
Binary Tree

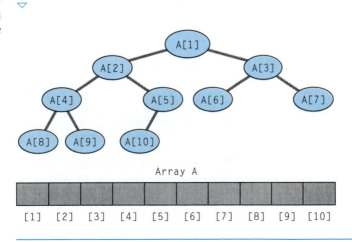

Array A

tally, the parent of any nonroot node having subscript I will have subscript I div 2. Our pointer implementation in Chapter 8 did not contain information about a node's parent.

Figure 9.4 shows the interface section for an object of type Heap. There are two private methods RestoreUp and RestoreDown, which are called by Insert and DeleteMax, respectively, to restore heap order following the insertion or deletion of elements from the heap. The implementation

Figure 9.4
Interface Section for Unit
HeapADT

Directory: CHAP 9
File: HEAPADT.PAS

```
unit HeapADT;
{
 Abstract data type Heap: contains declarations for data type
 Heap and its methods.

 Imports: HeapData from unit HeapDataADT;
}
interface

  uses HeapDataADT;

  const
    MaxHeap = 100;   {maximum heap size}

  type
    HeapRange = 1..MaxHeap;
    HeapArray = array [HeapRange] of HeapData;

  Heap = object
            procedure CreateHeap;
            function GetSize : Integer;
            function IsEmpty : Boolean;
            procedure Insert (El {input} : HeapData;
                            var Success {output} : Boolean);
            procedure DeleteMax
                        (var El {output} : HeapData;
                         var Success {output} : Boolean);
            procedure RetrieveMax
                        (var El {output} : HeapData;
                         var Success {output} : Boolean);
          private
            Size : Integer;
            Items : HeapArray;
            procedure Swap (var One, Two {in/out} : HeapData);
            procedure RestoreUp
                          (Root, Last {input} : HeapRange);
            procedure RestoreDown
                          (Root, Last {input} : HeapRange);
        end; {Heap}
```

of unit `HeapDataADT` would be similar to the version of `TreeDataADT` that we used for our binary search tree object (Programming exercise 1, Section 8.4).

Figure 9.5 shows the implementations of methods `CreateHeap`, `GetSize`, `IsEmpty`, and `RetrieveMax` are similar to the implementations of comparable methods in abstract data types that we discussed in previous chapters.

Figure 9.5
Implementations of Several
Heap Methods

Directory: CHAP 9
File: HEAPADT.PAS

```
implementation
  procedure Heap.CreateHeap;
  {
    Initializes heap instance to empty.
  }
  begin {CreateHeap}
    Size := 0
  end; {CreateHeap}

  function Heap.GetSize;
  {
    Returns number of elements housed in heap instance.
  }
  begin {GetSize}
    GetSize := Size
  end; {GetSize}

  function Heap.IsEmpty;
  {
    Returns true for empty heap and false otherwise.
  }
  begin {IsEmpty}
    IsEmpty := Size = 0
  end; {IsEmpty}

  procedure Heap.Swap (var One, Two {in/out} : HeapData);
  {
    Swaps values of One and Two.
  }
    var
      Temp : HeapData;

  begin {Swap}
    Temp := One;
    One := Two;
    Two := Temp
  end; {Swap}
```

▷ ▷ ▷ ▷ ▷ ▷

```
procedure Heap.Insert (El {input} : HeapData;
                          var Success {output} : Boolean);
{
 Inserts new element El into existing heap.
 Pre : Heap has been initialized.
 Post: El has been inserted into heap, heap order restored,
       and Success is True; or Success is False.
 Calls: RestoreUp.
}
begin {Insert}
  if Size < MaxHeap then
    begin
      {Place El in next available space}
      Size := Size + 1;
      Items[Size] := El;
      {Readjust heap - allow new value to rise if needed}
      RestoreUp (1, Size);
      Success := True
    end
  else
    Success := False
end; {Insert}

procedure Heap.DeleteMax (var El {output} : HeapData;
                          var Success {output} : Boolean);
{
 Removes heap root element and readjusts heap.
 Pre : Heap has been initialized, Items[1] is maximum.
 Post: Either El contains value of Items[Root], heap order
       restored, and Success is True; or Success is False.
 Calls: RestoreDown
}
begin {DeleteMax}
  if Size <> 0 then
    begin
      {save root data}
      El := Items[1];

      {move last leaf value to root}
      Items[1] := Items[Size];
      Size := Size - 1;
      {readjust heap - push root value down if needed}
      RestoreDown (1, Size)
    end
  else
    Success := False
end; {DeleteMax}

procedure Heap.RetrieveMax (var El {output} : HeapData;
                            var Success {output} : Boolean);
{
 Retrieves data store in heap root node.
 Pre : Heap is properly ordered and Items[1] is maximum.
```

▷ ▷ ▷ ▷ ▷

```
      Post: Either El contains data from heap root node and
            Success is True; or Success is False.
      }
      begin {RetrieveMax}
        if Size > 0 then
          begin
            {save root data}
            El := Items[1];
            Success := True
          end
        else
          Success := False
      end; {RetrieveMax}

end. {HeapADT}
```

To understand the implementations of methods `Insert` and `DeleteMax` requires us to trace the execution of methods `RestoreUp` and `RestoreDown`. Figure 9.6 shows the work performed by RestoreUp after the addition of the new heap element 9 to an existing heap. Notice that `Insert` places 9 in the rightmost position in the lowest level of the tree. Obviously, the order property is not satisfied, so we must rearrange the heap element. Color arrows show the heap elements that will be swapped by the next call to `RestoreUp`.

Figure 9.6
Insertion of a New Element into a Heap

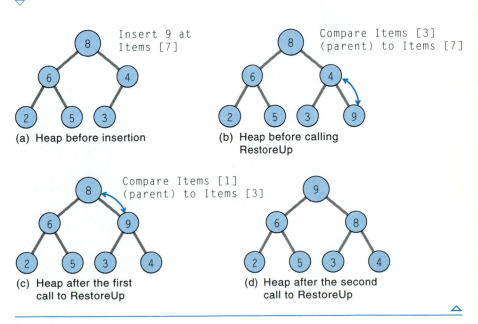

(a) Heap before insertion

(b) Heap before calling RestoreUp

(c) Heap after the first call to RestoreUp

(d) Heap after the second call to RestoreUp

`RestoreUp` is then called recursively to walk 9 up the tree to its proper position (see Fig. 9.7).

`RestoreUp` begins by comparing the values of `Last` and `Root` to see whether `Items[Last]` has a parent. If `Items[Last]` has a parent (`Items [Last div 2]`), their keys values are examined. If the key value associated with `Items[Parent]` is less than `Items[Last]` then the positions of the nodes in the heap are swapped. `RestoreUp` is called recursively to see if the new key value stored in `Items[Parent]` violates the heap order property.

Figure 9.8 shows the work performed by RestoreDown (see Fig. 9.9) after the deletion of the largest node in the heap. DeleteMax starts by moving the last node in the array to the root position temporarily. RestoreDown is then called recursively to walk the temporary root value to its final position in the heap. The color arrows in Fig. 9.8 show the heap elements that will be swapped by the next call to RestoreDown.

`RestoreDown` begins by computing the positions of the `Root` node's left (`Root * 2`) and right (`Root * 2 + 1`) children. If `Root` is not a leaf node, then the key values of its children are examined. `MaxChild` is the position of the `Items[Root]` child having the larger key value. If the key value associated with `Items[Root]` is less than the key value associated with `Items[MaxChild]`

```
procedure Heap.RestoreUp (Root, Last {input} : HeapRange);
{
 Restores heap order between Root and Last, working from
 node Last back to node Root.
 Pre : Assumes that element in position Last is the only
       element causing violation and that Last > Root.
 Post: Heap order has been restored between Root and Last.
}
  var
    Parent : Integer;       {parent index}

begin {RestoreUp}
  if Last > Root then
    begin
      {Last is not Root and Parent exists}
      Parent := Last div 2;

      if Items[Parent].LessThan(Items[Last]) then
        begin
          {Heap order property violated, swap values}
          Swap (Items[Parent], Items[Last]);
          {Restore heap between Root and Parent}
          RestoreUp (Root, Parent)
        end; {Heap order violation}
    end;
end; {Restoreup}
```

Figure 9.8

Deletion of the Largest
Element in a Heap

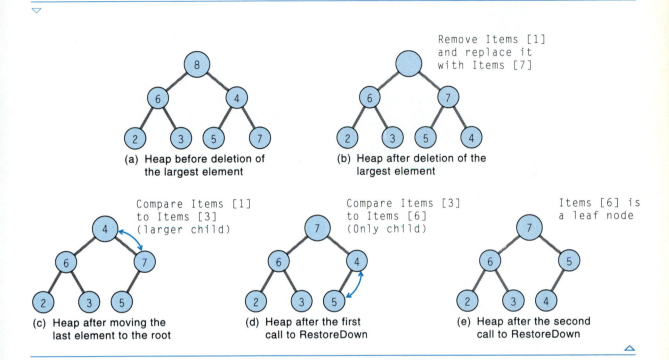

Remove Items [1]
and replace it
with Items [7]

(a) Heap before deletion of
the largest element

(b) Heap after deletion of the
largest element

Compare Items [1]
to Items [3]
(larger child)

Compare Items [3]
to Items [6]
(Only child)

Items [6] is
a leaf node

(c) Heap after moving the
last element to the root

(d) Heap after the first
call to RestoreDown

(e) Heap after the second
call to RestoreDown

the positions of these heap nodes is swapped. RestoreDown is called to see
if the new key stored in Items[MaxChild] violates the heap order property.

Priority Queues

A priority queue is an abstract data type in which only the highest-priority
queue element is accessible to client programs. The criteria for determining
which element has the highest priority is determined by the type of application
in which it is used. For example, an ordinary queue might be described as a
priority queue in which the highest-priority element is the element that has
been stored in the queue for the longest time. An ordered list might be described as a priority queue in which the highest-priority element is the element
that contains the largest (or smallest) key value. Operating systems may make
use of priority queues to determine which program to select for execution next.

   The primary operators associated with priority queues are concerned with
inserting new queue elements (Enqueue), deleting the largest queue element
(Dequeue), and retrieving the value of the largest queue element
(RetrieveMax). The other operators commonly associated with priority
queues would be similar to those we defined for our QueueADT in Chapter 6.

```
procedure Heap.RestoreDown (Root, Last {input} : HeapRange);
{
 Restores heap order between Root and Last, working down
 from Root.
 Pre : Assumes that element in position Root is the only
        element causing violation and that Last > Root.
 Post: Heap order has been restored between Root and Last.
}
  var
    MaxChild,           {index of larger child}
    Left,               {index of Root's left child}
    Right : Integer;    {index of Root's right child}

begin {RestoreDown}
  {compute indices of Root children}
  Left := Root * 2;
  Right := Root * 2 + 1;

  if Left <= Last then
    begin {Root is not a leaf node}
      {Determine index of larger child}
      if Left = Last then
        {only one Child}
        MaxChild := Left
      else
        {Root has two children}
        if Items[Right].LessThan(Items[Left]) then
          MaxChild := Left
        else
          MaxChild := Right;

      if Items[Root].LessThan(Items[MaxChild]) then
        begin
          {Heap order violation, swap values}
          Swap (Items[Root], Items [MaxChild]);
          {Restore heap between Max and Last}
          RestoreDown (MaxChild, Last)
        end {Heap order violation}
    end {Root is not leaf node}
end; {RestoreDown}
```

Heap Implementation of Priority Queues

Implementing a priority queue by using a heap is a very natural thing to do. We could describe our Heap object as being a priority queue whose elements are ordered by the key field defined in unit HeapDataADT. Method Heap.DeleteMax is equivalent to the priority queue dequeue operator. Heap.Insert is equivalent to the priority queue enqueue operator. Like-

wise, Heap.RetrieveMax is equivalent to the priority queue retrieve operator. We discuss the efficiency of these operators in the next section.

Analysis of Priority Queue Implementations

We have now examined four abstract data types that might be used to implement a priority queue. The average case efficiencies of these implementations are summarized in Table 9.2.

	Priority Queue Operation		
	Enqueue	*Dequeue*	*Retrieve*
Heap	$O(\log_2 N)$	$O(\log_2 N)$	$O(1)$
Linked list	$O(1)$	$O(N)$	$O(N)$
Ordered list	$O(N)$	$O(1)$	$O(1)$
Binary search tree			
Balanced	$O(\log_2 N)$	$O(\log_2 N)$	$O(\log_2 N)$
Skewed	$O(N)$	$O(N)$	$O(N)$

For the Retrieve operation, both the heap and ordered list implementations would have complexity of $O(1)$ or *constant complexity*, since the highest-priority element is stored in the first position of either data structure. On
the other hand, Search must be invoked to retrieve the highest-priority element in either the linked list implementation or the binary search tree implementation.

The ordered list implementation has constant complexity for deleting the
highest-priority element but requires a search to perform insertion of new
priority queue elements. An ordinary linked list implementation can have
constant complexity for insertion (at the left end) but requires a search of the
entire list for deletion of the largest element. For a balanced binary tree the
complexities of insertion and deletion are comparable to those for the heap
implementation (as they should be). However, if the tree is not complete,
it may degenerate to an ordinary linked list. The heap implementation has
the best average case complexity of these means of implementing a priority
queue if we assume that the number of Enqueue and Dequeue operations
will be similar.

Exercises for Section 9.1   ### Self-Check

1. Show the contents of the array housing the heap shown in Fig. 9.6 after
   adding the values 1 and 9 to the heap.
2. Show the contents of the resulting heap from Exercise 1 after removing
   its maximum heap element and restoring the heap.
3. Draw a picture of a heap containing the values 'A', 'B', 'C', 'D',
   'E', 'F', 'G', and 'H'.

Programming

1.   Implement unit `HeapDataADT`.

9.2   Balanced Binary Trees

In Chapter 8 we defined a balanced binary tree as a binary tree in which the heights of the left and right subtrees differ from one another by at most 1. Height-balanced binary search trees are also known as AVL trees (named after their inventors, Adelson-Velski and Landis). In this section we discuss how to balance the heights of binary search trees by using the AVL technique.

The basic strategy of the AVL technique is to monitor the shape of the binary search tree as nodes are inserted into and deleted from the tree. This requires an additional field in each tree node to hold the node's *balance factor* (computed as $H_L - H_R$, the difference of the left and right subtree heights). If any of the balance factors become larger than $+1$ or smaller than -1, the tree is no longer balanced. To rebalance the tree, some tree nodes must be rearranged or rotated to modify the balance factors of the offending nodes. The node rearrangement operations used are known as *AVL rotations*. Consider the tree in Fig. 9.10; before the insertion of the node containing 5, this was a balanced tree. Use of appropriate AVL rotations results in a balanced tree once more. Node insertions and deletions that do not cause a tree to become unbalanced do not need to be followed by AVL rotations.

There are two types of AVL rotations: single and double. Single AVL rotations may be either toward the left or toward the right. Figure 9.11 shows a single AVL rotation to the right. Insertion of the node 2 into the tree causes the balance factor at the node containing 6 to become $+2$ (H_L is 3, H_R is 1). To rebalance the tree requires 4 to become the parent of node 6. Because 6 is now the right child of 4, node 6 must adopt node 4's right subtree (node 5).

Figure 9.10
An Unbalanced Binary Search Tree

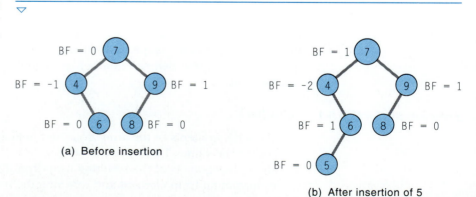

(a) Before insertion

(b) After insertion of 5

Figure 9.11
A Single AVL Rotation to
the Right

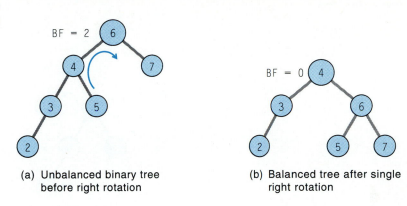

(a) Unbalanced binary tree
before right rotation

(b) Balanced tree after single
right rotation

Figure 9.12 shows a single right AVL rotation in a generic tree. Before rotation the heights of the left and right subtrees of node 4 (nodes 4_L and 4_R) are shown as h + 1 and h, respectively. Node 6 has a balance factor of 2 (H_L is h + 2, H_R is h). After rotation the tree is balanced, and for this tree the height has been reduced from h + 3 to h + 2. AVL rotations do not always reduce a tree's height. A single left AVL rotation would appear as the mirror image of the single right AVL rotation.

Consider the unbalanced tree in Fig. 9.13. To balance this tree requires a double rotation. Double rotations are similar to single rotations except that they involve four subtrees, not just three. The double rotation in Fig. 9.13 is known as a right-left double rotation because the first rotation that occurs is a right rotation about node 8 followed by a left rotation about node 3. Following the right rotation about node 8, node 8 must adopt node 5's right

Figure 9.12
Single AVL Rotation to
the Right

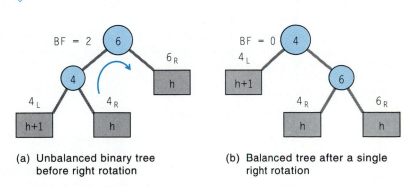

(a) Unbalanced binary tree
before right rotation

(b) Balanced tree after a single
right rotation

Figure 9.13
Right-Left Double Rotation

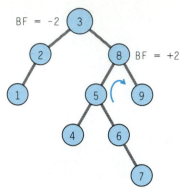

(a) Unbalanced binary tree before right rotation

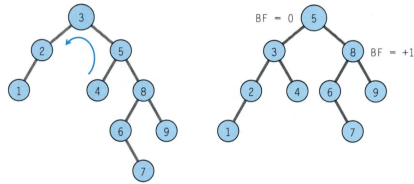

(b) After right rotation about node 8,   (c) After left rotation about node 3
    before left rotation

subtree. Following the left rotation about node 3, node 3 must adopt node 5's left subtree. A left-right double rotation would be used to rebalance a mirror-image tree.

Figure 9.14 shows this right-left double rotation in a generic tree. Following this double rotation the height of the AVL tree decreases from $h + 4$ to $h + 3$.

AVL Tree Operators

We can use our binary search tree operators on AVL trees for operations that do not change the contents of the tree. Binary tree operators that involve changing the shape of the AVL tree need to be written to take the node balance factors into account. For an AVL tree object, private methods would

Figure 9.14
Right-Left Double Rotation

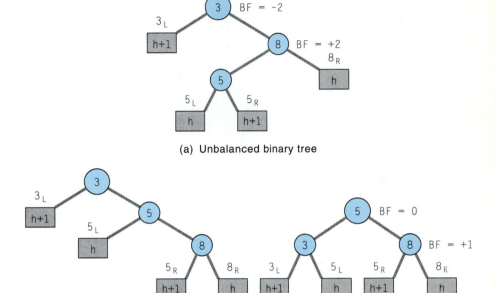

(a) Unbalanced binary tree

(b) After right rotation about node 8   (c) After left rotation about node 3

need to be written to accomplish the AVL rotations required to rebalance the tree following an insertion or a deletion.

In terms of efficiency, AVL trees can be shown to have a worst-case efficiency of $O(\log_2 N)$ for insertion, deletion, and search. For an unbalanced binary search tree the worst-case search efficiency can degenerate to $O(N)$. The increased search efficiency that comes with AVL trees comes at the cost of adding the storage required for the balance factor field to each tree node. The computational costs of maintaining the balance factors and rebalancing the trees must also be considered in deciding whether to use AVL trees for a given programming application. Despite the apparent benefits of using AVL trees, the costs of height-balancing binary trees are usually justified only when the binary search trees are badly skewed. This situation is often very hard to predict during the algorithm design stage. In Chapter 10 we will discuss B trees as another means of reducing the heights of tree type data structures.

Exercises for Section 9.2   **Self-Check**

1.   Compute the balance factors for each node in the following tree:

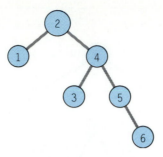

2.   Perform a single left AVL rotation about node 2 to rebalance the tree in Exercise 1.

9.3   General Trees

Not all trees are binary trees. Trees in which nodes have more than two descendants are sometimes known as *general trees* or just simply *trees*. Figure 9.15 contains an example of a general tree. Even though tree nodes may have any number of descendant nodes, each tree node may only have one parent. In the next section we will discuss a data type that allows nodes to have more than one parent or predecessor node.

It is difficult to determine the best representation for a node in a general tree, since each node may have a large number of descendants. One possibility would be to use an array of pointers to the node's descendants, as shown below:

```
const
  MaxChildren = 5;

type
  {insert declaration for TreeData here}

  ChildRange = 1..MaxChildren;
```

Figure 9.15
A General Tree

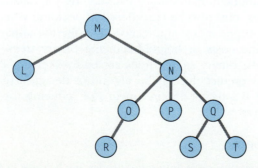

```
TreeNodePtr = ^TreeNode;
ChildNodes = array [ChildRange] of TreePtr;
TreeNode = record
              Info : TreeData;
              NumChildren : Integer;
              Children : ChildNodes;
           end; {TreeNode}
```

This node representation allows us to construct trees with nodes having at most five descendants; it does not let us represent trees having nodes with more than five descendants. Increasing the value of MaxChildren is not sufficient to let us use this node structure to represent trees in which nodes may have an arbitrarily large number of descendants. Figure 9.16 shows a representation for the node with key N in Fig. 9.15.

If any tree node can have a large number of descendants, some type of linked structure must be used to house the list of children. If the maximum number of tree nodes is determined in advance, then an array of records might be used to represent the tree. As shown in Fig. 9.17, one of the record fields contains the tree data value, and the other points to a linked list of descendant values. Each list node contains the subscript of the tree record housing the descendant node's data and a pointer to the next list record. Although this tree representation appears to allow each node to have a large number of descendants, it limits the total number of tree nodes to the number that may be anticipated at program compilation time.

A better alternative would be to link the list of tree nodes together as well. If we are careful about how we do this, we can use the following declarations:

```
type
  {insert declaration for TreeData}

  TreeNodePtr = ^TreeNode;
  TreeNode = record
              Info : TreeData;
              Child,                   {leftmost descendant}
              Sibling : TreeNodePtr    {next descendant}
           end; {TreeNode}
```

Figure 9.16

Node Containing N with Three Children

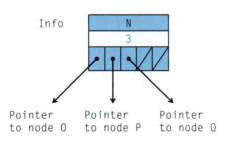

Info

N

3

Pointer to node O   Pointer to node P   Pointer to node Q

Figure 9.17

A General Tree
Implemented as an Array
of Records

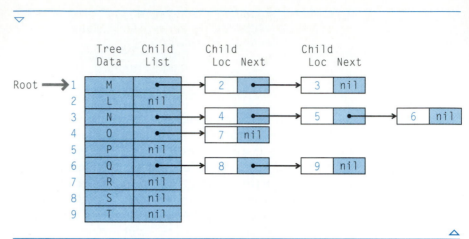

The nodes in this representation contain only two pointers, as in our binary tree implementation, and in fact could be defined by using the same node type as our binary tree object in Chapter 8. In our proposed general tree representation the tree node field Child points directly to a descendant tree node, like the Left pointer field in our binary tree implementation. In our proposed general tree representation the Sibling field points to the next node on the same tree level descended from the same parent node, rather than its own child on the next lower level as the Right pointer field does in our binary tree

Figure 9.18

Binary Representation of a
General Tree

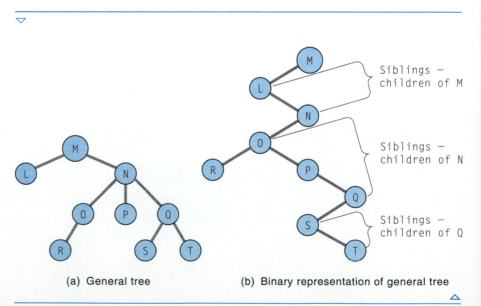

(a) General tree   (b) Binary representation of general tree

representation. Figure 9.18 shows how the general tree from Fig. 9.15 would be represented by using this binary tree type implementation.

This left child/right sibling representation of general trees allows us to use many of our binary search tree operators directly while still being able to recover the structure of our general tree when necessary. This type of flexibility is another example of why the binary tree is such an important abstract data type.

Exercises for Section 9.3   **Self-Check**

1. Draw a binary representation of the following general tree using the left child/right sibling representation.

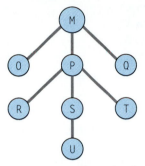

2. Write a pseudocode algorithm for a preorder traversal of a general tree.

9.4   Graph Abstract Data Type

One of the limitations of all tree data types is that they cannot be used to represent information structures in which data nodes have more than one parent. Also, tree data types cannot represent circular relations among data nodes.

In this section we introduce a data structure known as a *graph* that will allow us to overcome both these limitations. In a graph, any *vertex* (data node) can be related to any number of other vertices. In other words, each graph vertex can have an arbitrary number of predecessors and an arbitrary number of successors. Graphs are very general data structures that may be used to represent sets, trees, and lists.

A graph is a data structure that consists of a finite and nonempty set of *vertices* (data nodes) and a finite (but possibly empty) set of edges (relations) between pairs of vertices. The edges in a graph are *undirected*, meaning that if it is possible to travel from vertex A to vertex B, then it is also possible to travel from vertex B to vertex A. If a graph contains *directed* edges (*arcs*), it is known as a *digraph* (directed graph). In a digraph the existence of an arc from vertex A to vertex B does not guarantee the existence of an arc from vertex B to vertex A. Figure 9.19 shows both a graph and a digraph. Trees might be viewed as a special type of digraph (trees do not al-

Figure 9.19
A Graph with Undirected
Edges and a Digraph

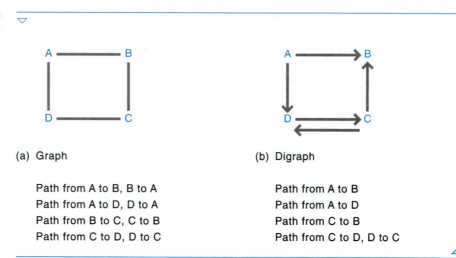

(a) Graph

Path from A to B, B to A
Path from A to D, D to A
Path from B to C, C to B
Path from C to D, D to C

(b) Digraph

Path from A to B
Path from A to D
Path from C to B
Path from C to D, D to C

low arcs in both directions). In this section we consider graphs as structures having only undirected edges.

A particular graph is frequently represented as a set of graph vertices (V) and a set of graph edges (E). For the graph in Fig. 9.19(a) we would have

```
Vertex set = V = {A, B, C, D}
Edge set   = E = {{A, B}, {B, C}, {C, D}, {A, D}}
               = {AB, BC, CD, AD}
```

The notation {A, B} or AB means that there is a path from A to B and from B to A. For the digraph in Fig. 9.19(b), we would represent the edge set as a set of ordered pairs as shown below:

```
Vertex set = V = {A, B, C, D}
Edge set   = E = {(A, B), (C, B), (C, D), (D, C), (A, D)}
```

The notation (A, B) means that there is a path from A to B.

The *size* of a graph is equal to the number of elements in its edge set. The *order* of a graph is equal to the number of elements in its vertex set.

Vertices A and B are said to be *adjacent* to one another if they are connected by an edge. Vertices A and B might also be described as *neighbors* if they are connected by an edge. An edge is said to be *incident* with the vertices that are its endpoints. Graphs that have more than one undirected edge connecting the same pair of vertices are known as *multigraphs* (Fig. 9.20). An edge connecting a single vertex with itself is known as a *loop*. We will not discuss multigraphs or graphs with loops in this chapter.

Graphs in which every vertex is connected to every other vertex are called *complete* graphs (Fig. 9.21). For a complete graph with N vertices, each vertex will have $N - 1$ adjacent vertices or neighbors, and its total

Figure 9.20
Multigraphs

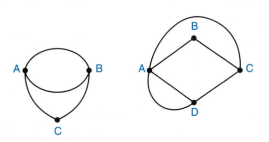

number of edges will be N * (N − 1)/2. Graphs in which it is possible to travel between any pair of vertices by following an alternating sequence of vertices and edges (known as a *walk*) are called *connected* graphs. Since we are not dealing with multigraphs in this chapter, we can describe a walk by simply listing its vertices in the order in which they are visited. One walk between vertices A and D for the graph in Fig. 9.22(c) might be represented as A, B, C, A, D. It is possible for a graph to be connected but not complete, as shown in Fig. 9.22(a). A walk between two vertices in which no vertex is listed more than once is called a *path*. One path between vertices A and D in Fig. 9.22(c) might be represented as A, C, D. A path that begins and ends at the same vertex is known as a *cycle*. One cycle that is present in Fig. 9.22(c) is given by the vertex sequence A, B, C, A. Graphs in which cycles are not possible are said to be *acyclic*. The graphs shown in Figs. 9.22(a) and 9.22(b) are both acyclic. Trees might then be described as connected, acyclic graphs.

Some graphs have names or *labels* associated with each edge, rather than just referring to each edge by using the vertex labels of its endpoints. Some graphs, called *weighted* graphs, have values associated with each edge. Of-

Figure 9.21
Complete Graphs

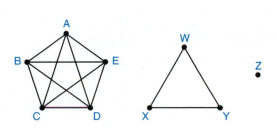

Figure 9.22
Examples of Connected
and Unconnected Graphs

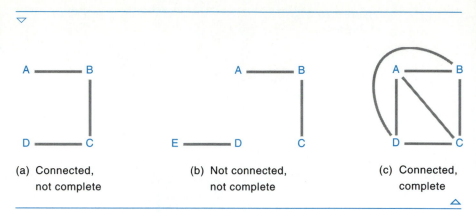

(a) Connected,
    not complete

(b) Not connected,
    not complete

(c) Connected,
    complete

ten, these values represent the distance between a pair of vertices or the cost of traversing the edge. Figure 9.23 shows a weighted graph that shows the roads and distances between several cities.

The major operations on graphs are concerned with graph creation, vertex insertion, vertex deletion, edge addition, edge deletion, testing for whether a vertex is in the graph, testing whether an edge is in the graph, and graph traversal. A graph traversal is similar to tree traversal in that each graph vertex is visited one time. For example, one traversal of the graph in Fig. 9.22.(c) would be A, B, C, D. There are several other operators that are implemented with graphs associated with particular programming algorithms. However, space does not allow us to discuss all these operators. We will consider the task of implementing our graph abstract data type in the next section.

Table 9.3 gives the full specification for a graph.

Figure 9.23
Weighted Graph

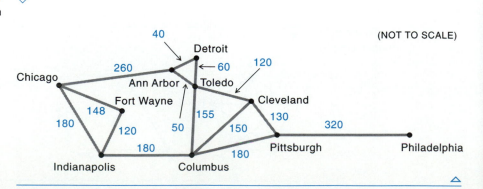

Structure

A graph is an unordered collection of distinct data values called vertices and an unordered collection of distinct relations called edges between two vertices. The graph header node contains a count of the number of vertices and edges that are present in the graph.

Operators

For the operator descriptions, assume the following parameters:

```
Vertex, FromVertex, and ToVertex have data type
VertexType.
Neighbors has type VertexTable.
Success is a Boolean flag indicating success (True) or
   failure (False) of an operation.
```

Graph.Create	Creates an empty graph. Must be called before any other operator.
Graph.IsEmpty	(function) Returns True if the graph contains no vertices and False otherwise.
Graph.GetNumVertices	(function) Returns the number of vertices that are currently in the graph.
Graph.GetNumEdges	(function) Returns the number of edges that are currently in the graph.
Graph.AddVertex (Vertex, var Success)	Adds Vertex to the graph vertex set and sets Success to True; otherwise, sets Success to False.
Graph.DelVertex (Vertex, var Success)	Deletes Vertex from the graph vertex set, removes all edges having Vertex as an endpoint, and sets Success to True; otherwise, sets Success to False.
Graph.AddEdge (FromVertex, ToVertex, var Success)	Adds the edge connecting FromVertex to ToVertex to the graph edge set and sets Success to True; otherwise, Success is set to False.
Graph.DelEdge (FromVertex, ToVertex, var Success)	Deletes the edge connecting FromVertex to ToVertex from the graph edge set and sets Success to True; otherwise, Success is set to False.
Graph.Traverse	Displays each vertex as defined by the graph edge set.
Graph.GetNeighbors (Vertex, var Neighbors, var Success)	Returns the set of vertices connected by an edge to Vertex and sets Success to True; otherwise, sets Success to False.

Table 9.3 Specification of Graph Abstract Data Type (*Cont.*)	***Graph.IsVertex (Vertex)***	(function) Returns True if Vertex is a member of the graph edge set and False otherwise.
	Graph.IsAdjacent (FromVertex, ToVertex)	(function) Returns True if the edge connecting FromVertex and ToVertex exists in the graph; otherwise, returns False.

Exercises for Section 9.4   **Self-Check**

1. How does a graph differ from a general tree?
2. Determine the vertex set and edge set for the following graph:

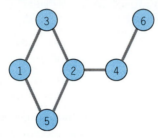

9.5   Implementing GraphADT

One very common way of representing the edges in a graph (or digraph) is by using an *adjacency matrix*. An adjacency matrix is a two-dimensional matrix of Boolean values in which the row and column subscripts are associated with the elements of the graph vertex set in some unique manner. If an edge exists in a graph, the array entry associated with vertex A and vertex B is set to True; otherwise, the entry is set to False. The adjacency matrix for a graph with undirected edges is symmetric about its main diagonal. Figure 9.24 shows a graph and its adjacency matrix representation.

Figure 9.24
A Graph and Its Adjacency
Matrix Representation

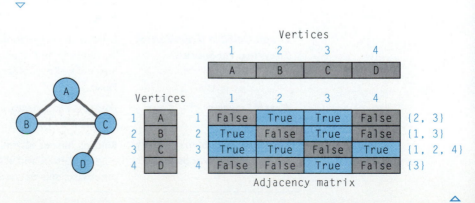

Figure 9.25
Graph Representation After
Adding a New Vertex

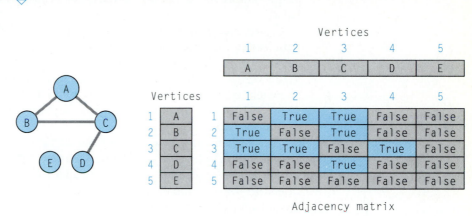

The adjacency matrix of a digraph is not guaranteed to be symmetric about its main diagonal. For a weighted graph, you might use the edge weight as the entry indicating the presence of an edge and use some sentinel value (e.g., 0 or `-Maxint`) to indicate the absence of an edge connecting the two vertices.

Figure 9.25 shows the effect of adding a new vertex E to the graph in Fig. 19.24. Notice that even though we have not added any edges to the graph, we need to activate an additional row and column in the adjacency matrix to allow edges between vertex E and the other four vertices. Once vertex E has been added to the graph, adding an edge between vertex A and vertex E requires us to set AdjacencyMatrix[1, 5] to True and AdjacencyMatrix[5, 1] to True.

Figure 9.26 shows the effects of deleting vertex C from the graph in Fig. 9.25. In addition to removing vertex C from the vertex table, we also need to delete all edges from the adjacency matrix. To delete edge AB from the

Figure 9.26
Graph Representation After
Deleting a Vertex

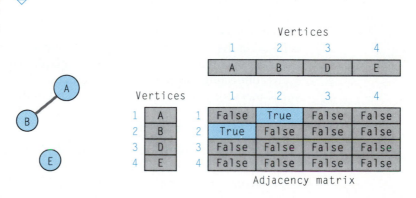

graph, simply set AdjacencyMatrix[1, 2] to False and AdjacencyMatrix[2, 1] to False.

Figure 9.27 shows the interface section for an object of type Graph. Unit `VertexDataADT` is similar to unit `TreeDataADT` from Chapter 8. Because one of the graph operators returns a list of vertices adjacent to a given vertex, we have also chosen to implement a type `VertexTable` as an object type of its own to provide restricted access to the vertex list by `GraphADT` client programs and to simplify the implementation of our graph operators.

The implementation section for our `GraphADT` unit is shown in Fig. 9.28. For our graph object we will define a `VertexTable` object and an adjacency matrix whose rows and columns parallel the `VertexTable` positions. The operators for our `VertexTable` object are easy to implement and will be discussed after Fig. 9.28. As new vertices are added to the vertex table, they are inserted in the `VertexTable` and the value of `NumVertices` is increased by one. When a vertex is removed from the `VertexTable`, the value of `NumVertices` is decreased by one.

Object Vertex Table

Object `VertexTable` houses the vertex list for a graph and contains a method for maintaining the list of vertices. Adding a vertex to an existing graph is accomplished by using method `VertexTable.AddVertex`. Adding an edge to a graph between two existing vertices is accomplished by calling method `VertexTable.VertexIndex` to determine the subscript values associated with the vertex names. Then we use these subscripts to set the appropriate adjacency matrix entries to True. Recall that in an undirected graph, every edge has two entries in the adjacency matrix. Removing an existing edge from the graph is handled by using method `VertexTable.VertexIndex` to determine which entries of the adjacency matrix to set to False. Deleting a vertex from the graph requires the use of method VertexTable.DelVertex to remove the vertex and the use of methods `VertexTable.VertexIndex` to determine which row and column to remove from the adjacency matrix. Method `Graph.DelVertex` must then move the rows up into the empty row position and move the columns to the left into the empty column position.

Our method `Graph.Traverse` applies procedure Visit to each vertex as it is found in the vertex table. Computer scientists have devised graph traversal algorithms that are designed to search graphs efficiently and identify good paths connecting any pair of graph vertices. We will look at one of these traversal methods in the case study at the end of this section.

Implementing VertexTableADT

Given the operators that are required to maintain an instance of object `VertexTable`, we could have used one of our linked list types from Chapter 7. However, for a graph with a small number of vertices, some savings in

Figure 9.27
Interface Section for Unit
GraphADT

Directory: CHAP 9
File: GRAPHADT.PAS

```
unit GraphADT;
{
 Abstract data type Graph: contains declarations for data type
 Graph and its methods.

 Imports: Object VertexData from unit VertexDataADT and
          object VertexTable from unit VertexTableADT.
}
interface

  uses VertexDataADT, VertexTableADT;

  type
    AdjacencyMatrix = array[VertexRange, VertexRange] of Boolean;

    ProcedureType = procedure (P : VertexData);

    Graph = object
                procedure CreateGraph;
                function IsEmpty : Boolean;
                function GetNumVertices : Integer;
                function GetNumEdges : Integer;
                procedure AddVertex
                        (Vertex {input} : VertexData;
                         var Success {output} : Boolean);
                procedure DelVertex
                        (Vertex {input} : VertexData;
                         var Success {output} : Boolean);
                procedure AddEdge
                        (FromVertex,
                         ToVertex {input} : VertexData;
                         var Success {output} : Boolean);
                procedure DelEdge
                        (FromVertex,
                         ToVertex {input} : VertexData;
                         var Success {output} : Boolean);
                procedure Traverse (Visit : ProcedureType);
                procedure GetNeighbors
                        (Vertex {input} : VertexData;
                         var Neighbors {output} : VertexTable;
                         var Success {output} : Boolean);
                function IsVertex (Vertex : VertexData) : Boolean;
                function IsAdjacent
                        (FromVertex,
                         ToVertex : VertexData) : Boolean;

            private
              Vertices : VertexTable;
              NumEdges : Integer;
              Edges : AdjacencyMatrix;
            end; {Graph}
```

Figure 9.28
Implementation Section for
Unit GraphADT

Directory: CHAP 9
File: GRAPHADT.PAS

```
implementation

  procedure Graph.CreateGraph;
  {
   Initializes graph instance to the null graph.
  }
    var
      I, J : Integer; {loop control}

  begin {CreateGraph}
    Vertices.CreateTable;
    NumEdges := 0;

    {initialize vertex adjacency matrix to empty}
    for I := 1 to MaxVertices do
      for J := 1 to MaxVertices do
        Edges[I, J] := False;
  end; {CreateGraph}

  function Graph.IsEmpty;
  {
   Returns true for empty graph and false otherwise.
  }
  begin {IsEmpty}
    IsEmpty := Vertices.IsEmpty
  end; {IsEmpty}

  function Graph.GetNumVertices;
  {
   Returns number of graph vertices.
  }
  begin {GetNumVertices}
    GetNumVertices := Vertices.GetNumVertices
  end; {GetNumVertices}

  function Graph.GetNumEdges;
  {
   Returns number of graph edges.
  }
  begin {GetNumEdges}
    GetNumEdges := NumEdges
  end; {GetNumEdges}

  procedure Graph.AddVertex (Vertex {input} : VertexData;
                              var Success {output} : Boolean);
  {
   Add Vertex to graph.
   Pre : Graph has been created and Vertex not already in graph.
   Post: Either Vertex added to graph vertex table and Success
         is true; or Success is false.
  }
```

▷ ▷ ▷ ▷ ▷ ▷

```
begin {AddVertex}
  Vertices.AddVertex (Vertex, Success);
end; {AddVertex}

procedure Graph.DelVertex (Vertex {input} : VertexData;
                               var Success {output} : Boolean);
{
 Removes Vertex from graph and all incident graph edges.
 Pre : Graph initialized and contains Vertex in vertex table.
 Post: Either Vertex removed along with all incident edges and
       Success is true; otherwise Success is false.
}
  var
    I, J,                  {loop control}
    NumVertices,
    VIndex : Integer;   {vertex index}

begin {DelVertex}
  {Save original number of vertices}
  NumVertices := Vertices.GetNumVertices;
  {Save table position before deletion}
  VIndex := Vertices.VertexIndex(Vertex);
  {Remove vertex from Vertices}
  Vertices.DelVertex (Vertex, Success);

  if Success then
    begin
      {Adjust NumEdges - for undirected graph only check row}
      for J := 1 to NumVertices do
        if Edges[Vindex, J] then
          NumEdges := NumEdges - 1;

      {Delete row VIndex from adjacency matrix}
      for I := VIndex + 1 to NumVertices do
       for J := 1 to NumVertices do
         Edges[I - 1, J] := Edges[I, J];

    {Delete column VIndex from adjacency matrix}
    for J := VIndex + 1 to NumVertices + 1 do
      for I := 1 to NumVertices do
        Edges[I, J - 1] := Edges[I, J]
  end
else
  Success := False
end; {DelVertex}

procedure Graph.AddEdge (FromVertex,
                            ToVertex {input} : VertexData;
                            var Success {output} : Boolean);
{
 Add edge [FromVertex, ToVertex] to graph.
 Pre : Graph has been created and that vertices FromVertex
       and ToVertex are already in graph.
```

▷ ▷ ▷ ▷ ▷ ▷

```
      Post: Either edge added to graph adjacency matrix and Success
            is true; or Success is false.
  }
    var
      FromIndex, ToIndex : Integer; {vertex indices}

  begin {AddEdge}
    Success := False;
    FromIndex := Vertices.VertexIndex(FromVertex);
    ToIndex := Vertices.VertexIndex(ToVertex);
    if (FromIndex <> 0) and (ToIndex <> 0) then
      {check for presence of edge in graph already}
      if not Edges[FromIndex, ToIndex] then
        begin {add new edge}
          {mark edge connecting FromVertex and ToVertex}
          Edges[FromIndex, ToIndex] := True;
          {for undirected graph also add reverse connection}
          Edges[ToIndex, FromIndex] := True;
          NumEdges := NumEdges + 1;
          Success := True
        end {add new edge}
  end; {AddEdge}

  procedure Graph.DelEdge (FromVertex, ToVertex {input} : VertexData;
                               var Success {output} : Boolean);
  {
    Delete edge [FromVertex, ToVertex] from graph.
    Pre : Graph has been created and edge [FromVertex, ToVertex]
          is already in the graph.
    Post: Either existing edge [FromVertex, ToVertex] removed from
          graph adjacency matrix and Success is true; or
          Success is false.
  }
    var
      FromIndex, ToIndex : Integer; {vertex indices}

  begin {DelEdge}
    Success := False;
    FromIndex := Vertices.VertexIndex(FromVertex);
    ToIndex := Vertices.VertexIndex(ToVertex);
    if (FromIndex <> 0) and (ToIndex <> 0) then
      {valid vertices}
      if Edges[ToIndex, FromIndex] then
        begin {delete existing edge}
          {remove edge connecting FromVertex and ToVertex}
          Edges[FromIndex, ToIndex] := False;
          {for undirected graph also remove reverse connection}
          Edges[ToIndex, FromIndex] := False;
          NumEdges := NumEdges - 1;
          Success := True
        end {delete existing edge}
  end; {DelEdge}
```

▷ ▷ ▷ ▷ ▷

```
procedure Graph.Traverse (Visit : ProcedureType);
{
 Apply procedure Visit to graph vertices.
 Pre : Graph is initialized; Visit defined in client program
       and compiled using Borland Pascal far call model.
 Post: Each vertex is visited in vertex table order
}
   var
     VIndex, Neighbor : Integer;    {loop control}
     Vertex : VertexData;           {vertex retrieved}
     Success : Boolean;             {retrieval flag}

begin {Traverse}
   for VIndex := 1 to Vertices.GetNumVertices do
     begin
       {Retrieve vertex information}
       Vertices.Retrieve (Vindex, Vertex, Success);

       {Display vertex}
       Write ('Vertex : ');
       Visit (Vertex);
     end {for}
end; {Traverse}

procedure Graph.GetNeighbors
                  (Vertex {input} : VertexData;
                   var Neighbors {output} : VertexTable;
                   var Success {output} : Boolean);
{
 Creates a table of vertices adjacent to Vertex.
 Pre : Graph is initialized and nonempty.
 Post: Either Neighbors contains the list of vertices adjacent
       to Vertex and Success is true; or Success is false.
}
   var
     I,                             {loop control}
     VIndex : Integer;              {vertex index}
     RetrieveOK, AddOK : Boolean;   {operator flags}

begin {GetNeighbors}
   Neighbors.CreateTable;
   VIndex := Vertices.VertexIndex(Vertex);
   if VIndex <> 0 then
     begin {vertex exists}
       for I := 1 to MaxVertices do
         if Edges[VIndex,I] then
           begin {edge exists}
             Vertices.Retrieve (I, Vertex, RetrieveOK);
             Neighbors.AddVertex (Vertex, AddOK);
             Success := RetrieveOK and AddOK;
           end {edge exists}
     end {vertex exists}
   else
```

▷ ▷ ▷ ▷ ▷ ▷

```
        Success := False
    end; {GetNeighbors}

    function Graph.IsVertex (Vertex : VertexData) : Boolean;
    {
     Determines whether Vertex is in graph vertex set or not.
     Pre : Graph is initialized and nonempty.
     Post: Returns true if Vertex is found and false otherwise.
    }
       var
         VIndex : Integer;

    begin {IsVertex}
       IsVertex := Vertices.InTable(Vertex)
    end; {IsVertex}

    function Graph.IsAdjacent (FromVertex,
                                ToVertex : VertexData) : Boolean;
    {
     Determines whether an edge connects FromVertex and ToVertex.
     Pre : Graph is nonempty and FromVertex and ToVertex are in
           the graph vertex table.
     Post: Returns true if edge exists and false otherwise.
    }
       var
         FromIndex, ToIndex : Integer; {vertex indices}

    begin {IsAdjacent}
       FromIndex := Vertices.VertexIndex(FromVertex);
       ToIndex := Vertices.VertexIndex(ToVertex);
       {check for legal vertices}
       if (FromIndex <> 0) and (ToIndex <> 0) then
         {check for presence of edge}
         IsAdjacent := Edges[FromIndex, ToIndex]
       else
         IsAdjacent := False
    end; {IsAdjacent}

end. {GraphADT}
```

both storage and execution time result from using an array implementation, as we have done in Fig. 9.29.

Linked Implementation of GraphADT

The adjacency matrix representation can be very wasteful of computer memory for graphs having a large number of vertices and a small number of edges. Consider a graph having 100 vertices; the adjacency matrix requires 10,000 storage locations, even for graphs having only 10 edges.

Figure 9.29
Unit `VertexTableADT`

Directory: CHAP 9
File: VERTEXTA.PAS

```
unit VertexTableADT;
{
 Implements object VertexTable to house vertex list for an
 undirected graph object.

 Imports: Object VertexData from unit VertexDataADT.
}
interface

  uses VertexDataADT;

  const
    MaxVertices = 20;    {maximum number of vertices}

  type
    VertexRange = 1..MaxVertices;
    VertexArray = array[VertexRange] of VertexData;

    VertexTable = object
                      procedure CreateTable;
                      function IsEmpty : Boolean;
                      function GetNumVertices : Integer;
                      procedure AddVertex
                              (Vertex {input} : VertexData;
                               var Success {output} : Boolean);
                      procedure DelVertex
                              (Vertex {input} : VertexData;
                               var Success {output} : Boolean);
                      procedure Retrieve
                              (Index : {input} Integer;
                               var Vertex {output} : VertexData;
                               var Success {output} : Boolean);
                      function VertexIndex
                              (Vertex : VertexData) : Integer;
                      function InTable
                              (Vertex : VertexData) : Boolean;

                    private
                      NumVertices : Integer;
                      Table : VertexArray;
                    end; {VerTextable}

implementation

  procedure VertexTable.CreateTable;
  {
   Initializes table instance to empty.
  }
  begin {CreateTable}
    NumVertices := 0;
  end; {CreateTable}
```

▷ ▷ ▷ ▷ ▷

```
function VertexTable.IsEmpty;
{
 Returns true for empty table and false otherwise.
}
begin {IsEmpty}
  IsEmpty := (NumVertices = 0)
end; {IsEmpty}

function VertexTable.GetNumVertices;
{
 Returns number of table entries.
}
begin {GetNumVertices}
  GetNumVertices := NumVertices
end; {GetNumVertices}

procedure VertexTable.AddVertex
                     (Vertex {input} : VertexData;
                      var Success {output} : Boolean);
{
 Adds Vertex to table.
 Pre :  Table has been created and Vertex is initialized and
        is not already present in Table.
 Post:  Either Vertex is added to vertex table and Success
        is true; or Success is false.
}
begin {AddVertex}
  if NumVertices < MaxVertices then
    begin
      NumVertices := NumVertices + 1;
      Table[NumVertices] := Vertex;
      Success := True
    end
  else
    Success := False
end; {AddVertex}

procedure VertexTable.Retrieve
                     (Index {input} : Integer;
                      var Vertex {output} : VertexData;
                      var Success {output} : Boolean);
{
 Retrieves table entry from position Index.
 Pre : Table has been initialized.
 Post: Either Vertex contains table entry and Success is True;
       or Success is False.
}
begin {Retrieve}
  if (Index > 0) and (Index <= NumVertices) then
    begin
      Vertex := Table[Index];
      Success := True
    end
```

▷ ▷ ▷ ▷ ▷ ▷

```
      else
         Success := False
end; {Retrieve}

function VertexTable.VertexIndex
                          (Vertex : VertexData) : Integer;
{
 Returns subscript of Vertex in VertexTable.
 Pre : Table has been initialized and is not empty and Vertex
       has been initialized.
 Post: Returns subscript if Vertex found; otherwise returns 0.
}
   var
      Index : Integer;      {vertex table position being checked}
      Found : Boolean;      {flag indicating Vertex found}

begin {VertexIndex}
   Found := False;
   Index := 1;
   while not Found and (Index <= MaxVertices) do
      {invariant:
         No value of Table[1..Index - 1] matches Vertex
         and Index < MaxVertices
      }
      begin
        if Table[Index].IsEqual(Vertex) then
          Found := True
        else
          Index := Index + 1
      end; {while}

   {assertion: either Vertex found or is not in vertex table}
   if Found then
      VertexIndex := Index
   else
      VertexIndex := 0
end; {VertexIndex}

procedure VertexTable.DelVertex
                       (Vertex {input} : VertexData;
                        var Success {output} : Boolean);
{
 Removes Vertex from table.
 Pre : Table initialized and contains Vertex and Vertex
       is initialized.
 Post: Either Vertex removed and Success is true; or
       Success is false.
}
   var
      I,                        {loop control}
      VIndex : Integer;      {vertex index}

begin {DelVertex}
   VIndex := VertexIndex(Vertex);
```

▷ ▷ ▷ ▷ ▷ ▷

```
      if VIndex <> 0 then
        begin
          {Remove Vertex from Table and close table gap}
          for I := VIndex + 1 to NumVertices do
            Table[I - 1] := Table[I];
          NumVertices := NumVertices - 1;
          Success := True
        end
      else
        Success := False
  end; {DelVertex}

  function VertexTable.InTable (Vertex : VertexData) : Boolean;
  {
   Determines whether Vertex is in table or not.
   Pre : Graph is initialized and nonempty.
   Post: Returns true if Vertex is found and false otherwise.
  }
    var
      VIndex : Integer;

  begin {InTable}
    VIndex := VertexIndex(Vertex);
    InTable := VIndex <> 0
  end; {InTable}

end. {VertexTableADT}
```

△

A linked representation (similar to our representations of general trees) could be used to represent connection information for graphs having a small number of edges or a large number of vertices. One alternative way of representing connection is to substitute a linked list for each row of the adjacency matrix. We can accomplish this by giving each vertex its own linked list whose elements are the names of its adjacent vertices. These lists are known as *adjacency lists.* Figure 9.30 contains an adjacency list representation for the graph in Fig. 9.24. If the graph vertices contain any additional information besides the vertex names, it is stored in the vertex table.

Alternatively, we could use a linked list to house our vertex table. We could choose to store array subscripts or pointer values in place of vertex names in the adjacency list nodes. The details of implementing a Graph object using adjacency lists are left as a programming project (see Programming Project 4 at the end of the chapter).

CASE STUDY   **Depth-First Search of a Graph**

We did not include a search method in our Graph object. Yet many graph problems involve searching a graph. Graph searching usually involves systematically traversing the graph edges. Finding a path through a maze (see

Figure 9.30
A Graph and Its Adjacency
List Representation

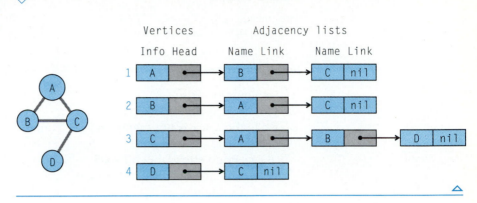

Chapter 4) can be recast as a problem in which we search for a path between two vertices in a graph. We can search a graph using a variation of our backtracking algorithm known as a *depth-first search*.

PROBLEM ▼

Given a graph and a pair of vertices, find a path between the vertices, if one exists, by using a depth-first search. If a path between the vertices exists, then each vertex will appear no more than once on the path. We can travel between two vertices only if they are connected by a pair of edges.

DESIGN OVERVIEW ▼

We need a systematic method for keeping track of the vertices that we have tried. With a depth-first search we see whether the starting vertex is connected to the final vertex directly; if it is, the search is over. If it is not connected directly, we need to check the vertices adjacent to the starting vertex. With a depth-first search we try to extend one path at time until we are successful or reach a dead end. If a path does not exist from the first vertex adjacent to our final vertex, we will try one of the others. We need to store untried adjacent vertices in a data structure that will allow us to backtrack when we reach a dead end on the current path. To avoid long backtracking sequences, we can house the untried vertices on a stack.

Data Requirements

Problem Inputs

```
The graph
The starting vertex
The final vertex
```

Problem Outputs

The names of all vertices tried on the final path in the order in which they need to be traversed

Initial Algorithm

1. Set Found to false
2. Push Start vertex on to a stack
3. while the stack is not empty and not Found do
    begin
        4. Pop vertex label off stack
        5. if vertex is Final vertex then
            begin
                6. Display vertex
                7. Set Found to True
            end
        else
            8. if vertex not marked as visited then
                begin
                    9. Mark vertex as visited
                    10. Display vertex
                    11. Get vertices adjacent to vertex
                    12. for each unvisited vertex
                        13. Push vertex on the stack
            end
    end
14. if not Found then
    15. Display message "no path exists"

Our DepthFirst algorithm begins by pushing the first vertex label onto the stack of untried vertices. The search for a path between vertex Start and vertex Final continues until the path is complete or there are no more untried vertex labels on the stack. Inside the while loop, a vertex label is popped off the stack. If this vertex label is not the label of vertex Final, we check to see whether this vertex has already been marked as visited. If we have not already visited this vertex, we mark it as visited, display its label, and find its adjacent neighbors. We push the label of each unmarked adjacent vertex onto the stack and continue our search.

For example, let's consider how our depth first algorithm would determine whether a path exists between vertex E and vertex C for the graph shown in Fig. 9.31. The first step is to push the starting vertex (E) onto the stack. Next, since the stack is not empty and we have not reached our final vertex (C), we pop the top vertex off the stack (E) and push its neighbors (B and D) onto the stack. Now, vertex D is popped off the stack and we push

Figure 9.31
Trace of Depth First
Algorithm

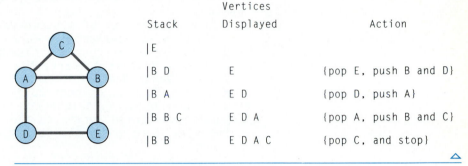

Stack	Vertices Displayed	Action
|E		
|B D	E	{pop E, push B and D}
|B A	E D	{pop D, push A}
|B B C	E D A	{pop A, push B and C}
|B B	E D A C	{pop C, and stop}

Figure 9.32
Procedure `DepthFirst`

Directory: CHAP 9
File: TESTDFS.PAS

```
procedure DepthFirst (G : Graph; Start, Final : VertexData);
{
 Use depth-first search to find path from Start to Final
 Pre : Graph G and vertices Start and Final are initialized;
       Graph G contains vertices Start and Final
 Post: Path between Start and Finish displayed if one exists;
       message indicating failure displayed otherwise.
}
  var
    Success,                    {operator success flag}
    Found : Boolean;            {search termination flag}
    S : Stack;                  {names of untried vertices}
    Marked : set of Char;       {set of visited vertices}
    Vertex : VertexData;
    VertexName : Char;
    Neighbors : VertexTable; {list of adjacent vertices}

begin {DepthFirst}
    Marked := [];
    S.CreateStack;
    Found := False;
    {Push the starting vertex label onto the stack}
    S.Push (Start.GetKey, Success);
    while not S.IsEmpty and not Found do
      begin
        {Get label of the next untried vertex}
        S.Pop (VertexName, Success);
        if VertexName = Final.GetKey then
          begin
            {Path complete, display final vertex label}
            WriteLn ('Vertex: ', VertexName);
            WriteLn ('Path is complete');
```

▷ ▷ ▷ ▷ ▷ ▷

```
                Found := True
            end {if}
        else if not (VertexName in Marked) then
            begin
                {Add vertex to set of visited vertices}
                Marked := [VertexName] + Marked;
                {Display label of vertex visited}
                WriteLn ('Vertex: ', VertexName);
                V.Init (VertexName);
                {Locate vertices adjacent to VertexName}
                G.GetNeighbors (V, Neighbors, Success);
                {Add each untried vertex to the stack}
                for I := 1 to Neighbors.GetNumVertices do
                    begin
                        Neighbors.Retrieve (I, Vertex, Success);
                        VertexName := Vertex.GetKey;
                        if not (VertexName in Marked) then
                            S.Push (VertexName, Success);
                    end;
            end {else if}
    end; {while}
    {Path did not end at vertex Final}
    if not Found then
        WriteLn ('No path exists between these vertices.');
end; {DepthFirst}
```

its only unvisited neighbor (A) onto the stack. Vertex A is then popped off the stack and vertices B and C are pushed onto the stack. Lastly, C is popped off the stack and because this is the final vertex our algorithm stops.

CODING ▼

Procedure DepthFirst is shown in Fig. 9.32. This procedure assumes that vertex labels are single characters so that a set (Marked) can be used to hold the vertices marked as visited. The stack element type is also declared to be of type Char.

TESTING ▼

To test procedure DepthFirst, we need to construct one or more test graphs. DepthFirst should be asked to find paths that require backtracking and paths that do not. We also need to test DepthFirst to be certain that it can determine correctly that no path exists between the two vertices.

Exercises for Section 9.5   *Self-Check*

1. What would be the complexity of an algorithm that displays the edges of a graph if connection information were stored in an adjacency matrix?

2. What would be the complexity of the algorithm from Exercise 1 if adjacency lists were used instead?
3. Which `Graph` methods would need to be modified to allow us to define a `Digraph` object as a descendant of our `Graph` object?

Programming

1. Write a recursive version of procedure DepthFirst.
2. Write a procedure that makes an exact copy of a graph.

9.6   Common Programming Errors

The implementations of the heap and graph objects discussed in this chapter contain array data fields. Subscript range errors are always possible in manipulating array subscripts, so you should guard against them. When recursive algorithms are used to implement operators, you need to be certain that these procedures do in fact terminate. Because our presentation of AVL trees and general trees suggested the use of linked implementations, you might wish to review the errors discussed in Chapter 7. For graph traversal algorithms you need to be careful that the path being followed is not really a cycle. If the path is cyclic, your traversal algorithm might not terminate.

CHAPTER REVIEW

In this chapter we discussed several tree and graph types. We described an implementation of a heap abstract data type and considered its usefulness for representing priority queues. We compared the relative efficiencies of several priority queue implementations. We discussed the use of height-balanced (AVL) trees as a means of improving binary tree search efficiency. We examined several general tree representations, including the binary tree left child/right sibling representation.

We introduced several graph types and described the operators for a graph abstract data type. We discussed the adjacency matrix as a means of representing graph vertex connection information. We described the implementation of a graph object and the depth-first search algorithm. We also introduced a linked representation of a graph.

Quick-Check Exercises

1. Does a heap need to be a complete binary search tree?
2. Is the following tree a balanced binary tree? What is the balance factor $(H_L - H_R)$ for each node?

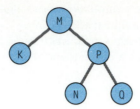

3. How does a general tree differ from a graph?

Use the following graph to answer Exercises 4 to 7.

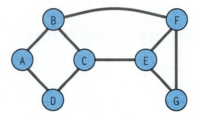

4. List the vertices adjacent to vertex E.
5. List the edges incident on vertex C.
6. Is this graph complete or connected or neither?
7. List the vertices in a path from vertex A to C.
8. If M is the adjacency matrix for a graph, does M[I, J] always equal M[J, I]? If M is a digraph?

Answers to Quick-Check Exercises

1. No
2. Yes; BF = 0 for nodes K, N, Q and BF = –1 for node M.
3. General trees do not permit the existence of cycles and do not allow data nodes to have more than one parent. Graphs are not rooted at any one vertex.
4. {C, F, G}
5. {BC, CE, CD}
6. Connected
7. {A, D, C} or {A, B, C} are two possible answers.
8. Yes; no

Review Questions

1. Assuming that H is an instance of object heap, E1 is type HeapELement, and OK is type Boolean, draw the heap resulting after the successful execution of the following operator sequence:

```
H.CreateHeap;
H.Insert (4, OK);
H.Insert (5, OK);
H.Insert (6, OK);
H.Insert (7, OK);
H.DeleteMax (E1, OK);
```

```
H.Insert (1, OK);
H.Insert (2, OK);
H.Insert (3, OK);
H.DeleteMax (E1, OK);
```

2. Draw the general tree represented by the following binary tree:

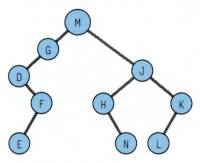

3. Describe the advantages and disadvantages of using AVL trees in place of binary search trees.

4. Write the adjacency matrix for the following graph:

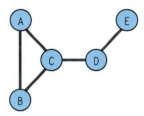

5. Draw a picture of a graph with

   ```
   Vertices: W, X, Y, Z
   Edges: WX, YZ, ZW, XZ
   ```

6. A graph S is said to be a subgraph of graph G if all the vertices and edges of S are in G. Write a new method IsSubGraph for our graph object. IsSubGraph should be implemented as a Boolean function that returns True if its argument S is a subgraph of the graph object.

7. One of the limitations of using a set to keep track of vertices marked as visited is that the vertex labels must be of some ordinal data type. Rewrite procedure DepthFirst to allow the use of strings as vertex labels by storing the visited vertex labels in a linked list.

Programming Projects

Directory: CHAP 9
File: PROJ9_1.PAS

1. Implement a priority queue object that is descended from our Heap object. Revise our bank simulation program from Chapter 5 so that it uses a priority queue to model the bank waiting line. The highest priority should be given to the person having the largest deposit, and the lowest priority should be given to the person making the largest withdrawal.

2. Write programs that will allow you to compare the ordered list and heap implementations of a priority queue. Determine the average number of comparisons

required to insert 100 elements into the priority queue and the average number of comparisons required to remove 100 elements from the priority queue. Use the Borland Pascal GetTime function from the DOS unit to determine the average execution times required to perform a single insert and a single deletion from each implementation.

3. Write programs to examine the relative efficiency of the adjacency matrix implementation of the graph abstract data type. Determine the average number of comparisons required to insert and remove 50 vertices from a graph. Determine the average number of comparisons required to insert and remove 100 edges from a graph. Use the Borland Pascal function GetTime to determine the average execution time for each operation.

**Directory: CHAP 9
File: PROJ9_3.PAS**

4. An alternative means of representing edge connection in graphs would be to substitute a linked list (called an adjacency list) for each row of the adjacency matrix (see Fig. 9.30). Modify our Graph object so that it uses an array of adjacency lists instead of an adjacency matrix. Redo Project 3 using your linked Graph object.

5. Write a menu-driven program for maintaining a graph in which the vertices contain a part name and its cost. Graph edges are used to indicate connections between parts. You should provide menu options to allow the user to add, remove, and replace part vertices and their connections. The user should also be able to display the part and connection information that is stored in the graph.

6. An alternative strategy for finding a path between two graph vertices, called a *breadth-first search,* uses a queue in place of a stack. Modify the algorithm shown in Section 9.5 so that the calls to stack operators are replaced by corresponding calls to queue operators, and write a program to implement a breadth-first search.

**Directory: CHAP 9
File: PROJ9_6.PAS**

CHAPTER TEN

Searching

We have written procedures for searching three data structures for a target key: an array, a linked list, and a binary tree. In this chapter we will investigate other techniques for search, starting with an array search that has similar behavior to that of a binary search tree. We will also consider three techniques that are used for searching very large collections of data: hashing, the use of indexes, and B-trees.

10.1 Sequential Search of an Array

In a *sequential search* of an array we compare array element keys in sequence to the target key, starting with the first array element. This section shows three different versions of an algorithm for sequential search.

The first algorithm examines all array keys and returns the position of the first occurrence of the target key. The for loop accesses each array element. The if statement compares the target key to the current key. If there is a match, Found is set to True, and the subscript of the current element key is stored in PosTarget. We always examine all array elements, regardless of where the target key is located.

Algorithm for Sequential Search

1. Set Found to False
2. for each array element do
   3. if target key matches current element's key and not Found then
      4. Set Found to True and set PosTarget to the current element's subscript.

It would be better to terminate the search process as soon as the target key is located rather than wait until we reach the end of the array. The second search algorithm does this.

Revised Algorithm for Sequential Search

1. Set Found to False and Cursor to 1.
2. while not Found and Cursor <= last array subscript do
   3. if the target key matches the current element's key then
      4. Set Found to True and set PosTarget to Cursor.
   else
      5. Advance Cursor to the next array element.

The search loop in Step 2 executes until the target key is located or the last array element is reached. On average we must make N/2 comparisons to locate a target key that is in the array. However, we must make N comparisons to determine that a target key is not in an array of N elements.

Often, we want to search an array whose elements are arranged in order by key field (analogous to an ordered list). We can take advantage of the fact that the array keys are in ascending order and terminate the search when an array key greater than or equal to the target key is reached. There is no need to look any further in the array; all other keys will be larger than the target key. After exiting the loop we can determine whether the current element's key matches the target key and set the search results accordingly.

Algorithm for Sequential Search of an Ordered Array

1. Set Cursor to 1.
2. while Cursor < last array subscript and
    the current element's key < the target key do
        3. Advance Cursor to the next array element.
4. if the current element's key matches the target key then
    5. Set Found to True and PosTarget to Cursor.
    else
    6. Set Found to False.

On average a sequential search of an ordered array requires N/2 comparisons to either locate the target key or determine that it is not in the array, so sequential search is an O(N) process. For this reason, sequential search is also called *linear search*. We will discuss a better way to search an ordered array next.

Exercises for Section 10.1   ***Self-Check***

1. If duplicate values of the target key are stored in an array, which key value position will be returned by each version of the sequential search algorithm?
2. Write a recursive version of the revised sequential search algorithm.

Programming

1. Implement the algorithm that you wrote for Self-Check Exercise 2.

10.2   Binary Search of an Array

Sequential search of a large array (e.g., N > 1000) can be very time consuming. In Chapter 8 we discussed searching of binary trees, and in Chapter 9 we described a technique for representing a binary tree by using an array. In this section we describe a *binary search algorithm* that combines these two ideas to give improved performance for large sorted arrays.

CASE STUDY   **Binary Search Algorithm**

PROBLEM ▼

Your employer has a directory of customers that she keeps in alphabetical order. Since business has been very good, this list has become too large to search efficiently by using a linear search. Write an improved search algorithm that takes advantage of the fact that the array is sorted.

DESIGN OVERVIEW ▼

The binary search algorithm, like a binary tree search, takes advantage of the fact that the array is ordered to eliminate half of the array elements with each probe into the array. Consequently, if the array has 1000 elements, it will either locate the target value or eliminate 500 elements with its first probe, 250 elements with its second probe, 125 elements with its third probe, and so on. Therefore a binary search of an ordered array is an $O(\log_2 N)$ process. We can use the binary search algorithm to find a name in a large metropolitan telephone directory using 30 or fewer probes, so this algorithm should be suitable for your employer.

Because the array is ordered, all we have to do is compare the target value with the middle element of the subarray that we are searching. If their values are the same, then we are done. If the middle value is larger than the target, then we should search the left half of the array next; otherwise, we should search the right half of the array.

The subarray to be searched has subscripts `First..Last`. The variable `Middle` is the subscript to the middle element in this range. The right half of the array (subscripts `Middle..Last`) is eliminated by the first probe as shown in Fig. 10.1.

`Last` should be reset to `Middle` − 1 to define the new subarray to be searched, and `Middle` should be redefined, as shown in Fig. 10.2. The target value, 35, would be found on this next probe.

The binary search algorithm can be stated clearly by using recursion. The stopping cases are as follows:

▶ The array bounds are improper (First > Last).
▶ The middle value is the target value.

In the first case the target key is missing; in the second case the target key is the middle element. The recursive step is to search the appropriate subarray.

Figure 10.1
First Probe of a
Binary Search

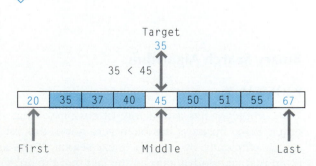

Figure 10.2
Second Probe of a Binary
Search

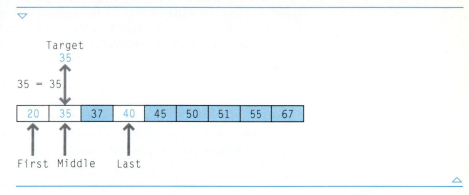

Data Requirements

Problem Inputs

Array to be searched (Table : SearchArray)
Target being searched for (Target : KeyType)
The first subscript in the subarray (First : Integer)
The last subscript in the subarray (Last : Integer)

Problem Outputs

The location of the Target value (Index : Integer)
A flag indicating success or failure (Success : Boolean)

Binary Search Algorithm

1. Compute the subscript of the middle element
2. if the array bounds are improper then
      3. Set Success to False
   else if the target is the middle value then
      4. Return the subscript of the middle element and set Success to True
   else if the target is less than the middle value then
      5. Search the subarray with subscripts First..Middle−1
   else
      6. Search the subarray with subscripts Middle+1..Last

For each of the recursive steps (Steps 5 and 6) the bounds of the new subarray must be listed as actual parameters in the recursive call. The actual parameters define the search limits for the next probe into the array.

CODING THE BINARY SEARCH ALGORITHM ▼

We will write the binary search algorithm as two procedures: `BinSearch` and a helper procedure `DoSearch`. Assuming that elements 1 through N of an array are being searched, Procedure `BinSearch` sets the search bounds (0 through N - 1) for the open array `Table`, which is searched by `DoSearch`.

Next, BinSearch calls DoSearch to perform the array search. If the target key is found, BinSearch adds 1 to the result returned by DoSearch. Bin-Search and DoSearch are shown in Fig. 10.3.

The assignment statement

```
Middle := (First + Last) div 2;
```

computes the subscript of the middle element by finding the average of First and Last. This value has no meaning when First is greater than Last, but it does no harm to compute it.

Figure 10.3
Procedures BinSearch and
DoSearch

Directory: CHAP 10
File: BINSEARC.PAS

```
procedure DoSearch (var Table {input} : Array of KeyType;
                    Target {input} : KeyType;
                    First, Last {input} : Integer;
                    var Index {output} : Integer;
                    var Success {output} : Boolean);
{
 Performs a recursive binary search of an ordered array
 with subscripts First..Last.
 Pre : The elements of Table are in ascending order by key
       field and First and Last are defined.
 Post: Returns through Index the subscript of Target if
       found in array Table; returns the search result (True
       or False) in Success.
}
  var
    Middle : Integer;       {the subscript of the middle element}

begin {DoSearch}
  Middle := (First + Last) div 2;
  {
   Determine if Target is found or missing or search next
   subarray.
  }
  if First > Last then
    Success := False                       {Target missing}
  else if Target = Table[Middle] then
    begin
      Index := Middle;                     {Target found}
      Success := True
    end {found}
    else if Target < Table[Middle] then
      DoSearch (Table, Target, First, Middle-1, Index, Success)
    else
      DoSearch (Table, Target, Middle+1, Last, Index, Success)
end; {DoSearch}

procedure BinSearch (var Table {input} : Array of KeyType;
                     Target {input} : KeyType;
```

▷ ▷ ▷ ▷ ▷ ▷

```
                        N {input} : Integer;
                        var Index {output} : Integer;
                        var Success {output} : Boolean);
    {
     Initiates a recursive binary search of an ordered array
     with subscripts 1..N. Calls DoSearch to perform the
     search.
     Pre : The elements of Table are in ascending order by
           key field.
     Post: Returns through Index the subscript of Target if
           found in array Table; returns the search result
           (True or False) through Success.
    }
    begin {BinSearch}
      DoSearch (Table, Target, 0, N-1, Index, Success);
      if Success then
        Index := Index + 1
    end; {BinSearch}
```

TESTING THE BINARY SEARCH PROCEDURES ▼

To test the binary search procedure, verify that it locates target values that are present in the array. Also verify that it determines when a target value is missing. Use target values that are within the range of values stored in the array. Also use a target value that is less than the smallest value in the array and one that is greater than the largest value in the array. Make sure that the binary search procedure terminates both when the target is missing and when it is found in the array. Also, the search procedure should terminate regardless of where the target is located if found.

Exercises for Section 10.2　**Self-Check**

1. Trace the search of the array shown in Fig. 10.1 in this section for a Target of 40. Specify the values of First, Middle, and Last during each recursive call.
2. What would be returned as the value of Index following the unsuccessful search of the array shown in Fig. 10.1 for a Target of 35?

10.3　Searching by Hashing

So far we have discussed the advantages of using the binary search technique to retrieve information stored in a large array. Binary search can be used only when the contents of the array are arranged in sequential order by key.

Figure 10.4
Computing a Hash Index

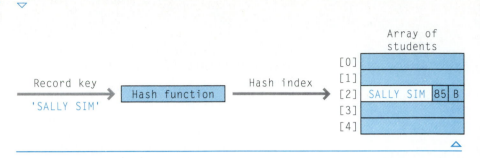

Another technique for storing data records in an array so that retrieval can be done in an efficient manner is called *hashing*. This technique consists of using a *hash function* to compute a *hash index* that corresponds to the record key. The hash index selects the particular array element where the new data will be stored during insertion. To retrieve the item at a later time, the hash function must recompute the hash index corresponding to the target key. This process is illustrated in Fig. 10.4, where the record key is a student's name and the hash function computes a hash index value of 2.

In function terminology the hash function is a mapping from the *domain* of all keys to the *range* of hash array subscripts (see Fig. 10.5). As implied by Fig. 10.5, the number of possible keys is normally much greater than the available subscripts (called *slots* or *buckets*) in the hash array. For example, if a person's Social Security number were used as a record key, there would be 10^9 possible keys. The subscript range would be based on the actual number of records to be stored and would need to be at least as large as the actual number of records to be stored.

Inserting a student record is accomplished by passing its key to function Hash and storing the record in the array element selected by Hash. After all records are stored in the array, we can retrieve a particular record by passing its key to function Hash and accessing the array element selected by Hash. The nice thing about all of this is that it will often take only one probe into the array to store or retrieve a particular record. Sometimes it will take more than one probe, as explained in the next subsection.

Figure 10.5
Mapping from Keys
to Subscripts

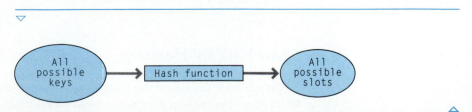

It is important to note that records will be stored in arbitrary order in a hash table. Therefore if we display the records in the order in which they are stored, starting with the record in the first position, their keys will not necessarily be in sequence. Also, empty slots will be intermixed with slots that contain actual records. For this reason you should not use hashing when it is important to access the records in sequential order by key.

Figure 10.6 shows an example of a hash table with 11 slots (numbered 0 through 10) that contains seven five-digit integer keys and four empty slots. As you can see, the keys are stored in arbitrary order. We are showing only the keys, but keep in mind that each slot could contain an entire record. In Section 10.3 we will describe the hash function that was used to store these keys.

Notice that the beginning of the table is more heavily populated than the end, so the records are not dispersed as well as we would like them to be. This phenomenon of keys being placed very near each other in the hash table is known as *clustering*. As we will describe later, a high degree of clustering in a hash table can lead to a decrease in search efficiency.

Collisions

Even if the record keys are unique, it is possible (even likely) for function Hash to return the same hash index value for two different keys. This is called a *collision*. We can store the first record in the slot selected by function Hash, but we will have to find another location for the second record. For example, in Fig. 10.6, keys 32145 and 13456 both had a hash index of 3. We placed the first key in slot 3 and the second key in slot 4. We will discuss in the next section why we did this.

When a record is stored in a slot other than the one selected by function Hash, *displacement* is said to have occurred. Displacement of records will

Figure 10.6
Hash Table with Seven Integer Keys

[0]	21098
[1]	87693
[2]	91236
[3]	32145
[4]	13456
[5]	
[6]	55567
[7]	
[8]	
[9]	
[10]	32108

also affect the efficiency of a hash table's operations, since we have to figure out where to look for a record (e.g., 13456) when we attempt a retrieval and find a different record key (e.g., 32145) in the slot selected by function Hash.

Self-Check

1. Under what circumstances would you expect hashing to outperform binary search as a means of searching an array for a target key?
2. Which problem (clustering or displacement) would you try to solve by using a different hash function?

10.4 Computing Hash Indexes and Resolving Collisions

The intention of this section is not to make you an expert on designing hash functions or resolving collisions, but to give you some idea of the issues involved and techniques used for handling them. We have stated that a good hash function should disperse the records uniformly throughout the table. A second characteristic of a good hash function is that it should be computationally efficient (i.e., not require too many operations to compute the hash index). Remember that our goal is efficient search and retrieval, so we don't want to lose the time saved due to fewer record key comparisons by spending a lot of time computing a hash index.

If the record key is a positive integer, Fig. 10.7 shows a very simple hash function (method HashData.Hash) that uses the *division-remainder method*. Function Hash divides the integer stored in data member Key by the table size and returns the integer remainder as the hash index. Figure 10.6 shows the results of using this function on a table with just 11 slots. With the exception of key 13456, each key is stored in the table slot selected by function Hash. We would normally use hashing with table sizes that are much larger than 11.

Function Hash in Fig. 10.7 is certainly computationally efficient, requiring only a single mod operation. If the keys are random integers, it will generally give reasonable average-case performance, since clustering is not likely to

---

Figure 10.7
Hash Function Using the
Division-Remainder
Method

Directory: CHAP 10
File: HASH.PAS

```
function HashData.Hash : Word;
{
  Computes the hash index corresponding to an integer key stored
  in data member Key using the division-remainder method.
}
begin {Hash}
  Hash := Key mod MaxSlots
end; {Hash}
```

occur. It is usually better if MaxSlots is a prime number, since this will tend to give a more uniform distribution of keys in the hash table.

What if the key is a string of characters instead of a numeric key? In this case we need to compute a hash index from the individual string characters. A simple hash function would just add up the ordinal numbers corresponding to the individual characters in the string and then perform a mod operation on the sum. For example, if the key is the string 'SAM', the decimal sum of the ordinal numbers is 225 (83 + 65 + 77).

There are two problems with this simple method. Because each ordinal number is less than 127, only the first 635 slots in a table would be used as hash indexes when storing five-character keys (5 × 127 is 635). If the table size were much larger than 635, the keys would all hash to indexes at the beginning of the table and would not be randomly dispersed. Another problem is that keys with the same letters but in different sequence (e.g., 'SAMMY' and 'MAMSY') would hash to the same table slot.

Figure 10.8 shows a hash function that multiplies each character's ordinal number by (32^{i-1}), where i represents the character's position in the string Key, counting from the right end. Multiplying by 32 is accomplished by shifting a binary number five bits to the left, so it is a very efficient operation. The only problem with this function is that for sufficiently long keys the leftmost characters are shifted out of the answer, and the result would be based on the rightmost characters. Also, for longer keys, integer overflow may occur. Both these deficiencies could be corrected by performing the mod operation after each addition, but that would increase the computation time significantly. Another approach for longer keys would be to skip every other character in the string Key.

It might not be obvious that function Hash in Fig. 10.8 multiplies each character's ordinal number by the required power of 32. However, if we

Figure 10.8
Hash Function for a
String Key

Directory: CHAP 10
File: HASH5TAB.PAS

```
function HashData.Hash : Word;
{
 Computes the hash index for a string key stored in
 data member Key.
}
   var
     K,
     HashSum : Word;

begin {Hash}
   HashSum := 0;
   for K := 1 to Length(Key) do
     HashSum := HashSum * 32 + Ord(Key[K]);
   Hash := HashSum mod MaxSlots
end; {Hash}
```

trace the loop in function `Hash` when the key is the string `'SAM'`, we get the result that

`HashSum = (Ord('S') * 32 + Ord('A')) * 32 + Ord('M')`

or

`HashSum := Ord('S') * 32² + Ord('A') * 32 + Ord('M')`

which is the desired result (`'S'` is in position 3 counting from the right end, `'A'` is in position 2, and `'M'` is in position 1). This result generalizes to keys of any length. Table 10.1 shows hash indexes computed by function `Hash` for some five-character string keys, assuming a table size of 997.

Table 10.1
Hash Indexes for Five-Character String Keys

Key	Hash Index
SAMMY	777
MAMSY	969
NORMA	888
CHRIS	911
KATIE	818
BENNY	836
MYLES	488

Other Techniques for Hashing

A variety of techniques have been proposed for improving hash function performance. As we discussed earlier, the objective of these techniques is to produce a uniformly distributed hash index, which will cause better dispersion of keys throughout the hash table. We discuss two of these methods here: midsquare and folding.

In the *midsquare method* the bit string for the key is multiplied by itself to form a much larger binary number. Next, the number of bits required to form a hash index is selected from the middle of the binary product. This can be done by logically "anding" the result with a bit string that contains 1s in the bit positions to be retained and 0 elsewhere. The net result is a relatively random hash index that is computed efficiently.

EXAMPLE 10.1 ▼

For convenience we will illustrate the midsquare method using decimal arithmetic. Assume that a record key is a four-digit decimal number and that the hash table contains 1000 slots. The square of record key 1120 is 1254400. If we retain only the "middle" three digits, the corresponding hash index is 544. ▲

In the *folding method* the bit string for a key is segmented into smaller substrings of equal size. Next, the substrings are combined by an addition or by an exclusive-or operation. For example, if the record key contains six-characters, we could form three substrings consisting of characters 1 and 2, characters 3 and 4, and characters 5 and 6. Each substring is represented by a bit string of length 16, so the result of an exclusive-or operation will be a bit string of length 16. If we use this bit string as the hash index, we will get table subscripts in the range 0 through 65535 (2^{16} − 1 is 65535). If the hash index is too large, we can use modular division to get the final hash index.

EXAMPLE 10.2 ▼

If we assume that the key is the string 'ABCD12', the three substring segments are 'AB', 'CD', and '12'. The 16-bit strings representing the substrings and their exclusive or follow:

```
        'AB'         01000001 01000010
        'CD'         01000011 01000100
        '12'         00110001 00110010
Exclusive or         00110011 00110100
```

Notice that the exclusive or has a 1 in column i when there is an odd number of 1 bits in column i. The binary result is equivalent to the decimal number 13108, which should be divided by the table size using modular division. ▲

Resolving Collisions

Regardless of how good the hash function might be, there will always be collisions as long as the range of key values is larger than number of hash table slots. Recall that a collision occurs whenever the same hash index is computed for two different record keys. To be able to complete a hash table storage or retrieval operation, we need to resolve this collision by selecting a new hash table index for one of the records. We discuss two methods of resolving collisions in this section: linear resolution (or probing) and quadratic resolution (or probing).

In *linear resolution* we adopt the straightforward policy of advancing to the next location in the hash table if the current slot is occupied by a record that has a key that is different from the target key. If that slot is also filled with a record whose key is not the target key, we access the next one after it, and so on. If we happen to reach the last slot of the table, we cycle back to the first slot (hash index of 0).

Figure 10.9 shows function `Rehash`, which computes the next hash index based on this algorithm assuming that `HashIndex` is the initial hash index (computed by function `Hash`). In attempting to insert or retrieve a key, `Hash` is called only once but `Rehash` may be called several times in succession. `Rehash` should be called when all prior attempts to insert (or retrieve) the current target key have resulted in a collision. The value of `Probe` represents the number of prior probes into the table. `Probe` should be set to 1 before

Figure 10.9
Function Rehash

Directory: CHAP 10
File: REHASH.PAS

```
function HashTable.Rehash (HashIndex, Probe : Word) : Word;
{
  Returns the next hash index assuming the slots at HashIndex and
  at all prior hash indexes computed by Rehash contain records
  with different keys from the target key.
  Pre : Probe >= 1 and 0 <= HashIndex <= MaxSlots
  Post: The function result is between 0 and MaxSlots
}
begin {Rehash}
  Rehash := (HashIndex + Probe) mod MaxSlots
end; {Rehash}
```

the first call to Rehash and should be incremented by 1 before each subsequent call to Rehash.

Function Rehash is very efficient in that it computes a new hash index using only an addition and a mod operation. However, experience shows that linear resolution can cause wide bands in the table where collisions become more likely to occur. Recall that this phenomenon is known as clustering. The reason for this is that linear resolution stores all keys with the same hash index in a contiguous band of filled slots rather than dispersing them uniformly throughout the rest of the table. Consequently, if three keys happen to have the same hash index, they will be stored in a contiguous band containing at least three filled table slots and possibly more. Now there will be a collision if a record key hashes to the original hash index or any of the other slots in that band. When this happens, the band size grows by one, and so on. A wide band of filled slots can lead to rather lengthy searches as the keys are displaced farther and farther from their original hash location.

As an example, let's look at the hash table from Fig. 10.6. Because the table wraps around, we can consider slots [10] through [4] to be a band of filled cells. If the next key to be inserted hashes to any slot in this band, there will be a collision, and that key will be stored in location 5. This can have dire consequences if the hash index of the new key happens to be 10. In this case, successive calls to Rehash will return the values 0, 1, 2, 3, 4, and 5 before an empty slot is reached. This means that a total of seven table locations have to be examined before the new key is inserted in slot 5, so we have a *search chain* of length 7. This search chain *overlaps* with the one for hash index 0 because they have several slots (0, 1, 2, 3, 4, and 5) in common. In the worst case, after many insertions and deletions the displacement problem can cause linear probing to degenerate to a sequential search of the entire hash table.

Quadratic resolution is an improved technique that disperses keys with the same hash index, thereby reducing the degree of clustering in a given hash table. In quadratic resolution the first key that hashes to HashIndex is

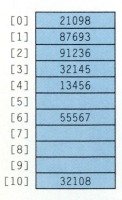

[0]	21098
[1]	87693
[2]	91236
[3]	32145
[4]	13456
[5]	
[6]	55567
[7]	
[8]	
[9]	
[10]	32108

stored in slot HashIndex, the second key in slot HashIndex + 1, the third key in slot HashIndex + 4, the fourth key in slot HashIndex + 9, and so on. The general rule for rehashing using quadratic probing is to try slots at positions

```
Key + Probe²
```

where Probe takes successive values from the sequence

```
{0, 1, 2, . . . }
```

Function Rehash is rewritten in Fig. 10.10 using quadratic probing. The net effect is that search chains do not overlap as much, and they are much shorter. However, the displacement problem is not eliminated.

Analysis of Resolution Methods

Extensive evaluation and comparison of these two methods are beyond the scope of this text. Computer scientists have determined that the expected (or average) number of probes required to locate a key that is known to exist in a hash table is

```
1/2 * (1 + 1/(1 - α))
```

for linear resolution and

```
-(1/α) * logₑ (1 - α)
```

for quadratic resolution, where α is the occupancy ratio (of filled slots to the total number of slots available) for the hash table. Table 10.2 shows the expected number of probes required to locate keys in tables with different ratios of filled to empty slots in the hash table. Comparing the two columns of Table 10.2, we see that quadratic probing leads to considerably shorter search chains when the occupancy ratio is high (70% or more).

Figure 10.10
Function Rehash Using
Quadratic Probing

Directory: CHAP 10
File: HASHTABL.PAS

```
function HashTable.Rehash (HashIndex, Probe : Word) : Word;
{
  Returns the next HashIndex assuming the slots at HashIndex and
  all prior values of Rehash contain records with different keys
  from the target key. Uses quadratic resolution.
  Pre : Probe >= 1 and 0 <= HashIndex <= MaxSlots
  Post: The function result is between 0 and MaxSlots
}
begin {Rehash}
  Rehash := (HashIndex + Probe * Probe) mod MaxSlots
end; {Rehash}
```

α	Linear Probing	Quadratic Probing
10%	1.06	1.05
20%	1.12	1.12
30%	1.21	1.19
40%	1.33	1.28
50%	1.50	1.39
60%	1.75	1.53
70%	2.17	1.72
80%	3.00	2.01
90%	5.50	2.56

One thing that should be obvious from Table 10.2 is that regardless of which method is used for hashing or collision resolution, the same hash function should lead to fewer collisions when there is more empty space in the hash table. Besides the techniques discussed in this section, there is another alternative for collision resolution called *bucket hashing*. We will discuss this approach in Section 10.6.

Exercises for Section 10.4   **Self-Check**

1. Assume that the ordinal number for the letter A is 1, that for B is 2, and so on, and MaxSlots is 12. Compute the hash indexes for the following names, and indicate where each name would be stored in the hash table: 'SAL', 'BIL', 'JIL', 'LIB', 'LAS', 'ROB'. Use linear probing to resolve collisions.
2. A modification to function Hash in Exercise 1 is proposed in which the ordinal number for each letter is multiplied by its position in the string (e.g., for 'SAL', multiply Ord('S') by 1, Ord('A') by 2, etc.). Where would the keys be placed? Why is this a better hash function?

10.5   Implementing a Hash Table ADT

Table 10.3 provides the specification for a hash table ADT. A hash table should be provided with methods for insertion, retrieval, and replacement of a table record. Because we don't want to break a search chain caused by a series of collisions, we will not provide a deletion method.

Table 10.3
Specification for Hash
Table ADT

Structure

A hash table is an array of records with a unique key field. The location of each record is determined by its hash index, which is computed from the record key (a string).

Operators

For the following descriptions, assume the parameters:

```
El (pronounced el) has data type HashData.
MaxSlots is a constant indicating the table size.
ASlot is type Word and is in the table subscript range.
Success is a Boolean flag indicating success (True) or
     failure (False) of an operation.
```

HashTable.CreateTable (MaxSlots)	Creates a hash table and initializes all elements to the empty record.
HashTable.Insert (El, var Success)	Inserts a record in the hash table. The value of Success indicates whether the insertion was successful.
HashTable.Retrieve (var El, var Success)	Retrieves a record from the hash table. The value of Success indicates whether the retrieval was successful.
HashTable.Replace (El, var Success)	Replaces the record with the same key as El in the hash table with El. The value of Success indicates whether the replacement was successful.
HashTable.Display	Displays the records stored in the hash table.
HashTable.IsFull	(function) Returns True if the hash table is full.
HashTable.GetSize	(function) Returns the number of records stored in the hash table.
HashTable.Search (El, var HashIndex, var Success)	Searches for record El starting at location HashIndex and returns through HashIndex the actual location of record El if found and sets Success to True. If record El is not in the hash table, returns the position of the empty slot where El should be stored and sets Success to False. If the hash table is full or no location is found for El, sets Success to False.

Figure 10.11 shows the interface section for `HashTableADT` written as a Borland Pascal object. We import data type `KeyType` from unit `HashDataADT`. Private function `Rehash` will be used to resolve collisions. You may be wondering why function `Hash` is not shown as a method. Because

Figure 10.11
Interface Section for Unit
HashTableADT

```
unit HashTableADT;
{
 Specification for a hash table abstract data type.

 Imports object HashData and constant MaxSlots from unit
 HashDataADT.
}
interface

  uses HashDataADT;

  const
    MaxSize = MaxSlots - 1;      {last table subscript}

  type
    HashRange = 0..MaxSize;      {range of table subscripts}
    InfoType = array [HashRange] of HashData;
    HashTable = object
                  procedure CreateTable;
                  function IsFull : Boolean;
                  function GetSize : Word;
                  procedure Insert
                          (El {input} : HashData;
                           var Success {output} : Boolean);
                  procedure Retrieve
                          (var El {in/out} : HashData;
                           var Success {output} :Boolean);
                  procedure Replace
                          (El {input} : HashData;
                           var Success {output} :Boolean);
                  procedure Search
                          (El {input} : HashData;
                           var HashIndex {in/out} :Word;
                           var Success {output} : Boolean);
                  procedure Display;

                private
                  Size : Word;       {number of records stored}
                  Info : InfoType;      {information records}
                  function Rehash
                          (HashIndex, Probe : Word) : Word;
                end; {HashTable}
```

the hashing operation depends on the structure of the record key, we will import it from HashDataADT.

Implementation Section for HashTableADT

Figure 10.12 shows methods CreateTable, IsFull, GetSize, and Display. CreateTable calls method HashData.CreateEmpty to store an "empty record" in each table slot. HashTable.Display displays the records stored in the hash table. For each table slot, it calls HashData.IsEmpty to determine whether that slot is filled, and if so, it calls HashData.Display to display its contents.

Method HashTable.Search

To find a target key in a hash table, we must first call function Hash to compute the hash index (HashIndex) for that key. There are three possibilities for the table slot with subscript HashIndex:

Figure 10.12
Methods CreateTable,
IsFull, GetSize, and
Display

Directory: CHAP 10
File: HASHTABL.PAS

```
implementation
  procedure HashTable.CreateTable;
  {
    Creates an empty hash table.
    Pre : None.
    Post: All records are "empty records".
  }
    var
      I : HashRange;

  begin {CreateTable}
    {Initialize all table elements to empty records}
    for I := 0 to MaxSize do
      Info[I].CreateEmpty;
    Size := 0
  end; {CreateTable}

  function HashTable.IsFull : Boolean;
  {
    Returns True if hash table is full.
  }
  begin {IsFull}
    IsFull := (Size = MaxSlots)
  end; {IsFull}

  function HashTable.GetSize : Word;
  {
    Returns number of records stored in hash table.
  }
    begin {GetSize}
      GetSize := Size
    end; {GetSize}

  procedure HashTable.Display;
  {
    Displays all records stored in hash table.
  }
```

▷ ▷ ▷ ▷ ▷

```
var
  I : Integer;

begin {Display}
  for I := 0 to MaxSize do
    if not Info[I].IsEmpty then
      begin
        WriteLn ('Slot ', I, ' contents:');
        Info[I].Display
      end
end; {Display}
```

▲

▶ The record at HashIndex contains the target key—the search is successful.
▶ There is no record stored at HashIndex—the search is unsuccessful.
▶ The key of the record stored at HashIndex is not the same as the target key—there is a collision.

In the first two cases we set Success to indicate the search result (True for case 1, False for case 2) and return from procedure Search. If there is a collision (case 3), we must look elsewhere in the hash table. We will use method Rehash (described in Section 10.4) to compute alternative locations to examine. The value (NewHash) returned by Rehash is based on the initial hash index and the number of probes made so far. We continue to search until any of the following occurs:

▶ We locate the target.
▶ We reach an empty slot. This means that the target key is not in the table.
▶ We have cycled back to the starting point (NewHash equals HashIndex). This means that the target key is not in the table and there is no slot available for record El.

When one of the above cases occurs, we replace the value in HashIndex with the last value computed by Rehash and set Success to indicate the search result (True for case 1, False for cases 2 and 3).

Figure 10.13 shows method HashTable.Search, which calls method HashData.IsEqual (tests for a key match) and method HashData.IsEmpty (tests for an empty record). The last statement in the while loop

```
Success := Info[NewHash].IsEqual(El)
```

sets the search result in the event of a collision. It sets Success to True when the search loop terminates because the target key is found.

Methods Insert, Retrieve, and Replace

Methods Insert, Retrieve, and Replace must first compute the HashIndex for record El and then call Search to find El's key or determine that El is not in the table. Insert must do nothing if El's key is found (no duplicate keys) and insert El if it isn't. Retrieve must extract the table record whose key matches El's key if found and do nothing if it isn't. Replace must replace the table entry whose key matches El's key with the new record in El if El's key is found. Figure 10.14 shows these

Figure 10.13
Method
HashTable.Search

Directory: CHAP 10
File: HASHTABL.PAS

```
procedure HashTable.Search (El {input} : HashData;
                            var HashIndex {in/out} : Word;
                            var Success {output} : Boolean);
{
 Searches for record El starting at hash table location
 HashIndex.
 Pre : HashTable is initialized; El and HashIndex are defined.
 Post: If El is found in hash table Success is set to True and
       HashIndex contains location of El; otherwise Success is
       set to False and HashIndex is set to location where El
       should be stored.
}
  var
    Probe                              {number of probes so far}
    NewHash : Word;                    {next hash index}

begin {Search}
  if Info[HashIndex].IsEqual(El) then
    Success := True                    {El's key at HashIndex}
  else if Info[HashIndex].IsEmpty then
    Success := False                   {No record at HashIndex}
  else
    begin {collision}
      {
       Find El's key or an empty table slot,
       whichever comes first.
      }
      Probe := 1;
      NewHash := Rehash(HashIndex, Probe);
      while not Info[NewHash].IsEqual(El) and
            not Info[NewHash].IsEmpty and
            (NewHash <> HashIndex) do
        {invariant:
           El's key not found yet and empty slot not found
           yet and haven't cycled back to HashIndex yet.
        }
        begin
```

▷ ▷ ▷ ▷ ▷ ▷

```
            Probe := Probe + 1;
            {Compute new location.}
            NewHash := Rehash(HashIndex, Probe)
          end; {while}

        {assert: Found El or an empty slot or out of slots.}
        HashIndex := NewHash;       {Return new hash index.}
        {Was El's key found?}
        Success := Info[NewHash].IsEqual(El)
      end {collision}
  end; {Search}
```

△

three procedures. Insert and Replace use method HashData.Init to
store a record, and Retrieve uses method HashData.Retrieve to extract
a record.

Figure 10.14
Methods Insert,
Retrieve, **and** Replace

Directory: CHAP 10
File: HASHTABL.PAS

▽

```
procedure HashTable.Insert (El {input} : HashData;
                                var Success {output} : Boolean);
 {
  Inserts El into hash table.
  Pre : Hash table is initialized and El defined.
  Post: Success set to True if insertion successful;
        Success set to False if no insertion performed.

 }
   var
     HashIndex : Word;

begin {Insert}
   if IsFull then
     Success := False    {table full - insertion not possible}
   else
     begin {not full}
       {
         Search for El's key or an empty slot starting
         at HashIndex.
       }

       HashIndex := El.Hash;    {compute hash index}
       {See if El is already in hash table}
       Search (El, HashIndex, Success);
       if Success then
         Success := False              {duplicate entry}
```

 ▷ ▷ ▷ ▷ ▷

```
      else if Info[HashIndex].IsEmpty then
        begin {empty slot}
          {Store El in empty slot.}
          Info[HashIndex].Init (El);
          Size := Size + 1;
          Success := True
        end {empty slot}
      end {not full}
  end; {Insert}

  procedure HashTable.Retrieve (var El {in/out} : HashData;
                                   var Success {output} : Boolean);
  {
   Retrieves hash table record with key matching El's key.
   Pre : Hash table initialized and El's key field defined.
   Post: Success set to True and hash table record returned as
         value of El; otherwise Success set to False.
  }
    var
      HashIndex : Word;

  begin {Retrieve}
    {Search for El's key or an empty slot starting at HashIndex}
    HashIndex := El.Hash;
    Search (El, HashIndex, Success);
    if Success then
      El := Info[HashIndex];        {copy table data to El}
  end; {Retrieve}

  procedure HashTable.Replace (El {input} : HashData;
                                   var Success {output} : Boolean);
  {
   Replaces hash table record whose key matches El's.
   Pre : Hash table is initialized and El defined.
   Post: Success set to True if replacement was successful and
         False otherwise.
  }
    var
      HashIndex : Word;

  begin {Replace}
    {Search for El's key or an empty slot starting at HashIndex}
    HashIndex := El.Hash;
    Search (El, HashIndex, Success);
    if Success then
      Info[HashIndex] := El            {store El in table}
  end; {Replace}

end. {HashTableADT}
```

Self-Check

1. What would be the consequences of deleting a record from the hash table by making its hash table location empty again?

Programming

1. Write unit HashDataADT assuming that hash table keys are strings of length three and that the maximum number of slots is 997.

10.6 Bucket Hashing

Before completing the discussion of hashing, we consider another hashing technique. In *bucket hashing,* we use separate buckets to store all records whose keys hash to the same hash index. One way to implement buckets is to use a hash table that consists of an array of pointers, each of which points to a linked list of records. If there are no records with a particular hash index, that table slot will contain a nil pointer. As shown in Fig. 10.15, the pointer at Table[i] points to the linked list of records whose keys have a hash index of i. In Fig. 10.15, there are no records with hash indexes 1 and 3, two records with hash index 0, and one record with hash index 2. The notation $record_{i,j}$ represents the jth record ($j >= 1$) with hash index i ($i >= 0$).

Figure 10.16 contains the interface section for a hash table implementation that makes use of linked list type buckets. You will notice that we no longer need the private method Rehash because we do not need to find an alternative slot in which to store the record that causes the collision. Since we are using our LinkListADT to implement the buckets, our hash table element is defined as being of type ListData. To display the hash table entries, we need to pass a procedure to method HashTable.Display that will be used by LinkList.Traverse to display the elements of each linked list bucket.

Figure 10.17 shows the implementation section of unit BucketHashTableADT. The implementations of most methods are fairly

Figure 10.15
Hash Table for
Bucket Hashing

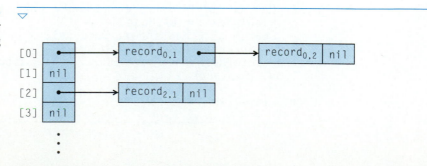

straightforward. Method `CreateTable` uses method `LinkList.CreateList` to initialize each bucket as an empty linked list. Method `IsFull` uses the Borland Pascal functions `MemAvail` and `SizeOf` to determine whether enough storage space is left in the heap to allocate a new list element.

To retrieve a record, we call function `Hash` to compute the hash index. Then we use method `LinkList.Search` to determine whether the target

Figure 10.16
Interface Section for Unit
BucketHashTableADT

Directory: CHAP 10
File: BUCKETHA.PAS

```
unit BucketHashTableADT;
{
  Specification for a hash table abstract data type.

  Imports object ListData and constant MaxSlots from unit
  ListDataADT and object LinkList from unit LinkListADT.
}
interface

  uses ListDataADT, LinkListADT;

  const
    MaxSize = MaxSlots - 1;        {last table subscript}

  type
    HashRange = 0..MaxSize;        {range of table subscripts}
    InfoType = array [HashRange] of LinkList;
    HashTable = object
                   procedure CreateTable;
                   function IsFull : Boolean;
                   function GetSize : Word;
                   procedure Insert
                              (El {input} : ListData;
                               var Success {output} : Boolean);
                   procedure Retrieve
                              (var El {in/out} : ListData;
                               var Success {output} :Boolean);
                   procedure Replace
                              (El {input} : ListData;
                               var Success {output} :Boolean);
                   procedure Search
                              (El {input} : ListData;
                               var HashIndex {in/out} :Word;
                               var Success {output} : Boolean);
                   procedure Display (Visit : ProcedureType);

                   private
                     Size : Word;       {number of records stored}
                     Info : InfoType;   {information records}
                   end; {HashTable}
```

key is stored in the bucket. If the bucket is empty or we cannot find the target key, the retrieval operation fails.

To insert a record, we call function Hash to compute the hash index. Next we use method LinkList.Search to determine whether the target key is already in the bucket. If we find the target, we have a duplicate entry, so the insertion operation fails. If the target key is not already present in the bucket, we insert the new record at the head of the bucket list.

Figure 10.17
Implementation Section for
BucketHashTableADT

Directory: CHAP 10
File: BUCKETHA.PAS

```
implementation
    procedure HashTable.CreateTable;
    {
     Creates an empty hash table.
     Pre : None.
     Post: All buckets are "empty".
    }
      var
        I : HashRange;

    begin {CreateTable}
      {Initialize all table elements to empty buckets}
      for I := 0 to MaxSize do
        Info[I].CreateList;
      Size := 0
    end; {CreateTable}

    function HashTable.IsFull : Boolean;
    {
     Returns True if hash table is full.
    }
    begin {IsFull}
      IsFull := MemAvail < SizeOf(ListData)
    end; {IsFull}

    function HashTable.GetSize : Word;
    {
     Returns number of records stored in hash table.
    }
    begin {GetSize}
      GetSize := Size
    end; {GetSize}

    procedure HashTable.Search (El {input} : ListData;
                                var HashIndex {in/out} : Word;
                                var Success {output} : Boolean);
    {
     Searches for record El starting at hash table location
     HashIndex.
```

▷ ▷ ▷ ▷ ▷ ▷

```
      Pre : HashTable is initialized; El and HashIndex are defined.
      Post: If El is found in hash table Success is set to True and
            HashIndex contains location of El; otherwise Success is
            set to False and HashIndex set to location where El
            should be stored.
}
begin {Search}
  Info[HashIndex].Search (El, Success)
end; {Search}

procedure HashTable.Insert (El {input} : ListData;
                                  var Success {output} : Boolean);
{
 Inserts El into hash table.
 Pre : Hash table is initialized and El defined.
 Post: Success set to True if insertion successful;
       Success set to False if no insertion performed.
}
   var
     HashIndex : Word;

begin {Insert}
  if IsFull then
    Success := False      {table full - insertion not possible}
  else
    begin {not full}
      HashIndex := El.Hash;            {compute hash index}
      {See if El is already in hash table}
      Search (El, HashIndex, Success);
      if Success then
        Success := False               {duplicate entry}
      else
        begin {insert El}
          {Store El at head of list}
          Info[HashIndex].InitCursor;
          Info[HashIndex].Insert (El);
          Size := Size + 1;
          Success := True
        end {insert El}
    end {not full}
end; {Insert}

procedure HashTable.Retrieve (var El {in/out} : ListData;
                                   var Success {output} : Boolean);
{
 Retrieves hash table record with key matching El's key.
 Pre : Hash table initialized and El's key field defined.
 Post: Success set to True and hash table record returned as
       value of El; otherwise Success set to False.
}
   var
     HashIndex : Word;
```

▷ ▷ ▷ ▷ ▷ ▷

```
    begin {Retrieve}
      {Search for El's key in bucket at HashIndex}
      HashIndex := El.Hash;
      Info[HashIndex].Search (El, Success);
      {Copy table data to El}
      if Success then
        Info[HashIndex].Retrieve (El, Success);
    end; {Retrieve}


    procedure HashTable.Replace (El {input} : ListData;
                                      var Success {output} : Boolean);
    {
     Replaces hash table record whose key matches El's.
     Pre : Hash table is initialized and El defined.
     Post: Success set to True if replacement was successful and
           False otherwise.
    }
      var
        HashIndex : Word;

    begin {Replace}
      {Search for El's key in bucket at HashIndex}
      HashIndex := El.Hash;
      Info[HashIndex].Search (El, Success);
      if Success then
        begin
          {Replace hash element with key matching El's key}
          Info[HashIndex].Delete;
          Info[HashIndex].InitCursor;
          Info[HashIndex].Insert (El)
        end {if}
    end; {Replace}


    procedure HashTable.Display (Visit : ProcedureType);
    {
     Displays all records stored in hash table.
     Pre : Visit is procedure with Listdata input parameter, which
           was compiled using the far call model in the client.
     Post: Visit applied to each bucket element starting with first
           bucket in hash table.
    }
      var
        I : Integer;

    begin {Display}
      for I := 0 to MaxSize do
        if not Info[I].IsEmpty then
          Info[I].Traverse (Visit)
    end; {Display}


end. {BucketHashTableADT}
```

To replace a record, we compute the hash index for the El's key and search that bucket for a record that has a matching key. If a matching record is found, method `LinkList.Delete` is used to delete the list element, and a new list element is inserted at the head of the bucket list by using method `LinkList.Insert`.

Comparison of Bucket Hashing with Regular Hashing

To compare bucket hashing with regular hashing, we must consider their relative search efficiencies and storage requirements. We would expect smaller search chains for bucket chaining. That is because we need to search only the records in the same bucket as the one with the target key, so search chains cannot overlap. In general, we would expect the average complexity of hash table operations involving bucket searching to be proportional to the average bucket size, which is

`(Number of keys housed in table)/(number of slots)`

The worst behavior would be O(N) in the case in which all N hash table keys were stored in the same bucket.

In terms of real execution time it should be quicker to traverse a search chain in regular hashing because array references tend to be a little faster than dereferencing pointer values. Therefore we can access a different table record just by changing the value of an array subscript. This is faster than following a chain of pointers.

With respect to storage an advantage of regular hashing is that we do not need to allocate extra storage space for pointers. In bucket hashing, we need to store a table of pointers as well as the records themselves, and we also need to store a pointer with each record. Therefore the extra storage required for bucket hashing consists of the memory required for the table of pointers plus the memory required to store one address with each record.

Even though extra storage is needed for the pointers, bucket hashing may require less overall storage space. This will be the case if the record size is large in comparison to the number of bytes in a memory address and if the hash table is sparsely populated. In regular hashing, each hash table entry must be large enough to store an entire record, and we need one table entry for each record plus extra storage capacity to reduce the chance of a collision. The hash table is allocated at compile-time, and the amount of storage allocated is the product of the table size and record size. In bucket hashing, storage for a record is allocated dynamically as needed.

EXAMPLE 10.3 ▼

Let's consider the storage requirements for a hash table with 1000 slots. Regular hashing requires 1000 × R bytes, where R is the record size in bytes. Assuming 4 bytes for storage of an address, bucket hashing requires 4000 + N × (R + 4) bytes, where N is the number of records actually stored and the table of pointers occupies 4000 bytes.

Table 10.4 shows the storage requirements for a 1000-slot table under regular hashing and bucket hashing with different values of N and R. The columns labeled 500 through 900 are for bucket hashing; the last column is for regular hashing, which is independent of the number of records actually stored. ▲

Table 10.4
Storage (in Bytes) Required
for Hashing

Number of Records Stored (N)

	Bucket					*Regular*
R	**500**	**600**	**700**	**800**	**900**	
4	8000	8800	9600	10400	11200	4000
8	10000	11200	12400	13600	14800	8000
16	14000	16000	18000	20000	22000	16000
32	22000	25600	29200	32800	36400	32000
64	38000	44800	51600	58400	65200	64000

Table 10.4 shows that a regular hash table always requires less storage space when the record size is 8 bytes or less because of the extra space used for pointers in bucket hashing. For larger records, bucket hashing uses less storage space than regular hashing when a small number of records is stored and more storage space when the number of records becomes sufficiently large. The break-even point is 600 records when the record size is 16 bytes, 800 records when the record size is 32 bytes, and 900 records when the record size is 64 bytes. Of course, the number of bytes (4) used for storing an address has a profound effect on this table.

Self-Check

1. Would it be more or less costly to implement buckets using an ordered linked list rather than an unordered linked list?
2. Would it be reasonable to implement a method for deleting elements from a regular hash table? Why or why not?

Programming

1. Determine the execution time required to store 500 records having integer type key fields in a hash table having 997 buckets and the execution

time required to store 500 records in a table having 997 slots using linear probing for collision resolution.

10.7   Searching with Indexes

There is another technique that may be used to improve the efficiency of searches of large arrays or tables. This technique uses an auxiliary data structure known as an *index* to establish the correspondence between key values and table location. As shown in Fig. 10.18, the index might be thought of as a collection of records whose field values contain a key and a pointer to the location of the record containing that key in the data table.

To locate the data table record containing the key value 'Sam', we search the index structure for the record whose key matches 'Sam'. We then use the location information to access the correct data table record. If the index contains fewer elements than the data table, the time required to search the index will be less than the time required to search for the record in the data table itself. This would be the case if some of the data records in the table were considered inactive (e.g., records with keys Stacy, Jane, Jeff in Fig. 10.19). An index does not need to be sparse, even though the data table that it indexes may contain several gaps between its active data records.

The record order in the index does not need to match the record order in the data table. There are times when we wish to access the elements of a data structure in an order that is different from the order in which the elements are physically placed in the data structure. For example, a library card

Figure 10.18
Table Index

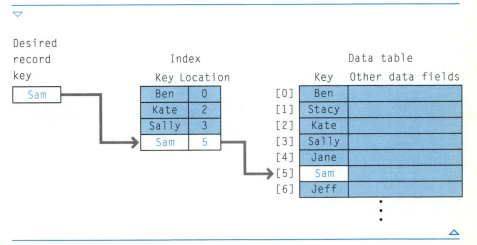

catalog (viewed as an index to books) allows you to search for books by author, title, or subject without being concerned about the placement of books on the shelves. As another example, we might like to produce a list of hash table elements arranged by key order rather than by slot or bucket order. An efficient technique for sorting a table is to sort its index without changing the positions of the records in the data table itself.

Another application of an index is to locate data records in *direct access* data files. Direct access data files are files in which each component may be accessed by specifying its location in the data file. Thus it is possible to read or write records anywhere in the data file. This means that a direct access data file can be treated like a very large array stored on disk. Borland Pascal provides procedures that allow us to work with direct access data files. We will describe the process of building an index for a direct access file in the case study at the end of this section. The index will often be small enough to fit in main memory, so we can search it efficiently, while the file cannot fit in main memory.

Sometimes an index itself may grow too large to search efficiently. This might be the case if the index contains inactive records. When this happens, we might decide to create an index for our index, as shown in Fig. 10.19. This new index is known as a *secondary index,* and the structure that it indexes is known as a *primary index.* The secondary index might contain keys for every 10th or 100th record in the primary index and therefore would be smaller. In file-processing applications the primary index might be stored in a direct access data file of its own, and the secondary index might be housed in the computer's memory.

Figure 10.19
Secondary Index

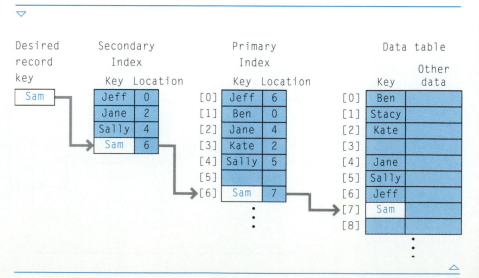

CASE STUDY   # Building a File Index

Searching a data file can be a very costly operation in terms of execution time. In file processing, one of the best ways to reduce the real execution time of an algorithm is to reduce the number of times the algorithm performs a physical read operation on the data file. By searching a file index that is held in the computer's memory to determine the location of a record in a direct access data file, the number of file read operations can be reduced to one.

PROBLEM ▼

We want to write an algorithm that will allow us to construct an index for a direct access file. The index will allow us to locate and retrieve records from the data file more efficiently.

DESIGN OVERVIEW ▼

We can use our ordered list abstract data type to house our index. Using an ordered list will allow us to maintain our index in primary key order. We will be able to create our index by reading the records of our data file one at a time and inserting a list element containing the record's key value and file location into our index. The records in the direct access file are not necessarily stored in key order.

Data Requirements

Problem Inputs

Direct access data file

Problem Outputs

Ordered list whose elements contain a record key and the relative location of that key's record within the data file

Algorithm for Building Index

1. open the data file for sequential input
2. set file location to 0
3. while not end of file do
  begin
    4. read data record from file
    5. store record key and location in list element
    6. insert list element in ordered list
    7. increment location counter by 1
  end

CODING `BuildIndex` ▼

We will write `BuildIndex` as a procedure having two parameters. The data file `MyData` will be processed sequentially by `BuildIndex` to create an index housed in ordered list `MyIndex`. Procedure `BuildIndex` is shown in Fig. 10.20. These type declarations were used in the program that created the direct access file:

```
type
   Item = record
               Name : KeyType;
               Rate : Real;
               Hours : Integer
             end; {Item}

   FileType = file of Item;
```

The type declarations for `KeyType` and `InfoType` used in unit `ListDataADT` are

```
type
   KeyType = string[15];
   InfoType = record
                  Key : KeyType;
                  Location : LongInt
                end; {InfoType}
```

```
procedure BuildIndex (var MyFile {input} : FileType;
                      var MyIndex {output} : OrderList);
{
  Builds index for direct access file MyFile.
  Pre : Direct access data file exists and has been associated
        with MyFile.
  Post: MyIndex is ordered list containing index for MyFile
}
  var
    OneEmp : Item;              {file data record}
    Location : Integer;         {data record location in file}
    IndexEntry : ListData;
    Success : Boolean;

begin {BuildIndex}
  Reset (MyFile);
  MyIndex.CreateList;
  Location := 0;                {initialize location counter}
  while not EOF(MyFile) do
    begin
      Read (MyFile, OneEmp);
      IndexEntry.Init (OneEmp.Name, Location);
      MyIndex.Insert (IndexEntry, Success);
      Location := Location + 1
    end {while}
end; {BuildIndex}
```

Once our index has been created, we can use it to access the data records in a random access data file. The following statements show how we would use our index to retrieve the data file record containing the key value stored in `IndexEntry` from the direct access data file `Employee`.

```
{Search index for entry with key matching IndexEntry}
MyIndex.Search (IndexEntry, Success);
if Success then
  begin
    {Retrieve record from index}
    MyIndex.Retrieve (IndexEntry, Success);
    {Determine record in location within file}
    Loc := IndexEntry.GetLocation;
    {Advance file pointer to record at position Loc}
    Seek (Employee, Loc);
    Read (Employee, OneEmp)
  end;
```

Seek is a Borland Pascal procedure that sets the binary file position pointer to point to the file component whose offset is passed to its second parameter. The first file component has offset 0, the second has offset 1, and so on. After calling Seek, procedure Read can be used to retrieve the file component. Alternatively, procedure Write can be used to replace the binary file component after calling Seek.

TESTING BuildIndex

To test procedure BuildIndex, we need to create a direct access binary file. After using procedure BuildIndex to construct the index we can use method LinkList.Traverse to display the contents of our index and see whether it agrees with a listing of the direct access file contents. We should see whether BuildIndex terminates properly when passed an empty file as input. We should also examine the index itself to be certain that values stored in its entries retrieve the correct records from the data file. As part of this testing we should use the index to retrieve the first and last records in the data file.

....

Exercises for Section 10.7 *Self-Check*

1. What are the advantages and disadvantages of using an ordered list to house an index?
2. Write an algorithm that could be used to construct an index for a regular hash table.

Programming

1. Write a client program that tests procedure BuildIndex.
2. By storing our index in an array of records, we can build it once and save it in a binary data file. Write a new version of procedure BuildIndex that stores the index in an array.

10.8   B-Trees

There is no reason why an index must be housed in a linear data structure. In Chapter 8 we showed how a balanced binary search tree could be searched more efficiently than a linked list. One problem with using a binary search tree is keeping it from becoming unbalanced. In Chapter 9 we introduced the AVL tree as a means of height balancing binary trees. In this section we introduce a technique for building a balanced general tree. The data structure that we will describe is known as a *B-tree,* and it is often the data structure that is used to house a data file index.

A *B-tree of order m* is a general tree that satisfies the following conditions:

▶ All leaf nodes are on the same level.
▶ The root node has at least two children and at most m children; all internal nodes have at least (m div 2) children and at most m children.
▶ The number of data items stored in each node is one less than the number of children. Values stored in the subtree to the left of a node data item have keys that are smaller than that item's keys. Values stored in a subtree to the right of a node data item have larger keys.

Figure 10.21 contains a B-tree of order 3. To search this tree for the node containing 20, we begin at the root and compare 20 to the items stored in the root. In this B-tree the root contains one data value (50). Since 20 is less than 50, it must be in the subtree to the left of 50. Since 20 is larger than 15 and less than 30, it must be in the subtree to the right of 15 and to the left of 30. We then find that the node containing 20 is located in the root of this subtree.

The basic step in constructing a B-tree is to start with a single node and insert key values until the node overflows. For a B-tree of order 3 this happens when we attempt to add the third value (the node capacity is m − 1 keys, where m is the order). When this happens, the node is split into two nodes. The median (middle) key value is promoted to a parent node, the values less than the median remain in the old node, and the values greater than the median are moved to a new node. If the original node has no par-

Figure 10.21
A B-Tree of Order 3

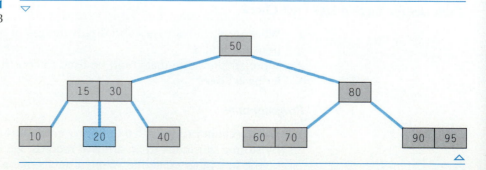

Figure 10.22
Inserting Three Keys into a
B-Tree

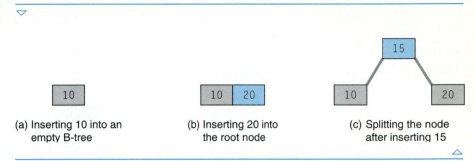

(a) Inserting 10 into an
empty B-tree

(b) Inserting 20 into
the root node

(c) Splitting the node
after inserting 15

ent, a new root node is created, and the median key is copied to this new node. Figure 10.22 illustrates this process when the integers 10, 20, and 15 are inserted in that order.

Suppose the next two values inserted are 30 and 40. As shown in Fig. 10.23, the 30 will be placed in the node containing 20. Node overflow occurs when we try to insert 40, so the node containing 20 is split. The median value 30 is promoted to the parent node, and a new node is created to house 40.

Sometimes inserting keys causes a tree to increase in height. We can insert 25 and 35 into the leaf nodes of the B-tree shown in Fig. 10.24. However, when we try to insert 50 into the node containing 40, overflow occurs, and we must split the node. When we try to promote 40 to its parent node, overflow occurs, and we must split this node too. A new root node is created, and the median key (30) is promoted to it.

Structure of a B-Tree Node

One data structure that could be used to house a B-tree node can be declared

```
const
    Order = 3;
    Size = Order - 1;

type
    Branch = ^BTreeNode;
```

Figure 10.23
Inserting Additional Values
into a B-Tree of Order 3

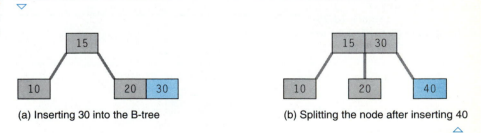

(a) Inserting 30 into the B-tree

(b) Splitting the node after inserting 40

Figure 10.24
Inserting Values
That Cause a B-Tree's
Height to Increase

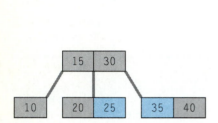

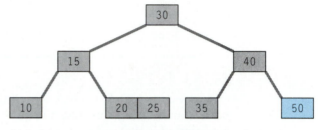

(a) Inserting 25 and 35 into the B-tree

(b) Splitting the root node after inserting 50 into a leaf node

```
ItemsIndex  = 1..Size;
ItemsArray  = array [ItemsIndex] of KeyType;

PointerIndex  = 0..Size
PointerArray  = array [PointerIndex] of Branch;

BTreeNode  = record
               KeyCount : Integer;
               Items : ItemsArray;
               Pointers : PointerArray
             end; {BTreeNode}
```

where `Items` is an array containing the values housed in the B-tree node and `Pointers` is an array containing the locations of the B-tree node's children. `KeyCount` contains a count of the number of keys housed in the B-tree node. Figure 10.25 shows the root node for the B-tree from Fig. 10.24(a).

Figure 10.25
Root node for the B-Tree in
Figure 10.25(a)

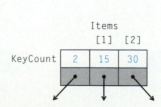

Analysis of B-Trees

B-trees are always balanced, so their search efficiency will be at least as good as that of binary search trees of the same height. Nodes in B-trees of order 3 or higher can have more than one data key stored in each node. This means that the height of a B-tree storing N data keys will generally be less than the height of a binary search containing the same nodes. Therefore the average search time will be less for a B-tree than for a binary search tree containing the same number of nodes.

In a large file-processing application the B-tree index itself may be stored in a direct access data file. To minimize the number of disk reads required to search the B-tree, we would try to make the B-tree size match the file block size as closely as possible. This allows us to read one whole B-tree node with a single disk access.

Exercises for Section 10.8 **Self-Check**

1. Insert the following keys into a B-tree of order 3, assuming that the keys are inserted in the order shown:

   `10, 20, 30, 40, 50, 60, 70, 35, 45, 65`

2. What would be the maximum number of data keys that could be stored in a B-tree of order 5 and height 3? What would be the minimum height of a binary search tree housing the same number of keys?

10.9 Common Programming Errors

One problem with search algorithms is the possibility of trying to access elements that are outside the bounds of the array. Be sure to enable range checking using {$R+} when debugging programs that manipulate arrays. When searching linked data structures, be certain that your algorithm halts properly when it reaches the end of the search path.

In writing collision-handling algorithms for hash tables, be certain that your algorithm tries every table position before deciding that the hash table has no free slots. Remember that it might not be possible to access hash elements in key order without the use of an index.

In debugging search procedures it is best to use relatively small arrays or lists (10 elements or fewer). This will make it easier to display the entire structure if something goes wrong.

CHAPTER REVIEW

We examined several search techniques in this chapter. We reviewed sequential searching algorithms for arrays that all had O(N) complexity. We described the binary search technique as a more efficient means of searching large sorted arrays. Binary search has complexity $O(\log_2 N)$. This means that the time required to perform binary search increases very slowly with increasing array size. For example, it takes only twice as long to perform binary search on an array with 256 elements ($\log_2 256$ is 8) as it takes to perform binary search on an array with 16 elements ($\log_2 16$ is 4).

We discussed using a hash table to provide quick access to data stored in an array. The record key is passed to the hash function, which computes an index to the array. In many cases, only one probe is required to access the desired record. We described three techniques for handling collisions (multiple keys with the same hash index values). Linear probing is a technique that examines successive hash table locations one at a time until the desired key is located or an empty table slot is reached. Quadratic probing was discussed as a means for reducing the clustering (tendency of filled slots to be near one another) problem often associated with linear probing. The use of linked list type buckets was introduced as a means of reducing the impact of the displacement problem (locating keys far away from their initial hash index location). The worst-case performance of hashing involving buckets is the size of the largest bucket. If the hash table has a large number of buckets relative to the number of keys stored in the bucket, we get very good searching performance when we use this technique.

Finally, we examined the use of an index as an efficient means of searching large, sparse data structures like direct access data files. We showed how to house an index in an ordered list and a B tree.

Quick-Check Exercises

1. What are three techniques for searching an array?
2. What are two techniques for searching an array whose elements are in order by key field?
3. Rate the three search algorithms in terms of time efficiency for a large array.
4. Rate the three search algorithms in terms of space efficiency for a large array.
5. What are three techniques for resolving hash table collisions?
6. Why is it important for a hash function to produce a uniform distribution of hash table locations?
7. What is an index?
8. A B-tree is another name for a binary tree. True or false?

Answers to Quick-Check Exercises

1. Sequential search, binary search, hashing
2. Sequential search of an ordered array, binary search
3. Hashing, binary search, sequential search
4. Sequential search and binary search, followed by hashing
5. Linear probing, quadratic probing, bucket hashing
6. To reduce the likelihood of clustering, which impairs the search efficiency of the hash table
7. A table containing keys and their locations in a larger data structure such as a direct access data file
8. False

Review Questions

1. Show how the following keys would be stored in a hash table with five slots, assuming the linear probing method of resolving collisions. Assume that the value returned by the hash function is shown after each key.

   `'Ace' 3, 'Boy' 4, 'Cat' 5, 'Dog' 3, 'Bye' 1`

2. Show how the keys in Question 1 would be stored in a hash table with seven slots, assuming that quadratic probing is used to resolve collisions.

3. Show how the following keys would be stored in a hash table with five linked list buckets if the hash function is defined by the expression (key mod 5).

   `10 12 8 6 7 13 15 16`

4. Write a function that recursively searches a string of 30 characters and returns the position of the first comma in the string. If the string does not contain a comma, the function should return 0.

5. Write an algorithm that makes use of the index produced by procedure `BuildIndex` (see Fig. 10.21) to replace the record in a direct access data file.

6. Insert the following keys into a B-tree of order 4, assuming that they are to be inserted in the order shown.

   `10 30 40 50 15 5 25 20 35 45 60`

Programming Projects

Directory: CHAP 10
File: PROJ10_1.PAS

Directory: CHAP 10
File: PROJ10_3.PAS

Directory: CHAP 10
File: PROJ10_4.PAS

1. Do Project 5 from Chapter 7 using a hash table with linked list buckets to maintain a passenger list. The main program should be menu driven and should allow its user to display the data for a particular passenger, display the entire list, create a list, insert a passenger entry, delete a passenger entry, and replace the data for a particular passenger.

2. Modify your program for Project 1 so that it maintains an index for the hash table to allow the passenger list to be displayed in alphabetic order.

3. Write a version of our hash table abstract data type that uses a direct access data file rather than an array as the hash table data type. Use linear probing to resolve collisions. Write a client program to test your hash table implementation.

4. Many supermarket checkout counters make use of computer equipment that allows the clerk to drag the item purchased across a sensor, which reads the bar code on the product container. After it reads the bar code, the store inventory database is examined, the item price and product description are located, counts are reduced, and a receipt is printed. Your task is to write a program that simulates this process. Your program will need to read the inventory information from the data file on disk into a hash table. The data in the inventory file is written one item per line, beginning with a four-digit product code, followed by a 30-character product description, its price, and the quantity of that item in stock. Your program will need to copy the information in the hash table to a new data file after all purchases are processed. Processing customers' orders involves reading a series of product codes representing each customer's pur-

chases from a second data file. A zero product code marks the end of each customer order. As each product code is read, the inventory hash table is searched to find a matching product code. Once it is located, the product price and product description may be printed on the receipt, and the quantity on hand is reduced by one. At the bottom of the receipt, you are to print the total for the goods purchased by the customer.

5. Binary search is not a useful technique for searching linked lists. Searching linked lists can be done more efficiently when the items that are retrieved frequently are housed near the beginning of the list. Two techniques may be used to accomplish this: *move to front* and *transposition*. With the move to front technique, every time the target item is located, it is moved in front of the first list element. With the transposition technique the item sought is moved in front of its predecessor after it is located. Write a Pascal program that stores 30 random integers in a linked list and then computes the average number of comparisons required to search this list 150 times for randomly chosen integers using each of these techniques. Be sure to begin with the same list each time and to include searches for numbers that do not appear in the list.

6. Write a procedure that accepts a B-tree of order 3 as an input parameter and performs an inorder traversal of it. Show the type declarations needed to implement your B-tree type.

CHAPTER ELEVEN

Sorting

In Chapter 2 we discussed one technique for sorting an array: selection sort. Because sorting is done so frequently, computer scientists have devoted much time and effort to developing efficient algorithms for sorting arrays. This chapter discusses several techniques for sorting an array and compares these algorithms with respect to their efficiency.

11.1 Selection Sort Revisited

The selection sort algorithm and its refinement shown below first appeared in Section 2.5. In this section we analyze the complexity of selection sort.

Selection Sort Algorithm

1. for Fill := 1 to N–1 do
>   **2.** Set PosMin to the subscript of the record with the
>   smallest key in subarray Fill..N.
>   **3.** if Fill is not equal to PosMin then
>   >   **4.** Switch the record at PosMin with the one at Fill.

Step 2 Refinement

2.1 Initialize PosMin to Fill.
2.2 for Next := Fill + 1 to N do
>   **2.3** if the key of record Next < the key of record PosMin then
>   >   **2.4** Reset PosMin to Next.

Steps 2 and 3 are performed $N - 1$ times. Step 3 performs an exchange of records if the record with the next smallest key is not in position `Fill`. Consequently, there are at most $N - 1$ record exchanges.

Step 2.3 involves a comparison of record keys and is performed $(N - Fill)$ times for each value of `Fill`. Since `Fill` takes on all values between 1 and $N - 1$, the following series computes the number of executions of Step 2.3:

$$(N - 1) + (N - 2) + \ldots 3 + 2 + 1$$

This series can be written in closed form as

$$\frac{N \times (N - 1)}{2} = N^2/2 - N/2$$

Therefore the total number of record key comparisons is

$$N^2/2 - N/2$$

For very large N we can ignore all but the most significant term in these expressions, so the number of comparisons is $O(N^2)$, and the number of exchanges is $O(N)$. Because the number of comparisons increases with the square of N, the selection sort is called a *quadratic sort*.

Exercises for Section 11.1 *Self-Check*

1. Write an expression that shows the total number of comparisons required by the recursive implementation of the selection sort algorithm (Fig. 4.14) to sort an array of N elements.

Programming

1. Determine the times required for the recursive and iterative implementations of selection sort to sort the same array of 1000 randomly chosen integers.

11.2   Bubble Sort

This section discusses another quadratic sorting algorithm, called the *bubble sort*. The bubble sort compares adjacent array elements and exchanges their values if they are out of order. In this way the smaller values "bubble" up to the top of the array (toward the first element) while the larger values sink to the bottom of the array; hence the name. The bubble sort algorithm follows.

Algorithm for BubbleSort

1. repeat
    2. for each pair of adjacent array elements do
        3. if the values in a pair are out of order then
            4. Exchange the values
  until the array is sorted

As an example, we will trace through one execution of Step 2, or one *pass* through an array being sorted. By scanning the diagrams in Fig. 11.1 from left to right we see the effect of each comparison. The pair of array elements being compared is shown in a darker color in each diagram. The first pair of values (M[1] is 60, M[2] is 42) is out of order, so the values are exchanged. The next pair of values (M[2] is now 60, M[3] is 75) is compared in the second array shown in Fig. 11.1; this pair is in order, and so is the next pair (M[3] is 75, M[4] is 83). The last pair (M[4] is 83, M[5] is 27) is out of order, so the values are exchanged, as shown in the last diagram.

The last array shown in Fig. 11.1 is closer to being sorted than is the original. The only value that is out of order is the number 27 in M[4]. Unfortu-

Figure 11.1
One Pass of a Bubble Sort
of Array M

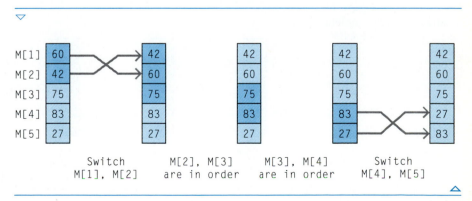

nately, it will be necessary to complete three more passes through the entire array before this value bubbles up to the top of the array. In each of these passes, only one pair of values will be out of order, so only one exchange will be made. The contents of array M after the completion of each pass are shown in Fig. 11.2; the portion that is sorted is shown in the darker color.

We can tell by looking at the contents of the array at the end of pass 4 that the array is now sorted; however, the computer can recognize this only by making one additional pass without doing any exchanges. If no exchanges are made, then all pairs must be in order. This is the reason for the extra pass shown in Fig. 11.2 and for the Boolean flag NoExchanges described below.

Local Variables for Bubble Sort

Flag to indicate whether or not any exchanges were made in a pass (NoExchanges : Boolean)
Loop control variable and subscript (First : Word)
Number of the current pass starting with 1 (Pass : Word)

Refinement of Step 2 of Bubble Sort

2.1 Initialize NoExchanges to True
2.2 for each pair of adjacent array elements do
    2.3 if the values in a pair are out of order then
        begin
            2.4 Exchange the values
            2.5 Set NoExchanges to False
        end

Step 2.2 is the header of a for statement. The for loop control variable, First, will also be the subscript of the first element in each pair; consequently, First + 1 will be the subscript of the second element in each pair. During each pass, the initial value of First is 1. The final value of First must be less than the number of array elements so that First + 1 will be in range.

Figure 11.2
Array M After Completion of Each Pass

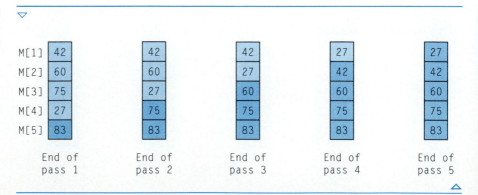

	End of pass 1	End of pass 2	End of pass 3	End of pass 4	End of pass 5
M[1]	42	42	42	27	27
M[2]	60	60	27	42	42
M[3]	75	27	60	60	60
M[4]	27	75	75	75	75
M[5]	83	83	83	83	83

For an array of N elements the final value of `First` can be `N - Pass`, where Pass is the number of the current pass, starting with 1 for the first pass. This is because at the end of pass 1 the last array element must be in its correct place, at the end of pass 2 the last two array elements must be in their correct places, and so on. There is no need to examine array elements that are already in place.

Procedure `BubbleSort` in Fig. 11.3 performs a bubble sort on an open array of integers.

Figure 11.3
Procedure `BubbleSort`

**Directory: CHAP 11
File: BUBBLESO.PAS**

```
procedure Switch (var Rec1, Rec2 {input/output} : Integer);
{
 Switches Rec1 and Rec2.
}
  var
    TempRec : Integer;                    {temporary record}

begin {Switch}
  TempRec := Rec1; Rec1 := Rec2; Rec2 := TempRec
end; {Switch}

procedure BubbleSort (var Table {in/out} : Array of Integer);
{
 Sorts the data in array Table.
 Pre : Table is defined and filled with data.
 Post: Array Table is sorted.
}
  var
    NoExchanges : Boolean;      {any exchanges in current pass?}
    First,                      {first element of a pair}
    Pass : Word;                {number of current pass}

begin {BubbleSort}
  Pass := 1;                                {start with pass 1}
  repeat
    {invariant:
       No prior array was sorted and
       elements after Table[High(Table) - Pass + 1] are
       in place.
    }
    NoExchanges := True;              {no exchanges yet}

    {Compare each pair of adjacent elements}
    for First := 0 to High(Table) - Pass do
      if Table[First] > Table[First+1] then
        begin {exchange}
          Switch (Table[First], Table[First+1]);
          NoExchanges := False              {Reset flag}
        end; {exchange}
```

▷ ▷ ▷ ▷ ▷

```
    Pass := Pass + 1                    {increment pass number}
    until NoExchanges

  {assert: Array is sorted}
end; {BubbleSort}
```

Analysis of Bubble Sort

Because the actual numbers of comparisons and exchanges performed depend on the array being sorted, the bubble sort algorithm provides excellent performance in some cases and horrible performance in other cases. It works best when an array is nearly sorted to begin with.

Since all adjacent pairs of elements are compared in each pass, the number of comparisons is represented by the series

```
(N - 1) + (N - 2) + ... 3 + 2 + 1
```

However, if the array becomes sorted early, the later passes and comparisons are not performed. In the worst case the number of comparisons is $O(N^2)$; in the best case the number of comparisons is $O(N)$.

Unfortunately, each comparison can lead to an exchange if the array is badly out of order. The worst case occurs when the array is *inverted* (i.e., the array elements are in descending order by key), and the number of exchanges is $O(N^2)$. In the best case, only one exchange is made during each pass ($O(N)$ exchanges), so the number of exchanges also lies between $O(N)$ and $O(N^2)$.

In estimating the worst-case performance of a sorting algorithm on a large array whose initial element values are determined arbitrarily, the definition of big-O requires us to be pessimistic. For this reason, bubble sort is considered a quadratic sort, and its performance is usually worse than selection sort because the number of exchanges can be $O(N^2)$ instead of $O(N)$ like selection sort.

We can use bubble sort to sort an array of records instead of an array of integer values. In this case we would compare record keys using the following if condition:

```
if Table[First].GetKey > Table[First+1].GetKey then
```

where method `GetKey` retrieves a record key. The parameters for procedure `Switch` should be changed from type Integer to a record (or an object) type. Because the time required to switch two records is proportional to the size of the records, bubble sort is generally not a good choice for sorting an array of large records.

Exercises for Section 11.2 *Self-Check*

1. How would you modify procedure `BubbleSort` to arrange an array of integer values in decreasing sequence?
2. How many passes of BubbleSort are needed to sort the following array of integers? How many comparisons are performed? How many exchanges? Show the array after each pass.

   ```
   40  35  80  75  60  90  70  75
   ```

3. How would you modify procedure `BubbleSort` to arrange an array of student records in decreasing sequence by exam score? Assume that each record has the form

   ```
   type
      Student = object
               . . .
               private
                  Name : string[20];
                  Score : Integer;
                  Grade : Char;
               end; {Student}
   ```

   with appropriate methods to retrieve the value in each data member. Also, modify BubbleSort to arrange the records in increasing sequence by letter grade and then alphabetically by name (i.e., all A students should be first, and they should be in alphabetical order; next should come all B students in alphabetical order; and so on).

11.3 Insertion Sort

Our next quadratic sorting algorithm is based on the technique used by card players to arrange a hand of cards. The player keeps the cards that have been picked up so far in sorted order. When the player picks up a new card, the player makes room for the new card and inserts it in its proper place.

The top diagram in Fig. 11.4 shows a hand of cards (ignoring suits) after three cards have been picked up. If the next card is an 8, it should be inserted between the 6 and 10, maintaining the numerical order. If the next card is a 7, it should be inserted between the 6 and 8 as shown in the bottom diagram of Fig. 11.4. This is also the technique that we used in Section 7.7 to insert new elements into an ordered list.

To adapt this *insertion algorithm* to an array that has been filled with data, we start with a sorted subarray consisting of the first element only. We then insert the second element either before or after the first element, and the sorted subarray has two elements. Next, we insert the third element where it belongs, and the sorted subarray has three elements, and so on. Figure 11.5 illustrates an insertion sort for a five-element array; the array ele-

Figure 11.4
Picking Up a Hand
of Cards

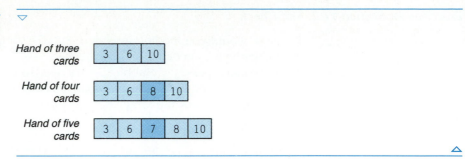

ments that have been inserted after each pass are in black, and the elements
waiting to be inserted are in grey.

Algorithm for Insertion Sort

1. for each array element after the first do
       begin
              2. Save the value of this element in NextVal.
              3. Make room for NextVal by shifting all larger
                     values down one position.
              4. Insert NextVal in place of the last value moved.
       end

Steps 3 and 4 are illustrated in Fig. 11.6. For the array shown on the left,
the subarray with subscripts 1..3 is sorted, and we want to insert the next element, 20, in its proper place. Since 30 and 25 are greater than 20, both these
values are shifted down one place. After the shift occurs (middle diagram),
there will temporarily be two copies of the value 25 in the array. The first of
these is overwritten when 20 is moved into its correct position—element 2 of
the four-element sorted subarray on the right. The shift and insert operations
should then be repeated to insert the new next value (28) where it belongs.

Figure 11.5
An Insertion Sort

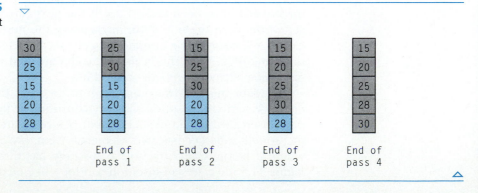

Figure 11.6
Inserting the Fourth Array
Element

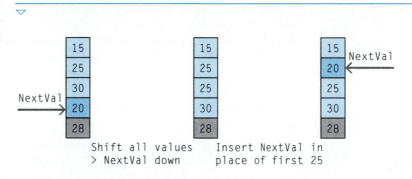

Shift all values   Insert NextVal in
> NextVal down   place of first 25

Figure 11.7
Procedure InsertSort

Directory: CHAP 11
File: INSERTSO.PAS

```
procedure InsertSort (var Table {input/output} : Array of Integer);
{
 Performs insertion sort on open array parameter Table.
 Pre : Table is defined and filled with data.
 Post: Table is sorted.
}
  var
    NextPos,        {subscript of next element to be inserted}
    NewPos : Word;        {subscript of element after insertion}
    NextVal : Integer;   {temporary storage for next element}

    {Insert ShiftBigger here}

begin {InsertSort}
  {Insert each array element, beginning with the second element}
  for NextPos := 1 to High(Table) do
    begin
      {invariant: subarray Table[0..NextPos - 1] is sorted}
      NextVal := Table[NextPos]; {Get next element to insert}

        {Shift all values > NextVal down one element}
      ShiftBigger (Table, NextPos, NextVal, NewPos);

      {assert: NewPos is the subscript of last value moved}

      {Insert NextVal in location NewPos}
      Table[NewPos] := NextVal
    end {for}
end; {InsertSort}
```

Procedure `InsertSort` is shown in Fig. 11.7 for an open array parameter with subscripts 0 through `High(Table)`. Procedure `ShiftBigger` is called to perform the shift operation and determine the correct position for the array element that is currently being inserted (`NextVal`).

Coding Procedure ShiftBigger

Procedure `ShiftBigger` must move all array element values that are larger than `NextVal`, starting with the array element at position `NextPos − 1`. If `NextVal` is the smallest value so far, the shift operation terminates after all array elements are moved. If `NextVal` is not the smallest value so far, the shift operation terminates when a value less than or equal to `NextVal` is reached. `NextVal` should be inserted in the position formerly occupied by the last value that was moved. The algorithm for `ShiftBigger` follows; the procedure is shown in Fig. 11.8.

Figure 11.8
Procedure ShiftBigger

Directory: CHAP 11
File: INSERTSO.PAS

```
procedure ShiftBigger (var Table {input/output} : Array of Integer;
                           NextPos {input} : Word;
                           NextVal {input} : Integer;
                           var NewPos {output} : Word);
{
  Makes room for NextVal in the subarray Table[0..NextPos]
  and sets NewPos as an index to the correct position of
  NextVal.
  Pre : Table[0..NextPos - 1] is sorted.
  Post: Shifts all values > NextVal in the subarray
        Table[0..NextPos - 1] by one position and sets NewPos
        to the subscript of the last element moved.
}
begin  {ShiftBigger}
  {Shift all values > NextVal. Start with element at NextPos - 1}
  while (NextPos > 0) and (Table[NextPos-1] > NextVal) do
    {invariant:
        NextPos >= 0 and
        all prior values tested in Table > NextVal
    }
    begin
      Table[NextPos] := Table[NextPos - 1]; {Shift value down}
      NextPos := NextPos - 1                  {Try next element}
    end; {while}

  {assert: Position of NextVal is found.}
  NewPos := NextPos
end; {ShiftBigger}
```

Algorithm for ShiftBigger

1. Start with the element in position NextPos − 1.
2. while first element not moved and element value > NextVal do
   begin
   3. Move element value down one position.
   4. Check next smaller element value.
   5. Define NewPos as original position of last value moved.
   end

The while statement in Fig. 11.8 compares and shifts all values greater than `NextVal` in the subarray `Table[1..NextPos - 1]`. The while condition

`(NextPos > 0) and (Table[NextPos - 1] > NextVal)`

could lead to an out-of-range subscript error if the order of the conditions were reversed or if short-circuit evaluation were not performed. Without short-circuit evaluation the second condition would be evaluated when `NextPos` becomes 0. When `NextPos` is 0, the array subscript is −1, which is outside the subscript range.

Analysis of Insertion Sort

Procedure `ShiftBigger` is called N − 1 times. In the worst case, `ShiftBigger` compares all elements in the subarray being processed to `NextVal`, so the maximum number of record key comparisons is represented by the series

`1 + 2 + 3 + ... + (N - 2) + (N - 1)`

which is $O(N^2)$. In the best case (when the array is already sorted), only one comparison is required for each call to `ShiftBigger` ($O(N)$). The number of record exchanges performed by `ShiftBigger` is one less than the number of comparisons or, when the new value is the smallest so far, the same as the number of comparisons. Also, each new record is copied into `NextVal` before the call to `ShiftBigger`, and `NextVal` is placed in the array after the return from `ShiftBigger` (two more exchanges). However, an "exchange" in an insertion sort requires the movement of only one record, whereas in a bubble sort or a selection sort, an exchange involves a temporary record and requires the movement of three records.

Exercises for Section 11.3 *Self-Check*

1. Sort the following array using an insertion sort. How many passes are needed? How many comparisons are performed? How many exchanges? Show the array after each pass.

   `40  35  80  75  60  90  70  75`

2. Explain how you would modify the insertion sort procedure to sort an array of student records. What changes would be needed to order the array elements as described in Exercise 3 of Section 11.2?

11.4   Comparison of Quadratic Sorts

Table 11.1 summarizes the performance of the three quadratic sorts. To give you some idea of what these numbers mean, Table 11.2 shows some values of N and N^2. If N is small (say, 100 or less), it really doesn't matter which sorting algorithm you use. However, if N is large, you should avoid using a bubble sort (particularly with large records) unless you are certain that the array is pretty nearly sorted to begin with. For most arrays, an insertion sort will provide better performance than a selection sort. Remember that an exchange in an insertion sort requires only one record assignment instead of three record assignments as in the other sorts.

Table 11.1
Comparison of
Quadratic Sorts

	Number of Comparisons		Number of Exchanges	
	Best	*Worst*	*Best*	*Worst*
Selection sort	$O(N^2)$	$O(N^2)$	$O(N)$	$O(N)$
Bubble sort	$O(N)$	$O(N^2)$	$O(N)$	$O(N^2)$
Insertion sort	$O(N)$	$O(N^2)$	$O(N)$	$O(N^2)$

Table 11.2
Comparison of Rates
of Growth

N	N^2	$N \times \log_2 N$
8	64	24
16	256	64
32	1,024	160
64	4,096	384
128	16,384	896
256	65,536	2,048
512	262,144	4,608

Since the time required to sort an array of N elements is proportional to N^2, none of these algorithms is particularly good for large arrays (i.e., N $\geq$ 100). The sorting algorithms discussed next provide N $\times$ $\log_2$ N average case behavior and are considerably faster for large arrays. In fact, one of the next algorithms that we will discuss has N $\times$ $\log_2$ N worst-case behavior. You can get a feel for the difference in behavior by comparing the last column of Table 11.2 with the middle column.

Exercises for Section 11.4 **Self-Check**

1. Indicate the best method to sort each of the following arrays in ascending order. Explain your choice.

   a. 10   20   30   50   60   80   70
   b. 90   80   70   60   50   40   30
   c. 20   30   40   50   60   70   10
   d. 30   50   10   40   80   90   60

2. Would your answers to Exercise 1 change if the values shown were sequences of key values from arrays of records?

11.5   MergeSort

The next algorithm that we will consider is called `MergeSort`. A merge operation is a common data processing operation that is performed on two files of data with the following characteristics:

▶ Both files have the same key field.
▶ The records of both files are in sequence by key field.

The result of the merge operation is to create a third file that contains all the records from the first two in sequence by key field. The algorithm for merging two files follows.

Algorithm for File Merge

1. Read the first record from both files.
2. while not at the end of either file do
      3. Compare the current records from each input file, write the smaller record to the output file, and read the next record from the input file whose record was just written.
4. while not at the end of input file 1 do
      5. Copy any remaining records from input file 1 to the output file.
6. while not at the end of input file 2 do
      7. Copy any remaining records from input file 2 to the output file.

The first while loop (Step 2) merges records from both input files to the output file. The current record from each input file is the one that has been most recently read but not yet written. Step 3 compares the two current records and copies the smaller one to the output file. If input file A's current record was the smaller one, the next record is read from file A and becomes its current record. If input file B's current record was the smaller one, the next record is read from file B and becomes its current record. After the end of either input file is reached, Step 5 or Step 6 copies the records from the other input file to the output file.

As an example, consider the file keys shown in Fig. 11.9. Steps 2 and 3 will first copy the records from file A with keys 234 and 311; then the records from file B with keys 324 and 415 will be copied; then the record from file A with key 478 will be copied. At this point the end of file A is reached, so the remaining records from file B will be copied to the output file by Steps 6 and 7.

Figure 11.9

File Merge Operation

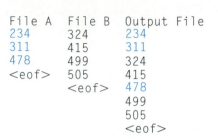

```
File A    File B    Output File
234       324       234
311       415       311
478       499       324
<eof>     505       415
          <eof>     478
                    499
                    505
                    <eof>
```

MergeSort works similarly to a file merge. Because we are attempting to sort a single array that is not ordered instead of two ordered files, we must first split the array into two halves, sort each half, and then merge the halves together to get a new sorted array.

We should get an overall improvement in performance because merging is an O(N) process, and Table 11.2 shows that sorting two smaller arrays takes less effort than sorting one large array. For example, even if we use a quadratic sort to sort each half of the original array, the effort required to sort and merge would be

$$c_1 * (N/2)^2 + c_2 * (N/2)^2 + c_3 * N$$

compared to N^2 to sort the entire array at once. For N = 100 the equation above evaluates to 5,100, while N^2 is 10,000 if we set the constants to 1. We will see that the actual improvement in performance is even more dramatic. The MergeSort algorithm follows.

Algorithm for MergeSort

1. Split the array into two halves.
2. Sort the left half.
3. Sort the right half.
4. Merge the two arrays together.

Figure 11.10 illustrates this process. An array with subscript type First..Last has been split into a left and a right subarray, both of which are sorted. Middle is the index of the last element in the left subarray. The two subarrays are merged to form a sorted array (shown at the bottom).

We can reformulate this algorithm using recursion. The stopping case is an array with one element. Since an array with one element is sorted by definition, we do nothing when the stopping condition (First = Last) is True. If the array has more than one element (First < Last), we want to sort subarray Table[First..Middle] and then sort subarray Table[Middle+1..Last]) using MergeSort. Next, we merge the sorted subarrays together.

Figure 11.10
Merging Two
Sorted Subarrays

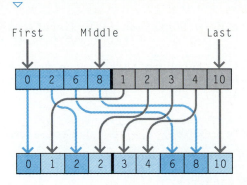

Procedure Inputs

The original subarray (Table : Array of Integer)
The leftmost subscript (First : Word)
The rightmost subscript (Last : Word)

Procedure Outputs

The sorted array (Table : Array of Integer)

Local Variables

The subscript of the middle element (Middle : Word)

Recursive MergeSort Algorithm

1. if First < Last then
        begin
        2. Set Middle to (First + Last) div 2
        3. MergeSort Table[First..Middle].
        4. MergeSort Table[Middle + 1..Last]
        5. Merge Table[First..Middle] with Table[Middle + 1..Last].
        end

Procedure `MergeSort` is shown in Fig. 11.11. When the recursive step executes, `MergeSort` calls itself first to sort the left subarray and then to sort the right subarray. Next, it calls procedure `Merge` (discussed next) to merge the two sorted subarrays together. If the array `Table` is filled with data, use the procedure call statement

```
MergeSort (Table, 0, High(Table))
```

to sort the array `Table`. If Table has N elements filled with data (N <= High(Table)), use the procedure call statement

```
MergeSort (Table, 0, N - 1)
```

```
procedure MergeSort (var Table {input/output} : Array of Integer;
                         First, Last {input} : Word);
{
  Recursive procedure to sort the subarray Table[First..Last].
  Pre : Table, First, and Last are defined.
  Post: Array Table is sorted.
}
  var
    Middle : Word;    {index of last element in right subarray}

  {Insert procedure Merge.}

begin {MergeSort}
  if First < Last then
    begin
      Middle := (First + Last) div 2;
      MergeSort (Table, First, Middle);
      MergeSort (Table, Middle + 1, Last);
      Merge (Table, Table, First, Middle, Last)
    end {if}
end; {MergeSort}
```

The two recursive calls to MergeSort in Fig. 11.11 will cause the MergeSort procedure to be applied to two smaller subarrays. If any subarray contains just one element, an immediate return will occur.

Coding Procedure Merge

At the end of each recursive step, the statement

```
Merge (Table, Table, First, Middle, Last)
```

calls procedure Merge to merge the two sorted subarrays. We stated earlier that merging two arrays is analogous to merging two files. In a file merge, two ordered files are merged to form a third file. Procedure Merge must merge two ordered subarrays of Table that are split at Middle into a new array. The purpose of the second array Table in the parameter list is to provide an output array for the result of the merge operation. When Merge is completed, elements Table[First..Last] will be in order. The algorithm for procedure Merge follows.

Local Variables for Merge

The index to the left subarray (NextLeft : Integer)
The index to the right subarray (NextRight : Integer)

Algorithm for Merge

1. Start with the first element of each subarray.
2. while not finished with either subarray do
   3. if the current element of the left subarray <
      the current element of the right subarray then
      4. Copy the current element of the left subarray to the
         merged array and advance to the next element in the
         left subarray and the merged array.
      else
      5. Copy the current element of the right subarray to the
         merged array and advance to the next element in the right
         subarray and the merged array.
   6. Copy the remaining elements from the unfinished array to the
      merged array.

Procedure `Merge` is shown in Fig. 11.12. Open array `TableIn` is a local copy of its array parameter (`Table`), which contains the two input subarrays. The variables `NextLeft` and `NextRight` are indexes to the two subarrays being merged; the variable `Index` is the index to the merged array, `TableOut`. `TableOut` is a variable parameter, so the merge results are stored directly in the actual array parameter (`Table`). `NextLeft` and `Index` are

Figure 11.12
Procedure `Merge`

Directory: CHAP 11
File: MERGESO.PAS

```
procedure Merge (TableIn {input} : Array of Integer;
                 var TableOut {output} : Array of Integer;
                 var First, Middle, Last {input} : Word);
{
 Merges TableIn[First..Middle] with TableIn[Middle + 1..Last].
 The result of the merge is stored in TableOut[First..Last].
 Pre : Table is defined and First <= Last and
       Middle = (First + Last) div 2.
 Post: Data in TableOut[First..Last] are sorted.
}
   var
     NextLeft,                {next element in left subarray}
     NextRight,               {next element in right subarray}
     Index : Integer;            {index to array TableOut}

begin {Merge}
  {Start with first element of all three subarrays}
  NextLeft := First;
  NextRight := Middle + 1;
  Index := First;
```

▷ ▷ ▷ ▷ ▷ ▷

```
{Perform the merge until one subarray is finished}
while (NextLeft <= Middle) and (NextRight <= Last) do
   if TableIn[NextLeft] < TableIn[NextRight] then
      begin {copy left element}
         TableOut[Index] := TableIn[NextLeft];
         NextLeft := NextLeft + 1;
         Index := Index + 1
      end {copy left element}
   else
      begin {copy right element}
         TableOut[Index] := TableIn[NextRight];
         NextRight := NextRight + 1;
         Index := Index + 1
      end; {copy right element}

{Copy any remaining elements in the left subarray}
while NextLeft <= Middle do
   begin
      TableOut[Index] := TableIn[NextLeft];
      NextLeft := NextLeft + 1;
      Index := Index + 1
   end; {while}

{Copy any remaining elements in the right subarray}
while NextRight <= Last do
   begin
      TableOut[Index] := TableIn[NextRight];
      NextRight := NextRight + 1;
      Index := Index + 1
   end {while}
end;   {Merge}
```

initialized to First; NextRight is initialized to Middle + 1, which is the first element in the right subarray.

Analysis of MergeSort

Our preliminary analysis indicated that MergeSort would be more efficient than a quadratic sort, but how much better is it? Procedure Merge copies data into an N-element array (array TableOut). An array copy is an O(N) process, so procedure Merge is also an O(N) process.

The remaining question to answer is: How many times is procedure Merge called? The answer is that Merge is called once for each execution of the recursive step in MergeSort. The recursive step splits the array into half each time it executes. From earlier splitting processes (e.g., binary search) we know that it requires $\log_2 N$ splits to reach the stopping state (N one-element subarrays). Therefore MergeSort appears to be an O(N $\times$ $\log_2$ N) process.

Table 11.2 shows that `MergeSort` provides significant improvement over a quadratic sort for a large array. Bear in mind that this analysis does not provide the whole picture. There is quite a bit of overhead for each recursive call to `Merge`. Also, in our implementation of `MergeSort`, each call to `Merge` allocates storage for a local array with the same number of elements as the original array. If the array being sorted is truly a very large array, the memory requirements of `MergeSort` could become a burden. Next we will discuss a sort with average case performance of $O(N \times \log_2 N)$ that moves elements around in the original array and does not require an auxiliary array.

Exercises for Section 11.5 **Self-Check**

1. Trace the execution of `MergeSort` on the following array. Show the values of `First`, `Last`, and `Middle` for each recursive call and the array elements after returning from each call to `Merge`. How many times is `MergeSort` called, and how many times is `Merge` called?

   55 50 10 40 80 90 60 100 70 80 20

11.6 QuickSort

The next algorithm that we will study is called `QuickSort`, and it works in the following way. Given an array with subscripts `First..Last` to sort, `QuickSort` rearranges this array so that all element values smaller than a selected *pivot value* are first, followed by the pivot value, followed by all element values larger than the pivot value. After this rearrangement (called a *partition*) the pivot value is in its proper place. All element values that are smaller than the pivot value are closer to where they belong as they precede the pivot value. All element values larger than the pivot value are closer to where they belong as they follow the pivot value.

An example of this process is shown in Fig. 11.13. We will assume that the first array element (44) is arbitrarily selected as the pivot. A possible result of the partitioning process is shown beneath the original array.

After the partitioning process, `PivIndex` is 5, and the fifth array element contains the pivot value, 44. All values less than 44 are in the left subarray (color background); all values greater than 44 are in the right subarray (grey background), as desired. The next step would be to apply `QuickSort` recursively to the two subarrays on either side of the pivot value. The algorithm for `QuickSort` follows. We will describe how to do the partitioning later.

Procedure Inputs

The array being sorted (Table : IntArray)
The first subscript (First : Integer)
The last subscript (Last : Integer)

Figure 11.13
First Partition of Array by
QuickSort

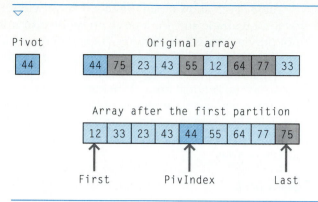

Procedure Outputs

The sorted array (Table : IntArray)

Local Variables

The subscript of the pivot value after partitioning
(PivIndex : Integer)

Algorithm for QuickSort

1. if First < Last then
   begin
   2. Partition the elements in the subarray First..Last so that the pivot value is in place (subscript is PivIndex)
   3. Apply QuickSort to the subarray First..PivIndex − 1
   4. Apply QuickSort to the subarray PivIndex + 1..Last
   end

A stopping case for `QuickSort` is an array of one element (`First` = `Last`), which is sorted by definition, so nothing is done. If `First` > `Last` is true, then the array bounds are improper (also a stopping case). If the array has more than one element, we partition it into two subarrays and sort the subarrays using `QuickSort`.

The implementation of procedure `QuickSort` is shown in Fig. 11.14. Use the procedure call statement

`QuickSort (Table, 0, High(Table))`

to sort the array `Table`.

The two recursive calls to `QuickSort` in Fig. 11.14 will cause the quick sort procedure to be applied to the subarrays that are separated by the value at `PivIndex`. If any subarray contains just one element (or zero elements), an immediate return will occur.

Figure 11.14
Procedure QuickSort

Directory: CHAP 11
File: QUICKSO.PAS

```
procedure QuickSort (var Table {input/output} : Array of Integer;
                          First, Last {input} : Integer);
{
  Recursive procedure to sort the subarray Table[First..Last].
  Pre : First, Last, and array Table are defined.
  Post: Table is sorted.
}
  var
    PivIndex : Integer; {subscript of pivot value}

  {Insert Partition here.}

begin {QuickSort}
  if First < Last then
    begin
      {Split into two subarrays separated by value at PivIndex}
      Partition (Table, First, Last, PivIndex);
      QuickSort (Table, First, PivIndex - 1);
      QuickSort (Table, PivIndex + 1, Last)
    end {if}
end; {QuickSort}
```

Coding Procedure Partition

Procedure Partition selects the pivot and performs the partitioning operation. When we are selecting the pivot, if the arrays are randomly ordered to begin with, it does not really matter which element is the pivot value. For simplicity we choose the element with subscript First. We then search for the first value at the left end of the subarray that is greater than the pivot value. When we find it, we search for the first value at the right end of the subarray that is less than or equal to the pivot value. These two values are exchanged, and we repeat the search and exchange operations. This is illustrated in Fig. 11.15, where Up points to the first value greater than the pivot and Down points to the first value less than or equal to the pivot value.

Figure 11.15
Locating First Values
to Exchange

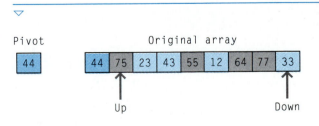

Figure 11.16
Array After the
First Exchange

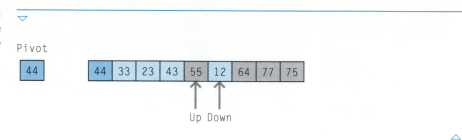

The value 75 is the first value at the left end of the array that is larger than 44, and 33 is the first value at the right end that is less than or equal to 44, so these two values are exchanged. The pointers `Up` and `Down` are then advanced from their current positions to the positions in Fig. 11.16.

The value 55 is the next value at the left end that is larger than 44, and 12 is the next value at the right end that is less than or equal to 44, so these two values are exchanged, and `Up` and `Down` are advanced again, as shown in Fig. 11.17.

After the second exchange, the first five array elements contain the pivot value and all values less than or equal to the pivot; the last four elements contain all values larger than the pivot. The value 55 is selected once again by `Up` as the next element larger than the pivot; 12 is selected by `Down` as the next element less than or equal to the pivot. Since `Up` has now "passed" `Down`, these values are not exchanged. Instead, the pivot value (subscript is `First`) and the value at position `Down` are exchanged. This puts the pivot value in its proper position (the new subscript is `Down`) as shown in Fig. 11.18.

The partitioning process is now complete, and the value of `Down` is returned as the pivot index (`PivIndex`). `QuickSort` will be called recursively to sort the left subarray and the right subarray. The algorithm for `Partition` follows and is implemented in Fig. 11.19.

Local Variables for Partition

The pivot value (Pivot : Integer)
Index to array elements larger than Pivot (Up : Integer)

Figure 11.17
Array After the
Second Exchange

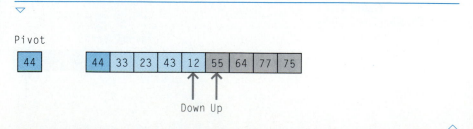

Figure 11.18
Array After the
Third Exchange

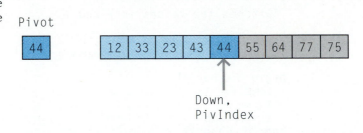

Index to array elements less than or equal to Pivot (Down : Integer)

Algorithm for Partition

1. Define the pivot value as the contents of Table[First].
2. Initialize Up to First and Down to Last.
3. repeat
　　4. Increment Up until Up selects the first element
　　　　greater than the pivot value.
　　5. Decrement Down until Down selects the first element
　　　　less than or equal to the pivot value.
　　6. if Up < Down then
　　　　7. Exchange their values.
　　　　　　until Up meets or passes Down
8. Exchange Table[First] and Table[Down].
9. Define PivIndex as Down.

Figure 11.19
Procedure Partition

Directory: CHAP 11
File: QUICKSO.PAS

```
procedure Partition (var Table {input/output} : Array of Integer;
                     First, Last {input} : Integer;
                     var PivIndex {output} : Integer);
{
 Partitions the subarray of Table with subscripts First..Last
 into two subarrays.
 Pre : First, Last, and array Table are defined.
 Post: PivIndex is defined such that all values less than or
       equal to Table[PivIndex] have subscripts <= PivIndex;
       all values greater than Table[PivIndex] have
       subscripts > PivIndex.
}
  var
    Pivot,                          {pivot value}
    Up,                             {index to values > Pivot}
    Down : Integer;                 {index to values <= Pivot}
```

▷ ▷ ▷ ▷ ▷ ▷

```
procedure Exchange (var X, Y {input/output} : Integer);
{
 Switches the values in X and Y
}
 var
   Temp : Integer;         {temporary cell for exchange}

begin {Exchange}
  Temp := X;
  X := Y;
  Y := Temp
end; {Exchange}

begin {Partition}
  Pivot := Table[First]; {Define leftmost element as the pivot}

  {Find and exchange values that are out of place}
  Up := First;        {set Up to point to leftmost element}
  Down := Last;       {set Down to point to rightmost element}
  repeat
    {Move Up to the next value larger than Pivot}
    while (Table[Up] <= Pivot) and (Up < Last) do
      Up := Up + 1;
    {assert: Table[Up] > Pivot or Up is equal to Last}

    {Move Down to the next value less than or equal to Pivot}
    while Table[Down] > Pivot do
      Down := Down - 1;
    {assert: Table[Down] <= Pivot}

    {Exchange out-of-order values}
    if Up < Down then
      Exchange (Table[Up], Table[Down])
  until Up >= Down;              {until Up meets or passes Down}

  {assert: Values <= Pivot have subscripts <= Down and
           values > Pivot have subscripts > Down}

  {Put pivot value where it belongs and define PivIndex}
  Exchange (Table[First], Table[Down]);
  PivIndex := Down
end; {Partition}
```

The two while loops in Fig. 11.19 advance pointers Up and Down to the left and right, respectively. Since Table[First] is equal to Pivot, the second loop will stop if Down happens to reach the left end of the array (Down is First). The extra condition (Up < Last) is added to the first while loop to ensure that it also stops if Up happens to reach the right end of the array.

Analysis of QuickSort

The QuickSort procedure works better for some arrays than it does for others. It works best when the partitioning process splits each subarray into two subarrays of almost the same size. The worst behavior results when one of the subarrays has zero elements and the other has all the rest except for the pivot value. Ironically, this worst-case behavior results when QuickSort is applied to an array that is already sorted. The pivot value remains in position First, and the rest of the elements will be in the subarray with subscripts 2..Last.

Procedure Partition compares each array element to the pivot value (an O(N) process). If the array splits are relatively even, the number of calls to partition is O($\log_2$ N). Therefore QuickSort is an O(N $\times$ $\log_2$ N) process in the best case. In the worst case there are N calls to Partition, and QuickSort degenerates to an O(N^2) process.

Because data values are usually distributed in random order in an array, QuickSort as presented will work quite well. A possible improvement is to use the average (median) of two or more array elements as the pivot value. This requires more computation time and also requires a modification to the algorithm because the pivot value is no longer an array element value. In the next section we will look at a sorting algorithm whose worst-case behavior is O(N $\times$ $\log_2$ N).

Exercises for Section 11.6 **Self-Check**

1. Complete the trace of QuickSort for the subarrays remaining after the first partition.
2. In the event an array contains some values that are the same, in which subarray (left or right) will all values that are equal to the pivot value be placed?
3. Trace the execution of QuickSort on the following array. Show the values of First and Last for each recursive call and the array elements after returning from each call. Also, show the value of Pivot during each call and the value returned through PivIndex. How many times is QuickSort called, and how many times is Partition called?

   55 50 10 40 80 90 60 100 70 80 20

   Which provides better performance: MergeSort or QuickSort? How do you think insertion sort would do in comparison to these two?

Programming

1. Determine the times required for MergeSort and QuickSort to sort the same array of 1000 randomly chosen integers.

Figure 11.20
Original Ordering of Array
Table Elements

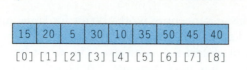

15	20	5	30	10	35	50	45	40
[0]	[1]	[2]	[3]	[4]	[5]	[6]	[7]	[8]

11.7 HeapSort

In Chapter 9 we described how an array can be used to store a heap. In this section we show how an unordered array can be made into a heap. We can then use this heap to help us sort the array using a process called HeapSort.

Consider the array Table shown in Fig. 11.20. We could arrange these array elements to get the heap shown in Fig. 11.21. If we wanted to sort the values stored in `Table` in ascending order, we could begin by switching the largest heap element (at `Table[0]`) with the value in the last position of `Table` (`Table[8]`). If we ignore the last element, we could rearrange the rest of Table (elements 0 through 7) to form a heap, and then switch Table[0] with Table[7], moving the second largest element in the heap to the second to last position of `Table`. If we continued moving the next largest heap element to the corresponding position in array `Table`, we would eventually end up with a sorted array containing the same elements as our heap.

To demonstrate how we might implement `HeapSort` without using a separate heap array, let's assume that the heap in Fig. 11.21 is housed in array `Table` itself. If we exchanged the values housed in `Table[0]` and `Table[8]`, we would have accomplished the task of placing the largest heap element in the last position of `Table`. As shown in Fig. 11.22(a), this ex-

Figure 11.21
A Heap Representation of
an Array Table

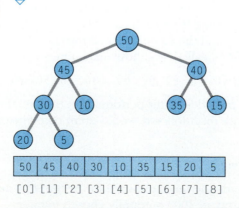

50	45	40	30	10	35	15	20	5
[0]	[1]	[2]	[3]	[4]	[5]	[6]	[7]	[8]

Figure 11.22
Cutting Two Elements from
a Heap

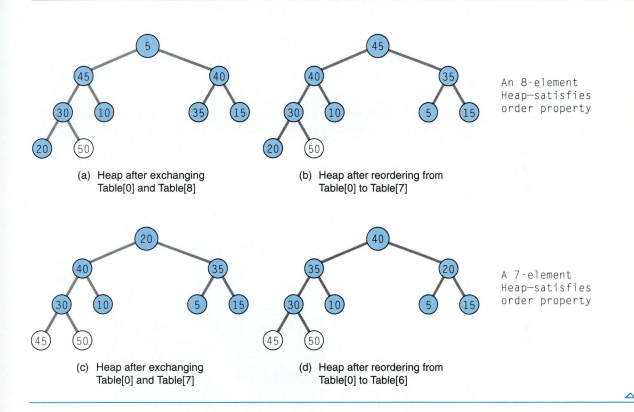

(a) Heap after exchanging
Table[0] and Table[8]

(b) Heap after reordering from
Table[0] to Table[7]

An 8-element
Heap—satisfies
order property

(c) Heap after exchanging
Table[0] and Table[7]

(d) Heap after reordering from
Table[0] to Table[6]

A 7-element
Heap—satisfies
order property

change violates the heap ordering property. However, if we reorder the
heap from `Table[0]` to `Table[7]`, as we will show in Fig 11.22(b), we will
end up with an eight-element heap whose largest element is stored in
`Table[0]`. In this diagram, the heap values are shown in color. The `Table`
element stored in the last array position, Table[8], has been cut out of the
heap. Now we can exchange the values housed in `Table[0]` and `Table[7]`
to place the next largest array element in its final location (Fig. 11.22(c)). We
now need to reorder the heap from `Table[0]` to `Table[6]` as shown in Fig.
11.22(d). If this process is continued, we will end up with a sorted array.

The algorithm for `HeapSort` follows. Notice that we begin by establishing
the heap order beginning with the longest path between a leaf node and the
root node (the first for loop). Next we move each element to its final location
in the heap, starting with the largest element, and rearrange the heap (the
second for loop).

Algorithm for HeapSort

1. for each array element from middle subscript downto the first
    2. restore heap order between current element and the first
3. for each array element from the last downto the second
    begin
        4. exchange the current element with the first
        5. restore heap from the first element to the position preceding
        the current position
    end

Figure 11.23 illustrates this process for array `Table`. After initializing the heap, we begin to move elements to their final positions and cut them out of

Figure 11.23
Trace of the
HeapSort Algorithm

	0	1	2	3	4	5	6	7	8
Initial array ordering	15	20	5	30	10	35	50	45	40
Initial heap	50	45	40	30	10	35	15	20	5
Swap Table[8] and Table[0]	5	45	40	30	10	35	15	20	50
Reorder Table [0..7]	45	40	35	30	10	5	15	20	50
Swap Table[7] and Table[0]	20	40	35	30	10	5	15	45	50
Reorder Table [0..6]	40	35	20	30	10	5	15	45	50
Swap Table[6] and Table[0]	15	35	20	30	10	5	40	45	50
Reorder Table [0..5]	35	30	20	15	10	5	40	45	50
Swap Table[5] and Table[0]	5	30	20	15	10	35	40	45	50
Reorder Table [0..4]	30	20	10	15	5	35	40	45	50
Swap Table[4] and Table[0]	5	20	10	15	30	35	40	45	50
Reorder Table [0..3]	20	15	10	5	30	35	40	45	50
Swap Table[3] and Table[0]	5	15	10	20	30	35	40	45	50
Reorder Table [0..2]	15	10	5	20	30	35	40	45	50
Swap Table[2] and Table[0]	5	10	15	20	30	35	40	45	50
Reorder Table [0..1]	10	5	15	20	30	35	40	45	50
Swap Table[0] and Table[0]	5	10	15	20	30	35	40	45	50
Reorder Table [0..0]	5	10	15	20	30	35	40	45	50

the heap. Notice that in Fig. 11.23, the heap gets smaller as the sequence of sorted elements grows larger at the end of the array.

Procedure HeapSort is shown in Fig. 11.24. We use an open array parameter to receive the array to be sorted. Inside procedure HeapSort we will need to assume that our array subscripts range from 0 to High(Table). We begin the sorting process by calling procedure RestoreDown repeatedly to create the heap. Then we begin cutting elements out of the heap. Procedure Exchange is called by both procedure HeapSort and procedure RestoreDown. We will describe procedure RestoreDown next.

Figure 11.24
Procedure HeapSort

Directory: CHAP 11
File: HEAPSORT.PAS

```
procedure Exchange (var X, Y {input/output} : Integer);
{
 Switches the values in X and Y
}
  var
    Temp : Integer;        {temporary cell for exchange}
begin  {Exchange}
  Temp := X;
  X := Y;
  Y := Temp
end; {Exchange}

procedure HeapSort (var Table {input/output} : Array of Integer);
{
 Performs heap sort on open array parameter Table.
 Pre : Table is defined and filled with data.
 Post: Table is sorted.
}
  var
    N,                    {largest array subscript}
    I : Integer;          {index to array values}

  {Insert procedure RestoreDown here}

begin {HeapSort}
  {Save value of largest Table subscript}
  N := High(Table);
  {Build the initial heap}
  for I := (N div 2) downto 0 do
    RestoreDown (Table, I, N);

  {Begin "cutting" values from heap}
  for I := N downto 1 do
    begin
      {invariant:
        Heap property holds for subarray Table[0..I] and
```

▷ ▷ ▷ ▷ ▷

```
              subarray Table[I + 1..N] are sorted in ascending order.
       }

       {Remove largest value from heap}
       Exchange (Table[0], Table[I]);
       {Reestablish heap property for remaining elements}
       RestoreDown (Table, 0, I - 1)
     end {for}
end; {HeapSort}
```

Coding Procedure RestoreDown

Procedure RestoreDown is shown in Fig. 11.25. The algorithm used in this procedure is the same as the one we used for method Heap.RestoreDown in Fig. 9.4. Procedure RestoreDown recursively pushes the element stored in Table[Root] to its final location in the subarray Table[Root..Last].

Analysis of HeapSort

What is the expected worst-case performance for HeapSort? The process of creating or reordering the heap requires the same amount of work as inserting a new element into the heap. In both operations the root element is compared successively to each of its descendants until it reaches its final location. In Chapter 9 we described this as an $O(\log_2 N)$ process. We repeat this process N/2 times to construct our initial heap. The task of constructing a heap from an unordered array is an $O(N \times \log_2 N)$ process. We must also reorder the heap N − 1 times as we cut elements from the heap. The task of cutting N − 1 items from the heap is also an $O(N \times \log_2 N)$ process. Therefore the whole HeapSort algorithm has an $O(N \times \log_2 N)$ worst-case performance.

HeapSort is an interesting algorithm because it has the same best-case, average-case, and worst-case performances. Experiments have shown that HeapSort may take a little more execution time on average to sort an array. However, given that the performance of HeapSort does not depend on the initial data ordering as that of QuickSort does, HeapSort is a better choice if there is a possibility that the array being sorted is close to being in order already (e.g., following the insertion of new array elements).

Exercises for Section 11.7   *Self-Check*

1. Trace the execution of HeapSort on the following array:

   55 50 10 40 80 90

   How many times is RestoreDown called directly by HeapSort? How many times does RestoreDown call itself recursively?

Figure 11.25
Procedure RestoreDown

Directory: CHAP 11
File: HEAPSORT.PAS

```
procedure RestoreDown (var Table {in/out} : Array of Integer;
                           Root, Last {input} : Integer);
{
 Restores heap order between Root and Last, working down
 from Root.
 Pre : Assumes that element in position Root is the only
        element causing heap violation and that Root < Last.
 Post: Heap order has been restored between Root and Last.
}
  var
    MaxChild,            {index of larger child}
    Left,                {index of Root left child}
    Right : Integer;     {index of Root right child}

begin {RestoreDown}
  {compute indices of Root children}
  Left := Root * 2;
  Right := Root * 2 + 1;

  if Left <= Last then
    begin {Root is not a leaf node}
      {Determine index of larger child}
      if Left = Last then
        {only one Child}
        MaxChild := Left
      else
        {Root has two children}
        if Table[Left] > Table[Right] then
          MaxChild := Left
        else
          MaxChild := Right;

      if Table[Root] < Table[MaxChild] then
        begin
          {Heap order property violated, swap values}
          Exchange (Table[Root], Table[MaxChild]);
          {Restore heap between Max and Last}
          RestoreDown (Table, MaxChild, Last)
        end {Heap order violation}
    end {Root is not leaf node}
end; {RestoreDown}
```

Programming

1. Determine the times required by HeapSort to sort an array containing
    1000 randomly chosen integers, 1000 integers arranged in ascending
    order, and 1000 integers arranged in descending order.

11.8 Common Programming Errors

One problem with sort procedures is the possibility of going beyond the bounds of a subarray. Make sure that you turn range checking on using the compiler directive {$R+} (or through the Options Menu) so that Borland Pascal will check for subscript range errors. In debugging a sort procedure it is best to use relatively small arrays (10 elements or fewer). You can use the Borland Pascal debugger to display the array after each pass through a sort procedure.

CHAPTER REVIEW

We analyzed several sorting algorithms; their performance is summarized in Table 11.3. Three of these, the selection sort, the bubble sort, and the insertion sort, are O(N²) or quadratic sorts. One of these, QuickSort, has average-case performance of O(N × log₂ N), but worst-case performance of O(N²). Two of these, MergeSort and HeapSort, have worst-case performance of O(N × log₂ N). For small arrays, either insertion or selection sort should generally be used; bubble sort is also a good choice when the array is likely to be nearly sorted. For larger arrays, use MergeSort, HeapSort, or QuickSort. Avoid MergeSort when storage space is likely to be limited. Avoid QuickSort when the array is nearly sorted.

Table 11.3
Comparison of
Sorting Algorithms

	Number of Comparisons		
	Best	*Average*	*Worst*
Selection sort	$O(N^2)$	$O(N^2)$	$O(N^2)$
Bubble sort	$O(N)$	$O(N^2)$	$O(N^2)$
Insertion sort	$O(N)$	$O(N^2)$	$O(N^2)$
Merge sort	$O(N \times \log_2 N)$	$O(N \times \log_2 N)$	$O(N \times \log_2 N)$
Quick sort	$O(N \times \log_2 N)$	$O(N \times \log_2 N)$	$O(N^2)$
Heap sort	$O(N \times \log_2 N)$	$O(N \times \log_2 N)$	$O(N \times \log_2 N)$

Quick-Check Exercises

1. Name three quadratic sorts.
2. Name two sorts with N × log₂ N worst-case behavior.
3. Which algorithm is particularly good for an array that is already sorted? Which is particularly bad? Explain your answers.
4. What determines whether you should use a quadratic sort or a logarithmic sort?
5. Which quadratic sort's performance is least affected by the ordering of the array elements? Which is most affected?

Answers to Quick-Check Exercises

1. Selection, insertion, bubble
2. `MergeSort`, `HeapSort`
3. Bubble sort and insertion sort are good; both require N − 1 comparisons with no exchanges. `QuickSort` is bad because the partitioning process always creates one subarray with a single element.
4. Array size
5. Selection sort; bubble sort

Review Questions

1. When does `QuickSort` work best, and when does it work worst?
2. Write a recursive procedure to implement the insertion sort algorithm.
3. What is the purpose of the pivot value in `QuickSort`? How did we select it in the text, and what is wrong with that approach for choosing a pivot value?
4. For the array

    30 40 20 15 60 80 75 4 20

    show the new array after each pass of an insertion sort and a bubble sort. How many comparisons and exchanges are performed by each?
5. For the array in Question 4, trace the execution of `MergeSort`.
6. For the array in Question 4, trace the execution of `QuickSort`.
7. For the array in Question 4, trace the execution of `HeapSort`.
8. The shaker sort is an adaptation of the bubble sort that alternates the direction in which the array elements are scanned during each pass. The first pass starts its scan with the first element, moving the larger element in each pair down the array. The second pass starts its scan with the next-to-last element, moving the smaller element in each pair up the array, and so on. Indicate what the advantage of the shaker sort might be.

Programming Projects

Directory: CHAP 11
File: PROJ11_1.PAS

1. Use the random number function to store a list of 1000 pseudo–random integer values in an array. Apply each of the sort procedures described in this chapter to the array, and determine how long it takes each procedure to sort the array. Make sure the same array is passed to each procedure. Refer back to Chapter 2 to find out about the timing functions in Borland Pascal.
2. Investigate the effect of array size and initial element order on the number of comparisons and exchanges required by each of the sorting algorithms described in this chapter. Use arrays with 500 and 1000 integers. Use three initial orderings of each array (randomly ordered, inversely ordered, and ordered). Be certain to sort the same six arrays with each sort procedure.

Directory: CHAP 11
File: PROJ11_3.PAS

3. The shell sort is a sorting technique that applies insertion sort to chains of elements in an array in which the elements in the chain are chosen by adding an increment value. The increment value decreases with each pass. For example, if an array has 15 elements, the initial increment value could be 5, and the five chains of elements listed below would be sorted in the "first pass." Each chain would be sorted by using insertion sort.

```
X[1], X[6], X[11]
X[2], X[7], X[12]
X[3], X[8], X[13]
X[4], X[9], X[14]
X[5], X[10], X[15]
```

If the next increment is 3, the three chains below would be sorted. Note that the chains increase in size as the increment shrinks.

```
X[1], X[4], X[7], X[10], X[13]
X[2], X[5], X[8], X[11], X[14]
X[3], X[6], X[9], X[12], X[15]
```

If the increment shrinks to 1, the whole array is sorted by using insertion sort. Implement the shell sort algorithm. Read the increment values for each pass into an array Increments before reading in the elements of the array to be sorted.

4. Implement the ShakerSort algorithm described in Review Exercise 8.

5. A variation of the MergeSort algorithm can be used to sort large sequential data files. The basic strategy is to take the initial data file, read in several (say, 10) data records, sort these records by using an efficient array-sorting algorithm, and then write these groups of sorted groups of records (runs) alternately to one of two output files. After all records from the initial data file have been distributed to the two output files, the runs on these output files are merged one pair of runs at a time and written to the original data file. After all runs from the output file have been merged, the records on the original data file are redistributed to the output files, and the merging process is repeated. Runs no longer need to be sorted after the first distribution to the temporary output files. Each time runs are distributed to the output files, they contain twice as many records as the time before. The process stops when the length of the runs exceeds the number of records in the data file. Write a program that implements MergeSort for sequential data files. Test your program on a file with several thousand data values.

Directory: CHAP 11
File: PROJ11_6.PAS

6. Write a procedure that sorts an ordinary linked list.

CHAPTER TWELVE

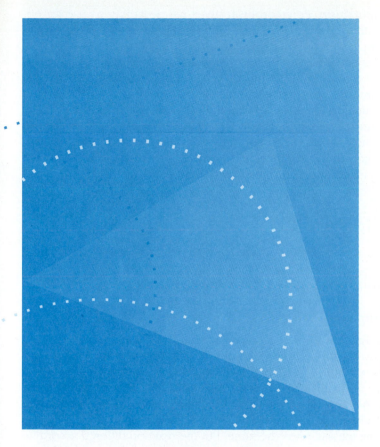

Object-Oriented Programming and Polymorphism

Object-oriented programming goes far beyond simply combining operator declarations and Pascal record type declarations to make a more compact object declaration. In Chapter 3 we demonstrated the ability of objects to *inherit* data and operators from previously defined object types. Inheritance has the potential to greatly reduce the effort required to implement new ADTs. For example, after defining a LinkList ADT we were able to implement a Stack ADT and a Queue ADT by simply allowing the new ADTs to obtain most of their necessary data and method members by inheritance.

This chapter explores another very important object-oriented programming technique: *polymorphism*. Polymorphism gives us the ability to use an object's methods without needing to know the object's exact type. This is analogous to allowing us to write functions and procedures that accept objects of varying data types as actual parameters. In object-oriented programming terminology, polymorphism gives us the ability to send the same message to instances of different object types, knowing that each will choose the correct method implementation to use in responding to the message. Borland Pascal allows us to write polymorphic methods by postponing the decision on which method implementation to use until run-time. In programming languages that do not allow polymorphic methods the decision as to which method to use is made during program compilation.

12.1   What Is Polymorphism?

In everyday terms, polymorphism is the ability to react differently to different stimuli. More specifically, different reactions are triggered when the source of the stimuli changes. Let's look at an everyday example.

Object Polymorphism

Consider what might have happened the last time you were driving a car and someone told you to slow down. If the person was one of your friends, you might have ignored him or her. If the person was your parent, you might have complained a bit, but you probably took your foot off the gas for a few moments to let the car decelerate slowly. If the person was a police officer who had pulled alongside your car, you probably hit the brakes.

In each case the message was the same, but the reaction differed according to the nature of the message sender. It is important to note that the driver's reaction to the request to slow down might be determined in part by the role he or she plays (friend, child, lawbreaker) as the recipient of this message.

In this example the driver of the car is analogous to a function or method that can be used with a wide variety of arguments. A method that is capable of polymorphism determines the type of the caller and uses this information to determine which object is the best recipient of the caller's message. In other words, the type of value that is returned by a function is determined by the argument types themselves. This is a little different from examples that we discussed in previous chapters, in which several unrelated object types simply had methods with the same names. Our next example should help to clarify the differences between these two situations.

Operator Polymorphism

We will look at an example of polymorphism found in many Pascal implementations. Operator polymorphism means that the same operator can be used with different object types and that the operator's response will be appropriate to its operand types. For example, the + operator has four distinct uses in Borland Pascal: string concatenation, integer addition, real addition, and set union, as shown:

```
'Hello' + ' world'
4 + 3
5.2 + 6.7
[a, b] + [c, d, e]
```

The compiler determines which operation is meant by + from the context in which it appears (e.g., the data types of its operands) and generates the code needed to perform the intended operation.

In this section we have looked at an example of Pascal's built-in polymorphism. In the remaining sections of this chapter we will discuss how to write your own polymorphic methods. Writing such methods involves a number of steps, and it is important that you begin with a firm understanding of what polymorphism is. You need to keep in mind that polymorphism means that you no longer have to decide at compile-time whether the particular method needed belongs to an object or one of its related types. With polymorphic methods you can defer this choice until run-time, when the caller's data type is known.

Polymorphism in Borland Pascal

To get dynamic type binding in Borland Pascal, we need to make use of pointer variables. Borland Pascal allows the declaration of pointers to instances of dynamic objects. Program PointerObjects, shown in Fig. 12.1, contains declarations for two object types, Applicant and Employee. Each object has a Display method and a constructor method. Object Applicant also has a destructor method. The Display methods are identified as being virtual. Constructors and destructors will be described in Section 12.2, and virtual methods will be described in Section 12.4.

Figure 12.1
Program
PointerObjects

Directory: CHAP 12
File: POINTERO.PAS

```
program PointerObjects;
{
  Program demonstrating limited dynamic type binding.
}
  type
    ApplicantPtr = ^Applicant;
    Applicant = object
                  constructor Init (N {input} : string);
                  procedure Display; virtual;
                  destructor Done;

                private
                  Name : string;
                  Next : ApplicantPtr;

                end; {Applicant}
```

▷ ▷ ▷ ▷ ▷

```
            EmployeePtr = ^Employee;
            Employee = object(Applicant)
                          constructor Init (N {input} : string;
                                            R {input} : Real);
                          procedure Display; virtual;

                        private
                          PayRate : Real;
                        end; {Employee}
var
  X, Y : ApplicantPtr;

constructor Applicant.Init (N {input} : string);
{
 Initializes objects of type Applicant.
 Pre : N is defined.
 Post: Name is assigned value from N and Next is nil.
}
begin {Init}
  Name := N;
  Next := nil
end; {Init}

procedure Applicant.Display;
{
 Displays Name field of object Applicant.
 Pre : Object has been initialized.
 Post: Name is displayed.
}
begin {Display}
  WriteLn ('Name is ', Name)
end; {Display}

destructor Applicant.Done;
{
 Reclaims heap storage used by object.
 Pre : Object has been initialized.
 Post: Object storage is reclaimed.
}
begin {Done}
end; {Done}

constructor Employee.Init (N {input} : string;
                           R {input} : Real);
{
 Initializes objects of type Employee.
 Pre : N and R have been defined.
 Post: Name is assigned value from N, PayRate gets value
       from R, and Next is nil.
}
begin {Init}
  Name := N;
  PayRate := R;
```

▷ ▷ ▷ ▷ ▷

```
   Next := nil
 end; {Init}

 procedure Employee.Display;
 {
  Displays Name and PayRate fields from object Employee.
  Pre : Object has been initialized.
  Post: Name and PayRate are displayed.
 }
 begin {Display}
   WriteLn ('Name is ', Name);
   WriteLn ('Pay Rate is $', PayRate :5:2)
 end; {Display}
begin {PointerObjects}
 {Allocate instance of object Applicant}
 X := New(ApplicantPtr, Init('John Smith'));
 {Allocate instance of object Employee}
 Y := New(EmployeePtr, Init('Jane Doe', 10.35));

 X^.Display;
 Y^.Display;

 {Call destructors to deallocate object storage}
 Dispose(X, Done);
 Dispose(Y, Done)

end. {PointerObjects}
```

The program body allocates two object instances, one of type `Applicant` and one of type `Employee`. Pointer variables `X` and `Y`, both of type `ApplicantPtr`, point to these new object instances. Notice that `Y` (type `ApplicantPtr`) can point to an object instance of type `Employee` because `Employee` is a descendant of `Applicant`. A pointer of type `EmployeePtr` would not be able to point to an object instance of type `Applicant`.

The call messages

```
X^.Display
Y^.Display;
```

display the data fields of each object instance. Notice that the correct version of `Display` is called each time. `X^.Display` activates `Applicant.Display`, and `Y^.Display` activates `Employee.Display`. This is the essence of polymorphism. The reason for this is that method `Display` is a virtual method. This means that the determination of which method `Display` to call is postponed until run-time, when the Borland Pascal system knows exactly what kind of object (`Applicant` or `Employee`) `X` and `Y` are pointing to. We will explain this further in Section 12.4.

Self-Check

1. List three different examples of operator polymorphism found in Pascal.
2. How does the caller's data type affect a polymorphic method?

12.2 Allocating and Deallocating Dynamic Objects

Dynamic (run-time) type binding and polymorphism are two features that set object-oriented programming apart from traditional Pascal programming. With polymorphism we may use a method to manipulate an object regardless of whether it is an instance of an ancestor object type or one of its descendants. Inheritance and the use of virtual methods provide much of the support that is required to ensure that the appropriate methods are used to manipulate a given object instance. The capability of deferring until run-time the binding of an object type to an instance identifier provides the remainder of the support that is required for methods to behave in a truly polymorphic manner.

Allocating Dynamic Objects

Dynamic data objects are allocated by using the standard identifier New. If the objects contain virtual methods, they also must be initialized using constructors. To facilitate this process, the New operation has been extended so that it can be called with two parameters: a pointer variable identifier as the first parameter and a constructor call as the second parameter, as shown:

```
New (X, Init ('John Smith'));
```

Note that the object instance X^ is not used to qualify Init in the extended form.

As a further extension, New may be called as a function that returns a pointer value. This is similar to typecasting, which we will discuss in Section 12.3. When used as a function designator, the first parameter passed to New is a type identifier for an object pointer rather than a pointer variable identifier. By this technique the next statement below has the same effect as that shown above.

```
X := New(ApplicantPtr, Init ('John Smith'));
```

There are times when the use of New as a function designator is more convenient (for example, passing object pointers as value parameters to procedures).

The object type passed to New must be assignment compatible with the pointer variable appearing on the left side of the assignment statement. Since objects of type Employee are descendants of objects of type Applicant, the following assignment statement is valid if Y is type ApplicantPtr or EmployeePtr.

```
Y := New(EmployeePtr, Init ('John Smith'));
```

The function form of New is used in Fig. 12.1.

SYNTAX DISPLAY

Using New with Object Pointers

Form: `type`
`    ptr obj type = ^obj type`

`New (pvar, constructor);`
`pvar := New(ptr obj type, constructor);`
Example: `New (X, Init('John Smith'));`
`        X := New(ApplicantPtr, Init('John Smith'));`
Interpretation: The standard identifier New can be used in one of two forms to allocate storage for dynamic objects. In the first form, procedure New may be passed actual parameters *pvar* of type *ptr obj type* and a call to a *constructor* method for *obj type*. In the second form, New is used as a function returning a pointer to the storage location for an object of type *obj type*. Function New is passed as arguments a pointer type identifier that is assignment compatible with *ptr obj type* and a call to a valid *constructor* for an object pointed to by *pvar*.

Deallocating Dynamic Object Storage

Storage allocated for dynamic objects is reclaimed by using the standard procedure Dispose. Dispose may be passed the name of a pointer to an object as an actual parameter. However, if the object contains fields that are pointers to other dynamic variables, more work may need to be done to reclaim all the storage that has been allocated to the object. This code would typically be collected in one or more special methods known as destructors. Destructors must be used to reclaim storage allocated to dynamic variables inherited from ancestor types. The object type Applicant has a method Done declared as a destructor. Destructors may be inherited. Though it is not required, destructors are usually declared as virtual methods.

The `Dispose` procedure has been modified to allow us to pass it a pointer variable identifier as a first parameter and a destructor call (e.g., Done) as a second parameter as shown:

`Dispose (X, Done);`

A destructor automatically returns all storage pointed to by an object's fields to the heap, including fields inherited from ancestor types.

SYNTAX DISPLAY

Using Dispose with Object Pointers

Form: `Dispose (pvar, destructor);`
Example: `Dispose (X, Done);`
Interpretation: The standard identifier Dispose can be used to reclaim storage allocated for dynamic objects. Dispose may be passed actual parameters *pvar* of some pointer type and call to a *destructor* method for an object pointed to by *pvar*.

Note: Dynamic objects must use destructors to free up any storage pointed to by its fields, in addition to using Dispose to deallocate the objects' storage.

Objects and Dynamic Data Structures

As we mentioned in our last example, it is possible to define pointers to an object with fields that are pointers to other dynamic data structures. When this happens, destructors need to be a bit more complex. For example, we might decide to use pointers to a linked list StackADT object that is similar to the one we discussed in Chapter 7. In this case we would want to write our destructor so that it disposed of the individual list nodes one at a time. For the examples that we discuss in this chapter we will not need to write destructors of this type.

Exercises for Section 12.2 **Self-Check**

1. Why do we need to use destructors in dealing with pointers to object instances?

Programming

1. Write a short program that creates a list of applicants and employees and then displays its contents.

12.3   Typecasting

We are getting closer to being able to do true object-oriented programming. In Section 12.4 we will examine the role that virtual methods play in the implementation of polymorphic methods. First, though, we need to examine one more technique: *typecasting*. Typecasting is the process of converting a data value from one data type to another. We saw one example of typecasting object pointer values using New in the previous section. It would be a good idea to review the typecasting facilities provided by Borland Pascal for its built-in data types.

Value Typecasts

In Pascal the Ord function can be used to convert any ordinal data to type Integer, and the Chr function can be used to convert an Integer value to type Char. The functions Ord and Chr may be regarded as inverses of one another. In standard Pascal it is not possible to convert from type Integer to any other data type except Char. However, in Borland Pascal it is possible to convert from one ordinal data type to another. These types do not even need to be assignment compatible. These conversions are accomplished by using the data type identifier as if it were a "function" or *value typecast*.

Table 12.1 shows the values of some type conversion "functions." The table entries assume the existence of an enumerated type Day declared as

```
type
  Day = (Sunday, Monday, Tuesday, Wednesday, Thursday,
         Friday, Saturday);
```

In Table 12.1 the first four lines show that the "function" Integer is equivalent to the function Ord for many argument values. Both functions convert their arguments to an integer value that represents the ordinal number of the argument (e.g., Integer(Sunday) is 0, and Integer(Monday) is 1).

Table 12.1
Type Conversion "Functions"

Typecast	Value
Ord(Monday)	1
Integer(Monday)	1
Ord('7')	55
Integer('7')	55
Boolean(0)	False
Boolean(1)	True
Boolean(Monday)	True
Day(0)	Sunday
Day(False)	Sunday
Day(1)	Monday
Day(True)	Monday

The "function" Boolean converts its argument to a value of type Boolean (False or True). Since both 1 and Monday have an ordinal value of 1 in their respective type (Integer and Day), they yield the same result (True) when passed as arguments to "function" Boolean. The result is True because True has an ordinal value of 1. The "function" Day converts its argument to a value of type Day.

Variable Typecasts

Borland Pascal also allows typecasting of one variable reference into another through a *variable typecast*. In typecasting, the data bits stored in the memory location associated with that variable are interpreted as if they are data bits representing a data value of the type specified by the typecasting "function." The only restriction imposed by Borland Pascal is that the size of the variable (number of bytes) must be the same as the size of the type denoted by the typecasting "function." As an example, consider the declarations in Fig. 12.2.

```
type
    IndexType = 1..2;
    IntArray = array [IndexType] of Integer;

    IntRec = record
                A, B : Integer
             end; {IntRec}

    IntObj = object
                A, B : Integer;
             end; {IntObj}

var
    X : IntArray;        {array of 2 integer elements}
    Y : IntRec;          {record of 2 integer data fields}
    Z : IntObj;          {object with 2 integer data fields}
```

In Fig. 12.2 we declare variable X as an array, variable Y as a record, and variable Z as an object. The data elements of each of the variables X, Y, and Z take up the same amount of storage. Under Pascal's rules for assignment compatibility, none of the assignment statements below are valid:

```
X := Y; {invalid}
Y := Z; {invalid}
X := Z; {invalid}
```

By using typecasting, each of the following represents a valid assignment statement:

```
Y := IntRec(X);       {copy array X to record Y}
IntArray(Y) := X;     {copy array X to record Y}
IntRec(X) := Y;       {copy record Y to array X}
Z := IntObj(X);       {copy array X to object Z}
IntArray(Z) := X;     {copy array X to object Z}
IntObj(X) := Z;       {copy object Z to array X}
```

The typecast IntRec(X) is treated like a record reference, and IntObj(X) is treated like an object reference, even though X is declared as an array type variable. A variable typecast may be followed by one or more qualifiers if appropriate for the data type. The typecast IntRec(X).A could be used to access the first data element of array X. The typecast IntArray(Z) [2] could be used to access the second data element of the object instance Z.

Some care must be taken in using variable typecasting because Borland Pascal requires only that the total size occupied by the two variables be the same. Borland Pascal does not require that the two variables involved have the same number of components or that the components have the same orderings. This can lead to very unusual results.

Typecasting and Descendant Objects

Extending variable typecasting to descendant object types is fairly straight-forward as long as you remember the rules about matching the components of structured data types using both size and declaration order. Consider the object declarations in Fig. 12.3. Object types One and Two are descended from the same ancestor object type Base. We can use typecasting to assign MyOne, which is an instance of object type One, to MyTwo, which is an instance of object type Two, as shown:

```
MyTwo := Two(MyOne);
```

This assignment statement has the effect of copying corresponding data field values from MyOne to MyTwo. It does not matter which two fields were inherited and which two were not. It is important that each field size matches the corresponding field size in both object types. Next we will show you how things change in dealing with pointers to descendant object types.

Typecasting Object Pointers

In Section 12.2 we discussed the use of New to initialize instances of dynamic objects. We can also use variable typecasting to initialize instances of descendant object types, as well as use it to convert instance variables from one data type to another. Let's consider what might be possible if we were to declare a type ExEmployee as a descendant of object type Applicant shown in Fig. 12.1. Assuming that the data needed for initialization are Name and Year, the object type declarations

Figure 12.3
Declarations for
Descendant Object Type
Instances

Directory: CHAP 12
File: TYPECAS2.PAS

```
type
  Base = object
            A : Integer;
            B : Real;
          end; {Base}

  IndexType = 1..2;
  IntArray = array [IndexType] of Integer;
  One = object(Base)
            C : IntArray;
          end; {One}

  Two = object(Base)
            D, E : Integer;
          end; {Two}

var
  MyOne : One;
  MyTwo : Two;
```

```
type
  ExEmployeePtr = ^ExEmployee;
  ExEmployee = object(Applicant)
              constructor Init (N {input} : string;
                                Y {input} : Integer);
              procedure Display; virtual;

          private
            Year : Integer;
          end; {Employee}
```

would accomplish this. If we were to declare variables Y and Z to be of type `ApplicantPtr`, then we could have Y point to an instance of object type Employee and have Z point to an instance of object type `ExEmployee`. One way to do this would be to use New as if it were a typecasting function, as we did in Section 12.2. The statements

```
Y := New(EmployeePtr, Init ('Jane Doe', 10.35));
Z := New(ExEmployeePtr, Init ('George Doe', 1992));
```

accomplish this. An equivalent way of doing the same thing would be to use the statements

```
New (EmployeePtr(Y), Init ('Jane Doe', 10.35));
New (ExEmployeePtr(Z), Init ('George Doe', 1992));
```

In these statements, explicit typecasts are used to initialize storage by using the data provided.

The key point to understand is that Init belongs to an object type and this type is passed as the first parameter in both cases. When New's first argument is cast to be of type EmployeePtr, Employee.Init will be called. When New's first argument is cast to be of type ExEmployeePtr, ExEmployee.Init will be called. Figure 12.4 diagrams the call to New to clarify its meaning.

There are two additional concepts to grasp here. First, when used in a call to New, the pointer (Y in Fig. 12.4) sets the type of the return value (an instance of Object Employee). Thus the call illustrated in Fig. 12.4 sets the type of variable Y to `EmployeePtr`, regardless of the fact that it was originally de-

Figure 12.4
Understanding a Call to
New with Typecast

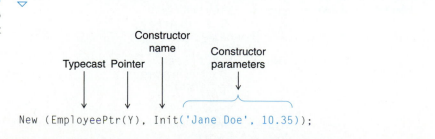

clared to be of type `ApplicantPtr`. The second concept, which is crucial to understanding polymorphism, is that since `EmployeePtr` is a pointer to an object descended from the object `Applicant`, `EmployeePtr` is of type `ApplicantPtr` as well.

Figure 12.5 attempts to make this a bit clearer. An object of type `Employee` has components inherited from `Applicant` (Name, Done) and components that are unique (`PayRate`, `Init`, `Display`). Therefore pointers to either the ancestor or the descendant object can point to an instance of the descendant object. In fact these two pointers may appear to be the same from the compiler's perspective. However, when `New` is called with a pointer to a descendant object, the run-time system defines an internal data member that automatically keeps track of which type of object is pointed to.

Typecasting between descendant object pointers is also allowed. For example, both of the statements

```
ApplicantPtr(Z) := Y;
EmployeePtr(Z) := EmployeePtr(Y);
```

have the effect of making `Z` point to an object of type `Employee`. It does not matter that `PayRate` is of type `Real` in object `Employee` and `Year` is of type `Integer` in object `ExEmployee`. There are no field size problems, as there would be if we tried to use a variable typecast between instances of `Employee` and `ExEmployee` objects.

The point to keep in mind is that a pointer to a descendant object is completely type compatible with a pointer to its ancestor type. The fact that a pointer to an instance of a descendant object type is also a pointer to its ancestor is what makes the implementation of virtual methods feasible. In the next section we will explain the role that virtual methods play in making it possible to implement polymorphic methods.

Figure 12.5
Pointer to Descendant
Object Type

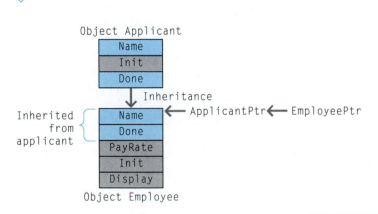

1. Would you expect a typecast between instances of types `Applicant` and `ExEmployee` to work? Why or why not?

Programming

1. Write a program that attempts all six typecasts among pointers to instances of object types `Applicant`, `Employee`, and `ExEmployee`. Are there any that do not work?

12.4 Understanding Virtual Methods

We discussed virtual methods briefly when we introduced object inheritance in Chapter 3. Virtual methods are methods that are likely to be redefined in some descendant object class or classes, such as the `Display` methods shown in Fig. 12.1. Methods `Applicant.Display` and `Employee.Display` have the same parameter lists but different implementation bodies. As we saw in Section 12.1, calls to virtual methods cannot be resolved during program compilation, because the data type of the object calling the method may not be known until run-time. In this section we explain how Borland Pascal knows which version of method `Display` to use at run-time. We also describe the role of virtual methods in developing polymorphic methods.

Using Case Statements with Implicit Arguments

In Chapter 8 we discussed the implementation of a binary expression tree ADT as an application of our binary tree ADT. Unlike an ordinary binary tree, a binary expression tree contains two different node types. We did not include the implementation of unit `TreeDataADT` that is necessary to use our binary expression tree ADT. However, given the information on object-oriented programming that we had presented up to that point in the text, we would have needed to use a variant record with a tag field as the data member of object `TreeData`, as shown in Fig. 12.6.

The implementations of `TreeData`'s methods are shown in Fig. 12.7. As you might expect, many of these methods make explicit checks of the variant record tag field to be able to process each type of tree node correctly. There is nothing wrong with this style of coding. However, consider what would need to happen if it becomes important to have both `RealOperand` nodes and `IntegerOperand` nodes in the same expression tree.

If we want to house both `RealOperand` and `IntegerOperand` nodes in the same expression tree node structure, we need to make several changes to our `TreeData` object:

Figure 12.6
Interface Section for Unit
TreeDataADT

Directory: CHAP 12
File: TREEDAT1.PAS

```
unit TreeDataADT;
{
  Implements object type TreeData for a binary tree whose
  nodes have an information field that is either an integer
  or character value.
}
interface

  type
    TagField = (Operator, Operand);
    InfoType = record
                 case Tag : TagField of
                   Operator : (OpChar : Char);
                   Operand : (OpVal : Real);
                 end; {InfoType}

    TreeData = object
                 procedure InitOperand (Item {input} : Real);
                 procedure InitOperator (Item {input} : Char);
                 function GetOperator : Char;
                 function GetVal : Real;
                 function IsOperator : Boolean;
                 procedure Display;

                 private
                   Info : InfoType;
                 end; {TreeData}
```

Figure 12.7
Implementation Section for
Unit TreeDataADT

Directory: CHAP 12
File: TREEDAT1.PAS

```
implementation

  procedure TreeData.Display;
  {
    Display operand or operator stored in tree node.
  }
  begin {Display}
    case Info.Tag of
      Operand : Write (Info.OpVal :2:1);
      Operator : Write (Info.OpChar)
    end
  end; {Display}

  procedure TreeData.InitOperand (Item {input} : Real);
  {
    Initialize operand type tree node.
  }
  begin {InitOperand}
    Info.Tag := Operand;
```

▷ ▷ ▷ ▷ ▷ ▷

```
      Info.OpVal := Item
  end; {InitOperand}

  procedure TreeData.InitOperator (Item {input} : Char);
  {
   Initialize operator type tree node.
  }
  begin {InitOperator}
    Info.Tag := Operator;
    Info.OpChar := Item
  end; {InitOperator}

  function TreeData.GetOperator : Char;
  {
   Return operator value stored in tree node.
  }
  begin {GetOperator}
    GetOperator := Info.OpChar
  end; {GetOperator}

  function TreeData.GetVal : Real;
  {
   Return operand value stored in tree node.
  }
  begin {GetVal}
    GetVal := Info.OpVal
  end; {GetVal}

  function TreeData.IsOperator : Boolean;
  {
   Tests value of tree node tag field; returns True if tree
   node is an operator node.
  }
  begin {IsOperator}
    IsOperator := (Info.Tag = Operator)
  end; {IsOperator}

end. {TreeDataADT}
```

1. We need to add `RealOperand` and `IntegerOperand` to type `TagField`.
2. We need to redefine `InfoType` to have three variant types.
3. We need to write two versions of `TreeData.GetVal` (one that returns an `Integer` and one that returns a `Real`).
4. We need to modify `TreeData.Display` to accommodate the new variants.
5. We need to find every location in `TreeDataADT`'s client modules where `TreeData` objects are referenced and decide what needs to be done differently for `Real` and `Integer` operands.

The first four tasks are not too difficult to accomplish. The last one is very difficult to do correctly. Not only is the last task very error-prone, but we might not actually have access to all the code that needs to be changed. If you are working on a large program with several other programmers, there may be case statements that reference `TreeData` objects that you have never seen. Therefore software maintenance using this technique would be very difficult.

Using Descendant Objects and Virtual Methods

The software maintenance problem discussed above could be greatly reduced by changing the nature of our implementation of `TreeData` so that it can exploit polymorphism. To do this, we need to use virtual methods, object pointers, pointer typecasting, and object inheritance. This makes the initial setup of `TreeData` a bit more complex, but the resulting object will allow much easier addition of new node types without needing to modify already written code. This is a huge gain in software quality (and hopefully productivity too).

Consider the interface section of the new unit `TreeDataADT` shown in Fig. 12.8. In this version we have implemented `TreeData` as an ancestor to descendant object types `RealOperand` and `Operator`. We also declared pointer types for each object. The reason that `TreeData` has no data fields of its own is that it is an example of an *abstract object*. This means that `TreeData` exists for the sole purpose of being used to declare descendant object types and to allow client programs to treat the descendant types as if they were of type `TreeData`. This also ensures that all objects descended from `TreeData` will have a constructor called `Init`, a destructor called `Done`, and procedural method `Display`.

Figure 12.8
Interface Section to New
`TreeDataADT`

Directory: CHAP 12
File: TREEDATA.PAS

```
unit TreeDataADT;
{
  Implements object type TreeData and descendant object types
  RealOperand and Operator, along with corresponding pointer
  types for use in a binary expression tree whose nodes have
  an information field that is either a real or character
  value.
}
interface

  type
    TreeDataPtr = ^TreeData;
    TreeData = object
                 constructor Init;
                 destructor Done; virtual;
                 procedure Display; virtual;
               end; {TreeData}
```

▷ ▷ ▷ ▷ ▷

```
RealOperandPtr = ^RealOperand;
RealOperand = object(TreeData)
                 constructor Init (Item {input} : Real);
                 function GetVal : Real;
                 procedure Display; virtual;

            private
               OpVal : Real;
            end; {Operand}

OperatorPtr = ^Operator;
Operator = object(TreeData)
                 constructor Init (Item {input} : Char);
                 function GetOperator : Char;
                 procedure Display; virtual;

            private
              OpChar : Char;
            end; {Operator}
```

By making `Display` a virtual method we allow `TreeData` clients to display the information stored in a node descended from `TreeData` without needing to know its exact data type. When a virtual method is declared in a descendant object type and a client program references this method with a pointer variable, the decision on which method to call (the ancestor's version or the descendant's version) is not made until run-time. The process of making this decision is called *binding* because its result is to tie (or bind) the calling statement to a specific method. If this decision is made at compile-time, it is referred to as *early binding*. If the decision is made at run-time, it is referred to as *late binding*.

Note that we have made destructor `Done` virtual too. Borland Pascal does not allow virtual constructors. There is a good reason for this. A constructor is called during object initialization, regardless of whether a pointer is involved or not. The type of the object or the object pointer must be known at compile-time. In the case of object pointers this may involve an explicit type-cast. Since the type is known at compile-time, there is never a need for constructors to be virtual. Once storage has been allocated for an object and initialized, its type is known. This is true even when object pointers are involved, so decisions about which method to call in an object hierarchy can be made at run-time. A destructor, on the other hand, is simply another method, and it may be virtual.

We have now defined the object hierarchy shown in Fig. 12.9. Objects `RealOperand` and `Operator` contain all of the data fields and methods that they inherit from `TreeData` plus their own constructors, their own versions

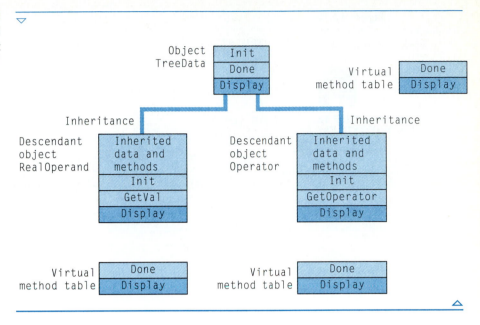

Figure 12.9
Object Hierarchy Defined
in New Unit
TreeDataADT

of the Display method, and methods for retrieving their own data fields. The presence of a virtual method in an object causes the compiler to set up a table location for each virtual method. Part of the constructor's initialization actions include storing in a table pointers to the methods that should be called for objects of that type. When the run-time system gets a call to a virtual method, it only has to determine the type of the object that made the call and execute the appropriate version of the method pointed to by the object's virtual method table.

The implementation of the methods for the object hierarchy defined in unit TreeDataADT is shown in Fig. 12.10. Since TreeData is an abstract object type, its methods have no code. We defined TreeData's methods to allow that every pointer to an instance of an object from this hierarchy can reference the three methods (Init, Done, Display), but in reality no instance of object TreeData is ever likely to be used in our binary expression tree (since TreeData nodes are neither operators nor operands). Notice that it is possible to add the methods for another descendant type IntegerOperand without needing to make any changes to any other previously defined methods. This is quite an improvement over our earlier implementation of TreeDataADT. In Section 12.5 we will develop a version of our binary expression tree ADT that uses our new TreeDataADT.

```
implementation

  constructor TreeData.Init;
  {
   Constructor for abstract tree node.
  }
  begin {Init};
  end; {Init}

  destructor TreeData.Done;
  {
   Provide clean-up services to descendants of type TreeData.
  }
  begin {Done}
  end; {Done}

  procedure TreeData.Display;
  {
   Abstract method for displaying tree node data contents.
  }
  begin {Display}
  end; {Display}

  constructor RealOperand.Init (Item {input} : Real);
  {
   Initialize real operand tree nodes.
   Pre : Item is defined.
   Post: Item stored as tree node data value.
  }
  begin {Init}
    OpVal := Item
  end; {Init}

  function RealOperand.GetVal : Real;
  {
   Returns value of real operand stored in tree node.
  }
  begin {GetVal}
    GetVal := OpVal
  end; {GetVal}

  procedure RealOperand.Display;
  {
   Displays value of real operand stored in tree node.
  }
  begin {Display}
    Write (OpVal :2:1);
  end; {Display}

  constructor Operator.Init (Item {input} : Char);
  {
```

▷ ▷ ▷ ▷ ▷ ▷

```
    Initialize operator tree nodes.
    Pre : Item is defined.
    Post: Item stored as tree node data value.
  }
  begin {Init}
    OpChar := Item
  end; {Init}

  function Operator.GetOperator : Char;
  {
    Returns operator character stored in tree node.
  }
  begin {GetOperator}
    GetOperator := OpChar
  end; {GetOperand}

  procedure Operator.Display;
  {
    Displays operator character stored in tree node.
  }
  begin {Display}
    Write (OpChar)
  end; {Display}
end. {TreeDataADT}
```

Exercises for Section 12.4 **Self-Check**

1. Explain the role of virtual methods in implementing polymorphism.
2. What are three disadvantages of using variant record types as a means of implementing the information portion of a binary expression tree node?

Programming

1. Write a unit ListData for a linked list object that is capable of housing nodes of types ApplicantPtr and EmployeePtr (Fig. 12.1).

12.5 Implementing Polymorphism

We have now developed all the tools that are needed to make use of polymorphism in a programming application. In this section we examine the changes that are needed to develop a binary expression tree that is capable of housing more than one type of data node. In our discussion we will consider only expression types having the two node types (RealOperand and Operator) that we discussed in Section 12.4. It would be very easy to extend our type hierarchy to include other node types as well.

Figure 12.11 contains the new interface section for unit `BinTreeADT`. The most significant change that we have made is the type of the `TreeNode` data field `TreeInfo` a pointer type (`TreeDataPtr`). This is necessary to allow the typecasting that is needed to implement polymorphism. Changing the type of `TreeInfo` requires us to make changes to several `BinTree` method headers. Any method header containing parameter `El` that is declared to be of type `TreeData` needs to be changed to parameter `ElPtr` of type `TreeDataPtr`. These are the only changes that are required in the interface section. We will not need to make changes like this again to allow for more node types in our binary expression tree.

Figure 12.11
New Interface Section for
Unit `BinTreeADT`

Directory: CHAP 12
File: BINTREEA.PAS

```pascal
unit BinTreeADT;
{
 Abstract data type BinTree: contains declarations for data
 type BinTree and its methods.
}
interface

  uses TreeDataADT;   {Import types a TreeData and TreeDataPtr}

  type
    TreePointer = ^TreeNode;
    TreeNode = record                        {a tree node}
                  TreeInfo : TreeDataPtr; {information part}
                  Left,
                  Right : TreePointer
                end; {TreeNode}

    ProcedureType = procedure (P : TreeDataPtr);

    BinTree = object                         {a binary tree}
                  procedure CreateTree;
                  function GetSize : Word;
                  function GetRoot : TreePointer;
                  function GetCursor : TreePointer;
                  function IsEmpty : Boolean;
                  procedure InsertAtRoot
                              (ElPtr {input} : TreeDataPtr;
                               var Success {output} : Boolean);
                  procedure InsertLeft
                              (ElPtr {input} : TreeDataPtr;
                               var Success {output} : Boolean);
                  procedure InsertRight
                              (ElPtr {input} : TreeDataPtr;
                               var Success {output} : Boolean);
                  procedure Retrieve
                              (var ElPtr {output} : TreeDataPtr;
                               var Success : Boolean);
```

▷ ▷ ▷ ▷ ▷

```
                procedure Replace (ElPtr {input} : TreeDataPtr;
                                   var Success : Boolean);
                procedure InitCursor (Ptr {input} : TreePointer);
                function HasLeftTree : Boolean;
                function HasRightTree : Boolean;
                procedure GoLeft;
                procedure GoRight;
                procedure InOrder (Visit : ProcedureType);

             private
                Root, Cursor : TreePointer;
                Size : Word;
                procedure DoInOrder (Next {input} : TreePointer;
                                     Visit : ProcedureType);

             end; {BinTree}
```

In the implementation section, each reference to `El` will need to be changed to `ElPtr` to reflect the fact that the method parameter name was changed. Changing the type of parameter `El` was essential to allow polymorphism. Changing the name of the parameter to `ElPtr` was done only to improve readability. If we added additional `TreeNode` descendants, we would not need to change `BinTreeADT` any more than we already have.

Figure 12.12 contains the interface section for our new unit `BinExpTreeADT`. The only change that is needed to the method declarations is the addition of a `Boolean` function method `IsOperator`. In Chapter 8, `IsOperator` was implemented as a method in `TreeDataADT`. We have implemented `IsOperator` as a `BinExpTree` method. The reason for this change is that we no longer need to store a `TreeNode` type code value in one of the `TreeData` object's data fields. If the node is a leaf node in a binary expression tree, it is an operand. If a node is not a leaf node in a binary expression tree, it is an operator.

Figure 12.12
New Interface Section for
Unit `BinExpTreeADT`

Directory: CHAP 12
File: BINEXPTR.PAS

```
unit BinExpTreeADT;
{
 Abstract data type BinExpTree: contains declarations for
 data type BinExpTree and its methods.
}
interface

   uses TreeDataADT, BinTreeADT; {Import object type TreeData}
```

```
type
  BinExpTree = object (BinTree) {descendant of binary tree}
                function Eval : Real;
                procedure InOrder (Visit : ProcedureType);
                function IsOperator
                            (Root : TreePointer) : Boolean;
               private
                procedure DoInOrder
                            (Root {input} : TreePointer;
                             Visit : ProcedureType);
                function DoEval (Root : TreePointer) : Real;
              end; {BinExpTree}
```

Figure 12.13 shows the new implementation section for unit `BinExpTree`. To implement method `BinExpTree.IsOperator`, we simply check to see whether the input node is a leaf node. A leaf node in a binary tree contains nil left and right pointers. In a binary expression tree, nonleaf nodes are operators. Since we have removed method `IsOperator` from object `TreeNode` and added it to object `BinExpTree`, we need to locate method calls of the form

`Root^.TreeInfo.IsOperator`

and replace them with method calls of the form

`IsOperator(Root)`

Methods `BinExpTree.DoInOrder` and `BinExpTree.DoEval` shown in Fig. 12.13 have been modified to reflect this change. We also need to make a change to method `BinExpTree.DoEval`. As shown in Fig. 12.13, the method call to `CurrentNode.GetEval` was replaced with a typecast. This was necessary to be able to return the correct result type for function `BinExpTree.DoEval`. The new return statement is

`DoEval := RealOperandPtr(CurrentNode)^.GetEval`

If we introduced an `IntegerOperand` object, this statement would need to be changed to get the correct version of `GetEval`.

Figure 12.14 contains a sample client program that builds, displays, and computes the value of the binary expression tree representing the expression

`(5 + 6)`

Observe how we use `New` with appropriate constructor calls to allocate storage for information to be housed in each tree node. As storage for each node is allocated, it is typecast as either an `Operator` or a `RealOperand` node. Each node is then placed in its correct position in the binary expression tree.

Figure 12.13
New Implementation
Section for Unit
BinExpTreeADT

```
implementation

  function BinExpTree.IsOperator
                        (Root : TreePointer) : Boolean;
  {
   Tests for operator tree node.
   Pre : Root is defined.
   Post: Returns True if Root does not point to expression
         tree leaf (operand) node and False if is does.
  }
  begin {IsOperator}
    IsOperator := (Root^.Left <> nil) and (Root^.Right <> nil)
  end; {IsOperator}

  procedure BinExpTree.DoInOrder (Root {input} : TreePointer;
                            Visit : ProcedureType);
  {
   Applies procedure Visit to each node in tree having root
   pointer Next.
   Pre : Tree initialized and Visit defined
   Post: Returns if Next is nil; otherwise, traverses left
         subtree, visits root to apply Visit, and traverses
         right subtree.
  }
  begin {DoInOrder}
    if Root <> nil then
      begin {recursive step}
        if IsOperator(Root) then
          Write ('(');
        DoInOrder (Root^.Left, Visit);  {Traverse left subtree}
        Visit(Root^.TreeInfo);          {Display root value}
        DoInOrder (Root^.Right, Visit); {Traverse right subtree}
        if IsOperator(Root) then
          Write (')')
      end {recursive step}
  end; {DoInOrder}

  procedure BinExpTree.InOrder (Visit : Proceduretype);
  {
   Applies procedure Visit to each tree element using an inorder
   traversal.
   Pre : Tree initialized; Visit defined in client program and
         compiled using Borland Pascal far code model.
   Post: Visit has been applied to each tree node.
  }
  begin {InOrder}
    DoInOrder (GetRoot, Visit)
  end; {InOrder}

  function BinExpTree.DoEval (Root : TreePointer) : Real;
  {
```

▷ ▷ ▷ ▷ ▷

```
   Computes value of expression stored in expression tree
   with root stored in Root.
   Pre : Binary expression tree is initialized.
   Post: If tree is empty returns 0.0. If CurrentNode is an
         operand the operand value is returned. If it is an
         operator, DoEval calls itself recursively to evaluate
         the left and right subtree of the tree whose root
         is stored in Root.
}
  var
    CurrentNode : TreeDataPtr;    {Point to current node data}
    LeftTreeVal,                  {Left subtree value}
    RightTreeVal : Real;          {Right subtree value}
    Success : Boolean;            {flag}

begin {DoEval}
  InitCursor (Root);                    {Set Cursor to tree root}
  Retrieve (CurrentNode, Success);      {Retrieve root data}
  if not Success then
    DoEval := 0.0                                {Tree is empty}
  else if not IsOperator(Root) then
    {Return operand's value}
    DoEval := RealOperandPtr(CurrentNode)^.GetVal
  else
    begin {operator}
      LeftTreeVal := DoEval(Root^.Left);
      RightTreeVal := DoEval(Root^.Right);
      {Determine which operator is stored in node}
      case OperatorPtr(CurrentNode)^.GetOperator of
        '+': DoEval := LeftTreeVal + RightTreeVal;
        '-' : DoEval := LeftTreeVal - RightTreeVal;
        '*' : DoEval := LeftTreeVal * RightTreeVal;
        '/' : DoEval := LeftTreeVal / RightTreeVal
      end {case}
    end {operator}
end; {DoEval}

function BinExpTree.Eval : Real;
{
 Computes value of expression stored in expression tree
 with root stored in Root.
 Pre : Binary expression tree is initialized.
 Post: If tree is empty returns 0.0. If CurrentNode is an
       operand the operand value is returned. If it is an
       operator, DoEval calls itself recursively to evaluate
       the left and right subtree of the tree whose root
       is stored in Root.
}
begin {Eval}
  Eval := DoEval(GetRoot)      {Start at tree root.}
end; {Eval}

end. {BinExpTreeADT}
```

Figure 12.14
Program UseBinExpTree

Directory: CHAP 12
File: USEBEXPT.PAS

```
program UseBinExpTree;
{
 Program builds a binary expression tree and displays the
 expression along with its value.
}
  uses TreeDataADT, BinTreeADT, BinExpTreeADT;

  var
    MyTree : BinExpTree;
    NextNode : TreeDataPtr;
    Success : Boolean;
    Result : Real;
    Next : TreePointer;

  procedure DisplayNodeInfo (InfoPtr {input} : TreeDataPtr); far;
  {
   Procedure to be applied to each list node by method
   BinTree.Traverse.
   Pre : InfoPtr is defined.
   Post: Display contents of one list node.
   Note: Parameter list must be compatible with declaration of
         ProcedureType in unit BinTreeADT.
  }
  begin {DisplayNodeInfo}
    InfoPtr^.Display
  end; {DisplayNodeInfo}

begin {UseBinExpTree}
  MyTree.CreateTree;

  {Insert operator at root}
  NextNode := New(OperatorPtr, Init ('+'));
  MyTree.InsertAtRoot (NextNode, Success);

  {Insert two operands as leaf nodes}
  MyTree.InitCursor (MyTree.GetRoot);
  Next := MyTree.GetCursor;
  NextNode := New(RealOperandPtr, Init (5.0));
  MyTree.InsertLeft (NextNode, Success);
  MyTree.InitCursor (Next);
  NextNode := New(RealOperandPTR, Init (6.0));
  MyTree.InsertRight (NextNode, Success);

  MyTree.InOrder (DisplayNodeInfo);           {display expression}

  Result := MyTree.Eval;                       {evaluate expression}
  WriteLn (' value is ', Result :3:2)
end. {UseBinExpTree}
```

It would be desirable to devise a method that was capable of building an expression tree automatically. We described one such method in Programming Project 5 at the end of Chapter 8. The important point to observe is that we have now built a basic framework to allow easier addition of new node types to our `BinTreeExpADT`. Reuse and extension of existing objects are one very important area of software development in which polymorphism is especially useful.

Exercises for Section 12.5 *Self-Check*

1. What changes need to be made to `BinTreeADT` and `BinaryExpADT` to allow nodes of both `RealOperand` and `IntegerOperand` in the same expression tree?
2. What changes need to be made to our `SearchTreeADT` to accommodate nodes containing `Applicant` or `Employee` information? Do we need to make changes to our new `BinTreeADT` (Fig. 12.14)?

Programming

1. Implement `IntegerOperand` as an object type descended from the object type `TreeData`.

12.6 Common Programming Errors

Many of the errors that programmers make when they work with objects come from incorrect use of pointer variables or failing to use constructors to initialize instances of object types. For example, using the assignment operator to copy object instances does not work properly unless both variables have been initialized as shown:

```
A.Init;
B.Init;
A := B;
```

When working with object types having virtual methods, you must use constructors to initialize instances of these types or any of their descendants. Constructors may not contain calls to virtual methods. It is likewise important to use destructors to reclaim any storage that is used by dynamic objects.

You should always define methods to manipulate object fields and avoid manipulating fields directly in a client program. Remember that typecasts may be necessary to access fields that are not declared locally by instances of descendant object types.

CHAPTER REVIEW

In this chapter we discussed polymorphism and object-oriented programming in Borland Pascal. We demonstrated how to implement polymorphism in Borland Pascal using typecasting, object pointers, virtual methods, and inheritance. We showed how objects could be used to implement a binary expression tree with more than one type of data node.

Quick-Check Exercises

1. Why are virtual methods needed to implement polymorphism?
2. What does a descendant object inherit from its ancestor?
3. What is operator polymorphism?
4. Object pointers cannot be typecast into one another. True or false?
5. Variable typecasts are allowed only between dynamic objects. True or false?
6. Late binding is essential in all object-oriented languages to be able to implement polymorphism. True or false?
7. What is an abstract object type?

Answers to Quick-Check Exercises

1. So that the decision as to which method is needed can be deferred until runtime when the object type is known.
2. The ancestor's fields and methods
3. The ability of an operator to base its response on the data types of its operands
4. False
5. False
6. True
7. An object type that is placed at the root of an object hierarchy to ensure type compatibility of its descendants

Review Questions

1. Describe the differences in the effects of a constructor method and a destructor method.
2. Explain how polymorphism can reduce the effort that is required to do software maintenance.
3. List the steps that are required to implement a polymorphic Display method for a set of related objects.
4. Explain why constructors do not ever need to be declared as virtual methods.
5. What happens when the variables involved in a typecasting operation are of different sizes?
6. Modify unit `TreeDataADT` so that it may be used in a binary search tree that houses `Applicants`, `Employees`, and `ExEmployees`.
7. Modify unit `SearchTreeADT` to allow it to use the version of `TreeDataADT` that you wrote for Review Question 6.

Directory: CHAP 12
File: PROJ12_1.PAS

Programming Projects

1. Complete the implementation of unit `BinExpTreeADT` discussed in Section 12.5. Write a method that stores an infix expression containing either integer or real operands in a binary search tree.

2. Modify our `ListDataADT` and `LinkListADT` unit so that they can be used by a client program to maintain and display a list of `Figure` type objects (see Chapter 3).

3. Implement a stack object type that can be used by client programs to house operators while converting infix expressions to postfix or operands in evaluating postfix expressions. Test your implementation by using the case study programs in Sections 5.3 and Section 5.5.

Directory: CHAP 12
File: PROJ12_4.PAS

4. Modify `HeapSort` from Chapter 11 so that it can sort an array of pointers to objects of types `Applicant`, `Employee`, and `ExEmployee` using `Name` as the key field.

5. Implement an object hierarchy for office supplies that contains polymorphic methods for reading and displaying objects of each descendant type. The supply objects consist of paper, ribbons, and labels. For paper the information stored is number of sheets per box, sheet length, and sheet width. For ribbons the information stored is width and color. For labels the information stored is number per box. Write a menu-driven program for maintaining a linked list of supply type items.

Directory: CHAP 12
File: PROJ12_5.PAS

A P P E N D I X   A

Borland's Turbo Pascal Integrated Environment

Borland's integrated Pascal development environment for MS-DOS (Microsoft Disk Operating System) is known as Turbo Pascal. In this appendix, we discuss the Turbo Pascal 7.0 programming environment.

All of the programs in the book will also run if you use Turbo Pascal with Microsoft Windows. However, you must insert the line

```
uses WinCrt;
```

just after the program statement.

A.1   The Turbo Pascal Integrated Environment

All Main menu items have menus of their own from which you can choose other tasks to perform or make changes in the way Turbo Pascal will compile your programs and link together previously compiled units. If a menu item is followed by ellipses (. . .), then choosing that item causes a dialog box to be displayed. Choosing an item followed by an arrowhead causes another menu to pop up. Unmarked commands are performed as soon as they are selected. Each Main menu item is described below.

The **File menu** provides the user with DOS file manipulation capabilities.

New Creates a new file in a new Edit window.

Open... Opens an existing file in an Edit window.

Save Saves the file displayed in the active Edit window.

Save as... Saves file in the active window using a new filename.

Save all Saves all modified files.

Change dir... Chooses new default directory.

Print Prints contents of active Edit window on system printer.

Printer setup... Chooses printer filter to use for printing.

DOS shell Exits to DOS. Type **exit** at DOS prompt to return.

Exit Exits Turbo Pascal.

The **Edit menu** undoes mistakes and manages the Clipboard.

Edit	
Undo	Alt-BkSp
Redo	
Cut	Shift-Del
Copy	Ctrl-Ins
Paste	Shift-Ins
Clear	Ctrl-Del
Show clipboard	

Undo   Undoes previous editor operation.

Redo   Redoes previous undone editor operation.

Cut   Moves selected block of text from Edit window to Clipboard.

Copy   Copies selected text from Edit window to Clipboard.

Paste   Moves selected text from Clipboard to Edit window.

Clear   Deletes selected text from Edit window or Clipboard.

Show Clipboard   Opens Clipboard window and makes it active.

The **Search menu** handles searching operations during editing.

Search	
Find...	
Replace...	
Search again	
Go to line number...	
Show last compiler error	
Find error...	
Find procedure...	

Find...   Allows user to search for text string in active Edit window.

Replace...   Allows user to search for and replace a text string.

Search again   Repeats last Find or Replace operation.

Go to line number...   Moves cursor to a specified line number.

Show last compiler error   Moves cursor to position of last error.

Find error...   Moves cursor to position of last run-time error.

Find procedure...   Searches for procedure or function header.

The **Run menu** manages program execution.

Run	
Run	Ctrl-F9
Step over	F8
Trace into	F7
Go to cursor	F4
Program reset	Ctrl-F2
Parameters...	

Run   Executes the current program.

Step over   Executes next statement stepping over functions and procedures.

Trace into   Executes next statement.

Go to cursor   Executes program, stops at Edit cursor position.

Program reset   Restarts debugging session, releases all program resources.

Parameters...   Sets command-line parameters passed to program.

The **Compile menu** handles program and unit compilation.

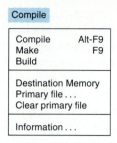

Compile   Compiles source file displayed in active Edit window.

Make   Compiles files that have been modified since last compile.

Build   Recompiles source file and all imported files.

Destination   Specifies whether source file is compiled to memory or disk.

Primary file...   Specifies file that is focus of Make and Build.

Clear primary file   Clears previously set primary file.

Information...   Displays status of program and system memory usage.

The **Debug menu** manages program debugging facilities.

Debug	
Breakpoints	
Call stack	Ctrl-F3
Register	
Watch	
Output	
User screen	Alt-F5
Evaluate/modify...	Ctrl-F4
Add watch...	Ctrl-F7
Add breakpoint...	

Breakpoints   Allows user to set, view, and edit breakpoints.

Call stack   Displays active subprogram calls.

Register   Opens the Register window.

Watch   Opens the Watch window.

Output   Opens the Output window.

User screen   Switches to full-screen user output.

Evaluate/modify...   Allows expression evaluation or variable modification.

Add watch...   Inserts a watch expression into the Watch window.

Add breakpoint...   Adds a program breakpoint.

The **Tools menu** allows user to run utility programs.

Tools	
Messages	
Track next	Alt-F8
Track previous	Alt-F7
Grep	Shift-F2
Turbo Assembler	Shift-F3
Turbo Debugger	Shift-F4
Turbo Profiler	Shift-F5

Messages   Opens the tool Message window.

Track next   Go to next line.

Track previous   Go to previous line.

Grep

Turbo Assembler

Turbo Debugger   } User-installed tools.

Turbo Profiler

The **Options menu** allows user to set integrated environment controls.

Options

Compiler...
Memory sizes...
Linker...
Debugger...
Directories...
Tools...

Environment ▶

Open...
Save
Save as...

`Compiler...` Allows user to set compiler directive defaults.

`Memory sizes...` Allows user to specify default stack and heap sizes for compiled programs.

`Linker...` Allows user to set linker options.

`Debugger...` Allows user to set debugger options.

`Directories...` Allows user to specify paths for units, include files, and object files.

`Tools...` Allows user to create or change tool menu entries.

`Environment` Allows user to change editor, mouse, and color.

`Open...` Loads previously saved options file.

`Save...` Saves current options settings in an options file.

`Save as...` Saves current options settings under new filename.

The **Window menu** provides window management capabilities from keyboard.

Window

Tile
Cascade
Close all
Refresh display

Size/Move   Ctrl-F5
Zoom   F5
Next   F6
Previous   Shift-F6
Close   Alt-F3

List...   Alt-0

`Tile` Arranges desktop windows so they do not overlap.

`Cascade` Arranges desktop windows so they do overlap.

`Close all` Closes all windows and clears all history lists.

`Refresh display` Redraws the desktop.

`Size/Move` Changes size or position of window.

`Zoom` Switches from full-screen to reduced window sizes.

`Next` Makes next window the active window.

`Previous` Makes the previously active window the active window.

`Close` Closes the active window.

`List...` Shows a list of all active windows.

The **Help menu** manages the online Help system.

Help

Contents
Index   Shift-F1
Topic search   Ctrl-F1
Previous topic   Alt-F1
Using help
Files...

Compiler directives
Reserved words
Standard units
Turbo Pascal Language
Error messages

About...

`Contents` Displays table of contents for online Help.

`Index` Displays index for online Help.

`Topic search` Allows user to select a topic for online Help.

`Previous topic` Redisplays last-viewed Help screen.

`Using help` Instructions on how to use online Help.

`Files...` Adds or deletes installed Help files.

`Compiler directives` Display help on compiler directives.

`Reserved words` Displays reserved words.

Standard units   Displays list of Turbo Pascal
   units.
Turbo Pascal Language   Shows help on Turbo
   Pascal Language.
Error messages   Displays error message help.
About...   Shows Turbo Pascal version and copy-
   right information.

The Edit Local Menu

There is one additional menu in the Turbo Pascal integrated environment called the Edit Local menu. This menu is displayed any time the mouse cursor is inside an Edit window and the right mouse button is clicked. The menu items are described below.

Cut	Shift-Del
Copy	Ctrl-Ins
Paste	Shift-Ins
Clear	Ctrl-Del
Open file at cursor	
Topic Search	Ctrl-F1
Toggle breakpoint	Ctrl-F8
Go to cursor	F4
Evaluate/modify...	Ctrl-F4
Add watch...	Ctrl-F7
Options...	

Cut   Moves selected block of text from Edit window to Clipboard.

Copy   Copies selected block of text from Edit window to Clipboard.

Paste   Copies selected text from Clipboard to Edit window.

Clear   Deletes selected text from Edit window or Clipboard.

Open file at cursor   Opens the file indicated by the Edit cursor.

Topic Search   Displays Help for topic under Edit cursor.

Toggle breakpoint   Enables or disables breakpoint at Edit cursor.

Go to cursor   Executes program, stops at Edit cursor position.

Evaluate/modify...   Evaluates an expression or modifies a variable.

Add watch...   Inserts a watch expression in the Watch window.

Options...   Allows user to specify editor option settings.

A.2 Windows and Dialog Boxes

The Turbo Pascal integrated environment makes extensive use of windows and dialog boxes in its user interface. Windows are screen areas that can be moved, resized, overlapped, opened, and closed. Dialog boxes are movable screen areas that contain fields that allow options to be viewed and set. Unlike windows, which remain on the desktop even when they are not active, dialog boxes are usually removed from the desktop once their options have been set.

Figure A.1
A Typical Window

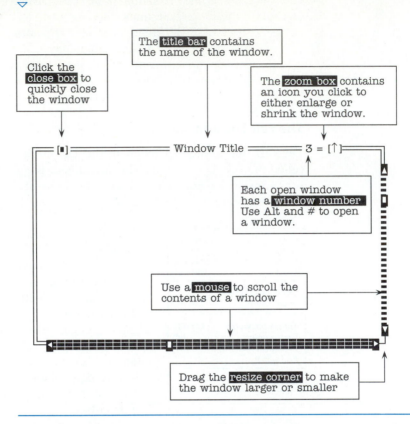

Windows

Turbo Pascal uses several types of windows. Most have the features shown in Fig. A.1. Edit windows are opened by the Open or New command in the File menu. Many other windows are opened by a Window menu command. You can have a number of windows open in the Turbo Pascal environment, but only one window is active at any one time. Most menu commands apply only to the active window. Turbo Pascal places a double-lined border around the active window. To activate a window, place your mouse cursor on the window and click the left button, or press the F6 key (Next window) repeatedly until the doubled-lined border appears around the window, or hold down the Alt key and type the number of the window (e.g., press Alt-3 for window 3).

To close the active window, press Alt-F3 or position your mouse cursor on the window's close box and click the left mouse button. To change the size of the window or its location, use the Window menu Size/Move command or your mouse. To move a window, position the mouse cursor on the window title bar and drag it (click and then hold the left mouse button while you move the mouse cursor) to the desired desktop position. The window will follow the mouse cursor. To resize a window, position the mouse cursor on the lower right corner and drag the corner until the window becomes the desired size.

If a window has been resized, you can expand it to occupy the full screen by pressing the F5 key. Pressing the F5 key a second time shrinks the window back to its reduced size. You can also achieve the same effect by positioning your mouse cursor on the zoom box and clicking the left button.

You can scroll the text that appears inside a window horizontally or vertically by using the appropriate scroll bars on the sides of the window. Position the mouse cursor on one of the scroll bar arrowheads and press and hold the left button to scroll the window in the desired direction. You can also position the mouse cursor on the scroll bar box, press the left button, and drag it to some other point in the scroll bar. The text will be quickly positioned to that relative point in the window. If you do not have a mouse, use the cursor arrow keys to scroll the window text.

Dialog Boxes

A dialog box provides a convenient means of viewing and setting multiple command options. A typical dialog box appears in Fig. A.2. Five basic types of controls may be present in a dialog box: radio buttons, check boxes, action buttons, input field boxes, and list boxes.

You can mark as many check boxes as you want in a dialog box. An X will appear when you activate a check box. You can mark only one radio button active in each group of radio buttons shown in a dialog box. To change the activation status of either a check box or a radio button, position the mouse cursor over the box or button and click the left mouse button. If you are not using a mouse, use the Tab key to select the desired check box or radio button and then press the Spacebar.

Figure A.2
Typical Turbo Pascal
Dialog Box

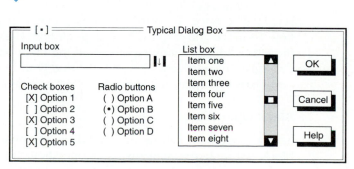

Action buttons are activated either by using your mouse or by using the Tab and Enter keys. The dialog box shown in Fig. A.2 has three action buttons: `OK`, `Cancel`, and `Help`. If you activate `OK`, the dialog box is closed and the command is executed. If you activate `Cancel` (or press the Esc key), the dialog box is closed and the command is not executed. Activating the Help button causes temporary exit to an appropriate Help screen.

Input field boxes require you to enter the appropriate text from the keyboard. If a box containing an arrow follows the input field box, a history list is associated with the input field. To access the history list, use your mouse and click on the arrow box or use the Down arrow key. You can use text that appears on the history list as your entry to the input field by using your mouse or the cursor keys to highlight and select the desired text. You can edit history list items before you make a selection.

You can make selections from a list box by using your mouse and the scroll bar or by using the cursor keys to highlight the desired item. Use the Enter key or the left mouse button to select the highlighted item.

A.3   Using the Turbo Pascal Editor

The Turbo Pascal editor is invoked when you open an Edit window. Turbo Pascal 7.0 allows you to have several Edit windows displayed on the desktop at once. The editor allows you to create new programs or to change existing ones. The editor uses special commands for moving the cursor in the Edit window, inserting text, deleting text, and searching for text. These commands are shown in Fig. A.3.

You can press one of the four arrow keys to move the Edit cursor. You can also position the Edit cursor by moving the mouse cursor to the desired character and clicking the left mouse button. Several additional commands are available to facilitate faster and more convenient movement in the Edit window. Pressing the Home key moves the cursor to column 1 of the current line. Pressing the End key moves the cursor to the last position in the current line. Typing Ctrl-Home or Ctrl-End moves the cursor to the top or bottom, respectively, of the Edit window.

As a program file grows larger, it may become too big to appear on the screen all at once. To move back to a previous page of text, press the PgUp key. To move ahead to the next page of text, press the PgDn key. To move the cursor to the beginning or end of the file, you would type Ctrl-PgUp or Ctrl-PgDn, respectively. You can also use your mouse and the Edit window scroll bars to display any portion of your program.

Block Operations

Several operations can be performed on an entire section of a file, called a block. Before performing any block operation, you must first designate a particular section of your program or file as a block. To use your mouse to mark

Figure A.3
Turbo Pascal Editor
Commands

▽

Cursor Movements

Character left	←	or	^S
Character right	→	or	^D
Word left	^←	or	^A
Word right	^→	or	^F
Line up	↑	or	^E
Line down	↓	or	^X
Scroll up	^W		
Scroll down	^Z		
Page up	PgUp	or	^R
Page down	PgDn	or	^C
To beginning of line	Home	or	^QS
To end of line	End	or	^QD
To top of window	^Home	or	^QE
To bottom of window	^End	or	^QX
To top of file	^PgUp	or	^QR
To end of file	^PgDn	or	^QC
To beginning of block	^QB		
To end of block	^QK		
To last cursor position	^QP		
To last error position	^QW		

Insert and Delete

Inset mode on/off	Ins	or	^V
Insert line	^N		
Insert compiler directives	^OO		
Delete line	^Y		
Delete to end of line	^QY		
Delete word right of cursor	^T		
Delete char under cursor	Del	or	^G
Delete char left of cursor	BkSp	or	^H

Block Commands

Mark block	Shift-arrow (↑, ↓, →, ←)
Mark block begin	^KB
Mark block end	^KK

Mark single word	^KT
Mark single line	^KL
Hide/display block	^KH
Copy block	^KC
Move block	^KV
Delete block	^KY	or	^Del
Read block from disk	^KR
Write block to disk	^KW
Cut to clipboard	Shift-Del
Copy to clipboard	^Ins
Paste from clipboard	Shift-Ins
Print block	^KP
Block indent	^KI
Block unindent	^KU

Miscellaneous Editing Commands

Abort operation	Esc
Autoindent on/off	^OI
Control char prefix	^P
Pair braces forward	^Q[
Pair braces backward	^Q]
Find	^QF
Find and replace	^QA
Find place marker	^Qn
Repeat last search	^L
Restore line	^QL
Save and edit	F2
Set place marker	^Kn
Tab	Tab	or	^I
Tab mode	^OT
Language help	^F1
Invoke Main menu	F10
Load file	F3
Optimal fill on/off	^OF
Unindent on/off	^OU
Close window	Alt-F3

Note: ^ means to hold the Ctrl key prior to typing the next key; n means any integer number.

△

a block of text, click the left button and drag the mouse cursor over the desired text. Release the left button when the entire block appears in inverse video.

Using the Clipboard

You can use the Edit menu to copy and move blocks of text. You do this by marking the desired block of text and then copying the marked block of text to the clipboard, using the `Copy` command from the Edit menu. Next, you position the Edit cursor at the location in the active window where the clipboard text is to be copied. Now you can copy the clipboard text by using the `Paste` command from the Edit menu.

Reserved Words, Standard Identifiers, Operators, Units, Functions, Procedures, and Compiler Directives

Reserved Words and Standard Directives

Reserved words are integral parts of Borland Pascal. They cannot be redefined and must not be declared as user-defined identifiers.

and	exports	mod	shr
asm	file	nil	string
array	for	not	then
begin	function	object	to
case	goto	of	type
const	if	or	unit
constructor	implementation	packed	until
destructor	in	procedure	uses
div	inherited	program	var
do	inline	record	while
downto	interface	repeat	with
else	label	set	xor
end	library	shl	

The following are Borland Pascal's standard directives. Unlike reserved words, you may redefine them, but we do not advise this.

absolute	far	near	virtual
assembler	forward	private	
external	interrupt	public	

private and public act as reserved words within object type declarations, but are otherwise treated as directives.

Selected Standard Identifiers

Borland Pascal defines a number of standard identifiers for predefined types, constants, variables, procedures, and functions. Any standard identifier may be redefined but it will mean loss of the facility offered by that identifier and may lead to confusion.

Units
  Crt, Dos, Graph, Overlay, Printer, System

Constants
  False, True, MaxInt, MaxLongInt

Types
  Boolean, Char, Text, Integer, ShortInt, LongInt, Byte,
  Word, Real, Single, Double, Extended, Comp

Files
  Input, Output

Functions
  Abs, ArcTan, Chr, Cos, Concat, Copy, EOF, EOLN, Exp,
  FileSize, Frac, Int, IOResult, Ln, Length, Odd, Ord, Pi, Pos,
  Pred, Random, Round, Sin, Sqr, Sqrt, Succ, Trunc, Upcase

Procedures
  Assign, Close, Delete, Dispose, Erase, Exit, Halt, Insert,
  New, Randomize, Read, ReadLn, Reset, Rewrite, Seek, Str,
  Val, Write, WriteLn

Operators

Table B.1 summarizes all the operators of Borland Pascal. The operators are grouped in order of descending precedence. If the Operand Type and Result Type columns contain Integer, Real, the result type is Real unless both operands are integers. *Scalar types* are all ordinal and Real data types.

Table B.1
Table of Operators

Operator	Operation	Operand Type(s)	Result Type
+ unary	Sign identity	Integer, Real	Same as operand
– unary	Sign inversion	Integer, Real	Same as operand
@	Operand address	Variable reference or procedure or function identifier	Pointer
not	Negation	Integer, Boolean	Same as operand
*	Multiplication	Integer, Real	Integer, Real
	Set intersection	Any set type	Same as operand
/	Division	Integer, Real	Real
div	Integer division	Integer	Integer
mod	Modulus (remainder)	Integer	Integer
and	Arithmetical and	Integer	Integer
	Logical and	Boolean	Boolean
shl	Shift left	Integer	Integer
shr	Shift right	Integer	Integer
+	Addition	Integer, Real	Integer, Real
	Concatenation	string or Char	string
	Set union	Any set type	Same as operand

−	Subtraction	`Integer, Real`	`Integer, Real`
	Set difference	Any set type	Same as operand
`or`	Arithmetical or	`Integer`	`Integer`
	Logical or	`Boolean`	`Boolean`
`xor`	Arithmetical xor	`Integer`	`Integer`
	Logical xor	`Boolean`	`Boolean`
`=`	Equality	Any scalar type	`Boolean`
		`string`	`Boolean`
		Any set type	`Boolean`
		Any pointer type	`Boolean`
`<>`	Inequality	Any scalar type	`Boolean`
		`string`	`Boolean`
		Any set type	`Boolean`
		Any pointer type	`Boolean`
`>=`	Set inclusion	Any set type	`Boolean`
	Greater than or equal	Any scalar type	`Boolean`
		`string`	`Boolean`
`<=`	Set inclusion	Any set type	`Boolean`
	Less than or equal	Any scalar type	`Boolean`
		`string`	`Boolean`
`>`	Greater than	Any scalar type	`Boolean`
		`string`	`Boolean`
`<`	Less than	Any scalar type	`Boolean`
		`string`	`Boolean`
`in`	Set membership	The first operand may be of any ordinal type, the second must be a set of elements of that type.	`Boolean`

Units

Borland Pascal is distributed with several predefined units, similar to those that you might define yourself, containing a large number of additional constants, types, functions, and procedures. Some of these predefined units are described in Table B.2. All but the `Graph` unit are stored in the file `TURBO.TPL`. The details of the contents of each unit are described in the *Borland Pascal Reference Guide* and also in the on-line help facility provided in the Borland Pascal integrated environment.

Unit	Description
`Crt`	Contains routines that allow you full control over the PC's screen display, keyboard, and sound
`Dos`	Supports several DOS functions, including date-and-time control, directory search, and program execution

Graph	Stored in the file GRAPH.TPU, contains a library of 50 graphics routines and device-independent graphics support for several display devices
Overlay	Contains the Borland Pascal unit overlay management routines, which allow units to be swapped between main memory and disk storage during program execution
Printer	Provides easy access to a printer connected to your computer system by declaring a Text file Lst and associating it with the DOS device LPT1
System	Contains run-time support routines for all standard identifiers and is used automatically by any program or unit, without requiring a reference in a uses statement

Functions

Some of the predefined functions of Borland Pascal appear in Table B.3. The functions following the dotted line are not part of standard Pascal.

Function	Returns
Abs(num)	Integer or real absolute value of its integer or real argument.
ArcTan(num)	Angle whose tangent is num. The result is expressed in radians.
Chr(num)	Character with ordinal number corresponding to the integer num.
Cos(num)	Cosine of real angle num, expressed in radians.
EOF(fil)	Boolean value indicating end of file status of file variable fil.
EOLN(fil)	Boolean value indicating end of line status of Text file fil.
Exp(num)	Value of e (2.71828) raised to the power indicated by its real argument.
Ln(num)	Logarithm base e of its real argument.
Odd(num)	True if its integer argument is an odd number; False if not.
Ord(ordinal)	Ordinal number corresponding to its ordinal type argument.
Pred(ordinal)	Predecessor of its ordinal type argument.
Round(num)	Closest integer to its real argument.
Sin(num)	Sine of real angle num, expressed in radians.
Sqr(num)	Square of its integer or real argument.
Sqrt(num)	Real number representing the positive square root of its integer or real argument.
Succ(ordinal)	Successor of its ordinal type argument.
Trunc(num)	Integer part of its real argument.

Table B.3 Table of Functions (*Cont.*)	

`Concat(st1, st2,...,stN)`	String formed by concatenating its argument strings in the order in which they appear.
`Copy(st, pos, num)`	Substring of `st` starting at position `pos` and consisting of `num` characters.
`FileSize(fil)`	Number of components contained in its file argument.
`Frac(num)`	Fractional part of its real argument `num`.
`High(arg)`	If argument is an open array, returns the largest subscript value relative to 0 as the smallest subscript. If argument is an ordinal type, returns the largest value for that type.
`Int(num)`	Real number representing the whole number part of its real argument.
`IOResult`	Number of input/output error (returns 0 if no input/output error has occurred since previous call).
`Length(st)`	Number of characters in its string argument `st`.
`Low(arg)`	Returns the smallest value for its ordinal type argument.
`New(ptype, constructor)`	A pointer to object storage is allocated on the heap.
`Pi`	Approximation to `Pi` (3.1415926536).
`Pos(subst, st)`	Starting position in `st` of first occurrence of the string contained in `subst` (returns 0 if `subst` does not appear in `st`).
`Random or Random(int)`	Real random number between 0.0 and 1.0 if no argument given; if integer argument is given, returns random integer greater than or equal to 0 and less than `int`. The procedure `Randomize` should be called prior to the first reference to `Random`.
`UpCase(ch)`	Uppercase equivalent of `Char` argument `ch`, if one exists.

Procedures

Some of the predefined procedures of Borland Pascal appear in Table B.4. The procedures following the dotted line are not part of standard Pascal.

Table B.4 Table of Procedures	

Procedure	**Effect**
`Dispose (p)`	Returns dynamic storage pointed to by pointer variable p to heap.
`New (p)`	Creates new dynamic variable and sets pointer variable p to point to its memory location.
`Read (f, variables)`	Reads data from file f to satisfy the list variables. If f is not a `Text` file, only one component can

Procedure	Description
	be read at a time. If f is not specified, data are read from file Input (the keyboard).
ReadLn (f, variables)	Reads data from Text file f to satisfy the list of variables; skips any characters at the end of the last line read.
Reset (f)	Opens file f for input and sets the file-position pointer to the beginning.
Rewrite (f)	Prepares file f for output and sets the file-position pointer to the beginning. Prior file contents are lost.
Write (f, outputs)	Writes data in the order specified by outputs to file f. If f is not a Text file, only one component may be written at a time. If f is not specified, data are written to Output (the screen).
WriteLn (f, outputs)	Writes data in order specified by outputs to Text file f; writes end-of-line marker after the data.
Assign (f, st)	Assigns name of external file contained in the string expression st to file variable f.
Close (f)	Closes file f.
Delete (st, pos, num)	Removes substring of string st starting at position pos and consisting of num characters.
Dispose (p, destructor);	If called with a destructor as second argument, Dispose can be used to return object storage to heap.
Erase (f)	Erases external file associated with file variable f from disk.
Exit	Halts execution of current block and returns control to the calling block.
Halt	Stops program execution and returns control to the operating system.
Insert (obj, targ, pos)	Inserts string obj into string targ starting at position pos in targ.
New (p, constructor)	If called with a constructor as second argument, New can be used to allocate and initialize heap storage for an object.
Randomize	Initializes the built-in random-number generator with a random value derived from the system clock.
Seek (f, recnum)	Moves file-position pointer for file f to component number indicated by LongInt argument recnum.
Str (numval, st)	Converts numeric value of numval to string stored in st. Form of st is specified by format part of numval.
Val (st, num, code)	If successful, converts string st to an integer or real value as determined by the type of num and code is set to 0. If not successful, code will be set to the position of first offending character in st.

Compiler Directives

A Borland Pascal compiler directive consists of an opening curly brace ({) followed by a dollar sign, followed by the option name (one or more letters), followed by the option value (+ or –) or parameters affecting the compilation of the program or unit, and is terminated by a closing curly brace (}). Spaces are not allowed before a dollar sign or between the option name and option value. At least one space must separate the option name from a parameter. Examples of several compiler directives appear below.

```
{$B-}
{$R+}
{$B-, $R+, $D-}        {3 compiler directives}
```

A plus sign as the value of a compiler option enables it (makes it active), and a minus sign value disables the option (makes it passive). The compiler directive

```
{$I INCLUDE.PAS}
```

includes the source code from file `INCLUDE.PAS` during compilation.

Table B.5
Compiler Option
Directives

Directive	Default	Effect
Align Data	{$A+}	Align variables on word boundaries.
Boolean Evaluation	{$B-}	Use short-circuit evaluation of Boolean expressions.
Debug Information	{$D+}	Generate debug information during compilation. Usually used with {$L+}.
Emulation	{$E+}	Links floating-point run-time library, which emulates the 80x87 numeric coprocessor.
Force Far Call	{$F-}	Allow Turbo Pascal to choose near or far call model for function and procedure calls, based on program context.
Generate 286 Instructions	{$G-}	Do not use any special 80286 processor instructions during code generation.
Input/Output Checking	{$I+}	Enables automatic generation of code to check the result of an input/output procedure call.
Local Symbol Information	{$L+}	Generate local symbol information during compilation. Must be used with {$D+}.
Numeric Processing	{$N-}	Perform all real-type calculations by calling the TP run-time library routines and not the actual 80x87 routines.
Overlay Code Generation	{$O-}	Disables overlay code generation.
Open Parameters	{$P-}	Disallows use of open string or array as declarations for function or procedure formal parameters.

Overflow Checking	{$Q-}	Disables generation of code to check for integer overflow during arithmetic operations. {$Q+} is often used with {$R+}.
Range Checking	{$R-}	Disables generation of code to check for range-checking and object initialization violations.
Stack-Overflow Checking	{$S+}	Enables generation of code at beginning of each procedure or function, which checks for enough stack space to meet local data needs of subprogram.
Typed @ Operator	{$T-}	Disables pointer type checking for @ result value.
Var-String Checking	{$V+}	Enables strict type checking for string variables passed to var parameters.
Extended Syntax	{$X+}	Enables support for special Turbo Pascal function and string capabilities.
Symbol Reference Information	{$Y+}	Enables generation of symbol reference information.

Borland Pascal Syntax Diagrams

program

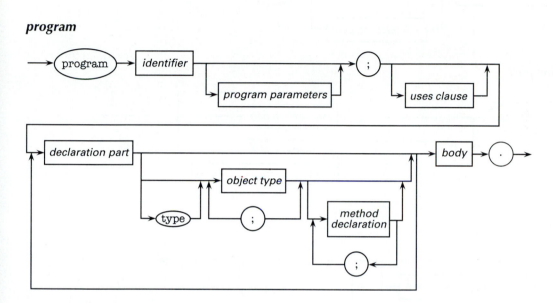

program parameters

body

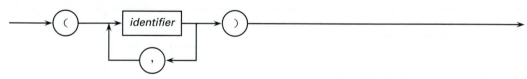

uses clause

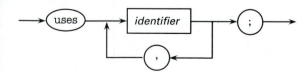

unit

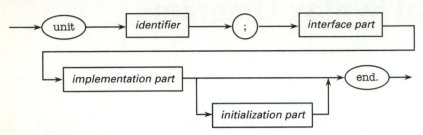

implementation part

interface part

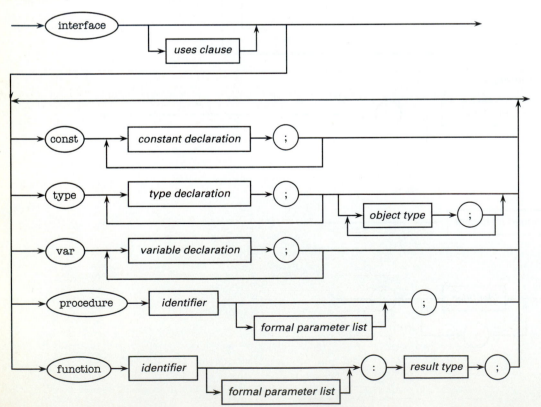

initialization part

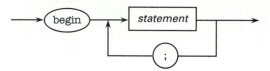

declaration part

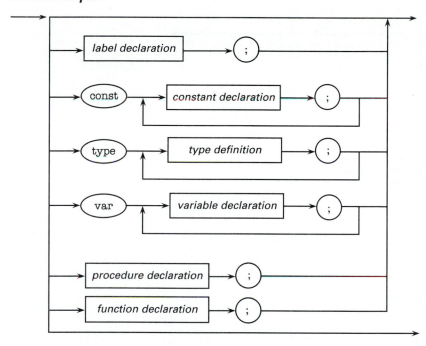

label declaration

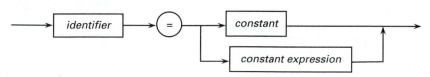

constant definition

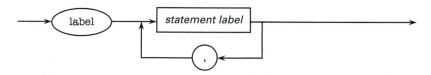

type definition

variable declaration

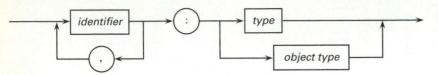

statement label

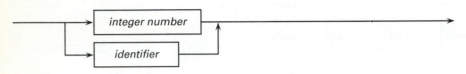

constant

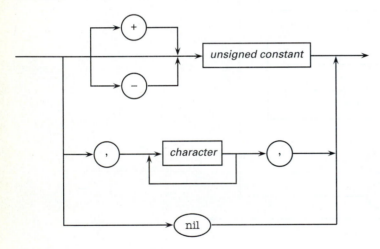

unsigned constant

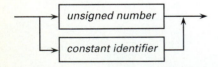

identifier

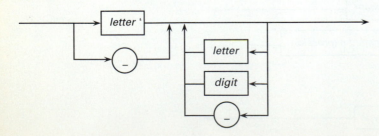

function declaration

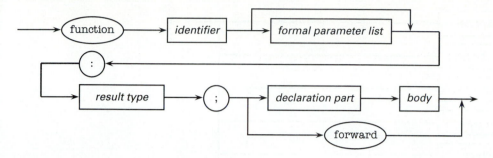

result type

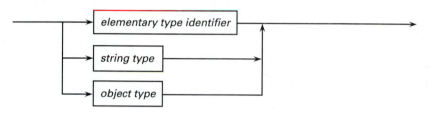

procedure declaration

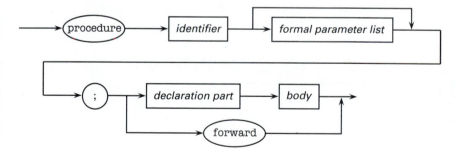

formal parameter list

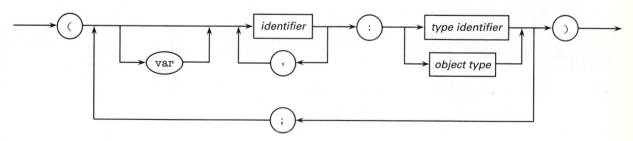

type

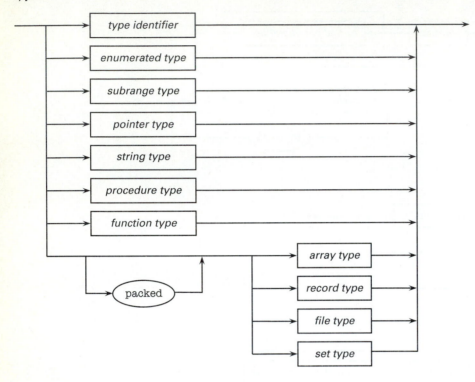

enumerated type

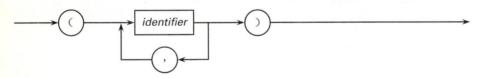

subrange type

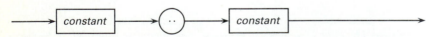

string type

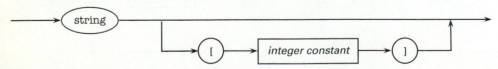

procedure type

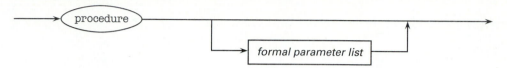

function type

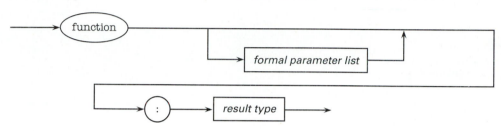

array type

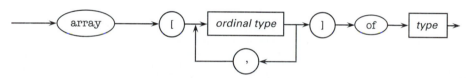

record type

field list

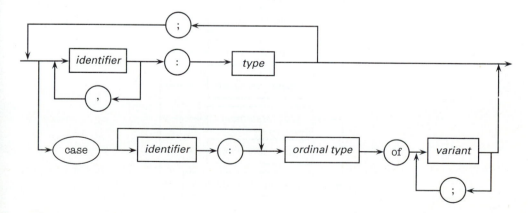

variant

file type

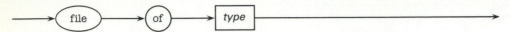

set type

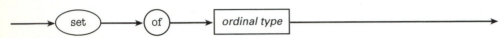

compound statement

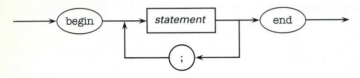

statement

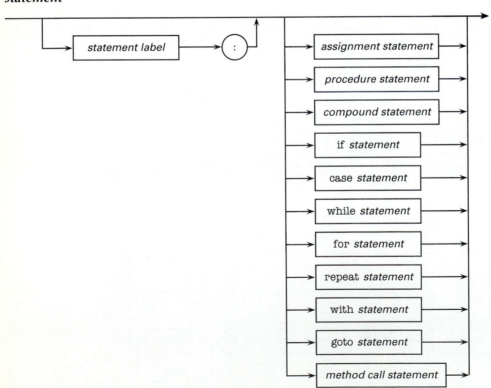

assignment statement

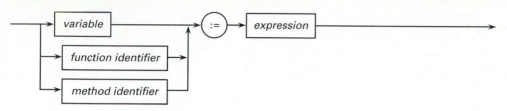

procedure call statement

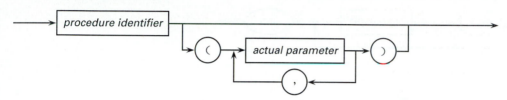

if statement

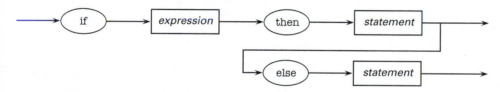

while statement

for statement

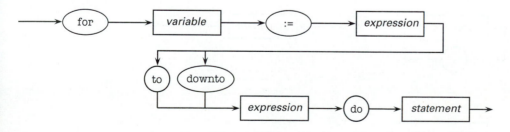

case statement

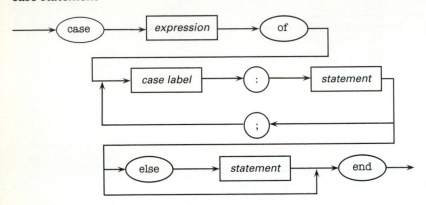

case label

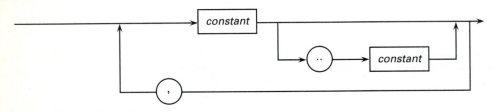

repeat statement

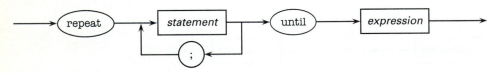

with statement

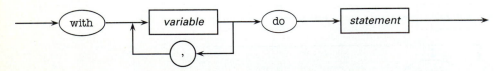

goto statement

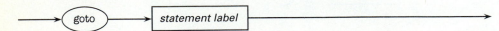

actual parameter

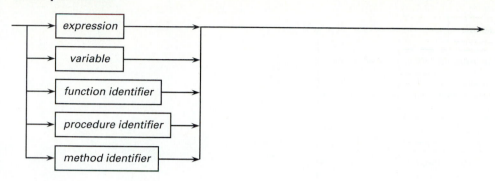

expression

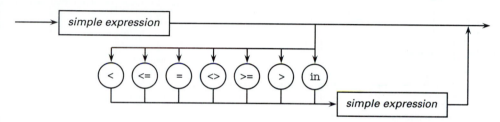

simple expression

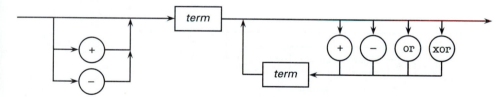

term

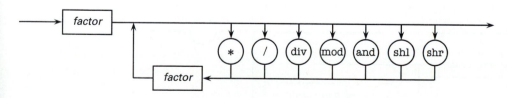

factor

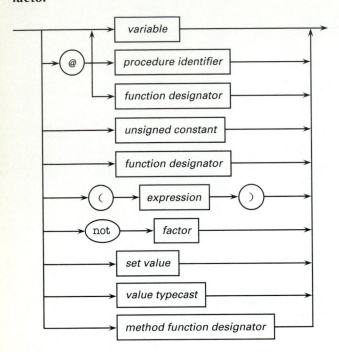

function designator

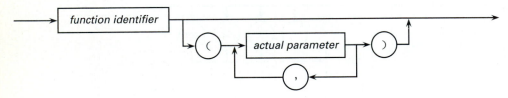

set value

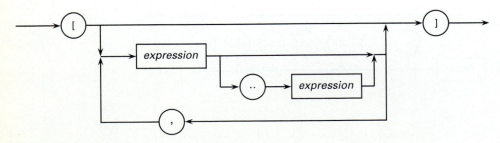

value typecast

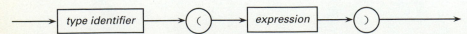

variable

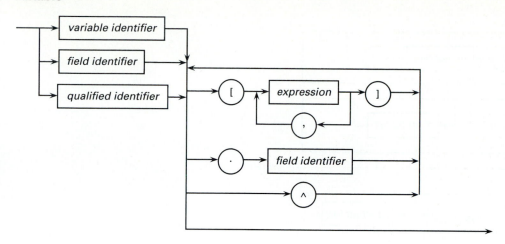

qualified identifier

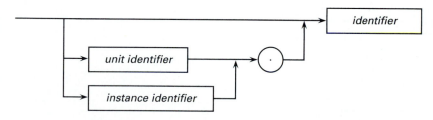

unsigned number

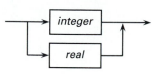

signed number

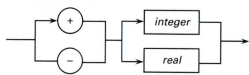

integer

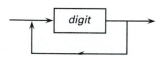

real

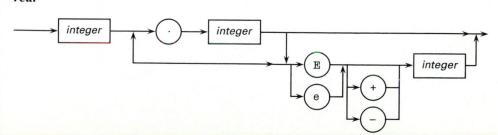

object type

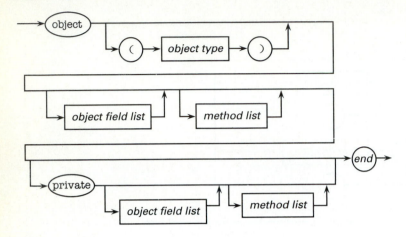

object field list

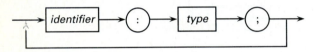

method list

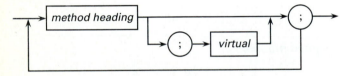

method heading

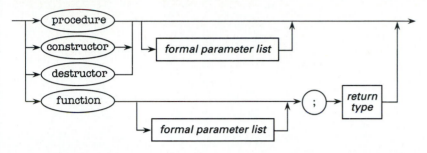

method declaration

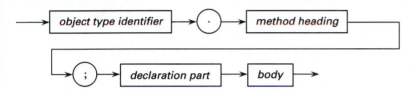

method call statement

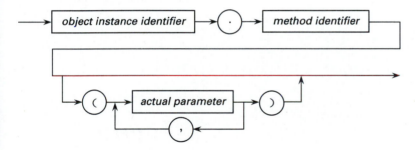

method function designator

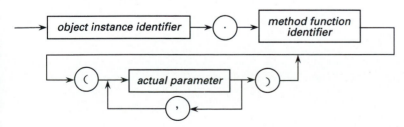

A P P E N D I X   D

Answers to Selected
Self-Check Exercises

CHAPTER 1

Section 1.2

1. The six phases of the Software Life Cycle are: (1) Requirements Specification, (2) Analysis, (3) Design, (4) Implementation, (5) Testing and Validation, (6) Operation and Maintenance.
The last phase, operation and maintenance, lasts the longest.

Section 1.3

1. Information hiding allows us to make use of a procedure without knowing anything about its implementation, as long as we understand its interface requirements.
2. The logical view of a data object describes what information is stored in it without being specific as to how the information is organized or represented. The physical view of a data object is its actual internal representation.

Section 1.4

1. A data object and its set of operators.
2. Information hiding allows us to make use of a data object and its operators without knowing anything about how it has been implemented. This allows us to makes changes in the data object implementation, without affecting the behavior of any of its clients, as long as we do not change its interface.

Section 1.6

1. In object-oriented design, there is no sharp division between the analysis and design phases. Testing is not a separate phase in object-oriented design.
2. It is difficult to restrict access to the Pascal data structure used to implement an ADT; the data structure element type cannot be changed without recompiling the unit; and one must use different operator names to allow two data structures with identical physical structures, but different element types, to exist in the same client program.

Section 1.7

1. To prohibit access to the data or method members of an object by a client module.
2. The preconditions tell a programmer what must be done before a method is called. The post conditions tell a programmer the effects of the method on the object's data members.

CHAPTER 2

Section 2.2

1. Programming team members may be able to identify design errors or bugs that may have been overlooked by the programmer because he or she is too close to the problem.
2. Passing the same actual parameter value as the minimum and maximum range end points. Passing (-MaxInt - 1) and MaxInt as the range endpoint values.

Section 2.3

1. Test data used during white box testing is designed to exercise every logic path within a given code segment or procedure. A procedure interface error would not be discovered until after the procedure has become part of a larger module or complete program and has been called at least once.
2. a. white box testing

MinN	MaxN	N
0	10	5
0	10	-3
0	10	25
5	5	5
-3	5	-3
-3	5	5
-MaxInt	MaxInt	3
5	3	4

b. black box testing

MinN	MaxN	N
0	10	5
0	10	-3
0	10	25
-3	5	-3
-3	5	5
5	3	4

Section 2.5

1.  ```
    {invariant:
       InRange = False and no all of N has been read satisfying
       the condition MinN <= N <= MaxN.
    }
    ```

    Use the following assertion after the while loop:

    ```
    {assert:
       either MinN <= N <= MaxN or
       MinN > MaxN and N is not defined.
    }
    ```

2. Add the following assertion after the if..then..else statement:

    ```
    {assert:
       MinN <= MaxN and an in range value for N has not been
       entered; or MinN > MaxN and it is not possible to
       enter a value of N in the interval MinN..MaxN.
    }
    ```

3. The inner for loop says that IndexOfMin contains the subscript of the smallest array element so far found in the unsorted portion of the array.

    ```
    [1] [2]          ...        [Fill-1] [Fill]   ...     Next      ...      [N]
    ```

Elements in increasing order	Elements > SArray [Fill - 1]

    ```
                                              [IndexOfMin]
    ```

4. This 5-element array requires 15 comparisons and four exchanges using SelectSort.
5. To sort in descending order, replace the > with < in the comparison statement.

Section 2.6

1. a. WriteLn executes N * N times; $O(N^2)$
    b. WriteLn executes N * 2 times; $O(N)$
    c. WriteLn executes $(N + (N - 1) + (N - 2) + ... + 2 + 1)$ times; $O(N^2)$

CHAPTER 3

Section 3.1

1. Using Pascal's built-in array type allows unrestricted access to the array elements by a client program.
2. To allow functions and procedures to manipulate arrays of any size, as long as they have the same element type.
    ```

Section 3.2
1. 21

Section 3.3
1. The second character of the Name field of the third record housed in the array MyClass.
2. In a two-dimensional array the row elements are all of the same data type; in an array of records the "rows" may contain fields of several different data types.

Section 3.4
1. Operations on variant record field references cannot be type checked during program compilation. Including a tag field allows the programmer to use a conditional statement to ensure that a field reference is appropriate to the record variant that is active.

Section 3.5
1. To ensure that an object containing virtual methods will make use of the correct method implementation at run-time.
2. To minimize the effort required to implement a new, but similar, object type and to allow addition of new abstract types without needing to recompile the units containing the declarations of the object's ancestors.

Section 3.6
1.   a. Store 'Abracadabara' in Magic.
     b. Return 11.
     c. Store 'Abracada' in HisMagic.
     d. Change Hismagic to 'Abrda'.
     e. Change Hismagic to 'AbAbrarda'.
     f. Return 5.
     g. Return 1.
     h. Store 1.234 in RealNum; Error is 0.
     i. Store '1.2' in RealStr.

2.
```
PosComma := Pos(',', Source);
Target := Copy(Source, 1, PosComma - 1);
LenFirstName := Length(Source) - PosComma - 1;
Destin := Copy(Source, PosComma + 2, LenFirstName);
```

Section 3.7
1. A null-terminated string is an arbitrarily long sequence of characters whose end is marked by the null character.
2. A variable length character string contains an extra field indicating the actual number of characters stored in the string.

CHAPTER 4

Section 4.1

```
2. Algorithm to Divide M by N
     if M < N then
         Return 0
     else
         Return 1 + value of (M - N) divided by N
```

Section 4.2

1. The actual parameter in the recursive call Palindrome (N – 1) is an expression and must correspond to a formal parameter that is a value parameter.

2. The screen output is: /–+*

First call:	N	4	Next	*
Second call:	N	4,3	Next	*,+
Third call:	N	4,3,2	Next	*,+,–
Fourth call:	N	4,3,2,1	Next	*,+,–,/
First return:	N	4,3,2	Next	*,+,–
Second return:	N	4,3	Next	*,+
Third return:	N	4	Next	*
Fourth return:	N		Next	

3.

			Result
Multiply(5, 4)	M|5	N|4	?
Multiply(5, 3)	M|5,5	N|4,3	?
Multiply(5, 2)	M|5,5,5	N|4,3,2	?
Multiply(5, 1)	M|5,5,5,5	N|4,3,2,1	?
return from (5, 1)	M|5,5,5	N|4,3,2	5
return from (5, 2)	M|5,5	N|4,3	10
return from (5, 3)	M|5	N|4	15
return from (5, 4)	M|	N|	20

Section 4.3

```
1. if Power = 0 then
       PowerRaiser := 1
   else
       PowerRaiser := Base * PowerRaiser(Base, Power - 1)
```

2. Program output: 3
   Program TestStrange calls a function Strange if it counts the number of times its argument can be divided by 2.

3. The recursion would go on forever. When N is 2, a recursive call to Fibonnaci(0) results. This causes calls to Fibonnaci(–1) and Fibonnaci(–2), and so on.

Section 4.4

```
1. X is 5,8,10,1        ┌─>X is 5,8,1,10        ┌─>X is 5,1,8,10
   N is 4               │  N is 3               │  N is 2
   X becomes 5,8,1,10   │  X becomes 5,1,8,10   │  X becomes 1,5,8,10
   SelectSort(X, 3)─────┘  SelectSort(X, 2)─────┘  SelectSort(X, 1)
```

For the last frame (not shown) N is 1, so an immediate return occurs.

```
2. X is 5,8,10,1       ┌─>X is 5,8,10,1      ┌─>X is 5,8,10,1      ┌─>X is 5,8,10,1
   N is 4              │  N is 3             │  N is 2             │  N is 1
   4 = 1 is False      │  3 = 1 is False     │  2 = 1 is False     │  1 = 1 is True
   Display 1           │  Display 10         │  Display 8          │  Display 5
   PrintBack(X, 3)─────┘  PrintBack(X, 2)────┘  PrintBack(X, 1)────┘  Return
```

Section 4.5

1.

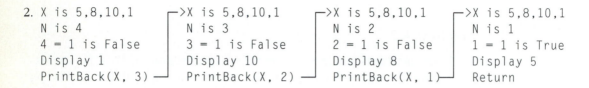

Subproblems of "Move two disks from peg A to Peg C"

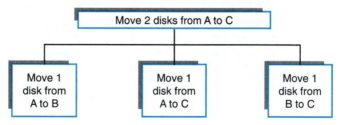

Subproblems of "Move three disks from peg A to Peg C"

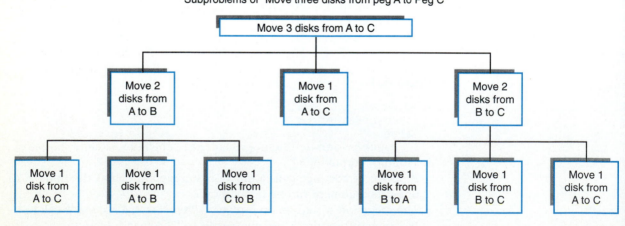

2. $2^6 - 1$, or 63

Section 4.6

1.

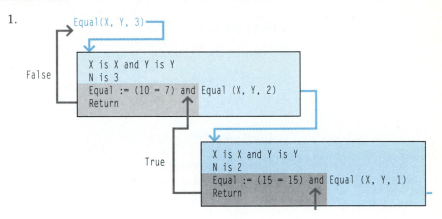

2. For BlobCount(1, 1), Grid[X, Y] is empty so 0 is returned. BlobCount(1, 2) has as its value the expression:

   1 + BlobCount(0, 3) + BlobCount(1, 3) + BlobCount(2, 3) +
   BlobCount(2, 2) + BlobCount(2, 1) + BlobCount(1, 1) +
   BlobCount(0, 1) + BlobCount(0, 2)

   An immediate return occurs with a value of 0 for all function designators except BlobCount(2, 1), which has as its value the expression:

   1 + BlobCount(1, 2) + BlobCount(2, 2) + BlobCount(3, 2) +
   BlobCount(3, 1) + BlobCount(3, 0) + BlobCount(2, 0) +
   BlobCount(1, 0) + BlobCount(1, 1)

   An immediate return with a value of 0 occurs for each function designator, so BlobCount(2, 1) returns 1 and BlobCount(1, 2) returns 1 + 1, or 2.

3. The order of the tests is critical. The first test checks for a cell that is off the grid and prevents the second from being evaluated for such cells, thus avoiding a subscript-range error.

Section 4.7

1. Solve would begin searching Maze[1, 1], move down to check Maze[2, 1], and then try to move to Maze[3, 1], which is not possible. Solve then backtracks to Maze[2, 1] and tries to move right to Maze[2, 2], which is blocked. Solve then backtracks to Maze[1, 1] and moves right to Maze[1, 2]. Solve then tries to move down to Maze[2, 2], which is blocked. Solve then moves right to Maze[3, 1], followed by moves to Maze[3, 2], and Maze[3, 3].
2. If the current path being explored reaches a dead-end it is not possible for the algorithm to explore other paths once bactracking begins.

CHAPTER 5

Section 5.1

1. |2+C/$ Success is True.
   |2+C/$–   Success is True.
   |2+C/$ NextCh is '–'; Success is True.
   |2+C/$ NextCh is '$'; Success is True.

Section 5.2

1. First expression:
   (Balanced is True.
   ({   Balanced is True.
   ({[Balanced is True.
   ({   Open is '[', Close is ']', Balanced is True.
   (Open is '{', Close is '}', Balanced is True.
            Open is '(', Close is ')', Balanced is True.
   (Open is '(', Close is ')', Balanced is True.
            Open is '(', Close is ')', Balanced is True.

   Second expression:
   (Balanced is True.
   ({   Balanced is True.
   ({[Balanced is True.
   ({   Open is '[', Close is '}', Balanced is False.

Section 5.3

1.
Expression	OpStack	NextCh	NewOp	Result
4 5 6 * 3 / + ^	|4	'4'	4	
4 5 6 * 3 / + ^	|4 5	'5'	5	
4 5 6 * 3 / + ^	|4 5 6	'6'	6	
4 5 6 * 3 / + ^	|4 30	'*'		30
4 5 6 * 3 / + ^	|4 30 3	'3'	3	
4 5 6 * 3 / + ^	|4 10	'/'		10
4 5 6 * 3 / + ^	|14	'+'		14

Section 5.4

1. const
   StringLen = 20;

```
    type
StringType = string[20];
Student = record
            Name : StringType;
            Score : Integer;|
            Grade : Char
          end; {Student}
```

```
StackElement = Student;
```

Yes, the stack operators in unit StackADT can be used.

Section 5.5

1. No.
2. Push, Pop.

CHAPTER 6

Section 6.1

1. Front   Rear

Watson Business 1	Carson FirstClass 2	Harris FirstClass 3

McMann was removed and three passengers remain in the queue.

Section 6.2

1. Front   Rear

Watson Business 1	Harris Economy 3

Section 6.3

1. Front is 2, Rear is 3, and Items[1..3] are 'Brown', 'Watson', 'Dietz' respectively.

2.
```
for I := 1 to size of queue do
    begin
        Remove first queue element.
        Display element just removed.
        Insert this element at end of the queue.
    end
```

Section 6.4

1. Because the precondition for StartServe requires that at least one of its input parameters needs to be a non-empty queue and calling Check-NewArrival before StartServe ensures this.

CHAPTER 7

Section 7.1

1. a. The string 'CA' is stored in the Current field of the record pointed to by R.
   b. The record pointed to by R is copied to the record pointed to by P.
   e. Pointer O value stored in Volts filed of record pointed to by R.
   f. Pointer P set to point to same record as R.
   g. String 'XY' is stored in Current field of the third record, where the first record is pointed to by R.
   h. The Volts field of the record pointed to by R is copied into the Volts field of the record pointed to by Q.
2. Exchange the values of the Current fields of the records pointed to by R and Q.

Section 7.2

1. A pointer to a memory cell that has been already been returned to the heap.

Section 7.3

1. AC 115
   DC   12

Section 7.5

1. Use method LinkList.InsertAtEnd in place of LinkList.Insert in the Fig. 7.10 program when building the list.
2. One strategy would be to define a LinkList method that returns as its value the memory location of the linked-list element which precedes the list insertion or deletion point.

Section 7.6

1. No, because Head and Cursor were declared as private in their ancestor object LinkList.
2. Yes, Stack and Queue objects have access to all inherited LinkList methods that were not redefined. Object inheritance (in Borland Pascal) does not let you hide methods from descendant classes without hiding them from client programs as well.

Section 7.7

1. Before inserting a new node into the list, search for the location of the first node whose key value is larger than the key value of the new node and then use method LinkList.Insert to perform the insertion.

2. Modify program RunPoly so that it includes a function IsLess that makes use of method ListData.LessThan to compare two list elements. Modify procedures InsertPoly and ReadPoly so that they pass function IsLess to method OrderList.Insert rather than function IsGreater.

Section 7.8

1. In a circular list, the successor of the last list node is the first list node. In a linear list, the successor field of the last list node is defined to be nil.

CHAPTER 8

Section 8.1

1. A + (B $\star$ – (C + D)) and (A $\star$ (X + Y)) $\star$ C
2. X $\star$ Y / (A + B) $\star$ C

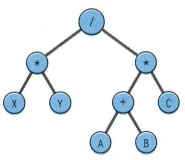

X $\star$ Y / A + B $\star$ C

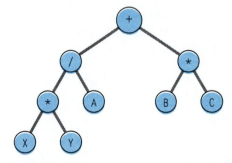

Section 8.2

1.
Prefix	Postfix
/ $\star$ X Y $\star$ + A B C	X Y $\star$ A B + C $\star$ /
+ / $\star$ X Y A $\star$ B C	X Y $\star$ A / B C $\star$ +

2.
Inorder	Preorder	PostOrder
A + B $\star$ – C + D	+ A $\star$ B – + C D	A B C D – $\star$ +
A $\star$ X + Y $\star$ C	$\star$ $\star$ A + X Y C	A X Y + $\star$ C $\star$

3. Inorder	Preorder	Postorder
B ∗ D ∗ X + − Y	∗ B + + D X − Y	B D X ∗ Y − + ∗

Section 8.4

1. Yes, by using a nil pointer as the value of the left child pointer in the node containing the unary minus.

Section 8.5

1. 30; root key (35) > rightmost child (30) in left subtree
2. Either 30 or 42 could be moved to the root as shown below.

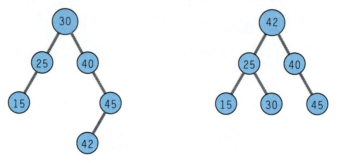

Section 8.6

1. We would also need to implement: CreateTree, GetSize, GetRoot, GetCursor, IsEmpty, InsertAtRoot, InsertLeft, InsertRight, Retreive, Replace, InitCursor, HasLeftTree, HasRightTree, GoLeft, GoRight, Inorder.

2.
```
function Height(tree)
    if three is empty then
      Height is 0
    else
      Height is 1 + maximum of Height (tree left subtree) and
      Height (tree right subtree).
```

Section 8.7

1.
```
if Parent is nil then
   Success is False
else if target key is in node Parent^ then
   begin
      DeleteNode (Parent^)
      Success is True
   end
else if target key > key of node Parent^ then
   TreeDelete (Parent^.Right, Target, Success)
else if target key < key of node Parent^ then
   TreeDelete (Parent^.Left, Target, Success)
```

2. In a binary tree the node keys are not ordered, so that the node being deleted may be replaced with any convenient node. In a binary search tree the deleted node must be replaced by the node's in-order successor.

Section 9.1

1.

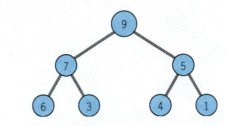

2.

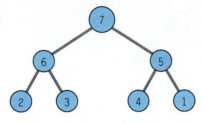

3.

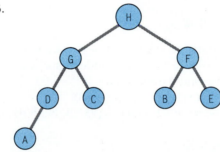

Section 9.2

1.

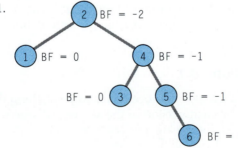

2.

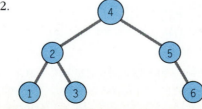

Section 9.3

1.

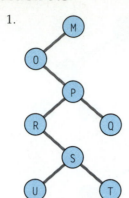

2. Visit root node.
   Traverse subtree with leftmost child as root.
   Traverse right subtree with next sibling as root.

Section 9.4

1. Graphs can contain cycles and general trees cannot. A graph node can have more than one predecessor, where a general tree node can only have one parent node.
2. Vertex set = {1, 2, 3, 4, 5, 6}
   Edge set = {{1, 3}, {1, 5}, {3, 2}, {5, 2}, {2, 4}, {4, 6}}

Section 9.5

1. $O(N^2)$, where N is the number of vertices in the graph.
2. $O(E)$, where E is the number of edges in the graph.
3. Methods Graph.AddVertex and Graph.DelVertex would need to be modified if object Digraph were defined as a descendant of object Graph.

Section 10.1

1. Only position of the first key matching the target key will be returned by each version of the sequential search algorithm.
2.
```
if Cursor > last subscript then
   Set Found to False
else if target key matches current element's key then
   begin
      Set Found to True
      Set PosTarget to Cursor position
   end
else
   Search (array, Successor(Cursor), Target, Found)
```

Section 10.2

1. DoSearch Call

	First	Last	Middle
First	0	8	4
Second	0	3	1
Third	2	3	2
Fourth	3	3	3

   Value returned by BinSearch is 4 (3 + 1).
2. Index is undefined and Success contains False.

Section 10.3

1. For hash tables in which the average search length is less than $O(\log_2 N)$.
2. Clustering.

Section 10.4

2. This is a better hash function because words that differ only in the permutation of their letters will hash to different positions. For example 'BIL' and 'LIB' will hash to different table positions.

Section 10.5

1. Finding an empty table position while searching for a displaced key terminates the search. Therefore, marking a table position as empty means that HashTable.Search will not be able to locate keys in the tail of the search chain.

Section 10.6

1. Insertions would be more costly for ordered list buckets (O(N)) than for unordered buckets (O(1)) on the average, while retrieving keys would have the same average case complexity.
2. No, because empty slots are used to terminate search chains.

Section 10.7

1. One advantage of using an ordered list to house an index is that the size of the index does not need to be known in advance. Another advantage is that it is very easy to add or remove index items without needing to move any other index items. One of the disadvantages of using an ordered list is that sequential search is necessary to locate index key values.
2. ```
Initial index structure
for hashtable positions 1 to Max do
   if hash table position is not empty then
      Store key value and hash table position in index
      structure
```
```

Section 10.8

1.

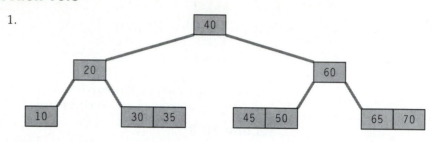

2. 624, $\log_2 624$

CHAPTER 11

Section 11.1

1. $N * (N - 1) / 2$

Section 11.2

1. Change the if statement to
   if Table[First] < Table[First + 1] then
2. 40 35 80 75 60 90 70 75   Pass   Comparison   Exchange
   35 40 75 60 80 70 75 90   1   7   5
   35 40 60 75 70 75 80 90   2   6   3
   35 40 60 70 75 75 80 90   3   5   1
   35 40 60 70 75 75 80 90   4   4   0
                                    Total   22   9
3. Change the data type of BubbleSort parameter Table to
   ```
   var Table {input/output} : Array of Student
   ```
   and the if statement in BubbleSort to something like
   ```
   if Table[First].GetGrade < Table[First + 1].GetGrade then
   ```
   In procedure Switch, the data types of parameter Rec1,
   parameter Rec2, and the local variable TempRec need to be
   changed to Student.

   The if statement should look something like:
   If (Table[First].GetGrade > Table[First + 1].GetGrade) or

((Table[First].GetGrade = Table[First + 1].GetGrade) and
(Table[First].GetName > Table[First + 1].GetName)) then

Section 11.3

1. 40 35 80 75 60 90 70 75	Pass	Comparison	Exchange
35 40	1	1	2
35 40 80	2	1	1
35 40 75 80	3	2	2
35 40 60 75 80	4	3	3
35 40 60 75 80 90	5	1	1
35 40 60 70 75 80 90	6	4	4
35 40 60 70 75 75 80 90	7	3	3
	Total	15	16

2. Change the declaration of InsertSort parameter Table to

```
     var Table {input/output} : Array of Student
```

and the type declaration of local variable NextVal to Student.

Change the declaration of ShiftBigger parameter Table to

```
     var Table {input/output} : Array of Student
```

and the type declaration of parameter NextVal to Student. You also need to change the while loop condition to use one of the Student methods to retrieve the value to use in the comparison like:

```
     while (NextPos >= 0) and
           (Table[NextPos - 1].GetName > NextVal) do
```

Section 11.4

1. a. bubble sort; would be sorted in one pass
   b. selection sort; array is inverted
   c. insertion sort; all elements except the last would be placed with one comparison

d. either insertion sort or selection sort; array order is relatively random
2. No

Section 11.5

1.

[1]	[2]	[3]	[4]	[5]	[6]	[7]	[8]	[9]	[10]	[11]	First	Mid	Last
55	50	10	40	80	90	60	100	70	80	20	1	6	11
55	50	10	40	80	90						1	3	6
55	50	10									1	2	3
55	50										1	1	2
55											1		1
	50										2		2
50	55										Result	of	Merge
		10									3		3
10	50	55									Result	of	Merge
			40	80	90						4	5	6
			40	80							4	4	5
			40								4		4
				80							5		5
			40	80							Result	of	Merge
					90						6		6
			40	80	90						Result	of	Merge
10	40	50	55	80	90						Result	of	Merge
						60	100	79	80	20	7	9	11
						60	100	70			7	8	9
						60	100				7	7	8
						60					7		7
							100				8		8
						60	100				Result	of	Merge
								70			9		9
						60	70	100			Result	of	Merge
									80	20	10		11
									80		10		10
										20	11		11
									20	80	Result	of	Merge
						20	60	70	80	100	Result	of	Merge
10	20	40	50	55	60	70	80	80	90	100	Result	of	Merge

Merge is called 10 times and MergeSort is called 21 times.

Section 11.6

```
1. [1] [2] [3] [4] [5] [6] [7] [8] [9]      First   Last   PivIndex
   [44  75  23  43  55  12  64  77  33]        1       9
   [12  33  23  43] 44 [55  64  77  75]      After partition 5
   [12  22  23  43]                            1       4
    12 [33  23  43]                          After partition 1
                                              1       0
       [33  23  43]                           2       4
       [23] 33 [43]                          After partition 3
        23                                    2       2
                 43                           4       4
             [44  55  64  77  75]             5       9
              44 [55  64  77  75]            After partition 5
                [55  64  77  75]              6       9
                55 [64  77  75]             After partition 6
                  [64  77  75]                7       9
                  64 [77  75]               After partition 7
                                              7       6
                [77  75]                      8       9
                [75] 77                      After partition 9
                   75                         8       8
                                             10       9
```

2. In the left subarray.

```
3. [1] [2] [3] [4] [5] [6] [7] [8] [9] [10][11]  First Last   PivIndex
   [55  50  10  40  80  90  60 100  70  80  20]     1    11
   [20  50  10  40] 55 [90  60 100  70  80  80]   After partition  5
   [20  50  10  40]                                 1     4
   [10] 20 [50  40]                               After partition  2
    10                                              1     1
           [50  40]                                 3     4
           [40] 50                                After partition  4
            40                                      3     3
                                                    5     4
           [90  60 100  70  80  80]                 6    11
           [80  60  80  70] 90[100]               After partition 10
           [80  60  80  70]                         6     9
           [70  60  80] 80                        After partition  9
           [70  60  80]                             6     8
           [60] 70 [80]                           After partition  7
            60                                      6     6
                   80                               8     8
                       100                         11    10
```

There are 12 calls to QuickSort and six calls to partition.
QuickSort would probably beat MergeSort. Because of the small
array size, insertion sort would be best.

Section 11.7

	[0]	[1]	[2]	[3]	[4]	[5]
1. Original array	55	50	10	40	80	90
Initialize Heap	90	80	55	40	50	10
Swap values Table[5] and Table[0]	10	80	55	40	50	90
Reorder Table[0..4]	80	55	50	40	10	90
Swap values Table[4] and Table[0]	10	55	50	40	80	90
Reorder Table[0..3]	55	50	10	40	80	90
Swap values Table[3] and Table[0]	40	50	10	55	80	90
Reorder Table[0..2]	50	40	10	55	80	90
Swap values Table[2] and Table[0]	10	40	50	55	80	90
Reorder Table[0..1]	40	10	50	55	80	90
Swap values Table[1] and Table[0]	10	40	50	55	80	90
Reorder Table[0..0]	10	40	50	55	80	90
Final Array	10	40	50	55	80	90

RestoreDown is called directly by HeapSort eight times.
RestoreDown calls itself recursively 12 times.

CHAPTER 12

Section 12.1

1. The – and ⋆ operators can be used with integer, real, and set type
   operands. The Sqrt function can be used with both integer and real arguments.
2. The caller's data type is used to determine which method implementation to call at run-time.

Section 12.2

1. Destructors are used to reclaim storage allocated to dynamic variables
   inherited from ancestor types.

Section 12.3

1. No, because instances of types Applicant and ExEmployee are not the
   same size.

Section 12.4

1. Virtual methods allow us to defer until run-time the decision as to
   which method implementation to call.
2. You must modify the original unit in which the variant record is defined to add new variants to the record type. You also need to either
   write new methods for the new variant or you need to modify each ex-

isting method to take the variants into account, and you need to examine each reference in the client modules that make use of the type to see if changes need to be made to take the new variant into account.

Section 12.5

1. Unit BinTreeADT would not require any further changes to accommodate nodes of type IntegerOperand and RealOperand in the same binary tree. In unit BinaryExpTreeADT we would need to be certain the calls to method GetEval called the appropriate version of the method (either RealOperand or IntegerOperand).
2. Unit SearchTreeADT would need to use pointers to objects, rather than attempt to reference objects directly in order to accommodate nodes of type Applicant and Employee in the same tree. BinTreeADT (Fig. 12.14) should not require any further changes.

INDEX